T0180495

Lecture Notes of the Institute for Computer Sciences, Social Informatics and Telecommunications Engineering   372

More information about this series at http://www.springer.com/series/8197

Sara Paiva · Sérgio Ivan Lopes ·
Rafik Zitouni · Nishu Gupta ·
Sérgio F. Lopes · Takuro Yonezawa (Eds.)

Science and Technologies for Smart Cities

6th EAI International Conference, SmartCity360°
Virtual Event, December 2–4, 2020
Proceedings

 Springer

Editors
Sara Paiva 🆔
School of Technology and Management
Escola Superior de Tecnologia e Gestão
VIANA DO CASTELO, Portugal

Rafik Zitouni 🆔
SIC Laboratory, INSEEC U
ECE Paris Graduate School of Engineering
PARIS, France

Sérgio F. Lopes 🆔
University of Minho
Guimarães, Portugal

Sérgio Ivan Lopes 🆔
Polytechnic Institute of Viana do Castel
Viana do Castelo, Portugal

Nishu Gupta 🆔
Vaagdevi College of Engineering
Telangana, India

Takuro Yonezawa
Nagoya University
Nagoya, Japan

ISSN 1867-8211   ISSN 1867-822X (electronic)
Lecture Notes of the Institute for Computer Sciences, Social Informatics
and Telecommunications Engineering
ISBN 978-3-030-76062-5   ISBN 978-3-030-76063-2 (eBook)
https://doi.org/10.1007/978-3-030-76063-2

This Springer imprint is published by the registered company Springer Nature Switzerland AG
The registered company address is: Gewerbestrasse 11, 6330 Cham, Switzerland

Preface

We are delighted to introduce the proceedings of the 6th edition of the EAI SmartCity360° International Convention (SmartCity360° 2020) which, due to the safety concerns and travel restrictions caused by the COVID-19 pandemic, took place online in a live stream performed via the Zoom platform. Taking into account the commitment of the entire team involved in this event, the technical and scientific quality was not affected in any way by the restrictions that this year imposed.

This volume of proceedings refers to seven of the conferences co-located at the convention in distinct areas of the smart cities field, which brought together researchers, developers, and practitioners from all around the world.

AISCOVID 2020 (the 1st International Conference on AI-assisted Solutions for COVID-19 and Biomedical Applications in Smart-Cities) received nine contributions to the current state of the art, reporting results for the AI techniques used in the computer network-assisted diagnosis of COVID-19 and similar diseases. It shed light on potential mobile Internet, big data, artificial intelligence, cloud computing, and other modern information technology applications that can build the required online and cost-efficient medical service platforms.

Edge-IoT 2020 (the 2nd International Conference on Intelligent Edge Processing in the IoT Era) received eight contributions. EdgeIoT was created as a flagship conference aiming at addressing the decentralization of contemporary processing paradigms, notably edge processing, focusing on the increasing demand for intelligent processing at the edge of the network, which is paving the way to the intelligent IoT era.

IC4S 2020 (the 2nd International Conference on Cognitive Computing and Cyber Physical Systems) received four contributions that presented fundamental principles for both the integration of cyber and physical elements and the infrastructure for building Cyber Physical Systems (CPS), highlighting the design, implementation, and investigation of CPS applications.

CICom 2020 (the 1st International Conference on Computational Intelligence and Communications) received six contributions. The tracks fcused on how to apply computational intelligence for big data, the Internet of Things, wireless networks, intelligent transportation systems, and cyber security.

S-CUBE 2020 (the 12th International Conference on Sensor Systems and Software) received five contributions that focused on the state of the art in the broad area of system development and software support for wireless sensors networks (WSN).

SmartGov 2020 (the 3rd International Conference on Smart Governance for Sustainable Smart Cities) received five contributions that addressed mainly the rapid change in the ways that cities and settlements have to be managed and also how emerging digital technologies offer new ways for local government to understand and monitor the dynamics of the city.

Finally, Urb-IoT 2020 (the International Conference on IoT in Urban Space) received five contributions focused on exploring the urban space and its dynamics within the scope of the Internet of Things and the new science of cities.

Coordination between all members of the entire team was fundamental to the success of this convention. A word of appreciation to the President of the European Agency Alliance, Prof. Imrich Chlamtac, to the Conference Team Supervisor, Karolina Marcinova, and all Conference Managers who have impeccably supported all the logistics of each of the conferences involved in the convention. A word of appreciation also to all Conference Chairs and to the entire Organizing Committee who have professionally contributed to the success and scientific quality of the publications that are part of this volume. To the reviewers, also a word of appreciation for the time they dedicated to making their precious contributions to further raise the scientific quality of the final version of the papers.

Finally, a special mention to the authors who submitted their work to the 6th edition of the EAI SmartCity360° International Convention. We believe that this convention provided and will continue to provide, in its next edition, an excellent forum to discuss science and technology, from several perspectives, aspects and domains, relevant to smart cities.

May 2021   Henrique Santos
                                                            Sara Paiva

Organization

AISCOVID 2020 Conference Organization

Steering Committee

Imrich Chlamtac   University of Trento, Italy

Organizing Committee

General Chair

Mustafa Kurt   Near East University, Turkey
Fadi Al-Turjman   Near East University, Turkey

Technical Program Committee Chair and Co-chair

Fadi Al-Turjman   Near East University, Turkey
Lakshmana Kumar   Hindusthan College of Engineering and Technology,
   Ramasamy   India

Workshops Chair

Enver Ever   Middle East Technical University, Turkey

Posters and PhD Track Chair

Mehmet Özsöz   Near East University, Turkey

Panels Chair

Sertan Serte   Near East University, Turkey
Krishna Doddapaneni   Amazon Web Services, USA

Publicity and Social Media Chair

Nedime Serakinci   Near East University, Turkey

Publications Chair

Fadi Al-Turjman   Near East University, Turkey

Technical Program Committee

Arafatur Rahman   Universiti Malaysia Pahang, Malaysia
Zaib Ullah   University of Camerino, Italy
Aziz Shah   Manchester Metropolitan University, UK

Shehzad Ashraf Chaudhry	Istanbul Gelisim University, Turkey
Enver Ever	Middle East Technical University, Turkey
Hadi Zahmatkesh	Oslo Metropolitan University, Norway
Masood Habib	Dalian University of Technology, China
Deepak Kumar Jain	University of Chinese Academy of Sciences, China
Syed Sabahat Hussain	Chonqing University, China
Muhammad Rashid Naeem	Sichuan University, China
Farhan Ullah	Comsats University Islamabad, Pakistan
Muhammad Farhan	Comsats University Islamabad, Pakistan
Manvinder Sharma	Chandigarh Group of Colleges, India
Bhoopesh Singh Bhati	Guru Gobind Singh Indraprastha University, India
Thompson Stephan	Amity University, India
Abdullahi Umar Ibrahim	Near East University, North Cyprus
Adedoyin Ahmed Hussain	Near East University, North Cyprus
Ilker Gelisen	Near East University, North Cyprus
Mehmet Ozsoz	Near East University, North Cyprus
Nedime Serakinci	Near East University, North Cyprus
Eser Gemikonakli	University of Kyrenia, North Cyprus
Ramiz Salama	Near East University, North Cyprus
Ersin Aytac	Near East University, North Cyprus
Sertan Serte	Near East University, North Cyprus

CICom 2020 Conference Organization

Steering Committee

Imrich Chlamtac	University of Trento, Italy
Manolo Dulva Hina	ECE Paris School of Engineering, France

Organizing Committee

General Chairs

Amar Ramdane-Cherif	University of Versailles – Paris Saclay, France
Manolo Dulva Hina	ECE Paris School of Engineering, France
Rafik Zitouni	ECE Paris School of Engineering, France

Technical Program Committee Chair and Co-chairs

Manolo Dulva Hina	ECE Paris School of Engineering, France
Seyedali Mirjalili	Torrens University, Australia
Jaouhar Fattahi	Université Laval, Canada
Amreesh Phokeer	AFRINIC and University of Cape Town, South Africa
Yassine Meraihi	Université de Boumerdes, Algeria
Ravi Tomar	University of Petroleum and Energy Studies, India

Workshops Chairs

Houda Chihi   Tunisie Télécom, Tunisia
Yassine Meraihi   Université de Boumerdés, Algeria
Seyedali Mirjalili   Torrens University, Australia

Sponsorship and Exhibits Chairs

Assia Soukane   ECE Paris School of Engineering, France
Amar Ramdane-Cherif   University of Versailles – Paris Saclay, France

Web Chair

Ravi Tomar   University of Petroleum and Energy Studies, Dehradun, India

Publicity and Social Media Chairs

Naila Bouchemal   ECE Paris School of Engineering, France
Nadir Bouchama   CERIST Research Institute, Algeria

Workshop Chairs

Houda Chihi   Tunisie Télécom, Tunisia
Yassine Meraihi   Université de Boumerdés, Algeria
Seyedali Mirjalili   Torrens University, Australia

Publications Chairs

Rafik Zitouni   ECE Paris School of Engineering, France
Brik Bouziane   Burgundy University, France
Max Agueh   EFREI Paris, France

Panel Chairs

Hongyu Guan   University of Versailles – Paris Saclay, France
Abderraouf Khezaz   ECE Paris School of Engineering, France

Tutorials Chair

Nadia Saadia   Université des Sciences et de la Technologie Houari-Boumédiène, Algeria

Demos Chair

Hongyu Guan   University of Versailles – Paris Saclay, France

Posters and PhD Track Chairs

Asma Gabis   Université de Boumerdes, Algeria
Aghiles Djoudi   ESIEE Paris and University of Gustave Eiffel, France

Local Chai

Leila Kloul	University of Versailles – Paris Saclay, France

Technical Program Committee

Naila Bouchemal	ECE Paris School of Engineering, France
Jae Yun Jun Kim	ECE Paris School of Engineering, France
Aakash Soni	ECE Paris School of Engineering, France
Atef Zaguia	Taif University, Saudi Arabia
Rolou Lyn Maata	Gulf College, Oman
Ali Awde	Cégep de Sainte-Foy, Canada
Hongyu Guan	University of Versailles – Paris Saclay, France

Edge-IoT 2020 Conference Organization

Steering Committee

Imrich Chlamtac	University of Trento, Italy

Organizing Committee

General Chair

Sérgio Ivan Lopes	Instituto Politécnico de Viana do Castelo, Portugal

General Co-chairs

Mauro Migliardi	University of Padova, Italy
Arnaldo Oliveira	Universidade de Aveiro, Portugal

Technical Program Committee Chair and Co-chair

Alessio Merlo	University of Genova, Italy
Luca Verderame	University of Genova, Italy

Sponsorship and Exhibit Chair

Jorge Ribeiro	Instituto Politécnico de Viana do Castelo, Portugal

Workshops Chair

Carlos Abreu	Instituto Politécnico de Viana do Castelo, Portugal

Publicity and Social Media Chair

Pedro Santos	Instituto Politécnico do Porto, Portugal

Publications Chairs

Paula Maria Castro	University of A Coruña, Spain
Pedro Pinto	Instituto Politécnico de Viana do Castelo, Portugal

Web Chair

Silvestre Malta	Instituto Politécnico de Viana do Castelo, Portugal

Technical Program Committee

Alberto Sillitti	Innopolis University, Russia
Alessandra De Benedictis	Università "Federico II" di Napoli, Italy
Alexandre Meslin	Pontifical Catholic University of Rio de Janeiro, Brazil
António M. R. Cruz	Instituto Politécnico de Viana do Castelo, Portugal
António Moreira	Instituto Politécnico do Cavado e do Ave, Portugal
Carlo Ferrari	Universita' degli Studi di Padova, Italy
Daniel Albuquerque	Instituto Politécnico de Viseu, Portugal
Fang-Ye Leu	Tunghai University, Taiwan
Felix Freitag	Technical University of Catalonia, Spain
Fernando J. Álvarez Franco	Universidad de Extremadura, Spain
Francesco Palmieri	Universita' degli Studi di Salerno, Italy
Ilsun You	Tunghai University, South Korea
José Lima	Instituto Politécnico de Bragança, Portugal
Josu Bilbao	IKERLAN Technology Center, Spain
Kangbin Yim	Soonchunhyang University, South Korea
Luigi Benedicenti	University of New Brunswick, Canada
Luís Ferreira	Instituto Politécnico do Cavado e do Ave, Portugal
Massimiliano Rak	Università della Campania Luigi Vanvitelli, Italy
Paula Fraga-Lamas	Universidade da Coruña, Spain
Paulo Leitão	Instituto Politécnico de Bragança, Portugal
Paulo Pedreiras	Universidade de Aveiro, Portugal
Pedro Miguel Moreira	Instituto Politécnico de Viana do Castelo, Portugal
Rómulo Antão	Univerdidade de Aveiro, Portugal
Riccardo Pecori	Università del Sannio, Italy
Teodoro Aguilera Benítez	University of Extremadura, Spain
Tiago Fernandez	Universidade da Coruña, Spain
Valentina Casola	Università "Federico II" di Napoli, Italy

S-CUBE 2020 Conference Organization

Steering Committee

Imrich Chlamtac	University of Trento, Italy
Henrique Santos	University of Minho, Portugal

Organizing Committee

General Chairs

Sérgio F. Lopes	University of Minho, Portugal
António Costa	University of Minho, Portugal

Technical Program Committee Chair

Henrique Santos	University of Minho, Portugal

Publications Chair

Sérgio F. Lopes	University of Minho, Portugal

Demos Chair

Hugo Silva	PLUX Wireless Biosignals, Portugal

Local Chair

António Costa	University of Minho, Portugal

Technical Program Committee

Hui Chen	City University of New York, USA
João Ferreira	Lisbon University Institute, Portugal
Bruno Dias	University of Minho, Portugal
Jose Cabral	University of Minho, Portugal
Joaquim Macedo	University of Minho, Portugal
José Afonso	University of Minho, Portugal
Jose Carlos Meireles Metrôlho	Polytechnic Institute of Castelo Branco, Portugal
Le Huy Trinh	Vietnam National University Ho Chi Minh City, Vietnam
Nikolaos Doulamis	National Technical University of Athens, Greece
Pedro Sousa	University of Minho, Portugal
Roberto Passerone	University of Trento, Italy
Sergio Monteiro	University of Minho, Portugal
Xinwei Fang	University of York, UK
Jaime Lloret	Universidad Politecnica de Valencia, Spain

IC4S 2020 Conference Organization

Steering Committee

Imrich Chlamtac	University of Trento, Italy

Organizing Committee

General Chair

Nishu Gupta — Vaagdevi College of Engineering, India, and University of Oviedo, Spain

General Co-chair

Tushar Khare — NEC Technologies, India

Technical Program Committee Chair and Co-chairs

Sarhan M. Musa — Prairie View A&M University, USA
Henrique Manuel Pires Gil — Polytechnic Institute of Castelo Branco, Portugal
Luís Barreto — Instituto Politécnico de Viana do Castelo, Portugal

Sponsorship and Exhibit Chairs

Emanuel Peres — University of Trás-os-Montes e Alto Douro, Portugal
Salviano Pinto — University of Trás-os-Montes e Alto Douro, Portugal

Workshops Chair

Raghavendra Pal — Madanapalle Institute of Technology & Science, India

Publicity and Social Media Chairs

Thet Thet Htew — University of Computer Studies, Myanmar
Zarine Cadersaib — University of Mauritius, Mauritius

Publications Chairs

Prakash Pareek — Vishnu Institute of Technology, India
Shubhanshu Gupta — Centre for Development of Advanced Computing, India

Web Chairs

Hendra Yufit Riskiawan — State Polytechnic of Jember, Indonesia
R. P. Ojha — GL Bajaj Institute of Technology and Management, India

Panels Chair

Parvesh Kumar — Vaagdevi College of Engineering, India

Technical Program Committee

Manuel Cabral Reis	University of Trás-os-Montes and Alto Douro, Portugal
Mahardhika Pratama	NTU Singapore, Singapore
Xicu Xabiel García Pañeda	University of Oviedo, Spain
Vitor Santos	NOVA University Lisbon, Portugal
Anil Gupta	Centre for Development of Advanced Computing, India
Ahmad Hoirul Basori	King Abdulaziz University, Saudi Arabia
Roberto García Fernández	University of Oviedo, Spain
Ariel Soares Teles	Federal Institute of Maranhão, Brazil
Thanos Kakarountas	University of Patras, Greece
Dimitrios G. Myridakis	University of Thessaly, Greece
David Melendi Palacios	University of Oviedo, Spain
Banishree Ghosh	A*STAR, Singapore

SmartGov 2020 Conference Organization

Steering Committee

Imrich Chlamtac	University of Trento, Italy

Organizing Committee

General Chair

Sara Paiva	Instituto Politécnico de Viana do Castelo, Portugal

Technical Program Committee Chairs

Ângela Ferreira	Instituto Politécnico de Bragança, Portugal
Ana Pereira	Instituto Politécnico de Bragança, Portugal
Gabriella Casalino	University of Bari, Italy
Mohd Abdul Ahad	Jamia Hamdard, India

Web Chair

Zdzislaw Polkowski	WSG University, Poland

Publicity and Social Media Chair

Ahmed J. Obaid	University of Kufa, Iraq

Workshop Chair

Gautami Tripathi	Jamia Hamdard, India

Sponsors and Exhibits Chair

Ahmed J. Obaid	University of Kufa, Iraq

Publication Chair

Mohd Abdul Ahad   Jamia Hamdard, India

Technical Program Committee

Tamanna Dalwai	Muscat College, Oman
Thomas Lampoltshammer	Danube University Krems, Austria
Marciele Berger	University of Minho, Portugal
Lorenzo Madrid	Smart City Business Institute, USA
Ricardo Matheus	Delft University of Technology, Netherlands
Jaime Meza	Universidad Técnica de Manabí, Ecuador
Adriana Reveiu	Bucharest University of Economic Studies, Romania
Shefali Virkar	Danube University Krems, Austria
Ralf-Martin Soe	Tallin University of Technology, Estonia
Teresa Pereira	Polytechnic Institute of Viana do Castelo, Portugal
Alejandro Sanchez	National University of San Luis, Argentina

Urb-IoT 2020 Conference Organization

Steering Committee

Imrich Chlamtac	University of Trento, Italy
Fahim Kawsar	Bell Labs, Belgium

Organizing Committee

General Chair

Rui José   University of Minho, Portugal

General Co-Chair

Helena Rodrigues   University of Minho, Portugal

Technical Program Committee Chair

Takuro Yonezawa   Nagoya University, Japan

Publicity and Social Media Chair

Yuuki Nishiyama   University of Tokyo, Japan

Publications Chair

Filipe Meneses   University of Minho, Portugal

Web Chair

Maria João Nicolau   University of Minho, Portugal

Local Chair

Adriano Moreira   University of Minho, Portugal

Technical Program Committee

Stefan van der Spek	Delft University of Technology, Netherlands
Till Riedel	Karlsruhe Institute of Technology, Germany
Kristof Van Laerhoven	University of Siegen, Germany
Julio Cezar De Melo Borges	Karlsruhe Institute of Technology, Germany
Florian Michahelles	Siemens, Germany
Ulf Blanke	ETH Zürich, Switzerland
Yoshito Tobe	Aoyama Gakuin University, Japan
Takeshi Iwamoto	Toyama Prefectural University, Japan
Jin Nakazawa	Keio University, Japan
Christopher Bull	Lancaster University, UK
Rossi Kamal	Kyung Hee University, South Korea
Antonio Costa	University of Minho, Portugal
Adriano Moreira	University of Minho, Portugal
Jorge Silva	University of Coimbra, Portugal
Matthias Budde	Karlsruhe Institute of Technology, Germany

Contents

Cognitive Computing and Cyber Physical Systems

Sensor Systems and Software

Smart Governance for Sustainable Smart Cities

IoT in Urban Space

Contents

AI-assisted Solutions for COVID-19 and Biomedical Applications in Smart-Cities

IoT and AI for COVID-19 in Scalable Smart Cities

Adedoyin A. Hussain[1,2(✉)], Barakat A. Dawood[1,2], and Fadi Al-Turjman[2,3]

[1] Computer Engineering Department, Near East University, 10 Mersin, Nicosia, Turkey
[2] Research Centre for AI and IoT, Near East University, 10 Mersin, Nicosia, Turkey
fadi.alturjman@neu.edu.tr
[3] Department of Artificial Intelligence Engineering, Near East University, 10 Mersin, Nicosia, Turkey

Abstract. COVID-19 which is also known as the novel coronavirus started from China. Motivated by continuous advancement and employments of the Artificial Intelligence (AI) and IoT in various regions, in this study we focus on their underlining deployment in responding to the virus. In this survey, we sum up the current region of AI applications in clinical associations while battling COVID-19. We moreover survey the component, challenges, and issues identified with these technologies. A review was made in requesting AI and IoT by then recognizing their applications in engaging the COVID-19. In like manner, emphasis has been made on a region that utilizes cloud computing in combating diverse similar diseases and the COVID-19 itself. The investigated procedures set forth drives clinical information examination with an exactness of up to 95%. We further end up with a point by point discussion about how AI utilization can be in an ideal situation in battling diverse diseases. This paper gives masters and specialists new bits of information in which AI and IoT can be utilized in improving the COVID-19 situation, and drive further assessments in ending the flare-up of the infection.

Keywords: COVID-19 · IoT · Artificial intelligence · Cloud computing · Deep learning

1 Introduction

The COVID-19 known as the novel coronavirus has changed the world inside and out, including its therapeutic administrations, money related perspectives, guidance, transportation, legislative issues, etc. [1]. In any case, there are no clinical antibodies to prevent the COVID-19 disease and unequivocal meds/helpful shows to fight this transmittable disorder [2, 3]. Another model is that a supercomputing system for inspecting similar diseases to the coronavirus was assembled [4]. As a result of the pandemic, a couple of merchants at present offer free access to articles, particular standards, and various reports related to the COVID-19-like contamination, while web recorded organizations cause a brisk association with assembling all to preprint related disease to COVID-19 [5]. To understand the coronavirus pandemic, various papers and exploration are being

S. Paiva et al. (Eds.): SmartCity360° 2020, LNICST 372, pp. 3–19, 2021.
https://doi.org/10.1007/978-3-030-76063-2_1

circulated for survey over the last couple of months [6]. The brisk rising of events over the globe has prompted the prerequisite without a doubt implementing counter-measures to check the effects of the coronavirus scene. To this stage, this surveys suggests the use of advanced headways, for instance, IoT, cloud, and AI with this, it will help ease the opposing effects of the coronavirus and help the recovery system [7]. Besides, before exploring the expected imaginative responses for the COVID-19 impact, we give a thorough study of the coronavirus, and its clinical features, assurance, prescription, and the impact of its scene.

1.1 Comparison to Other Works

A couple of months following the rise of the COVID-19, a couple of papers examining different pieces of the COVID-19 have been circulated [8–12]. Creators in [13] have thought about focal points, for instance, economics, signs, and appearances, and clinical history of the impressive number of patients to review their cases warily. Creators in [14] pondered a few people with the infection, 49 of them had a quick association with the fish showcase in Huanan Wuhan, which said to be the infection point of convergence. The epidemiological, clinical, and radiological characteristics of the infection being found have been explored. Concerning the disclosures, amid the patient's report that were inspected, 0.17 made serious respiratory difficulty issues (ARDS), and amid the patient, 0.11 passed on various organ brokenness conditions (MODS). Creators in [15] have investigated six circulated examinations seeing the clinical characteristics of the COVID-19. Their work has summarized these assessments and, doing such, gave a succinct chart of clinical features and meds of the infection. The makers of [16] have investigated the current composition of handled tomography (CT) qualities of the infection open on stages. The fundamental comparative issue between the works is that they review a little subset of much increasingly broad subject or item. The makers in [6, 17] give a succinct diagram of the infection scene in regards to its clinical features, neutralization, end, and medicine. Anyway, these diagrams put more knowledge into the current circumstance of the COVID-19 scene, they additionally give a short and confined idea concerning the particular condition. Concerning this overview, we set forth a thorough review of the COVID-19 circumstance which will help perusers with expanding a progressively significant perception of the current overall condition as a result of the COVID-19 pandemic. In Table 1, we set forth a correlation with other examinations.

1.2 Contribution and Scope of the Survey

As the passionate impact of the pandemic over the globe, a lot of attempts are being advanced to give answers to fighting the COVID-19 scene. Government undertakings are for the most part trustworthy to end the circumstance, for instance, shut down the locale to limit the boundless of sickness, ensuring the social protection structure can adjust to the scene and give crisis group to limit the impact on the national monetary perspectives and hold onto adaptable procedures as shown by the COVID-19 situation. At the same time, individuals are encouraged to stay sound and secure by following a couple of knowledge like putting on a cover at open zones, hands washing once in a

Table 1. Comparison to other research.

Reference	AI	IoT	Deep learning	Efficiency	Cloud
[8]	✓		✓	✓	
[9]	✓		✓	✓	
[10]	✓	✓		✓	✓
[11]			✓		✓
[12]	✓	✓	✓	✓	
[13]	✓			✓	✓
[14]	✓	✓	✓	✓	
[15]	✓		✓	✓	
[16]	✓		✓	✓	
[17]	✓	✓		✓	✓
[6]	✓	✓		✓	✓
Our survey	✓	✓	✓	✓	✓

while, keeping up the social expelling plan, and enumerating the latest sign informa-tion to the neighborhood prosperity network. The models referenced above are areas where AI and IoT are applied in checking defilements like the COVID-19 which have made outstanding accomplishments. Contrasting with the assessments referenced, for the convincing utilization of new AI methodologies. However, in like way be furnished considerations and self-reevaluating capacities to impel its accuracy which are dependent on assessment. The AI and IoT applications can help specialists by giving bleeding edge clinical information from papers, course books, and clinical endeavors to move fitting patient contemplations. Furthermore, the framework can help with decreasing legitimate and remedial slip-ups in the master clinical practices. Moreover, an AI structure ousts to have essential information gotten from patient to assist with impelling instigations for prospering dangers and flourishing result desire. In like way, our commitment can be depicted out as follows:

- The issues and troubles identified with IoT and AI are described.
- This study portrays a wide and effective review of IoT and AI in fighting against the COVID-19.
- We discuss open issues and challenges.
- We put forward reasonable courses of action using these systems against the COVID-19.
- The Motivations of utilizing AI in COVID-19 are described.
- Finally, the application of cloud computing against COVID-19 has been discussed.

The paper is described as follows. In Sect. 2 we present vital data on battling COVID-19 with AI and show fundamental motivations driving the usage of AI. At that point, utilizing IoT, and Cloud in combating the COVID-19 pandemic, for instance, examining the patients, following the COVID-19 erupt, making drug investigates, and improving the clinical treatment, are assessed and summarized in Sect. 3 and 4 as needs be. Section 5 highlights troubles and proposals picked up from this paper including the challenges that will be clarified later on. Ultimately, Sect. 6 wraps up this paper with the conclusion. Table 2 gives an overview of the pre-owned shortened forms and their significance.

Table 2. Used abbreviations.

Terms	Meaning
WHO	World Health Organisation
CDC	Centre of Disease Control
ML	Machine Learning
LIWC	Linguistic Inquiry and Word Count
CNN	Convolutional Neural System
DL	Deep Learning
SNN	Siamese Neural System
CT	Computed Tomography
AI	Artificial Intelligence
IoT	Internet of things
NN	Neural Networks
SIR	Susceptible Infected Removed
GIS	Geographic Information Systems

2   AI and COVID-19

This model is a prospering development for some brilliant applications in various fields. Some noticeable occurrences of AI are free vehicles, clinical finding and telehealth in therapeutic administrations, cybersecurity systems, picture handling, and normal language planning. Among various pieces of AI, two huge systems are profound learning and ML [18]. As shown by [19], profound learning has two guideline features, the ability to get acquainted with the right depictions gives one part of profound learning and profound learning licenses the system to take in the data in a significant way, various layers are used progressively to adjust dynamically noteworthy depictions. Man-made brainpower offers a helpful advantage for the fight to come against the pandemic. For example, the analysts in [20] developed a profound learning model to perceive existing and business drugs, finding a quick medicine method using existing meds that can be speedily applied to the defiled patients. This assessment is prodded by the way it takes a long effort to be adequately attempted before heading off to the market. Be that as it may, disclosures concerning this examination are correct now, regardless of everything to open better ways to deal with fighting the COVID-19. Creators in [21] proposed using the significant generative technique for calm divulgence that is portrayed as a route toward perceiving new meds. The infection protease structure made by the profound learning technique in this paper could furthermore be used for PC exhibiting and reenactments to obtain new substance against the COVID-19. Utilizing profound learning picture planning in figured tomography (CT), makers in [22] showed that the recommended technique after experimentation can achieve a precision of up to 90% with a positive insightful estimation of 84% and a negative farsighted estimation of 98%. This examination offers a snappy method to manage to recognize the affected patient, which may give remarkable associates in advantageous disconnect and clinical treatment. The last model uses AI for anticipating the polluted COVID-19 circumstance over an area [23]. Starting late, it is proclaimed by and by that they are giving an exploration dependent on cloud resource that has been set up on the COVID-19 database [24]. Likewise, it has grasped the proposed AI development for sedating divulgence, by which a few novel infection cases have been gotten, legitimately declared in [25]. We will talk about various territories where AI will be applied to in combating the COVID-19 underneath.

2.1 Bio Medics

The race is getting fruitful antibodies and clinical meds to fight the COVID-19 disease, which demands for liberal undertakings from prosperity tech just as programming building, with the help of AI and creating headways. Much the same as in [26] the creators have tended to this request and AI in biomedicine. In any case, the colossal proportion of biomedical data has set off the use of AI in various domains of the biomedicine and drug store. The earlier years have increased a more extensive extent of the utilization of AI to biomedicine analyzes like assistant science and calm revelation and repurposing [27, 28]. As a result of the earnestness of the COVID-19 pandemic, AI has found drug application in checking the heightening of the infection, that mostly revolve around protein structure, steady revelation, and repositioning prescription. The work in [29] utilizes a COVID-19 disease unequivocal dataset to set up a learning model. By then, this readied model is used to check a few financially available drugs and find potential inhibitors with high affinities. The work in [30] proposed a data-driven strategy for sedating repurposing by the blend of AI and quantifiable examination procedures. The ability of the inhibitor CVL218 finding is that it is affirmed to represents a security resemblance in monkeys and rodents. A comparative charming examination for sedating repurposing is [31], it utilizes the Siamese neural framework (SNN) to recognize the protein structure of the COVID-19 versus HIV-1 and the Ebola diseases. Focal points of the paper are the recommended DL strategy that can be set up with no prerequisite for a huge dataset and it works directly with available regular datasets as opposed to open datasets, which are not unequivocal about the COVID-19 contamination. Other than sedating repurposing, many have been resolved to calm exposure [32–34] and protein structure estimate [35–37] for battling the infection. For example, in [38] the work used a DL to learn particles that can tie protein contaminations, a while later using it to deliver candidate medicine for rewarding the COVID-19 disease.

2.2 Detection and Dialysis

Probably the most ideal method of fighting this infection is snappy treatment. On account of the COVID-19 disease, a couple of tries have been committed to improving this strategy [39] and for various alternatives [40]. These techniques are, regularly costly and repetitive, having low clear positive rates, and require unequivocal materials, equipment, and instruments. Additionally, most countries are encountering a nonattendance of testing units on account of the obstacle to spending plans and methodology. Thusly, the standard procedure isn't sensible to meet the requirements of the snappy area and following during the pandemic. An essential and insignificant exertion answer for the infection unmistakable evidence is using smart devices alongside AI structures [41, 42]. This is suggested as flexible prosperity or mHealth in the composing [43]. These works are ideal since splendid contraptions are step by step used for numerous reasons. Additionally, the improvement of the edge and cloud handling can effectively beat the limitation of player, storing, and figuring limits [44].

Concerning the battle against the pandemic, making profitable scientific and treatment procedures expect a noteworthy activity in reducing the impact of COVID- 19 disease [45]. In [46] they present a procedure reliant on DL to gauge varieties from the standard concerning the COVID-19 affliction. The commitment to the proposed learning method is a chest non contrasted pictures, while its yield is a genuine score. The proposed learning method, when arranged, it outlines critical results with the Pearson's relationship coefficient among reality and foreseen yield up to 97%. The result is exceptionally noteworthy as it achieves an exactness of 91%. Nonetheless, the fundamental finding from this examination is the real level which is progressively dependent on the features isolated from the right lung. In particular, the procedure relies upon the way that COVID-19 contamination is most likely going to have qualities from the basic pathomorphological changes. The execution of the model at a greater extension is correct presently compelled by a couple of issues, similar to the sum and nature of the datasets, and the nonappearance of clinical endorsement.

2.3 Epidemy Control

Until this point in time, most trustworthy information on the pandemic is dissipated on authentic destinations and channels of the clinical affiliations, and the administration of prosperity and government help with each country. Additionally, electronic medium and online stages have demonstrated their hugeness inflowing information related to the pandemic. Despite the nature and source, by media stage and the web is uncommonly accessible and perfect, so more examinations might be completed if the data might be assembled and dealt with properly. As an astounding resource for deal with an enormous proportion of data, AI has been utilized to have an unrivaled cognizance of the relational association components and to propel the infection situation. To layout the employments of AI in this pandemic, creators in [47] presented some veritable models like using online life data to follow the open direct, assessing the prosperity for the lead of the Ebola erupt, lastly open reaction towards the Chikungunya scene.

The proposed system licenses us to think about the COVID-19 risk in a specific region, thusly engaging the decision and appropriate exercises to restrain the impact of

COVID-19. Starting late, the makers in [48] proposed a novel procedure, to be explicitly augmented, to assess the number of confirmed cases inside 2 days ahead. The data is assembled from better places, official clinical explanations from Wuhan, Internet search works out, Cloud media news, and step by step evaluates achieved by the strategy proposed in [49]. In improving the dataset, each datum point is also augmented by including a sporadic Gaussian clatter with mean 0 and standard deviation 1. The results show that the proposed augmented system can defeat the benchmark models for most testing circumstances.

3 IoT and COVID-19

The Internet of Medical Things moreover otherwise called human administrations IoT, is the mix of clinical contraptions and programming applications serving expansive therapeutic administration benefits that are related to the social protection IT structures. Starting has of late, much like the IoT, in the clinical field has seen a flood in regards to the amount of its noteworthy usage [50]. The flood is credited to the way the growing amount of mobile phones is at present furnished with Near Field Communication (NFC) perusers which license these contraptions to help out IT structures [51]. Employments of clinical IoT consolidate checking patients from a far off territory, following medication demands, and using wearables in transmitting clinical information to the principle restorative administration specialists. Inferable from their ability to accumulate, separate, and transmit clinical data productively, the social protection division has comprehended the transformative capacity of clinical IoT progresses [52, 53]. Amid the advancing COVID-19 pandemic, a couple of pioneers, clinical affiliations, and government bodies are wanting to utilize IoT devices to lessen the weight on the restorative administration structures. In the going with the fragment, we explore diverse IoT propels which makes a noteworthy responsibility in checking, and therefore, managing the impact of the pandemic.

3.1 Smart Health

The demonstration of using clinical IoT headways to support far off patient checking is known as telehealth. The preparation licenses specialists to survey, break down and furnish patients with treatment without requiring any physical coordinated effort with the patient [54]. Following the eruption of the incredibly irresistible infection, a couple of IoT tech and telehealth stages have defied a quick flood in busy time gridlock. Starting late, an electronic business stage for therapeutic administration game plans has reported seeing an amazing climb for web interviews since the erupt of the infection [55]. The Civil Rights Office OCR and Medicaid Services CMS have conceded fundamental medicare laws for allowing experts to outfit their training with distant clinical capacity using telemedicine stages [56]. Following these rules, a Texas- based overall telehealth association has uncovered a giant addition for its telehealth courses of action. This flood has induced its offer expenses to rise by over 100% in a scope of barely any week [57]. In the past, very few months, a couple of telehealth mechanical assemblies like telehealth trucks, teleconsultation programming, and minimized tablets have exhibited their authenticity in the fight against the pandemic. Also, the authentic capacity of telehealth must be recognized while existing telehealth stages are used with various developments. The blend of these headways with existed telehealth stages can mull over a continuously exceptional therapeutic administration's natural framework that could enable distant watching and blocked off clinical thought of patients with smooth cases of the infection. Which the wide extent of the use, cases presented above shows the ability of IoT in lighting up the surprising challenges introduced by the COVID-19. Regardless, the mechanical assemblies discussed, above structure a little subset of significantly greater space that is IoT.

3.2 Quick Detection

A USA clinical advancement association had pushed web-related thermometers to examine people with solid fevers. Even though the thermometers from the outset were advanced to follow the ordinary flu, regardless, they are winding up being outstandingly significant in perceiving the potential COVID-19 gatherings all through the US. Following the COVID-19 erupt, they have passed on over a million sharp thermometers to nuclear families in various urban territories. The thermometers are associated with a flexible application, which allows the transmission of their outcomes to the association immediately. When gotten, this data is consumed to create step by step maps showing which of the USA territories are seeing an extension in high fevers, thusly allowing the USA pros to perceive likely hotspots. In the earlier years, the instinctive guides are exhibited to be significantly exact in the ideal desire for the transmission of flu around the USA, surpassing the CDC's genuine application to the extent of the briskness of estimate [58]. As countries and clinical affiliations everywhere throughout the globe fight to direct the transmission of the COVID-19, savvy gadgets are passed on to help in rewarding the patients, and accordingly, alleviating the sentiments of nervousness of the therapeutic administration's workers. Also, shrewd restrained noncontact brilliant UV face purifying procedures are in like manner being used to limit the trading of the disease using contaminated surfaces. Appeared differently about the demonstration of manual refinement, which incorporates the association of cleaning staff and henceforth places them at risk for getting the contamination, independent purging robots ensure fast and amazing cleansing of the premises, with for all intents and purposes zero human contact [59].

3.3 Smart Devices

To keep up high cleaning standards and cut off the amount of crisis facility picked up infections, a couple of clinical centers in Vancouver have presented battery-worked IoT gets [60]. These were planned for quick sending in any office, paying little heed to their size, to give brief alerts to the organization, seeing them of any sanitation or upkeep issue that may speak to a risk to open social insurance. An awesome segment of these gets is their opportunity on the external establishment, similar to their ability to stick to some arbitrary surface [61]. An association known for its Bluetooth territory reference focuses has starting late developed a ton of wearable contraptions to enable contact to catch up at the workplace, attempting to give delegates a progressively secure workplace condition. This wearable contraption licenses affiliation pioneers to screen the clinical status of their agents distantly and to follow any occurrence of infection transmission among them. This empowers an affiliation's boss to control the infirmity transmission before it moves fiercely inside the affiliation or outside it [62]. Right when the contraption is on, it channels for other comparable devices and spares any close by joint efforts inside them. This present devices' hardware fuses an idle GPS territory tracker despite Bluetooth controlled region sensor, ultra-wideband system, LTE, and the battery-fueled battery [63]. Moreover, every device has LED markers and gets, much equivalent to a smartwatch. With the inspiration driving these gets is to allow the laborers to go into their consistent clinical status. In this way, the individual wearing it can revive their prosperity status as interesting or affirmed corrupted. Exactly when the wearer revives their clinical position, it is spared in a central information stockroom that spares information for whatever length of time that about a month and a half. It contains three varieties, a stone-like device worn on the neck, and a versatile wrist-worn gadget, lastly a device as a card.

4   Cloud and COVID-19

The brunt of the pandemic on the cloud business is flighty. Particular cloud organizations and shippers have proclaimed seeing a huge expansion inactive time gridlock [64]. The epic degree utilization of system data transmission is being related to the associations' isolate endeavors that are obliged to training foundations to use web resources, and relationship to allow their operators to expand reality. Furthermore, the COVID-19 pandemic has left the cloud district frail. Like other cloud affiliations, a great deal of TSPs and ISPs have taken notes of a huge slide in their offer costs during the time recently. Overall Data's offer worth assessment of a piece of the top TSPs around the world [65]. The colossal level of an undertone of the pandemic on the general economy is credited to the inadmissible answer framework got after its key emit. Regardless of the way that the response to the pandemic are being framed than the responses to past scourges and pandemics, little troubles in the current pandemic structure answer remains [66]. These exercises are staggeringly applicable to other wellbeing related emergencies similarly as though there is a flood of the COVID-19 pandemic later on. The cloud is the blend of gadgets and programming applications that offer far-reaching cloud benefits that are identified with the human organization's IT structures. Beginning late, much like the IoT has seen a flood in the measure of its potential applications [50]. This flood is credited to the way that a developing number of cloud vendors that permit these contraptions to interface with IT frameworks [67]. Underneath we portray diverse material zones identified with cloud and COVID-19.

4.1   Dialysis

Despite the measure and spread using a cloud system, the cloud can help COVID-19 affirmation and prescription structures. Believe it or not, the limit of the cloud resource for diagnosing convincing issues like COVID-19 has been appeared through late victories, from early finding [68], the craving for treatment results, and building reliable devices for a clinical strategy. Concerning the infection and prescription, cloud asset has given a few blueprints as point by point in the structure. An assessment in [69] presented an energetic, delicate, express, and fundamentally quantitative course of action subject to multiplex polymerase chain responses that can separate the COVID-19. The model incorporates 172 courses of action of unequivocal establishments related to the SARS-CoV-2 genome which could be collected through china. The proposed Multiplex PCR plot is an able and clear procedure to separate Plasmodium falciparum contaminations, with high thought of up to 98%. Another examination in [70] executed a nuclear trademark model for genomic assessments of strains of the SARS-CoV-2, with a thought on concentrating on individuals from Australia which travelers with COVID-19 disease utilizing genome information. This assessment may give gigantic bits of data into viral reasonable arrangement and sponsorship COVID-19 end in districts with lacking genomic information. This progression can track and figure the chance of the ailment from the accessible information, electronic frameworks organization, and media stages, concerning the dangers of the debasement and its feasible transmission. Likewise, it can imagine the number of positive cases going in either zone. Cloud-based knowledge could help see the weakest zones, individuals, nations, and take the assessment in like the way [71].

4.2 Smart Applications

The clinical structures need an adaptable and safe cloud foundation to direct and keep up data with quick and adaptable exactness. During the COVID-19 pandemic, there is a certified need for progressions, for example circled figuring for the assessment of patients' information. As the measure of electronic thriving records is broadening, social insurance suppliers are turning into the utilization of adaptable and essentially secure limit cloud to think about a colossal number of cases. Private experts and restorative organization establishments are giving internet prompting amid nation lockdowns. The need for adaptable walking associations has expanded given the malady emit [71]. These working environments and associations need cloud-based correspondence and joint effort stages to improve operational ability and representative productivity. Human organization suppliers are making cloud-based applications to increase clinical experiences on COVID-19 and measure asset necessities, for example, ICU beds and ventilators. Hence, broadened information assessment and clinical getting necessities, and high spending on cloud-based application improvement and ERP blueprints amid the COVID-19 pandemic are making compensation open doors for cloud ace affiliations.

4.3 Infection Tracking

Another action of cloud and its enormous data is the going with of the infection transmission, it is a central vitality for human organization affiliations and countries in subduing satisfactorily the pandemic. Contrasts starting late making blueprints utilizing monster data are proposed to help the going with of the COVID-19 transmission. For instance, the assessment in [72] proposed a critical information- driven technique for following the COVID-19 transmission. Another direct model is amassed utilizing near to masses and air pioneers as evaluated factors that are essential to measure the distinction in revealed cases in urban systems. Significantly more unequivocally, the creators utilized a Spearman relationship appraisal for the normal client traffic from the spoiled city and the firm client traffic in this period with the measure of up to 49 arranged cases. Nonetheless, the quick yield gives a noteworthy association concedes the constructive affliction cases and the individual's populace. The creators in [73] thought about utilizing the epic data for spatial assessment strategies and Geographic Information Systems (GIS) progression that can stimulate asset securing and the mix of heterogeneous assets from thriving data assets, for example, countries, clinical labs, patients, and everyone. Cloud can engage and make a splendid stage for changed checking and want for the spread of this illness. Cloud- engaged virtualization can comparatively be made to clear the visual features of this infection, and this would help in the genuine checking and treatment of the affected individuals [74, 75]. This accompanies the restriction of offering common updates of the patients and offers reactions to be considered during the pandemic.

5   Challenges and Suggestions

As evaluated in the past territories, the advancements reviewed have found their exceptional prospects in the worldwide battle against the pandemic. Besides certain ideal conditions, there are still incites ought to have been discussed and watched out for later on. Additionally, we include a couple of activities that began from this overview and give a couple of propositions for the investigation systems and authorities.

5.1 Lack of Data

To make the advancements a trustful response for fighting the COVID-19 disease, a fundamental test develops through the nonappearance of the typical database. As investigated in the past sections, various AI estimations and colossal data were recommended, in any case, they are not taken a stab at using the proportional database. Regardless, we can't pick which estimation is better for the contamination revelation since two datasets with different amounts of tests were used. Additionally, most datasets found in the composing have been advanced on account of individual endeavors. To crush this test, the administration, firms, and clinical affiliations expect a key activity as they could agreeably perform for an extraordinary bore and huge database. A collection of data assets could be given by the components. For example, the COVID-19 dataset [24] has been made and driven for Security and various associates. As declared in [76], this structure has been used by more than a few centers in the Asian area by its stunning individual undertakings, a movement to administer an open database of the COVID-19 clinical pictures is available at [77] with an overall variety of open-get to stretches out on the COVID-19 is likewise open.

5.2 Protection

Right now, huge things are keeping people sound and in a little while controlling the condition; besides, how close data is secure and private is so far required and should be explored. A component of this test is the humiliation of the video application against its assurance and security troubles. During this pandemic, authorities may request their family to give their information, and step by step works out, which is relied upon to control the condition, make uncommon plans, and pick fast exercises. Data is a flat out need to guarantee the achievement of any of the above-studied innovations; albeit, commonly people would lean toward not to share their information, if not officially referenced. There is trade-off security and execution. These advances are open to handle the security and assurance troubles concerning the COVID-19 scourge. In any case, we perceive some normal plans underneath that could take care of in as investigation arranges later on.

5.3 Regulating the Spread

As the scene is impacting and the step by step number of attested cases increases stunningly, various strategies have been taken to control this erupt. Thusly, regulatory masters have a huge activity in describing game plans that can empower the relationship of occupants, analysts, and pros, similarly as mixing the techniques executed by different substances to avoid any blocks and obstructions in the strategy for preventing the COVID-19 disease. Concerning challenge, various undertakings have been delivered utilizing the principle confirmed COVID-19 to current condition. A model is from the confine technique in the Asian area. Even more expressly, all voyagers entering the nation are required to be disengaged for at any rate 14 days at selected areas or allowed workplaces. Likewise, all explorers are requested to perform step by step self-assurance two times each day a short time later sending the reports using self-investigation applications presented in their mobile phones. The knowledge watching structure is executed by the metropolitan power to, therefore, affirm the clinical conditions of the people who don't have no telephones or conceivably have not presented the self-finding applications [78–88].

6 Conclusion

As the grappling continues with the impact of the COVID-19 pandemic. Here, we have presented a review of the courses of action in the battle against the COVID-19 pestilence. Additionally, we gave an introduction of the COVID-19 disease, the essentials, and motivations of AI for finding fast and fruitful philosophies that can sufficiently fight the sickness. IoT and cloud rising progressions were discussed with an endeavor to help its impact against the disease. By then, we have examined the employments of AI for distinguishing proof and assurance, development and anticipating the scene, the study of disease transmission, and smart health. In like way, the AI strategy was used to amass the protein in the patient body from clinical notes. Thusly, a short period later the patient result was beneficial, which achieves over 91% exactness. Also, we have discussed the achievement of AI in fighting the COVID-19 pandemic. Also, a broad review of the IoT and cloud, where we research its clinical IoT and cloud organizations. A short time later, we portray the confronted difficulties and proposals. In any case, dynamically future examination is to be accomplished to guarantee that everybody offers and coordinates in a manner that abstains from missing any basic center interests. Moral contemplations will acknowledge a colossal action by helping us to go around likely snags in the social event of consistent thinking instruments in helping the condition. Along these lines, the rest of the requests that despite everything destroys them, for example, the subject of the sharing of commitments, should be tended to. We should join a conversation among all accessories pushed. Thusly, it has all the reserves of being extensively progressively fundamental to concentrate on quiet voices. Future solicitations can be considered to follow the emergency of COVID-19 at various scales. In like way, in making fitting treatment, cautious techniques, solution, and vaccination movement. The explored procedures put forward move clinical data assessment with a precision of up to 90%.

References

1. "Situation update worldwide, as of 9 April 2020," (2020). https://www.ecdc.europa.eu/en/geographical-distribution-2019-ncov-cases
2. "Coronavirus disease (COVID-19) pandemic," (2020). https://www.who.int/emergencies/diseases/novel-coronavirus-2019
3. "Coronavirus (COVID-19)," (2020). https://www.cdc.gov/coronavirus/2019-nCoV/index.html
4. "White House announces new partnership to unleash U.S. supercomputing resources to fight COVID-19," (2020). https://www.whitehouse.gov/briefings-statements
5. "arXiv announces new COVID-19 quick search," (2020). https://blogs.cornell.edu/arxiv/2020/03/30/new-covid-19-quick-search/
6. Sohrabi, C., et al.: World Health Organization declares global emergency: a review of the 2019 novel coronavirus (COVID-19). Int. J. Surg. **76**, 71–76 (2020)
7. Roser, M., Ritchie, H., Ortiz-Ospina, E., Hasell, J.: Coronavirus (COVID-19) Cases. (2020). https://ourworldindata.org/covid-cases
8. Fang, L., Karakiulakis, G., Roth, M.: Are patients with hypertension and diabetes mellitus at increased risk for COVID-19 infection? Lancet. Respir. Med. **8**(4), e21 (2020)
9. Wong, S.H., Lui, R.N., Sung, J.J.: Covid-19 and the digestive system. J. Gastroenterol. Hepatol. **35**(5), 744−748 (2020)
10. Baldwin, R., Tomiura, E.: Thinking ahead about the trade impact of COVID-19. In: Economics in the Time COVID-19, p. 59 (2020)
11. Surveillances, V.: The epidemiological characteristics of an outbreak of 2019 novel coronavirus diseases (COVID-19) China, 2020. China CDC Weekly **2**(8), 113–122 (2020)
12. Chen, H., et al.: Clinical characteristics and intrauterine vertical transmission potential of COVID-19 infection in nine pregnant women: a retrospective review of medical records. Lancet **395**(10226), 809–815 (2020)
13. Wang, D., et al.: Clinical characteristics of 138 hospitalized patients with 2019 novel coronavirus-infected pneumonia in Wuhan, China. J. Amer. Med. Assoc. **323**(11), 1061 (2020)
14. Chen, N., et al.: Epidemiological and clinical characteristics of 99 cases of 2019 novel coronavirus pneumonia in Wuhan, China: a descriptive study. Lancet **395**(10223), 507–513 (2020)
15. Jiang, F., Deng, L., Zhang, L., Cai, Y., Cheung, C., Xia, Z.: Review of the clinical characteristics of coronavirus disease 2019 (COVID-19). J. Gen. Intern. Med. **35**(5), 1545–1549 (2020). https://doi.org/10.1007/s11606-020-05762-w
16. Salehi, S., Abedi, A., Balakrishnan, S., Gholamrezanezhad, A.: Coronavirus disease 2019 (COVID-19): a systematic review of imaging findings in 919 patients. Am. J. Roentgenol. **215**(1), 87–93 (2020). https://doi.org/10.2214/AJR.20.23034

17. Singhal, T.: A review of coronavirus disease-2019 (COVID-19). Indian J. Pediatrics **87**(4), 281–286 (2020)
18. World Health Organisation (WHO): Novel coronavirus (2019-nCoV). Situation report-SS. (2020). https://www.who.int/docs/default-source/coronaviruse/situation-reports/20200315-sitrep-55-covid-19.pdf?sfvrsn=33daa5cb_6
19. Goodfellow, I., Bengio, Y., Courville, A.: Deep learning. MIT press (2016)
20. Beck, B.R., Shin, B., Choi, Y., Park, S., Kang, K.: Predicting commercially available antiviral drugs that may act on the novel coronavirus (2019-nCoV), Wuhan, China through a drug-target interaction deep learning model. Comput. Struct. Biotechnol. J. **18**, 784–790 (2020)
21. Zhavoronkov, A., et al.: Potential COVID-2019 3C-like protease inhibitors designed using generative deep learning approaches. ChemRxi (2020)
22. Zheng, C., et al.: Deep learning-based detection for COVID-19 from chest CT using weak label. MedRxiv (2020)
23. Hu, Z., Ge, Q., Li, S., Jin, L., Xiong, M.: Artificial intelligence forecasting of COVID-19 in China. arXiv preprint arXiv:2002.07112 (2020)
24. COVID-19 open research dataset challenge (CORD-19): An AI challenge with AI2, CZI, MSR, Georgetown, NIH & The White House. (2020). www.kaggle.com/allen-institute-for-ai/CORD-19-research-challenge
25. IBM releases novel AI-powered technologies to help health and research community accelerate the discovery of medical insights and treatments for COVID-19. (2020). https://www.ibm.com/blogs/research/2020/04/ai-powered-technologies-accelerate-discovery-covid-19/
26. Mamoshina, P., Vieira, A., Putin, E., Zhavoronkov, A.: Applications of deep learning in biomedicine. Mol. Pharm. **13**(5), 1445–1454 (2016)
27. Cao, C., et al.: Deep learning and its applications in biomedicine. Genomics Proteomics Bioinform. **16**(1), 17–32 (2018)
28. Ekins, S., et al.: Exploiting machine learning for end-to-end drug discovery and development. Nature Mater. **18**(5), 435 (2019)
29. Hu, F., Jiang, J., Yin, P.: Prediction of potential commercially inhibitors against SARS-CoV-2 by multi-task deep model. arXiv preprint arXiv:2003.00728 (2020)
30. Ge, Y., et al.: A data-driven drug repositioning framework discovered a potential therapeutic agent targeting COVID-19. BioRxiv (2020)
31. Savioli, N.: One-shot screening of potential peptide ligands on HR1 domain in COVID-19 glycosylated spike (S) protein with deep Siamese network. arXiv preprint arXiv:2004.02136 (2020)
32. Ton, A.T., Gentile, F., Hsing, M., Ban, F., Cherkasov, A.: Rapid identification of potential inhibitors of sars-cov-2 main protease by deep docking of 1.3 billion compounds. Molecular Informatics **39**(8), 2000028 (2020)
33. Hofmarcher, M., et al.: Large-scale ligand-based virtual screening for SARS-CoV-2 inhibitors using deep neural networks. SSRN 3561442 (2020)
34. Ong, E., Wong, M.U., Huffman, A., He, Y.: COVID-19 coronavirus vaccine design using reverse vaccinology and machine learning. BioRxiv (2020)
35. Jumper, J., Tunyasuvunakool, K., Kohli, P., Hassabis, D., Team, A.: Computational predictions of protein structures associated with COVID-19. DeepMind (2020)
36. Senior, A.W., et al.: Improved protein structure prediction using potentials from deep learning. Nature, **577**(7792), 706–710 (2020)
37. Strokach, A., Becerra, D., Corbi-Verge, C., Perez-Riba, A., Kim, P.M.: Fast and flexible design of novel proteins using graph neural networks. BioRxiv (2020)
38. Chenthamarakshan, V., et al.: Target-specific and selective drug design for COVID-19 using deep generative models. arXiv preprint arXiv:2004.01215 (2020)
39. Corman, V.M., et al.: novel coronavirus (2019-nCoV) by real-time RTPCR. Eurosurveillance **25**(3), 2020 (2019)

40. Fomsgaard, A.S., Rosenstierne, M.W.: An alternative workflow for molecular detection of SARS-CoV-2-escape from the NA extraction kit-shortage. medRxiv (2020)
41. Maghded, H.S., Ghafoor, K.Z., Sadiq, A.S., Curran, K., Rabie, K.: A novel AI-enabled framework to diagnose coronavirus COVID-19 using smartphone embedded sensors: design study. arXiv preprint arXiv:2003.07434 (2020)
42. Rao, A.S.S., Vazquez, J.A.: Identification of COVID-19 can be quicker through artificial intelligence framework using a mobile phone-based survey in the populations when cities/towns are under quarantine. Infect. Control Hosp. Epidemiol. **41**(7), 826-830 (2020)
43. Silva, B.M., Rodrigues, J.J., de la Torre Díez, I., López-Coronado, M., Saleem, K.: Mobile-health: a review of current state in 2015. J. Biomed. Inform. **56**, 265–272 (2015)
44. Pham, Q.-V., et al.: A survey of multi-access edge computing in 5G and beyond: fundamentals, technology integration, and state-of-the-art. CoRR arxiv.org/abs/1906.08452 (2019)
45. Afshar, P., Heidarian, S., Naderkhani, F., Oikonomou, A., Plataniotis, K.N., Mohammadi, A.: COVID-CAPS: a capsule network-based framework for identification of COVID-19 cases from X-ray images. Pattern Recogn. Lett. **138**, 638−643 (2020)
46. Chaganti, S., et al.: Quantification of tomographic patterns associated with COVID-19 from chest CT. arXiv preprint arXiv:2004.01279 (2020)
47. Ganasegeran, K., Abdulrahman, S.A.: Artificial Intelligence Applications in Tracking Health Behaviors During Disease Epidemics, pp. 141–155. Springer International Publishing, Cham (2020)
48. Liu, D., et al.: A machine learning methodology for real-time forecasting of the 2019–2020 COVID-19 outbreak using internet searches, news alerts, and estimates from mechanistic models. arXiv preprint arXiv:2004.04019 (2020)
49. Chinazzi, M., et al.: The effect of travel restrictions on the spread of the 2019 novel coronavirus (COVID-19) outbreak. Science **368**(6489), 395−400 (2020)
50. Hassija, V., Chamola, V., Saxena, V., Jain, D., Goyal, P., Sikdar, B.: A survey on IoT security: application areas, security threats, and solution architectures. IEEE Access **7**, 82721–82743 (2019)
51. Rouse, M.: What is IoMT (Internet of Medical Things) or Healthcare IoT?-Definition From WhatIs.com. IoT Agenda, (2015). https://internetofthingsagenda.techtarget.com/definition/IoMT-Internet-%of-Medical-Things
52. Deloitte Centre for Health Solutions. Medtech Internet Med. Things (2018). https://www2.deloitte.com/content/dam/Deloitte/global/Documents/Life-Sciences-Health-Care/gx-lshcmedtech-iomt-brochure.pdf
53. Rodrigues, J.J.P.C.: Enabling technologies for the Internet of health things. IEEE Access **6**, 13129–13141 (2018)
54. AMD Telemedicine. Telemedicine Defined. https://www.amdtelemedicine.com/telemedicineresources/telemedicine-defined.html. Accessed 20 Apr 2020
55. Hornyak, T.: What America Can Learn From China's Use of Robots and Telemedicine to Combat the Coronavirus. CNBC. (2020). https://www.cnbc.com/2020/03/18/how-china-isusing-robots-and-telemedic%ine-to-combat-the-coronavirus.html
56. Hinkley, G., Briskin, A., Waives, U.S.: Medicare and HIPAA Rules to Promote Telehealth. Pillsbury Law, (2020). https://www.pillsburylaw.com/en/news-and-insights/uswaivesmedicare-an%d-hipaa-rules-to-promote-telehealth.html
57. Makroo, S.: Technology and Business Order post COVID-19. Observer Research Foundation (ORF), (2020). https://www.orfonline.org/expert-speak/technology-and-business-order-postcovid-19-64471/
58. Mcneil, D.G.: Can smart thermometers track the spread of the Coronavirus? The New York Times, Mar. (2020). https://www.nytimes.com/2020/03/18/health/coronavirusfever-thermometer%s.html

59. Yang, G.-Z., et al.: Combating COVID-19-The role of robotics in managing public health and infectious diseases. Sci. Robot., **5**(40) (2020) Art. no. eabb5589. https://doi.org/10.1126/sci robotics.abb5589

60. Watson, J., Builta, J.: IoT Set to Play a Growing Role in the COVID-19 Response-Omdia. OMDIA. (2020). https://technology.informa.com/622426/iot-set-to-play-a-growin grole-in%-the-covid-19-response

61. D'mello, A.: First IoT Buttons Shipped for Rapid Response to Cleaning Alerts. IoT Now-How to Run an IoT Enabled Business, (2020). https://www.iot-now.com/2020/03/24/101940-rstiot-buttons-shipped-rapid-response-cleaning-alerts/

62. Burns, C.: Estimote wearables track workers to curb COVID-19 outbreak. SlashGear, (2020). https://www.slashgear.com/estimote-wearables-track-workers-to-curbcovid-19-out break-02615366/

63. Etherington, D.: Estimote launches wearables for workplace-level contact tracing for COVID-19. TechCrunch, (2020). https://techcrunch.com/2020/04/02/estimote-launcheswearables-for-workp%lace-level-contact-tracing-for-covid-19/

64. Deloitte: Understanding COVID-19's Impact on the Telecom Sector. Accessed: (2020). https://www2.deloitte.com/global/en/pages/about-deloitte/articles/covid19/understanding-covid-19-impact-on-the-telecom-sector.html

65. GlobalData: Telecom Sector Will Shine in Post Covid-19 Era, Says GlobalData. (2020). https://www.globaldata.com/telecom-sector-will-shine-in-post-covid-19-e%ra-says-globaldata/

66. Sohrabi, C., et al.: World health organization declares global emergency: a review of the 2019 novel coronavirus (COVID-19). Int. J. Surgery, **76**, 71–76 (2020)

67. Rouse, M.: What is IoMT (Internet of Medical Things) or Healthcare IoT. (2015). https://int ernetofthingsagenda.techtarget.com/definition/IoMT-Internet-of-Medical-Things

68. Garattini, C., Raffle, J., Aisyah, D. N., Sartain, F., Kozlakidis, Z.: Big data analytics, infectious diseases and associated ethical impacts. Philos. Technol. **32**(1), 69–85 (2019)

69. Li, C., et al.: High sensitivity detection of coronavirus SARS-CoV-2 using multiplex PCR and a multiplex-PCR-based metagenomic method. bioRxiv (2020)

70. Eden, J.-S., et al.: An emergent clade of SARS-CoV-2 linked to returned travellers from Iran. bioRxiv (2020)

71. Sohrabi, C., et al.: World Health Organization declares global emergency: a review of the 2019 novel coronavirus (COVID-19). Int. J. Surg. 76, 71–76 (2020)

72. Zhao, X., Liu, X., Li, X.: Tracking the spread of novel coronavirus (2019-ncov) based on big data. medRxiv (2020)

73. Zhou, C., et al.: COVID-19: challenges to GIS with big data. Geography Sustain. **1**(1), 77–87 (2020)

74. Haleem, A., Vaishya, R., Javaid, M., Khan, I.: Artificial Intelligence (AI) applications in orthopaedics: an innovative technology to embrace. J. Clin. Orthop. Trauma **11**, S80–S81 (2020). https://doi.org/10.1016/j.jcot.2019.06.012

75. Biswas, K., Sen, P.: Space-time dependence of coronavirus (COVID-19) outbreak. arXiv preprint arXiv:2003.03149 (2020)

76. How DAMO academy's AI system detects coronavirus cases. (2020). https://www.alizila.com/how-damo-academys-ai-system-detects-coronavirus-cases/

77. Kalkreuth, R., Kaufmann, P.: COVID-19: a survey on public medical imaging data resources. arXiv preprint arXiv:2004.04569 (2020)

78. Seoul introduces the COVID-19 AI monitoring call system. (2020). https://english.seoul.go.kr/seoul-introduces-the-covid-19-%E3%80%8Cai-monitoring-call-systemE3808D/

79. Hussain, A.A., Bouachir, O., Al-Turjman, F., Aloqaily, M.: AI techniques for COVID-19. IEEE Access **8**, 128776–128795 (2020). https://doi.org/10.1109/ACCESS.2020.3007939

80. Jin, J., Sun, W., Al-Turjman, F., Khan, M., Yang, X.: Activity pattern mining for healthcare. IEEE Access **8**(1), 56730–56738 (2020)
81. Ullah, Z., Al-Turjman, F., Mostarda, L., Gagliardi, R.: Applications of artificial intelligence and machine learning in smart cities. Elsevier Comput. Commun. J. **154**, 313–323 (2020)
82. Al-Turjman, F., Baali, I.: Machine learning for wearable iot-based applications: a survey. Wiley Trans. Emerging Telecommun. Technol. (2019). https://doi.org/10.1002/ett.3635
83. Srivastava, V., et al.: A systematic approach for the COVID-19 prediction and parameters estimation. Personal Ubiquitous Comput. J. (2020). 10.1007_s00779–020–01462–8
84. Karmore, S., et al.: IoT based humanoid software for identification and diagnosis of Covid-19 suspects. IEEE Sensors J. (2020). https://doi.org/10.1109/JSEN.2020.3030905
85. Kolhar, M., et al.: A three layered decentralized IoT biometric architecture for city lockdown during COVID-19 outbreak. IEEE Access **8**(1), 163608–163617 (2020)
86. Al-Turjman, F., Deebak, D.: Privacy-aware energy-efficient framework using internet of medical things for COVID-19. IEEE Internet of Things Mag. (2020). https://doi.org/10.1109/IOTM.0001.2000123
87. Rahman, M., et al.: Data-driven dynamic clustering framework for mitigating the adverse economic impact of covid-19 lockdown practices. Elsevier Sustain. Cities Soc. **62**, 102372 (2020)
88. Waheed, A., et al.: CovidGAN: data augmentation using auxiliary classifier GAN for improved covid-19 detection. IEEE Access **8**, 91916–91923 (2020)

Automated Segmentation of COVID-19 Lesion from Lung CT Images Using U-Net Architecture

Seifedine Kadry[1]([⊠]) ⓘ, Fadi Al-Turjman[2] ⓘ, and V. Rajinikanth[3] ⓘ

[1] Faculty of Applied Computing and Technology, Noroff University College, Kristiansand, Norway

[2] Artificial Intelligence Department, Research Center for AI and IoT, Near East University, Nicosia, Mersin 10, Turkey

[3] Department of Electronics and Instrumentation Engineering, St. Joseph's College of Engineering, Chennai, India

Abstract. Pneumonia caused by the novel Coronavirus Disease (COVID-19) is emerged as a global threat and considerably affected a large population globally irrespective of their age, race, and gender. Due to its rapidity and the infection rate, the World Health Organization (WHO) declared this disease as a pandemic. The proposed research work aims to develop an automated COVID-19 lesion segmentation system using the Convolutional Neural Network (CNN) architecture called the U-Net. The traditional U-Net scheme is employed to examine the COVID-19 infection present in the lung CT images. This scheme is implemented on the benchmark COVID-19 images existing in the literature (300 images) and the segmentation performance of the U-Net is confirmed by computing the essential performance measures using a relative assessment among the extracted lesion and the Ground-Truth (GT). The overall result attained with the proposed study confirms that, the U-Net scheme helps to get the better values for the performance values, such as Jaccard ($>86\%$), Dice ($>92\%$) and segmentation accuracy ($>95\%$).

Keywords: COVID-19 · Lung CT images · U-Net scheme · Segmentation · Performance validation

1 Introduction

Assessment of the disease in vital internal organ is very crucial and to assess the disease, considerable methodologies are followed including the bio-signal assisted procedures and bio-image assisted technique. The information existing in the bio-image based methodology is large compared to the signal based technique; and hence most of the diseases in the internal organs are widely assessed using the bio-image based methodologies. Due to its significance, a considerable number of bio-image modalities are developed and utilized to assess the disease in vital internal organs [1–3].

Lung is one of the vital internal organ; responsible to exchange the air between the atmosphere and other body sections. The disease in lung will severely affect the air

© ICST Institute for Computer Sciences, Social Informatics and Telecommunications Engineering 2021
Published by Springer Nature Switzerland AG 2021. All Rights Reserved
S. Paiva et al. (Eds.): SmartCity360° 2020, LNICST 372, pp. 20–30, 2021.
https://doi.org/10.1007/978-3-030-76063-2_2

exchange and this may cause very complicated situation, including the death. The abnormality in lung arises in various situations and pneumonia is one of the major causes of the lung abnormality and may cause very severe heath problem among the children (age < 5 years) and elderly people (age > 65 years). In humans, the pneumonia is caused due to a variety of reasons ranging from the climatic conditions to the virus/bacterium [4]. From the recent literature, it can be noted that, the infection due to COVID-19 causes a severe pneumonia in elderly people and the unrecognized and untreated COVID-19 will lead to death [5, 6].

From the literature, it can be noted that the COVID-19 infection is discovered only in December 2019, in China and due to the outbreak, the infection reached and affected almost all humans in the globe [7]. Even though a considerable number of precautionary measures are followed, the infection rate and the death rates are gradually rising till the date. The pneumonia due to the COVID-19 is discovered with; (i) RT-PCR test and (ii) Lung image assisted detection procedures [8–10]. The RT-PCR is a clinical trial, in which the samples collected from the infected patient is evaluated and confirmed with the possibility of the COVID-19 infection. When the RT-PCR test result is positive, then the patient is allowed to undergo the bio-medical imaging procedure using the imaging modality; Chest Radiograph (X-Ray) or the lung CT. From the earlier literature, it can be noted that, the assessment of the COVID-19 lesion with the lung CT is quite straight forward compared to the chest X-Ray [11, 12]. Hence, in most of the research works, the assessment of the lung CT is widely adopted compared to the chest X-Ray.

Due to its clinical significance, a considerable number of lung CT image examinations is proposed and implemented in the literature to detect the COVID-19 infection using the two-dimensional (2D) image slice of the chosen dimension. Every approach is implemented either a segmentation technique or a classification technique with the help of a chosen image examination technique. In the proposed research work, the examination of the COVID-19 lesion is assessed using the lung CT scan slices of the benchmark image dataset using a chosen segmentation technique.

In the proposed work, the COVID-19 infection is assessed using the lung CT images with the help of the Convolutional Neural Network (CNN) and the well-known CNN based segmentation technique called the U-Net is then employed to extract and evaluate the pneumonia infection from the chosen lung CT scan slices. The methodology implemented in the proposed work is as follows; (i) Collection of the 3D lung CT from the benchmark dataset, (ii) 3D to 2D conversion and resizing the 2D slices into images with dimension $572 \times 572 \times 1$ pixels, (iii) Implementation of the pre-trained U-Net architecture to extract the COVID-19 lesion, and (iv) Executing a comparative assessment among the extracted lung lesion and the GT and computing the performance measures to validate the performance of the U-Net scheme.

In the proposed work, 300 numbers of images are collected from the benchmark datasets [13, 14] available for the research purpose and the essential performance measures are computed to confirm the superiority of the proposed technique. The proposed technique is implemented using the MATLAB software and the segmentation binary image is then considered to confirm the superiority of the proposed technique based on the computed values of the Jaccard, Dice and segmentation Accuracy. The experimental result with the proposed research confirms that, proposed technique helped to achieve a better result on the considered lung CT images and extracts the COVID-19 infection with better segmentation accuracy.

The main contribution of the research work includes:

- Implementing U-Net to segment the COVID-19 lesion
- Considering the clinical-grade lung CT images for the experimental investigation
- Improved overall accuracy (>96%) is achieved

The remaining section of this paper is arranged as follows; Sect. 2 presents the context, Sect. 3 discusses the methodology implemented and Sect. 4 and 5 shows the results of the proposed work and the conclusion respectively.

2   Context

In recent days, due to its clinical importance, a number of lungs CT based COVID-19 evaluation proposals are discussed by the researchers with (i) Segmentation methods, (ii) Machine-Learning (ML) techniques and (iii) Deep-Learning (DL) approaches. The earlier works also substantiate that the lung CT assisted evaluation will offer a better diagnosis compared to the chest X-ray. Table 1 summarizes few earlier research works implemented with the lung CT to detect the COVID-19 lesion.

Table 1. Summary of COVID-19 infection assessment with lung CT scan slices

Reference	Implemented assessment technique
Ahuja et al. [8]	This research implemented a detailed comparative studies on well known DL schemes to examine the COVID-19 lesion using lung CT images. The proposed ResNet18 helped to attain a better classification accuracy (>98%) on the considered image dataset
Dey et al. [9]	This work proposed a ML scheme by combining the morphological segmentation and classification methods. In this work, the implemented segmentation offered an accuracy of >91% and the K-Nearest Neighbor (KNN) classifier helped to achieve a classification accuracy of >87%
Rajinikanth et al. [10]	Implementation of Otsu's thresholding based enhancement and watershed based segmentation is executed on the benchmark lung CT images and this work helped to propose a methodology to identify the COVID-19 infection rate
Kadry et al. [11]	This work implemented a ML scheme to examine the COVID-19 infection using the lung CT images and the Support Vector Machine (SVM) classifier helped to get a classification accuracy of >89%
Fan et al. [12]	This work proposed a novel segmentation scheme called the Inf-Net to segment the COVID-19 lesion from the lung CT images and achieved better segmentation accuracy on the considered images

(continued)

Table 1. (*continued*)

Reference	Implemented assessment technique
Ardakani et al. [15]	Development of a clinical computer-aided diagnosis system (COVIDiag) is proposed in this work. The developed COVIDiag is tested and validated on 612 patient's lung CT images and this system helped to attain an accuracy of >91%
Ardakani et al. [16]	This work implemented a detailed comparative study among ten DL schemes existing in the literature. In this work, 1020 lung CT images collected from 108 patients are evaluated and assessed
Chen et al. [17]	This work implemented a novel U-Net architecture to segment the COVID-19 lesions from the lung Ct images and the proposed scheme helped to attain a overall accuracy of 89%
Zhou et al. [18]	U-Net attenuation mechanism based segmentation is employed to extract the COVID-19 lesion from the lung CT images and this work helped to get a Dice score of 83.1%
Müller et al. [19]	Implementation of 3D U-Net is discussed in this work to segment the COVID-19 lesion from the lung CT images
Shi et al. [20]	This work presented a detailed review on the various artificial intelligence techniques employed during the collection, segmentation and classification of the lung images for the COVID-19 examination
Shoeibi et al. [21]	A detailed review on various DL system assisted COVID-19 lesion detection and forecasting using lung CT images are clearly presented and discussed

Table 1 confirms the availability of a considerable number of the image segmentation techniques to extract and evaluate the COVID-19 lesion using the lung CT images [20, 21]. Further, the CNN schemes, such as the U-Net architecture is also widely employed in the literature to extract and evaluate the COVID-19 lesion with better accuracy. The proposed research work in this paper also employed a traditional U-Net scheme to examine the lung CT images. The proposed technique is implemented using MATLAB software and the attained result (binary segmentation) is then considered to assess the performance of the proposed technique with the help of a comparative assessment with the existing Ground-Truth (GT) images.

3 Methodology

This section presents the methodology implemented in the proposed research work. Figure 1 depicts the various stages available in the proposed segmentation scheme.

The various phases existing in the proposed CT examination scheme is depicted in Fig. 1. Initially, the essential lung CT images (3D) are collected from the benchmark dataset. Assessment of 3D image needs major computation effort and hence, the 3D to 2D conversion is then executed using the ITK-Snap tool [22, 23]. The extracted 2D slices are then resized into $572 \times 572 \times 1$ pixels and the resized images are then considered to train

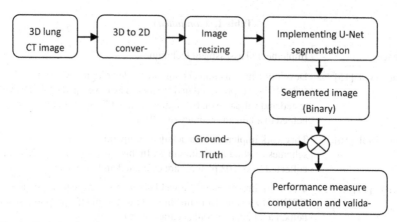

Fig. 1. Various phases involved in the proposed COVID-19 lesion segmentation system

and test the CNN based U-Net segmentation architecture. Initially, the U-Net scheme is trained with the original and augmented CT images and this procedure is repeated till the CNN trains completely to identify the COVID-19 lesion in the considered test image. The segmentation performance of the considered U-Net scheme is then confirmed based on a comparative assessment performed between the extracted COVID-19 lesion and the GT. During this comparison, essential image performance measures are computed and based on these values, the performance of the proposed technique is validated. The main need for the proposed approach is to extract the COVID-19 lesion automatically with improved accuracy. Based on the lesion dimension, the doctor can plan and implement the treatment to cure the infection.

3.1 Lung CT Image Collection

Due to its significance, a number of clinical grade lung CT images (healthy/COVID-19 class) are made available to the researchers. In this work, the COVID-19 class lung CT images available in [13, 14] is considered for the assessment. This dataset is one of the commonly adopted CT image dataset, since it has the clinical grade images collected from the real patients. Further, this database is available with the associated Ground-Truth provided by the image experts. Most of the benchmark lung CT images are available in 3D form and the assessment of the 3D images are quite complex compared to the 2D class. Hence, initially, ITK-snap tool is used to extract the 2D slice (Axial view) from the considered 3D images and the extracted 2D slices are resized into $572 \times 572 \times 1$. All the considered images are available along with the GT and 2D image of the GT (Axial view) is also extracted and resized into $388 \times 388 \times 1$. In the GT is a binary image in which the COVD-19 infection is assigned with a value of "1" and the background is assigned with a value of "0".

3.2 U-Net Segmentation

After preparing the essential test images (200 images from database 1 and 100 images from database 2) for the assessment, the traditional U-Net architecture is then employed to extract the COVID-19 infection with better accuracy. This work implements the U-Net architecture in MATLAB® environment using the workstation with the following specifications; Ryzen 5 quad core 2.1 GHz processor with 8 GB RAM and the implemented U-Net provides a segmentation result with a mean time of 107 ± 29 s.

Figure 2 shows the traditional U-Net architecture implemented in this research. The various stages of the scheme is clearly presented in this figure and from this scheme, it is clear that the input image given to this network is with a dimension of $572 \times 572 \times 1$ and the output image is with a dimension of $388 \times 388 \times 1$ pixels. To extract the essential information, this scheme implements both the down and the up convolution process and finally, it extracts the essential information from the image under study. In this work, the following initial parameters are assigned before training and testing the considered segmentation technique; number of iterations is assigned as 500, Number of Epochs are fixed as 50, the learning rate is assigned as 0.001. Initially, the considered images (original and augmented) are considered to test the segmentation performance of the U-Net and then all the considered original images are considered to test and validate the performance of the proposed scheme. The final outcome of the U-Net is a binary image with a dimension $388 \times 388 \times 1$ pixels and the extracted binary image is then compared against its GT and the essential image performance measures are then computed.

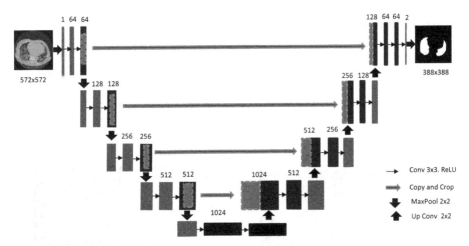

Fig. 2. Employed U-Net architecture considered to extract COVID-19 lesion

3.3 Performance Evaluation

The merit of any computer based image examination system is confirmed by computing the essential image performance measures. In this work, after extracting the COVD-19 lesion from the chosen test image, a comparison is then executed with the related GT and the essential performance measure is then computed.

The performance measures considered in this research is depicted in Eq. (1) to (6) [24–30]:

$$Jaccard = \frac{GT \cap SI}{GT \cup SI} \tag{1}$$

$$Dice = \frac{2|GT \cap SI|}{|GT| + |SI|} \tag{2}$$

$$Accuracy = \frac{TP + TN}{TP + TN + FP + FN} \tag{3}$$

$$Precision = \frac{TP}{TP + FP} \tag{4}$$

$$Sensitivity = \frac{TP}{TP + FN} \tag{5}$$

$$Specificity = \frac{TN}{TN + FP} \tag{6}$$

where GT is the ground-truth-image, SI is the segmented-image, TP, TN, FP and FN denotes true-positive, true-negative, false-positive and false-negative, respectively.

4 Result and Discussion

This section presents the experimental results and discussion attained in the proposed work. Initially the considered U-Net architecture is implemented on all the 300 images and the segmented COVID-19 lesion is then considered for the further assessment. Figure 3 presents a sample test image of the benchmark Database 1 and the corresponding result. Figure 3(a) and (b) depicts the test image and the binary GT. Figure 3(c) and (d) shows the saliency map and the binary SI respectively.

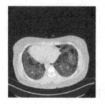  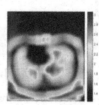 

(a) Test image   (b) Ground-truth   (c) Saliency map   (d) Extracted lesion

Fig. 3. Test image and various phase results attained using U-Net segmentation

Table 2 presents the outcome attained with the U-Net architecture for the test image depicted in Fig. 3(a). From this table, it can be noted that the accuracy will gradually rise when the number of iteration as well as the epoch rises and finally the U-Net produces the segmented image when the loss value equals to the assigned learning rate. Similar procedure is implemented on all other images of Database 1 [13] and Database 2 [14] considered in this study and the attained result are considered for further assessment.

Table 2. Sample results attained with the implemented U-Net scheme

Epoch	Iteration	Elapsed time (mm:ss)	Mini-batch		Learning rate
			Accuracy	Loss	
1	1	00:16	68.16%	3.1642	0.001
25	250	02.35	93.42%	0.6153	0.001
50	500	03.47	97.16%	0.0011	0.001

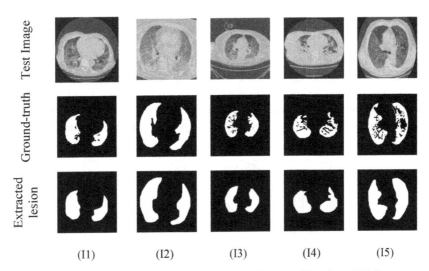

Fig. 4. Results attained with the sample test images of Database 2 [14]

Table 3. Preliminary image similarity measure

Image	TP	FP	TN	FN	Jaccard	Dice
I	6313	972	132938	528	0.8080	0.8938
I1	12333	339	127811	1304	0.8824	0.9375
I2	22392	635	108765	2060	0.8926	0.9432
I3	8284	304	132694	1381	0.8310	0.9077
I4	9519	243	128125	2130	0.8005	0.8892
I5	13796	761	113759	3546	0.7621	0.8650

Figure 4 depicts the sample test images, GT and extracted SI for the images of the database 2 and similar results are attained for all other test images. Tables 3 and 4 present the computed performance measures based on the comparison between the GT and SI. In these tables, the image I denotes the test image discussed in Fig. 3 and other images

Table 4. Essential similarity measure to confirm U-Net performance

Image	Accuracy	Precision	Sensitivity	Specificity
I	0.9893	0.8666	0.9228	0.9927
I1	0.9884	0.9732	0.9044	0.9974
I2	0.9799	0.9724	0.9158	0.9942
I3	0.9882	0.9646	0.8571	0.9977
I4	0.9831	0.9751	0.8172	0.9981
I5	0.9673	0.9477	0.7955	0.9934

are presented in Fig. 4. Table 3 and 4 confirms that, the performance measures, such as Jaccard, Dice and the segmentation accuracy is better for the considered images. Similarly, the performance measures for the images of database 1 and database 2 is separately compared as depicted in Fig. 5. This figure also confirms that, proposed CNN based segmentation technique works well on the considered lung CT images.

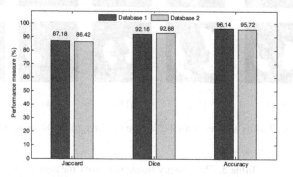

Fig. 5. Overall performance measures attained with U-Net segmentation

The experimental result of the proposed study confirmed that, the segmentation accuracy attained with the U-Net scheme is >95% and in future, the attained outcome can be compared with other traditional and CNN based segmentation techniques existing in the literature.

5 Conclusion

The proposed research work implemented a CNN supported segmentation to extract and evaluate the COVID-19 infection in lung CT images. The traditional U-Net scheme is employed to mine the COVID-19 lesion from the chosen test images. The proposed scheme help to process the images with $572 \times 572 \times 1$ pixels and after the processing, the implemented U-Net helps to offer a binary SI with a dimension of $388 \times 388 \times 1$ pixels. The procedure implemented on 300 test images offers a better overall performance measures, such as Jaccard (>86%), Dice (>92%) and Accuracy (>95%) is superior with the proposed automated segmentation technique. In future, a CNN classification can be included along with the U-Net in order to classify the lung CT images into normal/COVID-19 class. Further, the performance of U-Net can be improved using VGG16 architecture as the encoder section (VGG-Unet).

References

1. Khan, M.A., et al.: Computer-aided gastrointestinal diseases analysis from wireless capsule endoscopy: a framework of best features selection. IEEE Access **8**, 132850–132859 (2020)
2. Bakiya, A., Kamalanand, K., Rajinikanth, V., Nayak, R., Kadry, S.: Deep neural network assisted diagnosis of time-frequency transformed electromyograms. Multimedia Tools Appl. **79**(15–16), 11051–11067 (2018). https://doi.org/10.1007/s11042-018-6561-9
3. Fernandes, S.L., Rajinikanth, V., Kadry, S.: A hybrid framework to evaluate breast abnormality using infrared thermal images. IEEE Consum. Electron. Mag. **8**(5), 31–36 (2019)
4. Bhandary, A., et al.: Deep-learning framework to detect lung abnormality–a study with chest X-Ray and lung CT scan images. Pattern Recogn. Lett. **129**, 271–278 (2020)
5. Nishiura, H., et al.: Closed environments facilitate secondary transmission of coronavirus disease 2019 (COVID-19). *MedRxiv* (2020)
6. Satapathy, S.C., Hemanth, D.J., Kadry, S., Manogaran, G., Hannon, N.M., Rajinikanth, V.: Segmentation and evaluation of COVID-19 lesion from CT scan slices-a study with Kapur/Otsu function and cuckoo search algorithm (2020)
7. Zu, Z.Y., et al.: Coronavirus disease 2019 (COVID-19): a perspective from China. Radiology **96**, E15–E25 (2020)
8. Ahuja, S., Panigrahi, B., Dey, N., Rajinikanth, V., Gandhi, T.: Deep transfer learning-based automated detection of COVID-19 from lung CT scan slices. Appl. Intell. **51**(1), 571–585 (2020). https://doi.org/10.1007/s10489-020-01826-w
9. Dey, N., Rajinikanth, V., Fong, S., Kaiser, M., Mahmud, M.: Social group optimization–assisted Kapur's entropy and morphological segmentation for automated detection of COVID-19 infection from computed tomography images. Cogn. Comput. **12**(5), 1011–1023 (2020). https://doi.org/10.1007/s12559-020-09751-3
10. Rajinikanth, V., Dey, N., Raj, A.N.J., Hassanien, A.E., Santosh, K.C., Raja, N.: Harmony-search and Otsu based system for coronavirus disease (COVID-19) detection using lung CT scan images. arXiv preprint arXiv:2004.03431 (2020)
11. Kadry, S., Rajinikanth, V., Rho, S., Raja, N.S.M., Rao, V.S., Thanaraj, K.P.: Development of a machine-learning system to classify lung CT scan images into normal/COVID-19 class. arXiv preprint arXiv:2004.13122 (2020)
12. Fan, D.P., et al.: Inf-Net: automatic COVID-19 lung infection segmentation from CT images. IEEE Trans. Med. Imag. **39**(8), 2626–2637 (2020)
13. Database 1. https://zenodo.org/record/3757476#.X0Jztcgza6k
14. Database 2. https://medicalsegmentation.com/covid19/
15. Ardakani, A.A., Acharya, U.R., Habibollahi, S., Mohammadi, A.: COVIDiag: a clinical CAD system to diagnose COVID-19 pneumonia based on CT findings. Eur. Radiol. **31**(1), 121–130 (2020)
16. Ardakani, A.A., Kanafi, A.R., Acharya, U.R., Khadem, N., Mohammadi, A.: Application of deep learning technique to manage COVID-19 in routine clinical practice using CT images: results of 10 convolutional neural networks. Comput. Biol. Med. **121**, 103795 (2020)
17. Chen, X., Yao, L., Zhang, Y.: Residual attention U-Net for automated multi-class segmentation of COVID-19 chest CT images. arXiv preprint arXiv:2004.05645 (2020)

18. Zhou, T., Canu, S., Ruan, S.: An automatic COVID-19 CT segmentation based on U-Net with attention mechanism. arXiv preprint arXiv:2004.06673 (2020)
19. Müller, D., Rey, I.S., Kramer, F.: Automated chest CT image segmentation of COVID-19 lung infection based on 3D U-Net. arXiv preprint arXiv:2007.04774 (2020)
20. Shi, F., et al.: Review of artificial intelligence techniques in imaging data acquisition, segmentation and diagnosis for COVID-19. IEEE Rev. Biomed. Eng. **4**, 4–15 (2021)
21. Shoeibi, A., et al.: Automated detection and forecasting of COVID-19 using deep learning techniques: a review. arXiv preprint arXiv:2007.10785 (2020)
22. Yushkevich, P.A., Gao, Y., Gerig, G.: ITK-SNAP: an interactive tool for semi-automatic segmentation of multi-modality biomedical images. In: 2016 38th Annual International Conference of the IEEE Engineering in Medicine and Biology Society (EMBC), pp. 3342–3345. IEEE, August 2016
23. ITK-Snap. https://www.itksnap.org/pmwiki/pmwiki.php
24. Liu, X., Lin, C.C., Muhammad, K., Al-Turjman, F., Yuan, S.M.: Joint data hiding and compression scheme based on modified BTC and image inpainting. IEEE Access **7**, 116027–116037 (2019)
25. Al-Turjman, F.: AI-powered IoT for COVID-19 (2020)
26. Rahman, M.A., Zaman, N., Asyhari, A.T., Al-Turjman, F., Bhuiyan, M.Z.A., Zolkipli, M.F.: Data-driven dynamic clustering framework for mitigating the adverse economic impact of COVID-19 lockdown practices. Sustain. Cities Soc. **62**, 102372 (2020)
27. Ramchandani, A., Fan, C., Mostafavi, A.: DeepCOVIDNet: an interpretable deep learning model for predictive surveillance of COVID-19 using heterogeneous features and their interactions. arXiv preprint arXiv:2008.00115 (2020)
28. Nagasubramanian, G., Sankayya, M., Al-Turjman, F., Tsaramirsis, G.: Parkinson data analysis and prediction system using multi-variant stacked auto encoder. IEEE Access **8**, 127004–127013 (2020)
29. Stephan, T., Al-Turjman, F., Balusamy, B.: Energy and spectrum aware unequal clustering with deep learning based primary user classification in cognitive radio sensor networks. Int. J. Mach. Learn. Cybern. 1–34 (2020)
30. Rajinikanth, V., Joseph Raj, A.N., Thanaraj, K.P., Naik, G.R.: A customized VGG19 network with concatenation of deep and handcrafted features for brain tumor detection. Appl. Sci. **10**(10), 3429 (2020)

COVID-19 Patient Care: A Content-Based Collaborative Filtering Using Intelligent Recommendation System

B. D. Deebak[1](✉) ⓘ and Fadi Al-Turjman[2] ⓘ

[1] Schoool of Computer Science and Engineering,
Vellore Institute of Technology, Vellore 632014, India
deebak.bd@vit.ac.in

[2] Department of Artificial Intelligence Engineering, Research Center for AI and IoT,
Near East University, Nicosia, Mersin 10, Turkey

Abstract. COVID-19 is a more transferable illness caused by a new novel coronavirus. It is highly emerging with efficient biosensors such as sensitive and selective that afford the diagnostic tools to infer the disease early. It can maintain a personalized healthcare system to evaluate the growth of disease under proper patient care. To discover as a personalized technology, the healthcare system prefers collaborative filtering. It can effectively deal with cold-start and sparse-data to conduct useful extensions. Due to the continuous expansion of scaling data in a medical scenario, content-based, collaborative filtering, and similarity metrics are preferred. It relies on the most similar social users or threats when the information is large. Many neighbors gain importance to obtain a set of users with whom a target user is likely to match. Forming communities reveal vulnerable users and also reduce the challenges of collaborative filtering like data-sparsity and cold-start problems. Thus, this framework proposes content-based collaborative filtering using intelligent recommendation systems (CCF-IRS) based on high correlation and shortest neighbor in the social community. The result is shown that the proposed CCF-IRS achieves better accuracy than the existing algorithms.

Keywords: COVID-19 · Healthcare · Content-based · Collaborative filtering · Recommendation systems · Accuracy

1 Introduction

A novel coronavirus known as SARS-CoV2 has widely been transferred across Wuhan to other parts of the country. This transferrable infection was unacquainted until it had been a chain of occurrences at Wuhan in early December 2019 [1]. In the past nine months, it has been widely dispersed that reports 27 million as reported case, 18 million as recovered case, and 881,000 as the death case [2]. In general, it has some common symptoms such as fever, loss of strength and energy, nasal clog, sore throat, and dry cough. An elderly person with medical complexities such as diabetes, heart disease, and

S. Paiva et al. (Eds.): SmartCity360° 2020, LNICST 372, pp. 31–44, 2021.
https://doi.org/10.1007/978-3-030-76063-2_3

hypertension are bearing with a continual illness, whereas an individual with deprivation, cough, and fever must inquire for a proper health checkup [3]. This infection is so viral among the people when they are closely contacted. On the other hand, the people should keep up a minimum distance of 3 feet to control the spread out during sniffing or talking. This infectious virus may survive up to 72 h on the contact surfaces. Therefore, a protective system is recommended to measure the safety precautions including a face mask, handwash, and sanitization [4].

This has led to several strategical approaches such as self-isolation, lockdown, risk assessments, transport containment, and closure of provisional necessities. The SARS-CoV2 has been dominated as a global threat that affects thousands of people in various forms such as chest pressure, fatigue, repeated shaking with chills, and loss of taste. The healthcare and respiratory monitoring form a drone-based platform to meet the objectives of the defense department such as sensing temperature, crowd distancing, workforces, heart, and respiratory assistance [5]. A drone is generally represented as the aerial vehicle that aviates over a region like an aircraft without human intervention. It has specific hardware and embedded system to design a suitable aerial vehicle that tracks the payload to improve the information efficiency and accuracy [6]. It may be modernized to visualize the sourcing model that explores the concept of crowdsourcing to perform several societal activities such as work, information, opinion. In this pandemic, it is widely used to monitor the system functionalities including thermal scanning, food supply, alter system, and medication [7].

Any form of personal data may result in the outcome of electronic activities to categorize the information as personal or professional. It may protect the sensitive data of the people to preserve privacy rights. Of late, SARS-CoV2 has caused several causalities that is nowadays growing exponentially across the globe. World Health Organization (WHO) has declared the disease as a pandemic outbreak that essentially demands technological tools, intellectual mechanisms, and network resources to save the human's life [8]. It is severely affecting people living in terms of fever, dry cough, and tiredness. Approximately, 80% of people have developed a mild infection and recovered without hospitalization. However, the symptoms such as chest pain, pressure, suffocation, loss of moment are found to be more vulnerable. In addition, people with medical ailments namely diabetes, cancer, respiratory issue, and cardiovascular disease may have a severe illness causing sudden death. Unfortunately, this disease does not have any proper treatment or vaccination to examine potential threats. Due to a lack of medical procedures and treatment, people should proactively prevent the infection by frequent hand-wash, wearing-mask, and stay-home [9].

The drone-based system integrates the distinct features of mission-centric regions such as red, orange, and green zone to deploy thermal screening, sanitization, contact tracing, and patient tracking. A smart healthcare system collects the medical data to observe patient conditions using a recommendation system that uses the information filters to provide a better-personalized recommendation [10]. It can be available as a search engine that periodically examines the input queries to process a set of contextual information of the users. Accordingly, it can generate a ranking list for the precaution measures that suit the standard requirement of the public or government. Since the treatment case may grow exponentially due to more public threats, a suitable recommender is highly necessitated to maintain the threat list in terms of region-wise or state-wise. However, the online database should be properly handled to solve the issue of overloading and network mapping. To determine the relevant information in the massive dataset, a suitable strategy such as collaborative filtering may be applied. It allows the recommendation system to filter the relevant information quickly that improves the application loyalties to save human life.

It is intended to offer a suitable web forum or intelligent application that acts as a real-time entity to monitor the activities of the patient. This system may widely be implemented to serve the purpose of public communities including schools, colleges, airports, transport, shopping malls, government, and industrial sectors. It has a product of an intelligent recommendation system (I-RS) to motivate the researchers to categorize the filtering methods into content-based, collaborative-filtering, and hybrid. These methods rely on the personal information of the patient that has a problem of privacy leak to ensure a feature of credible preference to the medical analysis. It may demand a mutual trust to prevent the data leakage containing the collaborative filter that protects the identities of the patient and the systems. Thus, this paper presents content-based collaborative filtering using intelligent recommendation systems (CCF-IRS) to offer data privacy and confidentiality. The proposed CCF-IRS mitigates the error deduction rate to measure the data trust in terms of similarity and trusted-criterion.

The remaining sections are as follows: Sect. 2 discusses the similar collaborative techniques to signify the use of similarity models. Section 3 shows a drone-based smart intelligence to signify the essential characteristics of three computing platforms including edge, fog, and cloud. Section 4 presents content-based collaborative filtering using intelligent recommendation systems. Section 5 shows the examination results of the proposed CCF-IRS and other collaborative techniques. Section 6 concludes the research work.

2   Related Works

To support data confidentiality and reduce the system error rate, various solutions have been proposed. Generally, it can categorize the recommendation systems into five types such as cryptographic, perturbation, data mining, and trust-based in social communities. Erkin et al. [11] introduced a cryptographic algorithm to privatize data access. It uses a data encryption technique including public and private keys to protect data confidentiality. It relies on trusted third parties to generate a reliable private and public key to the users. As each user requires a unique public and private to generate a reliable key pair, it is consuming more time to complete the process of key generation. Ma et al. [12] designed a new Applet framework to preserve the user information that obtains the user status from the cloud environment. It uses Paillier encryption to calculate and store the user ranking in text format. However, this designed strategy cannot be more reliable to produce a key pair of public and private keys. Liu et al. [13] designed a homomorphic algorithm using elliptic-curve cryptography that generates public and private keys through trusted third parties to preserve data privacy. However, this technique is consuming more time to compute the complex operation. Shieh developed homomorphic encryption to generate a key pair between the real-time entities. Unfortunately, this method is consuming more time to deal with the error rate.

Soni and Panchal [14] introduced homomorphic encryption to preserve data privacy in the recommendation system. This mechanism uses trusted third parties to produce the key pairs that ensure data confidentiality. Patil and Jadhav [15] use collaborative-based homomorphic encryption to protect the privacy of the recommendation system. Kaur et al. [16] introduced a homomorphic method to generate the public and private through the knowledge of trusted third parties. Chen et al. [17] utilized a field of cryptography to create public and private keys. However, it could not be more reliable to cite in the referral systems. Li et al. [18] developed a randomized perturbation technique to offer privacy-preserving that demands the expectation levels of the recommendation systems. It uses noise-based perturbation to form collaborative filtering that generates a random number using perturbation to enhance the prediction rate. Dou et al. [19] introduced a privacy-preserving method that uses a perturbation technique to meet the requirements of the social networks. It has a core aspect of user activities to define the raging matrix that predicts the ranking of multimedia resources. It applies a perturbation function to guess the adversary activities. However, it cannot achieve a better privacy-preserving to improve system performance. Polatidis et al. [20] designed a multi-level method to preserve user privacy using collaborative filtering. It uses randomized perturbation to rate the server access in-network domains.

It is worthy to note that the randomness provides better security protection, but the rate prediction is a bit complex to penetrate the rating process. Liu et al. [21] and Xiong et al. [22] utilized differential privacy and randomized perturbation that uses a perturbation technique to release the private data. These methods apply a privacy-preserving technique to increase the accuracy rate of user privacy. Goyal et al. [23] combined classification and clustering to improve rating efficiency, but cannot protect user privacy. Ma et al. [24] proposed a lightweight privacy-preserving technique that applies a random trust relationship to analyze the attributes of the social network using the KNN algorithm. Heidari et al. [25] use a clustering method to categorize the attributes of the big data. It can reduce the error rate efficiency, but does not affect the data confidentiality.

3   Drone-Based Smart Intelligent Systems

This section presents a drone-based smart intelligence system that integrates artificial intelligence to include learning techniques such as machine learning and deep learning to analyze the real-time data effectively. The service-based networking includes the Internet of Things (IoT), Internet of Medical Things, Internet of Vehicle, and Internet of Drone that uses AI technology to process the data efficiently. Besides, it has network computing resources such as fog, cloud, and edge to functionalize data storage, location tracking, distance tracing, face mask, etc. The smart-driven technology associates with user profiling to monitor the commuter movement that cautiously analyses the activities such as testing, tracing, observing, treating, recovering, and monitoring during this pandemic situation. Figure 1 shows the proposed architecture of drone-based smart intelligence that regulates three key factors such as control, monitoring, and analytics to meet the objectives of the mission-intelligent systems. This smart system architecture has six technological components, which are as follows:

Thermal Imaging: It is an alternative strategy to deploy the sensory platform to examine the collective information. It uses a drone-based camera to capture and analyze people's information including thermal reading and distance measurement.

Wearable Sensory System: This architecture deploys the sensory platform to observe commuter environments including public transport, shopping mall, school, and college. It uses a wearable sensor or ground movement detector to examine the surveillance areas. It uses interconnected networks such as the wearable body area network, Internet of Things, and the Internet of Medical Things to collect, observe, and analyze the statistical data. A patient under observation can be regulated using a wearable sensory system. In specific cases, a drone-navigator can be deployed to collect the patient's movements including tracking, tracing, treating, and observing the activities of the patients. On the other hand, the patient movements are continuously monitored using multiple servers to store the activities in big data. It uses computing platforms such as edge, fog, and cloud to maintain data modeling, profiling, processing, and analyzing the real-time data. The collective data are regulated under the government policies to operate any system procedures in the medical boards. The proposed strategy endures to tackle the pandemic situation to govern the people activities such as person profiling, location tracking, and data observation that integrates the wearable sensory system to formulate the design strategy of Industrial IoT. It can interconnect the sensory systems with medical intelligence to process the clinical trails such as drug supply, patient tracking, consulting, storage, and analysis.

Edge Networking: This system standardizes the data modeling and decision-making process that saves the computing resources to maintain the collection of medical data. It uses a drone network to handle discrete decisions in real-time. It is more useful to operate the system instruction to address the key challenges such as time stipulation, system interconnection, and computing tasks. The proposed system considers the data transfer cost to increase the feature of scalability that requires system intelligence and network resources to transfer the network costs.

Fog Networking: The proposed system incorporates the system intelligence to handle user profiling that executes decision-making and data monitoring to maintain the patient profile including commuter trajectory.

Cloud Networking: The proposed system applies application-level to pattern the regulation policies such as patient recognition, tracking, decision making, distance measuring, and sanitization. It can handle high-end computing systems to provide a comprehensive analysis.

Drone System: It uses a closed-circuit television (CCTV) to cover the surveillance areas including thermal screening, drug delivery, scanning, and sanitization. It can integrate the resources such as biosensors, accelerometers, and microelectromechanical systems to constitute a large data transfer and analysis. There are few important drones such as Parrot Mambo and DJI Phantom 3 Pro to navigate the indoor hospital system. It may also use radar or optical system to avoid collision avoidance that has a large number of aerial vehicles or drones to regulate various computing services such as public movement, transportation, aviation, etc.

Control Room and Covid-19 Monitoring: This system regulates the data observation to monitor the hotspots remotely that executes the necessary actions to control the individual's movements.

Data Processing, Capturing, and Analytical Flow: The proposed system uses drone-based intelligence to monitor or capture the patient information. However, it is still challenging to address privacy and security concerns.

Confidence-Based Trust Model: It considers patient profiling and trusted network groups to design a trust model that assigns different trust values to the patients according to the risk of region vulnerabilities. To group the trusted users in any network, the trusted values play a crucial role that infers the nature of user vulnerability in terms of risk ranking. It is typically based on the community networks to represent whether the trusted users are known to each other or not.

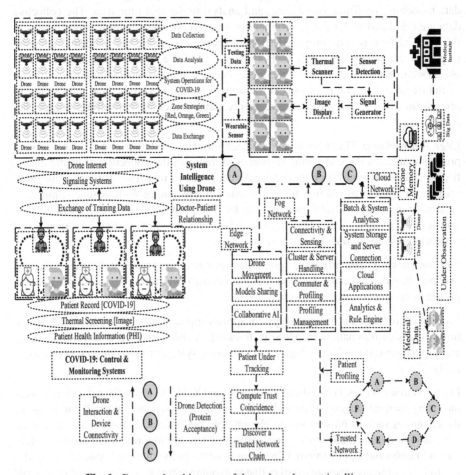

Fig. 1. Proposed architecture of drone-based smart intelligence

4 Proposed CCF-IRS

This section presents content-based collaborative filtering using intelligent recommendation systems with the detection of threat rates. The proposed CCF-IRS discusses content-based recommendation and collaborative filtering to mine the network communities in the trusted networks.

4.1 Content-Based Trust Recommendation

A content-based trust recommender has its own root to find the relevant information retrieval that applies a searching technique of information filtering. It can recommend similar items to the one that the user tries to prefer in the past. Most of the existing recommender systems focus on textual information including books, news, and documents. In any intelligent system, the content is generally labeled with keywords, thus informativeness of any keywords is measured using the weight of term frequency-inverse document frequency (TF-IDF). Any profiling document weights a keyword that denotes the term frequency (TF), while the weight of a keyword is defined as the inverse document frequency (IDF). However, content-based recommender has several limitations that are as follows:

Limited Content Analysis: The systems have difficulty applying the inherent problems with automatic feature extraction such as user profiling.

Overspecialization: The system has the recommended items to find the limitation of similar items, which are already rated by the users.

New User Problem: The content-based recommender uses preference settings to rate sufficient user profiling, hence it cannot recommend any user profiles with few user ratings.

4.1.1 Algorithm 1: Content-Based Rating, Offering by Social Community S_C for a Common Person P

In content-based vectorization, the social threats or items represent a rating mechanism that aims at user ranking r_u of a given user-item offering by S_C which is yet to rate in social networks. The formulation utilizes TF and IDF to recommend the nature of user profiling. It has a set of user items su and social threats T'_{su} to rank the social user su, which is yet to rate. While a score s is computed for the given unrated items u_i, Algorithm 1 gives careful consideration to two scoring strategies:

1. Firstly, it applies the cosine similarity score of all the social items in T'_{su}. It can aggregate k social items enduring the cosine similarity in the highest form. Later on, p is a parameter of the contention model to denote the approach as '$p - Approach$'.
2. Secondly, a single vectorization is represented to obtain a key parameter T'_{su} that achieves the $n - dimension$ vector to represent the social threat T'_{su}. It has an $n - dimensional$ vector centroid $T'_{su} = \langle vc_1, vc_2, vc_3, \ldots\ldots, vc_n \rangle$ in which each user entry defines its own relevance score to the corresponding term T_d averaging over the social items in T'_{su}:

$$T_d = \frac{1}{\left|T'_{S_u}\right|} \cdot \sum_{i \in T'_{S_u}} v_{id} \tag{1}$$

Then, the assigned score i defines the cosine similarity between vector i and centroid T'_{su}. It utilizes the relevance score to evaluate whether the representation of the individual items in T'_{su} adds a reasonable value over a reduced error rate.

4.2 Collaborative Filtering Techniques

This technique is widely used to build recommender systems that classify into memory-based and model-based approaches. In the former approach, the user-item matrix is applied to signify input and predicted user interest that directly uncovers the complex and unpredicted patterns from the past behavior of the recommended items. The users with similar interests and profiling preferences have a perfect combination to explore network communication in a social environment. It can find whether any user coincides with similar profiling agreed with each other in the past or not.

Table 1. Merit and key issues in memory-based approach

Name	Merits	Key Issues
User-based	• No content analysis • Domain-independent • Quality improves • Bottom-up approach • Serenity	• New user problem • New item problem • Popular taste • Scalability • Sparsity • Cold start problem
Item-based	• Focus on items; assume that the items rated similarly are probably similar. • It recommends items with the highest correlation	• New item problem • Popular taste • Sparsity • Cold start problem

It is more likely to agree with each profiling that randomly chooses the users in the future as well. The memory-based approach is typically divided into a user-based and item-based method. The former predicts the unknown threat rating from similar user profiling over the weighted average, whereas the latter predicts the threat rating from the user profiling over the average weighted rating by the same communities. However, it has some significant issues to tabulate (see Table 1). On the other hand, the item-based technique correlates the social threats using mining or similarity ratings before any threat is recommended newly (see Fig. 2). This technique deals with the 'cold start' problem because it is depended on sufficient user behavior from the past. When the systems execute the collaborative filtering technique for a while, this problem endures to emerge the rating when new users or items are newly added. On the one hand, the new users should give sufficient ratings for the social items in order to provide an accurate recommendation based on the user-based method. On the other hand, the new items should rate with a sufficient number of community users when any social items are under community threats. Additionally, it deals with the 'sparsity' upon the user action taken on the networks. Since these filtering techniques rely on community-driven information, community threats are supposed to be more common across the regions. The learners with an unusual threat may have less qualitative recommendations, while the learners with common threats are unlikely to classify the highly vulnerable threats.

Hence, the common problem of the filtering technique is scalability, thereby it cannot deal with large amounts of data to provide a proper recommendation to the global communities in real-time exceeding in 27.4 million.

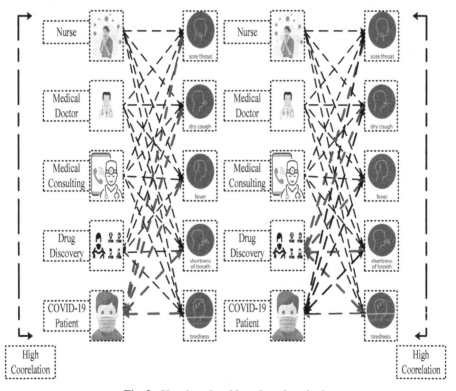

Fig. 2. User-based and item-based methods

To measure the correlations, several similarity measures are available listed below. It is assumed that $su = \{su_1, su_2, su_3, \ldots\ldots, su_N\}$ and $t = \{t_1, t_2, t_3, \ldots\ldots, t_M\}$ are the set of social users and threats respectively. The rating matrix of social-user-threat is denoted by $R = (r_{ij})_{NxM}$, where $i = 1, 2, 3, \ldots\ldots, N$ and $j = 1, 2, 3, \ldots\ldots, M$. The Pearson correlation coefficient (PCC) and cosine (CoS) similarities are the most widely used to measure the similarities in collaborative filtering. The formulas are defined as follows:

$$(su, v)^{PCC} = \frac{\sum_{t\in I}(r_{su,t} - \overline{r_{su}}) \cdot (r_{v,t} - \overline{r_v})}{\sqrt{\sum_{t\in I}(r_{su,t} - \overline{r_{su}})^2} \cdot \sqrt{\sum_{t\in I}(r_{v,t} - \overline{r_v})^2}} \tag{2}$$

$$(su, v)^{cos} = cos(\overrightarrow{su}, \overrightarrow{v}) = \frac{\overrightarrow{su} \cdot \overrightarrow{v}}{\|\overrightarrow{su}\| \cdot \|\overrightarrow{v}\|} \tag{3}$$

where I defines the set of common social rating threats by the social users $su, v.\overline{r_{su}}, \overline{r_{su}}$ and $\overline{r_v}$ are the average rating values of su and v respectively. $r_{su,t}$ and $r_{v,t}$ defines the rating of the social threats t given by su and v respectively. $\overrightarrow{su}$ and $\overrightarrow{v}$ are the rated social vector su and v respectively. $\| \|$ is the vector magnitude vector. However, few shortages exist in both PCC and CoS to improve similarity measures. In general, the scale of social ratings is unqualified to analyze the metrics in recommender systems. The system infers the social ratings as positive or negative to determine the social impact in any social community. Hence, the Constrained Pearson correlation coefficient (CPCC) is defined as follows:

$$(su, v)^{CPCC} = \frac{\sum_{t\in I}(r_{su,t} - r_{med}) \cdot (r_{v,t} - r_{med})}{\sqrt{\sum_{t\in I}(r_{su,t} - r_{med})^2} \cdot \sqrt{\sum_{t\in I}(r_{v,t} - r_{med})^2}} \tag{4}$$

where r_{med} defines the rating scale median. To find a similarity the user profiling, $(su, v)^{CPCC}$ is utilized. It can predict the profiling on social items using the average ratings defined in Eq. (1).

5 Proposed CCF-IRS

This section shows the process of the proposed CCF-IRS that includes content-based rating and collaborative filtering to analyze the rating of active users.

We prefer to use the available social threats which are primarily focused as a pandemic threat of COVID-19. It is attracting global attention as it is being viewed as a serious threat to the socio-economic impacts. The infection is so common across the globe with some cautious symptoms such as dry cough $\langle 1 \rangle$, fever $\langle 2 \rangle$, fatigue $\langle 3 \rangle$, sore throat $\langle 4 \rangle$, conjunctivitis $\langle 5 \rangle$ that gradually develops from mild to moderate illness ≈ 5 to ≈ 9 days. However, the infectious cause may even take up ≈ 14 days to mutate its form as S and L type. The mutation process may change from asymptomatic to severe pneumonia that reviews with some typical symptoms such as headache, nausea, congestion, and vomiting. Thus, the clinical presentation considers some universal precautions to prevent further transmission. This transferable disease demands the use of a face mask to reduce the transmission rate across the various communities and workplaces. To provide an effective measure, a preprocessing strategy is applied with a scale of 5-threats. Each social user experiences at least some threats to define the set of social users as communities. The social user rates the infectious rate to represent the sequence of events that represent the correlation between the infection rate (see Fig. 3).

It has two basic assumptions to visualize the quality measurement that performs the maximum modularity using the Gephi tool.

1. Social user su_1 rates social threat I_1 with 4
2. Social user su_2 rates social threat I_2 with 3

A total of 56 communities has been identified with maximum modularity of $Q = 0.549$. The quality metric such as modularity is considered to analyze the library function using igraph in R. The proposed CCF-IRS considers the analytical dataset to determine the impact of the training sets that recommend the qualities of the original samples. It uses a cross-validation technique to partition the dataset into $k - samples$. It considers one subsample to validate the testing model that has two scenarios such as 90% of social user ratings and 40% of rating instances to test the real-time scenario.

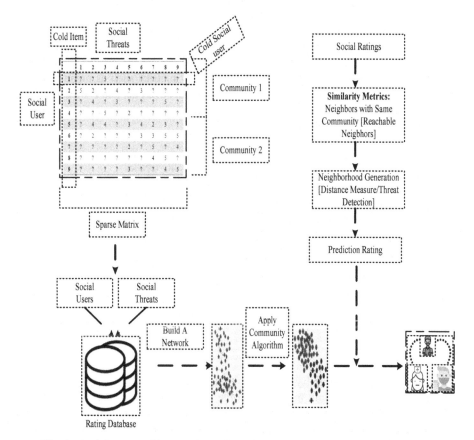

Fig. 3. Social communities and threats based collaborative recommendation system

In R Programming, the library known as recommender lab uses content-based collaborative filtering using intelligent recommendation systems that apply the quality metrics such as mean absolute error (MAE), root mean square error (RMSE), precision, coverage, and F-Measure to examine the prediction accuracy of the proposed CCF-IRS. The metrics are defined as follows:

$$MSE = \frac{1}{t} \cdot \sum_{Su,v} \left| R_{su,v} - \overline{R_{su,v}} \right| \tag{5}$$

$$RMSE = \sqrt{\frac{1}{t} \cdot \sum_{su,v} \left(R_{su,v} - \overline{R_{su,v}} \right)^2} \tag{6}$$

$$Precision = 1 - \frac{(RMSE)}{4} \tag{7}$$

$$Coverage = \frac{su}{N} \tag{8}$$

$$F - Measure = \frac{\langle 2 * Precision * Coverage \rangle}{\langle Precision + Coverage \rangle} \tag{9}$$

where $R_{su,v}$ represents the rating provided by social users over su and v, $\overline{R_{su,v}}$ represents the prediction rating, and t represents the cumulative tested ratings. Table 2 estimates the performance efficiencies of different quality metrics such as mean absolute error (MAE), root mean square error (RMSE), precision, coverage, and F-Measure. The examination reveals that the proposed CCF-IRS achieves better performance efficiency than other collaborative techniques.

Table 2. Performance of different quality metrics

Algorithms	$RMSE$	MAE	$Precision$	$Recall$	$F - Measure$
Item-based CF	1.271	0.942	0.844	0.7264	0.756
SNCF	1.254	0.887	0.896	0.742	0.796
Proposed CCF-IRS	1.243	0.872	0.912	0.889	0.861

6 Conclusion

In this paper, a typical drone-based smart intelligence has been proposed for COVID-19 patient care. It can mainly investigate some quality measures such as face masks, social distancing, sanitization, statistical analysis, and report analysis to control the infection rate. This framework gathers the sensitive data of the patient using wearable or movement sensors in any targeted area through thermal image-screening. It may apply a multi-layered architecture to examine the statistical data and to make any decision-making. Moreover, it has an edge, fog, and cloud computing to build technological intelligence before any decision is made. To improve the preferential measurement and quality recommendation, this paper has proposed CCF-IRS. It uses similarity models to validate the effectiveness of quality measures. The proposed CCF-IRS integrates content-based and collaborative filtering to resolve the issues of cold-start and sparsity-data. It can explore user profiling to infer the difficulties of the user communities that typically view the systematic flows of social threats. The experimental result reveals that the proposed CCF-IRS achieves better performance measures than other collaborative techniques. In the future, we will explore the similarity computation of trusted users pertaining to the same communities.

References

1. Suliman, K., et al.: Emergence of a novel coronavirus, severe acute respiratory syndrome coronavirus 2: biology and therapeutic options. J. Clin. Microbiol. **58**(5) (2020)
2. Kumar, A., Sharma, K., Singh, H., Naugriya, S., Gill, S., Buyya, R.: A drone-based networked system and methods for combating coronavirus disease (COVID-19) pandemic. Future Gener. Comput. Syst. **115**, 1–19 (2021). https://doi.org/10.1016/j.future.2020.08.046
3. Singer, M., Baer, H., Long, D., Pavlotski, A.: Introducing medical anthropology: a discipline in action. Rowman & Littlefield (2019)
4. World Health Organization. Water, sanitation, hygiene, and waste management for SARS-CoV-2, the virus that causes COVID-19: interim guidance, 29 July 2020 (No. WHO/COVID-19/IPC_WASH/2020.4). World Health Organization (2020)
5. Kuula, J.: The hyperspectral and smartphone technology in CBRNE countermeasures and defence. Jyväskylä Stud. Comput. **256** (2016)
6. Meier, L., Tanskanen, P., Heng, L., Lee, G.H., Fraundorfer, F., Pollefeys, M.: PIXHAWK: a micro aerial vehicle design for autonomous flight using onboard computer vision. Auton. Robot. **33**(1–2), 21–39 (2012)
7. Liang, T.: Handbook of COVID-19 prevention and treatment. The First Affiliated Hospital, Zhejiang University School of Medicine. Compiled According to Clinical Experience, 68 (2020)
8. Jeffery Reeves, J., et al.: Rapid response to COVID-19: health informatics support for outbreak management in an academic health system. J. Am. Med. Inform. Assoc. **27**(6), 853–859 (2020). https://doi.org/10.1093/jamia/ocaa037
9. Fong, S., Dey, N., Chaki, J.: Artificial Intelligence for Coronavirus Outbreak. Springer Singapore, Singapore (2021)
10. Manogaran, G., Varatharajan, R., Lopez, D., Kumar, P.M., Sundarasekar, R., Thota, C.: A new architecture of Internet of Things and big data ecosystem for secured smart healthcare monitoring and alerting system. Future Gener. Comput. Syst. **82**, 375–387 (2018)
11. Erkin, Z., Veugen, T., Toft, T., Lagendijk, R.L.: Generating private recommendations efficiently using homomorphic encryption and data packing. IEEE Trans. Inf. Forensics Secur. **7**(3), 1053–1066 (2012)
12. Xindi, M., et al.: APPLET: a privacy-preserving framework for location-aware recommender system. Sci. China Inf. Sci. **60**(9), 092101 (2017)
13. Liu, K., Giannella, C., Kargupta, H.: A survey of attack techniques on privacy-preserving data perturbation methods. In: Aggarwal, Charu C., Yu, Philip S. (eds.) Privacy-Preserving Data Mining, pp. 359–381. Springer US, Boston, MA (2008). https://doi.org/10.1007/978-0-387-70992-5_15

14. Soni, K., Panchal, G.: Data security in recommendation system using homomorphic encryption. In: Satapathy, S.C., Joshi, A. (eds.) ICTIS 2017. SIST, vol. 83, pp. 308–313. Springer, Cham (2018). https://doi.org/10.1007/978-3-319-63673-3_37

15. Patil K., Jadhav N.: Multi-layer perceptron classifier and Paillier encryption scheme for friend recommendation system. In: International conference on computing, pp. 1–5. IEEE (2017)

16. Kaur, H., Kumar, N., Batra, S.: An efficient multi-party scheme for privacy preserving collaborative filtering for healthcare recommender system. Future Gener. Comput. Syst. **86**, 297–307 (2018)

17. Chen, S., Rongxing, L., Zhang, J.: A flexible privacy-preserving framework for singular value decomposition under internet of things environment. In: Steghöfer, J-P., Esfandiari, B (eds.) IFIPTM 2017. IAICT, vol. 505, pp. 21–37. Springer, Cham (2017). https://doi.org/10.1007/978-3-319-59171-1_3

18. Li, D., et al.: An algorithm for efficient privacy-preserving item based collaborative filtering. Future Gener. Comput. Syst. **55**, 311–320 (2016)

19. Dou, K., Guo, B., Kuang, L.: A privacy-preserving multimedia recommendation in the context of social network based on weighted noise injection. Multimedia Tools Appl. **78**(19), 26907–26926 (2017). https://doi.org/10.1007/s11042-017-4352-3

20. Polatidis, N., Georgiadis, C.K., Pimenidis, E., Mouratidis, H.: Privacy-preserving collaborative recommendations based on random perturbations. Expert Syst. Appl. **71**, 18–25 (2017)

21. Liu, X., Liu, A., Zhang, X., Li, Z., Liu, G., Zhao, L., Zhou, X.: When differential privacy meets randomized perturbation: a hybrid approach for privacy-preserving recommender system. In: Candan, S., Chen, L., Pedersen, T.B., Chang, L., Hua, W. (eds.) DASFAA 2017. LNCS, vol. 10177, pp. 576–591. Springer, Cham (2017). https://doi.org/10.1007/978-3-319-55753-3_36

22. Xiong, P., Lefeng, Z., Tianqing, Z., Gang, L., Wanlei, Z.: Private collaborative filtering under untrusted recommender server. Future Gener. Comput. Syst. (2018). https://doi.org/10.1016/j.future.2018.05.077

23. Goyal, N., Aggarwal, N., Dutta, M.: A novel way of assigning software bug priority using supervised classification on clustered bugs data. In: El-Alfy, E.-S.M., Thampi, S.M., Takagi, H., Piramuthu, S., Hanne, T. (eds.) Advances in intelligent informatics. AISC, vol. 320, pp. 493–501. Springer, Cham (2015). https://doi.org/10.1007/978-3-319-11218-3_44

24. Ma, X., Ma, J., Li, H., Jiang, Q., Gao, S.: ARMOR: a trust-based privacy-preserving framework for decentralized friend recommendation in online social networks. Future Gener. Comput. Syst. **79**, 82–94 (2018)

25. Heidari, S., Alborzi, M., Radfar, R., Afsharkazemi, M., Rajabzadeh Ghatari, A.: Big data clustering with varied density based on MapReduce. J Big Data **6**(1), 1–16 (2019). https://doi.org/10.1186/s40537-019-0236-x

26. Al-Turjman, F., Deebak, B.D.: Privacy-aware energy-efficient framework using the internet of medical things for COVID-19. IEEE Internet of Things Mag. **3**(3), 64–68 (2020)

27. Deebak, B.D., Al-Turjman, F.: A novel community-based trust aware recommender systems for big data cloud service networks. Sustain. Cities Soc. **61**, 102274 (2020)

A New Blood Pressure Estimation Approach Using PPG Sensors: Subject Specific Evaluation over a Long-term Period

Franck Mouney[1,2]([✉]), Teodor Tiplica[1], Jean-Baptiste Fasquel[1], Magid Hallab[2], and Mickael Dinomais[3]

[1] LARIS Laboratory, Angers University, Angers, France
[2] Clinique Bizet, Service de Cardiologie, 23 Rue Georges Bizet, 75116 Paris, France
[3] CHU Angers, Angers, France

Abstract. In this paper, a new approach for predicting the blood pressure (BP) from the photoplethysmogram (PPG) signal is proposed related with a new original public dataset. The originality of the dataset is based on the fact that subjects are periodically monitored over weeks, while public datasets consider short acquisition periods. The proposed BP estimation approach uses key frequencies in the spectrum of the PPG signal isolated using the LASSO algorithm, then a predictive model is constructed as a patient-specific BP estimation model. The efficiency of the proposed methodology is evaluated on experimental data recorded over a long time period. Moreover, an evaluation of the various temporal markers of the PPG signal that have been proposed in the literature is conducted on the same data set. It is showed that only few of these temporal markers are useful for the estimation of the systolic and diastolic blood pressures. The results highlight that better blood pressure estimations are obtained when using the spectrum of the PPG signal rather than optimally selected temporal markers.

Keywords: Blood pressure estimation · LASSO · PPG · spectrum · Temporal markers · Dataset

1 Introduction

Arterial BP has always been a key physiological measurement in the frame of medical examination, being one of the most important bio-markers in clinical evaluation. Thus, continuously monitoring the BP in order to predict cardiovascular diseases is one of the major challenges for the next years.

Some recent surveys focus on the use of Ballistocardiogram signals [10], Electrocardiography (ECG) signals [20], or on both ECG and photoplethysmogram (PPG) signals [14,24] to predict BP. Many researchers focus their works on predicting cuff-less BP measurement from PPG signals only [16,19]. In this paper,

S. Paiva et al. (Eds.): SmartCity360° 2020, LNICST 372, pp. 45–63, 2021.
https://doi.org/10.1007/978-3-030-76063-2_4

one considers PPG-based BP estimation, because such an approach enables a non-invasive and continuous measurement from wearable sensors.

PPG based methods uses optical properties and the relationship between synchronous changes in the blood volume and the arterial BP [7]. Red or near infrared wavelengths are used for the PPG light source as they allow to correctly evaluate blood volume changes through absorption and reflection phenomenons of blood cells. Figure 1 illustrates the use of such sensor integrated in a wearable device (watch/band) for BP monitoring from a PPG signal.

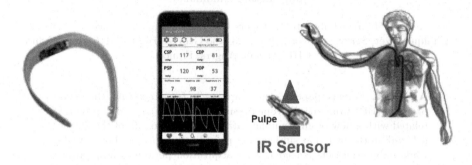

Fig. 1. Example of wearable device (watch) enabling to monitor PPG.

As it appears in the literature, BP estimation from PPG sensors has been mainly studied by considering time domain approaches [5,13,25]. Most of them involve signal pre-processing (smoothing, filtering, etc.), extraction of temporal features and finally data-based model for BP estimation.

Frequential features have been investigated for BP estimation. For instance, Fast Fourier Transform (FFT) has been recently considered to extract spectral information to estimate BP [30]. As recently underlined [19], spectral-domain-based techniques are more convenient as there is no need to detect pulse waves, compared to time-domain-based techniques. Note that some recent approaches combine both temporal and frequential information [2].

Besides BP estimation techniques, another crucial aspect concerns the PPG signal collection protocol to estimate the BP. According to Stergiou et al. [21], a new kind of validation protocols will be developed for continuous, cuff-less, and central BP monitors. The IEEE Std 1708^{TM} [1] was specifically studied to define the objective performance to evaluate wearable cuff-less BP measurement devices with different operating mode (e.g., to measure short-term, long-term, snapshot, continuous, beat(s)-to-beat(s) BP, or BP variability). An important underlying aspect regards the evaluation dataset that has to be representative enough.

In this context, we created a new data set for evaluating blood pressure estimation models. The originality of this dataset is that it concerns the long time period follow-up of a subject, with PPG and BP acquisitions (snapshot) regularly taken over several weeks. Existing datasets do not consider such acquisition protocol and are limited to short time acquisitions.

The originality of this paper concerns the evaluation of all existing temporal features on our original dataset and the proposition of a new efficient frequency-based BP estimation method.

Section 2 describes both the material and the proposed approach, including the methodology that is considered for comparing with time-based features. Section 3 presents the results. Before concluding, our work is discussed in Sect. 4.

2   Material and Method

2.1   Material

The acquisition protocol has been drawn in order to obtain clean and replicable data and most importantly the same physiological condition over several weeks. This protocol implies that the subject lies down for 5 min with the medical devices already positioned on him (avoiding physiological variations in the microvascular capillaries resulting from PPG clip positioned on the finger). Then, after 5 min, three consecutive measurements are made with 1 min interval between them. Both PPG signal and blood pressure are recorded at the same time.

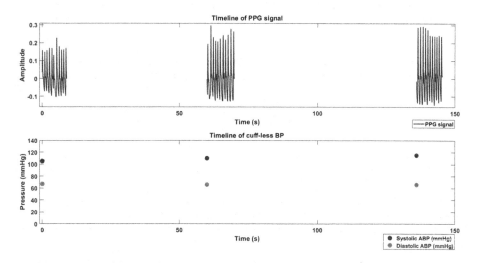

Fig. 2. Timeline of one day record.

We used a certified BP cuff Cardio Maxi[1] and a classic PPG sensors plug via pOpmetre device[2]:

---

[1] https://mon-materiel-medical-en-pharmacie.fr/tensiometres/669-tensiometre-cardio-maxi.html.

[2] https://www.axelife.fr/le-popmetre-en/.

– The blood pressure cuff is positioned on the left arm of the subject.
– The PPG clamp is positioned on the thumb of the subject's right hand.

We assume that there is no difference of PPG signals with respect to the selected arm, as studied by [9].

The measurements are usually done at the same time every day just before lunch in order to avoid other disturbance of the daily life (e.g. lunch, coffee, etc.). Every day, during 6 weeks, three consecutive measurements of 10 s PPG signals were recorded (sampling frequency 1000 Hz) together with the corresponding cuff-less BP (see Fig. 2). As a result, 84 PPG signals and their corresponding systolic and diastolic blood pressures were recorded on a period of 40 days. To capture the intrinsic blood pressure variation, even if all acquisitions are achieved in the same conditions, a long period monitoring is needed. This aspect is illustrated and discussed in Sect. 3, providing an overview of the distribution of measured blood pressures for the considered subject.

2.2   Method

The methodology used in order to predict the blood pressure from the PPG signal is illustrated by Fig. 3. The three main steps of the proposed method are detailed hereafter. Note that the proposed frequency-based method corresponds to the right part of Fig. 3, while the left part deals with the comparison with existing temporal features.

Data Processing: First, each PPG signal is standardized by substracting its mean value and by dividing by its standard deviation (Std), leading to PPG_s defined by:

$$PPG_s(t) = \frac{PPG(t) - Mean[PPG(t)]}{Std[PPG(t)]} \tag{1}$$

Then, the data processing is conducted separately in the time and frequency domains.

<u>**Time Domain**</u>: As previously mentioned, most of related works consider a pre-processing step (filtering) before extracting temporal features.

The pre-processing step is required to correct artefacts resulting from the acquisition [15,16]: motion artefact, loose of skin contact, power-line interference, irregular cardio-vascular rhythm, detection of signal saturation, etc.... In our case, no artefacts were detected during acquisition.

Frequential filtering is mostly used with cutoff frequency band usually set to [0.1–10] Hz [16]. However, in order to filter unrelated artefacts from BP variations, Kalman filtering can be considered [11]. The motivation for such an adaptive filtering is that PPG signal is subject related. Indeed, according to [11], non-stationary effects caused by breathing artefacts are affecting the PPG signal. In such a case, an adaptative filtering is required to take into account the

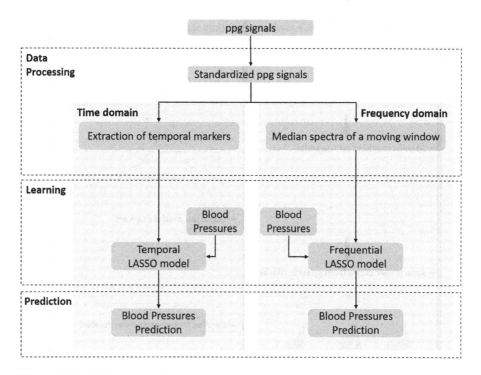

Fig. 3. Methodology used for predicting the blood pressure: the proposed frequency-based method corresponds to the right part, while the left one concerns the comparison with the use of temporal markers.

breathing time variation. Thus, the pre-processing filtering needs the ability to adapt its parameter over-time.

In [3], authors considered a classical band-pass filtering from 0.5 Hz to 5 Hz followed by a baseline drift removal. They used a sum of 2 Gaussian distributions to approximate the shape of each pulse (see Fig. 5). It allows the reduction of irregularities in the shape of the pulse captured by a smartphone. Note that [13] do not use any pre-processing at signal level but tried to reduce the noise during the recording from the camera of the smartphone by considering brightness, skin colour and position of the finger on the camera.

We use a low pass filter to suppress high frequencies in the signal with cutoff frequency 10 Hz which allows to suppress any power-line interference (50 Hz, 60 Hz, etc.). A smoothing is then applied by means of a digital filter with a polynomial order of three in order to have good quality of 1st and 2nd derivative of the signal.

Regarding time domain features present in the literature, there are different categories that have been tested to predict blood pressure (see Fig. 4). Note that related works use a combination of such temporal features. The categories and the corresponding published papers are:

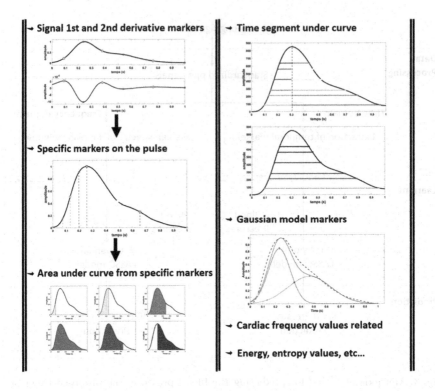

Fig. 4. Gaussian model method

- Specific markers on the pulse: [23, 29, 31].
- Area under curve from specific markers: [28, 29, 31].
- 1st and 2nd derivatives: [17, 22, 31].
- Time segment under curve: [11–13, 17, 25, 29].
- Cardiac frequency values related: [5, 11–13, 28, 31].
- Energy, entropy, skewness coefficient, etc.: [18].
- Gaussian model parameters: similar to [3].

We introduced new temporal features: 21 features from Gaussian model (see Fig. 5), energy of the signal, the slope of the upstroke, the skewness and kurtosis of the pulse. The 21 features built from the fitted Gaussian model [4] correspond to specific points, some of them being indicated in Fig. 5. Regarding the Gaussian model developed in this article, we extracted 21 parameters from this method which are mostly taken from some specific coordinate points (see Fig. 5). We use the method of maximum likelihood and the expectation maximization (EM) algorithm to make the sum of the two Gaussian to fit the closest possible the raw pulse [4]. Note that a similar approach has been considered for the analysis of noisy signals [3]. For sake of clarity, all features are not exhaustively described in this paper.

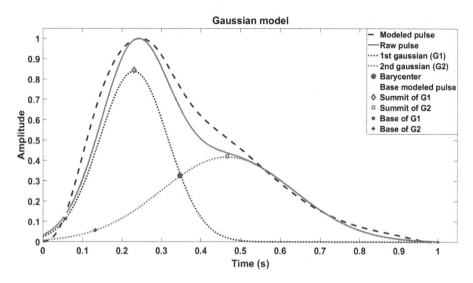

Fig. 5. Gaussian model and some key markers of the model.

In this study, we consider 153 temporal features (markers), including the newly introduced ones. Only relevant ones (leading to the best estimation) will be summarized in Sect. 3.

Frequency Domain: Given that acquisition of the PPG signals is not yet automatic (i.e. with a fixed and controled duration), the time length of the various PPG signals lies between 4.47 and 32.98 s. This is troublesome because the various spectra of the PPG signals depict different spectral resolutions. In order to overcome this problem, the PPG spectrum results from the computation of the median spectrum over sliding windows of 10 s, as illustrated by Fig. 6. Thus, the PPG signals having less than 10 s are not used in this study. That means that in our case only 56 PPG signals out of 84 are retained and their median spectra computed as described before.

Moreover, to increase the resolution of the PPG signal spectra, the PPG signal has been padded (adding zero values at end of the signal) up to 10^5 (equivalent of a temporal window of 100 s at 1 KHz sampling rate).

Learning: At this step, the temporal markers and respectively the median spectra of the PPG signals together with their corresponding systolic and diastolic blood pressures are considered to build a predictive model of the subject blood pressure. In both cases (temporal and frequential), the LASSO (Least Absolute Shrinkage and Selection Operator) algorithm [26] is used in order to build the predictive model. The LASSO is an L1 penalized regression technique that enjoys some of the proprieties of both subset selection and ridge regression. The main reason that motivated the choice of the LASSO algorithm in our study is the high number of predictive variables (153 temporal markers and respectively

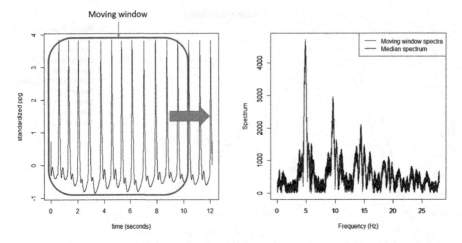

Fig. 6. Computing the median spectrum of a moving window on the PPG signal

700 frequencies) and the few number of observations (84 in the case of temporal markers and respectively 56 in the case of spectral descriptors). Indeed, the ordinary least squares estimates in a regression model are obtained by minimizing the residual squared error. This usually generates low bias estimators but having in counterparts large variance and thus poor estimation accuracy. The LASSO algorithm sets to zero some coefficients in order to reduce the variance of the predicted values and thus to improve the overall estimation accuracy. When a large number of predictors are initially taken into account in the predictive model, the LASSO algorithm keeps a smaller subset that exhibits the strongest effects and thus helps to interpret the resulting model easier. The interested readers can consult the following references [6,27] for more information on the LASSO algorithm. In this paper, we used the R software and the **lars** package (version: 1.2) proposed by Trevor Hastie and Brad Efron for computing the various results obtained.

Estimation: For the estimation of the blood pressure, the trained LASSO model is used. The LASSO model inputs takes the given temporal markers or the given median spectra of the PPG signal and the model realises the blood pressure estimation. The efficiency of the predictive model is evaluated through the Mean Square Error (MSE) indicator obtained by cross-validation. The leave-one-out cross validation method is used in this study. The graphics relevant to the predicted versus real BP additionally give an illustration about the quality of the predictive model, this being detailed in next Section.

3   Results

For the subject taken in consideration in this study, a summary of statistics concerning his blood pressure variation over the survey period of 6 weeks (28 days)

is given in Table 1. The patient is a healthy male of 21 years old (height 1.75 m and weight 50 kgs). Note that Q_{25} and Q_{75} represent the 1st and 3rd quartiles of the blood pressure distribution.

Table 1. Summary of statistics of the subject's blood pressure (in mm Hg)

Blood pressure	Min	Q_{25}	Median	Mean	Q_{75}	Max
Systolic	86	95	96.5	97.07	100.25	107
Diastolic	53	57	59	59.04	60.25	67

Figure 7 shows the spread of the blood pressures recorded over the 6 weeks of the survey. This illustrates the previously mentioned variability that can be observed over long time period, even though acquisitions are performed in the same conditions.

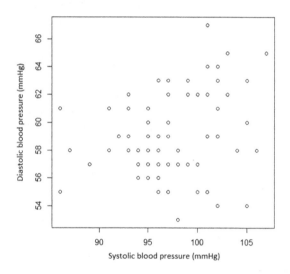

Fig. 7. Subject blood pressure variation over the survey period of 6 weeks

The results concerning the temporal and frequential LASSO models, respectively obtained from temporal markers and median spectra are presented in next Sections.

3.1   Temporal LASSO Model

The LASSO algorithm is used to identify the temporal markers that are useful for the blood pressure estimation. Figure 8 reports the leave-one-out cross-validated

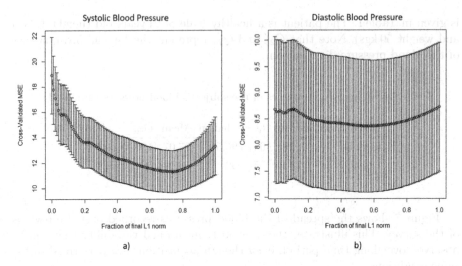

Fig. 8. The cross-validated mean squared estimation error of the lasso algorithm when using the temporal markers of the PPG signal: case of the systolic blood pressure (a) and the diastolic blood pressure (b)

mean squared estimation error of the lasso algorithm, for both systolic and diastolic blood pressures.

The lowest MSE of the blood pressure estimation is obtained with two sets of temporal markers, corresponding to either the systolic or the diastolic pressures.

In the case of the systolic blood pressure (newly introduced markers are those without reference in the literature):

- $ATG1$: Base amplitude of the first Gaussian model.
- ASM: Area under curve from start to summit of the pulse [31].
- $NCCP$: Number of consecutive pulse detected to evaluate cardiac frequency.
- $TUTE90$: Time width between up-stroke and down-stroke at 90% of amplitude under curve [3,5,25].
- TE: Time width mean of pulses detected [3,28,31].
- $Aa2D$: Amplitude of the 1st top of the signal's second derivative [17].
- HV: Variance of the spectral entropy of the signal. Note that the spectral entropy H has been used by [18].
- LgE: Energy of the signal (inspired from [18]).
- $KTEM$: Mean of the Kaiser-Teager energy of the signal [18].
- $SQIM$: Mean of the Skewness of the pulses in the signal [15].

In the case of the diastolic blood pressure (newly introduced markers are those without reference in the literature):

- $NCCP$: Number of consecutive pulse detected to evaluate cardiac frequency.
- TDP: Time width between start to diastolic peak (2nd maximum point) of the pulse [29].

- *AbP*: Amplitude of the 2nd minimum point of the signal's second derivative reported the pulse [17,22].
- *ASMMG*: Mean area under curve between start of the pulse to maximum amplitude extracted from Gaussian model (inspired from [31]).
- *AMDP*: Mean area under curve between start to diastolic peak (2nd maximum point) of the pulse [29].
- *Te2D*: Time width between start to the third top of the signal's second derivative of the pulse [17].
- *Tf2D*: Time width between start to the fifth top of the signal's second derivative of the pulse (Inspired from [17] and [22]).

The final predictive LASSO models for both the systolic and diastolic blood pressures are reported in Table 2.

Table 2. LASSO models for the estimation of the systolic (SBP) and diastolic (DBP) blood pressure when using temporal markers extracted from the PPG signal

SBP	ATG1	ASM	NCCP	TUTE90	TE	Aa2D	HV	LgE	KTEM	SQIM
	−5.56	−1460.55	2.36	−0.01	65.40	4331.39	−2.1e+07	−42.64	6.36e+05	−30.19
DBP	NCCP	TDP	AbP	ASMMG	AMDP	Te2D	Tf2D	-	-	-
	1.23	−39.26	−11294.59	988.39	220.86	0.05	−0.04	-	-	-

Figure 9 illustrates the predicted BP versus real BP when using the LASSO predictive models given in Table 2. The leave-one-out cross validated MSE for respectively predicting the systolic blood pressure and the diastolic blood pressure are respectively 11.31 and 8.36.

Blue points in Fig. 9 are the 56 measures that are retained in the frequential analysis (records where the duration of the PPG signal is more than 10 s). These points are highlighted for comparative purposes with the frequential approach detailed in next Section.

3.2 Frequential LASSO Model

Hereafter, the LASSO algorithm is used to identify frequencies of the PPG spectra that are useful for the blood pressure estimation. Figure 10 gives the leave-one-out cross-validated mean squared estimation error of the lasso algorithm for both systolic and diastolic blood pressures.

The LASSO model with the lowest MSE (18.07) used for the estimation of the systolic blood pressure estimation is given in Table 3.

The LASSO model with the lowest MSE (7.95) used for the estimation of the diastolic blood pressure is given in Table 4.

Figure 11 reports predicted versus real blood pressures when using LASSO predictive models given in Tables 3 and 4.

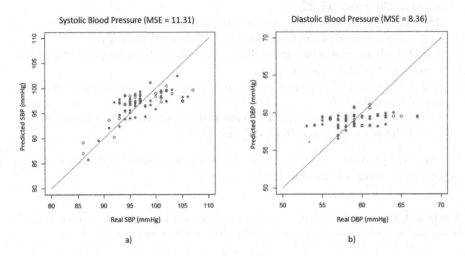

Fig. 9. Predicted versus real systolic blood pressure (a) and diastolic blood pressure (b) for the temporal LASSO model. Blue points correspond to the 56 measurements used for the frequential analysis.

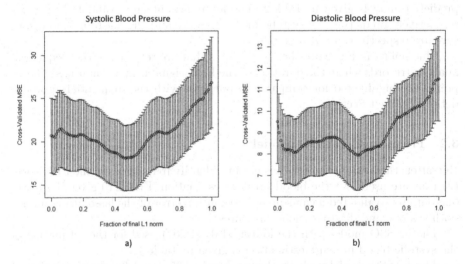

Fig. 10. The cross-validated mean squared estimation error of the lasso algorithm when using the spectra of the PPG signal: case of the systolic blood pressure (a) and the diastolic blood pressure (b)

Table 3. Coefficient of the LASSO model for the estimation of the systolic blood pressure when using the PPG signal spectrum

Frequency (Hz)	0.36	2.08	5.20	6.00	6.28	8.60	10.12	10.48
LASSO coefficients ($\times 10^{-4}$)	−31.32	6.66	7.10	5.54	31.10	−6.11	−25.08	64.51
Frequency (Hz)	10.88	10.92	14.64	15.68	16.52	17.20	17.24	17.76
LASSO coefficients ($\times 10^{-4}$)	−2.21	−22.47	−29.31	15.28	5.11	−5.97	−10.97	−54.22
Frequency (Hz)	18.08	18.36	19.88	20.00	20.24	20.56	20.60	22.60
LASSO coefficients ($\times 10^{-4}$)	22.98	−56.71	10.07	62.41	−35.46	6.20	20.26	20.74
Frequency (Hz)	22.64	25.32	25.56	26.60	27.20	27.56		
LASSO coefficients ($\times 10^{-4}$)	16.95	12.93	−32.07	65.43	24.03	22.43		

Table 4. LASSO model for the estimation of the diastolic blood pressure when using the PPG signal spectrum

Frequency (Hz)	0.04	1.76	2.12	2.60	2.88	5.24	5.76	5.80
LASSO coefficients ($\times 10^{-4}$)	−16.01	34.04	7.10	16.85	0.47	9.92	5.76	6.24
Frequency (Hz)	6.00	6.76	7.08	8.44	8.60	8.76	13.08	13.60
LASSO coefficients ($\times 10^{-4}$)	16.27	−1.24	3.08	−3.25	−0.01	−3.17	−8.06	−17.80
Frequency (Hz)	14.40	15.04	15.76	15.80	17.16	18.84	18.88	19.20
LASSO coefficients ($\times 10^{-4}$)	−2.99	−12.37	−13.61	−1.46	−27.77	−1.05	−7.54	−28.36
Frequency (Hz)	19.88	19.92	21.88	22.92	23.96	24.88	25.08	27.52
LASSO coefficients ($\times 10^{-4}$)	42.60	1.05	48.18	−6.56	21.96	38.08	15.75	198.89

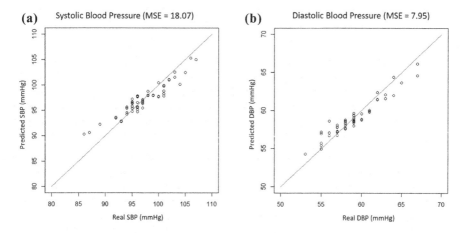

Fig. 11. Predicted versus real systolic blood pressure (a) and diastolic blood pressure (b) for the frequential LASSO model

4 Discussion

According to Table 1 and Fig. 7, it appears that the blood pressure variation is quite consequent even if the subject is always in the same position (lying down). Indeed, we noticed that the systolic blood pressure vary between 86 mmHg and 107 mmHg while the diastolic blood pressure fluctuates between 53 mmHg and 67 mmHg. Thus, a gradient of 21 mmHg on the systolic blood pressure and respectively of 14 mmHg on the diastolic blood pressure is observed over the 6 weeks of daily records. Therefore BP estimation methods should integrate this variability on the evaluation protocol, requiring long term datasets.

The first aspect that we want to discuss here aspect concerns the temporal markers of the PPG signal that are related to the blood pressure estimation. Despite the high number of temporal markers that have been proposed in the literature for predicting the blood pressure, to our knowledge, there is no comparative study of their performances. Indeed, in order to make an objective comparison of these temporal markers, an essential aspect that must be taken into account is obviously to use the same data set. Some public databases that can be used for the blood pressure estimation from the PPG signals like MIMIC [8] or Elgendi [15] have some drawbacks. Concerning the Elgendi dataset, very short PPG signals (2.1 s) are recorded, and only once. Regarding the MIMIC dataset, signals are recorded on subjects in intensive care unit, meaning that subjects might have been under medication or in very unstable states. Although signals are recorded over hours, we cannot extract the same type of information compared to daily records over several weeks as in our case.

The LASSO algorithm found that only 10 temporal markers are useful for the estimation of the systolic blood pressure (see Table 3). The estimation of the systolic blood pressure seems to fit quite well for low blood pressures (less than 95 mmHg) - see Fig. 9a. But, for higher pressures, a saturation effect appears in the estimation (the model can't correctly predict higher blood pressures and the output of the model seems to be a random variation around 97 mmHg). Concerning the diastolic blood pressure, only 7 out of 153 temporal markers seem to be related to the blood pressure. When looking to the Fig. 9b, one can easily notice that the diastolic blood pressure estimation is very poor even if the MSE seems to be acceptable. Indeed, the model can't predict efficiently the diastolic blood pressure variation and the estimations look like a random variation around 59 mmHg. Figure 12 better illustrates this observation over the different records (sessions). The real blood pressures are represented by the black points. The blue points are the estimations when the blood pressure is underestimated and the red points are the estimations when the blood pressure is overestimated. These points are linked to the black points by vertical blue and respectively red lines. It is obvious that less higher are the vertical lines and better is the estimation. It can be noticed that a lot of variation in the blood pressure remains unexplained especially for the diastolic blood pressure. This clearly shows that using just some indicators like MSE, RMSE (Root Mean Square Error), MAE (Mean Average Error), etc., is not sufficient in order to evaluate the quality of a estimation.

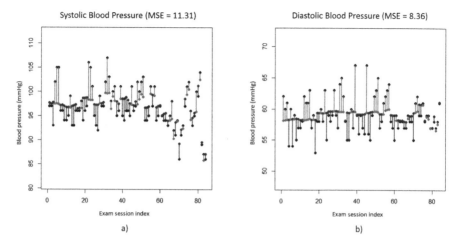

Fig. 12. Predicted systolic blood pressure (a) and diastolic blood pressure (b) for the temporal LASSO model

Concerning the frequential LASSO model used for the estimation of the blood pressure, it has to be noticed that we used only 30 frequencies in the case of the systolic blood pressure (see Table 3) and 32 frequencies in the case of the diastolic blood pressure (see Table 4). It appears that better estimations are obtained than in the case of the temporal markers. Indeed, one can easily visually observe that both predicted systolic and diastolic blood pressures better fit real blood pressures than in the case of temporal markers (see Fig. 11, to be compared with blue points in Fig. 9). It is clear that, in the spectra of the ppg signal, there are some frequencies that can be used to efficiently predict the entire spread of the blood pressure variation. The estimation of the diastolic blood pressure is highly better than in the case of the temporal markers. In the case of the systolic blood pressure, the model seems to slightly underestimate the high blood pressures and to slightly overestimate the low blood pressures. Anyway, the quality of the systolic blood pressure estimation is significantly improved compared to the use temporal markers because the saturation observed when the estimations are done in the temporal domain is not present in the spectral domain. Figure 13 better illustrates the higher quality of estimations in the spectral domain. Compared to the estimations based on temporal markers (see Fig. 12), the height of the vertical lines representing the difference between the real and the predicted is significantly reduced. Regarding the relevance of indicators such as the considered MSE, note that reported values such as 18.07 (frequential LASSO on Systolic pressure) and 11.31 (temporal LASSO on Systolic pressure), are not sufficient to reflect the efficiency of the approach: indeed, according to MSE (computed through a leave-one-out procedure), the temporal approach seems to outperform the frequential one. Nevertheless, as discussed hereabove, it is not the case, as illustrated by Figures (Figures report estimations, using trained models, on the entire dataset).

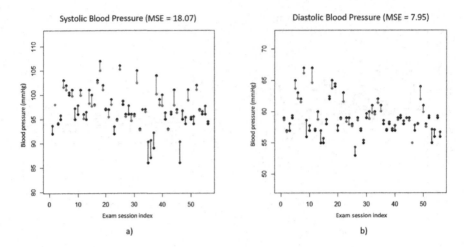

Fig. 13. Predicted systolic blood pressure (a) and diastolic blood pressure (b) for the frequential LASSO model

These results appears accurate enough to integrate the proposed algorithm into a medical device, although additional evaluations have to be performed on an extended dataset.

The last aspect to be pointed out is the size of dataset, limited to one subject with relatively few BP measurements for these preliminary experiments. Further experiments are planned with more subjects and more BP measurements per subject. Therefore, in this work, the limited number of BP measurements may involve a risk of over-fitting, even if one considers a cross-validation. Additionaly, LASSO models resulting from the cross-validation procedure may not keep the same set of (temporal or frequential) features for each cross-validated result: it would be interesting to study, on a larger database, whether the automatically selected set of features remains the same whatever the subdataset used to build the LASSO models. Concerning the evaluation procedure, one considers the standard leave-one-measurement out procedure, usually used in data analysis. It would be interesting to use a leave-one-day out procedure to evaluate the model performance over time, in adequacy with the nature of this dataset and of the considered application.

5   Conclusion

We propose a new data set to be used by researchers working in the field of estimation of the blood pressure from the PPG signal. This data set contains 84 measurements of the systolic and diastolic blood pressures related to PPG signals. Subject has been monitored over a period of 6 weeks, this being not the case any other public data set. We hope that more data set recording subjects over long time period will appear in the next few years as we found out that it enables better blood pressure estimation model to come out and as it enables to compare efficiently estimation approaches. We will add more content to our data set in the future encouraging researcher to do the same. The public data set is available online[3].

We objectively evaluated on this data set various temporal markers of the PPG signal that have been proposed in the literature for the estimation of the blood pressure. Based on our data set, few of them have been found to be useful for the blood pressure estimation. The estimation quality is relatively low, especially for the diastolic blood pressure.

We proposed a new subject specific blood pressure estimation approach based on the spectrum of PPG signals. Our approach exploits the LASSO algorithm for the selection of key frequencies to predict the blood pressure. Our method gives better results than in the case of time markers and variations appear correctly captured over the distribution of recorded blood pressures. An additional strength of this approach is its robustness regarding bad signal quality, compared to temporal approaches that are very sensitive to artefacts.

Some future works concern the test of the proposed approach on an extended dataset involving a new acquisition protocol where the subjects' blood pressures and their corresponding PPG signals are measured in different conditions: at rest lying down (the current dataset); at rest standing up; immediately after a physical effort and finally a short time after the physical effort. We hope that much more variation of the blood pressure will be available in this way. Data issued from this new protocol will be used for different purposes: identification of the subject profile when doing effort; calibration of the predicting model according to the subject profile; better estimation of the blood pressure in conditions that are closer to the real life activities of a person.

References

1. Association, I.S., et al.: IEEE standard for wearable Cuffless blood pressure measuring devices. IEEE Std. 1708–2014 (2014)
2. Baek, S., Jang, J., Yoon, S.: End-to-end blood pressure prediction via fully convolutional networks. IEEE Access **7**, 185458–185468 (2019)
3. Banerjee, R., Ghose, A., Choudhury, A.D., Sinha, A., Pal, A.: Noise cleaning and Gaussian modeling of smart phone photoplethysmogram to improve blood pressure estimation. In: 2015 IEEE International Conference on Acoustics, Speech and Signal Processing (ICASSP), pp. 967–971. IEEE (2015)
4. Bishop, C.M.: Pattern Recognition and Machine Learning. Springer, New York (2006)
5. Choudhury, A.D., Banerjee, R., Sinha, A., Kundu, S.: Estimating blood pressure using windkessel model on photoplethysmogram. In: 2014 36th Annual International Conference of the IEEE Engineering in Medicine and Biology Society, pp. 4567–4570. IEEE (2014)
6. Efron, B., et al.: Least angle regression. Ann. Stat. **32**(2), 407–451 (2004)
7. Elgendi, M.: On the analysis of fingertip photoplethysmogram signals. Curr. Cardiol. Rev. **8**(1), 14–25 (2012)

---

[3] https://www.kaggle.com/franckycash/cuff-blood-pressure-ppg-over-6-weeks.

8. Goldberger, A.L., et al.: Physiobank, physiotoolkit, and physionet: components of a new research resource for complex physiologic signals. Circulation **101**(23), e215–e220 (2000)

9. Jiang, X., et al.: Change of bilateral difference in radial artery pulse morphology with one-side arm movement. Artery Res. **19**, 1–8 (2017)

10. Kim, C.S., Carek, A.M., Inan, O.T., Mukkamala, R., Hahn, J.O.: Ballistocardiogram-based approach to cuffless blood pressure monitoring: proof of concept and potential challenges. IEEE Trans. Biomed. Eng. **65**(11), 2384–2391 (2018)

11. Kurylyak, Y., Barbe, K., Lamonaca, F., Grimaldi, D., Van Moer, W.: Photoplethysmogram-based blood pressure evaluation using kalman filtering and neural networks. In: 2013 IEEE International Symposium on Medical Measurements and Applications (MeMeA), pp. 170–174. IEEE (2013)

12. Kurylyak, Y., Lamonaca, F., Grimaldi, D.: A neural network-based method for continuous blood pressure estimation from a PPG signal. In: 2013 IEEE International Instrumentation and Measurement Technology Conference (I2MTC), pp. 280–283. IEEE (2013)

13. Lamonaca, F., et al.: Application of the artificial neural network for blood pressure evaluation with smartphones. In: 2013 IEEE 7th International Conference on Intelligent Data Acquisition and Advanced Computing Systems (IDAACS), vol. 1, pp. 408–412. IEEE (2013)

14. Landry, C., Peterson, S.D., Arami, A.: Nonlinear dynamic modeling of blood pressure waveform: Towards an accurate cuffless monitoring system. IEEE Sens. J. **20**(10), 5368–5378 (2020)

15. Liang, Y., Chen, Z., Liu, G., Elgendi, M.: A new, short-recorded photoplethysmogram dataset for blood pressure monitoring in china. Sci. Data **5** (2018)

16. Liang, Y., Elgendi, M., Chen, Z., Ward, R.: An optimal filter for short photoplethysmogram signals. Sci. Data **5** (2018)

17. Liu, M., Po, L.M., Fu, H.: Cuffless blood pressure estimation based on photoplethysmography signal and its second derivative. Int. J. Comput. Theory Eng. **9**(3), 202 (2017)

18. Monte-Moreno, E.: Non-invasive estimate of blood glucose and blood pressure from a photoplethysmograph by means of machine learning techniques. Artif. Intell. Med. **53**(2), 127–138 (2011)

19. Mouney, F., Tiplica, T., Hallab, M., Dinomais, M., Fasquel, J.B.: Towards a smartwatch for cuff-less blood pressure measurement using PPG signal and physiological features. In: International Conference on IoT Technologies for HealthCare (2019)

20. Simjanoska, M., Gjoreski, M., Gams, M., Madevska Bogdanova, A.: Non-invasive blood pressure estimation from ECG using machine learning techniques. Sensors **18**(4), 1160 (2018)

21. Stergiou, G.S., et al.: A universal standard for the validation of blood pressure measuring devices: association for the advancement of medical instrumentation/European society of hypertension/international organization for standardization (AAMI/ESH/ISO) collaboration statement. Hypertension **71**(3), 368–374 (2018)

22. Suzuki, S., Oguri, K.: Cuffless and non-invasive systolic blood pressure estimation for aged class by using a photoplethysmograph. In: 2008 30th Annual International Conference of the IEEE Engineering in Medicine and Biology Society, pp. 1327–1330. IEEE (2008)

23. Suzuki, S., Oguri, K.: Cuffless blood pressure estimation by error-correcting output coding method based on an aggregation of adaboost with a photoplethysmograph sensor. In: 2009 Annual International Conference of the IEEE Engineering in Medicine and Biology Society, pp. 6765–6768. IEEE (2009)
24. Tang, Z.: A chair-based unobtrusive cuffless blood pressure monitoring system based on pulse arrival time. IEEE J. Biomed. Health Inform. **21**(5), 1194–1205 (2016)
25. Teng, X., Zhang, Y.: Continuous and noninvasive estimation of arterial blood pressure using a photoplethysmographic approach. In: Proceedings of the 25th Annual International Conference of the IEEE Engineering in Medicine and Biology Society (IEEE Cat. No. 03CH37439), vol. 4, pp. 3153–3156. IEEE (2003)
26. Tibshirani, R.: Regression shrinkage and selection via the lasso. J. Roy. Stat. Soc. B **58**(1), 267–288 (1996)
27. Tibshirani, R.: The lasso method for variable selection in the cox model. Stat. Med. **16**(4), 385–395 (1997). https://doi.org/10.1002/(SICI)1097-0258(19970228)16: 4⟨385::AID-SIM380⟩3.0.CO;2-3
28. Visvanathan, A., Sinha, A., Pal, A.: Estimation of blood pressure levels from reflective photoplethysmograph using smart phones. In: 13th IEEE International Conference on BioInformatics and BioEngineering, pp. 1–5. IEEE (2013)
29. Xie, Q., Wang, G., Peng, Z., Lian, Y.: Machine learning methods for real-time blood pressure measurement based on photoplethysmography. In: 2018 IEEE 23rd International Conference on Digital Signal Processing (DSP), pp. 1–5. IEEE (2018)
30. Xing, X., Sun, M.: Optical blood pressure estimation with photoplethysmography and fft-based neural networks. Biomed. Opt. Express **7**(8), 3007–3020 (2016)
31. Yang, S., Zhang, Y., Cho, S.Y., Morgan, S.P., Correia, R., Wen, L.: Cuff-less blood pressure measurement using fingertip photoplethysmogram signals and physiological characteristics. In: Optics in Health Care and Biomedical Optics VIII, vol. 10820, p. 1082036. International Society for Optics and Photonics (2018)

5G Network Slicing Technology and Its Impact on COVID-19: A Comprehensive Survey

Bashir Abdirahman Hussein[1]([✉]) and Fadi Al-Turjman[2]

[1] Electrical and Electronic Engineering, Near East University, Mersin 10, Nicosia, Turkey
20194701@std.neu.edu.tr
[2] Artificial Intelligence Engineering Department, Research Center for AI and IoT, Near East University, Mersin 10, Nicosia, Turkey

Abstract. At the end of 2019, no one could have imagined how the world will dramatically change. A new outbreak has emerged causing millions of people to go into lockdown for their own safety. World Health Organization (WHO) has later announced this outbreak of Coronavirus Disease 2019 (COVID-19) as pandemic. This has caused huge stress to medical staff. The need for digital connectivity between communities and nations had arisen. Digital revolutionary services like telehealth, telemedicine, eVisit, etc. play a vital role in reducing the risk and fighting the spread of the pandemic.

The industry and academia accept 5G as the potential network capable of serving vertical applications of next generation with specific service needs. In order to achieve this dream, the physical network must be separated into several separate functional blocks of various sizes and systems devoted to specific kind of services depending on their needs (a full slice for large eHealth apps, healthcare servers, IoT apps, smart cities and so on).

Network slicing (NS) was described as the foundation of fast-growing 5G. Although, as its standardization advances and consolidation, few literatures which address main concepts, research challenges and service enablers, in a detailed way are available. In this paper these aspects should be provided and discussed. This study covers industry trends and requirements for 5G including both business drivers and performance requirements. Network slicing Key enabling technologies, architectures and implementations, standardization and future challenges will be discussed and briefly viewed.

Keywords: 5G · COVID-19 · Pandemic · Slicing · Telehealth · Telemedicine

1 Introduction

Over the ages people around the world has met with different epidemics [1]. On 31st December 2019, Hubei province of chine in Wuhan city has informed the World Health Organization (WHO) about what has been called Coronavirus disease 2019 (COVID-19) [2–4]. Later in the beginning of 2020, World Health Organization (WHO) has announced this universal event as pandemic [5]. Factors like staying home, social distancing and

© ICST Institute for Computer Sciences, Social Informatics and Telecommunications Engineering 2021
Published by Springer Nature Switzerland AG 2021. All Rights Reserved
S. Paiva et al. (Eds.): SmartCity360° 2020, LNICST 372, pp. 64–86, 2021.
https://doi.org/10.1007/978-3-030-76063-2_5

good hygiene has made possible by the reduction of transmitting the disease [6]. Furthermore, individuals that are not diagnosed by COVID-19, notably those Who seem to be at higher risk of contracting the disease (e.g. older people as well as those with medical conditions) can receive regular treatment in hospitals without the risk of exposure to other patients [7]. In addition, inappropriate staff, like professional therapists, firmly deny to reach the patient division of COVID-19 under strict infection control [8]. Natural disasters and pandemics cause additional barriers to health care delivery. As an outcome, to meet both the basic needs of COVID-19 patients and other individuals who need healthcare services, creative and transformative solutions are needed. Technological breakthroughs offer additional options in this regard [9]. The use of technologies like Internet of Medical things [10], telemedicine, telehealth and e-Education with the help of IoT during pandemic circumstances (COVID-19 outbreak) seems to have the ability to strengthen epidemiological studies, disease prevention, clinical case management and studying via online [11, 12].

The amount of Internet-connected devices is predicted to reach above 45 billion at some point from 2025 onwards [13, 14]. As the world adapts to a new norm of a global remote workforce due to COVID19, users and data transfers are growing very fast. The current mobile network generation does not give much versatility to independent manufactures which require a connection to link their devices. Such businesses, for most part, adjust their networking specifications to suit the multifunctional mobile network, thus leaving them attainable [15]. In smart interconnected networking landscapes, the fifth generation of mobile technology is supposed to assemble users, healthcare providers, devices, data, apps, and cities. Previous networks contemporarily face obstacles in providing the mentioned solutions [16–18]. NS has being suggested by academia and industry as a key enabler to facilitate personalized 5G technology resources for customers to incorporate multiple spatial-specific information in response to enhanced mobile broadband networks with the existing cellular network [19].

In 5G sense, NS is a set of technologies for the development of advanced, devoted logical networks as a service (NaaS) to facilitate the convergence of internet infrastructure and meet the globally competitive specifications of industry domains [20].

The NS idea has come as a result of the ongoing development in technology i.e. Software-Defined Networking (SDN) [21, 22]. SDN controllers configures SDN switch routing tables, and spectrum sharing for the RAN, In addition to that NFV which network functions are introduced by software and distributed to request on versatile hardware [23–25].

In NS a physical network is sliced into many logical networks, every slice should come up with tailored activities for a specific use case scenario [26]. In order to support multiple business-driven application scenarios concurrently over the same data centers, 5G NS posed through possibly autonomous and self-contained networks which are versatile and fully interactive. In order to effectively achieve planned network services, decomposing the current large monolithic network functions paired with different modern systems to various smaller modular network interfaces based on software with variable complexity is crucial. These cloud-native functional requirements would then be assembled upon request in versatile forms to produce various network segments that support various 5G standards. NS would allow companies in building various types of care for different vertical businesses, encouraging them better optimize everyone's services. [27, 28].

Table 1. List of abbreviations.

No.	Abbr.	Meaning of the words	No.	Abbr.	Meaning of the words
1.	5G	Fifth Generation of mobile communication	22	URLLC	Ultra-Reliable and Low Latency Connectivity
2.	4G	Fourth Generation of mobile communication	23	mMTC	massive Machine Type Communication
3.	3G	Third Generation of mobile communication	24	HD	High-Definition
4.	NS	Network Slicing	25	AR	augmented reality
5.	NaaS	Network As A Service	26	VR	virtual reality
6.	IoT	Internet of Things	27	FMC	fixed mobile convergence
7.	NFV	Network Function Virtualization	28	5GPPP	5th infrastructure public partnership project
8.	SA	Service and System Aspects	29	IMT	International Mobile telecommunication
9.	WG	Working Groups	30	QoE	Quality of Experience
10.	OSS	Operation Support System	31	RAN	Radio Access Network
11.	BSS	Business Support System	32	PLC	PlanetLab Central
12.	MANO	Management and Orchestration	33	NSF	National Science Foundation
13.	MEC	Multiple-Access Edge Computing	34	E2E	End-to-End
14.	IoV	Internet of Vehicle	35	MVNO	Mobile Virtual Network Operator
15.	SLAs	Service-Level Agreements	36	CriC	Critical Communications
16.	3GPP	3rd Generation Partnership Project	37	EV2X	Enhanced Vehicular to Everything
17.	KPI	Key Performance Indicator	38	MIoT	Massive Internet of Things
18.	eMBB	enhanced Mobile Broadband	39	WWRF	Wireless World Research Forum
19.	IETF	Internet Engineering Task Force	40	5GAA	5G Automotive Association
20.	ETSI	European Telecommunication Standardization Institute	41	COVID19	Coronavirus Disease 2019
21.	NGMN	Next Generation Mobile networks	42	IoE	Internet of Everything

1.1   Scope and Contributions of This Paper

This survey aims to offer and provide a deep understanding about the new advancements in network slicing which will give the readers a comprehensive, advanced and available solutions regarding NS in 5G that can be benefited during this COVID19 outbreak.

First, we will highlight how 5G can fulfill the demands of mobile network consumers and how effective is it. Then we will briefly define network slicing in order to provide the reader an idea about the concepts related to 5G network slicing in general and how will it enable a tremendous effect in the future of mobile networks. Before we deeply go to the main topic, we will give the service requirements of 5G in both business and quality drivers. We will also cover many aspects in this technology including 5G NS concepts, applications etc.

This paper as well presents 5G NS architectures and implementation by providing some projects. On the other side, standardization activities of 5G NS is given in this paper. Moreover, challenges in network slicing are given.

Generally, this survey aims to gather and highlight the critical architectural aspects which could be an interest to readers from all over the world, as well as service providers or industries. It gives multidimensional information to those who have desire in understanding the 5th generation's enabling technologies. It can also help to those who are in need to do research projects and implementations about this topic. For readers to have desired attention, this survey paper provides Table 1 that lists all abbreviations and their meanings.

1.2   Comparison to Similar Surveys

The technology related to 5G NS was firstly proposed by Next Generations of Mobile Networks (NGMN) [29]. Since then several survey studies have been carried and proposed. These papers include [26, 27, 30–34] and [35]. In paper [26] it proposes network slicing for 5G systems, it reviews some of the achievements of 3GPP, Service and system aspects (SA2) and RAN3 Working Groups (WG) which relates to the genesis of NS and previous 4th Generation of mobile network technical solutions. This paper proofs how NS shall be put into real networks and highlights some wanted steps to additionally contribute on this technology. The main goal of that article was to highlight the 4G endowment on NS and also evaluates the condition of 5G system standardization. Lastly it highlights the main open points in 5G standardization. On the other hand, another survey that carries similar topic has been proposed in [32] which gives a general view about how NS plays an important role in SDN and NFV. Some clear definitions of NS and its enabling ideas like SDN and NFV is provided, also the evolutionary values SDN and NFV for NS architectures are given in it. The paper also focuses on the architectural analysis of NS which includes OSS/BSS, (MANO) and operation and management.

In 2017 A study of NS in 5G was also proposed in [31] which the core of it is value is to provide a clear explanation about the existing knowledge of network slicing in 5G. The aim of the paper was to look other available works on NS in 5G ideology and also verifies the obstacles that need to be addressed. The authors also gave some 5G architectural proposals to highlight the crucial advantage that NS is predicted to play in providing the requirements of different use cases. In [30] Network slicing and softwarization survey was presented, which highlights some major aspects that identify network slicing as the backbone of the rapidly growing 5th Generation of mobile network technology. This study elaborates NS concepts by an end-to-end point which details the historical heritage, the main ideas, some of the empowering technologies and elucidations and different use cases of NS. The study has also given some details about particular slicing elucidations for different sections for 5G systems. Moreover, A review that is composed of architectures and future challenges about NS was proposed in [27]. The study provides survey about current solutions related to 5G NS, they have also provided a validation of 5G system softwarization and slicing patterns which includes some major theories, history and variety of Applications.

On the other hand, they have provided some tutorials regarding to 5G NS enablers that include SDN, NFV, Multiple-access Edge Computing (MEC) and many other. A comparison to different 5G architectural approaches was also presented. This study also evaluates the standardization of NS about 5G systems. In [33] NS as enablers of 5G service survey is proposed which provides a review of the standardization efforts of NS and identifies big obstacles for mobile operators. Another survey is presented in [34] this covers solutions for all network domains as well as management of network slices. Lastly a survey which is about resource slicing in virtual wireless networks was proposed in [35]. This study focuses definitions of problems, discussing challenges and analyzing how SDN and NFV can assist in the slicing. Below is a Table 2 which summarizes all similar studies with description.

1.3 Organization of the Paper

The remaining part of this article is arranged as the follows: Sect. 2 Covers all service requirements of 5G which will include in both quality requirements and business drivers of 5G. In Sect. 3 Network slicing concepts and use cases including definitions, history and applications will be covered. Network slicing architectures and implementation shall be covered in Sect. 4. In Sect. 5 standardization efforts in 5G network slicing will be covered which we shall look different standardizing efforts from different industries. Challenges and future work and conclusions will be given on Sects. 6 and 7 respectively. Figure 1 also gives a detailed summary about the organization of the paper and provides all the sections we will cover.

2 5G Industry Trends and Requirements

The 5G systems was not designed only as infrastructure to the "Internet of Things" (IoT), but as a way of giving rise to an enormous size of new technologies, instilling in forthcoming telecommunications an everlasting vitality. IoT needs funding for a variety of servicing categories like Telehealth, e-Health, e-Education, Internet of Vehicle (IoV), Smart Buildings, organizational Safety, Environmental checking etc. Such services would drive IoT's rapid growth and encourage the connectivity of billions of systems connected to the network, that on the other hand comes up with the "Internet of Everything (IoE)" dream particularly over the vertical markets [36].

5G service requirements are clustered mainly into these categories: a) performance requirements, including things like Speed, throughput, coverage, availability and so on, b) Functional requirements like service assurance, isolation, security e.t.c. c) Operational requirements like charging, billing, Key Performance Indicators (KPI) which is monitored to assure Service-Level Agreements (SLAs) [37].

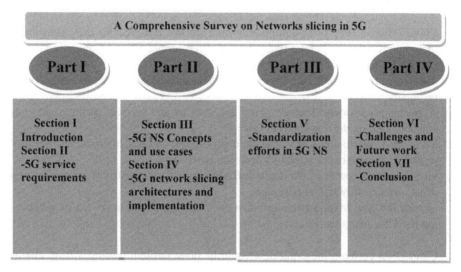

Fig. 1. Organization of the paper

2.1 Performance Requirements

The networks proposed in 5G period fell to three common schemes: Ultra-Reliable and Low Latency Connectivity (URLLC), enhanced Mobile Broadband (eMBB), and Massive Machine type communication system (mMTC). The eMBB specializes on broadband services such as HD clips, VR, augmented reality AR, and FMC networks.

URLLC works on services which are prone to latency, like self-driving, remote surgery or drone control. MMTC focuses on services with high link density specifications, like those popular in smart cities use cases. Each situation requires for a completely different network [38].

Summarizing all the requirements provided by 5GPP on 5G vision [39], IMT-2020 vision [40, 41] and [42] gives a conclusion to these points: Low latency (1 ms delay), 1000x bandwidth, Increase number of connected devices, Availability up-to 99.999%, Reliable Secure connection [43], Coverage perception of 100%, Service continuity [44], reduced energy usage in the network, Long-life battery up-to ten years [45] and Quality of Experience (QoE) [46–48].

2.2 Business Drivers and Vertical Industry Requirements

5G is expected to provide service into different business ecosystems which shall give innovative services and high network competence to the newly industry shareholders. Hence, it requires to adapt business models and new partnerships.

The role in which 5G will play in the market that it provides through virtualization and slicing include:

1. Cloud drivers: They offer computation and storage resources to their consumers including resources of cloud like Amazon's web service Elastic Computing cloud, Google Kubernetes and Linux's Openstack.
2. Infrastructure providers: Facilitate both physical network infrastructure and software resources.
3. Application providers: Provide many applications and services to their end consumers based on the demand they have.
4. Verticals: Cover many services to their third parties to utilize cloud and network resources from network operators and cloud providers.
5. virtual network operators: Works for infrastructure distributers to either compliments of its own capacity and/or coverage.
6. Service brokers: Mapping requests that came from application providers, it acts as mediator for mapping the services.

Connection between these partners could be done through resources from clouds and networks.

NS technology is one of the promising business enablers for 5G, providing increased network coverage to third party organizations in reliable way, promising an supplementary revenue for infrastructure, vendors and cloud distributors [30]. Table 3 also gives summarized information about the different requirements of 5G.

3 5G NS Concepts and Applications

3.1 NS History

Since IBM [49] has introduced it is first operating system (CP-40) in 1960s which supported virtual memory and time sharing, network slicing concepts is heavily linked to virtualization concepts [50, 51]. In computing, the design offered number of simultaneous users approximately up to 15 to individually use and work with separate hardware and software [52]. Hence, virtualization had generally adapted by data centres in 1970s and 1980s in which a virtual is created from a physical entity through methods of software then it introduced the idea of virtual networks through network resources, different platforms for computers and storage devices [50].

Overlay networks were proposed in the late 1980s Logical links linked network nodes to come with a Digital network running on growing fitness infrastructure. The overlaying systems were a previous way of cutting the network definition as they incorporate variety of tools of Control domains thus QoS is guaranteed to lastly end-users.

Table 2. Summary of available surveys

Ref	5G performance requirements	5G Business drivers and vertical industry requirements	NS concepts, history and principles	5G NS Standardization attempts	5G NS architectures and implementations	NS Impact on COVID-19
[26]	✗	✗	✗	✗	✓	✗
[32]	✗	✗	✗	✗	✓	✗
[33]	✓	✗	✗	✓	✓	✗
[31]	✓	✗	✗	✗	✗	✗
[34]	✗	✓	✗	✗	✗	✗
[35]	✗	✗	✓	✗	✗	✗
Our work	✓	✓	✓	✓	✓	✓

Since they are adjustable, overlay networks don't have control and network programming Reviews. Reviews. In the nineties and the beginning of 2000s, Active and programmable network with a centre operating system that could give frameworks for resource control was presented. After that various principles such as PlanetLab USA (2002) [53] was adopted MyPLC [54].

Software package that enables distributed virtualization giving users the ability to obtain isolated usage of a unique slice. In this scenario a definition is given to what a slice is, it a u nit with specific allocated resources, these resources can either be a computing power or storage on hosts or other resources remaining in namespaces.

The development didn't stop in there, National Science Foundation's (NSF) GENI project initiatives pushed forward testbed development [55] by advocating studies on a clean condition network in consideration of combined resources and mobile network territories. Researchers got opportunity to run their experiments after SDN technologies were come to hand in 2009.

3.2 Concepts and Principles of 5G NS

NS relates to splitting a real network into many networks; it can be adjusted to your needs and configured for certain application set, or customer set through using leverage technologies on cloud computing and virtualisation. Shared physical resources on the network could Be dynamically, effectively and logically planned Slices of networks that related to changes of user demands. A slice of 5G system contains a group of Combined system functions and conditions for a particular application or profession type.

Network slicing promotes multiple distributed self-contained infrastructures in addition to a usual physical infrastructure universal scale engaging a reliable stakeholder environment which enables technically and businesses advancement to embed physically and/or logically built network and cloud's resources into a configurable, open software-disposed multi-tenant network environment [56]. The general concept of 5G

NS architecture is to include specialized tasks required for the particular use case traffic to be handled. Network slices have customized capabilities necessary for the corresponding services, also it has the ability to reshape the changing needs.

In accordance to the definition provided by NGMN [3], NS is mainly composed of three layers:

a. Service Instance Layer: which stands as the end user services or trade services which could be supported. Every service represents a service instance.
b. Network Slice Instance Layer: encompasses the network slice instance which could be provided. A network slice instance gives the network features which are needed in the service instances.
c. Resource Layer: promotes virtual or physical resource and network function which is necessary to build network slice instances.

Network slicing have the following main ideas which shape the principles and associated operations with each principle filling a demand:

1. Automation: This principle allows an on-demand configuration of NS while there is no need for fixed contractual deal and manual involvement. This operation enables third parties to create and place a slice from the network with the desired capacity, latency, jitter, etc.
2. Isolation: this is a prime part of network slicing which provides a guaranteed security and performance for each slice tenant [57].
3. Customization: guarantees that the provided resources are efficiently utilized with the requirements of the tenant [58]. This would be realized from a network which considers the abstracted configuration, on a data plane tailored service network functions, o the control plane that considers the introduction of operations, protocols and policies, and lastly on a service with value added.
4. Resource elasticity: this principle is perceived using an successful non-disruptive re-provisioning structure in which the provided network resource is categorised as on or off. It promises that the needed SLAs are regardless of the specified geographical location [59].
5. Programmability: This gives third parties the ability to manage the given network slice resources which includes network and cloud resources [60].
6. End-to-End (E2E): the property of E2E provides delivery of the allocated network slice from the providers to the end-users.
7. Hierarchical Abstraction: this need the NS to introduce an additional layer of Abstraction. To achieve this a separate logical and physical set of network resource and virtual network function are created [61]. This then facilitates the provision of service from the slice service to be the prior one.

3.3 Applications and Use Cases of 5G NS

5G's main goal addresses many upcoming operations and business needs for the future, the 3GPP started a (SMARTER) called study in the 3GPPP Services Working Group

Table 3. Summary of 5G Service requirements and Business drivers.

	5G service requirements and business drivers	Objectives
Performance requirements	Speed and Latency	Features that provide instantaneous network connectivity with 10 Gbps data rates and low latency of 1 ms
	Security, Service continuity and coverage	Features that provide robust, reliable and resilient support of services for all consumers
	Connectivity	A Feature that provides wireless connections for sensor and actuator bearing hundreds of thousands of devices per cell
	Quality of Experience (QoE)	A feature that gives minimal interference, disruptions, and fluctuation in network quality and performance
	Reduced Energy usage and battery life	Features that will enable billions of cellular enabled IoT applications to be connected with minimal energy usage and longer battery life
Business drivers	Cloud providers	Facilitate consumers with enough cloud services, storage resources and computation
	Infrastructural providers	provide both Hardware and software services/Connectivity to different kinds of consumers
	Application providers	Propose high data rates application providers a performance that will meet their demands to make sure rewarding user adventures
	Vertical	Provides many services to non-telecom industries, utilizing networks and cloud resource from different vendors and cloud distributors
	Vertical network operators	Compliment their own capacity and/or coverage by hiring resources from infrastructure providers, they also gain network coverage if they don't have physical infrastructure
	Service brokers	Communicates with physical network, gathers expedient details and behaves as a medium mapping the service for request from vendors

SA1. Several applications targeting new trade departments or distinct business chances which should be opened with the advent of 5G were grouped and mentioned. These categories include;

i.   eMBB which provides high data rates to survive from vast traffic capacity and user equipment connections per area.
ii. Critical Communications (CriC) [62] that focuses on the critical mission services like the protection of people, management of disasters and emergencies, AR/VR and tactile Internet [63]
iii. Enhanced Vehicular to Everything (EV2X) which mainly supports on welfare linked issues like autonomous, collision avoidance, remote driving and vehicle platooning by giving them direct vehicular communication.
iv. Massive Internet of Things (MIoT) [64] that mainly focuses on the connectivity for multiple amount of devices which are stationary with non-time critical service requirements, yet though it needs security, configuration and operational simplicity.

A multi-tenant architecture linked using OpenFlow switches above a virtual overlay network is provided on Fig. 2. This application shows how multiple tenants can have a similar accessibility to virtual slices, each tenant for example Mobile Virtual Network Operator (MVNO) has an access to a network slice without an interference from others.

NGMN also shares a large number of use case that should take part the emerging 5G technologies that mainly focus on; Enhanced broadband access every place and in

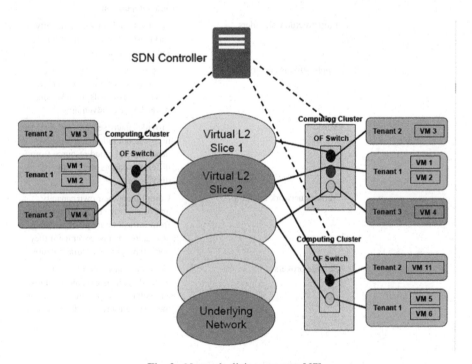

Fig. 2. Network slicing use case [67].

heavy traffic areas, higher customer mobilities, massive IoT, lifeline communication, acute real-time connection, ultra-reliable communication [65], broadcast-like services, light weight communication [66] and multi-connection.

3.4 Key Enabling Technologies of NS

The NS technology as mentioned in previous sections is among the key features of NFV and SDN. These two are the leading enhancing technologies that support network slicing.

Software Defined Networking (SDN)

Software-defined network (SDN) is a contemporary context of network design for the forthcoming time, these networks could be configured or controlled; two features can be managed and divided in the Internet and wireless communication and different areas, solving the problem in the network is not versatile and static, speeding up the new application of network implementation and online implementation [22]. SDN's key role is the ability to control network planning, open and versatile call forwarding separation and centralized control, the transfer of plane and control plane separation of network equipment, flexible scheduling and network traffic control, network automation and intelligent management.

Network Function Virtualization (NFV)

NFV was first presented by the biggest TOs in the world, such as AT&T, BT and DT. In line with ETSI, this concept of NFV was known as a network architectures that transform the behaviours that network are designed and managed by using existing IT virtualization ideas and integrating proprietary hardware-based networks into common business equipment [68].

4 NS Architecture and Implementation

4.1 Implementations and Architectures of NS

In a simple manner network slicing is to benefit from virtualization technologies, i.e. NFV or SDN for the architecture, partitioning, organization and optimization of physical infrastructure of communication and computation resources into multi-logical networks to enable a variety of services [69]. A 5G slice promotes a specific type of connection communication service in a unique method of solving the C- and U-plane for these services. For that purpose, a 5G slice consists of number of 5G network functions and specific RAT settings which are integrated for the specific case of use or business model [29]. Thus, a 5G slice will contain all domains of the network: software packages that attempt to operate on cloud nodes, specific transport network implementations that enable versatile placement of functions, a separate radio configuration or a unique RAT, along with configurations of 5G devices. Not most slices get the same functionality, but other functions might even be lacking in several of the slices that seem important for a mobile network today.

An example of several 5G slices operating on the same network concurrently is shown in Fig. 3. For example, by providing full-fledged functions distributed across the network, a 5G slice can be realized for regular smartphone use. It will be crucial for the safety, dependability and jitter of a 5G slice which serves autonomous use cases. At the cloud edge node, all necessary (and potentially devoted) software, such as the appropriate vertical model due to latency limitations, can be allowed. There are many devoted slices that can run simultaneously, and also as generic slice which offers easy connectivity with the maximum approach to reconcile with unknown use cases and congestion situations. The 5G technology will have flexibility which ensures end-to-end, and under all circumstances, operated and protected network operation, despite of the slices to be covered by the network. In order to achieve such a 5G architecture, the C- and U-plane functions must be clearly differentiated in compliance with SDN standards, with open interfaces established between the two. In addition, it is important to identify flexible interfaces among communication-specific and authenticate-agnostic functionality so that additional access technologies, including static and wireless, can easily be incorporated into 5G network in the coming years. Moreover, interaction across modules will allow multi-vendor reconfiguration of numerous uses.

4.2 5G Network Slicing Projects

Various collaborative research projects of 5G network slicing have been proposed and they are undergoing with each aiming to meet with the tremendous industry requirements that we have mentioned. Several standard bodies (i.e. IEEE, 3GPP, ITU), Associations (i.e. ETSI, TIA) alliances (i.e. NGMN and Wireless World Research Forum (WWRF) have admired some initiatives to running research on 5G and beyond future mobile networks. These research projects include: 5G Exchange (5GEx) [70], MATLIDA [71], SliceNet, 5GTANGO [72], 5GNORMA [73], SONATA, 5G-MoNArch, 5G!PAGODA [74], NECOS [75] and 5G-Transformer.

5 State-of-the-Art Standardization in 5G Network Slicing

Network effects prevail in telecommunications and thus systems must be interoperable in order to fully exploit the communications networks' capacity. In this context, technology standardization is crucial and the state-of-the-art standardization of network slicing must be analysed in such a way that both mobile operators and vendors know where to provide input covering their interested domains [33]. The current market discussions focused on the notion and demands of network slicing, evaluation of its impact on various levels or network stack layers (e.g., CN, the RAN, etc.). For example, from the vertical industry perspective; The 5G Automotive Association (5GAA) operates with several other automotive, technology, and telecommunications (ICT) companies to develop E2E ideas for sustainable mobility and transport solutions. To date, 5GAA WG5 has established the first workstream to Value the business model aspects of network slicing in the automotive sector. On the other hand, Manufacturing organization have been looking for the implementation and the development of smart Manufacturing solutions that are based on 5G.

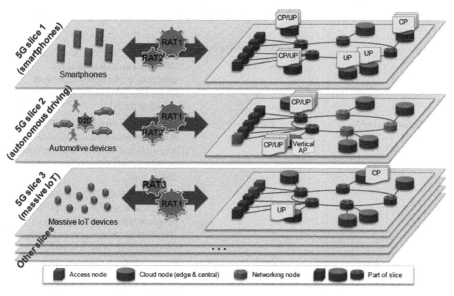

Fig. 3. 5G network slicing architectural implementation [29].

To cope with all these demands the operators were focusing on the exploration of the concepts, business drivers and high-level specifications of E2E Network slicing. The GSMA [15] Network Slicing Task Force (NEST) programme was started to reconcile slicing concepts, define slice types with distinctive advantages and simplify specifications for parameters and functionality. The NGMN [29] Alliance was the first to embrace the idea of network slicing as stated in its white paper, called "5G slicing" Since then the NGMN has established, consolidated, and communicated specifications for 5G network slicing and its architecture. As network slicing technology is among the forthcoming networking technologies, several organizations are associated with the standardization efforts. These efforts are generally categorized: i) Organizations approaching from the business point of view, Organizations approaching from technical aspects, Open-source organizations and Organizations that develop traditional standards. A summary of all standardizing bodies is provided in Table 4.

Table 4. Summary of standardization activities for 5G network Slicing.

	Standardizing bodies	Coverage
From business point of view	GSMA	GSMA primarily encourages compatibility and roaming between mobile operators by identifying standardized technologies and guiding business/relationship principles (e.g., charging principles and roaming agreements)

(continued)

Table 4. (*continued*)

	Standardizing bodies	Coverage
	NGMN	NGMN focuses on technology architectures (for example, network slicing Design) allowing each use case is identified for 5G
From Technical Aspects	TIP	Telecom Infra Project (TIP) [79] aims to make network infrastructure quite accessible and therefore concentrates on implementation rather than on holistic design
	TMF	TM Forum (TMF) [80] assesses business strategies and network slicing situations, and is therefore likely to contribute to architectures addressing customer needs in the near term
	BBF	Broadband Forum (BBF) is an infrastructure forum focused on intelligent and faster broadband networks. BBF offers a virtualisation conceptual model for business/residential purposes together with virtual gateways
	xRAN	extensible Radio Access Network (xRAN) covers the overall architectural design and fronthaul networks which are becoming even more meaningful to small cell proliferation. It also seeks to make the network infrastructure quite widely available and cost-effective
From Open-source communities	ONF	Open Networking foundation (ONF) is an open-source entity that leverages SDN principles and disaggregation, it uses open-source systems and structured Standards to build operator networks. it focuses on applying SDN and NFV on transport networks (backhaul or backbone) by providing Central Office Rearchitected as a Datacentre (CORD) platforms
	OpenStack	OpenStack is an open-source organization that creates a datacentre-wide platform and API for controlling and managing diverse pools of computing, storage, and network resources. Hence, OpenStack is focused on mobile network datacentre-like environments

(*continued*)

Table 4. (*continued*)

	Standardizing bodies	Coverage
	ONAP	Open Network Automation Platform (ONAP) ONAP is a project of the Linux Foundation, working with AT&T. It provides a complete platform for real-time, policy-driven orchestration of virtual and physical network services and automation. Additionally, ONAP focuses on key features of the network and MANO
From Traditional standard development Organizations	3GPP	3GPP is a significant player in wireless telephony as it defines the wireless network architectural design and technologies. in under 3GPP, the Service and System Aspects (SA), Radio Access Network (RAN) and Core Networks and Terminals (CT) standardize network slicing for mobile networks
	IETF	IETF is a massive outdoor international community of network operators, service providers, vendors and researchers involved in the transformation of internet architecture and the effective operation of the Internet. In network slicing, IETF concentrates on the rearchitecture of network features, network slicing management systems, as well as slice analysis and benchmarking
	ETSI	ETSI NFV plays a key role in network slicing. ETSI NFV offers the architectural basis for NFV and generates relevant and related specifications. The reports have moved from pre-standardization research to comprehensive requirements with early Proof of Concept (PoC) activities and interoperability events (Plug tests) since their introduction in November 2012

6   Future Challenges for Network Slicing

This section elaborates the challenges in achieving an E2E slice, which in-turn migrates from physical networks to virtual networks. To achieve an End-to-End slice with the interoperability of different slices, there will be several challenges, these challenges are discussed in the following sub-sections.

6.1   Radio Access Network Interoperability, Scalability and Roaming Manner

The end-to - end design, not even just the RAN, should be expected to manage ambiguities in the radio interface yet at the same time guaranteeing customers service levels as accepted through business deals. There are previous solutions regarding to these matters which have been promoted and researched by the academia like the one of Eurocom, which radio resources are able to maximize the unallocated network resources by satisfying as much requests as possible in a given time [76]. Another example is Orion [77], It exposes a base station hypervisor to the physical base station's transitional data plane and the virtual data plane of the slices, where the virtual Control plane is a logically separate case assigned to the tailoring and management of the unique slice for every slice. Another major difficult is the roaming of network slices. Roaming is more significant in the Internet of Things (IoT) era, as it unlocks the maximum potential of network slicing to allow communication technology (e.g., cars, asset management, monitoring and business development for multi-national corporations). Major telecom operators have proposed trials for testing roaming in the network slicing environment. So that, to achieve these slicing scenarios it is very difficult and challenging task which needs the consideration of more studies.

6.2   Software Functions and Hardware of Network Interoperability

The interoperability of network functions and hardware can be ensured when there are standard approaches for network slicing. Indeed, the precise statement of open interfaces between some of the 3GPP-specified network nodes facilitated a multi-vendor atmosphere that encouraged innovation and creativity within traditional mobile networks [78]. In the age of network slicing, cellular networks are no exception to this, and interfaces between network software functions, hardware and various layers of the virtualisation of the network should be transparent and interoperable. 5GPPP also underlines the significance of interoperability, since different types of network slices coexist in a mobile network reaching from one layer to the next. Also, in the interoperability GSMA suggests for scopes to ensure virtual network functions and Hardware's interoperability these include: Software upgrade. Vertical integration, service assurance and network service deployment.

The interoperability allowed by standardized format of various network components is very important in in maintaining a multi-vendor ecosystem. It is very challenging to resolve difficulties regarding the interoperability importance in vertically examining the impact of software upgrade.

6.3   Movement from Physical to Virtual Networks and Development of Innovative Features

Mobile networks are mainly physical and there have been a lot of arguments and descriptions that assume these networks will totally migrated to virtual. There is a big challenge in this migration and we need to consider a lot about these migrations to make mobile networks virtualized. For commercial mobile networks, it is indispensable to maintain a versatile migration that assures reliability and performance of mobile networks.

To migrate from physical to virtual, the traditional mobile network operator's community should consider different and numerous stakeholders in network slicing standardization activities. Finally, network carriers would have the option of migrating various layers (network function, infrastructure and operations & management) in relation or in diverse sequential order. While order will not seem to make much difference on the surface, real experiences suggest migrating first then the other layers of infrastructure.

The adaption of network slice will also relate to the aspects from techno-businesses. Therefore, in order for the mobile operators to quickly adopt network slicing, attributes beyond that of modern mobile networks still have to be tackled and embraced through network slicing. The attributes must also provide for the generation of Increased income, and/or incremental implementation costs are expected.

7 Conclusion

Network slicing will worth encouraging various 5G applications and use cases. Although, network slicing provides innovative networking technologies like Software Defined Networking (SDN) and Network Function Virtualization (NFV), the complexity of cellular networks will potentially increase and operators will face greater challenges. This is similar to the complexity in standardizing the network slicing.

This paper has provided a clear and understandable and updated information about 5G network slicing and the impact it could have on COVID-19, first we have drawn the requirements of 5G including both service and quality requirements from vertical industries and added the business key drivers of 5G. We also comprehensively provide a state-of-the art history, definitions, concepts and principles of 5G network slicing. In addition to these parts several applications and use case were added from several projects, also, the key enabling technologies of network slicing were mentioned which are SDN and NVF with each giving clear descriptions. Thus, the implementations and architectures of network slicing were presented in this study to give the readers a complete information from these technologies. Furthermore, a great deal of standardization efforts was summed up with other sections providing various standardizing bodies and their aims in this technology including 3GPP, IETF, ETSI, ONF, TMF, TIP NGMN, GSMA, OpenStack, xRAN and BBF. To conclude the study, state-of-the-art future challenge were presented by looking various aspects including Interoperability between mobile networks, scalability of radio access networks, Roaming, interoperability of software functions and hardware, migration from physical to fully virtual and the development of innovative features.

References

1. Abusaada, H., Elshater, A.: COVID-19 challenge, information technologies, and smart cities: considerations for well-being. Int. J. Commun. Well-Being **3**(3), 417–424 (2020). https://doi.org/10.1007/s42413-020-00068-5
2. AAP FactCheck: COVID-19 pandemic not a case of history repeating itself. AAP, 09 April 2020. https://www.aap.com.au/covid-19-pandemic-not-a-case-of-history-repeating-itself/

3. Srivastava, V., Srivastava, S., Chaudhary, G., Al-Turjman, F.: A systematic approach for COVID-19 predictions and parameter estimation. Pers. Ubiquitous Comput. (2020). https://doi.org/10.1007/s00779-020-01462-8

4. Karmore, S., Bodhe, R., Al-Turjman, F., Kumar, R.L., Pillai, S.: IoT based humanoid software for identification and diagnosis of Covid-19 suspects. IEEE Sens. J. 1 (2020). https://doi.org/10.1109/JSEN.2020.3030905

5. WHO: Coronavirus disease (COVID-19) pandemic WHO regional office for Europe, 12 March 2020. https://www.euro.who.int/en/health-topics/health-emergencies/coronavirus-covid-19/news/news/2020/3/who-announces-covid-19-outbreak-a-pandemic

6. Monaghesh, E., Hajizadeh, A.: The role of telehealth during COVID-19 out-break: a systematic review based on current evidence. BMC Public Health 20(1), 1193 (2020). https://doi.org/10.1186/s12889-020-09301-4

7. Smith, A.C., et al.: Telehealth for global emergencies: implications for corona-virus disease 2019 (COVID-19). J. Telemed. Telecare 26(5), 309–313 (2020). https://doi.org/10.1177/1357633X20916567

8. Li, W., et al.: Progression of Mental Health Services during the COVID-19 Out-break in China. Int. J. Biol. Sci. 16(10), 1732–1738 (2020). https://doi.org/10.7150/ijbs.45120

9. Wax, R.S., Christian, M.D.: Practical recommendations for critical care and anesthesiology teams caring for novel coronavirus (2019-nCoV) patients. Can. J. Anesth. Can. Anesth. 67(5), 568–576 (2020). https://doi.org/10.1007/s12630-020-01591-x

10. Al-Turjman, F., Deebak, B.: Privacy-aware energy-efficient framework using the internet of medical things for COVID-19. IEEE Internet Things Mag. 3(3), 64–68 (2020). https://doi.org/10.1109/IOTM.0001.2000123

11. Ohannessian, R.: Telemedicine: potential applications in epidemic situations. Eur. Res. Telemed. Rech. Eur. En Télémédecine 4(3), 95–98 (2015). https://doi.org/10.1016/j.eurtel.2015.08.002

12. Kruse, C.S., Krowski, N., Rodriguez, B., Tran, L., Vela, J., Brooks, M.: Tele-health and patient satisfaction: a systematic review and narrative analysis. BMJ Open 7(8), e016242 (2017). https://doi.org/10.1136/bmjopen-2017-016242

13. ITU: 5G - Fifth generation of mobile technologies. Challenges and Solutions: Building 5g Networks for the Future, December 2019. https://www.itu.int/en/mediacentre/backgrounders/Pages/5G-fifth-generation-of-mobile-technologies.aspx

14. Kolhar, M., Al-Turjman, F., Alameen, A., Abualhaj, M.M.: A three layered decentralized IoT biometric Architecture for City Lockdown During COVID-19 Outbreak. IEEE Access, 8, 163608–163617 (2020). https://doi.org/10.1109/ACCESS.2020.3021983

15. Soenen, T., Banerjee, R., Tavernier, W., Colle, D., Pickavet, M.: Demystifying network slicing: from theory to practice. In: 2017 IFIP/IEEE Symposium on In-tegrated Network and Service Management (IM), Lisbon, Portugal, pp. 1115–1120, May 2017. https://doi.org/10.23919/INM.2017.7987450

16. Agiwal, M., Roy, A., Saxena, N.: Next generation 5G wireless networks: a comprehensive survey. IEEE Commun. Surv. Tutor. 18(3), 1617–1655 (2016). https://doi.org/10.1109/COMST.2016.2532458

17. Andrews, J.G., et al.: What will 5G be? IEEE J. Sel. Areas Commun. 32(6), 1065–1082 (2014). https://doi.org/10.1109/JSAC.2014.2328098

18. Osseiran, A., et al.: Scenarios for 5G mobile and wireless communications: the vi-sion of the METIS project. IEEE Commun. Mag. 52(5), 26–35 (2014). https://doi.org/10.1109/MCOM.2014.6815890

19. Zhang, S.: An overview of network slicing for 5G. IEEE Wirel. Commun. 26(3), 111–117 (2019). https://doi.org/10.1109/MWC.2019.1800234

20. Peng,S., Chen, R., Mirsky, G., Qin, F.: Packet network slicing using segment routing draft-peng-teas-network-slicing-03. IETF, 16 February 2020. https://tools.ietf.org/pdf/draft-peng-teas-network-slicing-03.pdf

21. Benzekki, K., El Fergougui, A., Elbelrhiti Elalaoui, A.: Software-defined net-working (SDN): a survey: software-defined networking: a survey. Secur. Commun. Netw. **9**(18), 5803–5833 (2016). https://doi.org/10.1002/sec.1737

22. Horvath, R., Nedbal, D., Stieninger, M.: A literature review on challenges and effects of software defined networking. Procedia Comput. Sci. **64**, 552–561 (2015). https://doi.org/10.1016/j.procs.2015.08.563

23. Chowdhury, N.M.M.K., Boutaba, R.: Network virtualization: state of the art and research challenges. IEEE Commun. Mag. **47**(7), 20–26 (2009). https://doi.org/10.1109/MCOM.2009.5183468

24. Yi, B., Wang, X., Li, K., Das, S.K., Huang, M.: "A comprehensive survey of Network Function Virtualization. Comput. Netw. **133**, 212–262 (2018). https://doi.org/10.1016/j.comnet.2018.01.021

25. Li, Y., Chen, M.: Software-defined network function virtualization: a survey. IEEE Access **3**, 2542–2553 (2015). https://doi.org/10.1109/ACCESS.2015.2499271

26. Trivisonno, R., An, X., Wei, Q.: Network slicing for 5G systems: a review from an architecture and standardization perspective. In: 2017 IEEE Conference on Standards for Communications and Networking (CSCN), Helsinki, Finland, September 2017, pp. 36–41. https://doi.org/10.1109/CSCN.2017.8088595

27. Barakabitze, A.A., Ahmad, A., Mijumbi, R., Hines, A.: 5G network slicing us-ing SDN and NFV: a survey of taxonomy, architectures and future challenges. Comput. Netw. **167**, 106984 (2020). https://doi.org/10.1016/j.comnet.2019.106984

28. GSMA: Network-slicing-use-case-requirements-fixed.pdf., April 2018. https://www.gsma.com/futurenetworks/wp-content/uploads/2018/07/Network-Slicing-Use-Case-Requirements-fixed.pdf

29. NGMN: NGMN 5G White Paper, p. 125, February 2015

30. Afolabi, I., Taleb, T., Samdanis, K., Ksentini, A., Flinck, H.: Network slicing & softwarization: a survey on principles, enabling technologies & solutions, p. 24

31. Foukas, X., Patounas, G., Elmokashfi, A., Marina, M.K.: Network slicing in 5G: survey and challenges. IEEE Commun. Mag. **55**(5), 94–100 (2017). https://doi.org/10.1109/MCOM.2017.1600951

32. Chen, Q., Liu, C.-X.: A survey of network slicing in 5G. DEStech Trans. Comput. Sci. Eng., no. csma, December 2017. https://doi.org/10.12783/dtcse/csma2017/17318

33. Kim, D., Kim, S.: Network slicing as enablers for 5G services: state of the art and challenges for mobile industry. Telecommun. Syst. **71**(3), 517–527 (2018). https://doi.org/10.1007/s11235-018-0525-2

34. Kaloxylos, A.: A Survey and an Analysis of Network Slicing in 5G Networks. IEEE Commun. Stand. Mag. **2**(1), 60–65 (2018). https://doi.org/10.1109/MCOMSTD.2018.1700072

35. Richart, M., Baliosian, J., Serrat, J., Gorricho, J.-L.: Resource slicing in virtual wireless networks: a survey. IEEE Trans. Netw. Serv. Manage. **13**(3), 462–476 (2016). https://doi.org/10.1109/TNSM.2016.2597295

36. China Mobile Communications Corporation, Huawei Technologies Co, Deutsche Telekom, and Volkswagen, "5G Service-Guaranteed Network Slicing White Pa-per," no. V 1.0, February 2017. https://www-file.huawei.com/-/media/corporate/pdf/white%20paper/5g-service-guaranteed-network-slicing-whitepaper.pdf?la=en

37. El,A.: 5G Network Slicing Reference Model, White Paper (2019). https://doi.org/10.13140/RG.2.2.29838.82240

38. (GSA): 5G Network Slicing for Vertical Industries. September 2017. https://www.huawei.com/minisite/5g/img/5g-network-slicing-for-vertical-industries-en.pdf

39. 5GPP: 5G VISION: The 5G Infrastructure Public Private Partnership:the next generation of communication networks and services.".
40. IMT Vision – Framework and overall objectives of the future development of IMT for 2020 and beyond, p. 21
41. Elayoubi, S.E., et al.: 5G service requirements and operational use cases: analysis and METIS II vision. In: 2016 European Conference on Networks and Communications (EuCNC), Athens, Greece, June 2016, pp. 158–162. https://doi.org/10.1109/EuCNC.2016.7561024
42. Liu, G., Jiang, D.: 5G: Vision and requirements for mobile communication system towards year 2020. Chin. J. Eng. **2016**, 1–8 (2016). https://doi.org/10.1155/2016/5974586
43. 5G Americas: The evolution of security in 5G. 5G Americas whitepaper, October 2018. https://www.5gamericas.org/wp-content/uploads/2019/07/5G_Americas_5G_Security_White_Paper_Final.pdf
44. Noll, J., Chowdhury, M.M.R.: 5G: service continuity in heterogeneous environments. Wirel. Pers. Commun. **57**(3), 413–429 (2011). https://doi.org/10.1007/s11277-010-0077-6
45. Lauridsen, M., Berardinelli, G., Tavares, F.M.L., Frederiksen, F., Mogensen, P.: Sleep modes for enhanced battery life of 5G mobile terminals. In: 2016 IEEE 83rd Vehicular Technology Conference (VTC Spring), Nanjing, China, May 2016, pp. 1–6 (2016). https://doi.org/10.1109/VTCSpring.2016.7504476
46. Barakabitze, A.A., Sun, L., Mkwawa, I.-H., Ifeachor, E.: A novel QoE-centric SDN-based multipath routing approach for multimedia services over 5G networks. In: 2018 IEEE International Conference on Communications (ICC), Kan-sas City, MO, May 2018, pp. 1–7 (2018). https://doi.org/10.1109/ICC.2018.8422617
47. Banovic-Curguz, N., Ilisevic, D.: Mapping of QoS/QoE in 5G networks. In: 2019 42nd International Convention on Information and Communication Tech-nology, Electronics and Microelectronics (MIPRO), Opatija, Croatia, May 2019, pp. 404–408 (2019). https://doi.org/10.23919/MIPRO.2019.8757034
48. Mushtaq,M.S., Fowler, S., Augustin, B., Mellouk, A.: QoE in 5G cloud net-works using multimedia services. In: 2016 IEEE Wireless Communications and Networking Conference, Doha, Qatar, April 2016, pp. 1–6 (2016). https://doi.org/10.1109/WCNC.2016.7565173
49. IBM: IBM Systems Virtualization: Servers, Storage, and Software, p. 96, April 2008
50. Goldberg, R.P.: Survey of virtual machine research. Computer **7**(6), 34–45 (1974). https://doi.org/10.1109/MC.1974.6323581
51. Chiueh, S.N.T.: A survey on virtualization technologies, p. 42, January 2005.https://rtcl.eecs.umich.edu/papers/publications/2011/TR179.pdf
52. Lindquist, A.B., Seeber, R.R., Comeau, L.W.: A time-sharing system using an associative memory. Proc. IEEE **54**(12), 1774–1779 (1966). https://doi.org/10.1109/PROC.1966.5261
53. Peterson, L., Roscoe, T.: The design principles of PlanetLab. ACM SIGOPS Oper. Syst. Rev. **40**(1), 11–16 (2006). https://doi.org/10.1145/1113361.1113367
54. PlanetLab: MyPLC user's guide, PlanetLab. https://www.planet-lab.org/doc/myplc-3.3
55. Berman, M., et al.: GENI: a federated testbed for innovative network experi-ments. Comput. Netw. **61**, 5–23 (2014). https://doi.org/10.1016/j.bjp.2013.12.037
56. MGMN: Description of network slicing concept, 13 January 2016
57. Habiba, U., Hossain, E.: Auction mechanisms for virtualization in 5G cellular networks: basics, trends, and open challenges. IEEE Commun. Surv. Tutor. **20**(3), 2264–2293 (2018). https://doi.org/10.1109/COMST.2018.2811395
58. Samdanis, K., Costa-Perez, X., Sciancalepore, V.: From network sharing to multi-tenancy: the 5G network slice broker. IEEE Commun. Mag. **54**(7), 32–39 (2016). https://doi.org/10.1109/MCOM.2016.7514161
59. ONF: Applying SDN architecture to 5G slicing. ONF, April 2016. https://www.opennetworking.org/wp-content/uploads/2014/10/Applying_SDN_Architecture_to_5G_Slicing_TR-526.pdf

60. Kim, J., Kim, D., Choi, S.: 3GPP SA2 architecture and functions for 5G mobile communication system. ICT Express 3(1), 1–8 (2017). https://doi.org/10.1016/j.icte.2017.03.007
61. Ain Usmani, Z., Gupta, G.K.: ITU-T future networks and its framework of virtualization. Int. J. Recent Dev. Eng. Technol. 3(3) (2014). https://www.ijrdet.com/files/Volume3Issue3/IJRDET_0914_08.pdf
62. 3GPP TR 22.862: Feasibility Study on New Services and Markets Technology enablers for Critical Communications. 3GPP (2016)
63. Fettweis, G.P.: The tactile internet: applications and challenges. IEEE Veh. Technol. Mag. 9(1), 64–70 (2014). https://doi.org/10.1109/MVT.2013.2295069
64. 3GPP TR 22.861: Feasibility study on new services and markets technology enablers for massive Internet of Things. 3GPP, June 2016
65. Farris, I., T.T., Flinck, H., Antonio, I.: Providing ultra-short latency to us-er-centric 5G applications at the mobile network edge. Trans. Emerg. Telecom-mun. Technol. 2017. https://doi.org/10.1002/ett.3169
66. Taleb, T., Ksentini, A., Kobbane, A.: Lightweight mobile core networks for machine type communications. IEEE Access 2, 1128–1137 (2014). https://doi.org/10.1109/ACCESS.2014.2359649
67. Hakiri, A., Gokhale, A., Berthou, P., Schmidt, D.C., Gayraud, T.: Software-defined networking: challenges and research opportunities for Future Internet. Comput. Netw. 75, 453–471 (2014). https://doi.org/10.1016/j.comnet.2014.10.015
68. ETSI: Network function virtualization. SDN Openflow World Congr., no. Dusseldorf, Germany, Dusseldorf, Germany 2014. https://portal.etsi.org/NFV/NFV_White_Paper3.pdf
69. Wu, G., Mukherjee, U., Li, Q., Papathanassiou, A.: An end-to-end network slicing framework for 5G wireless communication systems. Netw. Internet Ar-chit. 13 (2016)
70. Biczok, G., Dramitinos, M., Toka, L., Heegaard, P.E., Lonsethagen, H.: Manufactured by software: SDN-enabled multi-operator composite services with the 5G exchange. IEEE Commun. Mag. 55(4), 80–86 (2017). https://doi.org/10.1109/MCOM.2017.1600197
71. Gouvas, P., et al.: Design, development and orchestration of 5G-ready applications over sliced programmable infrastructure. In: 2017 29th International Teletraffic Congress (ITC 29), Genoa, Italy, September 2017, pp. 13–18 (2017). https://doi.org/10.23919/ITC.2017.8065704
72. Parada, C., et al.: 5Gtango: a Beyond-mano service platform. In: 2018 European Conference on Networks and Communications (EuCNC), Ljubljana, Slove-nia, June 2018, pp. 26–30 (2018). https://doi.org/10.1109/EuCNC.2018.8443232.
73. Gramaglia, M., et al.: Flexible connectivity and QoE/QoS management for 5G Networks: the 5G NORMA view. In: 2016 IEEE International Conference on Communications Workshops (ICC), Kuala Lumpur, Malaysia, May 2016, pp. 373–379 (2016). https://doi.org/10.1109/ICCW.2016.7503816
74. Taleb, T., Mada, B., Corici, M.-I., Nakao, A., Flinck, H.: PERMIT: network slicing for personalized 5G mobile telecommunications. IEEE Commun. Mag. 55(5), 88–93 (2017). https://doi.org/10.1109/MCOM.2017.1600947
75. Silva, F.S.D., et al.: NECOS project: towards lightweight slicing of cloud federated infrastructures. In: 2018 4th IEEE Conference on Network Softwarization and Workshops (NetSoft), Montreal, QC, June 2018, pp. 406–414 (2018). https://doi.org/10.1109/NETSOFT.2018.8460008
76. Chang, C.-Y., Nikaein, N., Spyropoulos, T.: Radio access network resource slicing for flexible service execution. In: IEEE INFOCOM 2018 - IEEE Confer-ence on Computer Communications Workshops (INFOCOM WKSHPS), Honolu-lu, HI, April 2018, pp. 668–673 (2018). https://doi.org/10.1109/INFCOMW.2018.8407021

77. Foukas, X., Marina, M.K., Kontovasilis, K.: Orion: RAN slicing for a flexible and cost-effective multi-service mobile network architecture. In: Proceedings of the 23rd Annual International Conference on Mobile Computing and Net-working, Snowbird Utah USA, October 2017, pp. 127–140 (2017). https://doi.org/10.1145/3117811.3117831
78. GSMA: Considerations, best practices and requirements for a virtualised mobile network. GSMA (2017). https://www.gsma.com/futurenetworks/wp-content/uploads/2017/05/Virtualisation.pdf
79. TIP: "Telecom Infra Project. About us, 07 June 2019. https://telecominfraproject.com/
80. TMF: TM Forum. https://www.tmforum.org/about-tm-forum/. Accessed 09 Jun 2020

An Empirical Study of Trilateration and Clustering for Indoor Localization and Trend Prediction

Aarth Tandel[✉], Anvesh Chennupati, and Behnam Dezfouli

Department of Computer Science and Engineering, Santa Clara University,
Santa Clara, USA
{atandel,achennupati,bdezfouli}@scu.edu

Abstract. Localization via trilateration determines the location of moving objects using the distances between each object and multiple stations. Since low-power wireless technologies are the primary enablers of these localization methods, the technology's type and characteristics highly affect trilateration accuracy. In addition, pre-processing the collected data can also be used as an effective method to enhance system accuracy. This paper presents an effective way of tracking objects using trilateration in indoor environments. We analyze the data generated from the stations, including coordinates, timestamps, and identifiers. After running a clustering algorithm on the data, we infer information on the object's behavior, frequently visited places, and predict objects' location. Field testing results at Santa Clara University demonstrate that accuracy is increased in the range of 20 to 40% when applying the pre-processing method.

Keywords: Tracking · Clustering · Wireless · Trilateration · Gaussian mixture · BLE

1 Introduction

Indoor localization is the process of obtaining a device's location in an indoor environment. This type of localization has recently witnessed increased popularity due to the potential wide range of services it can provide by leveraging Internet of Things (IoT) technologies. A wide range of devices such as smartphones and wearable devices, which support Bluetooth Low Energy (BLE), has made indoor localization a reality.

An indoor localization system has a wide range of applications in the health sector, industry, disaster management, building management, surveillance and wholesale stores [1,2]. For example, to enforce social distancing while preserving user privacy, the location of people in an indoor environment can be frequently monitored to issue alarms when a distance is reaching a threshold value. Indoor localization in a nursing home can be used to identify the activity and movement pattern of residents. This information, for instance, can be used for identifying

S. Paiva et al. (Eds.): SmartCity360° 2020, LNICST 372, pp. 87–100, 2021.
https://doi.org/10.1007/978-3-030-76063-2_6

Table 1. Bluetooth devices shipped in billions

Categories	2015	2016	2017	2018	2019
Phone, Tablets and PC	2.0	1.96	2.02	2.05	2.08
Audio and Entertainment	0.77	0.94	1.1	1.2	1.3
Connected Devices	0.196	0.244	0.300	0.362	0.434
Smart Home	0.274	0.336	0.446	0.495	0.510

depression and dementia. In a doctor's room, localizing the doctor's position can be used to remind hand-washing when entering or leaving the room. As another example, if the clustered data for a customer is dense near a grocery store's eggs section compared to other sections, the customer can be presented with advertisements of bread or any product which matches egg's Jacobian similarity [5]. Similarly, clusters formed around a particular section in a store by different users can infer product popularity. This can be used to predict buying trends of the customers [14]. In disaster management, when a disaster such as a fire and earthquake occurs, an indoor localization technique can be very helpful for rescuing people from indoor environments where visibility is low due to smoke and rubble (Table 1).

Currently, wireless communication is the underlying mechanism used by most localization approaches. Long-range communication signals can estimate the global location of the device. These signals, which are transmitted from remote sources, have long wavelength (around 3 m), which means the signal strength does not dramatically change over short distances. Hence, long-range communication works better for large areas and cannot be used for indoor localization. Short-range communication technologies like Bluetooth can be used to estimate the relative indoor location of objects with respect to some reference points. The rapid growth of Bluetooth devices in handheld devices, entertainment devices, audio streaming and connected devices (as shown in Table 1 [21]) has made Bluetooth a popular choice for indoor localization.

Bluetooth Low Energy (BLE) is a low-power wireless technology used for connecting battery-powered devices. BLE can cover a range up to 70–100 m with higher energy efficiency compared to Bluetooth Classic [3]. BLE can be used with different localization techniques such as Received Signal Strength Indicator (RSSI), angle of arrival, and time of flight. For example, the iBeacon protocol has been proposed primarily for context-aware proximity-based services [4]. iBeacon allows a BLE enabled device to broadcast at periodic intervals, where the beacon message consists of 16 bytes Universally Unique Identifier (UUID). RSSI-based localization has been studied widely by the research community [8,9]. However, effective utilization of the data generated by the localization process has not been properly investigated. Specifically, pre-processing the data gathered from indoor localization is essential. Pre-processing involves identifying and removing unwanted data that might skew the results. After pre-processing, information such as coordinates, timestamps, and identifiers provide insights on most visited locations, behavior of the object, and predict the location of the object. Here, an object refers to an entity being tracked such as a person or a robot.

Several studies have been done to improve trilateration quality by using error correction algorithms [18,19]. Also, there are studies on mitigating main issues in indoor localization [20] such as multi-path fading, obstructions and effect of different materials on signal strength. In this paper, we propose a model to accurately predict users' behavior in an indoor locality using existing data mining algorithms and clustering algorithms. We also demonstrate how data flow is defined in the cloud and trilateration is used to determine user position. We further show how data is pre-processed using isolation forest [10] and then analyse the pre-processed data using Gaussian Mixture clustering algorithm [11]. Our results show accuracy enhancement in the range of 20 to 40%. Clustering algorithm is used to generate a model that can be used to predict users' behaviour by forming a heatmap. We validated system accuracy by testing the model in a Santa Clara University's indoor environment. Our results confirm that the clusters represent an average accuracy of 73% and 90% accuracy in best case scenario. This project is available in a GitHub repository[1].

In the subsequent sections of this paper, we detail the design and implementation of data collection system from BLE beacons and pre-processing model (Sect. 2), present testing results (Sect. 3), and then conclude the paper (Sect. 4).

2   Design and Implementation

In this section, we show how trilateration is achieved, define the data flow in the cloud, and analyze the data using data mining algorithms.

2.1   System Overview

In this study, we use an RSSI-based system. These systems are cost-efficient, easy to implement, and can be used by other RSSI-based technologies such as WiFi and ZigBee. We chose ESP32, which is a low-cost, low-power, integrated WiFi and dual-mode Bluetooth solution. We use the WiFi integrated in the ESP32 to connect to the Internet and transmit the data to the cloud. Each ESP32 device acts as a *station* and is used to receive BLE beacons and filter the scanned data.

Beacons are sent by *objects* that are being tracked. For the beacon we chose Blue Charm beacons [22], which is low-cost, secure, light weight and small in size (36 mm × 36 mm × 6 mm). Blue Charm beacons broadcasts data in iBeacon format, which makes it easy to identify using UUID. Beacons battery lasts up to 300 days and transmission power range is between -23 dBm to +4 dBm.

Since the data is transmitted periodically in short intervals (five seconds), we need an execution model where the cloud provider is responsible for executing a piece of code by dynamically allocating resources. Thus, we chose AWS (Amazon Web Services) serverless architecture, where the code is executed in a stateless container that can be triggered by a variety of events including HTTPS requests, database events or scheduled events.

---

[1] https://github.com/SIOTLAB/BLE-AWS-localization.git.

2.2   Trilateration

RSSI-based localization is one of the simplest and widely used approaches for indoor localization. RSSI is the received signal strength measured in decibel-milliwatts (dBm). It is used to estimate the distance between a station and a BLE beacon's source by using another constant known as the transmission power, which is the power emitted from the device. Increasing the transmission power results in a higher range.

Beacons do not broadcast data constantly, instead they broadcast data depending on the advertising interval. Advertising interval refers to how often the device enters the advertising state from the low power mode. Although a shorter interval enables the reception of a higher number of beacons during a given period, and therefore a higher accuracy localization, it also results in a higher energy consumption of the beacon source. Therefore, depending on the beacon transmitter's type of energy source, a trade-off between accuracy and lifetime needs to be established.

While RSSI-based approach is cost efficient, it suffers from multipath fading and noise, which may decrease the accuracy of localization. Different filters or averaging mechanisms can be used to mitigate these effects.

The distance d between a station and the BLE beacon source can be estimated using Eq. 1:

$$RSSI = -10n \log_{10} d + Tx \qquad (1)$$

where n is the path loss component and Tx is the measured power, both in dBm.

RSSI-based localization requires trilateration to determine indoor position. In Trilateration, positioning a point in Cartesian system requires measuring its distance in different alignments with respect to the base point (x, y). For 2-D positioning, a point's distance is measured, using the intersection formed by the three circles as shown in Fig. 1.

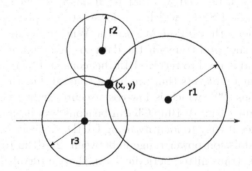

Fig. 1. Circles formed by three BLE beacon sources

Using the following formula, the intersection of the three circles in a Cartesian system, represented as coordinates (x, y), is computed as follows:

$$(X_1 - x)^2 + (Y_1 - y)^2 = (r_1)^2 \tag{2}$$

$$(X_2 - x)^2 + (Y_2 - y)^2 = (r_2)^2 \tag{3}$$

$$(X_3 - x)^2 + (Y_3 - y)^2 = (r_3)^2 \tag{4}$$

2.3   Data Acquisition and Transmission

For the trilateration to work, distance is needed from at least three stations to calculate the coordinates in a Cartesian plane. To reduce the processing on stations and collect data efficiently, data was transmitted to the cloud to calculate distance using RSSI and transmission power. Stations are placed at known locations throughout the venue. Once a station powers up, it searches for a pre-programmed SSID and connects to the Internet, after which it initiates connection to the server. When three or more Bluetooth stations detect the same beacon, the system can perform trilateration. While objects move and broadcast their identifiers, the stations collect the beacons and upload the data containing UUID, station identifier, RSSI, transmission power and time stamp, in JSON format to the cloud.

2.4   Cloud Architecture

The data transmitted by stations to cloud is via the MQTT protocol [17] and is updated in AWS shadow states, which is a JSON document used to store and retrieve the current state of stations. The Device Shadow service maintains a shadow for each device connected to AWS IoT. The shadow can be used to get and set the state of a device over MQTT. Once the data is reflected in shadow states, AWS Rules forward the data to AWS Lambda. AWS Rules provide the cloud with the flexibility to combine different data storage and processing options. AWS Lambda consists of the logic to calculate distance using RSSI and transmission power received from the stations. Entire cloud architecture is depicted in Fig. 2.

Once the distance from all stations is calculated using Eq. 1, the coordinates are calculated using Eq. 2, 3, and 4. The calculated coordinates are stored in a text file along with the UUID, time stamp, RSSI and transmission power.

2.5   Pre-Processing

The data consisting of X and Y coordinates of the BLE beacon is prone to anomalies as the values of RSSI can be affected by multipath fading, noise, and obstructions. An anomaly is an observation that deviates from other events which

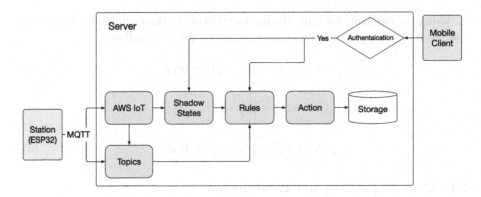

Fig. 2. AWS cloud server

raise suspicion that the data was generated by different means. If the anomalous data is processed by the clustering algorithm, the clusters generated is skewed by the anomalies. Figure 3 shows visualization of data, where red cross represents anomalies and green dot represents the correct observation which forms clusters.

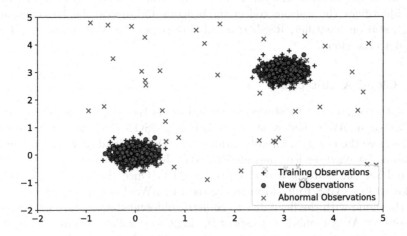

Fig. 3. Anomalies in data generates skewed clusters

We used *isolation forest* to clean the data obtained from stations. Isolation forest is an unsupervised learning algorithm that is based on the principles of decision trees. In these trees, partitions are created by randomly selecting a feature and then selecting a split value between minimum and maximum value of the selected feature. It is an algorithm with low linear time complexity and small memory requirements. It builds a performing model with a small number of trees using small sub-samples of fixed size, regardless of the size of the dataset.

2.6   Data Analysis

With enough data generated, choosing appropriate clustering algorithm is essential. We classified clustering algorithms according to geometry, use-cases and density estimation. When classifying clustering algorithms according to geometry, non-flat geometry is useful when the clusters have a specific shape. In an indoor environment, objects tend to move in linear paths, which forms clusters in elongated shapes. We excluded all the clustering algorithms which have use-cases in non-flat geometry and density estimation. Thus, according to the stated criteria, we analyzed the following clustering algorithms.

K-Means Clustering: K-means is an iterative algorithm that tries to partition the dataset into K pre-defined distinct non-overlapping subgroups (clusters) where each data point belongs to only one group. This results in separating the data into clusters.

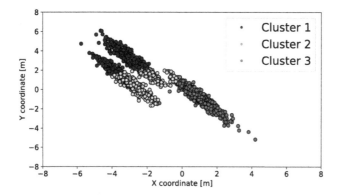

Fig. 4. Incorrect clusters formed by K-Means for elongated clusters

When analyzing the algorithm, we observed that the K-means clustering was not able to determine the clusters with elongated shapes. Specifically, it is ineffective when clusters are of varying density. As shown in Fig. 4, purple, yellow and cyan dots are the clusters formed by K-means. The predicted cluster 1 overlaps with cluster 2 as shown in Fig. 4, which is incorrect. This is because it aims to choose centroids that minimize the inertia [5,12]. Inertia makes the assumptions that the clusters are convex and isotropic, which causes K-means to respond poorly to elongated clusters. Hence, K-means is more suitable for even cluster shape where clusters are ball shaped.

Gaussian Mixture: Gaussian Mixture is an extension of K-Means clustering in which a probabilistic model assumes that all points are generated from a mixture of a finite number of Gaussian distributions with some unknown variables. It implements the expectation-maximum model for fitting the mixture of Gaussian model. Because of expectation-maximum model, Gaussian Mixture can effectively determine ellipsoids for multivariate models [13] and access the number of clusters in the data. Comparing Fig. 4 and Fig. 5 shows that the Gaussian Mixture performs better than K-means when dealing with elongated clusters.

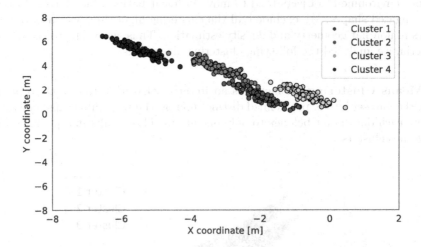

Fig. 5. Elongated clusters formed by Gaussian Mixture

2.7 Privacy Concerns

Since users' data is transmitted periodically to the server for data analysis, it is important to handle the data ethically and being transparent with the users regarding the collected data. First, the data is collected in a controlled environment such as hospitals and shopping complexes. Second, a simple mobile application can be developed to let the users enroll or opt out from their data being collected.

3 Testing and Results

Once the prototype was tuned and modified, it was tested in the field environment. By data collection and regression analysis, we determined the most effective value of n (path loss component) for Eq. 1 was 2. Then, several field tests were performed to determine how the system would perform in a real environment. One such testing took place in a building of Santa Clara University, located in Santa Clara, CA.

The indoor environment was divided into three areas namely *corridor*, *lecture hall*, and *sitting area*. Figure 6 shows the floor plan. The stations were kept in a

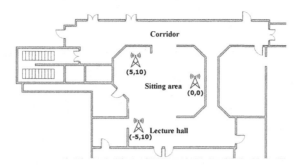

Fig. 6. Floor plan of Benson Center basement at Santa Clara University, Santa Clara, USA

triangular structure on an elevated position such that beacons were in the line of sight. This was done to minimize the obstruction from other objects. The coordinates of the stations are $(0, 0)$ $(-5, 10)$ and $(5, 10)$. Stations send their collected data to the cloud every five seconds.

After setting up the stations, the object was attached to the backpack of a student. The students was instructed to move anywhere within the area covered by the stations. The total testing duration was three hours: 60 min in lecture hall, 20 min in corridor, and 75 min in sitting area.

There were total of 1014 coordinates generated after trilateration, out of which 68 were anomalies, as shown in Fig. 7. In Fig. 7(b) all the red crosses (x) are anomalous coordinates and were removed from the dataset using the isolation forest technique. The blue circle denotes the correct coordinates. When we ran the Gaussian Mixture algorithm on the dataset without pre-processing, we found that 495 coordinates were incorrectly clustered. When calculating accuracy, 495 coordinates out of 1014 coordinates were incorrect, thereby resulting in about 52% accuracy, as Fig. 7(c) shows. Comparing Fig. 7(a) and Fig. 8(a), we observed there is a major change in the visualization of user's demographics after pre-processing.

Figure 8(b) shows clusters formed by Gaussian Mixture; red plus, green cross, and blue circles represent sitting area, corridor and lecture hall, respectively. The number of clusters were set to three as the entire area was divided into three sections. When analysing the data, we found that there were 92 coordinates which were incorrectly clustered in corridor, while these coordinates belonged to the sitting area. Apart from that, 854 coordinates were correctly categorized in their respective clusters of sitting area, lecture hall and corridor. Accuracy is calculated as the number of coordinates classified correctly. When calculating accuracy, 92 coordinates out of 946 were incorrect, thereby resulting in about 90% accuracy in best case scenario, as Fig. 8(b) shows. When doing regression testing, we achieved an average accuracy of 73% as shown in Fig. 8(c). When found that accuracy has increased by roughly 20% when applying pre-processing method.

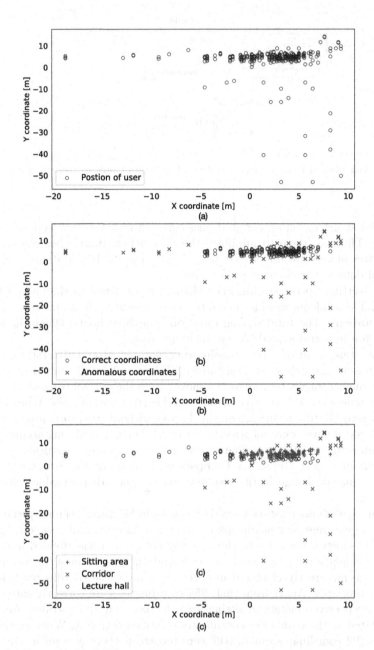

Fig. 7. (a) Demographics of the student, (b) anomalous and correct coordinates, and (c) accuracy without applying pre-processing. Out of 1014 coordinates, 495 were incorrect, thereby resulting in about 52% accuracy.

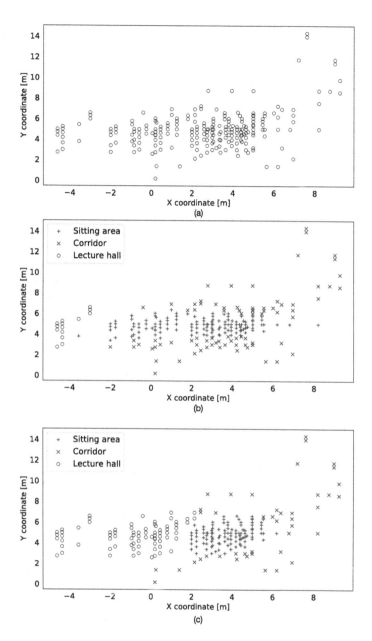

Fig. 8. Demographics of student (a) after removing anomalous data. (b) clusters formed after pre-processing. 92 coordinates out of 946 were incorrect, thereby resulting in about 90% accuracy. (c) clusters formed after pre-processing. 259 coordinates out of 946 were incorrect, thereby resulting in about 73% accuracy.

Our results demonstrate that the student spent the majority of his time in the sitting area and least in the corridor. Other information that can be derived is, the student spent a considerate amount of time in the sitting area before attending the lecture. Similar information can be deduced for people in a nursing home, where the number of clusters corresponds with the different areas and activities available to them.

3.1   Failure Modes

During the field testing, we found out obstruction causes the RSSI values to change drastically, which resulted in incorrect distance calculation. Incorrect or inconsistent measurements caused by obstruction could mislead users, cause device distrust, and negatively influence decision making. These potential failures can be mitigated in three ways. One way is to properly arrange the stations at a height so that all the beacons are in the line of sight with the nodes and there is less obstruction. Second way is to use fingerprinting technique, where features are collected in form of RSSI or CSI (Channel State Information) to estimate user's location. The third way is to use improved trilateration methods such as using error correction algorithms [15] and minimum generalization error [16].

4   Conclusion

In this paper we presented the design and development of a system that can effectively track objects in indoor environments using BLE devices. The system includes stations that extract RSSI from received beacons and communicates with a cloud platform to report data. We used isolation forest to remove anomalous data and then analyzed the pre-processed data with Gaussian Mixture algorithm to generate clusters to predict the behaviour of moving objects. Field testing results at Santa Clara University demonstrate that accuracy is increased in the range of 20 to 40% when applying the pre-processing method.

The Gaussian Mixture algorithm is not very scalable, considering its asymptotic time complexity of $O(NKD^3)$ for N data points, K Gaussian components and D dimensions, rendering it inadequate for high-dimensional data. If an algorithm's run-time complexity is less than $O(NKD^3)$, the system performance will increase and consume less resources.

We observed that the majority of errors occur due to faulty RSSI values caused by noise and interference. The impact of these erroneous values could be reduced by increasing beaconing rate and reception probability. From the stations point of view, however, since both BLE and WiFi use the same frequency band, concurrent operation of these radios would impact the ability of stations to receive beacons. Therefore, it is essential to minimize the operational time of WiFi radio. For this, a higher data transmission rate could be employed to reduce packet transmission duration.

References

1. Asimakopoulou, E., Bessis, N.: Buildings and crowds: forming smart cities for more effective disaster management. In: Fifth International Conference on Innovative Mobile and Internet Services in Ubiquitous Computing (IMIS), pp. 229–234. IEEE (2011)
2. Zelenkauskaite, A., Bessis, N., Sotiriadis, S., Asimakopoulou, E.: Interconnectedness of complex systems of internet of things through social network analysis for disaster management. In: Fourth International Conference on Intelligent Networking and Collaborative Systems, pp. 503–508. IEEE (2012)
3. Zafari, F., Papapanagiotou, I., Christidis, K.: Microlocation for internet-of-things-equipped smart buildings. IEEE Internet Things J. **3**(1), 96–112 (2016)
4. iBeacon. https://developer.apple.com/ibeacon/. Accessed 22 June 2017
5. Leskovec, J., Rajaraman, A., Ullman, J.D.: Mining of Massive Data Sets. Cambridge University Press, Cambridge (2020)
6. sumologic.com: How much data come from IoT?. https://www.sumologic.com/blog/iot-data-volume/. Accessed 22 Mar 2020
7. Yin, J., Yang, Q., Ni, L.: Adaptive temporal radio maps for indoor location estimation. In: Pervasive Computing and Communications, pp. 85–94 (2005)
8. Zegeye, W.K., Amsalu, S.B., Astatke, Y., Moazzami, F.: WiFi RSS fingerprinting indoor localization for mobile devices. In: IEEE 7th Annual Ubiquitous Computing, Electronics and Mobile Communication Conference (UEMCON), New York, NY, pp. 1–6 (2016)
9. Borenovic, M.N., Neskovic, A.M.: Comparative analysis of RSSI, SNR and Noise level parameters applicability for WLAN positioning purposes. In: IEEE EURO-CON, St.-Petersburg, pp. 1895–1900 (2009)
10. Liu, F.T., Ting, K.M., Zhou, Z.H.: Isolation forest. In: Eighth IEEE International Conference on Data Mining, ICDM, pp. 413–422. IEEE (2008)
11. Sridharan, R.: Gaussian mixture models and the EM algorithm (2014). http://people.csail.mit.edu/rameshvs/content/gmm-em.pdf
12. Vattani, A.: k-means requires exponentially many iterations even in the plane. Discrete Comput. Geom. **45**(4), 596–616 (2011)
13. Moon, T.K.: The expectation-maximization algorithm. IEEE Signal Process. Mag. **13**(6), 47–60 (1996)
14. Forbes.com: Is COVID-19 Coronavirus Leading to Toilet Paper Shortages? Here is the Situation. https://www.forbes.com/sites/brucelee/2020/03/06/how-covid-19-coronavirus-is-leading-to-toilet-paper-shortages/. Accessed 22 Mar 2020
15. Moradi Zaniani, M., Shahar, A.M., Abdul Azid, I.: Trilateration target estimation improvement using new error correction algorithm. In: 18th Iranian Conference on Electrical Engineering, Isfahan, pp. 489–494 (2010)
16. Liu, W., Xiong, Y., Zong, X., Siwei, W.: Trilateration positioning optimization algorithm based on minimum generalization error. In: IEEE 4th International Symposium on Wireless Systems within the International Conferences on Intelligent Data Acquisition and Advanced Computing Systems (IDAACS-SWS), Lviv, pp. 154–157 (2018)
17. Kumar, P., Dezfouli, B.: Implementation and analysis of QUIC for MQTT. Comput. Netw. **150**, 28–45 (2019)
18. Moradi Zaniani, M., Shahar, A.M., Abdul Azid, I.: Trilateration target estimation improvement using new error correction algorithm. In: 18th Iranian Conference on Electrical Engineering, Isfahan, pp. 489–494 (2010). https://doi.org/10.1109/IRANIANCEE.2010.5507021

19. Joshua, N.A., Randolph, L.M.: Sensor localization error decomposition: theory and applications. In: Proceedings of IEEE Statistical Signal Processing Workshop, pp. 660–664, August 2007

20. Grosicki, E., Abed-Meraim, K.: A new trilateration method to mitigate the impact of some non-line-of-sight errors in TOA measurements for mobile localization. In: Proceedings of IEEE International Conference on Acoustics, Speech, and Signal Processing, ICASSP 2005, Philadelphia, PA, 2005, vol. 4, pp. iv/1045–iv/1048 (2005). https://doi.org/10.1109/ICASSP.2005.1416191

21. Bluetooth.com: Bluetooth market update. https://www.bluetooth.com/wp-content/uploads/2019/03/. Accessed 22 Mar 2020

22. Amazon.com: Blue Charm Beacons. https://www.amazon.com/dp/B07FC5F MHW/. Accessed 21 June 2020

COVID-19 Detection on CT Scans Using Local Binary Pattern and Deep Learning

Sertan Serte[1]([envelope])[iD] and Fadi Al-Turjman[2][iD]

[1] Near East University, North Cyprus via Mersin 10, Nicosia, Turkey
sertan.serte@neu.edu.tr
[2] Research Center for AI and IoT, Near East University, Mersin 10, Nicosia, Turkey
fadi.alturjman@neu.edu.tr

Abstract. X-ray and CT scans show lungs, and images can be used to differentiate positive and negative cases. Analyzing these scans using an artificial intelligent method might provide fast and accurate COVID-19 detection. In this paper, a local binary pattern based deep learning method is proposed for the detection of COVID-19 infection on CT Scans. The proposed technique generates local binary pattern (LBP) representations of the CT scans, and then these representations are modeled using fine-tuned models. The fine-tuned models are AlexNet, VGG, ResNet-18, ResNet-50, MobileNetV2, and DensNet-121. We show that the proposed local binary pattern based deep learning model provides higher performance than classic deep learning models for COVID-19 detection. The classification performance of the method provides 90% AUC value for COVID-19 detection.

Keywords: Convolutional neural networks · Deep learning · Local binary pattern (LBP) · COVID-19

1 Introduction

A new respiratory disease, Coronavirus, appeared in Wuhan China in 2019, [27]. Coronavirus [14] is known as viral pneumonia, and this viral pneumonia can be group into COVID-19, SARS, and MERS. Bacterial and fungus types of pneumonia are non-COVID-19 pneumonia types. Streptococcus is a type of bacterial pneumonia, while pneumocystis is a type of fungus pneumonia.

Currently, people are catching this disease from each other, and there is no vaccine for COVID-19 disease. The only wave of avoiding infection is to isolate infected people from healthy ones. Therefore, regular COVID-19 tests are necessary for the identification of infection on people to separate them. Transcription-polymerase chain reaction (RT-PCR) tests mainly allow to detect people with COVID-19 in hospitals.

Computed tomography scan (CT scan) and X-ray images are alternative diagnostic tools for detecting COVID-19. Doctors image lungs and look for signs of COVID-19 deformations on the CT or X-Ray images. This process requires a certain amount of time for correct pneumonia type classification.

S. Paiva et al. (Eds.): SmartCity360° 2020, LNICST 372, pp. 101–107, 2021.
https://doi.org/10.1007/978-3-030-76063-2_7

However, convolutional neural networks (CNNs) might be used instead of or in conjunction with the doctors for faster and better diagnosis of COVID-19 on CT scans. CNNs include AlexNet [11], GoogleNet [25], VGG [24], MobileNetV2 [16], ResNet [6] and DenseNet [9]. These models have provided the classification of 1,000 objects in the ImageNet dataset [3]. The performance results show that these models are close to human-level object-level accuracy. These models also result in high classification performance in medical image classification. Recent studies in [10,17,20,22,23] used CNNs to model skin lesion detection. The authors [18,19,21] also proposed to detect eye disease on funds images.

The proposed deep learning model (Fig. 1) is different than previous works [12,27]. In this paper, a local binary pattern based deep learning model is proposed to detect COVID-19 on CT-scans. The proposed approach builds on obtaining local binary pattern representations [8,26] of CT scans, and then these LBP structures are used as inputs to the fine-turned models for COVID-19 classification. LBP allowed to creates local forms of COVID-19 related regions. Both image and structure-based models are evaluated on COVID19-CT dataset. Results show that local binary pattern based models outperform the classic image-based CNN models. The main novelties of this work are:

1. A new local binary pattern based deep learning model is proposed for COVID-19 detection on CT scans.
2. The ResNet18 convolutional neural network is proposed to model local binary pattern features of diagnosis of COVID-19 on CT exams.
3. The performance comparisons provide model evaluation for COVID-19 classification.

The organization of this paper is as follows. First, the information about recent works is given. Second, the proposed approach is introduced. Furthermore, the proposed deep learning method is presented. In addition, the performances of classic and local binary pattern based models are compared.

2   Related Work

Combining CNN and a Generative Adversarial Network (GAN) models is another way of achieving data-efficient models. GAN models [4,15,27,28], are known as creating synthetic images from a given set of images. This model architecture includes generator and discriminator networks. The generator is responsible for synthetic image generating while the discriminator compares real and synthetic images during this process. A review [28] reports all proposed GAN models.

Mei et al. [13] proposed to use the Resnet-18 convolutional neural network in conjunction with support vector machines for COVID-19 detection. In this work, the CNN model allows prediction on the CT image, while SVM provides COVID-19 prediction on non-image data. Authors combine ResNet-18 and SVM outputs to detect COVID-19.

Harmon et al. [5] utilized DensNet-121 deep learning architecture for classification of COVID-19 and pneumonia. The proposed method train and tested on a multi dataset for performance evaluation.

Bhandary et al. [1] use AlexNet in conjunction with support vector machines to classify COVID-19 and cancer on X-Ray and CT Scans. Authors also compare the SVM based Alexnet with AlexNet, VGG16, VGG19, and ResNet50.

Butt et al. [2] use ResNet-18 deep learning model for the classifying COVID-19, viral pneumonia, and normal CT scans. This method builds on creating 3D volumes of the CT scans and then extracting paths from these regions. Then these images were used as inputs to the ResNet-18 model for differentiating COVID-19, viral pneumonia, and normal CT scans.

3 Method

In the trainig part, image based fine-tuned AlexNet, VGG, ResNet-18, ResNet-50, MobileNetV2, and DensNet-121 models generated. A set of CT scans are augmented and used as inputs to the fined-tuned models for modeling COVID-19.

The structure-based fine-tuned LAlexNet, LVGG, LResNet-18, LResNet-50, LMobileNetV2, and LDensNet-121 models are also generated. A set of CT scans are transformed into LBP images [8,26]. Then transformed images are augmented and used as inputs to the fined-tuned models for training.

In the testing part, a test CT scan and LBP representation used as inputs to the image and structured based models, respectively. Each of the models provides output probabilities of COVID-19 and non-COVID19 predictions (Table 3).

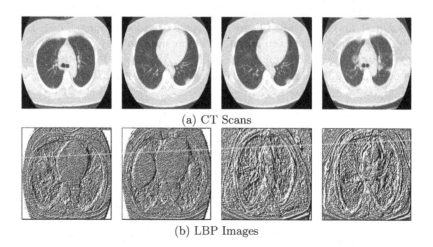

(a) CT Scans

(b) LBP Images

Fig. 1. Sample images from each dataset

Table 1. Total number of images in the datasets

CT-Scan	Dataset	Train	Test
COVID-19	COVID19-CT	324	40
Normal	COVID19-CT	293	37

Table 2. Total number of images in the datasets

Data	CT-Scan	Dataset	Train	Test
Image	COVID-19	COVID19-CT	1393	40
Image	Normal	COVID19-CT	1672	37
LBP	COVID-19	COVID19-CT	1393	40
LBP	Normal	COVID19-CT	1672	37

3.1   COVID19-CT Dataset

COVID19-CT dataset [7] includes 349 COVID-19 and 397 healthy CT scans. Figure 1 also shows the sample images from this dataset. The authors collected these CT-Scans from medRxiv3 and bioRxiv4 preprints. Images in the preprints show the COVID-19 finding on the images. Some of these findings can be seen clearly in the images.

3.2   Augmented Datasets

The fine-tuned models allow modeling COVID-19 and non-COVID-19 disease on the dataset. Since the available imaged are small in the dataset, the CT images are augmented, and then these images are used for model training. The CT scans of the training set are rotated to obtain an augmented dataset. Table 2 shows the number of augmented CT scans for COVID19-CT dataset. First, the dataset is split into training and testing sets. Then augmentation is performed on training images.

3.3   Model Generations

The fine-tuned models are generated for image and local binary pattern based deep learning methods. These fined-tuned models are the AlexNet, VGG, ResNet-18, ResNet-50, MobileNetV2, and DensNet-121.

All these models are pre-trained on the ImageNet dataset and the re-trained on CT scans and LBP images. The images are resized to 256×256 RGB images, and then these images are used as inputs to the CNN models. The $224 \times 224 \times 3$ random crops are extracted. The parameters of the convolutional layers are frozen, and only fully connected layers are estimated. To conclude, the proposed data-efficient models are fine-tuned for CT scans and LBP images of COVID-19 and non-COVID-19.

Table 3. Performance comparisons of single CNN models on COVID19-CT and Mosmed datasets.

Network	Data	AUC	ACC	SE	SP
AlexNet	Image	0.60	0.67	0.72	0.64
MobileNetV2	Image	0.71	0.73	0.82	0.69
Resnet18	Image	0.77	0.75	0.83	0.71
Resnet50	Image	0.71	0.77	0.86	0.72
Vgg	Image	0.65	0.75	0.86	0.70
Densenet121	Image	0.70	0.74	0.87	0.69
LResnet18	LBP	**0.90**	0.65	0.77	0.62
LResnet50	LBP	0.69	0.68	0.81	0.64
LVgg	LBP	0.63	0.67	0.80	0.63
LAlexNet	LBP	0.44	0.73	0.79	0.70
LDensenet121	LBP	0.45	0.65	0.71	0.63
LMobileNetV2	LBP	0.55	0.67	0.75	0.64

4   Performance Evaluation

Performance evaluation is performed using metrics as described follows. The area under the receiver operating characteristic (ROC) curve (AUC), accuracy (ACC), sensitivity (SE), and specificity (SP) performance merits are used to test the accuracy of the methods. We can describe accuracy, sensitivity, and specificity as:

$$\text{Accuracy} = \frac{\text{TP+TN}}{\text{TP+TN+FP+FN}} \tag{1}$$

$$\text{Sensetivity} = \frac{\text{TP}}{\text{TP+FN}} \tag{2}$$

$$\text{Specificity} = \frac{\text{TN}}{\text{TN+FP}} \tag{3}$$

where true positive, positive, true negative, false positive, and false negative are denoted as TP, TN, FP, and FN, respectively.

4.1   Image-Based Deep Learning Method

Table 3 reports the performances the AlexNet, VGG, ResNet-18, ResNet-50, MobileNetV2, and DensNet-121 deep learning models. These models only build on augmented data of the CT scans. These models are evaluated for on the COVID19-CT dataset.

4.2   Proposed Structure-Based Method

The performances of the proposed structure-based deep learning models are also evaluated in Table 3. Fine-tuned models build on LBP images of the CT scans. These fine-tuned models are AlexNet, VGG, ResNet-18, ResNet-50, MobileNetV2, and DensNet-121.

5   Conclusion

The image and local binary pattern based deep learning methods are proposed for COVID-19 detection on CT scans. The proposed methods build on both CT scans and LBP images of COVID19-CT dataset. This novel method allowed structuring available CT scans using LBP method. The fine-tuned The AlexNet, VGG, ResNet-18, ResNet-50, MobileNetV2, and DensNet-121 image-based models are generated. The LAlexNet, LVGG, LResNet-18, LResNet-50, LMobileNetV2, and LDensNet-121 LBP data based models also created. The results show that the proposed unified image and LBP-based model outperform image and structure-based models.

References

1. Bhandary, A., et al.: Deep-learning framework to detect lung abnormality - a study with chest x-ray and lung CT scan images. Pattern Recogn. Lett. **129**, 271–278 (2020)
2. Butt, C., Gill, J., Chun, D., Babu, B.A.: Deep learning system to screen coronavirus disease 2019 pneumonia. Appl. Intell. 1–7 (2020)
3. Deng, J., Dong, W., Socher, R., Li, L.J., Li, K., Fei-Fei, L.: ImageNet: a large-scale hierarchical image database. In: CVPR09 (2009)
4. Goodfellow, I.J., Shlens, J., Szegedy, C.: Explaining and harnessing adversarial examples (2014)
5. Harmon, S.A., Sanford, T.H., Xu, S., Turkbey, E.B., et al.: Artificial intelligence for the detection of COVID-19 pneumonia on chest CT using multinational datasets. Nat. Commun. **11**, 4080 (2020)
6. He, K., Zhang, X., Ren, S., Sun, J.: Deep residual learning for image recognition. In: 2016 IEEE Conference on Computer Vision and Pattern Recognition (CVPR), pp. 770–778 (2016)
7. He, X., et al.: Sample-efficient deep learning for COVID-19 diagnosis based on CT scans. medrxiv (2020)
8. Huang, D., Shan, C., Ardabilian, M., Wang, Y., Chen, L.: Local binary patterns and its application to facial image analysis: a survey. IEEE Trans. Syst. Man Cybernet. Part C (Appl. Rev.) **41**(6), 765–781 (2011)
9. Huang, G., Liu, Z., van der Maaten, L., Weinberger, K.Q.: Densely connected convolutional networks (2016)
10. Kaymak, S., Esmaili, P., Serener, A.: Deep learning for two-step classification of malignant pigmented skin lesions. In: 2018 14th Symposium on Neural Networks and Applications (NEUREL), pp. 1–6 (2018)

11. Krizhevsky, A., Sutskever, I., Hinton, G.E.: Imagenet classification with deep convolutional neural networks. In: Pereira, F., Burges, C.J.C., Bottou, L., Weinberger, K.Q. (eds.) Advances in Neural Information Processing Systems, vol. 25, pp. 1097–1105 (2012)
12. Loey, M., Smarandache, F., Khalifa, N.E.: Within the lack of chest COVID-19 x-ray dataset: a novel detection model based on GAN and deep transfer learning. Symmetry **12**, 651 (2020)
13. Mei, X., et al.: Artificial intelligence-enabled rapid diagnosis of patients with COVID-19. Nat. Med. **26**, 1–5 (2020). https://doi.org/10.1038/s41591-020-0931-3
14. Pereira, R.M., Bertolini, D., Teixeira, L.O., Silla, C.N., Costa, Y.M.: COVID-19 identification in chest x-ray images on flat and hierarchical classification scenarios. Comput. Methods Programs Biomed. **194** (2020)
15. Radford, A., Metz, L., Chintala, S.: Unsupervised representation learning with deep convolutional generative adversarial networks (2015)
16. Sandler, M., Howard, A., Zhu, M., Zhmoginov, A., Chen, L.: Mobilenetv 2: inverted residuals and linear bottlenecks. In: 2018 IEEE/CVF Conference on Computer Vision and Pattern Recognition, pp. 4510–4520 (2018)
17. Serener, A., Serte, S.: Keratinocyte carcinoma detection via convolutional neural networks. In: 2019 3rd International Symposium on Multidisciplinary Studies and Innovative Technologies (ISMSIT), pp. 1–5 (2019)
18. Serener, A., Serte, S.: Transfer learning for early and advanced glaucoma detection with convolutional neural networks. In: 2019 Medical Technologies Congress (TIPTEKNO), pp. 1–4 (2019)
19. Serener, A., Serte, S.: Geographic variation and ethnicity in diabetic retinopathy detection via deeplearning. Turk. J. Electr. Eng. Comput. Sci. **28**, 664–678 (2020)
20. Serte, S., Demirel, H.: Wavelet-based deep learning for skin lesion classification. IET Image Proc. **14**(4), 720–726 (2020)
21. Serte, S., Serener, A.: A generalized deep learning model for glaucoma detection. In: 2019 3rd International Symposium on Multidisciplinary Studies and Innovative Technologies (ISMSIT), pp. 1–5 (2019)
22. Serte, S., Demirel, H.: Gabor wavelet-based deep learning for skin lesion classification. Comput. Biol. Med. **113** (2019)
23. Serte, S., Serener, A., Al-Turjman, F.: Deep learning in medical imaging: a brief review. Trans. Emerg. Telecommun. Technol.
24. Simonyan, K., Zisserman, A.: Very deep convolutional networks for large-scale image recognition (2014)
25. Szegedy, C., et al.: Going deeper with convolutions. In: 2015 IEEE Conference on Computer Vision and Pattern Recognition (CVPR), pp. 1–9 (2015)
26. Tuncer, T., Dogan, S., Ozyurt, F.: An automated residual exemplar local binary pattern and iterative relieff based COVID-19 detection method using chest x-ray image. Chemom. Intell. Lab. Syst. **203** (2020)
27. Waheed, A., Goyal, M., Gupta, D., Khanna, A., Al-Turjman, F., Pinheiro, P.R.: Covidgan: data augmentation using auxiliary classifier GAN for improved COVID-19 detection. IEEE Access **8**, 91916–91923 (2020)
28. Yi, X., Walia, E., Babyn, P.: Generative adversarial network in medical imaging: A review. Med. Image Anal. **58** (2019)

Security and Privacy Issues Associated with Coronavirus Diagnosis and Prognosis

Vibhushinie Bentotahewa(✉) ⓘ, Chaminda Hewage ⓘ, and Jason Williams

Cardiff School of Technologies, Cardiff Metropolitan University, Llandaff, Campus, Western Avenue, Cardiff C5 2YB, UK
v.bentotahewa@outlook.cardiffmet.ac.uk

Abstract. The urgency of the need to manage and find a cure for the COVID-19 has made it necessary to share information. However, sharing information involves potential risks that are inevitably likely to infringe individual privacy. Therefore, whether permissible under extenuation circumstances or not, sharing and handling of information for medical diagnosis and prognosis need consideration without ignoring the need to protect privacy. This makes it important to strike a balance between protecting individual privacy and collecting information to combat the virus, the responsibility for doing so rests with the state. However, circumstances in which the COVID-19 pandemic appears to be accelerating, the medical professionals and the government seem to be focusing more on collecting information that could be used to limit the extent of the outbreak and mitigate the risks. Such a strategy overrides perception of the need to protect personal privacy. This paper discusses the security and privacy challenges associated with SARS-CoV-2 diagnosis and prognosis using case studies from different countries.

Keywords: Security · Privacy · Data protection · General data protection regulation · Coronavirus diagnosis · COVID-19

1 Introduction

In general, there is a wide public appreciation of their health privacy. The GPs (General Practitioners) and health clinicians take necessary measures to keep vast majority of sensitive information confidential. However, in unprecedented circumstances like COVID-19 pandemic, the privacy protection measures in the health sector may outweigh the risks to the public when measured against the privacy risk to the individual [1]. In such instances, the need to share patient information with research institutes and third parties can become necessary and can be justified, given that the overriding aim is to monitor and control the spread of the virus, and to provide guidance on preventive measure to keep the communities safe.

Over time, the General Data Protection Regulation (GDPR) has been reviewing the necessity for data processing in the interest of public health and, in recognition of the public interest, has accepted the need for lawful processing activities for the purpose of

S. Paiva et al. (Eds.): SmartCity360° 2020, LNICST 372, pp. 108–116, 2021.
https://doi.org/10.1007/978-3-030-76063-2_8

monitoring the spread of the epidemic. This provision has been endorsed in the article 9(2) (i) in the GDPR with an exemption to processing health related data that is otherwise considered sensitive and prohibited from processing [2]. However, concerns have already been raised about the measures taken by the government and the tech industry, and their response to the coronavirus outbreak, and the implications of the use of contact tracing apps and digital immunity passports on privacy, during and after COVID-19 pandemic. The use of technological solutions to combat COVID-19 is perceived with skepticism by the public and should remain vigilant of those using them.

2   Research Background (The Use of Personal Information During COVID-19)

European Data Protection Board issued a statement in March 2020, confirming that the GDPR contained a provision for legal grounds for enabling employers to process data in the context of epidemics such as COVID-19 without consent of the employees but obtaining consent in unforeseen circumstances will become necessary to comply with national legislations [3]. However, commercial organisations based in Italy or France do not conduct autonomous systematic collections of health data from employees [4]. That includes requesting information relevant to potential symptoms, temperature-taking requirements, or details of medical reports. As stated in the guidelines issued by the Italian data protection authority, the collection of COVID-19 associated health data must be left to the public health authorities [4]. Also, the French data protection authority has set out examples of unlawful processing of data, specifically for collecting daily temperature readings of the employees and the visitors, and for collecting medical files from all employees [4]. On the flipside, the employees in Italy and France are obliged to inform employers of any suspected symptoms of the coronavirus as a measure to protect health and safety of their work environment [4].

In general, countries such as Belgium, Luxemburg, Estonia, Netherlands, France and Peru prohibit collection of data in the form of temperature readings and medical questionnaires, and the disclosure of the identity of individuals who are suspected of carrying coronavirus or confirmed infected by it [5]. Philippines, China, Russia, European Union, Singapore, Hong Kong, South Africa, Ireland, Israel, Switzerland, Italy, United Kingdom, Japan, United States are less restrictive [5]. They acknowledge the need to process and disclose data without consent for the purpose of contact tracing, response measures. Also, according to the reports, the recorded data could be processed and exchanged among data controllers and law enforcement institutions [5]. The guidelines for data collection are more specific in Argentina, Australia, Iceland, Austria, Canada, Mexico, New Zealand, Norway, Czech Republic, Portugal, Finland, Germany, Greece, Sweden, Turkey, [5]. Personal information collected for COVID-19 prevention should be used for collected purpose only and should be deleted after the pandemic. The disclosure of the identity of the patient requires consent and processing is permissible only on a need basis to protect the vital interests of the individuals and the public [5]. Clearly different countries have different rules and regulations in place to combat the common enemy in coronavirus, therefore, over focusing on personal privacy should not divert attention away from the key objective to combat the virus, for the sake of personal privacy.

To mitigate the risks of spreading and worsening of the pandemic, scanning methods are being used to diagnose the presence of the virus whilst some countries are developing contact tracing apps. The google/apple apps provide a decentralised software architecture and save a log of the user contacts within the app without uploading to a government server [6, 7]. In contrast, the initially proposed NHS contact tracing app in the UK logged information of users in a centralised database of government servers [6, 7]. According to experts, centralised contact tracing system allows better management of the pandemic as data collected from all part of UK can be used for macro managements of the pandemic (e.g. enforcing local lockdowns). However, understandably, this method of holding personal data in a centralised database with access to government departments and law enforcement agencies makes the public jittery about how and when the said authorities would use personal information, they have access to. Therefore, public concerns about the use of surveillance operations on a scale never seen before stand to reason.

France is one of the few European countries to have opted for a centralized model for coronavirus contacts tracing. The French government has chosen to have user information fed into a central server. However, downloading and installation of the app is voluntary [7, 9]. UK also adopted a centralized approach to track and trace [6, 7], and to allay any public concerns about the contact-tracing app, those who developed the NHS app, gave assurances that collected data would not be shared with other government departments or private companies [7, 10]. However, UK discontinued the contact tracing app in use at the time and shifted to a model provided by Apple and Google [31].

The World Health Organisation (WHO) meanwhile has listed two diagnostic tests for emergency use during the COVID-19 pandemic. One is genesis Real-Time PCR and the second is cobras SARS-CoV-2 [11]. Aligning with WHO recommendations, two different types of tests are used in the UK. These tests include staff-administered regional test sites, mobile test units and self-administered home tests [12]. The testing process involves the collection of personal information of the targeted individual, such as the first and the last names, and even vehicle registration numbers. In the case of an individual taking the test at a regional test site, the information of other household members are also collected, and retained for further testing, if the person tested happened to be diagnosed positive [12]. That in effect is an infringement not only on individual privacy but also on everyone associated with the COVID-19 diagnosed person.

However, regardless of questionable infringement on personal privacy, the GDPR and the Data Protection Act 2018 provide a legal basis to justify collecting and withholding personal data. Article 6(1)(e) in GDPR states that processing is necessary to assess the performance of its official tasks that are carried out in the public interest, and to provide and manage a sustainable health service [2, 12]. Also, the Article 9(2) (i) in GDPR states that processing is necessary to serve in the interest of public health [2, 12]. The Data Protection Act 2018, Schedule 1, Part 1, (2) (2) (f) also states that the authorities can collect and process data for health or social care purposes [12].

3 Discussion and Recommendations

The world has been affected by the COVID-19 and is facing an unprecedented pandemic. With the rising demand for essential items and testing equipment, the health services call for urgent response to save lives. The biggest challenge the authorities faced was to prevent the spread of the virus going out of control. Given the urgency of the situation, number of states resorted to digital surveillance technologies for tracking and monitoring purposes.

The use of surveillance equipment infringes privacy of individuals even in the middle of a worldwide public health crisis, and the application of human rights laws stands regardless, and the states cannot simply turn a blind eye to privacy and freedom of expression. The human rights and civil society organisations around the world reacted with one voice calling all governments to adhere to human rights laws when employing digital surveillance technologies. In practice, the contact tracing app entails data gathering on an unprecedented level and that makes it open to unauthorised disclosure. Adding to the concerns, the Amnesty International UK director suggested that the Government should be looking at decentralised app models that do not store contact-tracing data on state run data bases [7, 13]. In response, the UK government released the current version of the app based on decentralised architecture, and Amnesty International UK welcomed this change of heart by the government [32]. Therefore, it is recommended to pursue privacy preserving contact tracing efforts to tackle privacy and security infringements during the global pandemic.

Healthcare professionals also do have a vital role to play in protecting privacy of individuals during this pandemic. U.S. Department of Health and Human Services posted a bulletin to remind health-care workers that information about 'an identifiable patient' may not be disclosed to the media or the public without 'written authorization of the patient' except in special circumstances [8], and issued a briefing page specifying how HIPAA relates to the COVID-19 outbreak. The health care providers including the doctors receive professional advice on restrictions barring the release of specific information about personal identity of the patients tested Coronavirus positive or negative without written authorization from the patient [14]. However, if it is deemed necessary to have patient information for monitoring or prevention purposes, the authorities can get 'de-identified' data (e.g., the use of anonymized and pseudonymized data). The Personal Information Protection and Electronic Documents Act (PIPEDA) is the national privacy law of Canada, and it regulates personal information disclosure. Under PIPEDA and, under provincial patient privacy legislation where it exists, consent is required to collect, use, or disclose an individual's personal health information [15]. Increased awareness about handling sensitive data focusing health professionals would reduce the impact of privacy and security risks.

In the prevailing pandemic environment, companies, employers, and public institutions face with unique privacy, data security, and cybersecurity implications are grappling with finding response solutions to the Coronavirus, and how to handle the legal implications of collecting and sharing health information of their employees and customers. Also, they are obliged to consider the circumstances under which the information about the employee health conditions and diagnosis could be disclosed to the workforce, and to the public health authorities. Given the exemption in Article 9 of GDPR for processing of health data, companies should track and follow the guidance provided by the data protection authorities in the applicable jurisdictions [2]. However, it has been reported, the overarching theme amongst the EU member states puts emphasis on the employers to focus on facilitating measures and encouraging voluntary self-reporting by the employees, instead of obligatory gathering of private medical information from them [4].

Data Minimization and Proportionality is one of the key principles in GDPR. Only the minimum data necessary should be collected, and processing activities should be proportionate to the legitimate interests of the company in responding to COVID-19. For instance, to maintain a safe and healthy workplace in the interests of the company, it may not be a requirement to share with other employees, the identity of an employee or identities of his family members with reported symptoms of COVID-19. Theoretically however, more data will provide greater knowledge beneficial to the organisations and the society but enforcing data minimisation will limit the success of the desired purpose. According to the GDPR, data minimization could be achieved by pseudonymization [16, 17]. However, one can argue that removing identifiers to achieve pseudonymization could potentially undermine the quality of the results derived as the data would be purposefully altered [16].

A report released by the General Medical Council in the UK states that passing information about notifiable diseases to the relevant authorities for communicable disease control and surveillance is of vital importance [18], and in the same context, it is important to gather patient information mostly for educational and training purposes. According to one of the key principles of the GDPR, the processed data should only be used for the purpose for which it is collected and should not be kept for longer than it is necessary [19]. However, the UK Government has informed that they would be using information about people for different purposes that are not directly relevant to healthcare [12]. These include research into COVID-19, planning of services or actions in response to COVID-19, monitoring progress and development of COVID-19 [12]. However, it has been emphasised that the information self-collected and provided by the public for COVID-19 testing will not be used for any other purpose that is not linked to COVID-19 [12]. The use of anonymised information by the authorities would be the better option to avoid any privacy implications (complications). However, if it deemed necessary to use patient identifiable information, or it became practically not feasible to anonymise information, the relevant authorities have the option to inform the patient and obtain explicit consent from the patient before disclosing information to anyone not involved in the provision of direct care to the patient. That will reassure the public that their privacy would remain confidential, and authorities and governments could expect public support with the knowledge that their privacy would not be compromised even for a good cause.

Apart from the medical professionals and governments, media also should play a responsible role when reporting on COVID-19 diagnosed individuals. The media has a responsibility to report facts and expose the truth to the public. They should also be aware of any distress that may be caused to the individuals when reporting on privacy issues. In South Korea, fears of a homophobic backlash are reported to be growing after a man infected with coronavirus had been spotted in clubs around Seoul's gay district [20]. Homosexuality is not illegal in South Korea and many Korean gay people manage to maintain anonymity and keep their sexuality discrete from family members and colleagues [20]. According to media reports, a 37-year-old IT engineer had been spotted in three clubs after staying away for months, and since had been in fear of losing his job, and even had been reluctant to come forward to take the test [20]. The privacy concerns arise from fear of being stigmatised, discriminated, and socially isolated. These prejudices have caused stress to gay community members and they have been in fear of identity exposure and retribution, also the social attitudes run so deep they would even lose their jobs. Irresponsible reporting by the media has led to this situation. It is unfortunate that lack of concerns for the gay community and open media reporting of their rights to individual to privacy has caused immense damage to a selected group of people for being different.

Also, similar cases of social stigmatisation of COVID-19 affected people, and infringements on their privacy have been reported in many parts of India. The names and addresses of 46 people (in Ajmer) suspected of having contacted the virus have been published in some local Hindi newspapers [21], and a report containing personal details of 300 people who were home-quarantined or confined to self-isolation [21], posted on a social media has gone viral. In Delhi and Chandigarh, posters carrying the names, quarantine period and the number of people in the family who had been asked to remain in isolation have been glued outside the homes of those suspected to carry the virus [21, 22]. The Mohali district administration has gone as far as publishing on its website, the names, phone numbers and residential addresses of not only those presumed to have been coronavirus positive but also the details of their family members, [21].

The repercussions of privacy violations through reporting could be long lasting and could leave people mentally affected for being stigmatised. This will also impact on those living in close knit communities. The unauthorised disclosure of privacy data compromises personal security and confidentiality of people, also it has a negative impact on medical ethics. Therefore, it is vitally important to implement necessary mechanisms to contain the pandemic and it is also equally important the government or the media organisations do not arbitrarily share data of COVID-19 positive case in the public domain. Some U.S. states (Ohio, Florida) took the same stand making patient privacy a priority [15].

There is also another security and privacy debate surrounding SARS-CoV-2 antibody tests and immunity passports. Those with low or no antibodies against SARS-CoV-2 are prohibited from returning to work until they were either immunised or hard evidence of immunity established [23]. Those with certified immunity to COVID-19 are provided with an immunity passport, and those without will be denied access to a workplace, school, or restaurant until scanned security clearance as applicable. Whether the disclosure of antibody protection information violates personal privacy issues or not is a big question. If governments were to use SARS-CoV-2 antibody tests to control access to the workplace, people will have to compromise their privacy, at least to some extent than before. It is a choice between protecting privacy and protecting the masses and, practically, it is difficult to maintain self-respect, dignity and protect privacy to a high standard whilst fighting the pandemic. The reality is the protection of one person's confidentiality endangers another's welfare or public health.

A recent report by artificial intelligence research group, Ada Lovelace Institute warned that the immunity passports would be of high risks in terms of social cohesion, discrimination, exclusion, and vulnerability [24]. However, China has been using the Alipay Health Code for a while, but this version is not explicitly called an immunity certificate, instead functions same as the immunity passport [24, 25]. Chile also has launched its own COVID-19 Immunity Card program [26]. Immunity certificates are still in their infancy, but as antibody testing becomes more widely available, more countries are likely to join in. U.S., UK, Italy, Chile, Germany have expressed interest in 'immunity passports' [27], a system of requiring people to present proof of immunity to COVID-19 to gain access to public spaces, work sites, airports, schools, and other venues.

It is envisaged that the digital form of immunity passport system could easily be expanded to check not just a person's immunity status, but also to check other personal information, such as age, gender, pregnancy, health records (e.g., HIV status), or criminal history if relevant [27]. In such circumstances, the chance of people being exposed to the danger of data breaches could be high. It is worth noting that even before the COVID-19 the world experienced data breaches when medical data was compromised by the hackers. One such incident is in 2019, an HIV database in Singapore leaked personal information of more than 14,000 individuals living with HIV [28].

It is crucially important to keep medical records securely stored in either paper or in electronic format [29]. As a solution to the question of security and privacy implications, the idea of blockchain has been suggested by some, particularly regarding the immunity passport. The blockchain technology (e.g., verifiable claims and Self Sovereign Identities (SSI)) could be the core innovation of digital immunity passport development. It will not only leave complete control of managing health data in the hands of the end user, but also give the employers and other stakeholders' peace of mind knowing that the data will not be unduly tampered with. [30] Looking ahead the same technology could be used for contact tracing, gathering and collating patient data, monitoring patients' movements and adherence to social distancing rules, whilst protecting their identity in doing so. Also, emerging technologies like Blockchain could device a platform that would directly or indirectly help future recurrences of an epidemic and manage it without compromising privacy and security of individuals.

4 Conclusion

The COVID-19 outbreak is an unwelcome unprecedented global pandemic threatening every aspect of human life across each continent of the world. The death toll continues to rise to an unimaginable level in some countries, whilst few have managed to contain it and minimise the impact. On top of that the economic costs are causing hardships and affecting livelihoods in every nation including the rich ones.

There are also other important issues emanating from the use of information of those tested positive and its impact on their privacy. Testing and tracing are considered necessary and essential to respond to the pandemic, and to prevent it spreading in the community. That requires personal data to be retained by the government and other authorities, inevitably raising a conflict between person's right to privacy and the need to log and share collected test results. Although technology has the capacity to contribute to pandemic combating strategy, it does also infringe privacy rights in circumstances where tracking and surveillance are used to monitor coronavirus affected individuals. The difficulty is to visualise the degree of surveillance and unexpected outcomes that will arise.

To start with, some countries have resorted to surveillance cameras and contact tracing apps to track the spread of COVID-19. That did raise public concerns about the use of such technology, but despite the concerns, the authorities continue with testing to identify those having the symptoms. The spectrum of data collected includes personal details of associates and those living with them. The latest development in the COVID-19 containment process will be the immunity passports that will make way for phased easing of restrictions towards normalising wider social interaction. Although the immunity passports look likely to compromise privacy, it fits the purpose. However, the researcher believes that the use of blockchain ledger will provide a compromised balance between health security and privacy of individual, as suggested by the experts.

Moving away from technology, people are becoming more concerned about the behaviour of media in reporting incidents related to COVID-19 and the media in many nations has come under scrutiny for failing to respect privacy of coronavirus affected individuals. The unethical insensitive reporting has caused distress to people and harmed them mentally, in some cases has treated disrespectfully and made them feel indignant. This supports the general belief that privacy is a sensitive issue and should not be open to violations. Therefore, the onus is on all parties, the government, healthcare professional and media to act in the public interest and protect their privacy. That said, it is also important to respond positively to extraneous circumstances which COVID-19 is one. Therefore, the use of technology and the measures taken to contain the pandemic can be justified given the risks of the incident developing into a crisis of unimaginable proportion in terms to loss to human life and the economic impact that will follow. It is equally important (for medical practitioners) to share patients' information for research purposes and to support the government in its effort to avoid a crisis. That underscores the importance of the need to strike a balance between privacy of individuals and the need to act positively in response to an unprecedented pandemic.

References

1. Theverge. https://www.theverge.com/2020/3/12/21177129/personal-privacy-pandemic-eth ics-public-health-coronavirus. Accessed 28 May 2020
2. Information Commissioner's office: Guide to the General Data Protection Regulation (GDPR). Information Commissioner's office, Government of United Kingdom (2018)
3. European Data Protection Board. https://edpb.europa.eu/news/news/2020/statement-edpb-chair-processing-personal-data-context-covid-19-outbreak_en. Accessed 5 June 2020
4. PrivSec Report. https://gdpr.report/news/2020/03/23/ccpa-covid-19-a-practical-guide-to-add ressing-privacy-and-data-security-implications-of-the-coronavirus/. Accessed 3 June 2020
5. JD Supra knowledge center. https://www.jdsupra.com/legalnews/global-regulatory-gui dance-for-covid-19-43117/. Accessed 25 May 2020
6. BBC. https://www.bbc.co.uk/news/technology-52441428. Accessed 2 May 2020
7. Info security magazine. https://www.infosecurity-magazine.com/next-gen-infosec/privacy-rights-covid19/. Accessed 15 June 2020

8. Institute of Medicine (US) Committee on Health Research and the Privacy of Health Information. Beyond the HIPAA Privacy Rule: Enhancing Privacy, Improving Health Through Research. National Academies Press, United States (2009)
9. ZDNet. https://www.zdnet.com/article/france-asks-apple-to-relax-iphone-security-for-cor onavirus-tracking-app-development/. Accessed 27 May 2020
10. The guardian. https://www.theguardian.com/technology/2020/may/05/uk-racing-to-imp rove-contact-tracing-apps-privacy-safeguards. Accessed 23 May 2020
11. World Health Organisation. https://www.who.int/news-room/detail/07-04-2020-who-lists-two-covid-19-tests-for-emergency-use. Accessed 14 May 2020
12. Department of Health and Social Care. https://www.gov.uk/government/publications/cor onavirus-covid-19-testing-privacy-information/testing-for-coronavirus-privacy-information. Accessed 15 June 2020
13. Daily Mail, Robinson. https://www.dailymail.co.uk/news/article-8288211/How-does-NHS-COVID-19-contact-tracing-app-work.html. Accessed 13 May 2020
14. Poynter. https://www.poynter.org/reporting-editing/2020/hipaa-and-coronavirus/. Accessed 3 June 2020
15. The conversation. https://theconversation.com/with-coronavirus-containment-efforts-what-are-the-privacy-rights-of-patients-131752. Accessed 8 June 2020
16. Info security magazine. https://www.infosecurity-magazine.com/next-gen-infosec/challe nges-gdpr-big-data/. Accessed 18 June 2020
17. Zarsky, T.Z.: Incompatible: the GDPR in the age of big data. Seton Hall Law Rev. 47(995), 995–1020 (2017)
18. General Medical Council: Confidentiality: disclosing information about serious communicable diseases, pp. 1–4. General Medical Council, United Kingdom (2020)
19. Goddard, M.: The EU general data protection regulation (GDPR): European regulation that has a global impact. Int. J. Market Res. 59(6), 1–4 (2017)
20. The guardian. https://www.theguardian.com/world/2020/may/08/anti-gay-backlash-feared-in-south-korea-after-coronavirus-media-reports. Accessed 14 June 2020
21. The Week. https://www.theweek.in/news/india/2020/03/22/privacy-of-covid-19-suspects-violated-names-addresses-made-public.html. Accessed 12 June 2020
22. The Hindu. https://www.thehindu.com/news/cities/Delhi/covid-19-poster-outside-west-delhi-house-keeping-people-away/article31176892.ece. Accessed 5 June 2020
23. The Scientist. https://www.the-scientist.com/news-opinion/opinion-public-health-trumps-pri vacy-in-a-pandemic-67429. Accessed 5 June 2020
24. Ada-Lovelace-Institute. Exit through the App store, pp. 5–19. Ada-Lovelace-Institute (2020)
25. Cl Net. https://www.cnet.com/health/covid-19-immunity-certificates-everything-to-know-about-this-controversial-solution/. Accessed 29 May 2020
26. Bloomberg. https://www.bloomberg.com/news/articles/2020-04-16/chile-to-start-controver sial-coronavirus-immunity-card-system. Accessed 12 June 2020
27. Electronic Frontier Foundation. https://www.eff.org/deeplinks/2020/05/immunity-passports-are-threat-our-privacy-and-information-security. Accessed 4 June 2020
28. BBC. https://www.bbc.co.uk/news/world-asia-47288219. Accessed 11 June 2020
29. Harman, L.B.: Electronic health records: privacy, confidentiality, and security. AMA J. Ethics 14(9), 712–719 (2012)
30. IT Pro Portal. https://www.itproportal.com/features/blockchain-can-answer-immunity-pas sport-security-concerns-but-any-roll-out-must-be-dictated-by-the-science/. Accessed 13 June 2020
31. BBC. https://www.bbc.co.uk/news/technology-53095336. Accessed 12 July 2020
32. Amnesty International UK. https://www.amnesty.org.uk/press-releases/amnesty-gives-cau tious-welcome-uk-government-u-turn-contact-tracing-app. Accessed 16 July 2020

Approach for the Development of a System for COVID-19 Preliminary Test

Ticiana Capris[1(✉)], Pedro Melo[1], Pedro Pereira[1], José Morgado[1], Nuno M. Garcia[2], and Ivan Miguel Pires[1,2,3]

[1] Computer Science Department, Polytechnic Institute of Viseu, Viseu, Portugal
{estgv17486,estgv18336,estgv10389}@alunos.estgv.ipv.pt,
fmorgado@estgv.ipv.pt
[2] Instituto de Telecomunicações, Universidade da Beira Interior, Covilhã, Portugal
ngarcia@di.ubi.pt, impires@it.ubi.pt
[3] UICISA:E Research Centre, School of Health, Polytechnic Institute of Viseu, Viseu, Portugal

Abstract. Nowadays, Coronavirus is the biggest challenge of medicine. This problem is divided into two sectors: health and economy. In relation to health, there has been an alarming exponential rise in deaths, those who do not belong to the risk group are precisely those who contaminate and lead to disease. The economy also bleeds globally, and companies are failing. Thus, thousands of people are out of work. This paper is focused on predicting whether an individual is possible with symptoms of COVID-19 and proposing the use of technology. In a context of ambient assisted living, it can save thousands of lives and builds the world economy. Therefore, a preliminary mobile diagnosis may provide a reduction in government costs and a potential alternative to the existing tests. In view of all that has been mentioned, sensors are the best solution to detect the symptoms of the disease. This project will try to identify different symptoms, such as high body temperature, breathing difficulties, and cough. The sensors that may be used to identify these symptoms are a thermometer, an electroencephalogram (EEG) sensor, an electromyography (EMG) sensor and an electrodermal activity (EDA) sensor.

Keywords: Sensors · Mobile devices · Pandemic situation · COVID-19 · Algorithms

1 Introduction

Due to limited health infrastructure, the fast diagnosis of COVID-19 is a challenge in different countries, especially in emerging ones [13, 23]. Sensors retain immense perspectives to collect data, which, after being filtered and processed, can identify symptoms related to the disease [4, 14, 21, 33]. Therefore, a low-cost solution is to use BITalino devices (see Fig. 1) with mobile devices, which it is a medical sensor kit that allows the development of technology, algorithms and artificial intelligence methods for the differential diagnosis in medicine field [3, 27].

© ICST Institute for Computer Sciences, Social Informatics and Telecommunications Engineering 2021
Published by Springer Nature Switzerland AG 2021. All Rights Reserved
S. Paiva et al. (Eds.): SmartCity360° 2020, LNICST 372, pp. 117–124, 2021.
https://doi.org/10.1007/978-3-030-76063-2_9

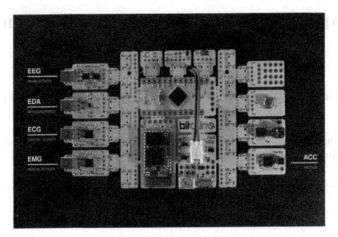

Fig. 1. BITalino device.

Coronavirus disease is a common virus that infects humans, and it is mainly related to an upper respiratory infection, commonly named as Severe Acute Respiratory Syndrome (SARS-CoV) [20]. Still, the Middle East Respiratory Syndrome (MERS-CoV) is another type of coronavirus [20]. The symptoms are like the flu, but it may cause a significant number of deaths than common flu. The air disseminates the coronavirus disease by coughing and sneezing, close personal contact, touching an object or surface contaminated with the virus and rarely, by faecal contamination [28]. The most common detailed symptoms are runny nose, sore throat, feeling unwell, cough, and fever [9].

Sensors allow the identification of different healthcare symptoms, such as high body temperature, breathing difficulties and cough [1, 2, 15, 18, 19]. The sensors that may be used are a thermometer, an electroencephalogram (EEG) sensor, an electromyography (EMG) sensor, and an electrodermal activity (EDA) sensor [10–12, 16, 24, 25, 30, 32].

The main objective of this paper is focused in the presentation of an approach for the development of a system that helps in the preliminar detection of COVID-19 with the use of different kinds of sensors embedded in the devices used daily. It was included in a summer course in 2020 that occurred in the Polytechnic of Viseu, Viseu, Portugal. The main contribution of this paper is the proposal of an architecture for a system that help in the detection of pandemic situations.

BITalino devices were created to solve a set of problems, with the premise of observing the need for medical solutions through technology [3]. It can be said that, due to this objective, results from these sensors are revolutionizing teaching, research and biomedical prototypes around the world [2, 6, 17, 26]. The success of this hardware is notorious since it has already been nominated for the Innovation Radar Prize 2017 [8]. This small hardware kit is essential for research and detecting possible patients with COVID-19, as it has the sensors previously mentioned. Therefore, it will collect the necessary data to recognize whether the person is sick or not [5, 15, 29, 31].

It is indisputable that artificial intelligence is currently the most explored concept in technology. Within this area, machine learning has been a concept with great potential being explored. Defining machine learning is essentially saying that a system can learn according to what has been trained, based on specific datasets and with minimal human interference. When establishing logical rules, the system itself can improve the performance of a task, that is, such practices are created based on the recognition of data patterns coming from the BITalino device, and it will be analyzed. The main objective here is to define the health standards of a particular individual and recommend, for example, that he check through a specific sensor to analyze any state of body imbalance.

As stated before, the goal is to get results that state changes in an individual's health. Thus, it is desired to obtain people's autonomy about their health, in other words, through the mobile application the user will have the ability to track some symptoms of COVID-19 and receive information about their status. Current health status. Furthermore, machine learning can be used to define health information more accurately.

The introductory section ends with this paragraph, and the remaining sections of this paper are structured as follows: Sect. 2 presents the description of the structure of the method implemented for the recognition of people with symptoms of COVID-19, including the sensors to be used with the proposed system. Section 3 presents the mobile application proposed. Finally, this article ends with the discussion and conclusions provided in Sect. 4.

2 Methods

The present methodology of this paper, presented in Fig. 2, can be elucidated mainly in three stages: data acquisition, processing and manipulation. Data acquisition will be made using BITalino sensors which are detailed in Sect. 3. After the data collection, possible noise filtering and data manipulation will be carried out. These procedures guarantee to eliminate false positives and through the algorithm exposed in Sect. 4. Thus, it is guaranteed that the systematic logic is obtained and therefore identify symptoms related to COVID-19.

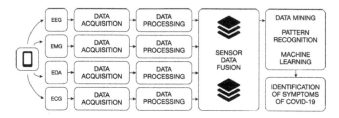

Fig. 2. Method for the identification of symptoms related to COVID-19.

There are several recent discussions about the concept of sensors and their importance for everyday life. Generally speaking, a sensor is a data monitoring device and is capable of verifying changes in a given environment. The use with an electronic system is efficient to measure various physical phenomena, such as heart rate and temperature. This device is intrinsically related to the internet of things (IoT), as they can detect conditions around which it is present. In summary, they are essential devices for IoT, in addition to measuring and indicating data related to light, heat, pressure, humidity and movement. Therefore, they will be used as the input data for analyzing the problem and baseline to identify patterns.

As far as BITalino device is concerned, mentioned in the introduction chapter, it is worth explaining that it is a low-cost, all-in-one hardware kit, an excellent development and research tool. Therefore, an inexpensive solution to measure the physiological signals evaluated to identify muscle contraction, temperature, electrical activity of the brain and measurement of skin activity. Given this training of BITalino device, it can verify common symptoms in people with COVID-19, which are: fever, dry cough, temperature, sweat and abnormal brain activity.

Additionally, discussions were performed about adequate measures to diagnose and detect severe cases of the disease. When using electroencephalogram (EEG), the studies reveal [22] that neurological abnormalities are being identified and that COVID-19 also involves brain investigation and nerves. Hence, the altered mental state is one of the symptoms that can manifest with those of fever, dry cough, tiredness and breathing difficulty.

When examining adult patients, the article published on NeurologyLive [33] experimented with 28 COVID-19 persons aged between 30 and 83 years old, of which 22 were positive for SARS-CoV-2 (63.6% men), and 6 were negative (33.3% men). Most were seriously ill, intubated due to acute respiratory failure (63.6% vs 100% in COVID-19 positive vs negative) and were already under sedatives or in anticonvulsant medications (86.4% vs 100% in COVID-19 affirmative vs negative). Because of the facts mentioned, it is clear that epileptiform abnormalities in the EEG of COVID-19 patients are relevant data that must be collected, thus seeking to prioritize possible severe cases of the disease.

For this reason, it stands out that processing and interpreting them is one more of the necessary filtering tools for possible symptom verification, so changes in mental status are an essential highlight to be measured. By observing the aspects mentioned, the predominance of frontal waves, bilateral symmetrical or asymmetrical, are the critical point and guide to the possibility of a frontal epileptiform focus and can be considered as evidence that this is the way that the virus the SARS- CoV-2 enters the CNS (via the nasopharyngeal mucosa or olfactory nerves).

EMG is the biggest sensor bet at the moment. Such a complementary exam consists of describing and evaluating muscle function, in an average session of 30 min. The preliminary exam designed for the mobile application, consists of using the sensor with Bluetooth connection to the cell phone and collects data from the electrodes, these non-invasively adhere to the skin to capture its ionic current.

The study of muscle activity can be applied to detect contractions in the chest and thus identify dry cough. Due to this aspect, when combining dry cough with other symptoms, it will be possible to alert the user of the mobile application that he has respiratory anomalies.

The electrothermal activity consists of verifying the peripheral response originated from the sympathetic nervous system [7]. Thus, an involuntary intervention moderated by the central nervous system. Given this activity, the sweat glands in the skin are activated, that is, sweat production. Such a method, being able to detect excessive sweating through empathic devices, soon detects one of the most common symptoms of coronavirus. The measurement is associated with two types, which are: phasic conductance response of the skin and tonic conductance level. The electrodes of the EDA sensor should be used on the palm, as the test will be done with the user awake and will result in a more significant signal. It should be noted that there is the advantage of doing a quick test, done several times over 24 h. EDA has data collected with greater efficiency in the long run, since it must be obtained through the average tonic level of an individual's skin.

3 Mobile Application

The algorithms will be essential to identify whether the individual is likely to be ill and suggest that he/she go to the doctor. As already explained briefly in Sect. 2, the algorithms are the sequence written logically, described in steps that will return an answer to the problem itself.

It was determined that applying algorithms is essential for the execution of what was proposed, *i.e.,* a COVID-19 symptom prediction tool. Given this proposal, the study (reference) that explored 2700 patients was examined, and many demographic and health parameters were collected associated with a higher risk of needing respiratory support. As a consequence of this, specific patterns were pointed out, namely: the body mass index in Kg/m^2 increased by 1.05 per unit, advanced age, fragility and possible relationship with the male sex. Such health parameters provide odds ratios and a 95% confidence interval.

By observing the overlooked aspects, an unsupervised time series was carried out in the group of patients, as well as being compared to 6 different groups of associated results. To visualize how the groups of infected people were distinguished, the authors used the reported average occurrence of a symptom each day and the Z-Score per event for each group concerning the presence of one of the 14 reported symptoms. Equivalent graphics for independent replication in the database are provided as supplementary material.

The data of the EMG activity should be analyzed and calculate the peaks and valleys to check if a patient has a dry cough. Therefore, the array is searched to search for all values, then the input value is checked against its predecessors and successors, that is, the next and the previous value. If this value is higher than both, then a local maximum is found, classified as a peak. Otherwise, a minimum is detected, this being the valley. However, to avoid false positives, the percentage difference between the absolute and a sample of possible false positives is then calculated. Another check to prevent false positives is to calculate the standard deviation, since this is a measure that expresses the degree of dispersion of a data set.

Consequently, with property to standardize data and make it more homogeneous. Taking advantage of this calculation, the percentage concept presented above applies for the same effect. Finally, this method allows you to increase the accuracy of the data and reduce noise.

4 Discussion and Conclusions

The proposed COVID-19 measurement system using sensors fulfils the requirement of being low-cost and allows the mobile application, through data processing and signalling of respiratory problems, COVID-19. In the face of such a typical scenario, the solution is efficient for non-invasive disease analysis and detection method is one of the most significant perspectives in modern medicine. Globally, such results mean preventing deaths, fast and cheap assistance. When individualizing data for a given user, it appears that the analysis will have higher precision and specific details, due to the identification of the daily data collected. Also, the relevant gain of what can be implemented allows for future improvements and to further increase the accuracy and to identify even more the rate of data acquisition is sufficient.

Through this paper, it was possible to demonstrate the usefulness of sensors associated with a mobile application, with the possibility of identifying respiratory problems, which in the current context are of high production and possibly effective in saving lives.

Also, using the algorithms and techniques outlined previously, to adapt to a set of usage scenarios and a class of mobile devices will make this methodology usable on most mobile platforms.

It is concluded that, given the methodology explained, it will be possible to present promising results with concrete numbers and corroborate the high relevance of the use of sensors in the health area. It is essential to use all technological resources and associate them with medicine, aiming at the evolution of human beings and enhancing their autonomy.

The proposed system has some limitations related to the use of sensors, because they are difficult to instrument in different people with different ages. In addition, it needs the constant Internet and Bluetooth connections in order to interconnect the different devices. The methods can be also developed with a large number of persons.

As future work, we intend to reduce the limitations of the system, creating machanisms to place the sensors in an easy manner, and the measurements should be improved and automated for the general people.

Acknowledgements. This work is funded by FCT/MEC through national funds and co-funded by FEDER – PT2020 partnership agreement under the project **UIDB/EEA/50008/2020** (*Este trabalho é financiado pela FCT/MEC através de fundos nacionais e cofinanciado pelo FEDER, no âmbito do Acordo de Parceria PT2020 no âmbito do projeto UIDB/EEA/50008/2020*).

This work is also funded by National Funds through the FCT - Foundation for Science and Technology, I.P., within the scope of the project UIDB/00742/2020.

This article is based upon work from COST Action IC1303–AAPELE–Architectures, Algorithms and Protocols for Enhanced Living Environments and COST Action CA16226–SHELD-ON–Indoor living space improvement: Smart Habitat for the Elderly, supported by COST (European Cooperation in Science and Technology). More information in www.cost.eu.

Furthermore, we would like to thank the Politécnico de Viseu for their support.

References

1. Amoh, J., Odame, K.M.: Technologies for developing ambulatory cough monitoring devices. Crit. Rev. Biomed. Eng. (2014). https://doi.org/10.1615/CritRevBiomedEng.2014010886
2. Appelboom, G., et al.: Smart wearable body sensors for patient self-assessment and monitoring. Arch. Public Health **72**, 28 (2014). https://doi.org/10.1186/2049-3258-72-28

3. Batista, D., Silva, H., Fred, A.: Experimental characterization and analysis of the BITalino platforms against a reference device. In: 2017 39th Annual International Conference of the IEEE Engineering in Medicine and Biology Society (EMBC), Seogwipo, pp. 2418–2421. IEEE (2017)
4. Bone, D., Lee, C.-C., Chaspari, T., Gibson, J., Narayanan, S.: Signal processing and machine learning for mental health research and clinical applications [perspectives]. IEEE Signal Process Mag. **34**, 196–195 (2017). https://doi.org/10.1109/MSP.2017.2718581
5. Cecilia, J.M., Cano, J.-C., Hernández-Orallo, E., Calafate, C.T., Manzoni, P.: Mobile crowd-sensing approaches to address the COVID-19 pandemic in Spain. IET Smart Cities **2**, 58–63 (2020). https://doi.org/10.1049/iet-smc.2020.0037
6. Collins, T., et al.: Version reporting and assessment approaches for new and updated activity and heart rate monitors. Sensors **19**, 1705 (2019)
7. Dawson, M.E., Schell, A.M., Filion, D.L., Berntson, G.G.: The electrodermal system. In: Cacioppo, J.T., Tassinary, L.G., Berntson, G. (eds.) Handbook of Psychophysiology, 3rd edn., pp. 157–181. Cambridge University Press, Cambridge (2007)
8. Desruelle, P., Nepelski, D.: The "innovation radar": a new policy tool to support innovation management. SSRN J. (2017). https://doi.org/10.2139/ssrn.2944104
9. Dong, X., et al.: Eleven faces of coronavirus disease 2019. Allergy **75**, 1699–1709 (2020). https://doi.org/10.1111/all.14289
10. Felizardo, V., et al.: E-Health: current status and future trends. In: Handbook of Research on Democratic Strategies and Citizen-Centered E-Government Services, pp. 302–326. IGI Global (2015)
11. Garcia, N.M.: A roadmap to the design of a personal digital life coach. In: Loshkovska, S., Koceski, S. (eds.) ICT Innovations 2015. AISC, vol. 399, pp. 21–27. Springer, Cham (2016). https://doi.org/10.1007/978-3-319-25733-4_3
12. Garcia, N.M., Rodrigues, J.J.P.C.: Ambient Assisted Living. CRC Press, Boca Raton (2015)
13. Gilbert, M., et al.: Preparedness and vulnerability of African countries against importations of COVID-19: a modelling study. Lancet **395**, 871–877 (2020). https://doi.org/10.1016/S0140-6736(20)30411-6
14. Huang, T., Lan, L., Fang, X., An, P., Min, J., Wang, F.: Promises and challenges of big data computing in health sciences. Big Data Res. **2**, 2–11 (2015). https://doi.org/10.1016/j.bdr.2015.02.002
15. Imran, A., et al.: AI4COVID-19: AI enabled preliminary diagnosis for COVID-19 from cough samples via an app. Inf. Med. Unlocked 100378 (2020). https://doi.org/10.1016/j.imu.2020.100378
16. Oniani, S., Pires, I.M., Garcia, N.M., Mosashvili, I., Pombo, N.: A review of frameworks on continuous data acquisition for e-Health and m-Health. In: Proceedings of the 5th EAI International Conference on Smart Objects and Technologies for Social Good, pp. 231–234. ACM (2019)
17. Oniani, S., et al.: Reliability assessment of new and updated consumer-grade activity and heart rate monitors. IARIA SensorDevices (2018)
18. Pantelopoulos, A., Bourbakis, N.G.: A survey on wearable sensor-based systems for health monitoring and prognosis. IEEE Trans. Syst. Man Cybern. Part C (Appl. Rev.) **40**, 1–12 (2010)
19. Patel, S., Park, H., Bonato, P., Chan, L., Rodgers, M.: A review of wearable sensors and systems with application in rehabilitation. J. NeuroEng. Rehabil. **9**, 21 (2012). https://doi.org/10.1186/1743-0003-9-21
20. Paules, C.I., Marston, H.D., Fauci, A.S.: Coronavirus infections—more than just the common cold. JAMA **323**, 707 (2020). https://doi.org/10.1001/jama.2020.0757

21. Perera, C., Zaslavsky, A., Christen, P., Georgakopoulos, D.: Context aware computing for the internet of things: a survey. IEEE Commun. Surv. Tutorials **16**, 414–454 (2014). https://doi. org/10.1109/SURV.2013.042313.00197

22. Petrescu, A.-M., Taussig, D., Bouilleret, V.: Electroencephalogram (EEG) in COVID-19: a systematic retrospective study. Neurophysiol. Clin. **50**, 155–165 (2020). https://doi.org/10. 1016/j.neucli.2020.06.001

23. Phua, J., et al.: Intensive care management of coronavirus disease 2019 (COVID-19): challenges and recommendations. Lancet Respir. Med. **8**, 506–517 (2020). https://doi.org/10. 1016/S2213-2600(20)30161-2

24. Pires, I.M., et al.: Android Library for Recognition of Activities of Daily Living: Implementation Considerations, Challenges, and Solutions (2018)

25. Pires, I.M.S., Garcia, N.M., Pombo, N., Flórez-Revuelta, F., Zdravevski, E., Spinsante, S.: A review on the artificial intelligence algorithms for the recognition of Activities of Daily Living using sensors in mobile devices (2018)

26. Ponciano, V., et al.: Smartphone-based automatic measurement of the results of the Timed-Up and Go test. In: Proceedings of the 5th EAI International Conference on Smart Objects and Technologies for Social Good, pp. 239–242. ACM (2019)

27. Ponciano, V., et al.: Machine learning techniques with ECG and EEG data: an exploratory study. Computers **9**, 55 (2020). https://doi.org/10.3390/computers9030055

28. Salehi-Abari, I., Khazaeli, S., Salehi-Abari, F., Salehi-Abari, A.: Practical guideline for screening the patients with SARS-CoV-2 infection and persian gulf criteria for diagnosis of COVID-19. Adv. Infect. Dis. **10**, 67 (2020). https://doi.org/10.4236/aid.2020.103008

29. Sethy, P.K., Behera, S.K.: Detection of Coronavirus Disease (COVID-19) Based on Deep Features. Engineering (2020)

30. Sousa, P. S., Sabugueiro, D., Felizardo, V., Couto, R., Pires, I., Garcia, N. M.: mHealth sensors and applications for personal aid. In: Adibi, Sasan (ed.) Mobile Health. SSB, vol. 5, pp. 265–281. Springer, Cham (2015). https://doi.org/10.1007/978-3-319-12817-7_12

31. Stojanovic, R., Skraba, A., Lutovac, B.: A headset like wearable device to track COVID-19 symptoms. In: 2020 9th Mediterranean Conference on Embedded Computing (MECO), Budva, Montenegro, pp. 1–4. IEEE (2020)

32. Villasana, M.V., et al.: Mobile applications for the promotion and support of healthy nutrition and physical activity habits: a systematic review, extraction of features and taxonomy proposal. TOBIOIJ **12**, 50–71 (2019). https://doi.org/10.2174/1875036201912010050

33. Yin, H., Jha, N.K.: A health decision support system for disease diagnosis based on wearable medical sensors and machine learning ensembles. IEEE Trans. Multi-Scale Comput. Syst. **3**, 228–241 (2017). https://doi.org/10.1109/TMSCS.2017.2710194

34. EEG Abnormalities in Acutely Ill Patients With COVID-19. In: Neurology Live. https:// www.neurologylive.com/clinical-focus/eeg-abnormalities-in-acutely-ill-patients-with-cov id19. Accessed 22 Aug 2020

Computational Intelligence
and Communications

Application of Distributed Generation for Reduction of Power Losses and Voltage Deviation in Electric Distribution System by Using AI Techniques

Takele Ferede Agajie[1]([✉]), Ghantasala Lakshmi Srinivas Rao[1], Engidaw Abel Hailu[1], Yayehyirad Ayalew Awoke[1], Tesfaye Meberate Anteneh[1], and Fsaha Mebrahtu Gebru[2]

[1] Debere Markos University, Debre Markos, Ethiopia
[2] Haramaya University, Haramaya, Ethiopia

Abstract. Distribution Electric power system is the largest and the most complex system made by the mankind. The distribution network power system is being encountered by quickly rising load demand and it is detected that under certain critical loading circumstances, the distribution system poses maximum power losses and poor voltage profile and collapse in convinced areas. To overcome these problems integrating distributed generation (DGs) on the grid near to the load center is the better solution as compared to others. Though, for the DG to serve its purpose, its location and size have to be determined optimally. In this paper, Grid-Based Multi-Objective Harmony Search Algorithm (GrMHSA) has been utilized to determine the size and location of DG in the distribution system in Debre Markos town. By placing DG optimally, in addition to the reduction of the power loss in the distribution network, the proposed mechanism improves the node (bus) voltage profile of the system under consideration. A MATLAB program is developed to mitigate power losses and improve the voltage profile by optimally sizing and placing a DG in the distribution network. After sizing and placing the DG in the network, the total voltage deviation, active and reactive power losses are reduced by 93.42%, 81.63% and 82.45% for Debre Markos Feeder 3 and 85.20%, 84.94% and 85.73% for Debre Markos Feeder 4 respectively. The performance comparison of GrMHSA and MOPSO has been made and GrMHSA has been found better in terms of reducing voltage deviation and power losses in the system.

Keywords: Distribution systems · GrMHSA · Distributed generation · Power loss reduction · DG location and size · Voltage deviation

1 Introduction

Distributed Generation is the source of electrical energy which is connected directly to distribution network without requiring high voltage power transmission network. As most of the DG sources are renewable energy, it produces a clean power. Typical energy

© ICST Institute for Computer Sciences, Social Informatics and Telecommunications Engineering 2021
Published by Springer Nature Switzerland AG 2021. All Rights Reserved
S. Paiva et al. (Eds.): SmartCity360° 2020, LNICST 372, pp. 127–139, 2021.
https://doi.org/10.1007/978-3-030-76063-2_10

sources of DG are solar and wind. Some of the desirable features of DG are better power system efficiency, better voltage profile, cost saving from additional power transmission line, improved power system reliability and usage of local energy resources. However, wrong DG location and capacity leads to more power loss and more cost than not having it [1, 2] and [3].

The penetration of DG into distribution systems has been increasing around the world. Moreover, developments in DGs have ready it a viable and smart choice for perfection [4, 5]. Distributed generations (DGs) are mostly used for active and reactive power injection in distribution networks. It is used also for power loss reduction and voltage profile improvement. The advantages of this kind of mechanism depends on how much and where to place the DGs in the radial distribution network system [6, 7] and [8].

Many optimization techniques have been utilized for optimal siting and sizing of the DG considering technical and economical performances [9–11] and [12]. Tools like heuristic, deterministic and hybrid techniques are capable and still sprouting in this field.

When connected to the distribution network, various DG technologies can lead to improved levels of power quality, reliability and security, if the DG units are in the best position and size [10, 11] and [12].

Various approaches and algorithms have been used for the siting and sizing of DGs; the majority of which are aimed to minimize active power losses and improve the voltage variations [13, 14]. The methods applied for solving the problems can be broadly divided as mathematical, heuristic, meta-heuristic, and hybrid types [15]. Mathematical methods include mixed integer linear programming [16, 17], mixed-integer second order cone programming [16] and multi-period optimal power flow [18]. In [19] and [20] power flow algorithm is used to determine the optimum DG size at all load buses assuming every load bus is connected to the DG source. Such a method is, however, inefficient due to a number of load flow computations. The genetic algorithm (GA) is used to determine the size and location of DG as presented in [21, 22] and [23]. GA is suitable for multi-objective problems like DG allocation and can give near-optimal results, but it is computationally demanding and slow in convergence. In [24], an analytical method to place DG in radial as well as meshed systems to minimize power loss of the system is presented. In this method, separate expressions for radial and meshed network systems are derived and a complex procedure based on phasor current is proposed to solve the location problem. However, this method only optimizes the location and considers the size of DG as fixed.

In this paper, the proposed optimization method for measuring and segregating DG components in an active distribution system is based on a Grid-based Multi-purpose agreement Harmony Search Algorithm (GrMHSA).

The remainder of this paper is organized as follows: in Sect. 2, test utility distribution network is discussed; In Sect. 3, the proposed optimization technique is discussed; Sect. 4 introduces the problem formulation and constraints; Sect. 5 presents the result and discussions; finally, the conclusions are drawn in Sect. 6.

2 Test Utility Distribution Network

In this paper, the case study is taken from Debre Markos distribution network and the data is collected and analyzed. The parameters of interest are node voltage and active and reactive power loss.

Debre Markos, is the capital town East Gojjam Zone in Amhara National regional state, Ethiopia. It's located at 10o21′N latitude and 37o43′E longitude.

The town is supplied from Debre Markos power Substation with two 15 kV feeders, namely Feeder 3 (Line 3) and Feeder 4 (Line 4) as shown from Fig. 1 in detail. The data including single line diagram of distribution network, current loading of the feeders and their branches, resistance and inductive reactance of the feeder lines were collected from local electric utility. These data were used to model the feeders for power flow study.

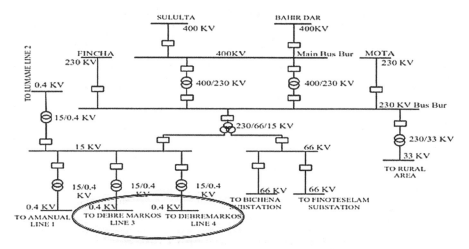

Fig. 1. Position of Feeder 3 (Line 3) and Feeder 4 (Line 4) in Debre Markos Power Substation

3 Implementation of Procedural Flow Charts for the Proposed GrMHSA Techniques

Stimulated by the managing process of music in search of perfect harmony sound, harmony Search algorithm is one of the merging meta-heuristic optimization algorithms [25, 26] and [27]. In this paper, a grid strategy is implemented as a secondary criterion for optimal siting and sizing of DGs. Among other heuristic algorithms, GrMHSA is preferred as it is simple for programming, faster in convergence and efficient in searching optimal solutions. The general flow chart of proposed algorithm of GrMHSA is shown in Fig. 2.

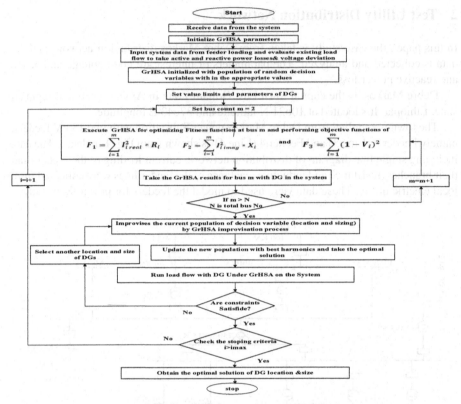

Fig. 2. Proposed GrMHSA algorithm for optimal DG sizing and placement

4 Formulation of Objective Functions and Constraints

The most important objective functions are total active power loss, total reactive power loss and total voltage deviation with constraints of voltage magnitude, branch thermal limits, and DG capacity limit. The objective functions are:

Total real power loss, P_1:

$$P_1 = \sum I_{i,real}R_i \tag{1}$$

Total reactive power loss, P_2:

$$P_2 = \sum I_{i,imag}X_i \tag{2}$$

Total voltage deviation, P_3:

$$P_3 = \sum |1 - V_j| \tag{3}$$

Where,

R_i: the resistance of branch i
I_i : the current magnitude flows in-branch i
X_i: the reactance of branch i
V_i : voltage of node j

A Backward-Forward Sweep Load Flow algorithm has been utilized to solve the distribution networks, and in the solution, the real and reactive power loss and voltage deviation need to be reduced.

The objective functions are to be minimized under the constraints presented from Eq. (4) to (7).

(i) **Node voltage constraint:**

$$0.95 \leq V_i \leq 1.05 \tag{4}$$

where, V_i is node voltage in p.u.

(ii) **Branch thermal limit constraint:**

$$I_{i,j} \leq I_{rated} \tag{5}$$

where,

$I_{(i,j)}$: Current carrying capacity of existing line branch between node i and j
I_{rated}: Thermal current carrying capacity of the line

(iii) **DG Capacity Limit:**
   The capacity of the DG to be connected to the existing distribution network should not be too high with respect to the feeder loading or too small to be economical. Therefore, selected DG must have the allowable size between the minimum and the maximum limits.

$$S_{DGm,i}^{min} \leq S_{DG,i} \leq S_{DG,i}^{max} \tag{6}$$

where:

$S_{DGm,i}^{min}$: Minimum power output limit of DG at node i
$S_{DG,i}^{max}$: Maximum power output limit of DG at node i
$S_{DG,i}$: actual The power output of DG at bus i

5   Results and Discussion

5.1   System Base Case and Comparison of Solution Algorithms

The GrMHS algorithm has been applied to find the optimal location and determine the optimal size of DGs in the distribution networks shown in Fig. 3 (Feeder 3) and Fig. 4 (Feeder 4).

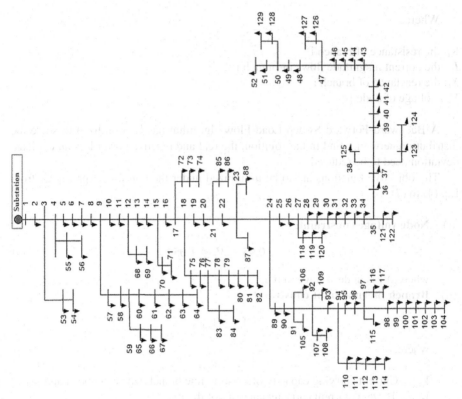

Fig. 3. Single line diagram of Feeder 3

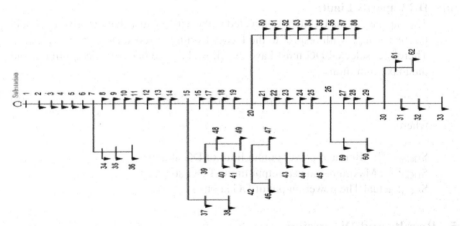

Fig. 4. Single line diagram of Feeder 4

On the distribution system shown in Fig. 3 and 4, the performance of the proposed algorithm, GrMHSA) is compared with multi-objective particle swarm optimization (MOPSO) by measuring its spread and time of convergence. MOPSO is chosen for comparison because it is more known by its ability to fast convergence and easy for implementation as compared to other algorithms [28].

A matlab code has been developed for GrMHS and MOPSO algorithms and both algorithms are executed with 50 populations for 110 iterations. The simulation spread is shown in Fig. 5, and it can be shown that efficient penetrating has been complete by GrMHSA over MOPSO in obtaining the best optimal solutions with respect to objectives functions of power losses (P_{loss} and Q_{loss}) and total voltage deviation (VD).

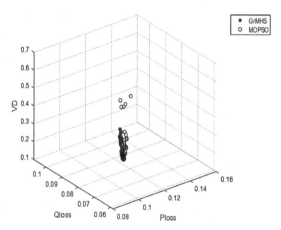

Fig. 5. Performance comparison of GrMHS with MOPSO algorithm

The load flow result for of the base case (the system with no DG) is shown in Table.

Table 1. Base case load flow result

Feeder	Feeder Current (A)	Connected Load (MVA)	Total real Power loss (kW)	Total reactive Power loss (kVAR)	Total Power loss (kVA)	Total Voltage deviation (p.u.)
Feeder 3	192.6	5.00	523.28	516.49	735.24	17.26
Feeder 4	128.3	3.33	472.97	410.43	626.22	6.85

The total power loss as a fraction of connected load to Feeder 3 and Feeder 4 is 14.70% and 18.81%, respectively. The overall efficiency of the distribution network is 16.34% considering only the reactive and active power losses on the conductors, which certainly tells one the system requires enhancement to reduce the power losses.

The node voltage profile of the base case system under consideration is shown in Fig. 6 and 7.

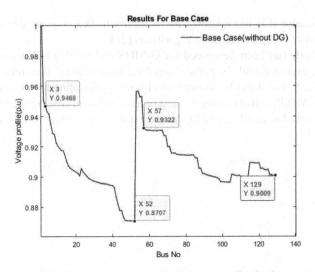

Fig. 6. Node voltage for the base case at Feeder 3

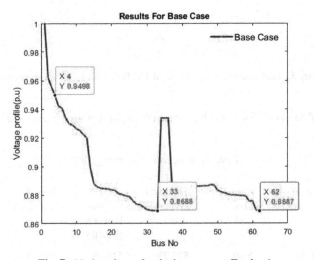

Fig. 7. Node voltage for the base case at Feeder 4

As it can be seen in Fig. 6 and 7, nodes 3–52 and node 57–129 for Feeder 3 and node 4–62 for Feeder 4 have voltage profile below 0.95p.u, which is below the standard [29]. The voltage profile at node 3, 52, 57 and 129 are 0. 9468 p.u, 0. 8707 p.u, 0.9322 p.u and 0.9009 p.u for Feeder 3 and the voltage profile at node 4, 33 and 62 are 0.9498 p.u, 0.8688 p.u and 0.8687 p.u for Feeder 4, respectively.

With node voltage levels less than 0.95 p.u, the actual node voltage will be less than 14.25 kV since the distribution voltage of the feeders are15 kV. Considering the voltage drops of low voltage lines and service transformers, the voltage at consumer premises will not be enough to run consumer electric and electronic appliances.

This implies that the system needs improvement to enhance at least the voltage profile at the nodes of the feeders and reduce active and reactive power losses in the system.

Hence, distributed Generation (DG) is proposed to mitigate the power loss and voltage deviation problems of the system.

5.2 Optimal Location and Size of DG with GrMHS and MOPSO Algorithms

The optimal sizes and location of DGs using GrMHS and MOPSO algorithms is presented in Table 2.

Table 2. Result of optimal sizing and placement of DG using GrMHSA and MOPSO

Feeder	Optimization techniques	DG location (@node)	Optimal DG size (MVA)	Real power loss (kW)	Reactive power loss (kVAR)	Total power loss (kVA)	Voltage deviation (p.u)
Feeder 3	GrMHSA	51	2.17	92.39	90.35	129.22	1.0642
	MOPSO	49	2.26	93.77	92.36	131.62	1.1852
Feeder 4	GrMHSA	30	1.88	65.27	60.68	89.12	0.8625
	MOPSO	27	1.96	67.33	63.86	92.80	0.9958

As shown in Table 2, with the GrMHS algorithm the required size of DG is optimally placed at node 51 for Feeder 3 and at node 30 for Feeder 4. However, MOPSO algorithm places the required DG size at node 49 (Feeder 3) and node 27 (Feeder 4). The optimal size of DG selected by MOPSO is 4.24% and 4.66% higher than that selected by GrMHSA for Feeder 3 and 4, respectively. Moreover, with GrMHSA algorithm, the total active and reactive power losses and total voltage deviation is lower than that obtained from MOPSO algorithm. This implies that GrMHSA chooses the most economical size of DGs and places them optimally resulting in the minimum power losses and voltage deviation.

Comparing total power losses (in kVA) presented in Table 1 and Table 2, when DG is sized and placed using GrMHSA, the power loss of Feeder 3 is reduced from 735.24 kVA to 129.22 kVA by 82% while the power loss of Feeder 4 is reduced from 626.22 kVA to 89.2 kVA by 86%.

The total voltage deviation (p.u) is also reduced by 94% for Feeder 3 and 87% for Feeder 4, respectively.

The comparison of node voltage profile of the base case, of a system with DG optimally sized and place with GrMHSA and MOPSO algorithms is shown in Fig. 8 and Figalso compared as it is shown in Fig. 8 and Fig. 9.

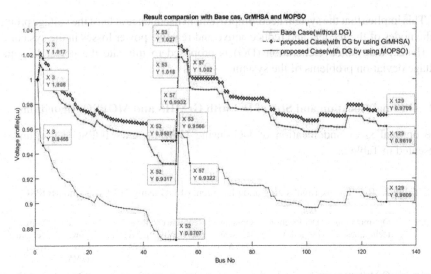

Fig. 8. Feeder 3 node voltage profile for the three cases (base case, with DG by MOPSO & DG by GrMHSA)

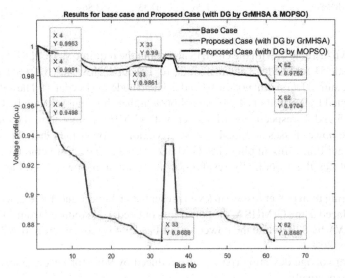

Fig. 9. Feeder 4 node voltage profile for the three cases (base case, with DG by MOPSO and GrMHSA)

As it is shown above in Fig. 8 and Fig. 9, the voltage profile of the system with DG selected by GrMHSA is better than the result by MOPSO. As can be seen from Fig. 8 and 9, the voltage at nodes 3, 52, 57 and 129 are increased from 0. 9468 p.u, 0. 8707 p.u, 0. 9322 p.u and 0. 9009 p.u to 1. 017 p.u, 0. 9507 p.u, 1. 002 p.u and 0. 9709 p.u for Feeder3. The voltage profile at nodes 4, 33 and 62 are increased from 0. 9498 p.u, 0.

8688 p.u and 0. 8687 p.u to 0. 9963 p.u, 0. 9900 p.u and 0. 9762 p.u for Feeder 4, respectively. The node voltages are now within the tolerable voltage limits (0.95 to 1.05 p.u) for both feeders after optimally sized DGs are placed in optimal locations.

6 Conclusion

The main challenges in distribution power networks are voltage deviation and power losses which lead to poor quality service and low efficiency of the system. There are different methods to tackle these problems, among thus are a reconfiguration of distribution network, incorporating capacitors into the network and adding DGs optimally into the distribution system. Integrating distributed generation (DG) into the system is one of the trending solutions which are done by many researchers. This paper has dealt with the sizing and location of DG in Debre Markos Feeder 3 and Debre Markos Feeder 4 of a distribution network system. Grid-based multi-objective harmony search algorithm (GrMHSA) has been used to size and find the optimal node for putting the DG. By placing of DG optimally, in addition to mitigating the power loss in the distribution network, the proposed mechanism enhances the voltage profile of the system under consideration. A MATLAB program is developed to mitigate power losses and improve the voltage profile by optimally sizing and placing a DG in the distribution network. After sizing and placing the DG in the network, the total voltage deviation, active and reactive power losses are reduced by 93.83%, 82.34% and 82.51% for Debre Markos Feeder 3 and 87.42%, 86.19% and 85.21% for Debre Markos Feeder 4 respectively. Moreover, the performance of the proposed algorithm, GrMHSA, is compared with Multi-Objective Particle Swarm Optimization (MOPSO), which has been made and GrMHSA has been found better in terms of reducing voltage deviation and power losses in the system.

References

1. Kayalvizhi, S., DM, V.K.: Optimal planning of active distribution networks with hybrid distributed energy resources using grid-based multi-objective harmony search algorithm. Appl. Soft Comput. **67**, 387–398 (2018)
2. Payasi, R.P., Singh, A.K., Singh, D., Singh, N.K.: Multi-objective optimization of distributed generation with voltage step constraint. Int. J. Eng. Sci. Technol. **7**(3), 33–41 (2015)
3. Ferede, A.T., Olalekan, S.A., Abel, H.E., Ayalew, A.Y.: Power loss mitigation and voltage profile improvement with distributed generation using grid-based multi-objective harmony search algorithm. J. Electr. Electron. Eng. (JEEE) **13**(2) (2020). P-ISSN 1844-6035
4. Nguyen, T.T., Truong, A.V.: Distribution network reconfiguration for power loss minimization and voltage profile improvement using cuckoo search algorithm. Int. J. Electr. Power Energy Syst. **68**, 233–242 (2015)
5. Awoke, Y.A., Agajie, T.F., Hailu, E.A.: Distribution network expansion planning considering DG-penetration limit using a metaheuristic optimization technique: a case study at Debre Markos distribution network. Int. J. Electr. Eng. Inf. **12**(2), 326–340 (2020)
6. Paliwal, P., Patidar, N.P., Nema, R.K.: Planning of grid integrated distributed generators: a review of technology, objectives and techniques. Renew. Sustain. Energy Rev. **40**, 557–570 (2014)

7. Pal, A., Chakraborty, A.K., Bhowmik, A.R.: Optimal placement and sizing of DG considering power and energy loss minimization in distribution system. Int. J. Electr. Eng. Inf. **12**(3), 624–653 (2020)
8. Agajie, T.F., Salau, A.O., Hailu, E.A., Sood, M., Jain, S.: Optimal sizing and siting of distributed generators for minimization of power losses and voltage deviation. In: 2019 5th International Conference on Signal Processing, Computing and Control (ISPCC), pp. 292–297. IEEE, October 2019
9. Singh, P., Bishnoi, S.K., Meena, N.K.: Moth search optimization for optimal DERs integration in conjunction to OLTC tap operations in distribution systems. IEEE Syst. J. **14**(1), 880–888 (2019)
10. Georgilakis, P.S., Hatziargyriou, N.D.: Optimal distributed generation placement in power distribution networks: models, methods, and future research. IEEE Trans. Power Syst. **28**(3), 3420–3428 (2013)
11. Kanwar, N., Gupta, N., Niazi, K.R., Swarnkar, A.: Simultaneous allocation of distributed resources using improved teaching learning based optimization. Energy Convers. Manag. **103**, 387–400 (2015)
12. Prabha, D.R., Jayabarathi, T.: Optimal placement and sizing of multiple distributed generating units in distribution networks by invasive weed optimization algorithm. Ain Shams Eng. J. **7**(2), 683–694 (2016)
13. Meena, N.K., Parashar, S., Swarnkar, A., Gupta, N., Niazi, K.R.: Improved elephant herding optimization for multiobjective DER accommodation in distribution systems. IEEE Trans. Industr. Inf. **14**(3), 1029–1039 (2017)
14. Ogunjuyigbe, A.S.O., Ayodele, T.R., Akinola, O.O.: Impact of distributed generators on the power loss and voltage profile of sub-transmission network. J. Electr. Syst. Inf. Technol. **3**(1), 94–107 (2016)
15. Hung, D.Q., Mithulananthan, N., Bansal, R.C.: Analytical expressions for DG allocation in primary distribution networks. IEEE Trans. Energy Convers. **25**(3), 814–820 (2010)
16. Mohan, N., Ananthapadmanabha, T., Kulkarni, A.D.: A weighted multi-objective index based optimal distributed generation planning in distribution system. Procedia Technol. **21**, 279–286 (2015)
17. Hung, D.Q., Mithulananthan, N.: Multiple distributed generator placement in primary distribution networks for loss reduction. IEEE Trans. Industr. Electron. **60**(4), 1700–1708 (2011)
18. Jamil Mahfoud, R., Sun, Y., Faisal Alkayem, N., Haes Alhelou, H., Siano, P., Shafie-khah, M.: A novel combined evolutionary algorithm for optimal planning of distributed generators in radial distribution systems. Appl. Sci. **9**(16), 3394 (2019)
19. Fandi, G., Ahmad, I., Igbinovia, F.O., Muller, Z., Tlusty, J., Krepl, V.: Voltage regulation and power loss minimization in radial distribution systems via reactive power injection and distributed generation unit placement. Energies **11**(6), 1399 (2018)
20. Quadri, I.A., Bhowmick, S., Joshi, D.: A comprehensive technique for optimal allocation of distributed energy resources in radial distribution systems. Appl. Energy **211**, 1245–1260 (2018)
21. Silvestri, A., Berizzi, A., Buonanno, S.: Distributed generation planning using genetic algorithms. In: PowerTech Budapest 99. Abstract Records (Cat. No. 99EX376), p. 257. IEEE, August 1999
22. Kim, K.H., Lee, Y.J., Rhee, S.B., Lee, S.K., You, S.K.: Dispersed generator placement using fuzzy-GA in distribution systems. In: IEEE Power Engineering Society Summer Meeting, vol. 3, pp. 1148–1153. IEEE, July 2002
23. Carpinelli, G., Celli, G., Pilo, F., Russo, A.: Distributed generation siting and sizing under uncertainty. In: 2001 IEEE Porto Power Tech Proceedings (Cat. No. 01EX502), vol. 4, pp. 7-pp. IEEE, September 2001

24. Naik, S.N.G., Khatod, D.K., Sharma, M.P.: Analytical approach for optimal siting and sizing of distributed generation in radial distribution networks. IET Gener. Transm. Distrib. **9**(3), 209–220 (2014)
25. Ala'a, A., Alsewari, A.A., Alamri, H.S., Zamli, K.Z.: Comprehensive review of the development of the harmony search algorithm and its applications. IEEE Access **7**, 14233–14245 (2019)
26. Ingram, G., Zhang, T.: Overview of applications and developments in the harmony search algorithm. In: Geem, Z.W. (ed.) Music-Inspired Harmony Search Algorithm, pp. 15–37. Springer, Heidelberg (2009). https://doi.org/10.1007/978-3-642-00185-7_2
27. Assad, A.: Recent advances in harmony search algorithm. In: Recent Advances in Harmony Search Algorithm, pp. 157–165 (2019)
28. Aghaei, J., Muttaqi, K., Azizivahed, A., Gitizadeh, M.: Distribution expansion planning considering reliability and security of energy using modified PSO (Particle Swarm Optimization) algorithm. Energy **65**, 398–411 (2014)
29. Gantayet, A., Mohanty, S.: An analytical approach for optimal placement and sizing of Distributed Generation based on a combined voltage stability index. In: 2015 IEEE Power, Communication and Information Technology Conference (PCITC), pp. 762–767. IEEE, October 2015

Non-linear Control Applied to a 3D Printed Hand

Sofiane Ibrahim Benchabane[1]($\boxtimes$) ![ORCID], Nadia Saadia[1], and Amar Ramdane-Cherif[2]

[1] University of Science and Technology Houari Boumediene, Bab Ezzouar, Algeria
[2] Versailles Saint-Quentin-en-Yvelines University, Versailles, France

Abstract. The dynamics of a prosthesis is an important parameter to consider in order to allow efficient use. In fact, the prosthesis should perform the desired task with enough precision under a controlled kinematics. To this aim, it is necessary to set up a control law which guarantees the operating of the structure according to a pre-established specification. A prosthesis like any mechatronic structure is a complex and dynamic system, based on parameters which can evolve as a function of interactions, physical conditions or time, for this it is necessary to use a robust control algorithm to address this issue. In this work we present a sliding mode control algorithm applied to an anthropomorphic prosthesis printed in 3D at the LRPE/LISV laboratories. The control structure used enables to overcome the modelling uncertainties and parametric variations of the mechatronic system such as the coefficients of friction in the joints and the coefficient of elasticity of cable-pull.

Keywords: Prosthetic control · Sliding mode control · Non-linear control

1 Adaptive Control

A linear system is a system whose output (s) are a linear combination of its input (s), in other words the system is represented by a linear transfer function where when the input of the system varies, the output varies similarly. The control of such a system is a task which consists in determining a control law constraining the response of the system to a desired dynamic. In order to synthesize this control law, it is generally sufficient to study the response of the system to a predefined set point (a step for example) thanks to the system's linearity its behaviour will be similar for any finite input (invariant causal system).

In the case where the system considered is linear but variable, that is to say that its parameters are not constant over time (aging, parameters sensitive to temperature, humidity, mechanical stress, etc.), the control law can turn out to be 'obsolete' and no longer guarantees the control of the system in all circumstances.

Several approaches can be implemented in the context of variable structure control such as: neural networks [1–8], fuzzy logic [9–11], the neurofuzzy approach [12–16], sliding mode control [17–21].

© ICST Institute for Computer Sciences, Social Informatics and Telecommunications Engineering 2021
Published by Springer Nature Switzerland AG 2021. All Rights Reserved
S. Paiva et al. (Eds.): SmartCity360° 2020, LNICST 372, pp. 140–155, 2021.
https://doi.org/10.1007/978-3-030-76063-2_11

The sliding mode control is a very popular strategy for control of nonlinear uncertain systems, with a very large frame of applications fields [22, 23]. The main drawback of the sliding mode control, the well-known chattering phenomenon [24, 25] is important and could damage actuators and systems. A first way to reduce the chattering is the use of a boundary layer: in this case, many approaches have proposed adequate controller gains tuning [26]. A second way to decrease the chattering phenomenon is the use of higher order sliding mode controller [27–30]. However, in both these control approaches, knowledge of uncertainties bound is required.

The Sliding Mode Control (SMC) is a command which is not sensitive to parametric variations as well as to modelling uncertainties, the approach also brings good results as regards resistance to disturbances.

The implementation of this method is relatively simple and does not affect the performance of the system in terms of response time. The SMC ensures the stability of the system by maintaining its state on the hyperplane S = 0, as illustrated in Fig. 1.

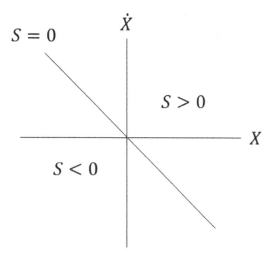

Fig. 1. Hyperplane S in the state space, when the system is on the right S = 0 it is in sliding mode

In the state space, we can define the line $S = \dot{X} + \sigma X, \sigma > 0$ where X is a state vector.

$$S = 0 \rightarrow \dot{X} = -\sigma X \rightarrow x(t) = Ce^{-\sigma t} \tag{1}$$

The Eq. (1) allows to affirm that the variable of state of the system tends towards 0 in a finite time, in other words the system will bring a finished response to a finished entry when $S = 0$ (system in sliding mode). Therefore, in order to ensure the stability of the system it is sufficient to maintain the system on the hyperplane $S = 0$. However, it is also necessary that the control law makes it possible to ensure the accuracy of the system by cancelling at the same time the system error e. By simply choosing to set $X = e$ when the system will be in sliding mode, we will therefore obtain that $e \rightarrow 0$, ensuring the precision and stability of the system. The control will therefore consist in evaluating S and acting on the setpoint of the system in order to bring it back on the hyperplane.

2   The Studied System

The studied system includes an EMG interface [31] who provides instructions for function enabling/disabling, i.e. determines which appropriate function to activate. Once this instruction is generated the system should execute it properly by driving it to a precise dynamic, as illustrated in Fig. 2.

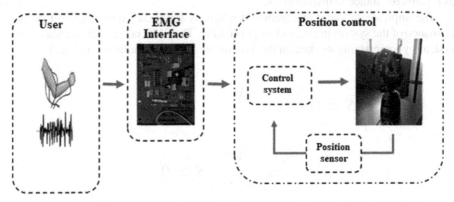

Fig. 2. Diagram of the different system's modules.

Beforehand, it is necessary to define the different components of the system as well as the specifications imposed on it. The system developed consists of the elements described below.

2.1   Setpoint Generator

In our system while the EMG module delivers a signal, the system remains operating (flexion or extension of the finger is held). To this end, the setpoint generator increments the desired angle every 200 ms while the activation signal at its input is present. Indeed, we require that a complete flexion or extension is performed in 20 steps of 4.5° each and in 4 s.

2.2   System to Control

The system to be controlled consists of the actuator (servomotor) and the prosthesis, an angular position sensor is incorporated on the servomotor lifter, which will be used to measure the angle provided by the actuator at the input of the mechanical device.

The setpoint generator will therefore indicate a desired angle to be reached (from the signal delivered by the EMG module), then the system (actuator, prosthesis) will have to satisfy this constraint. Figure 3 below illustrates the system:

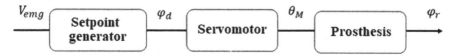

Fig. 3. Global diagram of the system to be controlled (servo + prosthesis)

The actuator is controlled by Pulse Width Modulation (PWM), namely is necessary to code the angle requested from the actuator by varying the duty cycle of the signal applied to it. For this reason, our system therefore incorporates a desired angle encoder, which will convert the setpoint angle into a signal "understandable" by the servomotor (modulated in pulse width).

2.2.1 The Desired Angle Encoder

The role of this module is to match the desired angle φ_d to a pulse width to be sent to the servomotor. In order to determine the pulse width which corresponds to a given angle, we apply a simple rule of three from the technical data sheet of the actuator:

$$180° \rightarrow 1 \ ms \ width$$

$$angle° \rightarrow t \ ms \ width$$

i.e.

$$t = \frac{angle}{180} 10^{-3} s \tag{2}$$

2.2.2 The Servomotor

The servomotor used in our system is the (SG90), producing a torque $T_u = 1.63$ Kg.cm.cm and a constant angular speed $\omega_{mot} = 600°/s$, under a supply voltage of 5 V. A servo motor is actually a DC motor with gears and a position control loop. In our approach, we consider the servomotor as the assembly of the following two modules:

A Pulse Width Converter: which corresponds to a variation in pulse width α of a DC motor operating time. Indeed, given that the motor rotates at a constant speed w_{mot} with a constant torque Tu, the position of the motor depends on the activation time of the latter. It is therefore necessary to establish the relationship between α is the operating time of the DC motor $t(\alpha)$ integrated in the servomotor.

A DC Motor: which delivers the position corresponding to the supply duration defined by the pulse width α. The engine is characterized by the electromechanical equations given below.

Figure 4 shows the SG90 and its various components:

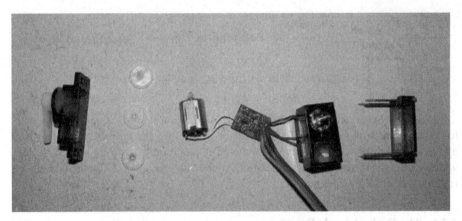

Fig. 4. The various constituents of SG90.

As shown in the Fig. 4, the servomotor is made up of: on the left the lifter and the reduction system, in the centre the direct current motor and its servo circuit, on the right the servomotor cover.

2.2.3 The Prosthetic Finger

The mechanical system (prosthesis) is the decoupled set of 5 fingers where each finger is an independent system, the control of our prosthesis therefore requires the control of each finger independently of the others.

The finger consists of 3 articulated phalanges, the angle of rotation of each joint is dependent on the angle of rotation of the motor as given below.

An angular position sensor linked to the servomotor lifter, delivers a voltage proportional to the measured angle of rotation, the sensor is positioned on the motor, and the flexion/extension angle of the finger and deduced from the relation $\varphi = f(\theta)$.

3 Specifications

The system developed is governed by specifications that we impose, as described in the following:

1. While the corresponding EMG function is active, the actuator is activated, and the finger is in motion.
2. 2. φ_r is the angle of flexion/extension of the finger identified from the end of the phalanx 3 to the carpus, $\varphi_r \in [0° - 180°]$.
3. A finger performs a complete flexion or extension in 4s.
4. A flexion or extension is completed in 20 steps of 4.5° each of the servomotor lifter (θ_M).
5. The movement of a finger is characterized by a constant dynamic (constant motor torque, constant motor angular speed).

4   Synoptic Diagram

In the dynamics that we impose on our system, a function remains activated while the EMG signal corresponding to its activation is present. This function is provided by a block which will be called the setpoint generator, which will deliver the duty cycle necessary to animate the structure according to the presence of the EMG signal.

Let T given in Eq. (3) be the transfer function of our open loop system, the block diagram according to Fig. 5 represents the open loop system.

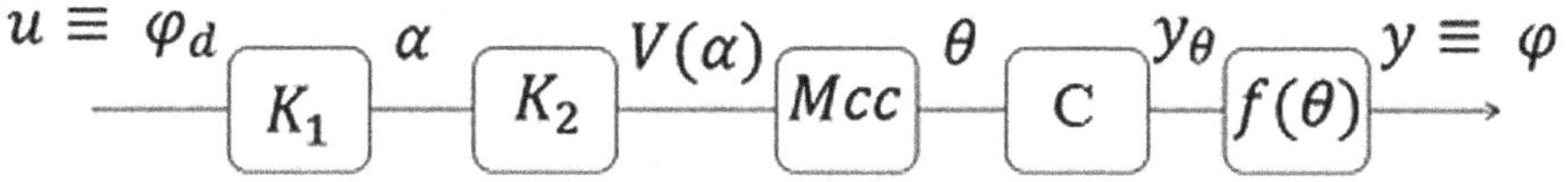

Fig. 5. Synoptic diagram of the sound system, including all the constituent segments of the system to be controlled

From the synoptic diagram we express the transfer function of the system in open loop:

$$T = K_1 K_2 MCC f(\theta) C \tag{3}$$

5   Transfer Functions

5.1   The Desired Angle Encoder (K_1)

Convert the input setpoint to PWM (α), α is calculated by a simple rule of three, indeed, a variation of the pulse width of 1 ms corresponds to an angle of 180° where the angle φ_d corresponds to a variation of pulse width of $\varphi_d \frac{0.001}{180}$.

i.e.

$$\alpha = \varphi_d 5.56 \text{ then } K_1 = 5.56 10^{-5} \tag{4}$$

5.2   Pulse Width Converter (K_2)

The pulse width converter translates α into voltage (supply time) at the input of the DC motor as illustrated by Eq. (5)

$$V_s = t(\alpha).E \tag{5}$$

Figure 6 illustrates the evolution of $t(\alpha)$.

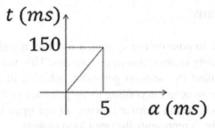

Fig. 6. The relation between α and the activation time required for the motor to reach the desired angle, knowing w_{mot}

From the Fig. 6 we have:

$$t(\alpha) = 30\alpha \qquad (6)$$

Therefore:

$$K_2 = 30E \qquad (7)$$

5.3 The DC Motor (MCC)

The DC motor is characterized by the following electromechanical equations:

$$\begin{cases} U = Ri + L\frac{di}{dt} + k\frac{d\theta}{dt} \\ J\frac{d^2\theta}{dt^2} = Tu = ki \end{cases} \qquad (8)$$

Given:

L, R, k, J the electromechanical parameters of the motor. We set $L \rightarrow 0$, from (8) we obtain:

$$U(p) = \frac{RJ}{k}p^2\theta(p) + kp\theta(p) \rightarrow \frac{\theta(p)}{U(p)} = \frac{k}{k^2p + RJp^2} \qquad (9)$$

The electrical resistance of the motor is determined experimentally, $R = 19\ \Omega$.

5.4 The Finger ($f(\theta)$)

The prosthesis is considered as a decouplable system or each finger can be ordered separately. A finger is a system with 3 pivot joints, as shown in Fig. 7.

From Fig. 7 we can summarize:

$$\begin{cases} x = x_1 + x_2 + x_3 \rightarrow x = L\sum_{i=1}^{3}\sin(i\theta) \\ y = y_1 + y_2 + y_3 \rightarrow y = L\sum_{i=1}^{3}\cos(i\theta) \end{cases} \rightarrow \tan\varphi = \frac{\sum_{i=1}^{3}\sin(i\theta)}{\sum_{i=1}^{3}\cos(i\theta)}$$

Therefore:

$$\varphi = Arctg\left(\frac{\sum_{i=1}^{3}\sin(i\theta)}{\sum_{i=1}^{3}\cos(i\theta)}\right) \qquad (10)$$

Figure 8 shows the plot of the angle φ as a function of the angle θ.

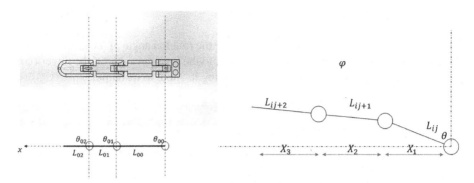

Fig. 7. Diagram illustrating $\varphi = f(\theta)$.

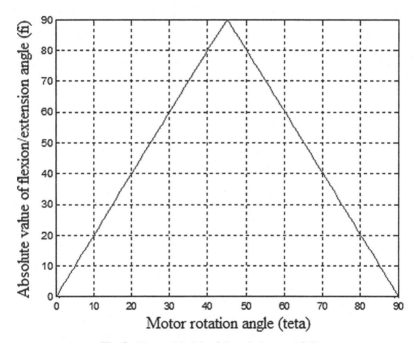

Fig. 8. Plot on Matlab of the relation $\varphi = f(\theta)$.

The negative slope part represents φ in the 3rd quadrant of the trigonometric circle $(3\pi/2)$. Figure 8 shows the relationship between the bending angle of the finger and the angle of rotation of the motor, when the motor rotates $90°$ the finger makes an angle of $180°$. From the figure we deduce the Eq. (11)

$$\varphi \approx 2\theta \tag{11}$$

The relation between φ and θ is approximated by a slope equal to 2.

5.5 Angular Position Sensor (C)

The angular position sensor allows us to measure the rotation angle of the motor, thanks to the Eq. (11) it is therefore possible to go back to the bending angle of the finger (φ). The sensor is characterized by the Eq. (12), linking its input to its output.

$$V_c = g(\theta) \rightarrow V_c = c.\theta \qquad (12)$$

c is the sensitivity of the sensor, the voltage delivered by the angular sensor is proportional to the angle of rotation measured. The sensor used in our application is a horizontal rotary potentiometer (1 kΩ, 20% tolerance), the calculation of the sensitivity goes through the development of the sensor conditioning circuit.

We deduce the angle of rotation from the output voltage delivered by the conditioning circuit, this is directly related to the value of the resistance of the potentiometer, which in turn depends on the position of the axis of 1 "adjustable (coupled to the axis of rotation of the servomotor). Conditioning requires a constant current source, in fact, so that the output voltage is proportional to the angle of rotation (therefore the value of the resistance) it is necessary that the current passing through the variable resistance is constant.

$$C = 0.13 \mp 20\% \qquad (13)$$

5.6 Open Loop and Closed Loop Transfer Functions

In open loop the system is the cascading of the different modules which constitute it (Fig. 5) so we get:

$$T = \frac{K_1 K_2 2ck}{k^2 p + RJp^2} = \frac{K'}{RJp^2 + k^2 p} \qquad (14)$$

The knowledge of the transfer function of the system in opened loop makes it possible to ensure an order insofar as it is possible to find the necessary setpoint, to be applied to the system in order to obtain the desired output. However, in this configuration it is not possible to be sure that the system output corresponds to the desired one, moreover if the output is affected by a disturbance no action can compensate the setpoint accordingly. It is then necessary to ensure the servo-control of the system by reporting its output to the set point (command in closed loop). The following block diagram (Fig. 9) represents the closed loop system:

The transfer function of the system when the output is brought back to the input is of the second order form and is given in the Eq. (14)

$$F = \frac{T}{1 + T}$$

$$F = \frac{K'}{RJp^2 + k^2 p + K'}$$

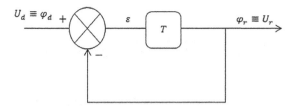

Fig. 9. Block diagram of the closed loop system

$$F = \frac{1}{\frac{RJ}{K}p^2 + \frac{k^2}{K}p + 1}$$

$$F = \frac{1}{9103.45p^2 + 3.096p + 1} \tag{15}$$

The system consists of modules whose parameters are subject to variation over time. Indeed, the parameters of the electric motor such as the armature resistance R, the flux constant k can change. The relation f (θ) is also sensitive to variations, this has been graphically approximated and can change over time, since it is strongly correlated to the fictions of the joints, to the stiffness of the return cable which can also evolve over time. The sensitivity of the sensor can also be affected by modelling uncertainty.

It is therefore wise to consider a robust control approach that is not very sensitive to parametric variation as well as to modelling errors. For this, we are oriented on an adaptive or variable structure control approach.

6   State-Space Representation of the System

We pass from the transfer function in closed loop of our system to its representation in the state space as follows:

From (14)

$$\frac{Y(p)}{U(p)} \rightarrow U(p) = c_1 p^2 Y(p) + c_0 p Y(p) + Y(p); c_1 = \frac{RJ}{K}, c_0 = \frac{k^2}{K} \tag{16}$$

$$(16) \rightarrow^{TL^{-1}} u(t) = c_1 \ddot{y}(t) + c_0 \dot{y}(t) + y(t)$$

By putting:

$$\begin{cases} x_1(t) = y(t) \\ x_2(t) = \dot{y}(t) \\ \dot{x}_1(t) = \dot{y}(p) \\ \dot{x}_2(t) = \ddot{y}(p) \end{cases} \tag{18}$$

The transition to the canonical form gives us:

$$\begin{cases} \begin{pmatrix} \dot{x}_1(t) \\ \dot{x}_2(t) \end{pmatrix} = \begin{pmatrix} 0 & 1 \\ -\frac{1}{c_1} & -\frac{c_0}{c_1} \end{pmatrix} \begin{pmatrix} x_1(t) \\ x_2(t) \end{pmatrix} + \begin{pmatrix} 0 \\ 1 \end{pmatrix} u(t) \\ y = (10) \begin{pmatrix} x_1(t) \\ x_2(t) \end{pmatrix} \end{cases} \tag{19}$$

i.e.:

$$\begin{cases} \dot{X} = AX + BU \\ Y = CX \end{cases}; A = \begin{pmatrix} 0 & 1 \\ -\frac{K'}{RJ} & -\frac{k^2}{RJ} \end{pmatrix}; B = \begin{pmatrix} 0 \\ 1 \end{pmatrix}; C = (1\ 0) \qquad (20)$$

Given:

$$a_0 = -\frac{K'}{RJ}; a_1 = -\frac{k^2}{RJ}$$

Figure 10 shows the state representation of our system:

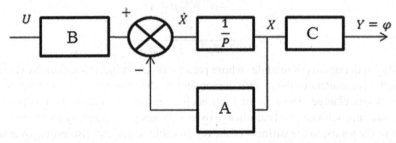

Fig. 10. Representation of the state of the system from its transfer function in LF, considering the angle φ as output from the system.

7 System Control

The sliding mode control (SMC) is a discontinuous and non-linear control technique, it belongs to the family of variable structure controls. SMCs are known for their robustness in the face of disturbances, modelling errors and parametric uncertainties.

The sliding surface is a function which represents the variation over time of the states of the system. The cancellation of the latter corresponds to the cancellation of the magnitude of state considered and the state of stability of the system.

The sliding surface denoted S is given in the following relation:

$$S = \dot{X} + \tau X \qquad (20)$$

When the sliding surface S cancels this ensures that the state variable tends towards 0 in a finite time, therefore the stability of the system is guaranteed as long as $S = 0$.

By setting $X = e$, with e: error of the system it is therefore possible to ensure the convergence of the error towards 0, consequently the system will respond in finite time and with an error tending towards 0 to a bounded input. For this reason, it is appropriate to choose $e = X$.

7.1 Stability in the Sense of Lyapunov

Let be the Lyapunov function V(S), in order to ensure the asymptotic stability of the solution of the equation $S(x) = 0$, it is necessary and sufficient that:

$$V(S) > 0; V(0) = 0; \dot{V}(S) < 0; \dot{V}(0) = 0 \qquad (21)$$

If the Lyapunov function satisfies the conditions cited, then the solutions of the equation $S(x) = 0$ is asymptotically stable.

By putting

$$S = Ge, G = (\gamma + 1), avec\ \gamma > 0 \tag{22}$$

Where e is the error

$$if\ S = 0;\ then\ e = 0$$

The Eq. (22) ensures the convergence of the system error towards a zero value guaranteeing the stability as well as the precision of the latter.

Let Lyapunov's function:

$$V(S) = \frac{S^2}{2} \tag{23}$$

$$\dot{V}(S) = S\dot{S} \tag{24}$$

Let's put:

$$\dot{V}(S) = -S^2 \tag{25}$$

From previous equations we get:

$$-S^2 = \dot{S}S \rightarrow S(\dot{S} + S) = 0 \tag{26}$$

From other part

$$S = G.e = (\gamma\ 1).(X_d - X),\ ou\ X = \begin{pmatrix} x_1 \\ x_2 \end{pmatrix} \tag{27}$$

$$\dot{S} = G(\dot{X}_d - \dot{X}) \tag{28}$$

From Eq. (26)

$$G(\dot{X}_d - \dot{X}) = -S \tag{29}$$

Hence

$$GX_d - GAX - GBu_c = -S$$

$$u_c = (S - GAX + GAX_d)(GB)^{-1} \tag{30}$$

$V(S)$, $\dot{V}(S)$ both satisfy Lyapunov's stability criteria, by applying the command u_c to our system, we will obtain that the latter is maintained on the hyperplane $S = 0$, canceling the error and ensuring in fact stability is the convergence of the system.

7.2 Control Law

u_c, is the command to be applied to the system in order to ensure that the latter is in sliding mode where S = 0, thus ensuring the cancellation of the system error in a finite time (stability and precision).

As shown in (16), $x_1(t)$ physically represents the output of the system (the angle φ), $x_2(t)$ represents the angular speed of the system φ', constant as stipulated in the specifications, $x_2(t)$ is therefore the angular acceleration of the system is worth 0. We will then have:

$$X_d = \begin{pmatrix} \varphi_d \\ \dot{\varphi} \end{pmatrix}; \dot{X}_d = \begin{pmatrix} \dot{\varphi} \\ 0 \end{pmatrix} = \dot{X} = \dot{\varphi} \tag{31}$$

The calculation of the u_c, command requires the evaluation of S, which is carried out from the relation in (27). From (27) and from (31) we simplify (30), in fact:

$$S = (\gamma\ 1)\begin{pmatrix} \varphi_d - \varphi \\ 0 \end{pmatrix} = \gamma(\varphi_d - \varphi)$$

By replacing in (30)

$$u_c = [\gamma w_{mot} - \varphi a_0 - \dot{\varphi}(a_1 + \gamma) + \gamma(\varphi_d - \varphi)]$$

$$u_c = [\dot{\varphi}a_1 - \varphi(a_0 + \gamma) + \gamma\varphi_d)] \tag{32}$$

It is important to remember that the system works as follows:

While the EMG interface provides an input, the setpoint generator increments φ_d by 4.5° (one step), the system must therefore cause φ to reach φ_d the Fig. 11 below shows the system control diagram.

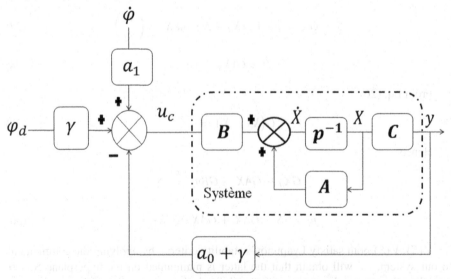

Fig. 11. System control diagram, the SMC controller generates the u_c command necessary to maintain the system in sliding mode from the setpoint φ_d the output φ, parameters a_0, a_1, and the speed $\dot{\varphi} = w_{mot}$ of the number γ.

The controller by sliding mode ensures the stability of the system considered, by choosing a sliding mode (a hyperplane) considering the system error e, the controller also ensures that e converges to a zero value. The SMC overcomes certain constraints, particularly those related to the variation over time of the parameters of the function modelling the system, modelling uncertainties as well as non-linearity.

8 Conclusion

The system presented is a system which can be divided into 2 main parts, the first concerns the determination of the user's intention via the EMG interface, as well as the consequent stimulation of the interactions of the mechatronic structure with its environment. The second part concerns the implementation of the user's intentions through the animation of the mechatronic system (prosthesis), during this the system must reach a position setpoint determined in the upstream part and this by ensuring the convergence of the system error towards a zero value in a finite time.

The control of the system consists in controlling the angle of flexion/extension (φ) of each finger of the prosthesis (independent) via the control of the angle of rotation (θ) delivered by the actuator, knowing the relation $\varphi = f(\theta)$. The block diagrams and the transfer functions illustrate the system and its operation, the angle of rotation of the motor is measured by an angular position sensor materialized by a rotary potentiometer, operated in a conditioning circuit so that the angle of rotation corresponds to a precise tension. The calculation of transfer functions can be subject to modelling uncertainties, as well as to parametric variations, in fact as explained above, certain parameters of the system can evolve or deteriorate over time, such as the value of resistances, the parameters of the engine, the friction of the finger joints, influencing the relation $\varphi = f(\theta)$ in an unpredictable way. For this, our choice fell on a control law which is robust to the constraints mentioned above.

In order to meet the constraints mentioned above, it is necessary to use a control architecture with a variable structure, namely a control law which is not sensitive to variations and to the non-linearity of the model. Several approaches can be envisaged in this context, nevertheless, our approach exploits the SMC, because this approach is relatively simple to implement and it brings satisfactory results in terms of stability and robustness of the system, the SMC was implemented in our approach so as to also ensure the accuracy of the system.

The main drawback when implementing control by sliding mode is what is called chattering, chattering is a vibrational phenomenon due to the switching of the u_c command according to the sign of the S function. indeed, in order to maintain the system in sliding mode (S = 0) it is necessary that the command compensates S in order to reduce its value to 0, if $S = K_S$ then u_c must make S vary from $-K_S$ in the case where S > 0 and of $+K_S$ in the contrary case, this phenomenon this manifest when the response time of the controller is greater than the response time of the controlled system, in fact, if the command u_c is not dosed correctly by the controller, S may exceed or not reach the hyperplane given the response time of the controller, the system output may reach relatively high values before the controller reacts, this is all the more true if the magnitude of a disturbance we are large where the significant modelling uncertainty.

The command proposed for our system takes into account (as evolving parameters) only the system setpoint as well as its output, relation (32) shows that the u_c command is generated as soon as the setpoint is present and the system responds ($y \neq 0$), there is therefore no delay generated in the response of the controller, thus avoiding the occurrence of chattering at significant amplitude, whatever the amplitude of the disturbances and the uncertainties on the model.

The correction solution provided is a good compromise between the simplicity of implementation and the robustness of the system, indeed, the corrector is simple to implement while guaranteeing the stability and the precision of the system.

References

1. Zhang, T., Ge, S.S., Hang, C.C.: Adaptive neural network control for strict-feedback nonlinear systems using backstepping design. Automatica **36**(12), 1835–1846 (2000)
2. Patre, P.M., Mackunis, W., Kaiser, K., et al.: Asymptotic tracking for uncertain dynamic systems via a multilayer neural network feedforward and RISE feedback control structure. IEEE Trans. Autom. Control **53**(9), 2180–2185 (2008)
3. Liu, Y.-J., Zeng, Q., Tong, S., et al.: Adaptive neural network control for active suspension systems with time-varying vertical displacement and speed constraints. IEEE Trans. Ind. Electron. **66**(12), 9458–9466 (2019)
4. Na, J., Wang, S., Liu, Y.-J., et al.: Finite-time convergence adaptive neural network control for nonlinear servo systems. IEEE Trans. Cybern. **50**(6), 2568–2579 (2019)
5. Shi, X., Cheng, Y., Yin, C., et al.: Design of adaptive backstepping dynamic surface control method with RBF neural network for uncertain nonlinear system. Neurocomputing **330**, 490–503 (2019)
6. Luan, F., Na, J., Huang, Y., et al.: Adaptive neural network control for robotic manipulators with guaranteed finite-time convergence. Neurocomputing **337**, 153–164 (2019)
7. Jia, C., Li, X., Wang, K., et al.: Adaptive control of nonlinear system using online error minimum neural networks. ISA Trans. **65**, 125–132 (2016)
8. Hayakawa, T., Haddad, W.M., Hovakimyan, N.: Neural network adaptive control for nonlinear uncertain dynamical systems with asymptotic stability guarantees. In: Proceedings of the 2005, American Control Conference, 2005, pp. 1301–1306. IEEE (2005)
9. Nguyen, A.-T., Taniguchi, T., Eciolaza, L., et al.: Fuzzy control systems: past, present and future. IEEE Comput. Intell. Mag. **14**(1), 56–68 (2019)
10. Zhang, Z., Liang, H., Wu, C., et al.: Adaptive event-triggered output feedback fuzzy control for nonlinear networked systems with packet dropouts and actuator failure. IEEE Trans. Fuzzy Syst. **27**(9), 1793–1806 (2019)
11. Qiu, J., Sun, K., Wang, T., et al.: Observer-based fuzzy adaptive event-triggered control for pure-feedback nonlinear systems with prescribed performance. IEEE Trans. Fuzzy Syst. **27**(11), 2152–2162 (2019)
12. Škrjanc, I., Iglesias, J.A., Sanchis, A., et al.: Evolving fuzzy and neuro-fuzzy approaches in clustering, regression, identification, and classification: a survey. Inf. Sci. **490**, 344–368 (2019)
13. Zahedi, F., Zahedi, Z.: A review of neuro-fuzzy systems based on intelligent control. arXiv preprint arXiv:1805.03138 (2018)
14. Khosravi, A., Koury, R.N.N., Machado, L., et al.: Prediction of wind speed and wind direction using artificial neural network, support vector regression and adaptive neuro-fuzzy inference system. Sustain. Energy Technol. Assess. **25**, 146–160 (2018)

15. Kamil, A., Rustamov, S., Clement, M., Mustafayev, E.: Adaptive neuro-fuzzy inference system for classification of texts. In: Zadeh, L.A., Yager, R.R., Shahbazova, S.N., Reformat, M.Z., Kreinovich, V. (eds.) Recent Developments and the New Direction in Soft-Computing Foundations and Applications. SFSC, vol. 361, pp. 63–70. Springer, Cham (2018). https://doi.org/10.1007/978-3-319-75408-6_6
16. Shihabudheen, K.V., Pillai, G.N.: Recent advances in neuro-fuzzy system: a survey. Knowl. Based Syst. 152, 136–162 (2018)
17. Li, H., Shi, P., Yao, D., et al.: Observer-based adaptive sliding mode control for nonlinear Markovian jump systems. Automatica 64, 133–142 (2016)
18. Plestan, F., Shtessel, Y., Bregeault, V., et al.: New methodologies for adaptive sliding mode control. Int. J. Control 83(9), 1907–1919 (2010)
19. Ferrara, A., Incremona, G.P.: Design of an integral suboptimal second-order sliding mode controller for the robust motion control of robot manipulators. IEEE Trans. Control Syst. Technol. 23(6), 2316–2325 (2015)
20. Huber, O., Acary, V., Brogliato, B.: Lyapunov stability and performance analysis of the implicit discrete sliding mode control. IEEE Trans. Autom. Control 61(10), 3016–3030 (2015)
21. Huber, O., Brogliato, B., Acary, V., et al.: Experimental results on implicit and explicit time-discretization of equivalent-control-based sliding-mode control (2016)
22. Slotine, J.-J.E., Li, W., et al.: Applied Nonlinear Control. Prentice Hall, Englewood Cliffs (1991)
23. Utkin, V., Guldner, J., Shi, J.: Sliding Mode Control in Electro-Mechanical Systems. CRC Press, Boca Raton (2009)
24. Boiko, I., Fridman, L.: Analysis of chattering in continuous sliding-mode controllers. IEEE Trans. Autom. Control 50(9), 1442–1446 (2005)
25. Boiko, I., Fridman, L., Pisano, A., et al.: Performance analysis of second-order sliding-mode control systems with fast actuators. IEEE Trans. Autom. Control 52(6), 1053–1059 (2007)
26. Choi, S.-B., Park, D.-W., Jayasuriya, S.: A time-varying sliding surface for fast and robust tracking control of second-order uncertain systems. Automatica 30(5), 899–904 (1994)
27. Levant, A.: Sliding order and sliding accuracy in sliding mode control. Int. J. Control 58(6), 1247–1263 (1993)
28. Bartolini, G., Ferrara, A., Usai, E., et al.: On multi-input chattering-free second-order sliding mode control. IEEE Trans. Autom. Control 45(9), 1711–1717 (2000)
29. Laghrouche, S., Plestan, F., Glumineau, A.: Higher order sliding mode control based on integral sliding mode. Automatica 43(3), 531–537 (2007)
30. Plestan, F., Glumineau, A., Laghrouche, S.: A new algorithm for high-order sliding mode control. Int. J. Robust Nonlinear Control: IFAC-Affiliated J. 18(4–5), 441–453 (2008)
31. Benchabane, S.I., Saadia, N., Ramdane-Cherif, A.: Novel algorithm for conventional myocontrol of upper limbs prosthetics. Biomed. Signal Process. Control 57, 101791 (2020)

To Beacon or Not?: Speed Based Probabilistic Adaptive Beaconing Approach for Vehicular Ad-Hoc Networks

Sarishma[1] ⓘ, Ravi Tomar[2](✉) ⓘ, Sandeep Kumar[3], and Mukesh Kumar Awasthi[4] ⓘ

[1] Graphic Era Deemed to be University, Dehradun, India
[2] School of Computer Science, University of Petroleum and Energy Studies, Dehradun, India
[3] IIMT College of Engineering, Greater Noida, India
[4] Department of Mathematics, School of Physical and Decision Sciences, BBAU, Lucknow, India

Abstract. Emergence of Wireless Sensor Networks provided the ability to connect, collect and disseminate information across various sensor nodes. Deploying this concept in the transportation domain evolved into the concept of Vehicular Ad-hoc Sensor Networks (VASNETs) or Vehicular Ad-hoc Networks (VANETs). VANETs turned out to act as a boon to enhance the safety and non-safety aspects of the transportation domain, giving way to the future of Intelligent Transport Systems. To generate cooperative awareness in the network, VANETs use beacons, which are small packets of information transmitted as BSMs (Basic Safety Messages). Beaconing was developed in the initial phases of development of VANETs and mainly suffers a trade-off between channel congestion and the level of accuracy of exchanged information. In this work, an adaptive speed based beaconing approach is proposed, the approach uses probability as a means to answer two key questions. First is whether to beacon or not and second is at what rate beaconing should be done to reduce channel congestion and increase the accuracy of information. The results are compared with an adaptive density-based approach and with normal static beaconing cases. Performance evaluation on Veins framework demonstrates that it gives better results as compared to both the other approaches. Further, the results concerning generated BSMs, received BSMs and total packet loss are compared. The simulation is modeled to make it as realistic as possible by introducing a vast heterogeneous network with random vehicle mobility trips.

Keywords: Wireless Sensor Networks (WSN) · Vehicular Ad-hoc Sensor Networks (VASNETs) · Vehicular Ad-hoc Networks (VANETs) · Intelligent Transport Systems (ITS) · Vehicular Ad-hoc Networks · Beacons · Adaptive beaconing · Basic safety messages · Veins

1 Introduction

Advancement in the field of Information and Communication Technology in the past couple of decades has tremendously increased. The incorporation of these technologies

© ICST Institute for Computer Sciences, Social Informatics and Telecommunications Engineering 2021
Published by Springer Nature Switzerland AG 2021. All Rights Reserved
S. Paiva et al. (Eds.): SmartCity360° 2020, LNICST 372, pp. 156–170, 2021.
https://doi.org/10.1007/978-3-030-76063-2_12

in the domain of transportation has opened a whole new arena of beneficial applications, ranging from safety to non-safety ones [1, 2]. VANETs are rapidly emerging with the constant effort being put by researchers leading to its enormous growth in the past decade itself. The advancement in VANETs is paving the way for the future of Intelligent Transport Systems [3].

Most of the vehicles come equipped with numerous technical modules out of which wireless communication system or module is of tremendous help in Vehicular ad-hoc networks. VANETs make use of this module to exchange information which is later on used in various ways to enhance user safety, user experience and lead to optimized utilization of resources.

VANETs are primarily composed of three major components which are Road Side Unit, On Board Unit and Application Unit [4]. Road Side Unit is a fixed device alongside roads, primarily used for infrastructure to vehicle communication. It is capable of providing strong compute services and communication services to the vehicles which are in range. On-Board Unit is a WAVE device mounted on the vehicle which provides resources for use via Resource Command Processor and communicates with the RSUs. Application Unit is a device used for running applications by using information provided by the OBU. It can be fixed or a mobile device such as Personal Digital Assistants.

The center of VANET based applications lies in maintaining updated information about the network in which any vehicle is present. This up to date information leads to the emergence of cooperative awareness in the network. Based on this cooperative awareness, realistic decisions can be made in real-time by the vehicles itself or by the users. VANETs make use of beacons to achieve cooperative awareness. Beacons are small packets of information which contain data such as the location of any vehicle, its ID, its moving direction and speed of motion [5]. The process of transmission and exchange of beacons in the network is termed as beaconing [6, 7].

Safety related messages in VANETs belong to either of the two categories: periodic messages or non-periodic messages [8]. Periodic messages are also known as heart beat messages or beacons which are responsible for maintaining updated information in the network. Non periodic messages comprise of information which need immediate attention or the one which is requested by user such as emergency information or audio/video requests by user.

There are two key aspects to spread information in the VANETs. One is beaconing and the other is information dissemination [9]. Beaconing is responsible for constructing the underlying knowledge base using which important information can be disseminated in a timely and efficient manner.

Wireless Access for Vehicular Environment or WAVE is a protocol stack used to provide wireless communication capability to VANETs. Its extension came out in the form IEEE 802.11p, which is a communication standard for VANETs [10]. Under IEEE 802.11p, beaconing is achieved by sending periodic BSMs or Basic Safety Messages on the CCH (control channel) which has a bandwidth of 10 MHz [11]. Beaconing has been mostly done by flooding the beacons in the network. Whenever a vehicle joins or leaves or moves across the network, it will constantly transmit the beacons generated by it. However, it does not turn out to be efficient in certain cases. When the vehicular density is high, the channel becomes congested by the constant traffic generated due to beacons. This also leads to wastage of channel bandwidth as the mostly the same information is going around in the network and somehow obstructs the path to more important information [12].

In the last decade, researchers have come up with the concept of adaptive beaconing, which has the potential to reduce unnecessary channel congestion in the network. The two types of adaptive approaches have come in the light as a result. First one is beacon generation rate adaptation where the rate of generation of beacons is adapted based on some custom defined parameters [13–17]. The other one is beacon transmission power adaptation where the transmission power of beacons is adjusted which materializes in the form of distance up to which the beacon will travel [18–20]. This work focus on the first approach, based on it the adaptive beaconing approach is proposed.

When vehicles move in the real world environment, the resulting network can be dense, relatively constant or sparse in terms of the number of vehicles on the road segment. A solution for beaconing is needed which can suit itself to all these three cases. Hence, an adaptive beaconing approach is proposed in this work, the proposed approach is based on the speed of vehicles in the network. The probability is calculated from the various parameters and it decides the frequency or transmission rate of the beacons in the network.

The work proposes two adaptive beaconing approaches, first is based on the density of one-hop neighbors of any vehicle at any instant, and the second is based upon both, the speed as well as the density around a vehicle. Both the proposed approaches are compared among them and with the static beaconing, which is configured to the frequency of 10ms. Further, it was observed that incorporating multiple parameters into the decision of beacon rate control yields more beneficial results as compared to using just one of the parameters or not at all.

The rest of the paper is organized as Sect. 2 highlights some of the key works done in this area of adaptive beaconing. Section 3 highlights the proposed work focusing on the algorithm, which contains a rule-based system for beaconing within it. Section 4 sheds light on the combination of simulators and why they have been chosen. Section 5 showcases the obtained results of the proposed approach based on three key parameters. Section 6 discusses the results and lastly, we conclude the work leaving the open future work.

2 Literature Review

This section is focused upon discussion of the works already been done in the domain of adaptive beaconing in VANETs:

A mobility prediction based adaptive beacon rate control (MPBR) is proposed in [21] where beacon rate is adjusted as per the predicted positions of the vehicles, rather than following the periodic beaconing scheme. As the location prediction may suffer from errors from time to time, they propose a threshold value crossing which beacon broadcasting will be initiated. The approach also classifies the traffic status on the road into categories, which makes it easier to determine the threshold value. However, when to comes to sparse network conditions, the approach does not work effectively resulting in a loss of coverage and a failure to disseminate data effectively.

ENeP-AB or Estimation of Neighbors Position privacy scheme with an Adaptive Beaconing approach proposes a modification in the pseudonym based on density and the predicted positions of the vehicles at any given point of time [22]. This scheme is extended to propose a protocol called E-ABRP standing for Adaptive Beaconing Rate Protocols, which aims at improving the quality of service while maintaining a steady beacon rate. This approach makes a modification by using the density as a parameter for beacon rate adjustment thereby covering the requirements of a sparse as well as a dense network. The algorithm proposed relies on spatial linking of vehicles and does not focus on the temporal aspect which might lead to congestion, thereby undermining the Quality of Service in the network.

A large solution space for adaptive beaconing is explored in [23, 24], where the focus is on several alternatives to determine the beacon rate. The work have proposed a situation based adaptive beaconing scheme where beacon rate can depend on either the vehicles own parameters or be altered by macroscopic or maybe microscopic elements of the network.

Beacon inter-reception time Ensured Adaptive Transmission is proposed in [18] for vehicle to vehicle safety communication. It is a congestion control algorithm for reducing contention occurring due to the beaconing. It leads to a supervised regulation of beacon rate intervals, thereby making it adaptive yet designed in a way to avoid channel congestion specifically. Extending this in [25], the usefulness of density as a parameter is judged by combining it with various other attributes. This leads to the conclusion that density based approaches give highly satisfactory results while calculating beacon rate control. The choice of parameters which must be ideal is not provided.

Use of ABC or Adaptive Beacon Control is proposed in [26], the authors used a new factor ρ called as danger coefficient with the help of which read end collisions are avoided in the VANETs. Leveraging this, the approach also propose a fully distributed beacon rate control scheme which uses a TDMA based MAC protocol to solve an NP-hard optimal problem by using a greedy heuristic algorithm. In [27], a collision based approach is provided to find the beacon rate but a collision in the network is needed for it to work. Both of the approaches fail to address the conditions where network is fast changing and collisions are not present. The calculated beacon rate has the potential to overuse the channel bandwidth, which will be counter effective during information dissemination.

Based on opportunistic routing and the nature of wireless channel used, authors in [28] have proposed a beacon rate adjusting scheme which focuses on estimated link-time between vehicles and the set of forwarding rules which will be active until some change in topology occurs.

Adaptive Beacon Rate Adjusting mechanism based on neural networks and back propagation is proposed in [8] where beacon rate adapts as per the QoS metric defined which includes delay and rate of packet loss. The proposed mechanism relies totally on the RSUs for the compute intensive work and assumes that vehicles are always connected to RSUs. It is unable to cope up with scenarios where connectivity is intermittent.

LIMERIC or Linear Message Rate Integrated Control algorithm is proposed in [29] where full precision controlled inputs are received from the wireless channel. These inputs lead to a deterministic value of beacon rate control and is aimed at avoiding the limit cycle which is inherent to binary control based approaches. The work establishes specific guidelines in order to implement their approach which makes its scope limited to practical applications.

3 Proposed Work

In this section, the proposed approach targeted towards optimizing the beaconing in vehicular ad-hoc networks is discussed in detail. This work proposes two approaches for adaptive beaconing, first is based on the density of one-hop neighbors, and the other incorporates speed of the vehicles. The validity of the proposed approach is established by comparing the two approaches with a static beaconing case and among each other. The following sub section discuss both the approach in details.

– Static beaconing:

In this approach, a fixed beacon rate value is taken. BSMs will be transmitted every x seconds by all the vehicles participating in the network. The static beacon frequency is selected from the following set containing 5 different values $\{0.1, 0.5, 1, 1.5, 2\}$ seconds.

– Adaptive beaconing with one-hop neighbour density:

The adaptive beaconing approach based on the one-hop neighbour density calculates its number of neighbours at any given point of time t and depending upon that decides an appropriate value using the rule-based system provided below. The density around the source vehicle is calculated by taking into account the nodes which are present in the range of 300 m. For the initial 10 s, when the vehicle joins the network, a beacon rate of 10 ms is assumed. During this interval, the vehicle records the information so as to become well aware of the network. Then the information from packets is divided and filtered to obtain the number of nodes which lie within range of the vehicle. This number is denoted as D (the density around that vehicle). This way all the vehicles keep on calculating their one hop neighbors every second. The value of D is then used to decide whether the network is sparse, dense or normal, details of which are given in Table 1. The appropriate beacon rate for the network is selected via the rule based system. The pseudo code to determine the adaptive beacon rate is given below:

Algorithm 1: Pseudocode for adaptive beacon rate

```
1:    Start at t=0
2:    While (t<10)
3:          Beacon rate = 0.1
5:    Record information till t=10
6:    Segregate the information as {Node ID, distance,
      speed}
7.    At t>10, for every node
8:          Calculate D which is the number of one-hop
            neighbours in the vicinity of the vehicle
9:          If D is less than 5
10:             BeaconRate = 20ms
11:         If D is between 5 and 10
12:             BeaconRate = 80ms
13:         If D is greater than 10
14:             BeaconRate = 1.2sec
15:     Else
16:         Do not beacon again
      Continue at t = t+1
17:   Exit when vehicle moves out of the network
18:   End
```

Table 1. Classes for the rule-based system (density)

Class	Density (D)	Beacon rate	Network type
I	D < 5	20 ms	Sparse network
II	5 < D < 10	80 ms	Normal network
III	D > 10	1.2 s	Dense network

This approach is implemented in the Veins framework, as discussed in the next section. Number of nodes participating are {800, 1100, 1400, 1800}. Going beyond this number was not possible as the computations grew much heavier due to an increased exchange of packets.

– Probability-based adaptive beaconing with speed and neighbor density:

The proposed adaptive beaconing approach is based on the speed and one hop neighbor density of the vehicles present in the network. When the speed of the source vehicle and the neighboring vehicles is high, then the network is assumed to be sparse or less dense. When the speed of the source vehicles and the neighboring vehicles is less, then we assume that the network is dense, thereby leading to an overall reduced speed in the network.

Two key parameters come into play, one is the density of vehicles in the network on a given road segment, and the other is the average speed of vehicles in that segment. Both of these parameters are considered to get a better adaptive beaconing rate. Based on the average speed of the vehicles and their neighbors within less than 300-m distance, the probability is calculated. Based on this probability, the decision needs to be made on whether beaconing is required or not and if it is required what should be the frequency for this.

When a vehicle receives a beacon, it records, in particular, the node ID, location and speed of the vehicle. The beacons are cumulatively stored in a table until the first 10 s of the introduction of the vehicle into the network. This time is needed to collect data based on which beacon rate will be adjusted. In these initial 10 s, the beaconing frequency is set to 0.1 s. After 10 s, the vehicle is ready to set and adapt its beacon rate as per the proposed approach. The vehicle calculates the number of one hop neighbors i.e. D. The speed of these vehicles within a range of 300 m is calculated and its average sum is taken as α. Using α, the β value is calculated by dividing it with the maximum speed attainable and by the vehicles in the network. The work fixes the max speed of the vehicle to 40 in the simulation environment. This assures that the value of β turns out to be less than 1, further the β is used to find out the Adaptive Beaconing Probability or ABP by subtracting it from 1. ABP is used as a catalyst to make the beacon rate more adaptive. This value when added to a pre-defined set of beacon rates gives a more adaptive and better result as it changes with respect to the change in the environment of the vehicle.

β cannot approach the value of 1 as it is practically impossible. All the vehicles cannot drive at their maximum speed in the network. Therefore, the value of 0.1 is selected as threshold, this value signifies that the vehicle speed in the network is high. On the other hand, value of ABP greater than 0.6 signifies that the network has becomes dense, and hence the increase the beacon interval is done. Similarly, as this value approaches 0.9, it signifies that the vehicle is about to come to a halt thereby inducing a stagnant state. And hence the values are chosen after much thought and trial demonstrations within the simulation. The values are chosen based on which were best suited. Based on the trial and run the resulting classification of the network is provided in the Table 2, that describe the selection criteria of the beacon rate.

The working of the proposed approach is explained in the form of pseudo code as:

Algorithm 2: Pseudocode for proposed approach

```
1:      Start at t=0
2:      While (t<10)
3:          Beacon rate = 0.1
5:      Record information till t=10
6:      Segregate the information as {Node
        ID, distance, speed}
7.      At t>10, for every node
8:          Discard Node ID with dis-
            tance>300m
9:          Calculate D= nodes < 300 m
            distance from the source node
```

$$\alpha = \frac{\sum_0^D speedVID}{D}$$

$$\beta = \frac{\alpha}{40}$$

```
12:         Close
13:     ABP = [1-β]
14:     If (ABP  is between 0.1 and 0.3)
15:         BeaconRate = 0.5+ABP
16:     ElseIf (ABP  is between 0.31 and
        0.59)
17:         BeaconRate = 1+ABP
18:     ElseIf (ABP  is between 0.6 and
        0.89)
19:         BeaconRate = 1.3+ABP
20:     ElseIf (ABP  <= 0.9)
21:         BeaconRate = 2+ABP
22:     Else
23:         Do not beacon again
24:     Continue at every t=t+1
25:     Exit when vehicle moves out of the
        network
26:     End
```

Table 2. Classes for a rule-based system

Class	Probability (ABP)	Beacon rate	Network type
I	0.1–0.3	0.5 + ABP	Sparse network
II	0.31–0.59	1 + ABP	Normal network
III	0.6–0.89	1.3 + ABP	Dense network
IV	>0.9	2 + ABP	Stagnant state

The realistic scenario from VEINS [30] framework has been taken for simulation in SUMO [31, 32] and VEINS. The numbers of vehicles were taken to be {800, 1100, 1400, 1800}. Having a large number of nodes in the network ensures the heterogeneity across the network and makes it more realistic where one vehicle can meet any particular vehicle multiple times in the same simulation. The following table shows some of the simulation parameters used for the testing (Table 3).

The following image shows the running simulation on the veins framework, where nodes are transmitting messages. These nodes are moving randomly in the network, entering from one end and leaving from another. The random mobility model is generated through the SUMO [31] (Fig. 1).

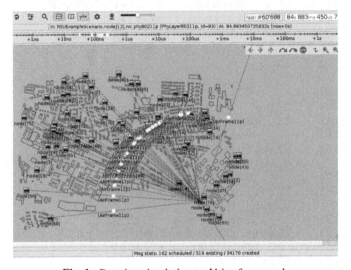

Fig. 1. Running simulation on Veins framework

Table 3. Simulation parameters

Parameter	Value
Playgroundsizex	3500 m
Playgroundsizey	3500 m
Playgroundsizez	50 m
Scalar-recording	True
Vector-recording	True
Sim-time-limit	1800
Accel	{2.6, 3.2, 4.1}
Decel	{3.7, 4.5, 5.7}
Mingap	2.5
Maxspeed	40
Random trips	trips.trips.xml

4 Implementation

This section describes the selected tools for the proposed work, as evaluating any of the proposed work in vehicular ad-hoc networking is a big challenge on its own. Real-world experimentation is extremely difficult to achieve because it requires rigorous labor and enormous hardware. The evaluation and implementation of any VANETs based approach requires majorly three tools the simulator, the mobility model and the framework. The network simulators allow us to test run the work in multiple scenarios like using random maps or custom generated maps, modifying the routes, beacon structure, applying a different set of algorithms for routing and so much more. To test the validity of the work, a combination of simulators and mobility model is used. The network simulator is OMNet++ [33, 34] is used and the proposed adaptive beaconing approach is deployed on the application layer of the IEEE 802.11p communication standard. The framework used on the simulator is VEINS[30].

The second tool is the mobility manager SUMO or Simulation for Urban Mobility [31, 35, 36] is an open-source, portable, microscopic road traffic mobility generator which is used mostly along with a network simulator. Its role is to populate the network with vehicles as entities whose properties and behavior can be custom-defined. The map, routes, type of vehicles, routes taken, intersection etc. all can be customized according to user demands, and it also works on real traffic data thereby making it more realistic in testing scenarios. The version which is used on top of the network simulator OMNet++ is SUMO 0.30.0 which is compatible with both the network simulator and VANET framework.

The final tool used is the framework for VANETs [37], the VANETs comprise of different property as compared to other network technologies. The network based customization can be done through the combination of the OMNet++ and SUMO. To incorporate specific VANET based environment, the VEINS framework [30] is selected, which already contains most of the common property required for a successful VANET such as a module specifically for the IEEE 802.11p standard. The proposed work utilizes the underlying VEINS framework to implement the customized beaconing and adaptive mode in the application layer.

5 Results

The proposed work is implemented in the Veins framework setup on top of OMNet++ 5.4.1 and SUMO 0.30.0. The number of generated BSMs, received BSMs and total packet loss are recorded in the scalar and vector files. The output files are further converted to csv files only containing the filtered data to be used for evaluation. Veins provide the ability to generate and segregate data allowing the creation of different graphs and other visualizing images, which can make analysis far better. The generated BSMs and received BSMs from the scalar application file are taken for each scenario. For calculating the total packet loss, the data from the vector file is taken. Total lost packets encompass of two types of packets, i.e. RxTx lost packets, and SNIR lost packets.

Figure 2 shows the number of generated packets vs number of nodes among different approaches. This parameter is crucial from the network load perspective. Higher the number of packet generated will result in the higher network load.

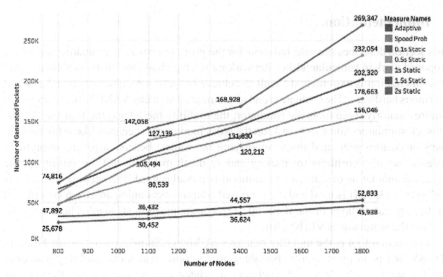

Fig. 2. Generated BSMs

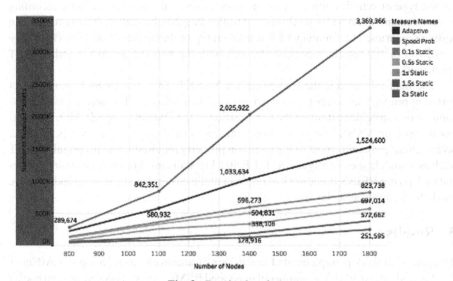

Fig. 3. Received packets

Similarly, in Fig. 3 the number of cumulative messages received on each nodes vs the number of vehicles is plotted. It is clear from the graph that the speed probabilistic is receiving higher messages as compared to all other nodes.

Figure 4 shows the lost packet on individual nodes vs the number of nodes, the lost packet is the parameter that is crucial in terms of the real-time application of VANETs. Higher the lost packet higher the chances of unreliable VANETs.

This can be observed from the graphs that the proposed approach works very optimally in all three aspects of the message generation, reception and loss.

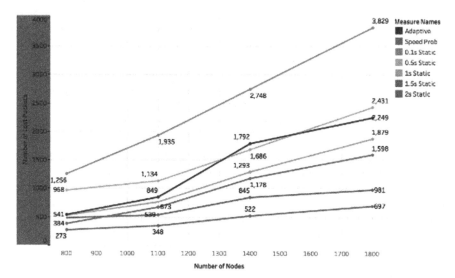

Fig. 4. Lost packets

6 Discussion

The number of generated BSMs is most significant in the case of static beaconing, where the beacon rate is 10ms and maximum is 2 s. This leads to constant generation and transmission of beacons by the vehicles in static beaconing cases. The result is channel congestion, bandwidth wastage and maybe refusal of transmission of critical information since the network is too crowded already. In the case of adaptive beaconing, however, the generated BSMs are comparatively lesser and fall within the range of 0.5 s to 1 s, which clearly demonstrates that adaptive beaconing is better than the static one in case of the number of generated BSMs. And, finally the speed based probabilistic approach where beacon rate is decided by considering the speed of the vehicles moving within the network. The number of generated BSMs is even lesser than adaptive beaconing, which means that the channel utilization has been optimized and there is less congestion in the network. Also, beacons are transmitted by the vehicles as determined by the procedure where the beacon rate is adapted concerning network state. This demonstrates that better coverage of the network is achieved. The decision to beacon or not also plays a major role in deciding whether to beacon recurrently or not, thereby leading to an optimized number of generated BSMs.

In case of several received BSMs, the static beaconing results show a lesser number of received beacons which mean there was unnecessary transmission by one end where no one was able to receive the messages at the other end. In case of adaptive beaconing based on mere density, the number of received BSMs is higher in comparison to all the static beaconing cases which yet again shows that adaptive beaconing is a better approach than the static one and has a better reach in practicality. Lastly, the adaptive approach based on speed and density has done well then both the adaptive and static beaconing. The number of received beacons gain momentum as the number of nodes increases in the network clearly representing that the performance is improving as the network becomes more complex and realistic.

Lastly, in terms of the number of packets lost, it can be observed that the packet loss is highest in the cases of static beaconing where beacon interval is less than 1 s. The corresponding number of generated BSMs is also high in static beaconing, and the number of received BSMs is less. Both of these factors reason out well with the highest number of packet loss in static beaconing. However, in the case of adaptive beaconing in both the scenarios, the number of lost packets is less due to the ability to adapt concerning changing environmental conditions in the network.

From the given graphs and charts, it can be observed that the adaptive beaconing approach outperforms static beaconing approach and also the one based solely on density. The speed-based probabilistic approach takes into account the density as well, though in a different manner, but the overall results have come out to be really promising.

7 Conclusion

Beaconing in Vehicular ad-hoc networks is used to generate cooperativeness in the network, which primarily helps in information dissemination when needed. This work have proposed a speed and density-based adaptive beaconing approach, which can be used to reduce network congestion and increased utilization of resources. Veins framework is used to implement the proposed technique, and the results are compared with density-based adaptive beaconing and static beaconing as is practiced in many standard works undergoing in VANETs. The results demonstrate that the proposed adaptive beaconing approach performs well as compared to static beaconing as to density-based adaptive beaconing as well. In future, the work can be extended by incorporating other parameters into the adaptive beaconing approach to make it more wholesome and optimized concerning the consumption of resources. The adaptive technique can also employ machine learning model, this work is identified for extension of this work.

References

1. Singhal, A., Sarishma, Tomar, R.: Intelligent accident management system using IoT and cloud computing. In: Proceedings of 2016 2nd International Conference on Next Generation Computing Technology, NGCT 2016, pp. 89–92 (2017)
2. Chang, B.-J., Liang, Y.-H., Yang, H.-J.: Performance analysis with traffic accident for cooperative active safety driving in VANET/ITS. Wireless Pers. Commun. **74**, 731–755 (2013). https://doi.org/10.1007/s11277-013-1318-2

3. Barrachina, J., et al.: Journal of network and computer applications VEACON: a vehicular accident ontology designed to improve safety on the roads. J. Netw. Comput. Appl. **35**(6), 1891–1900 (2012)
4. Aadil, F., Rizwan, S., Akram, A.: Vehicular Ad Hoc Networks (VANETs), Past Present and Future : A survey, January 2013
5. Adeel, S., et al.: Adaptive beaconing approaches for vehicular ad hoc networks: a survey. IEEE Syst. J. **12**, 1263–1277 (2016)
6. Van Eenennaam, M., Wolterink, W.K., Karagiannis, G., Heijenk, G.: Exploring the Solution Space of Beaconing in VANETs, pp. 1–8
7. Ghafoor, K.Z., Lloret, J., Bakar, K.A., et al.: Beaconing approaches in vehicular ad hoc networks: a survey. Wireless Pers. Commun. **73**, 885–912 (2013). https://doi.org/10.1007/s11277-013-1222-9
8. Feng, Y., Du, Y., Ren, Z., Wang, Z., Liu, Y., Zhang, L.: Adaptive beacon rate adjusting mechanism for safety communication in cooperative IEEE 802.11 p-3g vehicle-infrastructure systems. In: 2010 16th Asia-Pacific Conference on Communications (APCC), pp. 441–446 (2010)
9. Panichpapiboon, S., Pattara-Atikom, W.: A review of information dissemination protocols for vehicular ad hoc networks. IEEE Commun. Surveys Tutor. **14**(3), 784–798 (2011)
10. Jiang, D., Delgrossi, L.: IEEE 802.11 p: towards an international standard for wireless access in vehicular environments. In: VTC Spring 2008-IEEE Vehicular Technology Conference, pp. 2036–2040 (2008)
11. Qian, J., Jing, T., Huo, Y., Li, H., Ma, L., Lu, Y.: An adaptive beaconing scheme based on traffic environment parameters prediction in VANETs. In: Yang, Qing, Yu, Wei, Challal, Yacine (eds.) WASA 2016. LNCS, vol. 9798, pp. 524–535. Springer, Cham (2016). https://doi.org/10.1007/978-3-319-42836-9_46
12. Thaina, C., Nakorn, K.N., Rojviboonchai, K.: A study of adaptive beacon transmission on Vehicular Ad-Hoc Networks. In: 2011 IEEE 13th International Conference on Communication Technology, pp. 597–602 (2011)
13. Djahel, S., Ghamri-Doudane, Y.: A robust congestion control scheme for fast and reliable dissemination of safety messages in VANETs. In: 2012 IEEE Wireless Communications and Networking Conference (WCNC), pp. 2264–2269 (2012)
14. Egea-Lopez, E., Pavon-Marino, P.: Distributed and fair beaconing rate adaptation for congestion control in vehicular networks. IEEE Trans. Mob. Comput. **15**(12), 3028–3041 (2016)
15. Zrar, K., Abu Bakar, K., van Eenennaam, M., Khokhar, R.H., Gonzalez, A.J.: A fuzzy logic approach to beaconing for vehicular ad hoc networks. Telecommun. Syst. **52**(1), 139–149 (2013)
16. Hassan, A., Ahmed, M.H., Rahman, M.A.: Adaptive beaconing system based on fuzzy logic approach for vehicular network. In: 2013 IEEE 24th Annual International Symposium on Personal, Indoor, and Mobile Radio Communications (PIMRC), pp. 2581–2585 (2013)
17. Sommer, C., Tonguz, O.K., Dressler, F., Systems, C.: Traffic Information Systems : Efficient Message Dissemination via Adaptive Beaconing
18. Kloiber, B., Härri, J., Strang, T.: Dice the TX power—Improving awareness quality in VANETs by random transmit power selection. In: 2012 IEEE vehicular networking conference (VNC), pp. 56–63 (2012)
19. Ben Mussa, S.A., Manaf, M., Ghafoor, K.Z.: Beaconing and transmission range adaptation approaches in vehicular ad hoc networks: trends & research challenges. In: 2014 International Conference on Computational Science and Technology (ICCST), pp. 1–6 (2014)
20. Torrent-Moreno, M., Mittag, J., Santi, P., Hartenstein, H.: Vehicle-to-vehicle communication: fair transmit power control for safety-critical information. IEEE Trans. Veh. Technol. **58**(7), 3684–3703 (2009)

21. Li, F., Huang, C.: A mobility prediction based beacon rate adaptation scheme in VANETs. In: 2018 IEEE Symposium and Computing Communication, pp. 671–677 (2018)
22. Zidani, F., Semchedine, F., Ayaida, M.: Estimation of neighbors position privacy scheme with an adaptive beaconing approach for location privacy in VANETs ☆. Comput. Electr. Eng. **71**(July), 359–371 (2018)
23. Schmidt, R.K., et al.: Exploration of adaptive beaconing for efficient intervehicle safety communication, pp. 14–19 (2010)
24. Barbieri, D., Thibault, I., Lister, D., Bazzi, A., Masini, B.M., Andrisano, O.: Adaptive beaconing for safety enhancement in vehicular networks. In: 2017 15th International Conference on ITS Telecommunications (ITST), pp. 1–6 (2017)
25. Haouari, N., Moussaoui, S., Senouci, S.: Application reliability analysis of density-aware congestion control in VANETs. In: 2018 IEEE International Conference on Communication, pp. 1–6 (2018)
26. Lyu, F., et al.: ABC: adaptive beacon control for rear-end collision avoidance in VANETs. In: 2018 15th Annual IEEE International Conference on Sensing, Communication Network, pp. 1–9 (2018)
27. Chaabouni, N., Hafid, A., Sahu, P.K.: A collision-based beacon rate adaptation scheme (CBA) for VANETs. In: 2013 IEEE International Conference on Advanced Networks and Telecommunications Systems (ANTS), pp. 1–6 (2013)
28. Lee, K.C., Gerla, M.: Opportunistic Vehicular Routing
29. Bansal, G., Kenney, J.B., Rohrs, C.E.: LIMERIC: a linear adaptive message rate algorithm for DSRC congestion control. IEEE Trans. Veh. Technol. **62**(9), 4182–4197 (2013)
30. Sommer, C., Eckhoff, D., Brummer, A., Buse, D., Hagenauer, F., Joerer, S., Segata, M.: Veins: the open source vehicular network simulation framework. In: Virdis, Antonio, Kirsche, Michael (eds.) Recent Advances in Network Simulation. EICC, pp. 215–252. Springer, Cham (2019). https://doi.org/10.1007/978-3-030-12842-5_6
31. Krajzewicz, D., Hertkorn, G., Rössel, C., Wagner, P.: SUMO (Simulation of Urban MObility)-an open-source traffic simulation. In: Proceedings of the 4th middle East Symposium on Simulation and Modelling (MESM 2002), pp. 183–187 (2002)
32. Kaisser, F., Gransart, C., Kassab, M., Berbineau, M.: A framework to simulate VANET scenarios with SUMO. In: Opnetwork (2011)
33. Varga, A., Hornig, R.: An overview of the OMNeT++ simulation environment. In: Proceedings of the 1st International Conference on Simulation Tools and Techniques for Communications, Networks and Systems & Workshops, p. 60 (2008)
34. Varga, A.: OMNeT++. In: Wehrle, K., Günes, M., Gross, J.: Modeling and Tools for Network Simulation, pp. 35–59. Springer, Cham (2010). https://doi.org/10.1007/978-3-642-12331-3_3
35. Krajzewicz, D., Rossel, C.: Simulation of Urban MObility (SUMO). German Aerospace Centre (2007)
36. Behrisch, M., Bieker, L., Erdmann, J., Krajzewicz, D.: SUMO–simulation of urban mobility: an overview. In: Proceedings of SIMUL 2011, The Third International Conference on Advances in System Simulation (2011)
37. Tomar, R., Sastry, H.G., Prateek, M.: A V2I based approach to multicast in vehicular networks. Malaysian J. Comput. Sci. 93–107 (2020). ISSN 0127-9084. https://ejournal.um.edu.my/index.php/MJCS/article/view/27337. Accessed 11 Dec 2020

Reduce 802.11 Connection Time Using Offloading and Merging of DHCP Layer to MAC Layer

Vishal Bhargava and Nallanthighal S. Raghava[✉]

Delhi Technological University, Delhi 110042, India

Abstract. With the growth of Wi-Fi by the time, performance and quality are facing quite a lot of challenges. Wi-Fi works on the principle of the IEEE 802.11 based carrier sense multiple access – collision avoidance (CSMA/CA) to transmit packets and distributed coordination function (DCF) protocol based on Inter-frame spacing used to make the gap between two frames. In this manner, an 802.11 device gets limited time in the environment to finish its activity, with a rapid increase in the number of devices in the 802.11 environments. The important operation is always a connection of Wi-Fi device with another device, another device can be an Access point or any other Wi-Fi device (ad-hoc or Wi-Fi direct mode). Several researchers work on why connection time is more important and what factors affect its most [1, 2]. In this paper, we describe a way to reduce connection time with the use of cross-layer approach via offloading DHCP work to the MAC layer.

Keywords: 802.11 connection · DHCP · Authentication · Association · Offloading · Cross-layer approach

1 Introduction

In recent years 802.11 throughput acquires tremendous growth from 802.11b/g to 802.11n to 802.11ac to 802.11ax. With the growth of the throughput, the number of Wi-Fi devices increases exponentially (Fig. 1).

More than 1 billion access points were sold last year, and the station connected to an access point can be numerous. Wi-Fi devices connection is a standard process [4] defined by the IEEE 802.11 specification. Any Wi-Fi station device which wants to connect with an access point first performs a scanning operation. Earlier devices have 2.4 GHz band support only, but now mostly devices come with 5 GHz band support also, so scanning work increases for them. To save time, devices performs an active scan in comparison of passive scan (performed for DFS channels).

Figure 2 shows the Wi-Fi connection in open security mode. In the case of security mode (WPA/WPA2), additional 4-way handshake comes after the association process. In the connection process after scan DHCP process takes maximum time [2]. Connection sub phases are scan, authentication/association and DHCP assignment.

© ICST Institute for Computer Sciences, Social Informatics and Telecommunications Engineering 2021
Published by Springer Nature Switzerland AG 2021. All Rights Reserved
S. Paiva et al. (Eds.): SmartCity360° 2020, LNICST 372, pp. 171–187, 2021.
https://doi.org/10.1007/978-3-030-76063-2_13

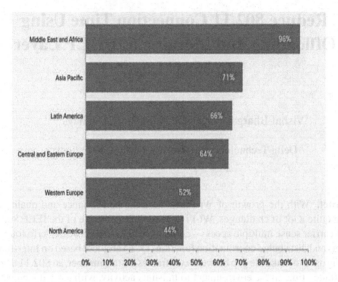

Fig. 1. Wi-Fi Data Traffic Growth in 2016 for different regions [3].

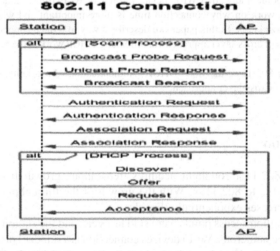

Fig. 2. Wi-Fi Connection between Station and Access Point.

1.1 Scan Phase

The scan is the process to find the desired Access point via station to which it wants to connect. There are mainly two types of scan: active scan and passive scan [4]. In active scan station device sends a frame which is called probe request frame to access point. Probe request can be unicast or broadcast. In response to the probe request, the Access point sends a probe response, which is used by a station to take connection related decision. In a passive scan, the station device wait for a special frame called beacon frame from the access point and connection decision taken according to that. A passive scan is a power saving technique but it is time-consuming in comparison to an active scan.

1.2 Authentication/Association Phase

After scan, now it is the turn of Wi-Fi station to show its capability to access point – whether it's a real authentic device to connect, and if yes, what it supports, what not, an access point takes the decision on the basis of these points, whether station can connect to access point or not. Four important frame exchange is done sequentially in this phase: authentication request, an authentication response, the association request an association response.

In the case of WPA/WPA2 security, additional 4-way handshake perform after the above four frame exchange.

1.3 DHCP Phase

Till now Wi-Fi device and Access point only interact with the perspective of the MAC layer. Now, it's application and IP layer's turn, a 1st station needs an IP address so the application can use it for communication with other devices.

After a successful association, the station device will interact with the DHCP server which can be inside of access point or can be a different entity. As an IP address is needed for communication, this phase is also considered in connection phase, actual real data transfer after this one.

Every network device has two types of addresses to communicate, so the wireless interface card also has two address. First one is the MAC address or physical address which is unique to device and second is a logical address also called IP address. IP address work on layer 3 (networking layer) so it can be considered as layer 3 address, while the MAC address is layer 2 address.

DHCP (Dynamic Host Configuration Protocol) is used to provide an IP address to a device. This IP address is provided by the remote server. DHCP works on a client-server model, where the device which needs IP address acts as a client and server assign an IP to the client.

DHCP mechanism is a combination of 4 processes (DORA). Stated below are the message exchanges between DHCP client and server.

- Discover
- Offer
- Request
- Acknowledgement

Below diagram shows the message exchange between the DHCP client and the Server (Fig. 3):

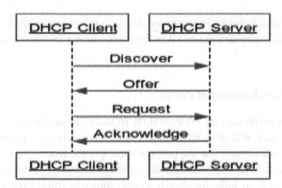

Fig. 3. DHCP Message Exchange between DHCP Client and DHCP Server.

Now let's go through every frame exchange between client & server with consideration of the OSI layer model, especially layer 2 i.e. data link layer and layer 3 i.e. networking layer.

Discover Frame or Message1

Device who is looking for an IP address sends a DHCP Discover message intended to search appropriate DHCP server. DHCP discover message is a layer 2 broadcast as well as layer 3 broadcast frame ((Figs. 4 and 5).

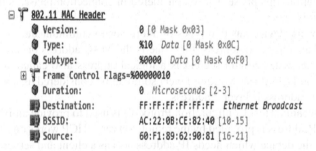

Fig. 4. Sniffer capture of DHCP Discover (MAC Layer Perspective).

```
⊟ IP Version 4 Header - Internet Protocol Datagram
    Version:              4 [32 Mask 0xF0]
    Header Length:        5  (20 bytes) [32 Mask 0x0F]
  ⊞ Diff. Services=0x10
    Total Length:         342 [34-35]
    Identifier:           0 [36-37]
  ⊞ Fragmentation Flags=%010
    Fragment Offset:      0  (0 bytes) [38-39 Mask 0x1FF
    Time To Live:         64 [40]
    Protocol:             17  UDP [41]
    Header Checksum:      0x3988 [42-43]
    Source IP Address:    0.0.0.0 [44-47]
    Dest. IP Address:     255.255.255.255  IP Broadcast
```

Fig. 5. Sniffer capture of DHCP Discover (IP Layer Perspective).

Offer Frame or Message 2

In response to Discover message, the DHCP server sends the DHCP offer message (Figs. 6 and 7).

```
⊟ 802.11 MAC Header
    Version:              0 [0 Mask 0x03]
    Type:                 %10  Data [0 Mask 0x0C]
    Subtype:              %1000  QoS Data [0 Mask 0xF0]
  ⊞ Frame Control Flags=%00000010
    Duration:             44  Microseconds [2-3]
    Destination:          60:F1:89:62:90:81 [4-9]
    BSSID:                AC:22:0B:CE:82:40 [10-15]
    Source:               AC:22:0B:CE:82:40 [16-21]
```

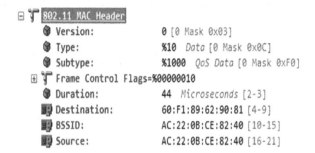

Fig. 6. Sniffer capture of DHCP Offer (MAC Layer Perspective).

```
⊟ IP Version 4 Header - Internet Protocol Datagram
    Version:              4 [34 Mask 0xF0]
    Header Length:        5  (20 bytes) [34 Mask 0x0F]
  ⊞ Diff. Services=0x00
    Total Length:         328 [36-37]
    Identifier:           19214 [38-39]
  ⊞ Fragmentation Flags=%000
    Fragment Offset:      0  (0 bytes) [40-41 Mask 0x1FFF]
    Time To Live:         64 [42]
    Protocol:             17  UDP [43]
    Header Checksum:      0xAAB6 [44-45]
    Source IP Address:    192.168.1.1 [46-49]
    Dest. IP Address:     192.168.1.143 [50-53]
```

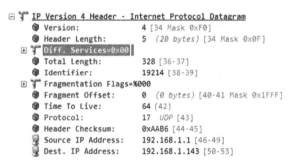

Fig. 7. Sniffer capture of DHCP Offer (IP Layer Perspective). Sniffer capture of DHCP Offer (IP Layer Perspective).

Request Frame or Message 3

After receiving the offer, DHCP client sends a DHCP Request message to the server, in which client either accept IP address given by server or it can request the new one. It can be seen at the mac layer as a unicast frame while broadcast on the IP layer and in this frame DHCP server provides an IP to the client (Figs. 8 and 9).

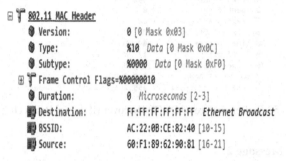

Fig. 8. Sniffer capture of DHCP Request (MAC Layer Perspective).

Fig. 9. Sniffer capture of DHCP Request (IP Layer Perspective).

Acceptance Frame or Message 4

After the request frame, the server sends an acceptance/acknowledge frame, whether it has accepted the client IP or denied it. The reason code is also mentioned in case of failure so a client can get information about why the DHCP server has rejected the request. This frame is unicast on both layers (Figs. 10 and 11).

Below figure shows complete sniffer capture for a station to access-point Wi-Fi connection in open security mode (Fig. 12):

The organization of this paper is as follows: Section 2 presents related work and research objectives. Our Simulation and Test Results and its conclusion is discussed in Sect. 3. Proposed work & feedback is described in Sect. 4 and finally, conclusions and future work are drawn in Sect. 5.

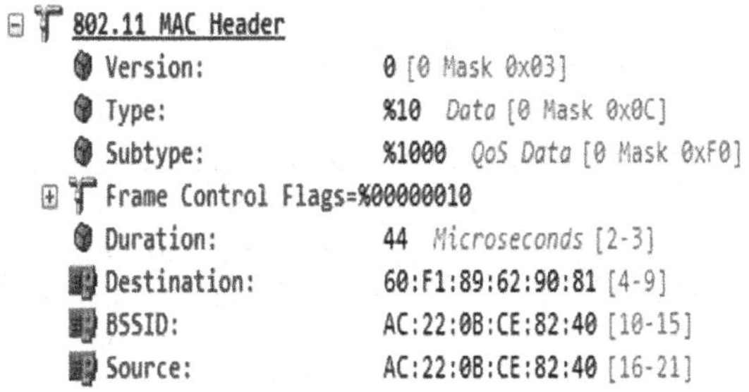

```
⊟ ⵀ 802.11 MAC Header
    ◉ Version:              0 [0 Mask 0x03]
    ◉ Type:                 %10  Data [0 Mask 0x0C]
    ◉ Subtype:              %1000  QoS Data [0 Mask 0xF0]
  ⊞ ⵀ Frame Control Flags=%00000010
    ◉ Duration:             44  Microseconds [2-3]
    ▓ Destination:          60:F1:89:62:90:81 [4-9]
    ▓ BSSID:                AC:22:0B:CE:82:40 [10-15]
    ▓ Source:               AC:22:0B:CE:82:40 [16-21]
```

Fig. 10. Sniffer capture of DHCP Acknowledge (MAC Layer Perspective).

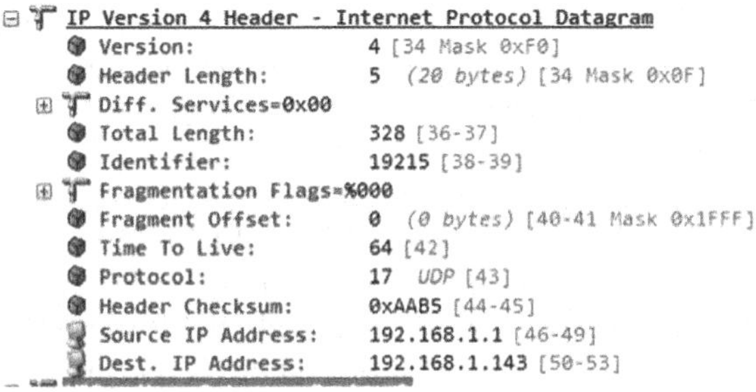

```
⊟ ⵀ IP Version 4 Header - Internet Protocol Datagram
    ◉ Version:              4 [34 Mask 0xF0]
    ◉ Header Length:        5  (20 bytes) [34 Mask 0x0F]
  ⊞ ⵀ Diff. Services=0x00
    ◉ Total Length:         328 [36-37]
    ◉ Identifier:           19215 [38-39]
  ⊞ ⵀ Fragmentation Flags=%000
    ◉ Fragment Offset:      0  (0 bytes) [40-41 Mask 0x1FFF]
    ◉ Time To Live:         64 [42]
    ◉ Protocol:             17  UDP [43]
    ◉ Header Checksum:      0xAAB5 [44-45]
    ▓ Source IP Address:    192.168.1.1 [46-49]
    ▓ Dest. IP Address:     192.168.1.143 [50-53]
```

Fig. 11. Sniffer capture of DHCP Acknowledge (IP Layer Perspective).

Packet	Source	Destination	BSSID	Flags	Channel	Signal	Data Rate	Size	Relative Time	Protocol	Decode: Message Type
1	60:F1:89:62:90:81	AC:22:0B:CE:82:40	AC:22:0B:CE:82:40	M	11	47%	1.0	45	0.000000	802.11 Auth	
3	AC:22:0B:CE:82:40	60:F1:89:62:90:81	AC:22:0B:CE:82:40	M	11	76%	1.0	45	0.001005	802.11 Auth	
4	60:F1:89:62:90:81	AC:22:0B:CE:82:40	AC:22:0B:CE:82:40	M	11	65%	1.0	90	0.009375	802.11 Assoc Req	
6	AC:22:0B:CE:82:40	60:F1:89:62:90:81	AC:22:0B:CE:82:40	M	11	76%	1.0	97	0.010746	802.11 Assoc Rsp	
8	0.0.0.0	IP Broadcast	AC:22:0B:CE:82:40		11	78%	1.0	378	0.422490	DHCP	1 Discover
9	192.168.1.1	192.168.1.143	AC:22:0B:CE:82:40		11	78%	54.0	366	0.422605	DHCP	2 Offer
10	0.0.0.0	IP Broadcast	AC:22:0B:CE:82:40		11	65%	36.0	392	0.454995	DHCP	3 Request
11	192.168.1.1	192.168.1.143	AC:22:0B:CE:82:40		11	78%	54.0	366	0.459353	DHCP	5 ACK

Fig. 12. Sniffer capture of Wi-Fi Connection in open mode.

2 Related Work and Research Objectives

At a broad level, fast operation and increased data throughput are a great challenge in a Wi-Fi environment and researchers are working to overcome these challenges. Users are increasing day by day using Wi-Fi and analyst are working on their behavior and problems [19]. Active scanning is also used to reduce connection time as shown in several research reports and also reduction of MAC layer handover time [8]. Partial scanning (perform channel scanning in chunks, not in one go) and special scanning algorithms [9, 10, 13] also works well in the fast handoff between the station and access point. Power consumption is also a challenging area especially for battery operated device [20] and offloading of features are performed to overcome this challenge in a small manner.

To make a fast connection, researchers used caching of previous connection information [5] or do fast sub-steps like authentication [6]. To improve connection time pre-allocation of DHCP also done [7]. In the case of roaming, authentication frame uses to share 4-way handshake information [11] for a fast connection.

3 Our Work, Simulation, and Results

To perform the test, we have used our own simulator system on windows operating system. We compile our driver and application by Visual Studio 2017 and use WinDDK to build the driver [17]. To perform our test, we developed a simple command line application and a windows WDM driver [15]. Here application acts as both DHCP Client & Server application for the station and access point respectively and this application talk with a simple WDM driver [16] using IOCTL. WDM driver works as the driver itself and as a virtual firmware and hardware device for a Wi-Fi device.

Here we assume access point has an embedded DHCP server. First, we tried to offload DHCP feature, like ARP or EAPOL offload (GTK rekey) performed in case of WoWLan (Wake on Wireless LAN) [13] feature. Offloading means instead of host/driver, the feature is performed by firmware. Mainly offloading is for the reduction of power consumption of device but it has saved a little time as driver-device latency reduced [12]. Later, we merge a DHCP frame with connection frames.

DHCP mainly IP layer procedure, and it is time-consuming also. If we talk from 802.11 perspectives, DHCP related frames are data frames, while connection frame like authentication & association is management frames. In our work, we have offloaded the DHCP feature and we have combined this feature with MAC layer connection frame via adding DORA [14] support in authentication/association frame. We have already discussed "connection and DHCP both have 4 frames respectively". So, we have done one to one mapping to create new frames which are shown in Table 1.

We have moved all the things to the MAC layer and at the MAC layer, Authentication Request is a unicast frame to AP, while DHCP discover is a multicast frame. Here we are assuming that access point has embedded DHCP server, so discover frame can be unicast as well.

Table 1. Proposed frames

Proposed frame	Direction	Combination
Authentication request	Station to AP	Authentication Request + DHCP Discover
Authentication response	AP to station	Authentication Response + DHCP Offer
Association request	Station to AP	Association Request + DHCP Request
Association response	AP to station	Association Response + DHCP Acceptance

Apart from discover frame, all other frames are unicast at mac layer, so it does not provide any problem.

The proposed Auth request frame have special IE (Information Element) present, which shows whether the device supports static IP or a dynamic IP and DHCP related (layer 3) information. If static set in station's auth request IE, AP's (inbuilt DHCP server) does not need to provide any IP to the station. Same in other connection frames: Auth response, Assoc request & Assoc response frame also have special IE which consists of DHCP related information.

Figure 13 shows the general device model about the layers a wifi device consist. Here firmware runs inside the device hardware, so we assume both are at the same layer (Fig. 14).

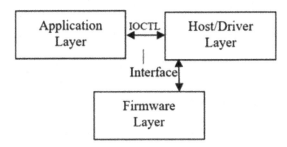

Fig. 13. General Device model.

To simulate the test, we have created two layers at user space and kernel space, Application runs at user space and driver & virtual firmware functionality runs at kernel space. The application works as a DHCP Client and DHCP server for station & access-point unit respectively. Application talks with the driver using IOCTL and a fixed interface delay gap are given between Host & Firmware function at the driver side. In a real device, an interface exists via which device is connected to the system, this interface can be USB, PCIe, SDIO or anything else, so an interface delay added between driver and firmware function.

Above figure shows our simulator model to perform the test. And below steps performed via every entity participate in this test:

1) Create connection command comes to application.
2) The application sends create connection OID to device driver with DHCP or Static IP support.
3) OID is handled by Client_Host function and it bypasses details to Client_Firmware function.
4) Now Client_Firmware sends proposed Auth Request frame to Server_Firmware function.
5) Server_Firmware process auth request frame and response back with auth response frame.
6) Client_Firmware receive Auth response frame and after successful processing, it sends back association request frame to server_firmware.

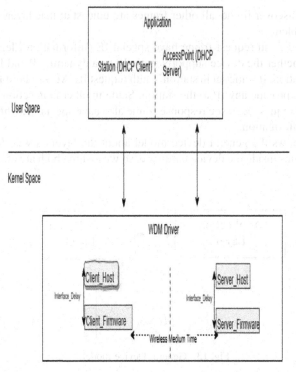

Fig. 14. Simulator Device Model in our test.

7) Finally, the association response frame is reverted back by Server_Firmware.
8) Respectively, Client_Firmware and Server_Firmware sync information with its respective application part via Client_Host&Server_Host bypass function.

In case of default behavior, DHCP works at the application layer and connection procedure works at the host or in some cases, at firmware side.

In our model, we have moved all the new frames to the firmware layer for fast execution. The application just provides required information to firmware via the host, so the new frame can be created at firmware side and send to access point as shown in Fig. 15.

Same at Access Point side, DHCP server & authentication works at firmware layer.

Below is the packet hex dump generated by our application. The color rule is followed to denote packet internally. Here Yellow color shows MAC Header, Green color shows connection Specific frame data (Auth or Association frame) and Pink color denotes DHCP Relative frame data. The default is the FCS field. In Auth Request, the red color is vendor command 0xDD followed by 0x0A, shown station support dynamic IP configuration instead of Static IP configuration.

For this test:

- AP MAC Address: 00:11:22:33:44:55

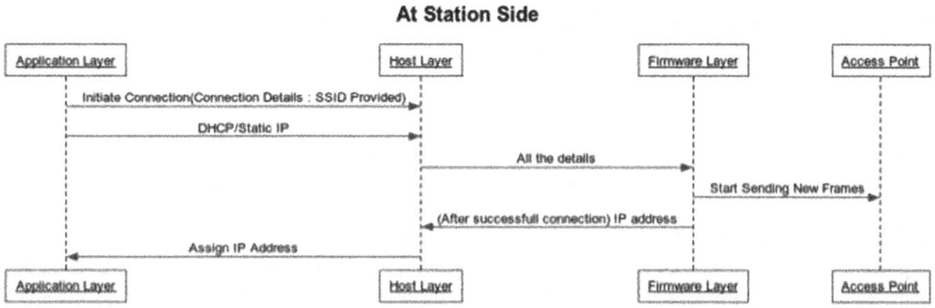

At Station Side

Fig. 15. Station side implementation. (Color figure online)

- Station MAC Address: 00:00:66:77:88:99

A. **Auth Request**:

> B0 00 3C 00 00 11 22 33 44 55 00 00 66 77 88 99 00 11 22 33 44 55 D0 0E 00 00
> 01 00 00 00 DD 0A DD 01 00 00 00 00 00 00 00 00 00 00 00 00 15 93 DE D9

B. **Auth Response:**

> B0 00 32 00 00 00 66 77 88 99 00 11 22 33 44 55 00 11 22 33 44 55 E0 94 00 00 02
> 00 00 00 DD 02 00 00 00 00 C0 A8 2B 2E C0 A8 2B BE A7 73 EB 4B

C. **Assoc Request:**

> 00 00 3C 00 00 11 22 33 44 55 00 00 66 77 88 99 00 11 22 33 44 55 E0 0E 11 01 0A
> 00 00 09 56 49 53 48 41 4C 5F 35 47 01 08 8C 12 98 24 B0 48 60 6C DD 03 00 00 00
> 00 00 00 00 00 00 00 00 00 32 04 C0 A8 2B 2E 4C 21 96 CE

D. **Assoc Response:**

> 10 00 32 00 00 00 66 77 88 99 00 11 22 33 44 55 00 11 22 33 44 55 F0 94 11 01 00
> 00 02 C0 01 08 8C 12 98 24 B0 48 60 6C DD 04 00 00 00 00 C0 A8 2B 2E C0 A8 2B
> BE 35 DE 27 67

After connection data, DHCP data start from 0xDD (Denotes vendor specific command). Here is the DHCP information inside packets which is exchanged between client and server.

- Message Type - 1 (Discover)

IP Address Known By Client: 0.0.0.0
Client IP Addr Given By Srvr: 0.0.0.0
Server IP Address: 0.0.0.0

- Message Type - 2 (Offer)

IP Address Known By Client: 0.0.0.0
Client IP Addr Given By Srvr: 192.168.43.46
Server IP Address: 192.168.43.179

- Message Type - 3 (Request)

IP Address Known By Client: 0.0.0.0
Client IP Addr Given By Srvr: 0.0.0.0
Server IP Address: 0.0.0.0
Requested IP Address
Option Code = 50
Option Length = 4
Address = 192.168.43.46

- Message Type - 4 (Ack)

IP Address Known By Client:0 .0.0.0
Client IP Addr Given By Srvr: 192.168.43.46
Server IP Address :192.168.43.179

It simply provides a reduction of 4 frames in the connection process. We have also performed a timing comparison between a normal connection procedure and our proposed procedure. Here is the timing variable used in the calculation.

- T_{MODE}: User Space to Kernel mode delay time
- $T_{INTERFACE}$: Interface Delay
- T_{TRANS}: Wireless Medium Time (Packet air travel time)

First, we will calculate DIFS (Distributed coordinator function Inter Frame Space), between two separate transmissions:

$$T_{SIFS} = 10\,\mu s \tag{1}$$

$$T_{SLOT} = 20\,\mu s \tag{2}$$

$$T_{SLOT} = 20\,\mu s \tag{3}$$

$$T_{DIFS} = T_{SIFS} + 2 \times T_{SLOT} = 10\,\mu s + 2 \times 20\,\mu s = 50\,\mu s \tag{4}$$

Coming on to the packet, it firstly consists of PHY header further consisting of PLCP preamble (144 bits) and header (48 bits). Here we have DSSS mode and assumed the packet transmission rate as 1Mbps. Therefore, time to transmit PHY header will be:

$$T_{PHY} = (144\,\text{bits})/(1\,\text{Mbps}) + (48\,\text{bits})/(1\,\text{Mbps}) = 192\,\mu s \tag{5}$$

Next up will be the MAC Header which is 24bytes (192 bits) which will also transfer at 1 Mbps. Therefore.

$$T_{FCS} = (32 \text{ bits})/(1\text{Mbps}) = 32 \,\mu s \tag{6}$$

Now payload will vary according to the packet, so now we will calculate FCS (Frame Check Sequence) which is 4 bytes (32 bits) long.

Also after each packet we have ACK (Acknowledgement frame) sent by the receiver. The MAC header of ACK frame is.

10 bytes (80 bits) long which will take 80 μs to transmit. Therefore ACK transmission time will be:

Using Eqs. (4) and (6).

$$T_{ACK} = T_{PHY} + 80 \,\mu s + T_{FCS} = 304 \,\mu s \tag{7}$$

As discussed, payload transmission time will be our variable and total time for complete transmission of any packet would be:

$$T_{TRANS} = T_{PHY} + T_{MAC} + T_{PAYLOAD} + T_{ACK} \tag{8}$$

Now we are ready to calculate the total time for each packet present in normal and our proposed model.

Let us first see the present model. T_{N_TOTAL} is total transmission time in normal scenario (Tables 2, 3, 4 and 5).

Table 2. Transmission time in normal scenario.

Payload	Length (bytes)	$T_{Payload}$ (μs)	T_{Trans} (μs)
Authentication Request	48	48	736
Authentication Response	48	48	736
Association Request	200	200	888
Association Response	128	128	816
DHCP Discover	2400	2400	3088
DHCP Offer	2700	2700	3408
DHCP Request	2400	2400	3088
DHCP ACK	2700	2700	3408
T_{N_TOTAL}			**16,168**

Now the proposed model: In our proposed model we have additional bytes to replace DHCP 4 packets exchange. These additional bytes will take additional time and is to be added in the total transmission time of each packet. T_{P_TOTAL} is total transmission time in proposed scenario.

To calculate the time between user mode & kernel mode we have used Dbgview.exe [18] and using print we got it.

Table 3. Transmission time in proposed scenario.

Payload	Length (bits)	Additional Length (bits)	$T_{Payload}$ (μs)	T_{Trans} (μs)
Authentication request	48	112	112	848
Authentication response	48	112	112	848
Association request	200	160	160	1048
Association response	128	112	112	928
T_{P_TOTAL}				**3,672**

For interface delay calculation assumption is interface equivalent to USB2.0, and practically USB 2.0 speed is around 40 megabytes per second (MBps) [21]. According to this, 112 byte takes around 2.46 μs.

Here is the value:

- $T_{INTERFACE}$ – 2.46 μs.
- T_{MODE} – 93 μs.

$$\text{Total time in all 9 steps} = 8 * T_{INTERFACE} + 5 * T_{MODE} + T_{P\_TOTAL} \qquad (9)$$

Table 4. Default behavior steps

S. No.	Step Detail	Time
1	Connection Request	T_{MODE}
2	Auth Request via station driver	$T_{INTERFACE} + T_{TRANS}$
3	Auth Response via AP driver	$T_{INTERFACE} + T_{TRANS}$
4	Assoc Request via station driver	$T_{INTERFACE} + T_{TRANS}$
5	Assoc Response via AP driver	$T_{INTERFACE} + T_{TRANS}$
6	DHCP Discover from application (Client side)	$T_{MODE} + T_{INTERFACE} + T_{TRANS}$
7	DHCP Offer from Application (Server side)	$T_{MODE} + T_{INTERFACE} + T_{TRANS}$
8	DHCP Request from application (Client side)	$T_{MODE} + T_{INTERFACE} + T_{TRANS}$
9	DHCP Acceptance from Application (Server side)	$T_{MODE} + T_{INTERFACE} + T_{TRANS}$

$$\text{Total time in all 6 steps} = 2 * T_{INTERFACE} + 2 * T_{MODE} + T_{N\_TOTAL} \qquad (10)$$

Table 5. Proposed behavior steps

S. No.	Step Detail	Time
1	Connection Request	$T_{MODE} + T_{INTERFACE}$
2	Auth Request via station driver	T_{TRANS}
3	Auth Response via AP driver	T_{TRANS}
4	Assoc Request via station driver	T_{TRANS}
5	Assoc Response via AP driver	T_{TRANS}
6	DHCP Discover from application (Client side)	$T_{INTERFACE} + T_{MODE}$

Total time in default behavior from Eq. 9.

$$= 8 * 2.46 + 5 * 93 + 16168 = 18463.24 \, ms.$$

Total time in proposed behavior from Eq. 10.

$$= 2 * 2.46 + 2 * 93 + 3672 = 4315.56 \, ms.$$

It is clearly visible that the proposed model saves connection time in the form of – reduced interface & IOCTL delay and change from 8 frame transmission to 4 frame transmission and it is around 1/4rd of default behavior.

4 Future Work and Conclusion

4.1 Future Work

Although the suggested approach significantly can reduce the wi-fi connection time, it still has some points which are to be taken care of in the future.

1) The current approach is tested in a simulator way, not in real time environment. So real-time implementation needs to done by Wi-Fi chip vendors.
2) This feature needs support from both side – station and access point, so backward compatibility case needs to tackle by both (Station & AP).
3) Every access point does not have an embedded DHCP server, so in that case, this feature development would be tough.
4) Auth Response and Assoc response consists of failure reason in case anything goes wrong from connection perspective. In case of DHCP failure more reason code needs tos be added in Auth Response and Assoc response specification.
5) In Simulation only success case is covered, it would be interesting to see if connection wise environment is fine but not for data exchange.

5 Conclusion

In this paper, through simulation and results, a new way is proposed for a fast Wi-Fi connection; Things moved from application to driver/firmware level and the number of frames reduced. The proposed solution shown is only for IPV4 but the same can be applied for IPV6 as well. Currently, the IEEE 802.11 specification does not define any of this type of combination frame as described in the paper. It is shown that the cross-layer and merging of the frame can significantly improve the Wi-Fi environment. In case of power saving of device, DHCP lease offloading can also be performed using the approach presented in the paper.

References

1. Seneviratne, S., et al.: Characterizing wifi connection and its impact on mobile users: practical insights. In: WiNTECH, pp. 81–88 (2013)
2. Pei, C., et al.: Why it Takes so Long to Connect to a Wi-Fi Access Point?, Cornell University Library, January 2017
3. Cisco vnireprot 2016. https://goo.gl/eqy2s2
4. Ieee standard 802.11. IEEE Std, 802:11 (2016)
5. US Patent US9204473B2 "Method and apparatus for accelerated link setup (2015)
6. Syahputri, R., Sriyanto, S.: Fast and secure authentication in IEEE 802.11i wireless LAN. In: 2012 2nd International Conference on in Uncertainty Reasoning and Knowledge Engineering (URKE), pp. 158–161 (2012)
7. Zuquete, A., Frade, C.: Pre-allocation of DHCP leases: a cross-layer approach. In: 4th IFIP International Conference on New Technologies, Mobility and Security https://doi.org/10.1109/NTMS.2011.5720663
8. Velayos, H., et al.: Techniques to reduce IEEE 802.11b mac layer handover time. Technical report (2003)
9. Ashraf, F., Kravets, R.H.: Making dense networks work for you. In: 2015 24th International Conference on Computer Communication and Networks (ICCCN), pp. 1–8 (2015)
10. Cicconetti, C., Galeassi, F., Mambrini, R.: Network-assisted handover for heterogeneous wireless networks. In: 2010 IEEE GLOBECOM Workshops (GC Wkshps), pp. 1–5 (2010)
11. Ieee standard 802.11. IEEE Std, 802:11r
12. Jia, J., Liu, G., Han, D., wang, J.: A Novel Packets Transmission Scheme Based on Software Defined Open Wireless Platform. Digital Object Identifier https://doi.org/10.1109/ACCESS.2018.2813007.
13. whitepaper Intel® Centrino® Mobile Technology Wake on Wireless LAN (WoWLAN) Feature
14. https://learningnetwork.cisco.com/thread/118328
15. Wu, A.H.: The Development of WDM Device Drivers Under Windows 2000/XP. Electronic Industry Press, Beijing (2005)
16. Walter, O.: Programming the Microsoft Windows Driver Model. Microsoft Press, America (1999)
17. Microsoft Windows 10 driver development kit documentation (2017)
18. https://docs.microsoft.com/en-us/sysinternals/downloads/debugview
19. Balachandran, A., Voelker, G., Bahl, P., Rangan, V.: Characterizing user behavior and network performance in a public wireless LAN. In Proceedings of ACM SIGMETRICS, Marina Del Rey, CA, June 2002

20. Balasubramanian, N., Balasubramanian, A., Venkataramani, A.: Energy consumption in mobile phones: a measurement study and implications for network applications. In: Proceedings of ACM IMC (2009)
21. https://www.cypress.com/file/139866/download

Hybrid Machine Learning Model for Traffic Forecasting

Khezaz Abderraouf[1,2(✉)], Manolo Dulva Hina[1], Hongyu Guan[2],
and Amar Ramdane-Cherif[2]

[1] ECE Paris School of Engineering, 37 quai de Grenelle, 75015 Paris, France
{abderraouf.khezaz,manolo-dulva.hina}@ece.fr
[2] Université Paris-Saclay, UVSQ, Laboratoire d'Ingénierie des Systèmes de Versailles,
78140 Vélizy-Villacoublay, France
{hongyu.guan,rca}@lisv.uvsq.fr

Abstract. Traffic prediction has been extensively studied in the past decades. Vehicle's speed is considered the main factor for traffic forecasting, but external parameters, such as the weather, can also have a strong impact. This is a case of a classification problem to which Machine Learning has shown to have strong solving potential, if trained properly. In this paper, we propose a two-level model related to traffic forecasting parameters: It is necessary that there is no missing data in the training set, then train a Neural Network able to accurately predict the traffic situation Three completion algorithms from different types (Machine learning, algebraic and statistical methods) are compared for the rebuilding of the training set. The set is then used to train a Convolutional Neural Network into predicting the state of the traffic the way a human would do. The model is evaluated on the two parts: How accurately it can complete the data set and how correct the predictions are. This work is part of the ongoing research on intelligent vehicles that are capable of determining the context of the driving environment.

Keywords: Traffic forecasting · Data augmentation · Convolutional Neural Network · K-Nearest Neighbour · Deep Learning

1 Introduction

As the number of road users increases, the number of traffic casualties does too. According to the 2020 World Health Organization (WHO) reports [1], 1.35 millions people die each year from traffic incidents, and cost most countries 3% of their gross domestic product. Noticing that those numbers have been slowly increasing over the years, the WHO response was the publication of a 60-pages documents detailing their studies and strategies in order to improve the situation. Amongst other things, they included a questionnaire for assessing the road safety situation in a country. The first component to be checked is "Data collection and systems", that addresses the availability, gathering system, quality and dealing of the data [18].

© ICST Institute for Computer Sciences, Social Informatics and Telecommunications Engineering 2021
Published by Springer Nature Switzerland AG 2021. All Rights Reserved
S. Paiva et al. (Eds.): SmartCity360° 2020, LNICST 372, pp. 188–199, 2021.
https://doi.org/10.1007/978-3-030-76063-2_14

This can be explained by the fact that the modern transportation environment has become a dynamic and complex network made of vehicles, infrastructure and pedestrians. This fast-changing environment compels drivers to have an acute perception of their surroundings and be focused on the event happening around them in real-time. Thanks to the surge of new technologies in Intelligent Transportation Systems (ITS), the vehicle can provide a valuable assistance to human users, and go as far as taking initiatives [8].

Fig. 1. Illustration of a traffic congestion situation. The weather, roadworks and speed limitations all contribute to the generation of a traffic jam

One of the many aspects of transportation that can be impacted by new technologies is traffic. The complex network of transportation made of vehicles does not have a determined speed-rate speed, and is more of an unpredictable and non-linear phenomenon. There is an increasing number of road users, and there is a proportional increase of risks on their lives too.

There are many unpredictable variables that can influence the state of Traffic at a given time, such as the weather or the presence of roadworks. The important amount of data generated by those factors can be too much to process by the driver alone, hence the idea of unloading this task to a smart agent embedded in the vehicle. With the computation power and the small size of intelligent components now present on cars, there is sufficient resources to build a model capable of analyzing and predicting the state of traffic in real-time. Setting up an intelligent architecture requires a reliable set of data for training and calibration, so this aspect should also be secured [9].

We propose a model that should be able to 1) Make sure the training set is accurate enough to be used for fitting and 2) A neural network that correctly predict the traffic situation according to a set of inputs. The model is briefly illustrated in Fig. 1.

The remainder of the paper is organized as follows: First a review of traffic forecasting works is presented in Sect. 2. In Sect. 3, the traffic forecasting data processing model is discussed in depths, including the gathering of data and their reconstructions, followed by the technical details of the model building and its validation. The paper is finally concluded by an analysis and a perspective of our future works (Fig. 2).

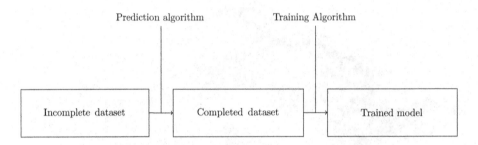

Fig. 2. A summary of the traffic forecasting model

2   Related Works

There have been many earlier works related to traffic forecasting. There have been many possible approaches to the problem; they all share the same objective – to be able to predict in the most accurate way the situation of traffic under specific conditions.

Traffic prediction has long been regarded as a statistical problem. In one of the earliest studies in 1991, Davis and Nihan [5] compared the simple univariate linear prediction a regression model in an empirical measuring of traffic congestion. They choose a Nearest-Neighbor approach and showed that this lazy-learning method was just slightly better than a classical parametric regression method. However, and as noted by the authors, the optimisation was not significant enough to be relevant, and the predictions were still not accurate enough, sometimes being up to 30% incorrect.

In 2003, with access to higher-quality traffic data, Clark [4] proposed a Non-parametric Regression model that would include other variable to speed, like the day of the week. Non-parametric regression is a form of regression that is based on the available data, rather than a pre-determined prediction function, hence being relevant in the traffic topic since there is not a single "fixed" behaviour. Their model showed great potential, but they did not have a database big enough to accurately train it, and were also lacking the computation power to properly calibrate it.

As pointed out by Vlahgioanni et al. [17], traffic forecasting has been studied for almost 3 decades now. In their literature review, they came out with 10 possible axis of improvement:

- Developing responsive algorithms and prediction schemes
- Freeway, arterial and network traffic predictions
- Short-term predictions: from volume to travel time
- Data resolution, aggregation and quality
- Using new technologies for collecting and fusing data
- Temporal characteristics and spatial dependencies
- Model selection and testing
- Compare models or combine forecasts
- Explanatory power, associations and causality
- Realizing the full potential of artificial intelligence

The last point has become the most interesting over the years. This review was made in 2014, a few months before the real surge of Deep Learning [10] and Artificial Intelligence. Many studies has since been focusing on the last improvement point proposed, i.e. building neural networks and using AI for traffic forecasting. In fact it is one of the approaches our own study is taking.

Artificial Intelligence have already been used in recent works for traffic forecasting. In 2015, Ma et al. [12] implemented a Long- short-term memory neural network to predict traffic situation. They used micro-wave detector to collect real-life data for a month and trained their model with them. They showed good results with 97% of accuracy on their predictions. Even though the model made very accurate predictions, the only input it had was the speed of cars that were going through the testing road, with no consideration of environmental data.

In 2011, Min et Wynter [14] developed a scalable method for traffic prediction up to 15 min in a dynamic environment. The mathematical model they proposed was built upon two variables: the distance and average speed of the vehicles. They showed excellent results but using only two parameters made the computation light enough to be fast. One of the possible improvements they mentioned was adding external parameters, such as "weather, incident data and roadwork, current or planned".

As stated before, most works have been focused on speed as the main traffic forecasting parameter. This paper will try to broaden the previous studies by considering a variety of other components into the prediction.

3   Traffic Forecasting Model Concept

3.1   Data Gathering

There are many types of data that can be used for traffic prediction. For this study we decided to focus on only 7 parameters and give them fixed possible values.

- **Weather**: Sunny, Cloudy or Rainy
- **Location**: City, Highway, Isolated Road
- **Day**: Weekday, Week-end
- **Time**: Rush hours, calm hours
- **Speed**: Up to 120 km/h
- **Roadwork**: Whether there are works on the road or not
- **Traffic Incident**: Whether there is a traffic incident or not

Those specific parameters were chosen after the literature review made in Sect. 2, which showed that traffic forecasting should at least include them. Data are either collected by the vehicle's sensors or the Smart City Broadcast, which is assumed to be by RF transmission of notable event. The data are also classified into 3 categories: Those related to the surrounding of the vehicles (Weather, Day and Time), the ones directly related to the car's behaviour (Speed and Location), and the events that can happen independently of the vehicle (Roadwork and traffic Incident). Those categories of data are respectively detailed in the Tables 1, 2 and 3. Based on the gathered information, we can predict the state of the traffic and categorize it into 4 different types: Light, Medium, Heavy and Extremely Heavy. The main parameters to define the output are the Roadwork and Traffic Incident variables, both being occasional and spontaneous events. They play an important role in traffic congestion, and coupled with the other parameters, such as the weather or the speed limitation, the traffic flow can be temporarily fully stopped.

Table 1. Environment parameters

Name of the parameter	Weather	Day	Time
Values of the parameter	Sunny, Cloudy or Rainy	Weekday, Week-end	Rush hours, calm hours
Gathering channel	Car sensors	Car system	Car sensors

Table 2. Car parameters

Name of the parameter	Position	Speed
Values of the parameter	City, Highway or Isolated road	up to 120 km/h
Gathering channel	Car sensors	Car sensors

Table 3. Event parameters

Name of the parameter	Roadwork	Traffic incident
Values of the parameter	Yes or No	Yes or No
Gathering channel	City broadcast	City broadcast

3.2 Data Cleaning

Once data are collected it is necessary to assure that necessary to assure that there is no missing information. For this part, three completion algorithms from different methods are compared: the algebraic SVD (Singular Value Decomposition), the statistical Mean Imputation and the learning-based classifier KNN (K-Nearest Neighbor).

– The dataset technically being an integer matrix, it is possible to use algebraic algorithms on it. One of those methods is the SVD decomposition, which has been proven to be used for matrix completion [13]
– Mean imputation is one of the easiest and most straightforward completion methods and consists of calculating the mean value of each column and using it as a replacement for the missing values. This method requires all the values to be numerical. [15]
– The KNN method takes an incomplete row of data and compares it to the most similar ones in order to predict the correct output. In this case it takes the road and traffic conditions as inputs and tries to find similar cases in the knowledge base and determine the traffic situation. [6]

These algorithms are evaluated based on the time they take to reconstruct the dataset and the accuracy of their outputs. The one with the best results is chosen as the optimal solution for the model.

3.3 Neural Network

Artificial Intelligence has become one of today's most rapidly growing technical fields, especially Machine Learning and Artificial Neural Networks (ANN). There are many different ANN architectures which efficiency depends on the task at hand, such as Recurrent Neural Networks (RNN), which requires considerable training resources but shows excellent results in time series treatment [19]. For example, one of RNN's sub-class known as Long Short-Term Memory (LSTM) [20] and using Deep-Learning methods, has been shown to even beat humans in high-level Real-Time Strategy videogames [2].

The particular case treated in this paper can be assimilated to a classification problem, to which Convolutional Neural Networks (CNN) have shown to be great solvers over the past years, in many fields such as image recognition [3] and audio recognition [7]. The second part of the model is the use of a Deep Neural Network to train the reconstructed dataset. It is expected to be able to correctly predict the output.

4 Model Implementation

4.1 Data Completion

The first step in building a model of traffic forecasting is the building of the dataset. A Python program was developed that would generate a 1000 set of events with their respective outputs. As described in Algorithm 1, the parameters are randomly assigned an integer value that corresponds to the state of the variable. For example, Weather = 0 means that the weather is sunny and presents no problem, whereas a value of 2 means it's a rainy day that can have a strong influence on the traffic. The traffic Situation output is computed by fusing the values of Weather, Location, Day, Time, Roadwork and traffic Incident. To simulate a more realistic situation where we could have a data loss, a complementary script was added that would go through the dataset and randomly delete an information, with a chance of 5%.

Once the incomplete dataset is ready, we started the augmentation phase. Data augmentation is the process where the initial dataset is reinforced and completed. We searched for the optimal algorithm to clean it. Three methods have been considered and tested: Mean Imputation, SVD and KNN classification methods. Table 4 shows a comparison of the three algorithms performance. The KNN requires calibration in finding the value of K, and the best results seem to be reached for K = 1, meaning the algorithm replaces a missing value with the closest set resembling it. This specific case of KNN, known as the 1-nearest-neighbour, has already been shown to have excellent results for low-dimension problems [16].

Algorithm 1: Complete Set

Input : None
Output: 1000*8 Training Set

Create Training Set;
Write the headers first;
for $i \leftarrow 0$ **to** 1000 **do**
    weather = randomValueOfWeather();
    location = randomValueOfLocation();
    speed = randomValueBetween[0:120] day = randomValueOfDay();
    time = randomValueOfTime();
    trafficIncident = randomBoolean();
    roadWork = randomBoolean();
    trafficSituation = trafficComputation(weather,location,speed,day,time, trafficIncident,roadWork);
    set = [weather,location,speed,day,time, trafficIncident,roadWork, trafficSituation]
    Write the vector *set* in row i of the Training Set
end

The SVD shows overall poor performances, which is not surprising considering that it must make complex operations on the dataset. KNN and Mean Imputation both shows overall similar results with an error rate of less than 1% and the KNN having a very small advantage, but the Mean Imputation is slightly faster. The difference of speed between both algorithms is small enough to be neglected, so it is decided to go with the KNN algorithm. The dataset being local, of 7 dimensions and of relatively small size, these conditions happens to be the most advantageous for the algorithm.

Algorithm 2: Incomplete Set

Input : 1000*8 Training Set
Output: 1000*8 Incomplete training Set

Import the Training Set;
for $i \leftarrow 0$ **to** 1000 **do**
$\quad j = \text{randomValueBetween}[0{:}100]$;
$\quad$ **if** $j > 95$ **then**
$\quad\quad$ | Random Cell from the row $i = NA$;
$\quad$ **end**
end
Save the new set as Incomplete Set;

Table 4. Comparison between the completion algorithms.

Algorithm	Execution time (in ms)	Performance
SVD	173	32%
Mean imputation	107	99,3%
KNN	132	99,5%

4.2 Neural Network Building

The new dataset will serve for training a classification model that will then be tested with different set of scenarios. To this end, a Convolutional Neural Network was built using the Keras tool for Python. The dataset is first split into a training and testing set, according to the common 80/20 split rule. The former is used for the training of the model whilst the latter is for validation purpose. The Network is made up of 5 fully-connected layers, following the recommendations of [11] for minimizing the effect of sparsity on the fitting. For the sake of clarity and to facilitate the replication of the presented approach, the details of the CNN are listed below.

- A 512 ReLU
- A 512 Linear
- A 64 ReLU
- A 64 Linear
- A 4 Softmax layer
- To avoid over-fitting, up to 40% of dropout is introduced between the layers.

This model takes a 7-dimensions dataset (containing only the inputs) and outputs a 4-dimension vector classifying each situation to one of the possible traffic Situation values (Light, Medium, Heavy, Very Heavy).

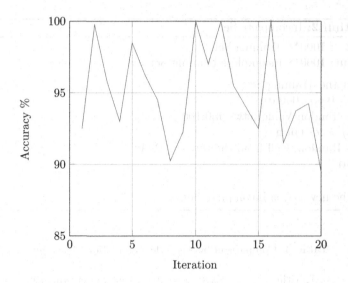

Fig. 3. Performances of the model over 20 iterations

A deep-learning architecture is described as "a multilayer stack of simple modules, all (or most) of which are subject to learning, and many of which compute non-linear input–output mappings" [10]. Our proposed network clearly matches this description, making our model a deep neural network.

In this work, the model is trained 1000 times. The fitting is done on an Ubuntu computed with an Intel *i7-8550* CPU and 16 BG of RAM memory and is made using the *ADAM* optimizer.

4.3   Model Validation

Once the CNN is built and fitted, the model is tested on different type of scenarios. Using the same algorithm as Algorithm 1, another batch of 400 sets is created and submitted to the model for classification. The intended goal is for the model to be able to predict the traffic situation the way a human would do. For example, if the weather is rainy and there is an accident on the road, a driver would automatically expect for the traffic to be heavy. On the contrary, on a sunny week-end day without any event, the traffic would be light.

When the dataset is ready, the inputs and outputs are separated, and we feed the former to the neural network. Since it is already trained, the *predict* function is used to have it classify each row of the testing set to a specific weather situation. Having saved the original outputs, they compare with what the model computed. The tests are 20 times and the results compared every time.

As shown in Fig. 3, the model shows good prediction results, averaging around 95,03% of success with a minimum of 89% and sometimes even reaching a full 100% accuracy.

Table 5. Details of the results

Iteration	Performance in %
1	92.5
2	99.75
3	95.75
4	93
5	98.5
6	96.25
7	94.5
8	90.25
9	92.25
10	100
11	97
12	100
13	95.5
14	94
15	92.5
16	100
17	91.5
18	93.75
19	94.25
20	89.5

5   Conclusion and Future Works

In this paper, a two-level model for traffic forecasting is presented. First, an incomplete data set of road conditions is built, then compared on 3 different completion algorithms: A soft-thresholded SVD, KNN and Mean imputation. The KNN was selected for this part because of the excellent results it produced.

A deep neural network made up of 5 hidden layers was then built and trained using this dataset. Once ready, generate another set of 400 data is generated and the inputs are fed to the model. They are then compared with the previously generated outputs. This operation is repeated over 20 iterations.

The model shows overall good performances, with around 95% of correct predictions. The average time to predict output is around 10 ms (fitting time not included) (Table 5).

There are still many ways to improve our model in the future. Amongst them are the following ones:

– Training with a bigger dataset
– Challenge the KNN with more completion algorithms

– Test the model in a real-life scenario

The authors are currently building a realistic driving simulator on Unity that would allow testing the model in harsher conditions.

Another improvement point is being considered is splitting the two parts of our model in different entities: Currently everything is done in one hardware, and the idea for the future would be to have a third-party gather and complete the data (i.e. a stationary drone), then send them to the vehicle which would do the prediction according to the received information.

References

1. Road traffic injuries. https://www.who.int/news-room/fact-sheets/detail/road-traffic-injuries
2. Arulkumaran, K., Cully, A., Togelius, J.: AlphaStar: an evolutionary computation perspective. In: Proceedings of the Genetic and Evolutionary Computation Conference Companion on - GECCO 2019, pp. 314–315 (2019). https://doi.org/10.1145/3319619.3321894. http://arxiv.org/abs/1902.01724
3. Cireşan, D., Meier, U., Masci, J., Schmidhuber, J.: Multi-column deep neural network for traffic sign classification. Neural Netw. **32**, 333–338 (2012). https://doi.org/10.1016/j.neunet.2012.02.023. https://linkinghub.elsevier.com/retrieve/pii/S0893608012000524
4. Clark, S.: Traffic prediction using multivariate nonparametric regression. J. Transp. Eng. **129**(2), 161–168 (2003). https://doi.org/10.1061/(ASCE)0733-947X(2003)129:2(161)
5. Davis, G.A., Nihan, N.L.: Nonparametric regression and short-term freeway traffic forecasting. J. Transp. Eng. **117**(2), 178–188 (1991). http://ascelibrary.org/doi/10.1061/
6. Hall, P., Park, B.U., Samworth, R.J.: Choice of neighbor order in nearest-neighbor classification. Annals Stat. **36**(5), 2135–2152 (2008). https://doi.org/10.1214/07-AOS537. http://arxiv.org/abs/0810.5276
7. Hershey, S., et al.: CNN architectures for large-scale audio classification. arXiv:1609.09430 [cs, stat] (2017)
8. Ingle, S., Phute, M.: Tesla autopilot : semi autonomous driving, an uptick for future autonomy. **03**(09), 4 (2016)
9. Jordan, M.I., Mitchell, T.M.: Machine learning: trends, perspectives, and prospects. Science **349**(6245), 255–260 (2015). https://doi.org/10.1126/science.aaa8415. https://www.sciencemag.org/lookup/doi/10.1126/science.aaa8415
10. LeCun, Y., Bengio, Y., Hinton, G.: Deep learning. Nature **521**(7553), 436–444 (2015). https://doi.org/10.1038/nature14539. http://www.nature.com/articles/nature14539
11. Lin, Z., Memisevic, R., Konda, K.: How far can we go without convolution: improving fully-connected networks. arXiv:1511.02580 [cs] (2015)
12. Ma, X., Tao, Z., Wang, Y., Yu, H., Wang, Y.: Long short-term memory neural network for traffic speed prediction using remote microwave sensor data. Transp. Res. Part C Emerging Technol. **54**, 187–197 (2015). https://doi.org/10.1016/j.trc.2015.03.014. https://linkinghub.elsevier.com/retrieve/pii/S0968090X15000935
13. Mazumder, R., Hastie, T., Tibshirani, R.: Spectral regularization algorithms for learning large incomplete matrices. J. Mach. Learn. Res. **11** 2287–2322 (2010)

14. Min, W., Wynter, L.: Real-time road traffic prediction with spatio-temporal correlations. Transp. Res. Part C Emerging Technol. **19**(4), 606–616 (2011). https://doi.org/10.1016/j.trc.2010.10.002
15. Scheffer, J.: Dealing with Missing Data **3**, 8 (2002)
16. Tibshirani, S., Friedman, H.: Valerie and Patrick Hastie p. 764
17. Vlahogianni, E.I., Karlaftis, M.G., Golias, J.C.: Short-term traffic forecasting: where we are and where we're going. Transp. Res. Part C Emerging Technol. **43**, 3–19 (2014). https://doi.org/10.1016/j.trc.2014.01.005. https://linkinghub.elsevier.com/retrieve/pii/S0968090X14000096
18. World Health Organization: Save LIVES: a road safety technical package. World Health Organization, Geneva (2017)
19. Zhang, J., Man, K.F.: Time series prediction using RNN. In: Multi-dimension Embedding Phase Space p. 6
20. Zhao, Z., Chen, W., Wu, X., Chen, P.C.Y., Liu, J.: LSTM network: a deep learning approach for short-term traffic forecast. IET Intel. Transport Syst. **11**(2), 68–75 (2017). https://doi.org/10.1049/iet-its.2016.0208

Labeling News Article's Subject Using Uncertainty Based Active Learning

Meet Parekh[1]($\boxtimes$) and Yash Patel[2]

[1] CBInsights, New York, USA
[2] New Jersey Institute of Technology, Newark, USA

Abstract. In Natural Language Processing, labeling a text corpus is often an expensive task that requires a lot of human efforts and cost. Whereas unlabeled text corpora in varying domains are readily available. For a couple of decades, research efforts have concentrated on algorithms that can be used for labeling the corpus, thus minimizing the number of articles required to be labeled manually. Semi-Supervised Learning and Active Learning have been a great promise for labeling the articles using a trained model. Also, Semi-Supervised learning algorithms and Active learning algorithms have strong theoretical guarantees. This study aims to tag 1183 articles from The New York Times and The Wall Street Journal with the subject (i.e. primary organization related to news articles) employing Active Learning algorithm. We used Active Learning algorithm which uses Random Sampling along with Uncertainty Based Querying. This Active Learning approach is used to train Naïve Bayes classifier using Bag of Words features. This classifier is used to tag 1183 articles of which only 167 required manual review, thus achieving reduction of 85.89% with 78.18% accuracy. Also, for verifying quality of labeled corpus, SVM classifier using same features was trained on labeled corpus giving accuracy of 74.45% on test data.

Keywords: Active learning · Natural language processing · Uncertainty sampling · Naïve bayes · SVM · Labeling

1 Introduction

While unlabeled text corpora are readily available, obtaining labeled corpus is a challenge confronting research community. The primary reason behind the scarcity of labeled corpus is the cost and human efforts incurred in labeling the corpus manually. Corpus used by Ng et al. [11] took university undergraduates one working year to label the corpus. Similarly, Tamas Vardi [12] took four years of efforts to construct Hungarian National Corpus. The Penn Chinese Tree Bank (CTB) [13] took four years to release its first edition CTB-I (annotated Chinese corpus) of 100,000 words. Thus labeling a corpus is a time-consuming effort and also requires high funding as subject experts have to dedicate a considerable amount of time for labeling a corpus.

© ICST Institute for Computer Sciences, Social Informatics and Telecommunications Engineering 2021
Published by Springer Nature Switzerland AG 2021. All Rights Reserved
S. Paiva et al. (Eds.): SmartCity360° 2020, LNICST 372, pp. 200–208, 2021.
https://doi.org/10.1007/978-3-030-76063-2_15

Year wise distribution of news articles

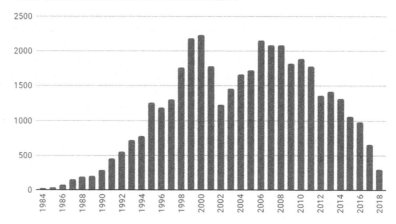

Fig. 1. Year wise distribution of News Articles

To address this issue, researchers have focused on devising algorithms for training models that can label articles. Different algorithms have been proposed by various studies that focus on minimizing the number of articles required to be labeled manually. Another goal for these algorithms is to produce high quality labeled corpus, as the accuracy of models highly depends on the underlying corpus. Thus different aspects of the quality of the corpus must also be taken into consideration while evaluating these algorithms. Literature alludes to semi-supervised learning [14] and Active Learning [1] for labeling unlabeled corpus.

Semi-supervised learning, an extension to supervised learning, can be defined as a model that trains itself on labeled dataset to predict the unlabeled dataset. The basic requirement of applying a Semi-Supervised learning is that unlabeled data should be much more than labeled data, else Supervised method could give the necessary output. The primary objective of Semi-Supervised learning is to train a classifier from both labeled and unlabeled data, such that it is better than the supervised classifier trained on the labeled data alone. Nigam et al. [23] showed that unlabeled data, when used in conjunction with a small amount of labeled data, can produce considerable improvement in learning accuracy. A classifier learns a function based on the provided labeled data, and extends this model to unlabeled data. The learning can be done in one of the many ways including self-training, probabilistic generative models, co-training, graph-based models, semi-supervised support vector machines, and so on.

Active Learning defers from Semi-Supervised learning in labeling unlabeled data, where Active Learning tries to determine most informative examples and queries them for manual review. Cohn et al. [1] defines Active Learning as learning in which learning algorithm has some form of control over which examples it will be trained on. Generally in Active Learning, learner selects a set of examples to be labeled and based on the learning strategy it sends some examples for manual review. Strategies can be devised to reduce cost, improving accuracy of learner, selecting most informative example, selecting examples that learner is uncertain about etc. Most of these strategies can be categorized into two broad categories viz. 1. Query based Committee and 2. Uncertainty based sampling which are described in further detail in Sect. 2. Although Active Learning reduces human efforts in labeling the unlabeled data [15,16,20,22], yet certain degree of human intervention is required in both.

Also, some Active Learning algorithms are shown to have strong theoretical guarantees. Mellow Active Learner have shown to have upper bound for the separable data [2], Agnostic Active Learning algorithm have been shown to have upper bound [3–6] as well as lower bound [7].

This study focuses on labeling subjects (i.e., the organization which is the primary subject of the article) of the News Paper articles using Active Learning algorithm. Generally, headlines are the subject of newspaper articles; however, nouns mentioned in the headline may not necessarily have relevance with the rest of the article, whereas on the other hand nouns not mentioned in the headline might have relevance with the article. For example, an article mentions "Microsoft" in its headline, but the article primarily focuses on the product launched by "Google". On the contrary, headlines of some of the articles may not mention "Microsoft", but the article may very much relate to it. Such a labeling can be useful if one wishes to use this corpus to perform sentiment analysis about a particular organization.

For this study, articles containing the word "Microsoft" at least once were extracted from The New York Times and The Wall Street Journal. These articles were labeled by Active Learning algorithm using Random Uncertainty Sampling [27] with Naïve Bayes classifier. We used Bag of Words model to train Naïve Bayes classifier. Accuracy of classification was measured on a separate test data, and it was measured as the function of number of articles labeled manually. Also to evaluate the quality of labeled corpus, SVM classifier using same features i.e. Bag of Words was trained on labeled corpus and evaluated on test data.

Outline of this paper is as follows, Sect. 2 describes details about Active Learning and other related work, Sect. 3 gives a description of corpus used, Sect. 4 describes Design and Implementation of the study, Sect. 5 underlines the Results, Sect. 6 highlights Future Works that could follow and Section Acknowledges the support received for this study.

2   Related Work

Active learning is learning in which learning algorithm has some form of control over which examples it will be trained on. In Active Learning, learner selects a set of examples to be labeled manually based on learning strategy. General motivation behind selecting examples is to select those examples which are most informative.

Based on this motivation different strategies can be devised to select examples. One basic motivation behind selecting examples is to reduce the cost incurred in labeling the articles. While many studies assumes that cost for labeling each example is same, this may not always be the case [32]. Thus a separate heuristic may be required to estimate the cost of labeling an example. Haertel et al. [17] devised cost sensitive heuristic function to measure the hourly cost incurred in labeling articles and used this heuristic to select articles which incurred low cost, thus achieving 73% reduction in hourly cost over random selection. Ringger et al. [21] further improvised heuristic function developed by Haertel et al. [17] by estimating the parameters for heuristic function based on a statistical study.

Another strategy is to select examples that possibly boosts up the accuracy of the classifier. This would be particularly useful if the purpose of the study is just to train classifier and use it for some task. Becker et al. [19] have used f-complement score to select examples that can potentially increase the f-1 score of classifier. On the similar lines, Thompson et al. [24] selected examples that would help maintain f-1 score of classifier.

At its base, general motivation is selecting examples that can be considered most informative for classifier. General strategies to achieve this purpose can be broadly categorized in two categories viz. 1. Query Based Committee and 2. Uncertainty Sampling [27].

In Query Based Committee methods, committee of classifiers are trained. These committee of learners are inquired to label examples. If there is disagreement within committee then this example is considered to be difficult and thus can be highly informative for classifier. Hachey et al. [16] used Query Based Committee method to determine examples that would need manual review, and found that examples selected by query based methods also had disagreement amongst group of annotators. Thus proving that these examples are complex and can be difficult to learn on. Dagan and Engelson [25] have used Query Based Committee method and found that it reduces cost of annotation. Similarly, Song et al. [33] considered examples on the margin of SVM to be the most informative examples, as they could change the separating hyper-plane.

In Uncertainty Sampling method, classifier gives certainty score for each example along with the label. If certainty score is below certain threshold then example is queried for manual review. Reason for selecting examples that the classifier is uncertain about, is that these examples can indeed be highly informative as they form boundary for probability based classifiers [26]. Lewis et al. [27] selected examples having probability of classification near 0.5 for manual review. In this study we have used Uncertainty Sampling along with Naïve Bayes classifier to determine examples that would be queried for manual review. Analogous to Uncertainty Sampling is Confidence Based Sampling, where learning algorithm requests manual review for examples for which confidence of classifier is low [30].

3   Dataset Description

Corpus containing 40144 news articles was constructed from The New York Times and The Wall Street Journal. All of these articles contained word "microsoft" either in metadata or body or headline of the article. Articles of The New York Times and The Wall Street Journal were extracted from ProQuest library, additionally articles of The Wall Street Journal were also extracted from Factiva Library. Each article contained a headline, publishing date, miscellaneous metadata, text, author, acknowledgments, and copyright details.

Figure 1 shows the distribution of these news articles over the years. It was observed that the majority of these articles i.e., 34750, were published between 1995–2015. Due to limitations in resources, we only focused on labeling articles for the year of 1996, which contained 1183 articles.

For initial training of classifier, 19 articles were labeled manually by subject experts. On top of that 55 articles from year 1998 were labeled manually by subject experts which were then used as test data.

4   Design and Implementation

Figure 2 shows the setup for this study. This section describes details about different steps of our experimental setup.

As described in Sect. 3, each articles in corpus contained headline, publishing date, miscellaneous metadata, text, author, acknowledgments, and copyright details. However much of these details were not required for the purpose of this study, so required data needed was extracted from these articles. Also text was required to be broken into tokens which would be needed in the Bag of Words model.

Firstly headline, publication data, and article text were extracted for each articles ignoring rest of information. Also date for each articles were in different format, so it was converted to standard yyyy-mm-dd format.

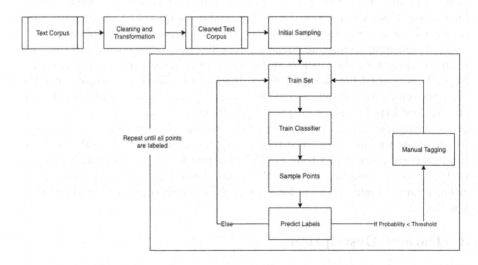

Fig. 2. Experimental setup

Thereafter NLTK [10] PUNKT [28] tokenizer was used to split article text and headline into tokens. Also NLTK "stopwords" corpus was used to remove tokens that were stop words. Remaining tokens were then used to create Bag of Words model where for each word corresponding frequency of occurrence of word were stored.

Once Bag of Words data was ready, Naïve Bayes classifier from sklearn [29] was trained on initial 19 labeled articles. Once classifier was trained we used Random Uncertainty Sampling to query articles for manual review which classifier was uncertain about.

To achieve this we randomly shuffled unlabeled data and fed it into classifier one by one. Articles that classifier was uncertain about were queried for manual review. Lewis et al. [27] used points having probability of certainty near 0.5 for manual review. Lewis et al. reasoned that these were the points that classifier was most uncertain about and formed sort of boundary for probabilistic classification, and if classifier was trained on these examples with correct label then classifier would be able to adjust its boundaries of classification. On similar lines we used the threshold of 0.6, such that if probability of majority class was less than 0.6 then it was queried for manual review. While rest of the articles having probability of classification above 0.6 were directly assigned respective labels. And this labeled articles were incorporated in training data.

After each manual review, classifier was retrained on new training data which included both, articles that were manually reviewed and articles that were directly assigned labels by the classifier. And then accuracy of classifier was measured on test data and plotted as a function of number of articles that were manually reviewed as shown in Fig. 3.

All 1183 articles of the corpus were labeled using this method. Another concern with Active Learning method is the quality of labeled corpus, i.e. how well would other classifiers work on corpus labeled with Active Learning [31]. To address this concern, we trained SVM classifier on this corpus using same features i.e. Bag of Words. We then evaluated accuracy of SVM on test data, results of which are described in Sect. 5.

5   Results

Figure 3 plots accuracy as a function of number of articles labeled manually. It can be observed from Fig. 3 that maximum accuracy achieved by Naïve Bayes on test data model was 78.18%. Also, learning process required 167 articles to be reviewed and labeled manually i.e. 14.11% required manual labeling. Thus model achieved reduction of 85.89% in labeling articles manually.

To measure the quality of labeled corpus, we trained SVM on labeled corpus using same features i.e. Bag of Words and measured its accuracy on test data. SVM gave accuracy of 74.45% on test data which is comparable with maximum accuracy achieved by Naïve Bayes i.e. 78.18% while labeling the corpus. This reflects that the labeling of the corpus is of good quality.

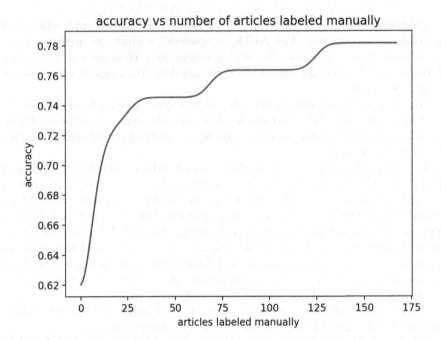

Fig. 3. Accuracy vs Number of articles tagged manually

6 Future Works

Random Sampling was used in this study to generate samples for training. Although reduction of 85.89% was observed using this method, there are few studies which suggests that purely Random Sampling may not be very effective strategy [17,19]. Thus, in future works we would like to further investigate different heuristics for selecting samples for training, and compare its result with pure Random Sampling.

For the purpose of this study, we evaluated the quality of labeled corpus by measuring the accuracy of SVM trained using same features i.e. Bag of Words. However for future studies, we would like to investigate training classifier using different features from the one used by classifier in Active Learning algorithm.

Also, we would like to use this strategy to label all 40144 articles and then use articles related to Microsoft for performing sentiment analysis, thus evaluating sentiments for Microsoft over a timeline of 24 years.

Acknowledgments. We want to thank New York University Library, ProQuest, and Factiva for making this news article corpus open to students for academic research. We would also like to thank our colleagues Manthan Shah of Pace University and Amod Panchal of Rutgers University, for manually tagging news articles.

References

1. Cohn, D., Atlas, L., Ladner, R.: Improving generalization with Active Learning. Mach. Learn. **15**(2), 201–221 (1994)
2. Hanneke, S.: Teaching dimension and the complexity of active learning. In: Bshouty, N.H., Gentile, C. (eds.) COLT 2007. LNCS (LNAI), vol. 4539, pp. 66–81. Springer, Heidelberg (2007). https://doi.org/10.1007/978-3-540-72927-3_7
3. Balcan, M.F., Beygelzimer, A., Langford, J.: Agnostic active learning. J. Comput. Syst. Sci. **75**(1), 78–89 (2009)
4. Dasgupta, S., Hsu, D.J., Monteleoni, C.: A general agnostic Active Learning algorithm. In: Advances in Neural Information Processing Systems, pp. 353–360 (2008)
5. Koltchinskii, V.: Rademacher complexities and bounding the excess risk in Active Learning. J. Mach. Learn. Res. **11**, 2457–2485 (2010)
6. Hanneke, S.: A bound on the label complexity of agnostic Active Learning. In: Proceedings of the 24th International Conference on Machine learning, pp. 353–360, June 2007
7. Beygelzimer, A., Dasgupta, S., Langford, J.: Importance weighted Active Learning. In: Proceedings of the 26th Annual International Conference on Machine Learning, pp. 49–56, June 2009
8. Settles, B.: Active Learning. In: Synthesis Lectures on Artificial Intelligence and Machine Learning, vol 6. no. 1, pp. 1–114 (2012)
9. Manning, C.D., Surdeanu, M., Bauer, J., Finkel, J.R., Bethard, S., McClosky, D.: The Stanford CoreNLP natural language processing toolkit. In Proceedings of 52nd Annual Meeting of the Association for Computational Linguistics: System Demonstrations, pp. 55–60, June 2014
10. Bird, S., Klein, E., Loper, E.: Natural Language Processing with Python: Analyzing Text With the Natural Language Toolkit. O'Reilly Media Inc., Sebastapol (2009)
11. Ng, H.T., Lee, H.B.: Integrating multiple knowledge sources to disambiguate word sense: An exemplar-based approach. In: Proceedings of the 34th Annual Meeting on Association for Computational Linguistics, pp. 40–47. Association for Computational Linguistics, June 1996
12. Váradi, T.: The Hungarian National Corpus. In: LREC (2002)
13. Xue, N., Chiou, F. D., Palmer, M.: Building a large-scale annotated Chinese corpus. In: COLING 2002: The 19th International Conference on Computational Linguistics (2002)
14. Board, R.A., Pitt, L.: Semi-supervised learning. Mach. Learn. **4**(1), 41–65 (1989)
15. Tomanek, K., Wermter, J., Hahn, U.: An approach to text corpus construction which cuts annotation costs and maintains reusability of annotated data. In: Proceedings of the 2007 Joint Conference on Empirical Methods in Natural Language Processing and Computational Natural Language Learning (EMNLP-CoNLL), pp. 486–495, June 2007
16. Hachey, B., Alex, B., Becker, M.: Investigating the effects of selective sampling on the annotation task. In: Proceedings of the Ninth Conference on Computational Natural Language Learning (CoNLL-2005), pp. 144–151, June 2005
17. Haertel, R.A., Seppi, K.D., Ringger, E.K., Carroll, J.L.: Return on investment for Active Learning. In Proceedings of the NIPS Workshop on Cost-Sensitive Learning, vol. 72, December 2008
18. Zhu, X.J.: Semi-supervised learning literature survey. University of Wisconsin-Madison Department of Computer Sciences (2005)

19. Becker, M., Hachey, B., Alex, B., Grover, C.: Optimising selective sampling for bootstrapping named entity recognition. In: ICML-2005 Workshop on Learning with Multiple Views, pp. 5–11, August 2005
20. Ringger, E., et al.: Active learning for part-of-speech tagging: accelerating corpus annotation. In: Proceedings of the Linguistic Annotation Workshop, pp. 101–108, June 2007
21. Ringger, E.K.: Assessing the costs of machine-assisted corpus annotation through a user study. In: LREC, vol. 8, pp. 3318–3324, May 2008
22. Ngai, G., Yarowsky, D.: Rule writing or annotation: cost-efficient resource usage for base noun phrase chunking. In: Proceedings of the 38th Annual Meeting on Association for Computational Linguistics, pp. 117–125. Association for Computational Linguistics, October 2000
23. Nigam, K., McCallum, A., Thrun, S., Mitchell, T.: Using EM to classify text from labeled and unlabeled documents (No. CMU-CS-98-120). Carnegie-Mellon Univ Pittsburgh PA School of Computer Science (1998)
24. Thompson, C.A., Califf, M.E., Mooney, R.J.: Active learning for natural language parsing and information extraction. In: ICML, pp. 406–414, June 1999
25. Dagan, I., Engelson, S.P.: Committee-based sampling for training probabilistic classifiers. In: Machine Learning Proceedings 1995, pp. 150–157. Morgan Kaufmann (1995)
26. Engelson, S.P., Dagan, I.: Minimizing manual annotation cost in supervised training from corpora. In: Proceedings of the 34th Annual Meeting on Association for Computational Linguistics, pp. 319–326. Association for Computational Linguistics, June 1996
27. Lewis, D.D., Gale, W.A.: A sequential algorithm for training text classifiers. In: SIGIR 1994, pp. 3–12. Springer, London (1994). https://doi.org/10.1007/978-1-4471-2099-5_1
28. Kiss, T., Strunk, J.: Unsupervised multilingual sentence boundary detection. Comput. Linguist. **32**(4), 485–525 (2006)
29. Pedregosa, F., et al.: Scikit-learn: machine learning in Python. J. Mach. Learn. Res. **12**, 2825–2830 (2011)
30. Li, M., Sethi, I.K.: Confidence-based Active Learning. IEEE Trans. Pattern Anal. Mach. Intell. **28**(8), 1251–1261 (2006)
31. Baldridge, J., Osborne, M.: Active learning and the total cost of annotation. In: Proceedings of the 2004 Conference on Empirical Methods in Natural Language Processing, pp. 9–16, July 2004
32. Settles, B., Craven, M., Friedland, L.: Active learning with real annotation costs. In: Proceedings of the NIPS Workshop on Cost-sensitive Learning, pp. 1–10, December 2008
33. Song, H., Yao, T., Kit, C., Cai, D.: Active learning based corpus annotation. In: CIPS-SIGHAN Joint Conference on Chinese Language Processing, Chicago (2010)

Intelligent Edge Processing in the IoT Era

Environment Monitoring Modules with Fire Detection Capability Based on IoT Methodology

Thadeu Brito[1,2](✉)(iD), Beatriz Flamia Azevedo[1](iD), Antonio Valente[3,4](iD),
Ana I. Pereira[1,5](iD), José Lima[1,4](iD), and Paulo Costa[2,4](iD)

[1] Research Centre in Digitalization and Intelligent Robotics (CeDRI), Instituto
Politécnico de Bragança, Campus de Santa Apolónia, 5300-253 Bragança, Portugal
{brito,beatrizflamia,apereira,jllima}@ipb.pt
[2] Faculty of Engineering of University of Porto, Porto, Portugal
paco@fe.up.pt
[3] Engineering Department, School of Sciences and Technology, UTAD,
Vila Real, Portugal
avalente@utad.pt
[4] INESC TEC - INESC Technology and Science, Porto, Portugal
[5] Algoritmi Research Centre, University of Minho, Campus de Gualtar,
Braga, Portugal

Abstract. Worldwide, forests have been devastated by fires in recent years. Whe- ther by human intervention or for other reasons, the history of burned areas is increasing year after year, degrading fauna and flora. For this reason, it is vital to detect an early ignition so that firefighters can act quickly, reducing the impacts caused by forest fires. The proposed system aims to improve the nature monitoring and to assist the existing surveillance systems through Wireless Sensor Network. The network formed by the set of sensors has the potential to identify forest ignitions and, consequently, alerts the authorities through LoRaWAN communication. This work presents a prototype based on low-cost technology, which can be used in areas that require a high density of modules. Tests with a Wireless Sensor Network made up of nine prototypes demonstrate its effectiveness and robustness in terms of data transmission and collection. In this way, it is possible to apply this approach in Portuguese forests with a high level of forest fire risk, transforming them into Forests 4.0 concept.

Keywords: WSN · IoT · Fire detection · Sensor Modules · Wildfires

1 Introduction

Portugal is the European country with the highest incidence of vegetation fires, not only in terms of number but also in the burnt area. This ecological disturbance occurs every year and causes dangerous social, economic and environmental damage [1,2]. The historical data indicates that in the last decades, there

S. Paiva et al. (Eds.): SmartCity360° 2020, LNICST 372, pp. 211–227, 2021.
https://doi.org/10.1007/978-3-030-76063-2_16

has been an increase in the occurrence and also in the severity of wildfires. In 2017, reports show that there were more than 15000 rural fires, corresponding to a burnt area close to 2400 km². The resulting devastation were directly responsible for the deaths of more than 100 people [3,4]. In the following year, in 2018, there were about 9700 rural wildfires, scoring a burnt area of approximately 380 km², with the Bragança region as the second district with the highest burnt area [3].

In this sense, monitoring the Portuguese forests is a fundamental action for our future, not only to observing flora and fauna but also to warn of possible fire ignition. By early warning of forest fire ignition, combat teams can act to minimize fire impacts. The project Forest Alert Monitoring System (SAFe) aims to contribute to the improvement of nature monitoring and to support the existing surveillance systems. The SAFe project implements a set of innovative operations that allow to identify a forest ignition and also will monitoring the fauna, such as sensors modules. The application of sensor modules for forest data acquisition will be implemented in the Bragança region, in the Serra da Nogueira territory. Due to the characteristics of this forest, spreading the modules across the whole would be chaotic and hard to understand the data [5]. Therefore, it is necessary to develop a strategy for fixing the modules regarding the vegetation type.

Some factors are deterministic for the choice of these points, such as forest type, history and estimation of areas at hazard of flame, areas that have been burned over the years, terrain elevation and forest density. Each of these maps provide essential data and finding the point that connects all of these maps is a possible solution for the insertion of each sensor modules. However, as a starting point for the SAFe project to find this point in common, it is necessary to obtain the operation of the fire detection modules in real situations. By attaching to each pair of modules in nearby regions, it is possible to determine the quality of communication and possible interference that the environment may cause in data collection.

This work will detail the modules' development that makes the detection of forest fires, as well as the small scale formation of the Wireless Sensor Networks (WSN) to obtain his behavior in real situations. In this way, the proposed sensor modules can provide the SAFe project with the necessary information from the developed modules to determine the optimal fixing points. Thus, the SAFe project could use the annual maps reported by the "Instituto da Conservação da Natureza e das Florestas" (ICNF) [6], and allocate the necessary number of sensors for each region with high fire risk.

This paper is organized as follows. After an introduction in Sect. 1, related work about fire detection techniques applied in Portuguese forests is presented in Sect. 2. In Sect. 3, SAFe system architecture is described. The sensor modules description is shown in Sect. 4, next is demonstrated in Sect. 5 the module assembled. The obtained results are presented in Sect. 6. Finally, Sect. 7 concludes the paper and points some future work direction.

2   Related Work

Wildfires are considered complex events in terms of causes, intensity, behavior, variability, hard to control, size and severity, their early detection is essential [7,8]. In this context, the maximum time interval, from ignition to the alert response of firefighters, should not exceed 6 min [9,10]. In addition to early detection capabilities, estimating the direction of propagation and the fire speed also crucial in extinguishing fires [11]. For these purposes, there are several methods: human observation towers [4]; systems that employ Charge-Coupled Device (CCD) [12,13] and Infrared detectors [14]; satellite systems and images [15] and WSN systems [16].

In the national plan, named "Plano Nacional de Defesa da Floresta Contra Incêndios" (PNDFCI) created by ICNF [6], it establishes myriad strategies to avoid wildfires. It is emphasizing on the existence of observation towers distributed throughout the national parks. However, the unreliability in the observation towers that are managed by human operators and their performance does not go beyond 10% in more unfavorable areas [7,17]. This reason pointed to use others technologies, as well as the use of surveillance cameras in the spectrum from the visible to the infrared. Even so, the accuracy of these systems depends on the type of topography, time of day, and other environmental conditions [18,19].

On the other hand, with the development of new technologies within the scope of Industry 4.0, the forestry sector can be digitized in terms of solving issues such as rural fires [20,21]. Integrating several systems, making them collaborative is a possible solution since there is still no type of operating system to alert wildfires based on these new approaches in Portuguese forests. For example, the service provided by [22], this company can provide forest ignitions in up to 4 min through modules that measure temperature, humidity, and CO_2 levels. In this sense, the literature does not present studies with developed techniques for forest fire alerts through the use of low-cost sensors that transmit information through long-range communication. This process would be possible with the implementation of sets of heterogeneous sensors that would work collaboratively, strategically located in forests with high fire risks. Therefore, the data can be analyzed by algorithms to predict regular situations based on forest history, and also identify abnormalities. Thus, an in-depth study is needed to integrate all these techniques that are available in the context of Industry 4.0 and apply in rural regions.

3   System Architecture

As already mentioned in the previous section, the SAFe project aims to install a set of innovative activities to be developed in regions with potential for ignition of fire in the district of Bragança. Therefore, SAFe is planned to follow an integration strategy with some tools that can work collaboratively. The union of these tools form the architecture of the system, illustrated in Fig. 1. Where a region with a greater risk of forest fire should be monitored according to its characteristics, such as identifying areas with greater or lesser irregularities in the soil. In this way, the forests in the Bragança region will benefit from these sets of components and applications proposed to identify forest ignitions.

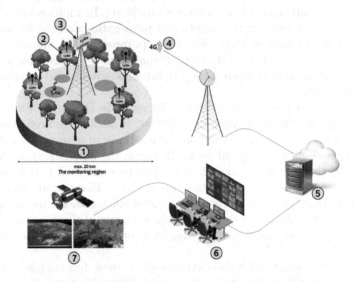

Fig. 1. Illustration of SAFe system architecture [23,24]. ① The monitoring region, ② Wireless sensor module, ③ LoRaWAN gateway, ④ 4G/LTE link, ⑤ Server, ⑥ Control center, and ⑦ Detection support system.

The proposed system can be divided into four essential elements: the monitoring region, the set of sensor modules, the communication system and the control center. The integration of these four elements together with a management system, based on artificial intelligence, will empower efficient and intelligent analysis of the data. This data analysis will generate the creation of forest ignition alerts, and consequently, should also alert the rescue and combat teams (such as firefighters, civil protection or city hall). These alerts must be parameterized and presented in a personalized way, according to each organization involved. It is still possible to fragment these four elements into smaller components, through categories. Therefore, it is possible to define eight categories that work collaboratively, identified by Fig. 1, they are:

- The monitoring region (represented by ①) is the region where the set of Wireless Sensor Modules will be placed to collect data. The choice of these regions should take into account the annual fire risk map provided by the ICNF [6].
- The WSN sets (represented by ②) are responsible for the data acquisition at the forest in real-time. The location of each Sensor Module is defined through an optimization procedure that considers the hazard fire in each coordinate,

and must also consider the forest characteristics, such as soil type, cover tree density, terrain relief, among others;

- The LoRaWAN Gateway (③) receives data from each sensor module by radio frequency communication, and then forward the data through a 4G/LTE link (or by Ethernet where available) to a server (represented by ④);
- The Control Center (represented by ⑥) receives all information, computes the data and sends alerts for hazardous situations or forest fire ignitions to the surveillance agent in the region. Therefore, this control center has a Server (represented by ⑤) that stores all collected data along over years, and perform artificial intelligence procedures to correlate data from sensor modules with external data (represented by ⑦); such as satellite image, local scale real-time fire hazard indexes, availability fuel content, weather data and moisture content of the vegetation.

Due to the complexity in the description and development of each of these items, this work will focus only on low-cost sensor modules. In this sense, the development stages of these modules are presented, with their respective considerations. The modules were designed to create a WSN, this network in turn will collect data from the region at risk of forest fires and inform the server. In order to form the WSN, many modules are necessary, and for that reason all the development was thought about the best cost benefit. In addition, it is also expected that these modules are easy to assemble and integrate with communication network, since the fixation sites are in the middle of dense forests. All these concepts is described, respectively, in the next section.

4   Wireless Sensor Modules

In the search to minimize the damage caused by forest fires, the PNDFCI plan determines what each region of Portugal must do [4]. These strategies have already shown that they are significant when compared to what has been implemented over the years. However, when comparing data from more recent years, it is noticeable that the areas affected by forest fires continue to grow. A possible justification is that the plan needs new approaches to complete the ones that are already being carried out. In this sense, considering that the plan only determines actions on a macro scale, it is necessary to take care of Portuguese forests with more attention to regional characteristics.

We are in a new technology paradigm, where digitization is revolutionizing industrial, medical and even educational sectors. Given this, it is possible to take advantage of and use the same technology to combat the fire. The Internet of Things (IoT) arises in a friendly way since the "thing" could be installed in the forests to detect fire ignitions and warn the fire-fighting teams. Therefore, each device needs to have unique characteristics to meet the most diverse scenarios found in Portuguese forests.

The development of these devices needs to consider a series of restrictions, such as size, battery autonomy, low cost (both in implementation and communication), being flexible for the addition of new sensors. Thus, the Fig. 2 illustrates in a simplified way the device proposed in this work. Each module components will be detailed in the next subsections.

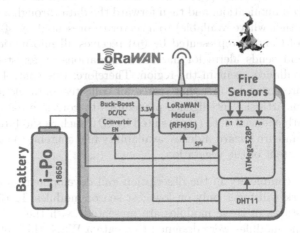

Fig. 2. The main architecture illustration of the proposed device [23].

4.1   The Core

This module was developed considering the characteristics that make it useful for forest situations, such as the ease installation and integration with WSN, and also low-cost for the use with WSN's high density. Besides, it can be placed in places where theft or vandalism may occur, such as the forest's edge regions. This module is also prepared to perform several measurements, in the case, to change or add more sensors for future approaches.

The central element of the module is the ATmega328p [26] microcontroller, hardware widely used by developers who want cost-benefit in their projects. It can be configured through the Arduino platform, either through the USB port or using the pin-outs RX and TX [25]; the latter is the means used in this work for the firmware update or configurations. Besides it is a well-known microcontroller, ATmega328p was chosen to be used in the modules because it has enough I/O analog and digital ports to support the sensors and the desired interfaces such as SPI to the LoRa module and it can be powered between 2.7 V and 5.5 V which is compatible with the Li-Po battery voltages.

4.2   Power Supply

Based on this, this module is powered by a 18650 lithium-ion cell battery that will power the entire system. The battery can supply a voltage of up to 4.1 V, so it can affect the operation of other components that operate in the 3.3 V region. To maintain the operating range of all sensors and transceivers used in

3.3 V, a buck-boost converter is applied. Therefore, this converter will ensure that no sensor changes its acquisition values during battery discharge and will also not damage the RFM95 transceiver. In this way, the 18650 battery is directly connected to the converter and the ATmega328p, and everything else is powered by the output of the DC-DC converter. Figure 3 presents the block diagram of the power supply system. Therefore, before entering the energy-saving mode, it is necessary to disable the converter through this digital pin. When it is necessary to collect and send data, it is required to activate this pin.

On the other hand, when the battery voltage reaches levels below 3.0 V, the converter stops working. In this case, the sensors and the transceiver will not work either, but the ATmega328p will continue to function because it is still in the operating voltage range. To avoid this case, one of the ATmega328p's analog ports is used to measure battery levels before performing the data collection and sending process. If the battery voltage is below 3.1 V, the sensor module sends a signal to the control center that the battery level is critical, then the microcontroller turns off the converter and the **Power Down** mode is triggered. The microcontroller will remain in **Power Down** mode and will no longer measure the sensors' values.

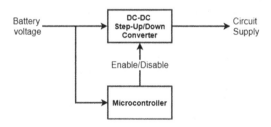

Fig. 3. DC-DC converter diagram used in each module.

4.3   Sensors

As already mentioned, the sensor modules are designed to be flexible in terms of sensor replacement or addition. It is possible to insert sensors with SPI and I2C interface (digital and analog), as long as it respects the limits of the ATmega328p. For this work, flame sensors and a device that acquires the temperature and relative humidity of the air were chosen.

These sensor modules read the ambient temperature and humidity through the DHT11 component [27]. Other temperature and humidity sensors could be used, but DHT11 was chosen to be implemented in the prototype due to the low cost, digital output, low installation complexity and also because it has a relatively small measurement tolerance ($\pm 5\%$ humidity and $\pm 2°$ temperature). In addition to the temperature and humidity measurement, there are five analog inputs that are used to acquire the commercial flame sensors values. Several flame sensors are being evaluated and will be addressed in future work. These values, both for flame and temperature and humidity, are measured over a sampling period of about 60 s. Then, they are transmitted to the control center to process these data.

4.4   LoRa Communication

The communication method to transmit the data collected from the forest must be based in low consumption (to enhance the sensor modules autonomy), long-range (due to the extensions of Portuguese forest reserves) and low-cost of implementation and operation (to maintain a good cost-benefit). Therefore, the LoRaWAN protocol emerges as a communication solution that satisfies all the listed requirements.

Among the available devices found on the market, RFM95 is the one used to approach this work, as presented in Fig. 4 a typical LoRa TM transmit sequence. This transceiver has a Long Range (LoRa) based modem, with interference immunity (which minimizes current consumption during transmission). Developed by Hope RF, this device makes it possible to achieve a sensitivity above 148 dBm, making it suitable for use in various industrial and agricultural sectors [28].

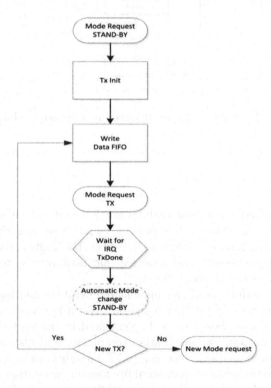

Fig. 4. RFM95/RFM96 applied in each module [28].

The RFM95 is powered by 3.3 V supplied by the DC-DC converter, so it will only be turned on after the ATmega328p microcontroller exits energy-saving mode. In this sense, the RFM95 is connected via SPI to receive from the microcontroller the data that the sensors have collected, and consequently, send to the LoRaWAN Gateway.

5   Sensor Module Assembled

Taking advantage of the tools mentioned in the previous section, a Printed Circuit Board (PCB) was created to aggregate all the tools in order to compose the sensor module. This PCB can be seen from different angles in Fig. 5, with ATMega328p used as the core, the DC-DC converter, the 18650 battery, the RFM95, the electronic components and the sensors. In which Fig. 5a indicates through a top view, the sectors distributed within the PCB, where the DC-DC converter is placed as close as possible to the battery and the microcontroller.

With an isometric view in Fig. 5b, there is a demonstration of the peripherals that need to be arranged on the edge of the board, such as serial communication for the firmware configuration, the DHT11 sensor needs to have contact with the ambient air to perform the measurement, RFM95 communication antenna to avoid signal blockages, and flame sensors cannot be blocked by other components.

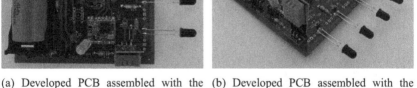

(a) Developed PCB assembled with the components (Top view).

(b) Developed PCB assembled with the components (Side view).

Fig. 5. Developed sensor module assembled in PCB.

The Fig. 6 shows the proposed low-cost prototype module finalized and deposited in a 3D printed box, with dimensions: 100 mm × 40 mm × 90 mm. There was a necessity to reorganize some peripherals, such as the arrangement of flame sensors. These were removed from the PCB and connected by wires, then they were fixed to all sides of the box, except the top and back of the sensor module.

There was no fixation on these faces because the idea is to attach these low-cost modules to the tree trunks (rear face), and also because it is not necessary to point to the sky (upper face). Another peripheral that demanded to be moved is DHT11, as it could not be inside the box. Therefore, a grid was created at the box bottom so that DHT11 could adequately measure the temperature and relative humidity air. As it is a prototype, the modules developed in this work do not yet consider the Ingress Protection (IP) standards. This standard indicates a protection scale for solids from 1 to 6 and liquids from 1 to 8. In this sense, it is necessary to dedicate a study only to determine the module structures' IP code, and therefore it will not be detailed in this work and will be further addressed.

Fig. 6. Developed sensor module in the 3D printed case.

6   Results

This section will present the results of the module developed by performing a WSN, regarding acquisition, transmission and registration. First, nine modules were assembled equal to the one described in the previous section. In this way, all modules have a DHT11 sensor and also five flame sensors aimed at each box side (except the rear and upper face). Then, the nine modules were separated in pairs, forming four sets of 2. And a module was chosen to be fixed alone. Thus, in total, five points are selected on the map to create the WSN shown in Fig. 7.

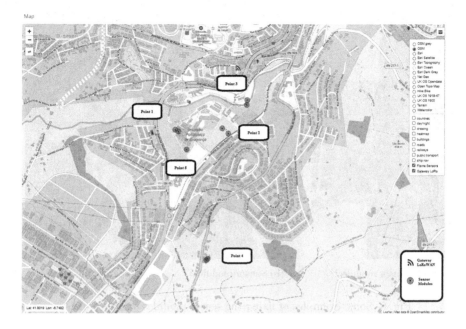

Fig. 7. Map with the sensor modules distribution forming the WSN.

The five fixation points were chosen according to the soil type and tree around the Polytechnic Institute of Bragança (IPB) campus. In this sense, the pair formed by modules 1 and 2 are joined to trees close to buildings. Module 3 and 4 are attached to tree trunks in a small orchard, and modules 5 and 6 are positioned to medium-sized trees around the Fervenza River that crosses the campus. On the other hand, modules 7 and 8 were fixed off-campus, in reserve with a high level of tree cover density. And the last module 9 is set on a tree that is planted on a yard; that is, it does not share other elements around it.

As the objective is to analyze the WSN's behavior, it was not considered the modules' positioning concerning the sun or other factors that are around the trees chosen to receive them. Just as it was not regarded as climatic events, like rainy days. However, as shown in Fig. 8, the modules were fixed on branches considered to be free, that is, branches that have their smooth surface and that would not interfere with leaves or other branches. The following subsection shows the data collected from DHT11 sensors and also from flame sensors.

(a) Sensor module 1.   (b) Sensor module 5.   (c) Sensor module 9.

Fig. 8. Some examples of fixing the sensor modules on tree trunks.

6.1   WSN Data

In order to verify the functioning of the WSN, the time interval of 60 s was configured in the firmware of each module. That is, at each time interval, the module checks the battery level, collects the environment data through the sensors and sends them to the LoRaWAN Gateway. Next, it goes into a power-saving state until the next time interval starts. The value configured for the time interval is the limit allowed according to the Things Network (TTN) server usage policies. In this way, all data is copied from the TTN to a local server and stored according to each ID, created individually for each module. The results are divided in temperature and humidity values at the beginning and for flame sensor values at the end of this subsection.

Temperature and Humidity. In Fig. 9, is shown the data collected during 24 h from the pair of sensors located at Point 1 (Module 1 and Module 2). Similarly, the graph in Fig. 10 exposes the data collected from Module 3 and Module 4 (Point 2).

As already mentioned, Point 3 and Point 4 are monitored, respectively by pairs Modules 5 and 6, and Module 7 and 8. The humidity and temperature data of these two points can be viewed through the graphs in Figs. 11 and 12.

The data reported from Module 9, inserted in Point 5, can be seen in Fig. 13. The amount of data collected during the 24 h was the same for all graphs displayed, that is, each graph has 1440 samples. This means that all WSN modules were able to carry out the monitoring procedure without losing information.

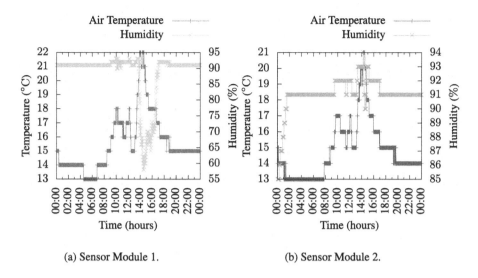

Fig. 9. Data collected from Point 1.

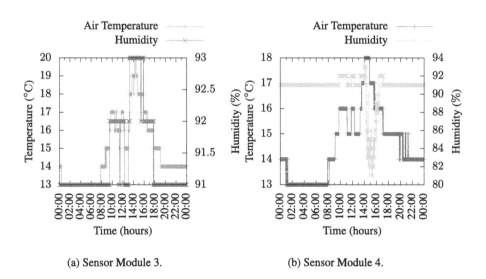

Fig. 10. Data collected from Point 2.

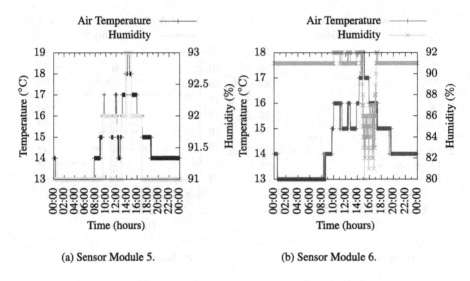

(a) Sensor Module 5.   (b) Sensor Module 6.

Fig. 11. Data collected from Point 3.

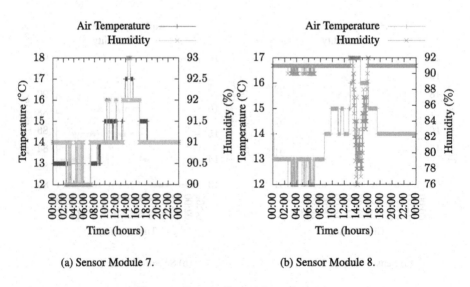

(a) Sensor Module 7.   (b) Sensor Module 8.

Fig. 12. Data collected from Point 4.

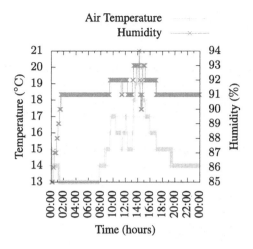

Fig. 13. Sensor Module 9, in Point 5.

Flame Sensor. As previously addressed, the developed module is equipped with five flame sensors. The results of the acquisition for modules 7 and 8, as example, are presented in Figs. 14. During the night period, the measured values are constant 1023. During the day, the acquired value decreases by an average of 1000. In fact it is true that the sunlight affects a little bit the flame sensor, but a fire ignition will be detected with lower values (around 400). It can be concluded that the modules should be placed in shadow places covered by the trees.

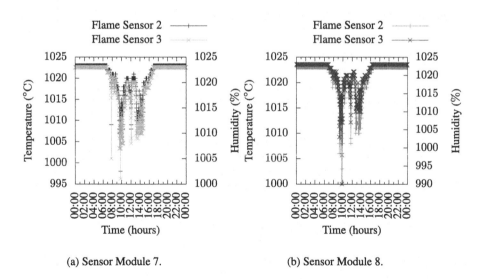

(a) Sensor Module 7.   (b) Sensor Module 8.

Fig. 14. Data collected from Point 4, Flame sensors in shadow area.

7   Conclusions and Future Work

The Forest Alert Monitoring System (SAFe) project proposes the development of innovative operations to minimize the alert time for forest fire ignitions. This project will contribute to real surveillance systems, improving firefighters and civil protection with more details and real-time information. As a basis for this project, the acquisition and communication modules, which will be spread across the forest, will gather information on various data relevant to the efficient characterization of existing forest conditions. This work addressed the developed modules that acquire and transmit the date through LoRaWAN. The hardware for these modules are presented and validated in real scenario. As future work, a new firmware will be developed to decrease the transmission rate while ensuring rapid fire detection and a battery consumption reduction. Furthermore, different flame sensors will be evaluated.

Acknowledgements. This work has been supported by Fundação La Caixa and FCT—Fundação para a Ciência e Tecnologia within the Project Scope: UIDB/5757/2020.

References

1. Amraoui, M., Pereira, M.G., DaCamara, C.C., Calado, T.J.: Atmospheric conditions associated with extreme fire activity in the Western Mediterranean region. Sci. Total Environ. **524**, 32–39 (2015)
2. Pereira, M.G., Calado, T.J., DaCamara, C.C., Calheiros, T.: Effects of regional climate change on rural fires in Portugal. Climate Res. **57**(3), 187–200 (2013)
3. ICNF - 6.° Relatório Provisório de Incêndios Rurais - 2018: 01 de Janeiro a 15 de Setembro. http://www2.icnf.pt/portal/florestas/dfci/Resource/doc/rel/2018/6-RIR-1jan-15set2018. Accessed 14 Sept 2020
4. Sistemas de Videovigilância de Prevenção de Incêndios a Partir de 2017 com apoio PO SEUR. https://poseur.portugal2020.pt/media/4140/plano_nacional_defesa_floresta_contra_incendios.pdf. Accessed 14 Sept 2020
5. Lloret, J., Garcia, M., Bri, D., Sendra, S.: A wireless sensor network deployment for rural and forest fire detection and verification. Sensors **9**(11), 8722–8747 (2009)
6. ICNF - Plano Nacional de Defesa da Floresta Contra Incêndios. http://www2.icnf.pt/portal/florestas/dfci/planos/PNDFCI. Accessed 14 Sept 2020
7. Rego, F.C., et al.: Análise da Rede Nacional de Postos de Vigia em Portugal. Relatório Final do Projecto. ADISA/CEABN-INESC/INOVAÇÃO. Iniciativa Incêndios Florestais, COTEC Portugal (2004)
8. Catry, F.X., Rego, F.C., Bação, F.L., Moreira, F.: Modeling and mapping wildfire ignition risk in Portugal. Int. J. Wildland Fire **18**(8), 921–931 (2010)
9. Silva, J.S., Rego, F.C., Fernandes, P., Rigolot, E.: Towards integrated fire management. Outcomes of the European Project Fire Paradox (2010)
10. Catry, F. X., Moreira, F., Pausas, J. G., Fernandes, P. M., Rego, F.: Cork Oak Vulnerability to Fire: The Role of Bark Harvesting. Tree Characteristics and (2012)
11. Marques, S., et al.: Assessing wildfire occurrence probability in Pinus pinaster Ait. stands in Portugal. Forest Syst. **21**, 111–120 (2012)
12. Kaur, H., Sood, S.K.: Soft-computing-centric framework for wildfire monitoring, prediction and forecasting. Soft. Comput. **24**(13), 9651–9661 (2020)

13. Sahin, Y. G.: A sensor selection model in simultaneous monitoring of multiple types of disaster. In Geospatial Informatics IX (Vol. 10992, p. 109920C). International Society for Optics and Photonics (2019)
14. Fukuhara, T., Kouyama, T., Kato, S., Nakamura, R., Takahashi, Y., Akiyama, H.: Detection of small wildfire by thermal infrared camera with the uncooled microbolometer array for 50-kg class satellite. IEEE Trans. Geosci. Remote Sens. **55**(8), 4314–4324 (2017)
15. Kyzirakos, K., et al.: Wildfire monitoring using satellite images, ontologies and linked geospatial data. J. Web Semant. **24**, 18–26 (2014)
16. Aslan, Y.E., Korpeoglu, I., Ulusoy, Ö.: A framework for use of wireless sensor networks in forest fire detection and monitoring. Comput. Environ. Urban Syst. **36**(6), 614–625 (2012)
17. Relvas, P., Almeida, J., Rego, F. C., Catry, F.: Estudo para implementação de um sistema de videovigilância florestal no Distrito de Viseu. In Silva, R., Páscoa, F. (eds.) Actas do 5° Congresso Florestal (2005)
18. Verde, J.C., Zêzere, J.L.: Assessment and validation of wildfire susceptibility and hazard in Portugal. Nat. Hazards Earth Syst. Sci. **10**(3) (2010)
19. Verde, J. C.: Wildfire susceptibility modelling in mainland Portugal (Doctoral dissertation, Universidade de Lisboa (Portugal)) (2015)
20. Müller, F., Jaeger, D., Hanewinkel, M.: Digitization in wood supply-a review on how Industry 4.0 will change the forest value chain. Comput. Electron. Agricult. **162**, 206–218 (2019)
21. Ghobakhloo, M.: Industry 4.0, digitization, and opportunities for sustainability. J. Clean. Prod. **252**, 119869 (2020)
22. LAD Sensors https://www.ladsensors.com/. Accessed 14 Sept 2020
23. Brito, T., Pereira, A.I., Lima, J., Valente, A.: Wireless sensor network for ignitions detection: an IoT approach. Electronics **9**(6), 893 (2020)
24. Brito, T., Pereira, A. I., Lima, J., Castro, J. P., Valente, A.: Optimal sensors positioning to detect forest fire ignitions. In: Proceedings of the 9th International Conference on Operations Research and Enterprise Systems, pp. 411–418 (2020)
25. Payne, E.K., Lu, S., Wang, Q., Wu, L.: Concept of Designing Thermal Condition Monitoring System with ZigBee/GSM Communication Link for Distributed Energy Resources Network in Rural and Remote Applications. Processes **7**(6), 383 (2019)
26. ATmega328p - Microchip. http://ww1.microchip.com/downloads/en/DeviceDoc/ATmega48A-PA-88A-PA-168A-PA-328-P-DS-DS40002061B.pdf. Accessed 14 Sept 2020
27. Singh, A., Singh, G.: Review on temperature & humidity sensing using IoT. Int. J. Adv. Res. Comput. Sci. Software Eng. **6**(2), 234–240 (2016)
28. RFM95 and RFM96 - Hope RF. https://www.hoperf.com/data/upload/portal/20190801/RFM95W-V2.0.pdf. Accessed 14 Sept 2020

NetButler: Voice-Based Edge/Cloud Virtual Assistant for Home Network Management

Diogo Martins[1,2], Bruno Parreira[2], Pedro M. Santos[1,3(✉)] (iD),
and Sérgio Figueiredo[2]

[1] Universidade do Porto, Faculdade de Engenharia, Porto, Portugal
[2] Altran Portugal, Porto, Portugal
{diogo.leitemartins,bruno.parreira,sergio.figueiredo}@altran.com
[3] CISTER Research Center, Instituto Politécnico do Porto, Porto, Portugal
pss@isep.ipp.pt

Abstract. Virtual assistants (VA) are becoming a standard tool in many aspects of our daily lives that require technical support. Voice-based VAs in particular, such as Amazon Alexa and Google Assistant, have become common in smart phones and domestic IoT devices (e.g., Google Home, Amazon Echo), replying to user inquiries (e.g., weather forecast) or performing simple services (e.g., play music). Through dedicated interfaces, VAs can be used or extended to support new services, and one particular area typically requiring assistance is the management of home networks. Activating specific features or troubleshooting connectivity problems may be difficult or impossible for users that are not tech-savvy. In this paper we introduce NetButler, a voice-based virtual assistant tailored to support the management of home networks, that leverages a third-party cloud-based voice service (Alexa) and dedicated routines at the home gateway. Offered functionalities are the setup of a guest network and diagnosis of connectivity problems, by quantifying the signal strength of the devices in the local network and performing a throughput test to an external server. We evaluate the user experience with the NetButler system with 8 test users. We report an average of up to 15 s to set up a guest network and between 30 to 60 s to diagnose various problems, and we find overall user satisfaction to be 3.75 in a 1-to-5 scale by means of a after-interaction questionnaire.

Keywords: Virtual assistant · Voice recognition/synthesis · Home network management

1 Introduction

A relevant share of the clients of residential broadband services have limited knowledge about the operation of modern communication networks and their own domestic network. Addressing issues or enabling additional functionalities

S. Paiva et al. (Eds.): SmartCity360° 2020, LNICST 372, pp. 228–245, 2021.
https://doi.org/10.1007/978-3-030-76063-2_17

- which are apparently hidden or out-of-reach - in their domestic network often involves contacting a support call center. This entails a number of inconveniences for both service provider and client: the service provider needs to assign human resources to customer service; it is hard to debug the problem with the imperfect information provided by the client; and the client may grow impatient or frustrated with the unfruitful interaction with another person. The problem is further aggravated by the relentless growth of the ecosystem of Internet-of-Things (IoT) devices, whose world market is estimated to reach US$ 135.3 billion by 2025 [7]. As home networks become crowded with personal devices and household appliances requiring Internet connection, clients that are not tech-savvy are increasingly more exposed to non-trivial connectivity problems.

Virtual assistants (VA) may offer an alternative to the traditional customer support processes, specifically first-line customer support. VAs are becoming increasingly relevant as they offer an intuitive and streamlined interaction experience with humans, whether through static interfaces (questionnaires), text messaging (*chatbots*), or voice interaction. On the latter category, voice-activated VAs are already offered as an embedded service or app in the smart phones and domestic IoT products of most major manufacturers of consumer electronics: some prominent examples include Amazon Alexa, Google Assistant, Apple Siri, and Microsoft Cortana. To offer some insight on their relevance, it is estimated that by 2027 the market size of VAs will be worth US$ 45.1 billion [6]. VAs allow a number of functionalities such as playing music, control smart devices, inform the user about various subjects (e.g., weather information), and even the possibility of hotel room reservation [13]. However, the potential of these systems for transforming household connectivity management into a more straightforward process for regular users has still not been properly exploited

In this paper we present **NetButler**, a voice-activated VA that helps the user enable functionalities and solve connectivity problems in the domestic network. The user communicates with the VA via smart phone, presenting the need/problem in question; the VA then applies the necessary actions at the home gateway or local-network router (typically, in households, these two network devices are in the same physical device provided by the ISP, so we use both terms interchangeably). Internally, the VA is composed by a third-party voice recognition/synthesis service, a cloud-hosted VA manager, and an agent at the home gateway to carry out the necessary routines. In its current version, the VA is able, based on the user's voice inputs, to set up a Wi-Fi *Guest* network and perform network diagnostics such as detecting wireless devices with poor signal strength in the WLAN network and testing bandwidth to external servers.

Our contributions are the following:

- Identification of scenarios of human-VA interaction towards diagnosing problems/activating features in home networks and their associated lexical field;
- Design of the VA architecture and implementation of its components in the home gateway and in third-party cloud services, whose entry point is the user's smart phone;

– Evaluation of the system with real users, that report low interaction times and overall positive experience.

The remainder of the article is as follows. In Sect. 2 we review the relevant works and technology related with voice-based virtual assistants. The system architecture and implemented use-cases are presented in Sect. 3. In Sect. 4, we describe an evaluation of the user experience with human testers. Final remarks are drawn in Sect. 5.

2   State-of-the-Art

Home Automation Systems (HAS): Several projects were carried out with the aim of designing and implementing an architecture control equipment in a domestic environment. In [3], a message-based middleware platform was implemented to connect different types of IoT devices to monitor the energy used by household appliances. The interface is made through the Telegram application (application for text messages and multimedia content), in which the user interacts with an chatbot assistant. Energy consumption in KWh and cost for various timescales (per day, month, etc.) are shown through a ThingSpeak dashboard. The authors of [1] propose an architecture that supports remote control equipment through a web interface, in addition to virtual assistant control. The architecture includes sensors placed in several rooms measure temperature and humidity and actuators to control light intensity in the rooms, and integrates several types of open-source services: Firebase for the database, Google's Web-Speech for speech recognition, and DialogFlow for integrating Natural Language Processing (NLP) with the IoT system. The authors report that about 70% of the response time is spent by the NLP module, while the remaining is spent on processing in microcontrollers and communication between modules. In [12], a Home Automation System (HAS) controlled by an Android application communicates with the equipment in the house and with a web server is reported. The system receives voice commands through the mobile device and a VRS (Voice Recognition System) tool interprets and forwards the commands, in text form, to the microcontroller and the web server.

Systems Implementing and Using Voice-Based Assistants: In [14], a virtual assistant prototype that reacts to the emotion displayed by the user is proposed. The key points on the user face (eyes, nose and mouth) are monitored to extract the associated emotion. While emotion identification is satisfactory, the intensity of the emotion is quite harder to identify. In [8], an webpage-based assistant interacts with university students and clarifies doubts regarding features/services. Through data collected at a satisfaction questionnaire at the end of the interaction, high rates of approval by the students were registered. The authors of [15] report a virtual assistant developed to assist users in online purchasing. The assistant is divided into agents responsible for 4 different stages in the interaction with the user. Finally, a virtual assistant to support human-human interaction in virtual environments is reported in [9]. The assistant offers suggestions of conversation topics in order to promote interactions between people from different cultures. Successful tests have been performed with interactions between Americans and Japanese.

Voice-Based Virtual Assistants: Commercially available voice-based virtual assistants include Amazon Alexa, Google Assistant, Apple Siri, and Microsoft Cortana. The performance indicators of a virtual assistant (e.g., naturalness the accuracy of the response) often depend on the functionality being evaluated [13]. Open-source virtual assistants are also available and offer flexibility in order to be adapted to the particular needs of the target application. The Mycroft virtual assistant[1] is a community-supported virtual assistant; users can purchase additional features from an online marketplace. The Snips virtual assistant [4] is similar to Mycroft, i.e., it is community-supported, available for various platforms and offers a vast library of features online. A major difference is that this assistant can perform offline processing (without access to a cloud); this reinforces security (as no personal data is sent to the cloud) but requires a domestic hosting device powerful enough to host the speech recognition/synthesis technologies. This tool has been discontinued due to acquisition by another firm[2].

Systems for Voice-Based Network Interactions: Limited research has been realized on enabling voice-enabled network management systems. Authors in [2] proposed a wireless home automation system which automatically translates spoken words into text commands using MATLAB, which are then transmitted to a microcontroller controlling the household appliances via their corresponding relays. Rajalakshmi et al. [11] proposed a system to connect and control IoT devices using voice. The solution integrated: i) Alexa Voice Service for developing a customized skill for connecting IoT devices and publishing them; ii) Amazon Web Services (AWS) IoT service as centralized management platform for the multiple IoT devices; and iii) AWS Lambda service trigger to process voice commands from the user. The authors also suggest possibilities regarding the extension to computer networking and data monitoring.

3   NetButler: A Virtual Assistant for Domestic Networks

The system architecture and components are the following (depicted in Fig. 1):

- **Voice Recognition/Synthesis (VRS) Service:** natural language processor responsible for mapping user voice utterances (i.e., spoken words or sentences) into *intents* that the system can act on, and convert system replies into speech;
- **User Equipment:** microphone/speaker-equipped device through which the user interacts with the VRS (e.g. smart phone);

---

[1] https://mycroft.ai/.
[2] https://snips.ai/.

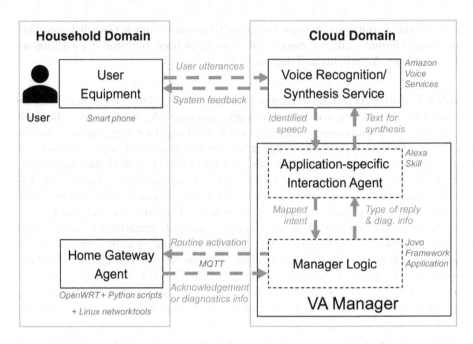

Fig. 1. Architecture of the voice-based home gateway assistant. Conceptual elements in black; technological elements (in the current version) in gray; data flows in orange.

- **VA Manager:** component that handles the interaction with the user (through a sub-component, the **application-specific interaction agent**) and commands the execution of the necessary actions at the home gateway based on the user inputs (through a second sub-component, the **manager logic**);
- **Home Gateway Agent:** component running on the home gateway/router that carries out the necessary actions as commanded by the VA manager.

We would like to highlight that the VRS service (and the VA Manager) could, in principle and in alternative to the present architecture, be hosted locally, i.e., at the user's premises. However, at the time of the execution of this project, the use of a third-party cloud-based VRS system was found to be the only viable option; we provide additional details at the end of Sect. 3.2.

The system's generic operation is as follows.

1. The user always initiates the interaction with the system through the user equipment (i.e., a smart phone in the current implementation), by instantiating the interface of the voice recognition/synthesis service (in smart phones, typically a service pre-installed in the device's OS, but possibly also an after-market app);
2. The cloud-based VRS service transforms the user's utterances into text, that in turn is processed by the application-specific interaction agent to extract the underlying intent;

3. The VA manager will map the received intent into one of several use-case workflows (described in the following subsection). In all such workflows, the VA manager signals the home gateway to initiate routines to implement/debug the identified need/problem. In some workflows, the VA may have to request additional information from the user before initiating those routines.

4. After the setup/debugging routines have been carried out at the home gateway, the home gateway replies to the VA manager with relevant confirmation or diagnostic information. The VA manager may instruct the application-specific interaction agent to forward a reply to the user (through the VRS service), with or without query-specific information.

5. Depending on the user reply, the interaction may be terminated or continue, in case the prior setup/resolution attempts were not successful and the use-case workflow encompasses additional steps for feature setup/debugging.

The following subsection describes the two use-cases developed for this system, and we conclude the section with a description of the current NetButler implementation.

3.1 NetButler Use-Cases and Respective System Operation

The voice-based assistant provides support to two main classes of needs/ problems, and offers execution of stand-alone functions. We now describe them in two dimensions: from the user's perspective, and in terms of the system's internal workflow.

Use-Case 1 (UC1) – Creation of Guest Network: This use case aims at allowing the user to create a *Guest* network, without password and isolated through a firewall from the household network, at the time of the request or at a scheduled time, i.e. activating the network at a specific time and/or during a certain period. Some utterances associated to this use case are *"Share my Internet"*, *"Turn on the Guest Wi-Fi"* and *"Activate the Wi-Fi for my guests"*.

Internally, after the user requests the provisioning of network connectivity for guests, the VRS forwards the text/intent to the VA manager, that in turn commands the home gateway agent to activate the *Guest* network. The VA manager then sends a reply to the VRS system confirming that the network will be available within a few seconds, or at a time in the future, if it is being scheduled. A similar procedure is available to disable the network. Figure 2 describes the procedure to activate a *Guest* network.

Use-Case 2 (UC2) – Diagnosis of Connectivity Issues: In this use case, the user informs the system he/she is experiencing limited connectivity to the Internet or a poor quality connection, thus hampering the use of online services. It is presumed that the user does not know the cause of such issues; the system will help the user identify the reason and offer suggestions to troubleshoot the

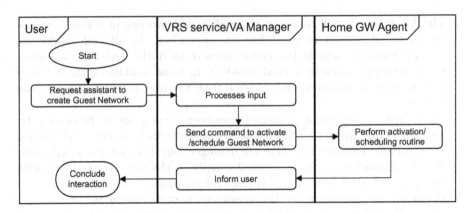

Fig. 2. System workflow to create a guest network.

problem. The utterances associated to this use-case are, for example, *"I am having Internet problems"*, *"I am having problems watching a video"* and *"I can't access the internet"*.

Internally, NetButler addresses this as follows. The user initiates the interaction with NetButler, through the third-party VRS service. The VA manager acts on the intent detected from the user's utterance, initiating a diagnostic routine at the home gateway to ascertain the cause of the problem. Once the routine is complete, results are sent back to the VA manager that in turn builds a reply to the user and instructs the VRS to synthesize it. This procedure is shown in Fig. 3.

Table 1. Selected queries and predefined replies to stand-alone functions.

Function	Query	Reply
Speedtest	Run a speed test Check my internet speed How fast is my internet? Measure my internet speed What is my latency?	The results of the speed test are the following: your download speed is [x] megabits per second, your upload speed is [y] megabits per second, and your latency is [z] milliseconds
Reboot	Reset the router Restart the router Reboot the router Turn the router off and on again	Your router will reboot in a few seconds
#devices	How many devices are connected? How many devices are using Internet? Count devices connected to the network	You have [x] devices connected to your network

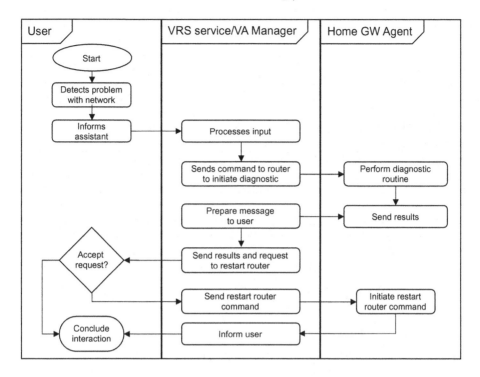

Fig. 3. System workflow to diagnose connectivity issues.

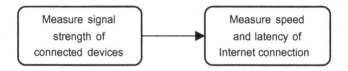

Fig. 4. Sub-routines of the diagnostic routine.

The routine checks for two possible causes, by measuring and reporting related metrics back to the user. In both cases, a threshold is defined for the system to decide whether the user should be informed of that potential cause or not. Even if an issue is detected and reported, NetButler always inquires the user if he/she wishes to proceed with the diagnostic routine. The assistant always terminates the interaction by inquiring the user whether the home gateway should be rebooted; this operation is typically performed by first line customer support as it solves many common problems. The sub-routines and tested causes are presented next following order (and summarized in Fig. 4 for convenience):

Poor signal quality: the system provides the user with the signal strength of wireless devices in the local network. We enforce a threshold of $-80\,\mathrm{dBm}$ to decide whether a device as *good* or *poor* signal strength; NetButler informs that at least one device with weak signal strength was found. System replies are as follows:

At least one device with below-threshold signal strength: *I detected at least one device with low WI-FI signal. If your device is far away from the router you might get Internet issues. Check your devices signal strength and get closer to the router if you find your signal low. If your device has good signal strength I can run a speed test to finish the diagnosis. Can I run it?*

All devices with above-threshold signal strength: *I don't detect any problems with the signal power on your devices. Can I run a speed test to finish the diagnosis?*

External bandwidth limitation: the system performs a connection speed test to a cloud server from the home gateway. We apply a threshold of 25 Mbit/s (based on Netflix's recommended connection speed[3]) to classify the Internet connectivity as *acceptable* or *poor*. The possible replies are:

Poor service (low throughput) observed: *I figured that your Internet speed is very low at the moment, there is nothing you can do since the problem is external. Can I reboot the router?*

Acceptable service/throughput observed: *The results of the speed test show me that you should be able to use your Internet with no problem. If you are having any issues check the other connected devices for any possible activity regarding the usage of your Internet. You might want to interrupt any download or video streams on other devices. Do you wish to reboot the router?*

Stand-Alone Functions: NetButler offers the user the option to execute some stand-alone functions (i.e., outside the context of a diagnostic routine), namely: (i) run an Internet speed and latency test (**Speedtest**); (b) reboot the device (**Reboot**); and (iii) count the number of devices in the local network (**#devices**). Table 1 presents some possible queries and the predefined replies for the stand-alone functions.

3.2   Technological Components and Integration

The different system components were implemented with the following technologies:

- Voice Recognition/Synthesizer Cloud Service: **Amazon Alexa**
- VA Manager: **Alexa Skills Kit & Jovo Framework**
- Home Gateway Agent: **Linux Networking Tools**

---

[3] https://help.netflix.com/en/node/306.

Additionally, to support the communication between the VA manager and the home gateway agent, MQTT is used. We now motivate these options and explain the interaction between components that enables the system's operation.

Amazon Alexa: Amazon Alexa offers cloud-based speech interpretation and synthesis services that can be integrated with external applications. External applications use Alexa through *Alexa Skills*, that can be viewed (in some sense) as an application-specific instance of Alexa. The programming of a Skill involves providing a list of utterances and corresponding intentions related to the target application, alongside some configurations to establish a connection to the external application. After a Skill is set up, the following occurs: (a) the generic Alexa interaction agent is capable of identifying a user's request for the target application (e.g., NetButler), hence forwarding all subsequent user-Alexa interaction (for that session) to the related Skill; (b) the Skill interprets user inputs to verify if they match utterances defined in the Skill configuration, and forwards the corresponding intention to the external application components, namely Jovo; (c) as the external application components provides feedback, the Skill triggers the speech synthesis of the reply provided by the external application components through Alexa Voice Services. The smart phone component to connect to the cloud-based speech processor is also provided by Amazon.

Alexa Skills Kit and Jovo Framework: The Skills described earlier are offered by Alexa Skills Kit[4] (ASK). Alexa's Skills can be programmed with a dedicated SDK or through a third-party platform such as Jovo Framework. Jovo[5] allows to develop and run applications that use the voice interaction services from third-party providers (e.g., Amazon Alexa, Google Assistant and Samsung Bixby). The use of the Jovo Framework was partly responsible for the option of using Amazon Alexa; from the three options mentioned earlier, Amazon Alexa was chosen as it features the largest presence in households [5].

The Jovo Framework offers abstraction to the programming of Alexa Skills. Applications are programmed in Node Javascript, and the association with the Alexa online console is made through a *webhook* created by the framework. The Jovo application can be executed in any machine where the Jovo framework is installed (in our implementation we used a standard personal computer, but it could be equally deployed in a cloud server). The application's source code files can be binned into two categories: the user input mapping files and the VA manager logic. In the first category, user inputs are organized in a data structure within a JSON file. Within the file are all voice commands that may be recognized during the interaction of the user with the system. These phrases are organized in categories called **intents**, i.e., the idea or will that the user wants to transmit when interacting with the assistant. For example, the phrases *"Run a speed test"* and *"How fast is my Internet?"* belong the same intent,

---

[4] https://developer.amazon.com/en-GB/alexa/alexa-skills-kit.
[5] https://www.jovo.tech.

which would be *Speed test.* It also allows for slots to be filled in by the user, e.g., the time for scheduling the creation of the *Guest* network.

The VA manager logic handles the requests and subsequent interaction with the user. Once the VA manager receives from the VRS service the user utterance in text form, the VA manager searches the user input mapping files for a related utterance and identifies the corresponding intent. Depending on the identified intent, the system proceeds to follow one of the workflows described in Figs. 2 and 3 or to execute one of the stand-alone functions. To that end, the VA manager prepares MQTT messages to be transmitted to the home gateway agent indicating the operations to be realized, to which the home gateway agent will reply with confirmation messages or the requested data. In that line, the VA manager also carries out a initial setup to subscribe the topics for which the router publishes and present some error messages in case the connection to the broker fails. The support for MQTT communication in the Jovo application is provided by the dedicated library MQTT.js[6]. The set of pre-defined replies to be offered to the user by NetButler is also stored in the VA manager logic.

Linux Networking Tools: The home gateway/router can be equipped with OpenWRT[7], a well-established open-source Linux-based operating system tailored for routers and network devices. Recall that we assume the home gateway and local-network router to be located in the same physical device, hence we use both terms are used interchangeably. In the scope of our system, the agent hosted at home gateway is composed of two elements: the agent itself, programmed in Python scripts and resorting to Linux commands and packages when necessary, and a MQTT broker that supports the communication with the VA manager. The home gateway agent starts by subscribing all topics on which the VA manager posts messages and vice versa. Topics are aligned with the particular features/problems being tackled by the system, e.g., *Guest Network.*

Upon reception of a new message, the agent has routines to perform all the functionalities described in Sect. 3.1: activate/deactivate of the *Guest* network; measure signal strength of devices; measure Internet speed and latency; reboot the device; and count number of devices. The creation of the *Guest* WLAN network is performed using Unified Configuration Interface (UCI), an interface provided by OpenWRT for editing the router settings. The created *Guest* network is detached from the remainder of the local network, forwarding the clients' traffic directly to the WAN (Wide Area Network) port. The speed and latency tests, as well as device counting and signal strength measurements, are performed by the Python module *speedtest-cli*[8]. There is also a support routine to encode the data to send to the assistant: due to the fact that the Alexa platform does not allow text inputs to contain numbers as numerals, a third-party library is used to transform numerals into their names[9]. For reference, development and implementation of the home gateway agent were carried out in a Linksys WRT-1200 router.

---

[6] https://www.npmjs.com/package/mqtt.

[7] https://openwrt.org/.

[8] https://github.com/sivel/speedtest-cli.

[9] https://github.com/collin5/python-n2w.

As a remark about the adopted architecture, in early design stages we set as desirable features: (i) the use of an open-source virtual assistant; (ii) implement an architecture that would be local to the user's network, i.e., not requiring a cloud component; (iii) avoid the need for additional hardware/devices. However, at the time of this work, there were no readily-available open-source products that would allow this architecture to be implemented. The Snips virtual assistant [4], suited for deployment in Android phones, would allow for the system to be independent of any connection to the Internet, but the service has been discontinued in January 2020. We tried installing the alternative open-source voice-based VA, Mycroft, in the home gateway with the aid of external memory, but this approach proved unsuccessful due to the gateway's limited capabilities. The only remaining solution to offer a fully-local experience would be to deploy an additional physical device in the user's household to run Mycroft, a compromise that we considered to be extremely burdensome and outweighing the disadvantages incurred by waiving the first two desired features.

4 Performance Evaluation

The objective of this section is to evaluate the user experience when using the proposed virtual assistant. For that, three dedicated tests were designed and carried out by eight test users. At the end of the tests, the users are asked to fill a questionnaire to assess the quality of the interaction and outcomes.

4.1 Tests Description and Evaluation Metrics

The three tests map directly into the two use-cases of user-system interaction presented in Sect. 3.1, aiming at evaluating the use-case workflows under controlled conditions. The second use-case, *Diagnosis of Connectivity Issues*, was assigned two independent tests as the system is able to identify two potential causes for connectivity problems.

The sequence of steps is common to all tests: the user interacts with the system, that in turn replies with information about the problem and/or suggestions to address it. Some tests require may subsequent user-system interaction, or specific preparation to set up the conditions necessary for the test. In all cases, user-system interaction is performed using a smart phone.

Test 1 (T1) – Activation and Deactivation of Guest Network: There are no prerequisites for this test. The user interacts with a virtual assistant and the system enables the *Guest* network; in turn, the user checks the successful creation of the *Guest* network in the smart phone. In a second stage, the user interacts with the assistant to disable the network; a new check is made on the user's smart phone to confirm the *Guest* network has been disabled. We break down this test in two parts: **T1/On** (turning on the *Guest* network) and **T1/Off** (turning off).

Test 2 (T2) – Weak Device Signal: The prerequisite for this test is that the user must be at distance from the home gateway such that the signal strength of the user's smart phone reaching the home gateway is low (less than -80 dBm). The user initiates the interaction with NetButler through the smart phone, indicating issues in accessing the Internet. The system performs the first of the two diagnostic sub-routines described in Fig. 4 – measurement of the device's signal strength – and identifies the cause of the problem at the end of the first sub-routine – poor signal strength. The system suggests the user to bring the device closer to the gateway to experience higher signal strength and, consequently, improve service quality.

Test 3 (T3) – Low Internet Speed: In this test, the user simulates to be experiencing low Internet speed, that the system addresses by measuring the throughput and latency of a connection to an external server. As a prerequisite, the user's device must be within range of the home gateway to obtain good signal strength. The user starts the test by complaining about the quality of Internet service to the virtual assistant, that then initiates the two-stage diagnostic routine. After the device's signal strength is deemed appropriate in the first sub-routine, the system proceeds to measure throughput and latency and provides feedback on whether observed throughput is acceptable or poor. As this is the final stage of the diagnostic routine, the system always terminates the interaction after this feedback. Hence, the interaction time does not change considerably whether an actual bandwidth limitation is in place or not (and hence we did not enforce it as a prerequisite).

We evaluated the quality of the system-user interaction through an quantitative metric – the duration of the interaction – and a qualitative analysis – identification of difficulties throughout the interaction, such as misunderstandings by the user and/or system of the counterpart's intentions or feedback, respectively. Additionally, we carried out a subjective evaluation through a questionnaire filled by the users regarding their experience with the virtual assistant. The 6 questions are presented in Table 2 (note that questions were posed in Portuguese; a translation is presented). Testers were asked to reply on a Likert scale [10] of 1–5 (1 being the least positive feedback and 5 the most positive feedback).

4.2   Evaluation

The pool of available test users was limited to eight people and composed mostly of young people (below 30 years old), due to the restrictions imposed by the COVID-19 situation; we intend to expand our set of system testers in the future to obtain more representative results. The eight users were binned into the following categories:

- *Adult:* 2 males with 45 and 53 years and a female with 50 years, background on engineering and accountancy;
- *Young adult with IT background:* 2 males of 19 and 23 years;

Table 2. Questionnaire posed to testers (translated from Portuguese).

Questions	Scale and Options
1. How do you classify the clarity and objectivity of the answers presented by the system?	1-Unclear; 3-Sufficient; 5-Clear
2. How do you classify the degree of technical terminology in the speech?	1-High; 3-Intermediate; 5-Low
3. How do you classify the suitability of the proposed solutions to your problem/need?	1-Inadequate; 3-Helpful; 5-Ideal
4. How do you classify the speed with which the system identified the problem/need?	1-Slow; 3-Appropriate; 5-Fast
5. Overall, how do you classify your experience with the virtual assistant?	1-Bad; 3-Average; 5-Good
6. Do you consider that virtual assistants can help in managing home networks?	1-No; 3-Maybe; 5-Yes

Table 3. Duration of interaction (in seconds).

	T1/On	T1/Off	T2	T3
Avg. μ	14.3	13.1	31.4	68.6
Std. dev. σ	1.030	0.661	1.323	1.580

– *Young adult with non-IT background:* 2 females with 22 and 23 years and a male with 25 years.

All users were Portuguese, albeit queries to the system must be made in English. The users were instructed about each use-case, but were not given any indications about the format and/or terminology that their query should follow. Some examples of posed questions per test are: **T1:** "I want to share my Internet."; **T2:** "I don't have Internet."; **T3:** "My Internet connection is slow". Each one of the 8 users performed all three tests, totalling 24 tests.

Interaction Duration and Issues: Table 3 reports the average duration (and respective standard deviation) for all tests. Tests T1/On & T1/Off, that address a well-defined functionality, took 14.3 s and 13.1 s in average respectively. In turn, tests T2 and T3 relate to troubleshooting use-cases and hence last more due to the diagnostic routine – 31.4 s & 68.6 s respectively. In fact, T3 takes more time simply because both steps of the diagnostic routine are performed. Test duration among the eight users was very similar, as standard deviation is fairly small; this shows that the system offers a consistent user experience.

The values presented for the interaction duration consider only the tests in which the system correctly identified the target issue from the initial user input. Throughout the 24 tests, there were a total of 4 occurrences in which the initial user input did not succeed in starting the interaction. In two of the cases, the

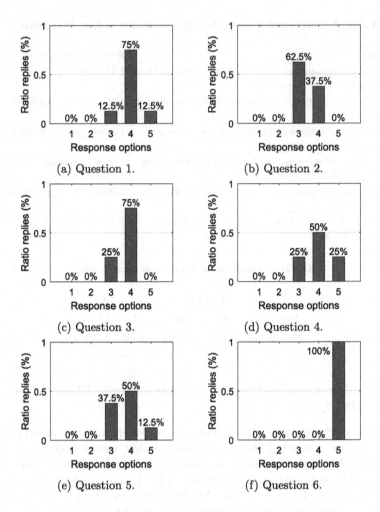

Fig. 5. Replies to user experience questionnaire.

users did not mastered the English language, and the query had to be rephrased; in the other two cases, the user utterance was not recognized by the system.

User Experience and Satisfaction: Figure 5 presents the replies to the questionnaire performed at the end of the tests. The clarity of the responses provided by the system was judged to be of level 4 (out of 5, with 3 being *Sufficient* and 5 being *Clear*) by 75% of the users. The level of technical terminology was deemed *Intermediate* by 62.5% of the users, with the remainder of the users considering it to be tendentially *Low*. This shows that the users experienced a natural interaction with the VA and understood the replies it provided; this can be considered an advantage given that the system aims to support non-tech-savvy users. The pertinence of the proposed solutions and speed of the resolution were also perceived as positive by the users: users reporting a level of 4 out 5 amounted to 75% regarding perceived pertinence and 50% regarding speed. Finally, we observed an overall good appreciation of the system, as shown by the answers to Question 5 (*"Overall, how do you classify your experience with the virtual assistant?"*), with 62,5% of the users reporting a satisfaction level of 4 or higher.

5 Conclusion

We present **NetButler**, a voice-based virtual assistant that helps clients of residential broadband services to address needs and problems in their domestic networks. The system leverages Amazon's natural language processing (NLP) service Alexa and operates routines in the home gateway through Linux/OpenWRT networking tools; a cloud-hosted VA manager orchestrates user interaction and home gateway operations. We evaluate the user experience and perception of the system under three use-cases: creation of a guest network, poor signal quality, and poor Internet service due to external causes. In evaluation with 8 non-technical users, the system was able to address all user requests with interaction time greatly inferior to those that a call to a support center would entail. Half the users reported an experience satisfaction level of 4 in a 1-to-5 Likert scale, with 5 being the most positive.

All test users highlighted, in the final question of questionnaire (*"Do you consider that virtual assistants can help in managing home networks?"*), the tremendous potential of the virtual assistants. This motivates us to pursue follow-up work to the current version of NetButler. First, we plan to carry out larger-scale user experience tests, as the pool of users in the current work was fairly limited and biased towards younger users. A particular issue to be addressed is the identification of the user's own device: while the home gateway is able to report MAC addresses, NetButler is currently not able to learn the MAC address of the user's device (as communication between the smart phone and VA Manager is done through the third-party Alexa tool) nor offers the option for the user to input it. This feature would be helpful to provide more meaningful indications to the user regarding his/her own device. We will continue to explore the possibility of a local solution, i.e., to have the voice-assistant deployed at the user's home (e.g., in the home gateway or smart phone), so that no connection to the Internet is required. Additional features, such as dynamic bandwidth adjustment, will be studied; and support for other languages will be incorporated, given that we observed this aspect to be critical to the naturalness of the interaction.

Acknowledgements. This work was partially supported by National Funds through FCT/MCTES (Portuguese Foundation for Science and Technology), within the CISTER Research Unit (UIDB/04234/2020).

References

1. Alexakis, G., Panagiotakis, S., Fragkakis, A., Markakis, E., Kostas, V.: Control of smart home operations using natural language processing, voice recognition and IoT technologies in a multi-tier architecture. Designs **3**, 32 (2019). https://doi.org/10.3390/designs3030032
2. Amrutha, S.R., Aravind, S., Mathew, A., Sugathan, S.: Voice controlled smart home. Int. J. Emerg. Technol. Adv. Eng. **5**(1) Jan 2015
3. Chilcañán, D., Navas, P., Escobar, M.: Virtual assistant for IoT process management, using a middleware. In: Proceedings of the 2018 2nd International Conference on Algorithms, Computing and Systems, pp. 209–213 (2018)
4. Coucke, A., et al.: Snips voice platform: an embedded spoken language understanding system for private-by-design voice interfaces. CoRR (2018). http://arxiv.org/abs/1805.10190
5. eMarketer: Alexa, say what?! Voice-enabled speaker usage to grow nearly 130% this year, May 2017. https://www.emarketer.com/Article/Alexa-Say-What-Voice-Enabled-Speaker-Usage-Grow-Nearly-130-This-Year/1015812. Accessed July 2020
6. Grand View Research: Intelligent virtual assistant market size, share & trends analysis report by product (chatbot, smart speakers), by technology, by application (BFSI, healthcare, education), by region, and segment forecasts, 2020–2027, April 2020. https://www.grandviewresearch.com/industry-analysis/intelligent-virtual-assistant-industry. Accessed July 2020
7. Grand View Research: Smart home market with COVID-19 impact analysis by product (lighting control, security & access control, HVAC control, entertainment, home healthcare), software & services (proactive, behavioural), and region - global forecast to 2025, June 2020. https://www.marketsandmarkets.com/Market-Reports/smart-homes-and-assisted-living-advanced-technologie-and-global-market-121.html. Accessed July 2020
8. Harvey, P.H., Currie, E., Daryanani, P., Augusto, J.C.: Enhancing student support with a virtual assistant. In: Vincenti, G., Bucciero, A., Vaz de Carvalho, C. (eds.) eLEOT 2015. LNICST, vol. 160, pp. 101–109. Springer, Cham (2016). https://doi.org/10.1007/978-3-319-28883-3_13
9. Isbister, K., Nakanishi, H., Ishida, T., Nass, C.: Helper agent: designing an assistant for human-human interaction in a virtual meeting space. In: Proceedings of the SIGCHI Conference on Human Factors in Computing Systems (CHI 2000), pp. 57–64. Association for Computing Machinery, New York (2000). https://doi.org/10.1145/332040.332407
10. Likert, R.: A technique for the measurement of attitudes. Arch. Psychol. **140**, 1–55 (1932)
11. Rajalakshmi, A., Shahnasser, H.: Internet of Things using Node-Red and Alexa. In: 2017 17th International Symposium on Communications and Information Technologies (ISCIT), pp. 1–4, September 2017. https://doi.org/10.1109/ISCIT.2017.8261194
12. Tharaniya Soundhari, M., Brilly Sangeetha, S.: Intelligent interface based speech recognition for home automation using android application. In: 2015 International Conference on Innovations in Information, Embedded and Communication Systems (ICIIECS), pp. 1–11, March 2015. https://doi.org/10.1109/ICIIECS.2015.7192988
13. Vtyurina, A., Fourney, A.: Exploring the role of conversational cues in guided task support with virtual assistants. In: Proceedings of the 2018 CHI Conference on Human Factors in Computing Systems (CHI 2018). Association for Computing Machinery, New York (2018). https://doi.org/10.1145/3173574.3173782

14. Wang, Z., Cheng, N., Fan, Y., Liu, J., Zhu, C.: Construction of virtual assistant based on basic emotions theory. In: Tao, J., Tan, T., Picard, R.W. (eds.) ACII 2005. LNCS, vol. 3784, pp. 574–581. Springer, Heidelberg (2005). https://doi.org/10.1007/11573548_74

15. Xu, B., Pan, Z., Yang, H.: Agent-based model for intelligent shopping assistant and its application. In: The First Conference on Affective Computing and Intelligent Interaction, Beijing, pp. 306–311 (2003)

Low-Cost LoRa-Based IoT Edge Device for Indoor Air Quality Management in Schools

António Abreu[1], Sérgio I. Lopes[1,2(✉)], Vitor Manso[3], and António Curado[4]

[1] ADiT - Instituto Politécnico de Viana do Castelo, Viana do Castelo, Portugal
[2] IT - Instituto de Telecomunicações, Campus de Santiago, Aveiro, Portugal
sil@estg.ipvc.pt
[3] Digiheart - Serviços em Tecnologias de Informação, Viana do Castelo, Portugal
[4] Prometheus - Instituto Politécnico de Viana do Castelo, Viana do Castelo, Portugal

Abstract. Indoor Air Quality (IAQ) is an essential requirement for improving building sustainability. In fact, indoor pollution creates serious problems for human health and occupants' well-being. Considering that Europeans spend on average 90% of their time inside buildings, IAQ plays a decisive role in human health, especially for the most vulnerable groups such as the elderly and children. Concerning children and youth, due to the presence for long periods of time in school classrooms, they tend to be more susceptible to developing chronic diseases such as asthma, allergies, and respiratory problems or make these problems more increased. In these circumstances, to prevent the occurrence of these specific illnesses, it is essential to improve the school environment, namely, classroom ' indoor air quality. This research aims to specify both the design and development processes of a LoRa-based IoT Edge device for classroom IAQ monitoring, by using low-cost commercial off-the-shelf components, capable of measuring relevant IAQ parameters specifically selected for a specific case-study analysis, namely the following: carbon dioxide (CO_2), particle matter, and volatile organic compounds (VOC). At last, the prototype is delivered and assessed under controlled conditions. It is also worth highlighting that the prototype's overall cost is approximately 150€.

Keywords: IAQ · IoT · Edge computing · LoRa

1 Introduction

Humankind spends most of their time in enclosed places [1], especially people living in urban areas, who are estimated to spend about 80–90% of their time in households, offices, school buildings, shopping centers, malls, and supermarkets [2]. This is particularly sharp for the school-age population (children and adolescents), who spend an extremely high percentage of their time in these areas [1]. Therefore, well-ventilated spaces providing fresh air are fundamental to improve indoor environmental quality, which includes not only Indoor Air

© ICST Institute for Computer Sciences, Social Informatics and Telecommunications Engineering 2021
Published by Springer Nature Switzerland AG 2021. All Rights Reserved
S. Paiva et al. (Eds.): SmartCity360° 2020, LNICST 372, pp. 246–258, 2021.
https://doi.org/10.1007/978-3-030-76063-2_18

Quality (IAQ) but also other physical and psychological variables of people's life indoor, just like thermal comfort, lighting, acoustics, etc. [3]. Given the importance of the theme, IAQ has been put on the environmental agenda in the last few years [4], with a particular focus on school buildings [3]. In fact, new specific legislation for all European countries has been providing appropriate recommendations to tackle indoor air quality problems within school environments [3], emphasizing both the need of reinforcing ventilation rates through natural or mechanical schemes to dilute pollutants and to reduce the number of airborne contaminants and particles generated indoors. The list of atmospheric pollutants to be taken into consideration for IAQ assessment and management includes gases (carbon monoxide, radon, volatile organic compounds, etc.), particulates, and microbial contaminants (mold, bacteria). These pollutants are associated with harmful health impacts, which can even be fatal [3] and cause significant socioeconomic effects by reducing the productivity levels in schools and work environment [4]. In school buildings' classrooms it is possible to find various types of gases and particle matter (PM) that negatively impact pupils' health and attention, such as carbon dioxide, radon, particle matter (PM1, PM2.5, and PM10), volatile organic compounds (VOCs), among others. As for PM, it is proved that the finer the particles, the more serious the effects on human health [5]. Despite its regular presence in indoor environments, the amount of these contaminant substances can change throughout the year. In fact, in colder months, during the winter season, the pollutant emission is generally higher, due to the increase in human activities and the warming of the environment. Likewise, high relative humidity rates associated with the low air renovation during winter blocks aerosol elimination or removal. In the summer season due to the positive effect of natural ventilation, the indoor air pollutant concentration is lower. However, cooking on stoves (frying mainly), burning garbage, smoking indoors, and vehicle traffic are, for both seasons, the main sources of particle matter emissions [4]. Additionally, other factors contribute to IAQ degradation, such as the proximity to pollutant factories and combustion activities on the building surroundings, among others [6]. Furniture and decoration accessories can be responsible for IAQ deterioration since wooden materials emit formaldehyde, and both new paints and flexible plastics are associated with respiratory problems and allergies, especially prevalent in children [7].

IAQ monitoring and control are therefore mandatory for school classrooms since it is of the utmost importance to offer a healthy, safe, comfortable, and productive environment for the entire academic community [1]. In fact, high concentrations of air pollutants in school classrooms, aggravated by inadequate ventilation conditions, is generally associated with poor student performance [8], and higher rates of school absenteeism [1]. The lack of ventilation tends to aggravate problems related to high formaldehyde concentrations due to the high density of furniture [3–9], incrementing therefore the risk of asthma and reducing academic performance in school-age children.

Thereby, school classroom IAQ monitoring is one of the top priorities for a Smart Campus since it contributes, both to improve students' learning ability, and to increase teachers' productivity [10]. Thus, IAQ assessment by performing a continuous classroom ' monitoring is a path to create healthy and comfortable schools, and to reduce energy consumption. [2]. At the same time, it will help to increase students' school performance while preventing possible negative impacts on their health [1].

In this article, a prototype of an integrated IAQ monitoring system is presented, more specifically, its design and overall architecture. In this prototype, an IoT Edge device is designed to assess indoor air temperature and relative humidity in a school classroom, as well as several IAQ parameters, such as CO_2, VOC, and PM, which were specifically selected for school IAQ assessment.

The collected data can also be used to infer the classroom occupancy, cf. [11,12], which can contribute to increasing its energy efficiency. For instance, the detection of an unoccupied school classroom with a heating system in operation may lead to an important energy saving.

This document is organized as follows: Sect. 2 introduces several related studies regarding IAQ in schools; Sect. 3 introduces the overall system architecture; Sect. 4 is dedicated to the design and detailed implementation of the IoT Edge Device; Sect. 5 presents the preliminary results; and finally, in Sect. 6 conclusions are undertaken and a final discussion is put forward.

2   Related Works

In [9], authors developed a study to assess IAQ in daycare centers due to the high vulnerability of children exposed to indoor air pollution and contamination. Daycare centers are public spaces, where you children spend part of their day while waiting for their parents. In this study, special attention was paid to particulate material, which is one of the most dangerous pollutants by causing very serious respiratory diseases in children, such as asthma. The objectives of the study were to assess, firstly, the indoor air concentrations in particulate material (PM1, PM2.5, PM10, and PMtotal) in different indoor environments, such as classrooms and canteen, for three different daycare centers on weekdays and weekends. External measurements of PM10 were also undertaken to obtain an I/O (Indoor/Outdoor) ratio. The results obtained showed that PM concentrations were particularly higher in the assessed classrooms, especially in the class of finer particles, reaching a maximum of $145\,\mathrm{mg/m^3}$ for PM1.0 and $158\,\mathrm{mg/m^3}$ for PM2.5. Both values are above the limits recommended by the World Health Organization (WHO), which allows concluding that room' ventilation with outdoor air affected indoor air quality, thus increasing PM accumulation. Therefore, it was concluded that daycare centers should increase air renovation rate after rooms' occupation, and must prevent air filtering to improve IAQ.

A study developed by Fraga et al. presented in [13], aims to analyze a possible correlation between IAQ and allergic and respiratory pathologies in students attending public schools in Porto, Portugal. The investigation carried out an in-situ assessment to evaluate relative humidity, CO_2, and VOC in a set of nine secondary schools. To complement in situ measurements, a representative sample of 1607 students were invited to answer a survey concerning demographic, social, and behavioral issues. This investigation applied the International Study of Asthma and Allergie in Childhood (ISAAC) questionnaire to assess respiratory symptoms. The attained results allowed concluding that for CO_2 concentration above 2100 ppm, students showed symptoms of cough, phlegm and wheezing, during exercise, and had a cough at night. Additionally, in the schools with higher VOC levels, the prevalence of asthma is higher, along with symptoms of wheezing and nocturnal cough.

In [14], authors present a system for indoor air monitoring and quality control in school building offices. To validate the system, four eight-hour tests in three distinct rooms were carried out under different ventilation conditions. The monitoring system allowed assessing CO_2, CO, relative humidity, and indoor air temperature. The authors concluded that the impact of air insufflation on indoor air quality is higher than the impact of air extraction.

3 IAQ in the Classroom

In Subsect. 3.1, the selected IAQ parameters to be assessed will be shortly described, as well as their implications regarding human health, including mitigation actions that must be undertaken when the regulated limits are exceeded. In Subsect. 3.2, the general system architecture will be explained and detailed.

3.1 IAQ Parameter Selection

By considering the related studies synthesized in Sect. 2, all focused on the relation between indoor air quality and allergic and respiratory pathologies in school classrooms, three parameters will be selected for assessment:

- **CO_2:** causes respiratory problems, eye irritation, flu and allergic rhinitis [15];
- **VOC:** affects the nervous system, causes headaches, liver problems and lack of memory [16];
- **PM2.5/PM10:** responsible breathing problems, such as asthma and bronchitis [17].

All selected parameters have negative effects on human health. To control its impact, there are regulatory limits that help to manage its indoor air concentration. For carbon dioxide, the legal limit is 1250 ppm [18]. When this value is exceeded, natural (or mechanical) ventilation actions must be performed to increase the air change rate in the classroom. The limit for VOC indoor air concentration is $600 \mu g/m^3$ [18]. When this limit is exceeded, the room air change rate must be increased to improve air renovation. This can be easily achieved through natural ventilation actions, such as windows opening, which can be seen as the most basic natural ventilation method offering a very simple and low-cost solution to providing ventilation. Windows opening can provide background ventilation allowing to adapt the ventilation rate when required. Finally, the PM2.5 legal limit is $25 \mu g/m^3$, which, when exceeded, means that the room must be cleaned and sanitized.

3.2   Conceptual Architecture

Figure 1 illustrates the conceptual architecture used for integrated IAQ management in a school building. Each classroom is equipped with an IoT edge device that collects several IAQ parameters. The acquired data is then transmitted periodically using LoRaWAN communications, that can be available at a building or city level. LoRaWAN is a MAC protocol used for low power and long-range wide area networks that runs on top of the LoRa Modulation [19]. A LoRaWAN server is used to enable effective and transparent communication between the LoRaWAN network, the analytics engine, and the application server, simplifying the integration on the client-side.

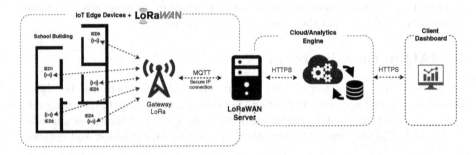

Fig. 1. Conceptual architecture with the core elements identified.

LoRaWAN protocol uses end-to-end security communications that rely on AES cryptographic algorithms. These algorithms have been widely adopted for securing constrained networks and devices [22–24]. For this, LoRaWAN uses three 128 bits AES security keys. Each LoRaWAN device is distinguished by a unique 128 bit AES Application Key (AppKey) and a globally unique device identifier (DevEUI), both used during the device authentication stage. After a device joins the LoRaWAN network, an Application Session Key (AppSKey) and a Network Session Key (NwkSKey) are generated. The AppSKey is kept private and the NwkSKey is shared with the network. Both keys are only used during the current session.

Additionally, the system includes a web-based app with a rich data visualization dashboard generated with the Grafana framework. Grafana is open-source software that provides a powerful interface for exploring time series data with native integration with several database types, turning it the standard for the visualization and analysis of this type of data. More details about the architecture in use can be found in [20, 21].

4   IoT Edge Device

Figure 2 depicts the block diagram of the IoT edge device, where it is possible to visualize its three main blocks: 1) sensing, 2) processing, and 3) communications. The sensing block is composed of three digital interfaced sensors specified based on the selection previously introduced in Sect. 3.1 to measure the following parameters: relative humidity, temperature, CO_2, TVOC, and PM2.5/PM10. Note that each sensor is capable of measuring more than one parameter. Processing is guaranteed by an ESP32 microcontroller that includes, although not used, built-in Wi-Fi and Bluetooth connectivity, as well as several interface modules such as I2C, UART, PWM, ADC, DAC, among others. Communications block is guaranteed by a LoRa RFM95W modem, that can be configured to operate in the 868/915 MHz bands. With this radio module, it is possible to configure the device to operate as a client or even as a LoRa gateway. We included an additional RGB Led for user interface purposes.

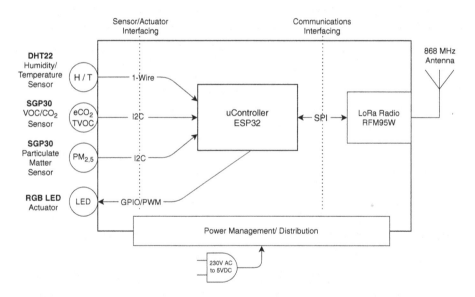

Fig. 2. IoT Edge device block diagram.

4.1   Hardware Development

Since educational institutions may have dozens of classrooms and offices, the cost is a critical factor, and a core requirement in the hardware design is to be low-cost and based on commercial off-the-shelf components. The sensor market is very competitive, with multiple manufacturers presenting low-cost solutions at the cost of reduced accuracy, making it often difficult for designers and engineers to choose the components that best meet the specific application requirements.

For the development of this device, the choice of the sensors was mainly focused on the cost-benefit regarding the component price versus its accuracy.

The DHT22 sensor was used to measure the relative humidity and temperature of indoor air. The DHT22 is a low-cost sensor that has an error of $\pm 0.5\,^\circ C$ for temperature and $\pm 2\%$ for relative humidity, which suggests that the sensor has a high degree of accuracy. It can work with a voltage of 3.3 V to 6 V, thus communicating with the microcontroller through a 1-wire interface [25].

The SGP30 is a metal-oxide (MOX) gas sensor developed by Sensirion for Indoor Air Quality applications that features multiple sensing elements in one chip. It is equipped with an I2C interface and is capable of detecting a wide variety of volatile organic compounds (VOCs). However, the sensor returns the value of the Total VOC (TVOC), and the carbon dioxide equivalent (eCO$_2$), an indirect measure, that although not highly accurate, after calibration turns out to be a very reliable estimate that allows to effectively infer the CO$_2$ trend on a budget. The SGP30 can be used with 3.3 V or 5 V [26].

The SPS30 is an optical PM developed by Sensirion for the measurement of particle matter (PM). This sensor has a lower limit detection size of $0.3\,\mu m$ and allows the measurement of the mass of particles up to sizes PM1.0, PM2.5, PM4 and PM10, and the number of particles up to sizes PM0.5, PM1.0, PM2.5, PM4 and PM10. In the previous notation, the lower number represents the maximum size in μm measured or counted, respectively. The sensor can communicate via I2C or UART and can operate using either 3.3 V or 5 V TTL levels [27].

The sensors previously introduced are wired to the ESP32 through I2C protocol, cf. Fig. 2, except for DHT22, which connects through a digital 1-wire interface. In terms of power, only the SPS30 needs to be powered with 5 V.

4.2   Firmware Development

Figure 3 depicts the flowcharts that represent the device drivers implemented for each sensor. As for DHT22, there is a library that can be used with all existing DHT models. Based on this library the DHT22 *readHT* function was implemented to perform a sequential read starting with the relative humidity in percentage and followed by the temperature in degrees celsius.

The SGP30 *readGAS* function allows TVOC, eCO$_2$, raw H$_2$ and raw ethanol values to be obtained sequentially. First, it starts by trying to measure the concentration of TVOC and eCO$_2$. If the measurement fails, it will return an error message. Then, a set of raw measurements, raw H2, and raw ethanol, is performed. After all measurements, a counter is incremented, and if it reaches thirty, a hexadecimal baseline is returned. This value is then used in a function provided by the SGP30 library for calibration purposes. The SGP30 uses a tinny metal-oxide element that, when exposed to organic compounds, changes its electrical resistance [26]. However, due to the variation of the environmental and operational conditions such as temperature and humidity, the resistance baseline changes, which demands a new baseline calibration to enable the measurement of absolute values.

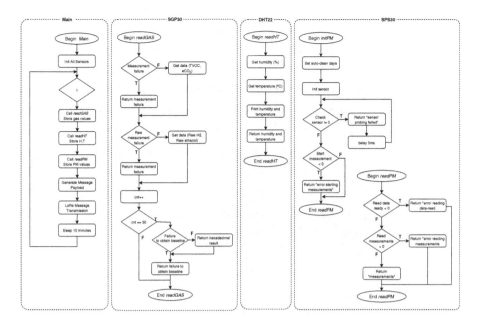

Fig. 3. Embedded firmware flowcharts.

The SPS30 sensor is used to measure particle matter and was configured to communicate with the microcontroller through I2C. Due to its normal operation, the SPS30 sensor accumulates dust inside, which must be released regularly. For this, the *initPM* function starts with the configuration of the number of days that the sensor will use to perform the internal automatic cleaning. The purpose of this initial step is to measure the concentration of particles, which are considered as dust. Finally, the SPS30 is then checked to verify that it is operating correctly. As for the *readPM* function, it aims to read the PM1, PM2.5 and PM10 particle concentrations and return the respective results.

4.3 Prototype

Figure 4 depicts the alpha version of the prototype where is possible to observe, the ESP32 microcontroller, the LoRa radio is below, all the sensors DHT22, SGP30, and the SPS30. Due to the COVID-19 pandemic situation, a PCB-based version was not implemented due to the current restrictions on accessing the laboratory. Nevertheless, at the writing of this paper, a more compact PCB version is being designed to increase the prototype robustness, allowing its evolution to a beta version for easy replication and deployment in classrooms. The dimensions are 95 mm × 70 mm × 35 mm with all components assembled and the total cost of the prototype is approximately 150€.

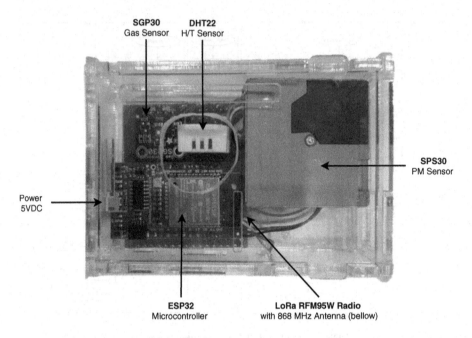

Fig. 4. IoT Edge prototype (Alpha version).

5 Preliminary Results

Due to the current pandemic situation regarding COVID-19, the validation tests had to be carried out at home, more precisely, in a bedroom, with approximately $28\,m^2$ for 48 h. Figure 5 presents the evolution of the acquired parameters and its relation with some specific annotated events, i.e. cleaning, window opening, and human occupancy. The 48-h average obtained for PM1.0 was around $15\,\mu g/m^3$; for PM2.5 and PM10, the values reached in both approximately $20\,\mu g/m^3$, being within the regulatory limits [18].

These results can be justified by the fact that the room where the data was collected is part of a non-smoking house, as well as that the house is cleaned daily, thus reducing the accumulation of particulate material.

As for the results obtained for VOCs, the measurements never exceeded 50 ppb. One of the tests that were performed, to check the sensor response, consisted of opening a bottle of acetone at a distance of 20 cm from the sensor. The values, after this action, immediately increased to around 150 ppb, not exceeding regulatory limits [18].

Regarding eCO_2, the values were around 400/450 ppm, given that the windows of the space were open. On the other hand, when closed, after some time, the results started to increase around 600/700 ppm, thus not meaning that the air was polluted.

Regarding the temperature and humidity, several measurements were acquired and compared with a digital calibrated hygrometer that was installed in the room. It was observed that the values obtained were in agreement with the sensor tolerance, as introduced in Sect. 4.1.

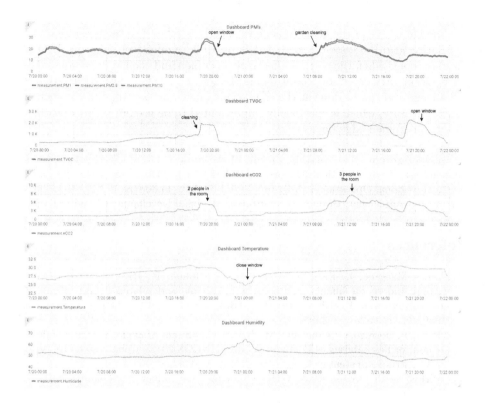

Fig. 5. Data obtained during a 48 h period in a regularly occupied classroom. The plots are annotated with relevant events, such as window state, outdoor events, number of people in the room and cleanings.

6 Conclusion and Future Work

Today's society organizes much of its daily life in closed spaces, in which IAQ needs to be assessed and managed for improvement. Thus, there are a significant number of health problems, such as asthma, irritation of the eyes, nose, and throat, among others. Schools and school spaces are no exception. In these environments, there is usually no adequate ventilation, in addition to cleaning rooms and offices, sometimes this may not be done daily. This ends up affecting the health, well-being, and success of the educational community.

The accomplishment of this work resulted from the fact that it is essential to obtain low-cost solutions for IAQ management in schools. The proposed IoT Edge device was designed for low-cost IAQ assessment in schools, presenting the ability to acquire several parameters, such as CO_2 equivalent, TVOC, $PM_{1.0}$, $PM_{2.5}$, PM_{10}, temperature, and humidity. The device uses a LoRaWAN network to push data to a cloud-based server and a web-based app with a rich data visualization dashboard generated with the Grafana framework.

Therefore, one of the goals to achieve shortly is related to the activation of a ventilation grid (or system), so that it is possible to effectively improve IAQ in the classrooms when the room is effectively occupied and the IAQ is evaluated as poor. Occupancy detection/counting and IAQ assessment performed together is a challenge and can be done at the edge using a machine learning library, such as Tensorflow Lite, which is specifically implemented to be used in microcontroller-based constrained edge devices [28].

Acknowledgment. This work is a result of the project TECH - Technology, Environment, Creativity and Health, Norte-01-0145-FEDER-000043, supported by Norte Portugal Regional Operational Program (NORTE 2020), under the PORTUGAL 2020 Partnership Agreement, through the European Regional Development Fund (ERDF).

References

1. Annesi-Maesano, I,. Baiz, N., Banerjee, S., Rudnai, P., Rive, S., SINPHONIE Group: Indoor air quality and sources in schools and related health effects. J. Toxicol. Environ. Health B Crit. Rev. **16**(8), 491–550 (2013). https://doi.org/10.1080/10937404.2013.853609
2. Ginga, J., Borrego, C., Coutinho, M., Nunes, C., Morais-Almeida, M.: Qualidade do ar interior nas habitaçães Portuguesas. In: CINCOS 2012 - Congresso de Inovação na Construção Sustentável, pp. 1–10 (2012)
3. World Health Organization: WHO Guidelines for Indoor Air Quality: Selected Pollutants. World Health Organization, Geneva (2010)
4. Massey, D., Kulshrestha, A., Masih, J., Taneja, A.: Seasonal trends of PM10, PM5.0, PM2.5 & PM1.0 in indoor and outdoor environments of residential homes located in North-Central India. Build. Environ. **47**, 223–231 (2012). ISSN 0360-1323 (2012). https://doi.org/10.1016/j.buildenv.2011.07.018
5. Schwartz, J., Neas, L.M.: Fine particles are more strongly associated than coarse particles with acute respiratory health effects in schoolchildren. Epidemiology **11**(1), 6–10 (2000). https://doi.org/10.1097/00001648-200001000-00004
6. Heudorf, U., Neitzert, V., Spark, J.: Particulate matter and carbon dioxide in classrooms - the impact of cleaning and ventilation. Int. J. Hyg. Environ. Health **212**(1), 45–55 (2009). https://doi.org/10.1016/j.ijheh.2007.09.011
7. Mendell, M.: Indoor residential chemical emissions as risk factors for respiratory and allergic effects in children: a review. Indoor Air **17**(4), 259–277 (2007). https://doi.org/10.1111/j.1600-0668.2007.00478.x
8. Fisk, W.: The ventilation problem in schools: literature review. Indoor Air **27**(6), 1039–1051 (2017). https://doi.org/10.1111/ina.12403
9. Branco, P., Alvim-Ferraz, M., Martins, F., Sousa, S.: Indoor air quality in urban nurseries at Porto city: particulate matter assessment. Atmos. Environ. **84**, 133–143 (2014). ISSN 1352-2310. https://doi.org/10.1016/j.atmosenv.2013.11.035
10. Lee, S., Chang, M.: Indoor air quality investigations at five classrooms. Indoor Air **9**(2), 134–138 (1999). https://doi.org/10.1111/j.1600-0668.1999.t01-2-00008.x

11. Lopes, S.I., Pereira, F., Vieira, J.M.N., Carvalho, N.B., Curado, A.: Design of compact LoRa devices for smart building applications. In: Afonso, J.L., Monteiro, V., Pinto, J.G. (eds.) GreeNets 2018. LNICST, vol. 269, pp. 142–153. Springer, Cham (2019). https://doi.org/10.1007/978-3-030-12950-7_12
12. Pereira, F., Lopes, S.I., Carvalho, N.B.: Design of a cost-effective multimodal IoT edge device for building occupancy estimation. In: IEEE International Smart Cities Conference (ISC2), Casablanca, Morocco, vol. 2019, pp. 122–128 (2019). https://doi.org/10.1109/ISC246665.2019.9071717
13. Fraga, S., et al.: Indoor air quality and respiratory symptoms in Porto schools. Revista Portuguesa de Pneumologia (English Edition) 14(4), 487–507 (2008)
14. Fernandes, S., Igrejas, G., Feliciano, M.: Monitoring and control indoor air quality in school offices. Revista de Ciências Agrárias 40, 274–281 (2017)
15. Azuma, K., Kagi, N., Yanagi, U., Osawa, H.: Effects of low-level inhalation exposure to carbon dioxide in indoor environments: a short review on human health and psychomotor performance. Environ. Int. 121, 51–56 (2018). https://doi.org/10.1016/j.envint.2018.08.059
16. US EPA: Volatile organic compounds' impact on indoor air quality. US EPA (2020). https://www.epa.gov/indoor-air-quality-iaq/volatile-organic-compounds-impact-indoor-air-quality. Accessed 23 July 2020
17. Sacks, J., et al.: Particulate matter-induced health effects: who is susceptible? Environ. Health Perspect. 119(4), 446–454 (2011). https://doi.org/10.1289/ehp.1002255
18. Portaria n° 353-A/2013 de 4 de Dezembro. Diário da República n° 235 - I Série. Ministérios do Ambiente, Ordenamento, do Território e energia, da Saúde e da Solidadriedade, Emprego e Segurança Social
19. Sornin, N., Luis, M., Eirich, T., Kramp, T., Hersent, O.: LoRaWAN specification, v1.0, January 2015
20. Lopes, S.I., et al.: On the design of a Human-in-the-Loop Cyber-Physical System for online monitoring and active mitigation of indoor Radon gas concentration. In: IEEE International Smart Cities Conference (ISC2), Kansas City, MO, USA, vol. 2018, pp. 1–8 (2018). https://doi.org/10.1109/ISC2.2018.8656777
21. Lopes, S.I., Moreira, P.M., Cruz, A.M., Martins, P., Pereira, F., Curado, A.: RnMonitor: a WebGIS-based platform for expedite in situ deployment of IoT edge devices and effective Radon Risk Management. In: IEEE International Smart Cities Conference (ISC2). Casablanca, Morocco, vol. 2019, pp. 451–457 (2019). https://doi.org/10.1109/ISC246665.2019.9071789
22. Sultan, I., Mir, B.J., Banday, M.T.: Analysis and optimization of advanced encryption standard for the Internet of Things. In: 2020 7th International Conference on Signal Processing and Integrated Networks (SPIN), Noida, India, pp. 571–575 (2020). https://doi.org/10.1109/SPIN48934.2020.9071380
23. Dao, M., Hoang, V., Dao, V., Tran, X.: An energy efficient AES encryption core for hardware security implementation in IoT systems. In: 2018 International Conference on Advanced Technologies for Communications (ATC), Ho Chi Minh City, pp. 301–304 (2018). https://doi.org/10.1109/ATC.2018.8587500
24. Dang, T.N., Vo, H.M.: Advanced AES algorithm using dynamic key in the Internet of Things System. In: 2019 IEEE 4th International Conference on Computer and Communication Systems (ICCCS), Singapore, pp. 682–686 (2019). https://doi.org/10.1109/CCOMS.2019.8821647
25. Liu, T.: Digital-output relative humidity & temperature sensor/module DHT22. Aosong Electronics (2013)

26. Datasheet SGP30: Indoor air quality sensor for TVOC and CO2eq measurements, Version 0.9, August 2017
27. Datasheet SPS30: Particulate matter sensor for air quality monitoring and control, Version 1.0, D1 March 2020
28. TensorFlow Light Guide. https://www.tensorflow.org/lite/guide. Accessed 14 July 2020

Technologies for Industrial Internet of Things (IIoT): Guidelines for Edge Computing Adoption in the Industry

Ralf Luis de Moura[1]([⊠]) , Tiago Monteiro Brasil[2] , Ludmilla Bassini Werner[1] ,
Claudio José Barcelos Dal' Col[2] , Alexandre Gonzalez[3] , and Sajjad Quadri[4]

[1] Vale S.A., Vitória 29990-900, Brazil
{ralf.moura,ludmilla.werner}@vale.com
[2] Vale S.A., Nova Lima 34006-270, Brazil
{Tiago.brasil,claudio.dalcol}@vale.com
[3] Vale S.A., Rio de Janeiro 22250-145, Brazil
alexandre.gonzalez@vale.com
[4] Vale S.A., Toronto M5J2K2, Canada
sajaad.quadri@vale.com

Abstract. The industrial sector is reinventing itself to find improved production processes. Industry 4.0 brings opportunities for growth productivity with the IIoT. There is a range of IIoT-related technologies to manage vast volumes of data that should be stored and processed for the decision-making process. Cloud computing is a reliable option for remote storage and data processing. However, in situations where the requirement is response time, intermittent connectivity, and low latency, edge computing processing is a more suitable option. Any device with computational resources can implement an edge computing capability with functions like gateway and data aggregator capabilities. These devices need to be classified to avoid an uncontrolled proliferation of appliances in the enterprise's environment, which easily create cybersecurity vulnerabilities and transform device management into chaos. This study proposes a taxonomy for edge computing and defines industrial application guidelines as a strategy to facilitate their sustainable implementation.

Keywords: Edge computing · Guidelines · Taxonomy · Industrial Internet of Things

1 Introduction

The Internet of Things (IoT) is considered a new technological paradigm where any device or machine may interact with each other [1]. The Industrial Internet of Things (IIoT) is the application of IoT in the industry. It is part of the Industry 4.0 concepts that transform many segments in enterprises and challenging industries to rethink their production processes on an unprecedented scale. The IIoT emphasizes the idea of consistent

© ICST Institute for Computer Sciences, Social Informatics and Telecommunications Engineering 2021
Published by Springer Nature Switzerland AG 2021. All Rights Reserved
S. Paiva et al. (Eds.): SmartCity360° 2020, LNICST 372, pp. 259–273, 2021.
https://doi.org/10.1007/978-3-030-76063-2_19

digitization, combining the strengths of traditional industry technologies with internet and cloud capabilities [7].

Many IIoT solutions have cloud-based applications as a central computational infrastructure to store and process data generated by different sources. This model assumes the existence of stable connectivity with low latency and acceptable response times for an ever-increasing demand for IIoT data.

The majority of IIoT literature is based on the reactive computing paradigm that data computing starts after the data task is offloaded to the central processing node. However, stringent latency and reliability constraints in networks often are not considered. The high volume and fast velocity of data streams generated by IIoT devices may consume a massive amount of network bandwidth. Since the remote cloud is physically distant from IIoT devices that send application requests and await the results to be processed and generated in the remote cloud, the response time for these requests may not be adequate. This delay can be especially unbearable, considering sensitive IIoT applications [5]. Due to these networks' distributed nature, having computing resources closer to the edge network enables personalized and robust computational services [4].

The concept of edge computing is predicated on moving some computational load to the network edge [3], enabling, for example, processing on-premise, next to where the data is being generated [1].

Several types of devices may process data on-premises. In general, any device with computational capability may receive data from various "things" and process them locally. This situation may provoke the enterprise dissemination of many distinct electronic devices with different characteristics. Its heterogeneity can produce management issues when maintaining and supporting these devices—for example, critical services such as things diagnosis and failure alarms [1].

Cyber-security is another critical point; edge devices, in the IIoT context, interact with various access technologies, such as Wi-Fi, Bluetooth, LoRaWAN, and LTE. It makes the edge infrastructure prone to several cybersecurity attacks. For example, Denial-of-Service (DoS) and Man-in-the-middle attacks, furthermore, attackers could access the information stored in the edge [6]. It shows how imperative it is to create specific rules for adopting adequate edge computing devices, to avoid reliability, management, and cyber-security issues.

There is a growing interest in using IIoT edge computing technologies in various industries [13], but one of the biggest challenges is choosing the right technology for adoption. There are a plethora of edge computing solutions, making their way into the industry [14]; however, the industry has specific technological features that need to be considered before choosing the right technology.

This study proposes an edge computing taxonomy and defines rules for their adoption in each category previously defined here. It assumes that edge devices need to be appropriately classified, and rules should be created before the industry's adoption. Device standardization is useful to avoid the proliferation of mixed solutions, simplify the management, and mitigate cyber-security attacks, facilitating these devices' adoption.

2   Industrial Internet of Things

Internet of Things – IoT can be considered as a "… group of infrastructures, intercon-
necting connected objects and allowing their management, data mining and the access to
data they generate" where connected objects are "sensor(s) and/or actuator(s) carrying
out a specific function that can communicate with other equipment" [8]. The Industrial
Internet of Things (IIoT) is the application of these technologies in manufacturing [5].
IIoT can be considered a physical network of things, objects, or devices for sensing and
remote control, in an industrial context, that allowing greater integration between the
physical and cyber world [5].

Boyes et al. [9] conceptualize the Industrial Internet of Things as "a system comprising networked smart objects, cyber-physical assets, associated generic information
technologies and optional cloud or edge computing platforms, which enable real-time,
intelligent, and autonomous access, collection, analysis, communications, and exchange
of process, product or service information, within the industrial environment, to optimize
overall production value."

The use of these technologies results in generating huge volumes of data to be stored,
processed, and presented in a friendly and interpretable way [6]. This large amount of
data requires information technology services with diverse and sufficient capacity to
support the growing demand, typically offered by cloud computing services [10].

Cloud computing is an internet-based computing paradigm that provides on-demand
services through a configurable set of computing resources [5]. The Cloud computing
platform delivers virtually endless capabilities and services that meet the various IIoT
demands [8, 9]. However, cloud computing may not always be the best strategy for
industrial applications, and sometimes, the computing needs to be performed closer to
the source of the data to improve the service delivered [18].

IIoT combines the application of machine-to-machine communication and smart
machines capable of delivering data that can be used for future analysis. IIoT requires
the application of several connectivity options due to the diversity of scenarios with varied
requirements in remote locations related to physical distance, latency/jitter, infrastructure, installation environments, and energy consumption [7]. These features demand
on-premises devices and particular communication protocols to provide robustness
and redundancy, considering that remote locations typically do not have the proper
communication infrastructure [10].

One technology that should be adopted by the industry is edge computing, in some
situations replacing cloud-based applications due to the network dependency and latency.
Real-time and near real-time systems need fast response time, for example, when applied
in industrial equipment. However, the application of these devices imposes challenges
that need to be adequately addressed.

3   Challenges in Edge Computing

Although the term edge computing is relatively new in the context of IIoT, its function has
been known and applied for many years, and it can be found in almost every segment of
human activity [23]. It is a variation of distributed computing [25] applied in the industry

through distributed control systems in which the process intelligence takes place closer to the factory floor. Generally, any equipment that does any processing close to the origin point of data can be considered edge computing.

ARC Advisory Group [14] defines the Industrial IoT edge as the place where physical devices, assets, machines, processes, and applications intersect with internet-enabled portions of the architecture. Industrial IoT edge devices provide input to, and may receive output from, industrial internet-enabled systems, applications, and services but reside outside of clouds and local data centers.

Koustabh and Datta [2] defines Edge Computing as "The delivery of computing capabilities to the logical extremes of a network to improve the performance, operating cost, and reliability of applications and services." Gartner defines edge computing as "solutions that facilitate data processing at or near the source of data generation" [3].

Edge computing refers to enabling technologies that allow computation to be performed at the edge of the network. It is any computing and network resources located between the data sources and the central storage and processing unit, such as a cloud data center [1]. An edge device can perform computing offloading, data storage, data aggregation, data filtering, caching, and processing and distribute requests and delivery services [1, 7, 10].

Edge computing is one of the IIoT devices that most interact with other devices [10]. The implementation of edge computing devices can bring several advantages, such as network traffic reduction, faster response rate, and lower network connection reliability [24].

An edge computing device can be responsible for consolidating data from multiple sources and forwarding it to a central storage and processing unit. Local processing, such as advanced analysis, can also be performed on the edge device. It is also responsible for handling outages, storage, and data forwarding. Additionally, it enables the orchestration of other devices from different vendors using different protocols [7, 10]. Those tasks at the edge of the network introduce risks and become a challenge for industry adoption.

Edge computing requires further research work to comprehend all potential benefits [23] and limitations. From the industry perspective, some key concerns need to be addressed to enable a sustainable implementation, like, for example, device management [15], reliability [17], security, and privacy protection [13].

3.1 Management Concerns

Some edge devices provide little or no visibility into their state and composition, including the identity of any external services and systems they interact with, and little or no access to their software and configuration. Their proliferation may difficult to access, managing, and monitoring those devices. This challenge can generate some issue that should be addressed [15]:

- Lack of management features: The administrator may not be able to fully manage an edge device, including firmware, operating systems, and applications.
- Complexity regarding management at scale: An edge device may not support standardized mechanisms for centralized management.

- Wide variety of software to manage: Extensive variety of software used by edge devices, including firmware, standard, and real-time operating systems, and applications, can complicate software management tasks such as configuration and patch management.
- Lack of inventory capabilities: Edge devices included in the IIoT technology environment may not be inventoried, registered, and otherwise provisioned via regular IT processes. **Sample Heading (Third Level).** Only two levels of headings should be numbered. Lower level headings remain unnumbered; they are formatted as run-in headings.

3.2 Reliability Concerns

IoT devices are usually not designed to be used in unpredictable and variated industrial environments [17]. Unlike traditional IoT devices, IIoT devices are generally used in harsh environments exposed to dust, electromagnetic noise, humidity under a wide variety of temperatures, along with other physical risks raising concerns regarding reliability and unexpected or premature failures.

Edge computing devices often employ embedded systems, variability in circuit parameters due to the nature of the manufacturing process, signal integrity issues arising from internal and external noise sources, and accelerated aging of the devices are essential categories of reliability concerns facing embedded design systems hardware [16].

3.3 Cyber-Security Concerns

According to NIST SP 800-37 [13], cybersecurity risk and privacy risk are related but distinct concepts. For privacy, the risk is "a measure of the extent to which a potential circumstance or event threatens an entity, and typically is a function of (i) the adverse impact or magnitude of the harm, that would arise if the circumstance or event occurs; and (ii) the likelihood of occurrence." For cybersecurity, the risk is about threats—the exploitation of vulnerabilities by threat actors to compromise device or data confidentiality, integrity, or availability.

As an IIoT device, Edge computing generally faces the same types of cybersecurity risks compared to conventional IT devices [11]. Edge devices interact with the physical world through the IIoT sensor data. In the physical world, effective IIoT data management is essential to mitigate physical attacks on sensor technology. Such attacks are usually performed through wireless signals [11, 12].

Edge computing can contribute to the aggregation of data collected by many sources used for future decision-making. When misused, these capabilities can affect the decision-making process or lead to revel private information. Edge devices with IIoT actuators can make changes to physical systems and thus affect the physical world. In a worst-case scenario, a compromise could allow an attacker to use an IIoT actuator to endanger human safety, damage or destroy equipment and facilities, or cause major operational disruptions [11, 12].

Edge network interfaces often enable remote access to physical systems. It may put the physical systems accessible through the IoT devices at much higher risk. Another important aspect is the operational requirements that devices must meet in various environments and use cases. Many devices must comply with stringent requirements for performance, reliability, resilience, safety, and other objectives. These requirements may be at odds with cybersecurity and privacy rules [11].

4 Challenges in Edge Computing

Edge computing is usually treated generically as if all edge devices perform the same function. However, this is not a reality in all use cases. The capabilities of edge computing devices range from event filtering to complex-event processing or batch processing, and more specialized edge computing devices can act as gateways or data aggregators [20].

4.1 IIoT Edge Gateway Data Capture

The first category of edge computing devices is Gateway Data Capture. Edge Gateway Data Capture (EGDC) provides connectivity for other IIoT devices, usually using wireless non-IP network protocols like LoRaWAN (Long Range Wide Area Network), Zigbee or, even IP networks like Wi-Fi. It works as a data aggregator from many sources and as a single point of store and forward.

Scripts can be created using high-level languages, python, for example, to execute during the receiving data process. These scripts can perform basic data filtering or basic data processing. EGDCs commonly are placed between network zones, for example, an access zone and another zone with internet connectivity, as showed in Fig. 1.

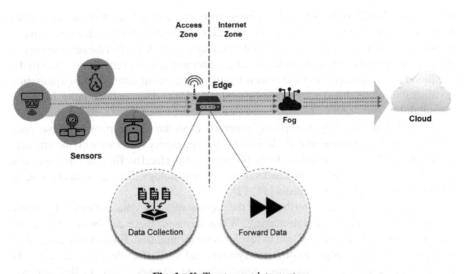

Fig. 1. IIoT gateway data capture.

These devices' primary role is data collection, usually working as a translator between access network protocols and internet protocols. Eventually, these devices can act as a local database, storing data locally when the internet connection is unavailable and forwarding data when the connection is available.

4.2 IIoT Edge Data Processing

The second category of edge computing devices is Edge Data Processing. Edge Data Processing (EDP) is a specialized device that enables a first pass data filtering, making it possible to reduce the amount of data transmitted, running batch processing, stream analytics [7, 22], and data cleaning [2], as shown at Fig. 2.

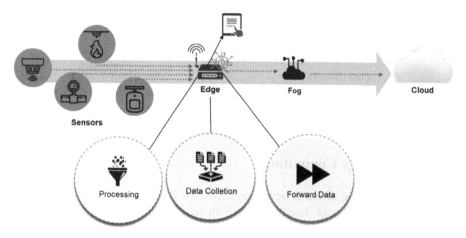

Fig. 2. IIoT gateway data processing.

The fundamental difference between Edge Gateway Data Capture and Edge Data Processing is the role that it plays in the data life cycle. For Edge Data Processing, sophisticated computational models are usually embedded and self-sufficient to the point of performing all complex processing functions locally as batch processing or stream analytics. After the processing, the row data is still needed in the cloud, but only to update the computational models' quality.

Those devices can sometimes manipulate physical variables, acting in equipment or triggering alarms. In some situations, Edge Data processing allows human interaction through human-machine interfaces (HMI), using screens, tablets, or mobile phones, for example [21].

Those two types of devices require different attention points, as they have different functions and characteristics (Table 1).

Some features are shared between the two types of devices, such as Basic Data Filtering, Storage and Forward, and Basic Data Processing, but others are different, generating different recommendations.

Table 1. Edge computing characteristics

Characteristics	EDP	EDGC
It is usually placed between network zones	No	Yes
Multiples protocols	No	Yes
Basic data filtering	Yes	Yes
Storage and forward	Yes	Yes
Basic data processing	Yes	Yes
Human machine interface	Yes	No
Embedded computational model	Yes	No
Complex data processing	Yes	No
Stream analytics	Yes	No
Data cleaning	Yes	No
Batch processing	Yes	No
Act on physical variables	Yes	No

5   Rules for Edge Computing

After the classification of the devices, it is necessary to establish rules for their adoption. Some rules are generic to adhering to both taxonomies, and some are specific to each type of edge. The rules are defined according to the concerns previously aborded: Management, Reliability, and Cybersecurity.

5.1   IIoT Edge Data Processing

With the proliferation of edge devices, it is essential to have a centralized management capability preferred to maintain all devices' control. For centralized processing to be implemented, each edge device must implement specific functions. Edge devices should enable remote management, including manipulating maintenance, monitoring, and inventory information [15].

For maintenance, the device should have the ability to:

- Upload firmware or operating system and to track the status of remote software/firmware update.
- Update applications or embedded code.

For monitoring, the device should have the ability to:

- Remotely collect health information.
- Real-time tracking of the physical location.
- Remotely collect diagnostic and error information.

For an inventory, the device should have the ability to:

- Provide information about hardware, versions, model, manufacturer.
- Provide information about time in operation, time on.

For EGDC-type devices, these features can be implemented through all protocols that the device has available, wireless or not. EDGC-type devices can also deliver information regarding other devices (things) to which they are connected to extend the same management functions. The device can be integrated into a centralized and agnostic device management system by supporting all management functions.

5.2 Reliability Rules

Tolerant electronics, as well as long life survivability, are critical capabilities required for IIoT. Approaches to harsh environments focus on component level robustness, and hardening should be considered. Moreover, the product can be designed to adapt to the changing use of environments to maintain target reliability.

Edge computing devices should be adequately designed with redundancy implemented that includes characteristics that mitigate environmental effects [16]:

- Edge devices should incorporate power optimizations and deploy techniques such as dynamic voltage scaling.
- Edge devices should use circuit techniques that generate less noise, improving circuit noise immunity, or suppressing noise without circuit modification.
- Redundancy should be provided for the edge device's subparts prone to failure.
- Industrial protection certification (water and dust resistance).
- Edge devices in IIoT networks are constrained many times. The computing capabilities should be enough for the processing suitable for the required processing load.

Harsh areas with difficult accessibility to IIoT Edge devices are very demanding on the lifespan of devices. Reliability characteristics should be present in both edge-type devices, but some of them can be relaxed if the device is installed in a location with external physical protection (panel, for example). By supporting all reliability rules, devices can be better prepared to support their tasks.

5.3 Cyber-Security Rules

To mitigate the risks of attacks on edge devices, specific rules needed to be established. By working with multiple protocols, Edge Gateway Data Capture devices may be more vulnerable to cyber-attacks. Communication protocols on access networks must be secure to prevent an attacker from taking control of an edge device or subtracting or modifying data.

Special attention needs to be given to EDP-type devices that act directly on physical variables. Devices of this type cannot be allowed to be invaded and manipulated by attackers.

Cyber-security topics should be addressed to cover fundamental security principles: for confidentiality to ensure only the data proprietor can access the edge computing information. For integrity, to assure the proper and steady transmission of data to the accredited device without unauthorized modification of the data. For availability to assure the authorized party manages to access the edge services for access control and authentication to ensure that an individual device's identification is accredited [24].

In general, an edge computing device should have:

- A registration process.
- An initial provisioning process regarding software, components, and configurations.
- Authentication mechanisms.
- Encryption mechanisms.
- A decommissioning strategy, including revocation of access, certificates, and deletion of sensitive data
- Control and restrict access to devices individually or in a group.

Device management systems implemented through the management rules can assist in the cybersecurity requirements since real-time monitoring can allow for halting attempts at hacking quickly.

By supporting all cyber-security rules, devices can be less vulnerable. These requirements are necessary for both edge computing devices, especially to EGDC-type due to the multiple options of connection and to EDP-type devices that manipulate physical variables.

5.4 IIoT Computing Placement Strategy

An IIoT edge device should be appropriately positioned in network infrastructure, and its data flow should be segregated to prevent mixing it with the TI data flow. This guidance is necessary for two main reasons, the first for security, preventing an attacker from taking over a smart device, or even the edge computing device to gain access to the corporate network. The second reason is related to the use of the corporate network only for traditional IT services, avoiding an overload or improper use of the infrastructure.

For economic reasons, the physical IT infrastructure, in some situations, may be used for IIoT data flow, but it should be logically segregated. Figure 3 shows an example of network segregation, using a DMZ as an intermediate zone between data collection at the source and the final destination of data in the cloud or an on-premises database. DMZ is the first line of defense to protect the internal infrastructure from external threats [26]. The figure shows a typical EGDC device; however, positioning can be applied to any type of edge computing device.

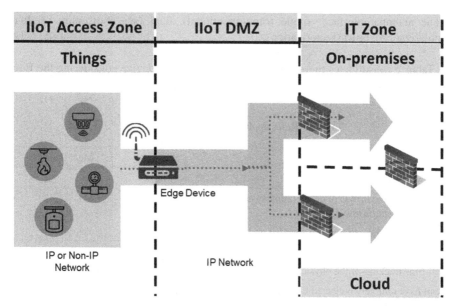

Fig. 3. IIoT edge placement

6 Study Case of Edge Computing Devices

Two case studies are presented in this section to illustrate the edge computing devices rules comprehensively. First, it was analyzed an EGDC-type device that uses LoraWAN protocol. Second, an EDP-type device for local data processing.

Both devices are available in the market and are considered relevant, and they can be easily acquired for IIoT applications. The manufacturers' names will not be revealed; only each one's main characteristics will be addressed.

6.1 IIoT Edge Gateway Data Capture

The EGDC-type device is part of the global Long-Range Radio fixed network to provide an M2M connectivity link between low power end-point and Internet access. The EGDC-type device has the following general characteristics:

- CPU Module, which includes: Power management, CPU, Memories and, GNSS receiver (GPS)
- WAN Module
- Backup battery
- 4G modem
- LoRa module
- Ethernet or GPRS/EDGE/HSPA/CDMA/LTE
- The unlicensed band (ISM)
- Ingress protection IP66 / EN 60529

- The antenna interface: single (omnidirectional), dual (space diversity or dual-polarization), or tri (sectorization).

Table 2 consolidates the analysis for the EDGC-type device considering the Edge computing rules.

Table 2. Rules applied to an EDGC-type device

Rules	Meet the rule
Management rules	
It can upload the firmware or operating system and track the status of remote software/firmware update	Yes
It can update applications or embedded code	Yes
It can have remotely collected health information	Yes
Real-time tracking of the physical location	Yes
It can have remotely collected diagnostic and error information	Yes
Provide information about hardware, versions, model, manufacturer	Yes
Provide information about time in operation	Yes
Reliability rules	
Incorporate power optimizations and deploy techniques such as dynamic voltage scaling	Yes
Use circuit techniques that generate less noise, improving circuit noise immunity, or suppressing noise without circuit modification	Yes
It has redundancy	Yes
Industrial protection certification	Yes
Processing capacity	Yes
Cybersecurity rules	
It has a registration process	Yes
It has an initial provisioning process regarding software, components, and configurations	Yes
It has authentication mechanisms	Yes
It has encryption mechanisms	Yes
It has a decommissioning strategy, including revocation of access, certificates, and deletion of sensitive data	Yes
Control and restrict access to devices individually or in a group	Yes

The EGDC-type device meets all defined rules regarding management, cybersecurity, and reliability and is ready to be applied in the industry context.

6.2 IIoT Edge Data Processing

The EDP-type device is a small computer-implemented in a single board that can use an operating system like Linux or Windows IoT. The device is mostly used in IoT applications due to its flexibility and low cost. The software can be developed installed to manage data from other devices. The EDP-type device has the following general characteristics:

- CPU: Quad-core 64-bit ARM Cortex A53 clocked at 1.2 GHz.
- Memory: 1 GB SDRAM
- Network: 10/100 Mbps Ethernet and 802.11n Wireless LAN.

Table 3 consolidates the analysis for the EDP-type device considering the Edge computing rules.

Table 3. Rules applied to an EDP-type device

Rules	Meet the rule
Management rules	
It can upload the firmware or operating system and track the status of remote software/firmware update	Yes
It can update applications or embedded code	Yes
It can have remotely collected health information	Yes
Real-time tracking of the physical location	No
It can have remotely collected diagnostic and error information	Yes
Provide information about hardware, versions, model, manufacturer	Yes
Provide information about time in operation	Yes
Reliability rules	
Incorporate power optimizations and deploy techniques such as dynamic voltage scaling	No
Use circuit techniques that generate less noise, improving circuit noise immunity, or suppressing noise without circuit modification	No
It has redundancy	No
Industrial protection certification	No
Processing capacity	Yes
Cybersecurity rules	
It has a registration process	Yes
It has an initial provisioning process regarding software, components, and configurations	Yes
It has authentication mechanisms	Yes
It has encryption mechanisms	Yes
It has a decommissioning strategy, including revocation of access, certificates, and deletion of sensitive data	Yes
Control and restrict access to devices individually or in a group	Yes

The EDP-type device does not meet all rules regarding reliability and management in the real-time tracking location. This device can only be applied in particular situations in which adequate physical/electric protection. A hardening process is necessary to reduce its vulnerability. In order to mitigate the absence of location tracking, this edge device should be used only in stationary applications.

7 Conclusion

Edge computing devices are pervasive and increasing their presence in industrial operations. To make an edge function, a device needs to have computational and communication capabilities obtained in countless ways with many devices. This context provides the risk of uncontrolled spread of devices that are not fully prepared to operate in industrial environments and can lead to human life and cybersecurity.

These devices must follow some minimum rules to be appropriately adopted in the industry. Standardization and attention to particular prerequisites can be the difference between a sustainable implementation and chaos.

This study established criteria for identifying two types of Edge devices used in the industry in the context of IIoT, called Edge Gateway Data Capture and Edge Data Processing.

Both types of devices have specific functions and characteristics that make them more adapted to certain data capture and data processing functions. However, both need to have specific characteristics that make them more suitable for industrial adoption, given factors such as reliability, management, and cyber-security. By establishing and following these rules, the industry can better prepare for the fourth industrial revolution's consequences.

References

1. Shi, W., Cao, J., Zhang, Q., Li, Y., Xu, L.: Edge computing: vision and challenges. IEEE Internet Things J. 3(5), 637–646 (2016)
2. Koustabh, D., Datta, S.K.: Comparison of edge computing implementations: fog computing, cloudlet, and mobile edge computing. In: Global Internet of Things Summit (GIoTS), pp. 1–6. IEEE, Geneva (2017)
3. Blesson, V., et al.: Challenges and opportunities in edge computing. In: 2016 IEEE International Conference on Smart Cloud (SmartCloud). IEEE, New York (2016)
4. Mohammed, E.S., Bennis, M., Saad, W.: Proactive edge computing in latency-constrained fog networks. In: 2017 European Conference on Networks and Communications (EuCNC). IEEE, Oulu (2017)
5. Fan, O., Ansari, N.: Application-aware workload allocation for edge computing-based IoT. IEEE Internet Things J. 5(3), 2146–2153 (2018)
6. Shirazi, S.N., et al.: The extended cloud: review and analysis of mobile edge computing and fog from a security and resilience perspective. IEEE J. Sel. Areas Commun. 35(11), 2586–2595 (2017)
7. Moura, R.L., Ceotto, L.D.L.F., Gonzalez, A.: Industrial IoT and advanced analytics framework: an approach for the mining industry. In: 2017 International Conference on Computational Science and Computational Intelligence (CSCI), pp. 1308–1314. IEEE Xplore, Las Vegas (2017)

8. Dorsemaine, B., et al.: Internet of Things: a definition and taxonomy. In: NGMAST 2015 9th International Conference on Next Generation Mobile Applications, Services and Technologies, pp. 72–77. IEEE, Cambridge (2015)
9. Boyes, H., et al.: The industrial Internet of Things (IIoT): an analysis framework. Comput. Ind. **101**, 1–12 (2018)
10. Moura, R.L., et al.: Industrial Internet of Things (IIoT) platforms-an evaluation model. In: 2018 International Conference on Computational Science and Computational Intelligence (CSCI), pp. 1002–1009. IEEE, Las Vegas (2018)
11. Boeckl, K., et al.: Considerations for managing Internet of Things (IoT) cybersecurity and privacy risks. US Department of Commerce, National Institute of Standards and Technology (2019)
12. Megas, K., Fagan, M.: Subject: NISTIR 8259, core cybersecurity feature baseline for securable IoT devices: a starting point for IoT device manufacturers (2019)
13. Ross, R.S., et al.: Guide for the security certification and accreditation of federal information systems. No. Special Publication (NIST SP)-800–37 (2004)
14. Polsonetti, C.: Industrial Edge 2.0. https://www.arcweb.com/blog/industrial-iot-edge-20. Accessed 03 May 2020
15. Moura, R.L., et al.: Industrial Internet of Things: device management architecture proposal. In: 2019 International Conference on Computational Science and Computational Intelligence (CSCI), Las Vegas, NV, USA, pp. 1174–1178 (2019)
16. Narayanan, V., Xie, Y.: Reliability concerns in embedded system designs. Computer **39**(1), 118–120 (2006)
17. Ahmad, M.: Reliability models for the Internet of Things: a paradigm shift. In: 2014 IEEE International Symposium on Software Reliability Engineering Workshops, Naples, pp. 52–59. IEEE, Washington DC (2014)
18. Varghese, B., et al.: Challenges and opportunities in edge computing. In: 2016 IEEE International Conference on Smart Cloud (SmartCloud). IEEE (2016)
19. Van der Meulen, R.: What edge computing means for infrastructure and operations leaders. https://www.gartner.com/smarterwithgartner/what-edge-computing-means-for-infrastructure-and-operations-leaders/. Accessed 05 Nov 2020
20. Wang, T., et al.: Big data cleaning based on mobile edge computing in industrial sensor-cloud. IEEE Trans. Ind. Inform. **16**, 1321–1329 (2019)
21. Liang, B., et al.: Mobile edge computing. Key technologies for 5G wireless systems, vol. 16, no. 3, pp. 1397–1411 (2017)
22. Calo, S.B., Touna, M., Verma, D.C., Cullen, A.: Edge computing architecture for applying AI to IoT. In: IEEE International Conference on Big Data (Big Data), pp. 3012–3016. IEEE (2017)
23. Stankovski, S., et al.: Using micro/mini PLC/PAC in the edge computing architecture. In: 19th International Symposium INFOTEH-JAHORINA (INFOTEH), pp. 1–4. IEEE, Jahorina (2020)
24. Mocnej, J., et al.: Impact of edge computing paradigm on energy consumption in IoT. IFAC-PapersOnLine **51**(6), 162–167 (2018)
25. Alrowaily, M., Lu, Z.: Secure edge computing in IoT systems: review and case studies. In: IEEE/ACM Symposium on Edge Computing (SEC), pp. 440–444. Virtual (2018)
26. El-Sayed, H., et al.: Edge of things: the big picture on the integration of edge, IoT and the cloud in a distributed computing environment. IEEE Access **6**, 1706–1717 (2017)
27. Dadheech, K., Choudhary, A., Bhatia, G.: De-militarized zone: a next level to network security. In: Second International Conference on Inventive Communication and Computational Technologies (ICICCT), pp. 595–600. IEEE, Coimbatore (2018)

Scalable Approximate Computing Techniques for Latency and Bandwidth Constrained IoT Edge

Anjus George[✉] and Arun Ravindran

University of North Carolina at Charlotte, Charlotte, NC 28223, USA
{ageorg28,aravindr}@uncc.edu

Abstract. Machine vision applications at the IoT Edge have bandwdith and latency constraints due to large sizes of video data. In this paper we propose approximate computing, that trades off inference accuracy with video frame size, as a potential solution. We present a number of low compute overhead video frame modifications that can reduce the video frame size, while achieving acceptable levels of inference accuracy. We present, a heuristic based design space pruning, and a Categorical boost based machine learning model as two approaches to achieve scalable performance in determining the appropriate video frame modifications that satisfy design constraints. Experimental results on an object detection application on the Microsoft COCO 2017 data set, indicates that proposed methods were able to reduce the video frame size by upto 71.3% while achieving an inference accuracy of 80.9% of that of the unmodified video frames. The machine learning model has a high training cost, but has a lower inference time, and is scalable and flexible compared to the heuristic design space pruning algorithm.

Keywords: Edge computing · IoT · Approximate computing · Machine learning · Machine vision

1 Introduction

Internet-of-Things (IoT) applications increasingly utilize machine vision for a variety of challenging tasks including autonomous driving, pedestrian safety, public security, and occupational health and safety. Such machine vision applications require continuous stream of video data generated by multiple cameras deployed in the field of operation. Due to latency and bandwidth constraints, the machine vision applications that process these video frames operate at the Edge of the network (Edge computing [3,4,19,28,29]). Transferring large amount of data generated by the cameras at the Edge in real-time results in high demand on the network bandwidth. Additionally many of these vision applications are latency sensitive - that is timely recognition of objects and their activity is important since events need to be responded within tight deadline constraints.

S. Paiva et al. (Eds.): SmartCity360° 2020, LNICST 372, pp. 274–292, 2021.
https://doi.org/10.1007/978-3-030-76063-2_20

Due to cost and ease of installation reasons, IoT devices deployed at the Edge make use of wireless technologies (WiFi (802.11ac) and Bluetooth (BLE)) as communication medium to transfer large amount of real-time video data. Data transmitted in the wireless channel (operating in the unlicensed bands) is prone to large variations in the latency due to interference, both from peer video cameras and unrelated external sources. The interference causes the data transfer network latency to exceed real-time response times and hence application set real-time bounds. Achieving a bounded latency in the face of unpredictable latency variations will require the ability to vary the information content transmitted from the cameras so as to match the channel conditions. However, varying the information content in the data (video frames in case of machine vision applications) will impact the application object/event detection accuracy as well.

In this paper we propose the use of approximate computing to meet dynamic network latency and bandwidth constraints at the Edge. Approximate computing is based on the idea that in some applications, selective inaccuracies in computation can be tolerated to achieve gains in efficiency [24]. Machine vision applications can potentially make use of approximate computing since they can tolerate compromises on object/event detection accuracy resulting from selective loss of video frame quality. We use this observation to investigate multiple video frame quality modification techniques (tuning knobs) so that the resulting reduction in data size satisfies latency and bandwidth constraints. Further we present two algorithms - the first based on a heuristic pruning of the large search space, and the second based on machine learning, to determine the settings of the tuning knob that simultaneously satisfy video frame size, and detection accuracy requirements. Experimental results indicate that for object detection vision application based on EfficientNet [31,32] Deep Learning architecture on the Microsoft COCO 2017 [20] dataset, we obtain an average video size reduction of 71.33% with an inference accuracy of 80.93% of that of the unmodified video frames.

This paper makes the following contributions -

- Investigates the applicability of approximate computing by characterizing the impact of video frame quality on machine vision accuracy.
- Identifies multiple video frame quality modification techniques (tuning knobs) that reduce video frame size.
- Presents pruning heuristic and machine learning based approaches to rapidly determine the settings of the tuning knob that simultaneously satisfy video frame size, and detection accuracy requirements.
- Presents extensive experimental evaluation of the approaches presented for object detection machine vision application using the EfficientNet Deep learning architecture on the Microsoft COCO 2017 dataset.

The rest of the paper is organized as follows - Sect. 2 provides a brief overview of related work in approximated computing, machine learning and video filtering at the Edge. In Sect. 3 we present the study of impact of video frame size on network latency. Section 4 lists multiple video frame quality tuning knobs and characterizes their impact on machine vision application inference accuracy.

Section 5 describes two scalable algorithms to identify tuning knobs that satisfy video frame size and application inference accuracy constraints. Section 6 experimentally evaluates the algorithms using publicly available dataset and machine vision application. Section 7 discusses the applicability of these algorithms in light of a representative Edge computing system. Section 8 concludes the paper.

2   Related Work

In this Section, we present the state of the art work done on application of machine learning, video filtering at the Edge and application of approximate computing.

In [25], Pakha et al. introduce the idea of control knobs such as frame selection and area cropping to parametrize a custom video protocol that streams videos from cameras to Cloud servers to perform neural-network-based video analytics. They developed a server driven video transmission protocol called SimpleProto that utilizes the tradeoffs between bandwidth usage and inference accuracy. In [6] Canel et al. proposes a new edge-to-cloud system called FilterForward that backhauls only relevant video frames from cameras to datacenter applications with the help of lightweight edge filters. However, unlike our approach, they perform computationally expensive Deep neural network based object detection at the client node.

Machine learning has been widely used at the wireless Edge for various applications such as resource management, networking, mobility management and localization [8,11,21,30,34]. In [34] Zhu et al. introduces a set of new machine learning-driven communication techniques. In [21] Mao et al. presents a taxonomy of applications of Deep Learning at different layers of wireless networks. Some of them include channel resource allocation, traffic prediction and link evaluation in data link layer and session scheduling and OS resource management for upper layers in the network stack. In contrast to these works where machine learning is applied at the lower layers of the network stack, our focus is on the application of machine learning at the application layer.

In [24], Mittal provides a survey of approximate computing techniques. Strategies for approximation at the code level such as loop perforation, and at the architecture level such as reduced precision operations are discussed. Regarding applications of approximate computing to Deep Learning, Chen et al. [7] use approximate computing to accelerate network training, while Ibrahim et al. [16] explore the use of approximate computing to realize Deep Learning networks on resource constrained embedded platforms. While our focus is on the use of approximate computing to satisfy network latency, and bandwidth constraints, in these works approximate computing is targeted towards reducing the computational load.

3   Impact of Video Frame Size on Network Latency

Size of video frames varies depending on the information content present in them. We initially explored the latency experienced by video frames with different sizes in the Wi-Fi channel using an IoT Edge testbed.

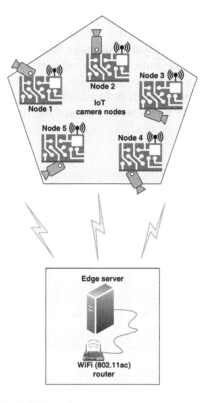

Fig. 1. IoT Edge test bed. IoT nodes equipped with cameras record and transmit video frames to an Edge server through a WiFi (802.11ac) wireless router. The Edge server runs machine vision algorithms on the received video frames for object detection, tracking and event prediction.

Figure 1 shows the IoT Edge test bed set up for Wi-Fi latency characterization purpose. The test bed consists of low power embedded boards (with 8-core ARMv8.2 based CPU) equipped with cameras, and a workstation furnished with an Nvidia GeForce 1060 GPU. The embedded boards and the workstation are termed as IoT camera nodes and Edge server respectively. Both IoT camera nodes and Edge server run Linux. The wireless link consists of a NETGEAR Nighthawk XR700 access point that uses 802.11ac (5 GHz) Wi-Fi standard. The Edge server is connected to the access point through Ethernet, while the IoT camera nodes connect to the access point through the 802.11ac Wi-Fi link. The IoT camera nodes are placed at 6m from the access point.

We characterized the Wi-Fi latency of video frames when they are transmitted from a test camera node to the Edge server. We use the term network latency to denote the latency experienced by video frames over the Wi-Fi channel when they are transmitted from IoT cameras nodes to the Edge server. This setup emulates an operational scenario where cameras produce variable size video frames depending on the scene dynamics in the area of observation.

Figure 2 shows the variation in network latency at different video frame sizes. The video frames of different sizes are chosen from publicly available vision dataset [26] and each measurement is taken as the average of 10 measurements. From this measurements, we note that the network latency shows an approximately linear variation with video frame size. Video frames with reduced size can be potentially transmitted with reduced network latency. Similar reductions in bandwidth requirements are possible by reducing the video frame size.

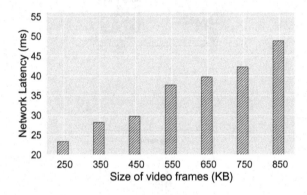

Fig. 2. Characterization of the impact of video frame size on video frame transfer network latency.

We note that the latency and bandwidth requirements are specified by the application, the wireless technology used, and cost constraints. Additionally, dynamically varying channel conditions due to interference, results in further constraint on bandwidth availability.

4   Video Frame Quality Tuning Knobs

As seen in Sect. 3, latency and bandwidth constraints can be satisfied by changing the video frame size. In this section we explore multiple video frame quality modification techniques which when applied on video frames reduce the frame size. Further, we investigate the impact of the reduced frame size on the machine vision application inference accuracy. The techniques, referred to as tuning knobs, are described below.

1. **Knob1 - Colorspace modifications:** Video frames can be converted from one colorspace to another resulting in total size reduction. We select 8 such colorspace modifications which are BGR $\leftrightarrow$ Gray, BGR $\leftrightarrow$ XYZ, BGR $\leftrightarrow$ HSV, BGR $\leftrightarrow$ HLS, BGR $\leftrightarrow$ LAB, BGR $\leftrightarrow$ LUV, BGR $\leftrightarrow$ YUV and BGR $\leftrightarrow$ CrCb. Our choice of color space modifications can reduce the video frame size by as much as 60%.

2. **Knob2 - Blurring:** Video frames can be blurred by passing them through various low pass filters. We chose the filter kernel sizes of 5, 8, 10, 15 and 20 as possible knob settings. Blurring the video frames can reduce the video frame size by as much as 75%.

3. **Knob3 - Denoising:** Noise content in video frames can be removed by passing them through denoising filters. The 5 knob settings selected for this knob are denoising filter strengths of 3, 10, 15, 20 and 30. Denoising knob can reduce the frame size upto 67%.

4. **Knob4 - Contrast stretching:** Contrast stretching can be done on video frames by performing range normalization over the frame pixel array. The norm values for range normalization are chosen from 0.3 to 0.9 with intervals of 0.1. Contrast stretching using these knob settings can achieve upto 70% size reduction.

5. **Knob5 - 2D filtering:** The 2D filtering approach convolves a video frame with a kernel and removes the noise in the frame. This knob could reduce the frame size as much as 68% when filter kernel sizes of 5, 6, 7 and 8 are applied on the video frames.

6. **Knob6 - Gaussian filtering:** A video frame can be convolved with a Gaussian kernel to remove Gaussian noise from the video frame. Selected kernel sizes are 5, 11, 21, 31 and 51 and achieved size reduction is 79%.

7. **Knob7 - Median filtering:** The median filtering technique computes the median of all the pixels under a kernel window and the central pixel is replaced with this median value. This technique is highly effective in removing salt-and-pepper noise from video frames. By choosing the knob settings as 5, 9, 11, 13 and 19, frame size reduced upto 72%.

8. **Knob8 - Bilateral Filtering:** Bilateral filtering removes noise in video frames while preserving the sharp edges in them. For this knob the filter sizes are chosen to be 10, 30 and 50 and filter sigma values are chosen as 70, 150 and 200. Upon application of this knob video frames reduced in its size by 64%.

9. **Knob9 - Erosion:** Erosion is a type of morphological transformation that erodes away the boundaries of objects in video frames and is useful in removing small white noises. Choosing erosion filter kernel sizes to be 5, 10 and 15 we could achieve size reduction of 62%.

10. **Knob10 - Dilation:** Dilation is another type of morphological transformation which is the opposite of erosion. This knob dilates video frames using a kernel structure. The kernel structure sizes chosen are 5, 8 and 10 with size reductions of upto 52%.

Note that each of these knobs can be set independent of the other knobs potentially resulting in a large ($\approx$22 million) search space.

4.1   Impact of Tuning Knobs on Application Inference Accuracy

Reducing the information content by applying these tuning knobs on video frames could impact the object/event detection inference accuracy of machine vision applications consuming these video frames. In general, the impact is dependent on the particular machine vision application. We choose object detection as the machine vision application since it is widely used, and is a basis of other computer vision tasks such as object tracking, and activity detection. The object detector EfficientDet [31] is based on EfficientNet [32], a deep learning neural network developed by Google brain team. It achieves state-of-the-art accuracy while being up to 9x smaller than competing models and using significantly less computation. Microsoft COCO [20] is a publicly available vision dataset consisting of 91 object categories (classes) with a total of 2.5 million labeled instances in 328K images. We input the original and modified video frames from COCO 2017 dataset to EfficientDet to generate object detections on video frames with bounding boxes drawn around the objects.

In order to evaluate these detections, each ground truth bounding box for that frame (publicly available) is matched exclusively to the outputted bounding box based on highest Intersection over Union (IoU) overlap. Positive matches with an IoU greater than a threshold are considered True Positives; result bounding boxes without ground truth matches are considered False Positives; and each unmatched ground truth box is considered a False Negative. These records are utilized for mAP (Mean Average Precision) calculation.

For object detection, we utilize the mAP metric with an Intersection-over-Union (IoU) threshold of 0.5. Equation 1 defines the calculation for mAP. Precision is $\frac{TP}{(TP+FP)}$ and Recall is $\frac{TP}{(TP+FN)}$, where TP, FP, and FN are the number of True Positives, False Positives, and False Negatives respectively. Average Precision calculated at a single IoU threshold (0.5 in our case) for a single object class is denoted as, $AP^{IoU=.5}$. Finally, mAP is obtained by averaging $AP^{IoU=.5}$ over different classes in the chosen dataset.

$$mAP = \frac{1}{\#classes} \sum_{class \in classes} AP^{IoU=.5}[class] \qquad (1)$$

where $\#classes$ represents number of classes of objects in the video frames and $AP^{IoU=.5}[class]$ represents $AP^{IoU=.5}$ for a specific object class.

Figures 3 and 4 show the impact of application of tuning knobs, blurring and denoising (Knobs 2 and 3) on and video frame size and mAP. The mAP of unmodified (without the application of any tuning knob) video frame is considered as the baseline mAP. The mAP values obtained after applying tuning knobs on video frames are normalized with respect to the baseline mAP. This characterization corresponds to mAP generated (using EfficientDet-D0 [2] model) on 300 images chosen from COCO 2017 dataset.

Figures 3 and 4 demonstrate that the application of these tuning knobs can reduce the video frame size 75% and application inference accuracy as much as 47%. A similar trend for video frame size reduction and accuracy degradation can be observed for other tuning knobs (Knobs 1 and 4–10) as well.

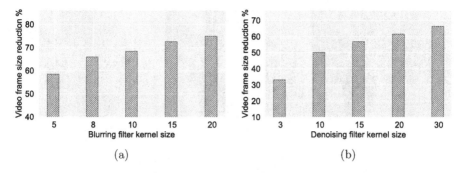

Fig. 3. Characterization of the impact of application of tuning knobs, (a) blurring (knob 2) and (b) denoising (knob 3) on video frame size.

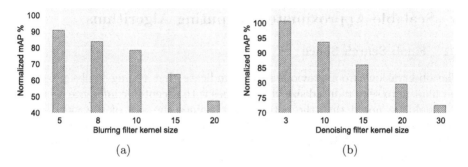

Fig. 4. Characterization of the impact of application of tuning knobs, (a) blurring (knob 2) and (b) denoising (knob 3) on mAP (application inference accuracy).

From Fig. 4, note that setting 1 of knob 2 reduced the mAP to 90.8% of the baseline and setting 2 of knob 3 reduced mAP to 93.5% of baseline. Figure 5 shows the visual impact of application of setting 1 of knob 2 and setting 2 of knob 3 on object detections. Because of the effect of quality modification, both the video frames have missed detections for a few objects. But note that both the modified video frames (Figs. 5b and 5c) still preserve most of the true detections for object categories such as person and bicycle.

This observation can be used to exploit the trade off between video frame size and video frame quality (approximate computing) inherent in machine vision applications. Approximate computing exploits the gap between the extent of accuracy needed by the applications and provided by the computing system for achieving various optimizations [24]. A lower quality video frame has a smaller size, and hence can be transferred with lower network latency and bandwidth requirements. If a lower quality frame can provide acceptable machine vision application inference accuracy, then a lower quality frame could be transferred from the IoT camera node to the Edge server satisfying network performance constraints.

(a)   (b)   (c)

Fig. 5. Visual impact on object detections before and after the application of tuning knobs. (a) Unmodified video frame, video frame after applying (b) blurring knob with a kernel size of 5 and (c) denoising knob with a kernel size of 10.

5 Scalable Approximate Computing Algorithms

5.1 Knob Search Space

The observations from previous section indicate that tuning knobs provide a mechanism to send reduced size video frames with acceptable inference accuracy. It should be noted that the network determines the size of the video frame that needs to be transmitted, while the machine vision application decides the inference accuracy metric (for e.g. mAP for object detection). To select the knob settings that constitute the targeted frame size and target inference accuracy metrics, all combinations of settings of identified knobs need to be characterized. However, combining the knob settings for different tuning knobs results in a combinatorial explosion of the design space as seen in Eq. 2. For tuning knobs from 1 to n, this number can be represented using the equation,

$$k_{total} = k_1 \times k_2 \times \ldots \times k_i \times \ldots \times k_n \qquad (2)$$

where k_{total} represents the total number of knob combinations and k_i represents number of knob settings for the ith knob. For the 10 tuning knobs identified in Sect. 4 this results in a total number of 22,394,880 knob combinations. Computing and storing the resulting frame size (by applying knob combinations sequentially on video frames) and the machine vision inference metric (by feeding the modified video frames to the machine vision application) become prohibitively expensive.

We therefore explore two scalable algorithms to solve the combinatorial explosion problem - a design space pruning heuristic algorithm, and a machine learning based algorithm.

5.2 Pruning Heuristic Algorithm for Knob Selection

We use pruning heuristic algorithm to successively filter out knob combinations that result in lower performance on the inference metric. In this algorithm we consider the k_{total} knob combinations of Eq. 2 as the heuristic decision space of the problem. The algorithm works as follows. The search space consists of n tuning knobs with each tuning knob i consisting of k_i tuning knob settings. In the first step of this algorithm we change the knob setting for a single tuning knob (while keeping settings of other knobs at their defaults) and calculate the frame size and inference metric. We repeat this process for all the knob settings independently for each knob. We then filter out knob settings that results in a low performance on the inference metric (lower than a application specified threshold). This completes the first step of the algorithm. In the second step, we choose pairs of knob combinations from distinct knob combinations obtained from the first step. A filtering step similar to the first step is then applied to weed out knob combinations with lower performance on the inference metric. This completes the second step of the algorithm. The process is repeated next considering 3 distinct knob combinations from the knob setting obtained from step 2. The algorithm terminates when all n distinct knob combinations are considered in the n-th step. Each step i, prunes the design space by eliminating low performing knob combinations.

The algorithm for the pruning heuristic knob selection is outlined in the pseudo code shown in Listing 1.

Algorithm 1: Pruning heuristic algorithm

Result: Video frame quality knob settings
InferenceAccuracy = $Iacc$;
InferenceAccuracyThreshold = $Iacc_{Thres}$;
numKnobs = n ;
$step_i = 1$;
while $step_i <= n$ **do**
    from n knobs, choose i settings = nC_i ;
    for *each setting k_i in nC_i* **do**
        apply setting k_i on video frame;
        calculate video frame size;
        calculate $Iacc$ on video frame;
        if $Iacc < Iacc_{Thres}$ **then**
            discard setting k_i;
    end
    increment $step_i$ by 1
end

5.3   Machine Learning Algorithm for Knob Selection

In contrast to pruning the entire knob space to identify useful knobs using the pruning heuristic algorithm, a machine learning algorithmic approach can be used predict video frame size and inference accuracy. To build the model, we first collect the input data required to train the model. We sample a small subset of knob combinations from the total possible set of knob combinations, and evaluate the video frame size and machine vision application inference accuracy for the sampled knob combinations. We then develop a machine learning model and train it using the sampled knob data to predict the size and inference accuracy for remaining knob combinations. The detailed steps of the algorithm are described below.

The first step of the algorithm is the data collection process. Here the data represents tuning knob combinations identified using Eq. 2, the resulting video frame size after applying tuning knobs, and the associated inference accuracy of machine vision application. Since the knob sample space is large calculating the frame size and inference accuracy for all the knob combinations is a time consuming process. Therefore we select a representative set of samples from the knob search space using a sampling method. A Latin Hypercube Sampling (LHS) [22,23] method can be used to generate near-random samples from the multi-dimensional search space of knobs. LHS with a 'maximun' criteria is specifically chosen to avoid the correlation between samples by maximizing the minimum distance between samples [17].

The next step is to modify the video frames by applying the sampled knob combinations, and recording the resulting video frame sizes. The modified video frames are fed to the machine vision application to generate the inference accuracy for each knob combination. At the end of this step for each knob combination we have a frame size and inference accuracy value.

We aim to two build two models - one to predict frame size and another to predict inference accuracy values; we consider the knob combinations as common input features to both models. We note that all the input features (knob combinations) have their dependent variable values (frame size and inference accuracy) labeled. Hence we conclude that a supervised learning method needs to be used for this kind of labeled data samples. Another observation is that both the dependent variables are real-valued quantities that need to be predicted. Therefore a regression model would be best suited for this type of data. Also we observed that knobs have a non-linear dependence on both frame size and inference accuracy. Additionally, video frames with same size map to different inference accuracy values. Due to the complex dependence of knobs on frame size and inference accuracy, we chose to proceed with a non-linear machine learning model to estimate the dependent variables.

We experimented with multiple non-linear models such as polynomial regression, Support vector machine [13], Random forest regression [5] and Decision tree regression [27]. But none of the models could provide sufficient level of prediction accuracy. Then we explored a recently proposed model called CatBoostRegressor [12] from open source gradient boosting library CatBoost [1] because of the categorical nature of the input features (knob combinations). Models from CatBoost library outperforms state of the art gradient boosting libraries such as XGBoost [9] and LightBGM [18] in terms of model quality and training speed. CatBoost is a decision tree based library that uses two phases to predict the next tree.

In CatBoost the second phase is performed using traditional Gradient Boosting Decision Tree (GBDT) [14] scheme and for the first phase a modified version of GDBT is used.

6 Implementation and Results

In this section we present the experimental evaluation of the scalable approximate computing algorithms described in Sect. 5.

6.1 Pruning Heuristic Algorithm

We implemented all the knobs identified in Sect. 4 using open source computer vision library OpenCV [33]. The video frames were chosen from Microsoft COCO 2017 dataset. A set of 300 video frames belonging to object classes person, bicycle, car and traffic light were selected for the experimental evaluation. We chose the object detector model EfficientDet [31] (based on EfficientNet [32]) as the machine vision application to evaluate its inference metric (mAP) on modified video frames. EfficientDet model D0 was chosen among models D0 to D7 because it is least complex model (has low number of model parameters and low computation latency) and is suited for resource constrained Edge devices.

A set of 146 knob combinations was identified using the pruning heuristic algorithm from the 22 million knob search space explained in Sect. 5.1. To identify these knob combinations we set the inference accuracy threshold (mAP) of the EfficientDet object detector to be >80% of the baseline mAP. Note that the application of all 146 combinations of the knobs identified above result in different sizes of video frames, all lower than the original.

Figure 6 shows the plot of the normalized mAP expressed as a percentage vs. video frame size for video frames (from COCO dataset) modified using the filtered knob combinations. The video frame size buckets in Fig. 6 corresponds to different combinations of the knob settings with different resulting mAP. Note that higher mAP indicates higher inference accuracy for EfficeintDet. (The reason for size bucket 100–120 showing a max normalized mAP greater than 100% is because of the effect of knob setting 1 of knob3-denoising, which actually caused the mAP to become slightly higher than baseline mAP.)

Using the pruning heuristic algorithm we could identify knob settings that achieved 71.33% video frame size reduction with mAP score of as much as 82.37% of the baseline mAP. This key observation enables transmission of smaller sized images with less mAP from the IoT camera nodes to the Edge server when subjected to network latency and bandwidth constraints.

Figure 7 shows the visual impact of application of tuning knobs (colorspace modification, denoising, contrast stretching and gaussian filtering) resulting in a normalized mAP of 82.37% and size reduction of 71.33%. We note that the object detections in Fig. 7b contains most of the true detections (from unmodified video frame) except a few missed detections such as a bicycle, a parking meter, one car

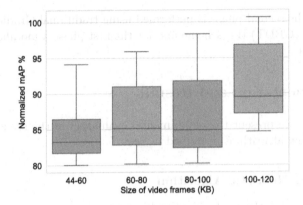

Fig. 6. Normalized mAP expressed as a percentage for EfficientDet mAP for video frames from COCO dataset. Note that each video frame bucket corresponds to different combinations of the knob settings with different resulting mAP.

and two traffic lights. Two wrong detections resulting here are a bicycle detected as vase, and a person detected as car.

Using Eq. 2 we estimate the total number of knobs need to be evaluated to be 354 by executing the pruning heuristic algorithm (Listing 1) for steps from 1 to 4 and using the 10 knobs and their settings identified in Sect. 4. The application set inference accuracy threshold was set to be >80% of the baseline mAP. The computation time taken to evaluate mAP scores (using EfficientDet-D0 on an Nvidia GeForce 1060 GPU) for 354 combinations for 300 video frames from COCO dataset is 10.03 h. The total time taken for evaluations escalates substantially when number of knobs and/or settings for each knob increase.

(a)   (b)

Fig. 7. Visual impact on object detections before and after the application of tuning knobs. (a) unmodified video frame and (b) video frame after applying knobs - colorspace modification, denoising, contrast stretching and gaussian filtering.

6.2   Machine Learning Algorithm

We sampled 1000 knob combinations (using Latin Hypercube Sampling) from the knob sample space to generate the input data for the model. Next, the sampled knob combinations are applied to video frames to calculate the video frame size. All the knob settings are represented as categorical features before feeding into the model. We then divided the samples into train and test samples using an 80–20% split. As explained in Sect. 5.3, we chose the machine learning model CatBoostRegressor [12] model from open source library for gradient boosting library catboost [1]. We trained the model and predicted the frame sizes for the knob combinations from the test sample set. We obtained train and test Root Mean Square Errors (RMSEs) for this model as 0.74 KB and 1.5 KB respectively.

Next we take knob settings along with their video frame sizes as input features to construct a model to predict the machine vision application inference accuracy. The inference accuracy metric chosen for EfficientDet is mAP. With knob settings represented as categorical features, we use the CatBoostRegressor model to predict mAP scores for test knob combinations. For this model we achieved train and test RMSEs as 0.51% and 1.6% (normalized mAP) respectively.

Using the machine learning algorithm we could identify knob settings that achieved 71.37% video frame size reduction with mAP score of as much as 80.93% of the baseline mAP.

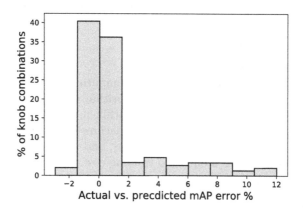

Fig. 8. Histogram showing the distribution of error between actual and predicted mAP scores for percentage of knob combinations chosen to test the mAP ML model. 82.19% of the knob combinations have predicted mAP error variation of only ±3% of actual mAP.

Figures 8 and 9 show the percentage variation of actual and predicted mAP and video frame size with respect to percentage of knob combinations in test sample. Video frame size histogram (Fig. 9) shows 78.08% of the knob combinations fall within ±10% of video frame size error. The mAP histogram (Fig. 8) shows that 82.19% of knob combinations fall within ±3% of mAP error. Since we could predict accurately (with less than 10% error) most of the knob combinations' video frame size and inference accuracy using the constructed models, we conclude that the models are sufficiently accurate. The computation time taken to evaluate mAP scores (using EfficientDet-D0 on an Nvidia GeForce 1060 GPU) for 1000 knob combinations (used for training and testing the models) for 300 video frames from COCO dataset is 28.33 h.

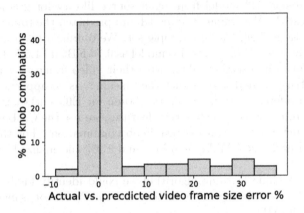

Fig. 9. Histogram showing the distribution of variation between actual and predicted video frame size for percentage knob combinations chosen to test the video frame size ML model. 78.08% of the knob combinations have predicted frame size error variation of only ±10% of actual frame size.

Comparing the two scalable approximate computing algorithms, the Categorical boost machine learning model based algorithm achieves comparable accuracies to the pruning heuristic algorithm (within ±3% error for mAP model, and ±10% for video frame size model). The machine learning approach is more scalable both in terms of the number of knobs, and the number of settings for each knob, since it only has a one time training cost.

7   System Integration

In the previous section we described how pruning heuristic and machine learning algorithms can be used to characterize video frame size and machine vision application inference accuracy for different combinations of video frame quality modifications. In this section we describe the applicability of these algorithms in a IoT Edge vision system.

Consider a multi-camera Edge vision system similar to the one shown in Fig. 1 deployed in a public space such as a traffic intersection for detecting pedestrians. The IoT nodes equipped with cameras stream live videos of the area under observation to the Edge server through a wireless network (for example

Wi-Fi). The Edge server aggregates the individual video streams from multiple cameras and run machine vision application to detect pedestrians to ensure road safety. The pedestrian detection application is latency sensitive and requires video frames from the cameras to be processed with in a short time window to meet the real time deadlines. The application informs real time latency and inference accuracy requirements to the IoT camera nodes. The camera nodes monitor current Wi-Fi channel conditions by sensing latency (varies depending on the channel interference) of video frame transmission in the channel. If the current latency exceeds the latency target set by the application video frames have to be modified by applying the tuning knobs describe in Sect. 4, hence reducing their size to meet target latency.

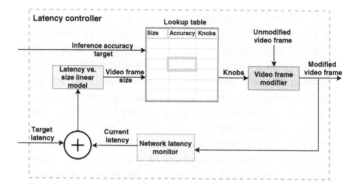

Fig. 10. Design of a latency controller for the Edge that uses knob selection algorithms explained in Sect. 5 to construct frame size, inference accuracy, knobs lookup table.

Video frame size that satisfy a latency value can be calculated from the latency characterization of Sect. 3. While reducing the size, the inference accuracy demand from the application also needs to be met. To facilitate the size reduction process in real time the IoT camera nodes can store the candidate knob combinations resulting from the algorithms described in Sect. 5 in a simple lookup table. The lookup table entries will be the frame size, inference accuracy value and the settings of the individual image modification knobs. The entries in the lookup table can then be used to search for the tuning knob combination that satisfy both the latency and inference accuracy demands. A controller operating at the camera node can potentially perform latency control of video frames in real time [15]. Figure 10 shows the block diagram of a possible closed loop control.

Alternately, the machine learning model could be evaluated in real-time to predict the inference accuracy, and frame size resulting from a given knob combination. In this case the machine learning models act as objective functions that need to be minimized or maximized in a multi-objective optimization space [10]. The goal would be to find a set of solutions (knob combinations) as close as possible to the conflicting objectives. The resulting knob combinations can then be used to populate the lookup table when the controller is operated in the real time. For instance the objectives can be video frame size upper bound that need to be minimized and inference accuracy lower bound that need to be maximized. Note that the network conditions determines the video frame size constraint whereas the machine vision application determines the inference accuracy constraint.

8   Conclusion

In this work we explored the problem of latency and bandwidth constrained operation at the IoT Edge for machine vision applications through the technique of approximate computing. We observe that despite reducing video frame sizes, acceptable inference accuracies are possible. We identified a number of video frame transformation techniques, that can result in reduced frame size, and effectively acts as latency/bandwidth tuning knobs for the application. Since the design space suffers from a combinatorial explosion problem precluding exhaustive characterization of knob combinations, we investigated scalable algorithms to facilitate our approximate computing approach. We experimentally evaluated two approaches - a heuristic based pruning algorithm of the design space, and a Categorical boost machine learning model based algorithm. Both approaches were able to reduce the video frame size by upto 71.3% while achieving a inference accuracy of 80.9% of the inference accuracy of the unmodified video frames. The lower frame size can facilitate operation in a bandwdith constrained environment, as well as results in a lower communication latency. The machine learning model has a fixed training cost compared to the heuristic based pruning algorithm, while being inherently more scalable. We also briefly discuss how the tuning knobs resulting from the two algorithms could be integrated in a latency controller in an autonomous system targeted at latency sensitive IoT Edge machine vision applications.

Among future work directions, we could incorporate the approximate computing based algorithms proposed in the paper in latency and bandwidth constrained Edge and Cloud computing systems. We have targeted object detection in this work, since it is a basic kernel in many machine vision tasks. We could also explore the use of the proposed techniques on other machine vision tasks such as object tracking, image segmentation, and activity detection.

References

1. Catboost. https://catboost.ai/. Accessed 12 Sep 2020
2. Efficientdet. https://github.com/google/automl/tree/master/efficientdet. Accessed 12 Sep 2020
3. Bonomi, F., Milito, R., Natarajan, P., Zhu, J.: Fog computing: a platform for Internet of Things and analytics. In: Bessis, N., Dobre, C. (eds.) Big Data and Internet of Things: A Roadmap for Smart Environments. SCI, vol. 546, pp. 169–186. Springer, Cham (2014). https://doi.org/10.1007/978-3-319-05029-4_7

4. Bonomi, F., Milito, R., Zhu, J., Addepalli, S.: Fog computing and its role in the Internet of Things. In: Proceedings of the First Edition of the MCC Workshop on Mobile Cloud Computing, MCC 2012, pp. 13–16. Association for Computing Machinery, New York (2012). https://doi.org/10.1145/2342509.2342513

5. Breiman, L.: Random forests. Mach. Learn. **45**(1), 5–32 (2001). https://doi.org/10.1023/A:1010933404324

6. Canel, C., et al.: Scaling video analytics on constrained edge nodes. In: Proceedings of the 2nd SysML Conference (SysML 2019), Palo Alto, CA, pp. 1–5 (2019)

7. Chen, C., Choi, J., Gopalakrishnan, K., Srinivasan, V., Venkataramani, S.: Exploiting approximate computing for deep learning acceleration. In: 2018 Design, Automation Test in Europe Conference Exhibition (DATE), pp. 821–826 (2018)

8. Chen, M., Challita, U., Saad, W., Yin, C., Debbah, M.: Artificial neural networks-based machine learning for wireless networks: a tutorial. IEEE Commun. Surv. Tutor. **21**(4), 3039–3071 (2019)

9. Chen, T., Guestrin, C.: XGBoost: a scalable tree boosting system. In: Proceedings of the 22nd ACM SIGKDD International Conference on Knowledge Discovery and Data Mining, KDD 2016, pp. 785–794. Association for Computing Machinery, New York (2016). https://doi.org/10.1145/2939672.2939785

10. Deb, K., Kalyanmoy, D.: Multi-Objective Optimization Using Evolutionary Algorithms. Wiley, USA (2001)

11. Deng, S., Zhao, H., Fang, W., Yin, J., Dustdar, S., Zomaya, A.Y.: Edge intelligence: the confluence of edge computing and artificial intelligence. IEEE Internet Things J. **7**(8), 7457–7469 (2020)

12. Dorogush, A.V., Ershov, V., Gulin, A.: CatBoost: gradient boosting with categorical features support. ArXiv abs/1810.11363 (2018)

13. Evgeniou, T., Pontil, M.: Support vector machines: theory and applications. In: Paliouras, G., Karkaletsis, V., Spyropoulos, C.D. (eds.) ACAI 1999. LNCS (LNAI), vol. 2049, pp. 249–257. Springer, Heidelberg (2001). https://doi.org/10.1007/3-540-44673-7_12

14. Friedman, J.H.: Greedy function approximation: a gradient boosting machine. Ann. Stat. **29**(5), 1189–1232 (2001). https://doi.org/10.1214/aos/1013203451

15. George, A., Ravindran, A.: Latency control for distributed machine vision at the edge through approximate computing. In: Zhang, T., Wei, J., Zhang, L.-J. (eds.) EDGE 2019. LNCS, vol. 11520, pp. 16–30. Springer, Cham (2019). https://doi.org/10.1007/978-3-030-23374-7_2

16. Ibrahim, A., Osta, M., Alameh, M., Saleh, M., Chible, H., Valle, M.: Approximate computing methods for embedded machine learning. In: 2018 25th IEEE International Conference on Electronics, Circuits and Systems (ICECS), pp. 845–848 (2018)

17. Joseph, V.R., Hung, Y.: Orthogonal-maximin Latin hypercube designs. Statistica Sinica **18**(1), 171–186 (2008). http://www.jstor.org/stable/24308251

18. Ke, G., et al.: LightGBM: a highly efficient gradient boosting decision tree. In: NIPS (2017)

19. Lee, E.A., et al.: The swarm at the edge of the cloud. IEEE Des. Test **31**(3), 8–20 (2014)

20. Lin, T.-Y., et al.: Microsoft COCO: common objects in context. In: Fleet, D., Pajdla, T., Schiele, B., Tuytelaars, T. (eds.) ECCV 2014. LNCS, vol. 8693, pp. 740–755. Springer, Cham (2014). https://doi.org/10.1007/978-3-319-10602-1_48

21. Mao, Q., Hu, F., Hao, Q.: Deep learning for intelligent wireless networks: a comprehensive survey. IEEE Commun. Surv. Tutor. **20**(4), 2595–2621 (2018)

22. McKay, M.D., Beckman, R.J., Conover, W.J.: A comparison of three methods for selecting values of input variables in the analysis of output from a computer code. Technometrics **21**(2), 239–245 (1979). http://www.jstor.org/stable/1268522
23. McKay, M.D.: Latin hypercube sampling as a tool in uncertainty analysis of computer models. In: Proceedings of the 24th Conference on Winter Simulation, WSC 1992, pp. 557–564. Association for Computing Machinery, New York (1992). https://doi.org/10.1145/167293.167637
24. Mittal, S.: A survey of techniques for approximate computing. ACM Comput. Surv. **48**(4), 1–33 (2016). https://doi.org/10.1145/2893356
25. Pakha, C., Chowdhery, A., Jiang, J.: Reinventing video streaming for distributed vision analytics. In: Proceedings of the 10th USENIX Conference on Hot Topics in Cloud Computing, HotCloud 2018, p. 1. USENIX Association, USA (2018)
26. Rasouli, A., Kotseruba, I., Tsotsos, J.K.: Are they going to cross? A benchmark dataset and baseline for pedestrian crosswalk behavior. In: 2017 IEEE International Conference on Computer Vision Workshops (ICCVW), pp. 206–213 (2017)
27. Rokach, L., Maimon, O.: Decision trees. In: Maimon, O., Rokach, L. (eds.) Data Mining and Knowledge Discovery Handbook. Springer, Boston (2005). https://doi.org/10.1007/0-387-25465-X_9
28. Satyanarayanan, M., Bahl, P., Caceres, R., Davies, N.: The case for VM-based cloudlets in mobile computing. IEEE Pervasive Comput. **8**(4), 14–23 (2009)
29. Shi, W., Cao, J., Zhang, Q., Li, Y., Xu, L.: Edge computing: vision and challenges. IEEE Internet Things J. **3**(5), 637–646 (2016)
30. Sun, Y., Peng, M., Zhou, Y., Huang, Y., Mao, S.: Application of machine learning in wireless networks: key techniques and open issues. IEEE Commun. Surv. Tutor. **21**(4), 3072–3108 (2019)
31. Tan, M., Pang, R., Le, Q.V.: Efficientdet: scalable and efficient object detection. In: 2020 IEEE/CVF Conference on Computer Vision and Pattern Recognition (CVPR), pp. 10778–10787 (2020)
32. Tan, M., Le, Q.: EfficientNet: rethinking model scaling for convolutional neural networks. Proceedings of Machine Learning Research, vol. 97, pp. 6105–6114. PMLR, Long Beach (09–15 June 2019). http://proceedings.mlr.press/v97/tan19a.html
33. Vision, O.S.C.: OpenCV documentation (2019). https://docs.opencv.org
34. Zhu, G., Liu, D., Du, Y., You, C., Zhang, J., Huang, K.: Toward an intelligent edge: wireless communication meets machine learning. IEEE Commun. Mag. **58**(1), 19–25 (2020)

Collaborative Task Processing
with Internet of Things (IoT) Clusters

Jorge Coelho[1,2]([✉]) and Luís Nogueira[1]

[1] School of Engineering (ISEP), Polytechnic Institute of Porto (IPP),
Porto, Portugal
jmn@isep.ipp.pt
[2] LIACC Research Centre – University of Porto, Porto, Portugal

Abstract. We propose a framework for a collaborative processing of resource intensive services among Internet of Things (IoT) devices. Our goal is to optimize the use of this type of devices, particularly those being underutilized. The infrastructure bellow our framework is typically built with heterogenous appliances that have specific functions and the idea is to minimize the need for software updates and other changes, trying to use their spare resources with minimal interference. We base our solution in a pragmatic approach to task offloading based in the Erlang programming language.

Keywords: Edge computing · Computational offloading · IoT · Functional programming · Erlang

1 Introduction

Given the ubiquity of Internet of Things (IoT) devices and their strong proliferation [3] many opportunities appear in exploring their potentialities, namely their connectivity and computational power [11]. The quantity of data produced by a variety of data sources and sent to end systems to further processing is growing significantly, increasingly demanding more processing power. The challenges become even more critical when a coordinated content analysis of the data sent from multiple sources is necessary. Thus, with a potentially unbounded amount of stream data and limited resources, some of the processing tasks may not be satisfyingly answered, guaranteeing a desired level of performance.

Computation offloading is recognized as a promising solution by migrating a part or an entire application to a remote server in order to be executed there. Various models and frameworks have been proposed to offload resource intensive components of applications for a more efficient execution [7,9,13]. These solutions rely on the concept of offloading to the cloud. However, due to the increase of hardware capabilities of IoT devices and their proliferation, making it common to have several of these devices in the same area, offloading to the cloud is not always a necessity if the available resources of these devices are wisely used.

© ICST Institute for Computer Sciences, Social Informatics and Telecommunications Engineering 2021
Published by Springer Nature Switzerland AG 2021. All Rights Reserved
S. Paiva et al. (Eds.): SmartCity360° 2020, LNICST 372, pp. 293–304, 2021.
https://doi.org/10.1007/978-3-030-76063-2_21

The study of scenarios where heterogeneous nodes with unknown resources are aggregated in a collaborative effort to achieve some goal was the subject of works such as [10] where some sort of data analysis is needed to estimate each node capacity and distribute work wisely.

Functional programming is an established approach to implement parallel and distributed systems [2]. The minimization of the need of a shared state enables code distribution and parallel processing which fosters the development of easily scalable systems. Due to the rise of multicore and distributed systems, functional programming spread its influence through many mainstream languages [14,15] and is used in major cloud infrastructures such as the AWS Lambda [4]. In particular, Erlang [1] due to its simplicity and strong support for fault tolerant distributed programming, is seen as a promising language for IoT applications [8].

In this paper, we propose an Erlang-based framework for parallel processing of tasks in a cluster of IoT devices. These devices are able to communicate and report their resource availability, accepting computational tasks for execution. The goal is to have one of the connected devices requesting to offload tasks and relying on a module that coordinates all the communication process and does a balanced scheduling of tasks based on their estimate computational cost and the device's availability in terms of computational power.

Distributing tasks implies knowing what nodes are available for this collaborating process, the amount of resources each node can offer and the approximate complexity of each task. These information will allow us to decide which node is the best one to process a given task. Note that we want to keep the changes at the node level minimal in order to not compromise its original function. Thus, we consider the use of resource reservation approaches [5,12] at the operating system level. A paradigm based on resource reservation can endow applications with timing and throughput guarantees independent of the behavior of other applications, and can be employed across all system resources including processor cycles, communication bandwidth, disk bandwidth, and storage. This way, IoT devices can cooperate and execute offloaded tasks while being able to establish the maximum amount of resources that can eventually be at use by the proposed framework.

This paper is organized as follows. In the next section, we introduce the system model with the formal definitions for the network, communication protocol and scheduling behavior. Then, we describe the implementation of our system, and finally, we evaluate the results and conclude the paper.

2   System Model

Here we describe the system model of our framework by introducing formal definitions along with several considerations about its behavior. It is important to note that it is the programmer's responsibility to identify decomposable problems that can be used in this scenario. Our system is presented in a very simplified high level description in Fig. 1 and described next:

Data decomposition and assignment of data to nodes: Work is decomposed in several pieces, where the number of pieces is a function of the number of available nodes, and their size is proportional to each node's performance index.

Communication and failure management: There is the need to send data to process to chosen nodes, wait for the results and manage their eventual failures. Whenever a node fails, the work that was not processed goes back to the decomposition phase as a new instance of the process.

Mapping of results: Final result computation and its return to the application.

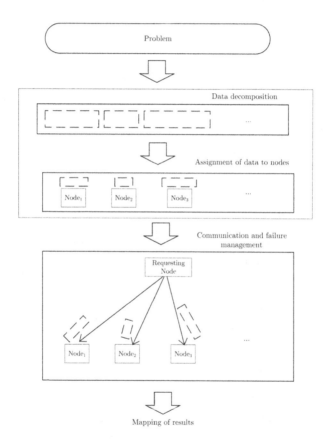

Fig. 1. Cooperative task execution overview

We now proceed with some definitions.

Definition 1 (Task). *We define a task t_i as a λ function. By nature, it will have no side effects and can be executed in parallel with other λ functions.*

In the remaining of this paper we will use the term task and lambda function for describing the same unit of execution and we use the term IoT device and node with the same meaning.

A device that needs to offload tasks to others can rely on a cluster of IoT devices for accomplishing this goal. We now define a cluster which is the set of nodes currently available, meaning they are currently accepting tasks to execute.

Definition 2 (Cluster of IoT devices). *Given an IoT device, we represent it by a node n_i. A cluster has a number of nodes which can be variable during the execution of a computational intensive application and is defined as $S = \{n_1, \ldots, n_k\}$, where $k \geq 1$ and $n_i \in S$ is one of the nodes currently available. The nodes can enter and leave the cluster at anytime as result for example of power failure (in case of leaving) or a new device is turned on (in case of entering).*

Computation platforms now integrate hundreds to thousands of processing cores, running complex and dynamic applications that make it difficult to foresee the amount of load they can impose to those platforms. Therefore, resource allocation is one of the most complex problems in large multi-processor and distributed systems, and in general it is considered NP-hard.

Elementary combinatorics provides us with evidence of the problem of scale. For a simple formulation of the problem of allocating jobs to processors (one-to-one allocation), one can see that the number of allocations grows with the factorial of the number of jobs and processors.

To cope with dynamism, a dynamic approach to resource management is the most obvious choice, aiming to dynamically learn and react to changes to the load characteristics and to the underlying computing platform. A static allocation decided before deployment based on the (nearly) complete knowledge about the load and the platform, is not viable. It is then evident that optimal resource allocation algorithms cannot cope with this type of problem, and that lightweight heuristic solutions are needed. A comprehensive survey of the kinds of resource allocation heuristics that can cover different levels of dynamicity, while coping with the scale and complexity of high-density many-core platforms is available in [5].

A cluster of nodes can be ordered from the more powerful to the less powerful by evaluating their capabilities in terms of processing power and memory. Our option was to adopt a pragmatic approach, by implementing a simple heuristic function that relates clock speed, available CPU, number of cores and available RAM. Details on how we get this data are described in the implementation section. We now define the device performance index.

Definition 3 (Device Performance Index). *We define function $\mathcal{P}$ that given a node n_i, its CPU speed Cs_{n_i} measured in Ghz, the number of cores Cc_{n_i}, the available CPU capacity Ca_{n_i} (measured in a number between 0 and 1), the available RAM M_{n_i} measured in Gigabytes and the remaining battery B_{n_i} (measured in a number between 0 and 1), returns the value $\mathcal{P}(n_i)$ that is a numerical estimate for n_i performance based on the following formula:*

$$\mathcal{P} = \alpha * (Cs_{n_i} * Cc_{n_i} * Ca_{n_i}) + \beta * M_{n_i} + \delta B_{n_i}$$

This is an easy to compute value that, even if it is a relatively rough approximation, is enough to distinguish node capacity without the burden of online benchmarking. It is also a programmer responsibility to define adequate values for the α, β and δ to produce adequate value for his/her application.

Example 1. Given a node n_0 reporting the following data: $Cs_{n_0} = 1.4$, $Cc_{n_0} = 4$, $Ca_{n_0} = 0.6$, $M_{n_0} = 0.37$ and without battery information and given $\alpha = \beta = 0.5$, the application of the formula results in:

$$\mathcal{P} = 0.5 * (1.4 * 4 * 0.37) + 0.5 * 0.6 = 1.336$$

Example 2. Given a node n_1 reporting the following data: $Cs_{n_1} = 1.5$, $Cc_{n_1} = 4$, $Ca_{n_1} = 0.15$, $M_{n_1} = 0.54$, the application of the formula results in:

$$\mathcal{P} = 0.5 * (1.5 * 4 * 0.54) + 0.5 * 0.15 = 1.695$$

Knowing each node's performance index, we now define how to decompose the problem in order to distribute it in a balanced manner.

Definition 4 (Simple Problem Decomposition). *Given a problem $\mathcal{D}$ and given a cluster of available nodes $\mathcal{S} = \{n_1, \ldots, n_k\}$, then the problem must be decomposable in k parts and defined as $\mathcal{D} = \{d_1, \ldots, d_k\}$ such that each part's computational cost is proportional to the assigned device performance index.*

Example 3. Given nodes $n_0, \ldots, n_5$ and a problem of summing 100000 numbers, the calculated performance index, the percentage of the computational power each node represents and the assigned partition of the problem is presented in the following table:

Node	Performance Index ($\mathcal{P}_i$)	Percentage of system power (p_i)	Assigned partition
n_0	2.013	21%	21000
n_3	1.965	20%	20000
n_1	1.695	18%	18000
n_4	1.472	15%	15000
n_2	1.336	14%	14000
n_5	1.125	12%	12000

A strict decomposition can be a bad solution if the computational cost of processing data is unevenly distributed. A small interval of data can be harder to process than a larger one. The approach we purpose includes the option to split the work in a bounded number of parts that are processed sequentially by the cluster of nodes. We now define the enhanced problem decomposition.

Definition 5 (Enhanced Problem Decomposition). *Given a problem $\mathcal{D}$ and given a cluster of available nodes $\mathcal{S} = \{n_1, \ldots, n_k\}$, then the problem must be decomposable in n parts and defined as $\mathcal{D} = \{D_1, \ldots, D_n\}$ and for each $D_i \in \mathcal{D}$, it is possible to decompose it further in k parts and defined as $D_i = \{d_{i1}, \ldots, d_{ik}\}$ such that each part's computational cost is proportional to the assigned device performance index. Thus, given a node n_i with a percentage of system power p_i then the size of the part D_i it will process is given by $p_i * sizeof(D_i)$.*

Example 4. Given the example 3, if we choose to have 5 partitions then we get:

D_1	D_2	D_3	D_4	D_5

l-elements

Here, each node n_i will process $p_i * l$ elements of each D_i corresponding to:

Node	Performance Index ($\mathcal{P}_i$)	Percentage of system power (p_i)	Part D_k size
n_0	2.013	21%	4200
n_3	1.965	20%	4000
n_1	1.695	18%	3600
n_4	1.472	15%	3000
n_2	1.336	14%	2800
n_5	1.125	12%	2400

Given the previous concepts, we now define the assigned problem.

Definition 6 (Assigned Problem). *Given a cluster of nodes $\mathcal{S} = \{n_1, \ldots, n_k\}$, where each node n_i has a performance index $\mathcal{P}_i$ and the problem $\mathcal{D}$ which is decomposed in k different parts we define an assigned problem as a set of triples, $\mathcal{A}_P = \{(n_1, \mathcal{P}_1, d_1) \ldots (n_k, \mathcal{P}_k, d_k)\}$.*

Communication between nodes is done using asynchronous message passing. There is a permanent link between the node requesting the work and the nodes executing that work. When this link is broken it signals a loss of communication and the node is removed from the list of available ones.

Definition 7 (Link set). *Given a cluster of available nodes $\mathcal{S} = \{n_1, \ldots, n_k\}$ we define $\mathcal{L} = \{l_1, \ldots, l_k\}$ as the list of links to the nodes such that the connection to node n_k is done by link l_k.*

Failure during the execution of a task results in rescheduling the unfinished task to the closest available node in terms of performance index. More formally, we define task reassignment.

Definition 8 (Task Reassignment). *Given a cluster of nodes* $\mathcal{S} = \{n_1, \ldots, n_k\}$, *where each node* n_i *has a performance index* $\mathcal{P}_i$, *the problem* $\mathcal{D}$ *decomposed in* k *different parts proportional to each of the nodes and the assigned problem* $\mathcal{A}_P = \{(n_1, \mathcal{P}_1, d_1) \ldots (n_k, \mathcal{P}_k, d_k)\}$. *When a link* l_j *assigned to a node* n_j *such that* $(n_j, \mathcal{P}_j, d_j) \in \mathcal{A}_P$ *fails then, the task* d_j *is reassigned to the node* n_m *such that* $(n_m, \mathcal{P}_m, d_m) \in \mathcal{A}_P \setminus (n_j, \mathcal{P}_j, d_j)$ *and* $\mathcal{P}_m \geq \mathcal{P}_n$ *for any* $(n_n, \mathcal{P}_n, d_n) \in \mathcal{A}_P \setminus (n_j, \mathcal{P}_j, d_j)$.

3 Implementation

Although the idea is to have a general purpose solution for IoT devices, at this moment, we decided to focus on a specific type of hardware/software to develop a proof of concept with all the properties we believe that are relevant in this domain. Our nodes are all single board computers, namely Raspberry Pi devices [6]. They all run a Linux distribution, an Erlang virtual machine and RPI-Monitor[1].

Although single board computers (SBC) are just one type of IoT devices, they enjoy enormous popularity due to the high performance for their price range and the vast number of scenarios where they can be used [6]. It is possible to have several Raspberry Pi SBCs in the same area each with a different purpose. With our framework we enable the optimization of devices that are many times sitting idle.

The computation of a node's performance index relies on the use of the RPI-Monitor utility, a general-purpose monitoring application that allows the extraction of several metrics from the Raspberry Pi. These metrics can be obtained by querying the device thought HTTP.

A node can be a slave (accepting work), a master (offloading work) or both. The code deployed to a slave node is initially minimal and consists in a simple process that processes execution messages and is described in Listing 1.1

```
task_executor()->
    receive
        { From, execute , Mod, Fun, Param } ->
            From ! { B,E,Mod:Fun(Param) },
        task_executor();
        _ ->
            task_executor()
    end .
```

Listing 1.1. Slave node main code

Function *task_executor*/0 waits for messages instructing the node to execute code (function *Fun* from module *Mod* with parameters *Param*) and the result of the execution is returned to the requesting node.

---

[1] https://xavierberger.github.io/RPi-Monitor-docs/index.html.

The master node coordinates the offloading process and, typically, nodes can be both a master and a slave. The main master Erlang function is succinctly described in Listing 1.2.

```
master (Mod, Fun, DataSize , NPart)  ->
    NodesList = initialize_cluster(),
    c : nl (Mod),
    Parts_Node = distribute (NodesList , DataSize , NPart),
    Results = execute (Mod, Fun, Parts_Node),
    reschedule (Results , Parts_Node).
```

Listing 1.2. Master node main code

Function *master*/4 receives the name of the module (*Mod*) with the code and data that must be distributed, the main function processing the data *Fun*, size of the data being processed (*DataSize*) and the number of partitions (*NPart*) that should be used in the distribution of the work. Next, function *initialize_cluster*/0 finds nodes in the local network area that are to collaborate (execute the slave function described before), and adds them to the *NodesList* establishing a link. Code and data is then distributed by the available nodes with the Erlang builtin function *c* : *nl*/1 and *distribute*/3 determines which parts of the data partition must be processed by which nodes. In case *NPart* is one, the process is a simple problem decomposition, if *Npart* > 1 then the process is an enhanced problem decomposition. The next step is to send the data for remote execution and gather all the results in the *Results* list. Finally, function *reschedule*/2 compares the results obtained from nodes with the requests that were made. In case it detects unanswered requests (resulting from nodes failing during execution), tasks related with those requests are rescheduled to available nodes as described in the System Model.

4   Evaluation

To evaluate the performance gain of our approach, we implemented an exhaustive set of benchmarks. For the sake of space, we present one benchmark based in a theoretically simple but still challenging problem, *i.e.* finding prime numbers in a given interval. We use a cluster of 4 IoT devices as described in Table 1.

Table 1. Cluster setup

Node	Device	CPU	Clock	RAM
n_1	Raspberry Pi 3 B+	quad-core	1.4 GHz	1.0 GB
n_2	Raspberry Pi Zero W	single-core	1.0 GHz	0.5 GB
n_3	Raspberry Pi 3 B+	quad-core	1.4 GHz	1.0 GB
n_4	Raspberry Pi Zero W	single-core	1.0 GHz	0.5 GB

The interval we use in this test is $\mathcal{I} = \{1, \ldots, 50000\}$ with a total of 5133 prime numbers. Note that the primes are not evenly distributed in this interval and higher ones are considerably more difficult to find than lower ones. We started with one device and added devices to the cluster measuring the gain in performance. Since the problem is not easy to break in balanced partitions we use the enhanced problem decomposition solution and break it in several partitions (1,5,10 and 20). Each of the partitions is then split by the available nodes accordingly with their reported performance index. We choose the node n_1 to be the master, although it also executes code as a slave. The calculation of the primes on $\mathcal{I}_1$ took an average of 26.07 s. We don't get any advantage in using more than one partition with one device since the implementation already uses multiple processes to optimize the use of the available cores of the device. The results of distributing data by two nodes (n_1 and n_2) are presented next:

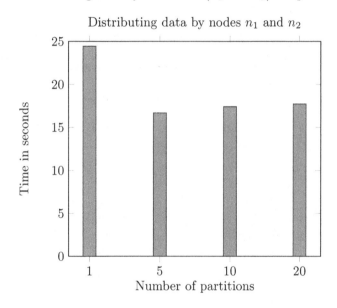

Even with only one partition, the time needed to compute all the primes decreases from an average of 26.07 s to an average of 24.43 s. The performance increases as we divide chunks of work by the devices. With 5 partitions, we achieve the best result of an average 16.67 s. The increase in the number of partitions is not alone a factor of enhancement in performance since the more partitions we have, the more messages we need to exchange. Next, we present the results of adding n_3 to the cluster. Here, the performance increases considerably, which seems normal since n_3 is a powerful node in this context.

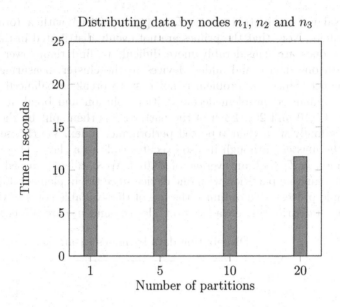

Distributing data by nodes n_1, n_2 and n_3

Finally, we present the results of adding all the nodes:

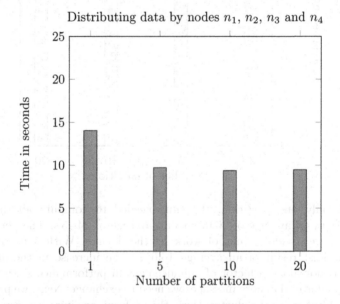

Distributing data by nodes n_1, n_2, n_3 and n_4

As a summary, we present the next graphic detailing the gain of having one device (no devices added to help), with one, two and three devices added. These values are the ones for the configuration with best performance in each of the scenarios.

Result of adding devices to n_1

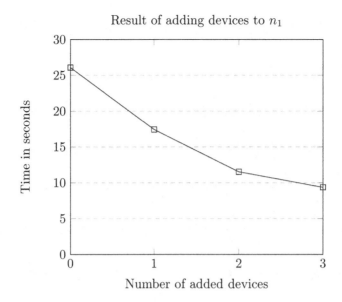

Number of added devices

By adding one node (n_2) to the cluster, one gets an increase in performance of $\sim 33\%$. By adding two devices (n_2 and n_3), one gets an increase in performance of $\sim 55\%$ and finally by adding three devices (n_2, n_3 and n_4), one gets an increase in performance of $\sim 64\%$. We also experimented with failure in nodes and consequent rescheduling. The impact of such operation is highly dependent on the capacity of the node or of the nodes failing. Failing node n_4 has a considerable higher impact than failing node n_2, due to their different capacity and thus the amount of work that is distributed to them. Nevertheless, with a small number of failures, the cooperative distributed computation still has a better performance when compared to the single problem solving solution.

5   Conclusions

A cooperative execution of resource intensive services among heterogeneous IoT nodes is a promising solution to address the increasingly demanding requirements on resources and performance. In this paper, we presented a framework for IoT devices based in Single Board Computers and the Erlang programming language. The goal is to maximize the collaborative power of these devices with a minimal setup.

The obtained results make us believe that it is possible to use the spare computational power of each of these devices such that their cooperation enables the solution of computationally complex problems, which are difficult to solve in single devices with an acceptable performance. We intend to add more features to the framework and foresee the creation of a distributed solution for computation that uses available power of simple devices replacing larger systems.

Acknowledgments. This work was partially supported by LIACC (UIDB/00027/2020) through Programa de Financiamento Plurianual of FCT (Portuguese Foundation for Science and Technology).

References

1. Armstrong, J.: A history of erlang. In: Proceedings of the Third ACM SIGPLAN Conference on History of Programming Languages, pp. 6-1–6-26. HOPL III, ACM, New York, NY, USA (2007). https://doi.org/10.1145/1238844.1238850
2. Cesarini, F., Vinoski, S.: Designing for Scalability with Erlang/OTP: Implement Robust, 1st edn. Fault-Tolerant Systems. O'Reilly Media Inc., Sebastopol (2016)
3. Cheng, C., Lu, R., Petzoldt, A., Takagi, T.: Securing the internet of things in a quantum world. IEEE Commun. Mag. **55**(2), 116–120 (2017). https://doi.org/10.1109/MCOM.2017.1600522CM
4. Hausenblas, M.: Serverless Ops. O'Reilly Media Inc., Sebastopol (2016)
5. Indrusiak, L., Dziurzanski, P., Singh, A.: Dynamic Resource Allocation in Embedded. High-Performance and Cloud Computing. River Publishers, Gistrup (2016). https://doi.org/10.13052/rp-9788793519077. http://www.sciencedirect.com/science/article/pii/S0167739X18301833
6. Johnston, S.J., et al.: Commodity single boardcomputer clusters and their applications. Future Gener. Comput. Syst. **89**, 201–212 (2018)
7. Khan, M.A.: A survey of computation offloading strategies for performance improvement of applications running on mobile devices. J. Netw. Comput. Appl. **56**, 28–40 (2015). https://doi.org/10.1016/j.jnca.2015.05.018
8. Kopestenski, I., Van Roy, P.: Erlang as an enabling technology for resilient general-purpose applications on edge IoT networks. In: Proceedings of the 18th ACM SIGPLAN International Workshop on Erlang, pp. 1–12. Erlang 2019, Association for Computing Machinery, New York, NY, USA (2019). https://doi.org/10.1145/3331542.3342567
9. Kumar, S., Tyagi, M., Khanna, A., Fore, V.: A survey of mobile computation offloading: applications, approaches and challenges. In: 2018 International Conference on Advances in Computing and Communication Engineering (ICACCE), pp. 51–58, June 2018. https://doi.org/10.1109/ICACCE.2018.8441740
10. Meurisch, C., Gedeon, J., Nguyen, T.A.B., Kaup, F., Muhlhauser, M.: Decision support for computational offloading by probing unknown services. In: 2017 26th International Conference on Computer Communication and Networks (ICCCN), pp. 1–9 (2017)
11. Nogueira, L., Coelho, J.: Self-organising clusters in edge computing. In: Silhavy, R., Silhavy, P., Prokopova, Z. (eds.) Intell. Syst. Appl. Softw. Eng., pp. 320–332. Springer International Publishing, Cham (2019)
12. Nogueira, L., Pinho, L.M.: A capacity sharing and stealing strategy for open real-time systems. J. Syst. Archit. **56**(4–6), 163–179 (2010). https://doi.org/10.1016/j.sysarc.2010.02.003
13. Noor, T.H., Zeadally, S., Alfazi, A., Sheng, Q.Z.: Mobile cloud computing: challenges and future research directions. J. Netw. Comput. Appl. **115**, 70–85 (2018). https://doi.org/10.1016/j.jnca.2018.04.018
14. Terrell, R.: Concurrency in.NET: Modern Patterns of Concurrent and Parallel Programming, 1st edn. Manning Publications Co., Greenwich (2018)
15. Warburton, R.: Java 8 Lambdas: Pragmatic Functional Programming. O'Reilly Media Inc., Sebastopol (2014)

An Energy Sustainable CPS/IoT Ecosystem

Haris Isakovic[1]([✉]), Edgar Azpiazu Crespo[2], and Radu Grosu[1]

[1] Technsiche Universität Wien, Vienna, Austria
{haris.isakovic,radu.grosu}@tuwien.ac.at
[2] Mondragon University, Mondragon, Spain
edgar.azpiazu@alumni.mondragon.edu,
http://ti.tuwien.ac.at

Abstract. This paper provides a short overview on methods and technologies necessary to build smart and sustainable Internet-of-Things (IoT). It observes IoT systems in a close relation with data centered intelligence and its application in cyber-physical systems. With the current rate of growth IoT devices and supporting CPS infrastructure will reach extremely high numbers in less than a decade. This will create an enormous overhead on world's supply of electrical energy. In this paper, we propose a model extension for estimation of energy consumption by IoT devices in next decade. The paper gives a definition of CPS/IoT Ecosystem as a mutually codependent heterogeneous multidisciplinary structure. Further we explore a set of methods to reduce energy consumption and make CPS/IoT Ecosystem sustainable by design. As a case study we propose energy harvesting sensor node implemented as a wildfire early detection system.

Keywords: Internet-of-things · Energy consumption · Sensor networks · Energy harvesting

1 Introduction

The rapidly expending world of internet-of-things (IoT) is changing technological landscape for civil, industrial and social projects. It is projected that the number of IoT devices is going to reach 100 billion until year 2025 [40]. An average energy consumption of Raspberry Pi 3 devices is between 1 Wh and 5 Wh [37]. To approximate average energy consumption of IoT application to about 4 Wh in the next 10 years we used following estimation formula, based on the models described in [7].

$$E_{IoT} = (E_{IoT_a} \times AR + E_{IoT_p} \times (1 - AR)) \times T \times D_{IoT} \times (\frac{100\% - ER\%}{100})^n \quad (1)$$

(E_{IoT_a}, E_{IoT_p}) are projected average consumption per device for an active and passive (i.e. sleep mode) operation.

S. Paiva et al. (Eds.): SmartCity360° 2020, LNICST 372, pp. 305–322, 2021.
https://doi.org/10.1007/978-3-030-76063-2_22

(*AR*) provides the ratio between active and passive operation of a device, we chose three arbitrary cases as best, average and worst.
(D_{IoT}) is projected number of IoT devices.
(*ER*) is projected energy efficiency increase as proposed by [7].
(*T*) is time in operation over a year.
(*n*) provides projection period in years.

Table 1. Different case scenarios depending for IoT device activity related to energy consumption. With the energy consumption projection of IoT devices in 2030.

Case	AR	D_{IoT} (10^9)	ER(%)	T(h)	Period	E_{IoT_a}(Wh)	E_{IoT_p}(Wh)	$E_{IoT_{2030}}$(TWh)
Best	0.01	100	5%	8640	10	4	2	**532**
Avg	0.3	100	4%	8640	10	4	2	**1493**
Worst	1	100	1%	8640	10	4	1	**3125**

IoT revolution will bring enormous influx of devices that are not always designed in energy efficient way as they are not considered as major energy consumers. However, if the quantity of these devices reaches the levels mentioned above it could create enormous overhead in energy consumption. Table 1 also provides three projections of energy consumption based on the Eq. 1 in year 2030. In addition, there is energy consumed by cloud infrastructure as the number of cloud applications will increase accordingly. Cloud server infrastructures are already consuming enormous amounts of electrical energy, with up to 1.5% of total worldwide consumption [35]. With the influx of new IoT applications, data and emerging applications as a result it is evident that the cloud server capacity needs to be increased. Authors in [7] provide an estimate of cloud infrastructure energy consumption in range of 1000 TWh up to 8000 TWh. In addition there is a consumption required for communication. This approximation intends to show possible scale of the IoT energy consumption overhead. It is evident that energy efficiency of new devices will improve but the quantity of possible devices is still overwhelming. To put this in a perspective an average energy production of European Union (EU) is not around 3400 TWh over past couple of years [8]. Sustainability of the IoT applications and infrastructure depends on an energy efficient methodological design of IoT devices and applications, optimizing existing devices and applications, communal use of infrastructure, and energy harvesting capabilities.

In this paper, we are exploring energy aware design of IoT devices as a requirement for constitution of sustainable CPS/IoT Ecosystems. We define CPS/IoT Ecosystem as "a heterogeneous structure of hardware devices, and corresponding software components distributed over tree intertwined scopes of operation: cloud, fog/edge, and sensor/actuator nodes" [30]. These systems are distributed over different platforms and infrastructural facilities such as a power grid, the Internet, or a mobile grid. It is extremely difficult to maintain oversight on energy consumption over the whole composition. We propose technologies and methods that can be used to ensure energy efficient and sustainable design from the perspective of sensor nodes. First, we will explore a set of methods that can be applied from the hardware design and up to ensure most beneficial performance to energy consumption ratio. Further, we will show examples on how to design a sensor node for IoT with low or completely neutral energy signature. Finally we will show how to optimize existing systems by introducing methods such as hardware acceleration.

In Sect. 1 we explore a problem of energy consumption overhead created by IoT devices and supporting CPS infrastructures. We propose an extended power consumption estimation model for IoT devices. Section 2 gives an overview of related activities on the topic. In Sect. 3 we provide a definition of CPS/IoT Ecosystem. Section 4 gives methodological steps towards energy aware CPS/IoT Ecosystem. Further, Sect. 5.5 proposes a sensor node that utilizes energy harvesting methods. Section 6 gives a short overview on a use case that can be realized with the described energy harvesting sensor node. Last two sections conclude the paper and provide due acknowledgements.

2 Related Work

The problem of the rapidly growing IoT market among with its energy needs, requires focussing on possible solutions for an efficient energy use on all the CPS/IoT Ecosystem's scopes. In this context, different approaches have been tried to reduce the energy consumption of sensor networks as, for example, trying alternative routing schemes to achieve a network lifetime increase as well [43]. Moreover, in traditional networks, the network configuration is not changed after initialization, but energy consumption improvements are noticed by adaptive network configuration where, if the distance between two sensors is calculated, the transmission power can also be adjusted avoiding the use of unnecessary power [48]. Further, analysing the architecture of a sensor, the main components that affect to their lifetime are identified so that aggressive energy optimization can be performed [38]. Nonetheless, the data centers used for cloud computing are an important point to consider regarding energy consumption. These centers can host up to several thousands of servers and they reach 1.1% to 1.5% of the total electricity use worldwide and is likely to rise [35]. In this context, an efficient cloud computing is crucial for which diverse hardware and software strategies can be adopted in all the levels that compose a data center [17, 25, 32]. An efficient operation can also be achieved for the Edge scope's components such as cloudlets balancing the workload across the nodes or adapting their configuration to manage latency and energy consumption [47].

In addition to managing the energy consumption, a wide range of energy harvesting methods can be used as an extra power source [28]. One of the main energy harvesting techniques is based on vibration energy scavenging. Its applications range from railway vehicles [26] to supplying hearing aids [6]. Other main method focuses on the solar energy which can be used to power sensors on both outdoor and indoor environments [22, 27, 39]. However, the energy source this paper focuses on is the thermal by using thermoelectric generators. The usages cover industrial applications to recover waste heat from engines and increase the vehicle's overall efficiency [16,24,31] as well as using an aircraft's fuselage varying temperature to power autonomous sensors and perform diverse measurements [41]. As a human body constantly generates heat, several studies have also been carried out to take advantage of it to power autonomous wearable electronics like watches, medical devices or other types of sensors [12,33,34]. However, the need to make the energy scavenging unobtrusively limits the power that can be obtained.

These autonomous sensors can be placed in inaccessible places where battery replacements are not possible so they only rely on the temperature gradient across the thermoelectric generator to work. Additionally, a wireless transmission module can be added to their structure to track the measurements remotely [9, 14,15]. These sensors will perform the programmed tasks as long as a minimum temperature gradient is achieved. Nevertheless, alternative storage elements like supercapacitors can be employed to manage the generated power and keep the system working even if this power is discontinuous [42]. A similar approach is presented in this paper, but an event detection circuit is introduced so the measurements are performed only under certain circumstances and the generated energy is just stored otherwise.

3   CPS/IoT Ecosystem

In Sect. 1 we structurally defined CPS/IoT Ecosystem, in this section we will give a motivational overview and functional description of this concept. The IoT allows us to connect physical environment with a digital infrastructure, collect its data and store it for the purpose of later or runtime analysis. CPS is a collection of practical and theoretical methodologies that allow us to interpret physical data, create models of physical environments using this data, recognize and extract emerging behaviours and use them to optimize system in question. We observe two concepts as separate disciplines but highly dependent on each other. We conceptualize CPS/IoT Ecosystem structurally in three scopes of operation:

Cloud. The cloud infrastructure provides the ability to construct computational units based on computational performance or storage requirements in an automated and scaleable fashion. It can compute and store enormous amounts of data and made it available to large number of users at the same time. This is an essential requirements for the large scale data analysis. Cloud servers are located at remote locations and accessible exclusively through internet.

Fog/Edge. The concept of fog and edge computing describes platforms with ability to perform computing and storage tasks in relative proximity to a physical environment and with extremely low response rates [11]. Fog hosts time sensitive tasks such as control loop execution where it is required to perform complex calculation based on historical data with low latency. Fog and edge devices are located within the same facility and are communicating using local area network from one side and the Internet to communicate with cloud level if necessary.

Sensor and Actuator. There are two basic types of devices that allow to interact with the physical environment, either by observing it or manipulating it. The sensors and actuators are implemented using low energy, low performance devices that are deployable in an imminent proximity to the observed object. The number of these devices is manifold of what is required on the upper levels and although they use less energy it needs to be considered based on the quantity. These devices are often placed in inaccessible locations with limited maintenance capabilities and their energy supply relies on energy storage devices such as batteries, or on their ability to harvest energy from the environment.

4   An Energy Aware CPS/IoT Ecosystem

CPS/IoT Ecosystem is a concept that allows to transform real data from a physical environment into valuable information, in order to increase efficiency of a system in different ways. This process requires number of layers of technology from hardware and software perspective. It relies on massive data collection and processing, learning statistical and mathematical paterns, applying optimizations and novel applications for forthcoming and legacy systems. The scale of this undertaking will require a massive number of devices from sensor to cloud level. In Table 1 possible energy consumption scenarios for IoT, plus overhead on Fog and Cloud infrastructure as shown in Sect. 1. This is why it is necessary to reduce its energy footprint by adopting various methods that increase overall efficiency and reduce energy consumption in all scopes of operation. In this section we will discuss methodological approach that would outperform commonly used approaches.

Energy aware design for CPS/IoT Ecosystem has multiple dimensions. It doesn't depend on hardware or software alone, it is rather a "full stack" problem starting from a system model to the final application artefacts.

Standardized IoT Model. One of the major obstacles in development of IoT systems is lack of standardization. IoT is building on top of embedded programming that has a significant number of libraries. A model based approach to development of IoT would ensure use of verified code that can be configured between energy and performance optimal instance. A model based approach would be realized in multiple aspects such as hardware platform model, service model, network model, application model and eventually wrapper model to unify all above mentioned cases. This would increase oversight and traceability of the system, reduce maintenance cost and increase resource utilization.

HW/SW Co-design. CPS/IoT Ecosystem applications are dependant on full range of devices from a cloud server with high-power CPU, to microcontrollers in embedded devices and custom designed hardware for networking solutions.

Use of FPGA or hybrid architectures is widely accepted, and its application in CPS/IoT applications is more than beneficial. Molding HW/SW platform to specific needs provides the advantages of a dedicated platform such as resource utilization and performance and flexibility of a COTS platform. Both IoT and CPS can profit from custom designed accelerators or IP blocks. Both ends of the CPS/IoT Ecosystem can benefit from a targeted application acceleration. Using hybrid architectures such as Intel Arria 10 [2] or Xilinx Znyq [3] applications have access to a standardized CPU architecture and FPGA device within the same platform. The FPGA is ideal for acceleration of mathematical tasks, network routing, security tasks or other application specific IP. Study presented in [29] showed massive acceleration for tasks such as matrix multiplication up to 5 times and reduced energy consumption up to 4 times. This comes with a cost of flexibility and programmability but with application of high level synthesis tools it can be significantly reduced.

Energy Harvesting. IoT is a leading industry in propagation of energy harvesting solutions from a piezzo electric auto-charging switches to solar driven fog and/edge stations. By adding energy harvesting capabilities use of electrical power from grid can be significantly reduced or completely neutralized as shown in Sect. 5.5. Environmental sources for energy harvesting are [10]: a) mechanical energy in form of vibration or movement with examples of piezzo-electric generators, wind and water turbines, b) Solar energy generated by the sun with examples of photo-voltaic generators or thermal generators, c) Thermal energy generated by environment with example of thermoelectric generator (TEG), electromagnetic energy generated by surrounding electromagnetic fields and converted into electricity by electromagnetic induction.

5   Energy Harvesting Sensor Nodes

In this section we propose an energy harvesting sensor node for remote data collection over narrow-band communication network. It is a sensor device that can use any of the above mentioned energy harvesting sources and can be deployed in a remote place with little to none maintenance. The sensor device is designed to track a specific event such as abrupt temperature rise or extreme kinetic forces in the environment. It is an environmental friendly device with no chemical batteries and low energy storage.

The sensor device shown in Fig. 1 is based on thermo-electric generator, which produces an electric power on a temperature gradient in the surrounding environment. It powers a microcontroller centered device over a power management unit (PMU). The power management unit uses a supercapacitor as an energy storage element and gives a stable regulated voltage necessary for MCU to perform its tasks. As an interface between MCU and PMU an event detection circuit is placed. It tracks outside event and releases power to the MCU when the stable voltage is reached. The MCU is further interfaced with a Sigfox transceiver and two sensors, a temperature sensor and a global positioning sensor. When

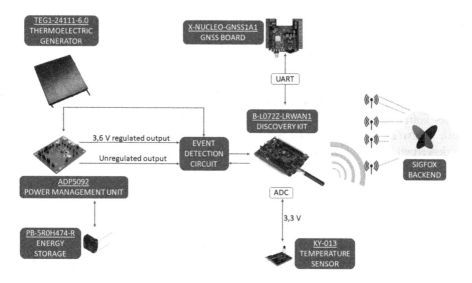

Fig. 1. Designed system's architecture

the temperature of the environment reaches threshold it will generate enough power to wake the MCU, acquire data from sensors and transmit the message over Sigfox network.

5.1 Thermoelectric Generator (TEG)

The selected TEG device for this application is the TEG1-24111-6.0 manufactured by Tecteg MFR [36]. As high temperatures may be reached during an event detection and its processing, it is important that the TEG module can work in that range so the chosen module is designed with high temperature bonding materials allowing it to withstand temperatures of up to 320 °C and offers superior performance when its hot side is over 150 °C.

5.2 Power Management Unit

The output obtained from the TEG module is a varying irregular voltage so that it cannot be used to power the MCU. Therefore, a treatment stage is added making use of the ADP5092 [19]. This is an ultralow power energy harvester PMU which offers a wide range of configurations so it can be configured in accordance with the energy harvesting source and the connected load requirements.

The board offers a Maximum Power Point Tracking (MPPT) control which can set the maximum power point ratio for the energy harvester obtaining the maximum available power from it. This is configured in its dynamic sensing mode and adjusted for a TEG harvester.

Rechargeable batteries, capacitors or other storage elements can be charged with the obtained energy so it can later be used to power the load when needed.

In this case we are using the Eaton's PB-5R0H474-R [23] supercapacitor with 0.47 F and 5 V. Less environmental friendly option would be a battery supported device that can easily be integrated in the device.

The PMU provides two power outputs, an unregulated power output for charging of the supercapacitor, and a regulated power output for direct supply of the microcontroller. The unregulated output is connected to the storage element so its voltage changes with the supercapacitor's charge. The regulated output with a current limit of 150 mA is available, which is sufficient to run the MCU as described in Sect. 5.4. The output voltage is set to 3.6 V but can be regulated from 1.5 V to 3.6 V. The regulated output is used to power the load in this approach while the unregulated output is directed to the event detection circuit as explained in Sect. 5.3.

Additionally, a couple of control features are used by the MCU to make a more efficient use of the PMU: RF interference are avoided by temporarily shutting down the boost regulator when a Sigfox message is going to be sent and the quality of the regulated output is checked before performing a cycle's actions.

In order to get an easy way to evaluate the ADP5092, the ADP5092-1-EVALZ evaluation board [21] has been chosen. This board provides a default working configuration which can be easily adjusted replacing any necessary component and making use of the provided jumpers.

5.3   Event Detection

As one of the key steps is the event detection to know when to perform the measurements and data transmission, a circuit has been designed to ensure a correct detection.

In this case event detection is fully corelated with the energy generation event. This means that the sensor node is triggered when the enough energy is generated. To start energy generation TEG device requires a temperature gradient between exposed and isolated side of the device. The design of the device provide us with physical means to ensure the gradient necessary to generate enough power. For the current version a required gradient is 50 °C. This will correspond to aproximate 2 V regardless of the working temperature, so this is the threshold of the desired event. Figure 2 represents the designed circuit to detect events over the defined threshold.

The thermoelectric generator is connected to the PMU and a 3.6 V regulated output is obtained to power the board. The board should be powered just when an event is detected and shut down otherwise so to control this, a comparator based circuit has been designed. This comparator compares the TEG output to the defined event threshold. To get this fixed voltage, the unregulated output of the PMU is directed through a low-dropout (LDO) regulator. The regulated output is used as the positive power supply for the comparator while the negative supply is connected to ground.

When the TEG output is higher than the threshold, the comparator gives a low output. Otherwise, when the TEG output is below the threshold, a high

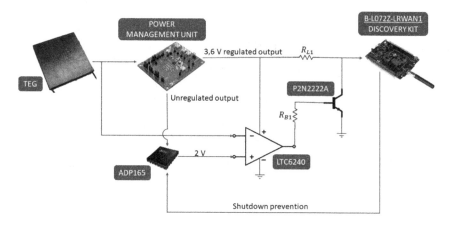

Fig. 2. Event detection circuit

output is generated. In order to control the board supply with this output, a transistor that acts as a switch is used. The comparator's output is connected to the transistor's base through a resistor (R_{B1}, so a low comparator output causes the transistor to work in its cut-off region leading to power the board, and a high output causes it to enter its saturation region resulting in a board shutdown.

Additionally, a shutdown prevention connection has been added to ensure the board is supplied until it finishes all its process. Otherwise, the TEG output could drop below the detection threshold causing a sudden board shutdown even if enough energy is still available in the PMU. This prevention is achieved by controlling the ADP165 voltage.

The ADP165 is a very low quiescent current, LDO, linear regulator [18]. Although an event detection threshold has been defined, the adjustable output option has been chosen over a fixed output to have some flexibility if any change is needed in the future. Figure 3 represents the used configuration.

To set the output voltage, R_1 and R_2 are adjusted. Additionally, the regulator can be enabled or disabled by means of the EN pin which is used for the board's shutdown prevention using a similar approach as before with a transistor. So, the regulator is working when the board is not powered but it is disabled after an event is detected. This means the regulator gives a low output forcing the TEG's comparator input to be always higher. The ADP165CP-EVALZ [20] evaluation board that simplifies the testing process has been used to try the configuration.

5.4 Microcontroller

The B-L072Z-LRWAN1 discovery kit [44] has been used in this project. It is a development tool which includes the CMWX1ZZABZ-091 open module by Murata allowing to use LoRa and Sigfox technologies. Being powered by an STM32L072CZ microcontroller which offers an ultra low power consumption makes it a great choice for IoT and energy harvesting applications.

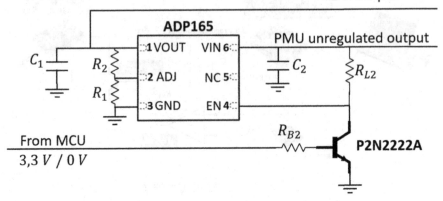

Fig. 3. ADP165 voltage regulator circuit

Location Acquisition. One of the relevant data to be acquired is the current location of the board for which the X-NUCLEO-GNSS1A1 module has been used which represents an easy-to-use, GNSS solution [46]. Both UART and I2C interfaces are available to establish a connection but UART is used in this case. It is compatible with the Arduino UNO R3 connector also present in the B-L072Z-LRWAN1 making it easy to connect them and allowing to stack extra components.

Temperature Sensor. The temperature is another important parameter to track as it conditions the performance of the whole system. The sensor chosen to read it is the analog low power consumption STLM20W87F by STMicroelectronics [45]. However, the analog KY-013 module has been used for testing purposes. It consists of a NTC thermistor whose resistance changes with the temperature leading to an output voltage variation. The sensor is connected using the Arduino UNO R3 [1] connector of X-NUCLEO-GNSS1A1 since it is stacked. Then, the real temperature is obtained using the ADC.

Operating Mode. Different possible operating modes for the board have been identified. The chosen operating cycle is shown in Fig. 4.

Increase in outside temperature creates a temperature gradient that generates electrical potential. When the power management unit detects this event it releases current and activates the board. This could be a short term event and take up to few seconds at most, so the energy is stored in the supercapacitor. The power management unit releases the energy from supercapacitor to power up the board.

Once powered up, the quality of the supply voltage is checked making use of the REG_GOOD pin in the PMU. If a high signal is read, the board reads the

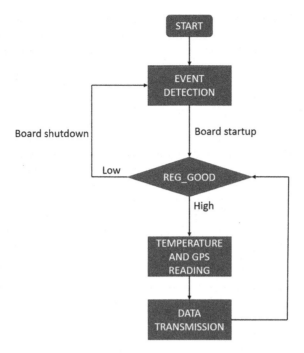

Fig. 4. Flowchart of the MCU's operating cycle

temperature and location measurements to, finally, send the data. Otherwise, the board is powerd down and until next event.

As the detected event may still be active after the first data is transmitted, and some energy may be available yet, the measurement and data transmission steps are repeated until there is not enough energy to repeat the process or a low signal is read in REG_GOOD. Like that, a complete event tracking and analysis is done.

Another option that we considered is to enter the standby mode and stay there until an event is detected. At that point, an interruption that wakes up the device is triggered, and the measurements are performed before the device goes back to standby mode. The main reason for the cycle selection is the uncertainty of the available harvested energy amount. As it is not known when an event will happen, the amount of time the device can stay in standby mode is undefined and, although its power consumption is very low, it needs a continuous supply which may not be available. Taking this into account, the selected mode fits better, powering the board just to track an event once it is detected.

Power Consumption. A rather pessimistic estimation for the power consumption of each step as well as the time spent on it is shown in Table 2. It is worth noting that the estimation has been done considering a supply voltage of 3.3 V.

Table 2. Execution cycle steps' power consumption.

Power mode	Stage	Power consumption	Time	CPU/Bus frecuency
Run	Board start-up, REG_GOOD checking	8.12 mA	500 μs	32 MHz
Run	Location acquisition	33.11 mA	8 s	32 MHz
Run	Temperature reading	18.11 mA	25 μs	32 MHz
Run	Signal Tx	128.11 mA	2.1 s	32 MHz

Taking this data into account, an average current consumption of 52.86 mA is obtained.

5.5   Sensor Node Evaluation

Energy harvesting sensor node was implemented in an experimental setup. It was used to test individual behaviour of components and the sensor as a whole. However, the TEG output was simulated making use of a power supply.

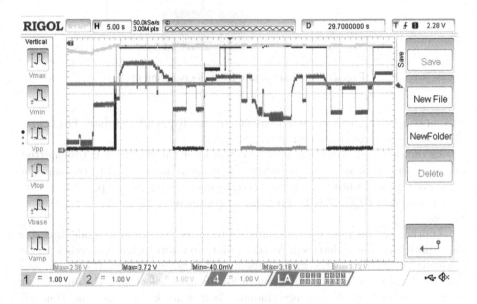

Fig. 5. System testing results

While testing the whole system, the following points were measured with an oscilloscope:

- Channel 1: Board power supply.
- Channel 2: TEG output simulation, V_{in}.
- Channel 3: Regulated output from the PMU.
- Channel 4: ADP165 output.

The captured results can be seen in Fig. 5. First, V_{in} increases until it gets higher than the ADP165 output. The comparator makes the transistor work in its cut off mode forcing a high board supply. Then, V_{in} gets lower than the ADP165 output, so the board's supply gets low. Later, the ADP165 output drops to a low voltage when the shutdown prevention is activated. At this point, as V_{in} is higher, a high board supply is obtained always. After the shutdown prevention is deactivated, it returns to its initial operation.

If the shutdown prevention is activated, because the board is working, and V_{in} drops to low, the supercapacitor's voltage will also start to drop. When it discharges enough, the regulated output will go low forcing a low board supply as well. Whether the supercapacitor is charged, a high output will be present again. This behaviour is shown in Fig. 6.

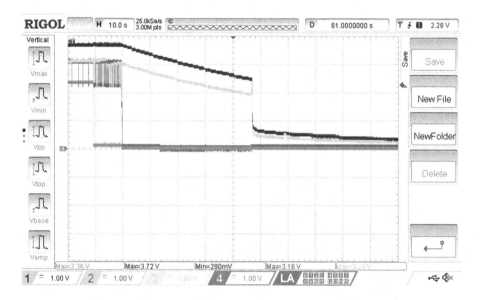

Fig. 6. System discharge testing

6 Energy Harvesting Use Case

The sensor node described in Sect. 5.5 can be applied in number of use cases. We are currently testing a prototype for a wildfire detection device. Despite all warning systems and services 100 people are confirmed dead during wildfires in Greece in 2018 [4]. In United States in the state of California an area of 7664,39 km^2 was caught in one of the largest recorded wildfires in the US, 89 people are confirmed dead [5]. In addition, the economic and environmental impact of these natural catastrophes is colossal. The damages to infrastructure, public and private properties are measured in billions. Furthermore, damages to wildlife and environment are enormous and areas affected will require years to recover. The proposed wild-fire detection device would provide both localized and global early warning system for wild-fires. When combine with current early warning systems it would be able to increase precision and timeliness of detected fires on a large scale. With approximately 800 sensors we would be able to cover up to 50 km^2. In addition to satellite based detection systems such as [13] this could be extended even further. To cover the area burned down in California it would take about 160000 devices. However, it is not necessary to cover the whole area, instead it would be enough to create a mash based on geographical parameters or protect residential, industrial or agricultural zones. The cost for the deployment of wildfire energy harvesting sensor nodes is almost insignificant to the amount of damage created by the fire. The devices showed in Fig. 7 can be placed on the endangered area with a distribution pattern that will complement other detection methods. This area should be covered with the low-band communication network, in this case we used Sigfox. The advantage of the radio based networks is the large coverage range and low power compared to other wireless communication networks. The device can stay dormant for years until a activation events occurs. In this case the activation event is a high temperature (or temperature gradient) generated by the fire. The sensor device will be triggered and sends a burst of alert messages containing temperature and location via narrow-band communication network to the cloud. Monitors in the

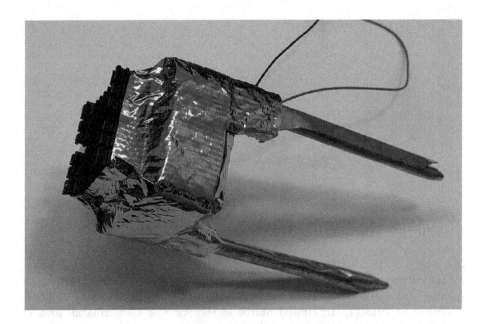

Fig. 7. Energy harvesting IoT node

cloud will notify authorities and provide them with the early detection necessary for a rapid response.

Table 3. Cost structure for the prototype.

Resource	Quantity	Unit cost (€)	Total (€)
TEG1-24111-6.0	1	50.00	50.00
X-NUCLEO-GNSS1A1	1	32.76	32.76
KY-013	1	1.00	1.00
B-L072Z-LRWAN1	1	43.52	43.52
ADP5092-1-EVALZ	1	44.00	44.00
ADP165CP-EVALZ	1	35.00	35.00
PB-5R0H474-R	1	4.47	4.47
LTC6240	1	1.89	1.89
P2N2222A	2	0.22	0.22
Various resistors	9	0.50	4.50
Case	1	25.00	25.00
Total			242.58

Figure 7 shows a package prototype of the energy harvesting node for the use case above. This design utilizes slow changing temperature of the ground in contrast to the air temperature, that changes rapidly in case of wildfire. The isolation layers divide hot and cold side of the TEG and ensure temperature gradient is achieved necessary to power up the sensor node. The cost of the prototype is given in Table 3 this can be reduced significantly in a serial production. This would make the platform highly viable and affordable considering the cost of the damages made by wildfires.

7   Conclusion

The number of IoT devices and supporting infrastructure used for CPSs is already affecting energy consumption and energy production models. This trend is continuing to grow and energy aware solutions are necessary to balance out the burden. In this paper, we proposed a model of estimating energy consumption for IoT devices and supporting infrastructure. We provided a set of methodological and design measures that could reduce energy consumption in CPS and IoT significantly. Finally, we proposed an energy harvesting method that is simple to produce and could be used to increase effectiveness of active early wildfire detection systems. They could be used by individuals to protect their property and also by official institutions to protect certain agricultural or forest resources.

Acknowledgments. This work has been conducted within projects that has received funding from the Austrian Government through the Federal Ministry Of Education, Science And Research (BMWFW) in the funding program Hochschulraum-Strukturmittel 2016 (HRSM). This work is part of a project that has received funding from the European Union's Horizon 2020 research and innovation programme under grant agreement No 871319.

References

1. Arduino Uno Rev3 — Arduino Official Store. https://store.arduino.cc/arduino-uno-rev3
2. Intel Arria 10 FPGA. https://www.intel.com/content/www/de/de/products/programmable/fpga/arria-10.html
3. Zynq-7000 SoC. https://www.xilinx.com/products/silicon-devices/soc/zynq-7000.html
4. Waldbrände in Attika 2018, July 2019. https://de.wikipedia.org/w/index.php?title=Waldbr%C3%A4nde_in_Attika_2018&oldid=190577400. Page Version ID: 190577400
5. California wildfires, May 2020. https://tinyurl.com/y7nmnesb. Page Version ID: 956440002
6. Amor, N.B., Kanoun, O.: Investigation to the use of vibration energy for supply of hearing aids. In: 2007 IEEE Instrumentation Measurement Technology Conference IMTC 2007, pp. 1–6 (2007)
7. Andrae, A.S.G., Edler, T.: On global electricity usage of communication technology: trends to 2030. Challenges 6(1), 117–157 (2015). https://doi.org/10.3390/challe6010117. https://www.mdpi.com/2078-1547/6/1/117. Multidisciplinary Digital Publishing Institute
8. BP: BP Statistical Review of World Energy 2017 p. 52, June 2017
9. Carmo, J.P., Goncalves, L.M., Correia, J.H.: Thermoelectric microconverter for energy harvesting systems. IEEE Trans. Industr. Electron. 57(3), 861–867 (2010)
10. Chalasani, S., Conrad, J.M.: A survey of energy harvesting sources for embedded systems. In: IEEE SoutheastCon 2008, pp. 442–447 (2008). https://doi.org/10.1109/SECON.2008.4494336. ISSN 1558-058X
11. Chiang, M., Zhang, T.: Fog and IoT: an overview of research opportunities. IEEE Internet Things J. 3(6), 854–864 (2016). https://doi.org/10.1109/JIOT.2016.2584538
12. Colomer-Farrarons, J., Miribel-Catala, P., Saiz-Vela, A., Puig-Vidal, M., Samitier, J.: Power-conditioning circuitry for a self-powered system based on micro pzt generators in a 0.13-μm low-voltage low-power technology. IEEE Trans. Ind. Electron. 55(9), 3249–3257 (2008)
13. Commission, E.: EFFIS - Active Fire Detection, January 2018. https://effis.jrc.ec.europa.eu/about-effis/technical-background/active-fire-detection/
14. Dalola, S., Ferrari, M., Ferrari, V., Guizzetti, M., Marioli, D., Taroni, A.: Characterization of thermoelectric modules for powering autonomous sensors. IEEE Trans. Instrum. Meas. 58(1), 99–107 (2009)
15. Dalola, S., et al.: Autonomous sensor system with RF link and thermoelectric generator for power harvesting. In: 2008 IEEE Instrumentation and Measurement Technology Conference, pp. 1376–1380 (2008)
16. Kwok, D.W., Huang, F.P.: Skorupa, J.A., Smith, J.W.: US9018512B2 - Thermoelectric generation system - Google Patents, April 2015. https://patents.google.com/patent/US9018512B2/en
17. Dayarathna, M., Wen, Y., Fan, R.: Data center energy consumption modeling: a survey. IEEE Commun. Surv. Tutor. 18(1), 732–794 (2016). https://doi.org/10.1109/COMST.2015.2481183
18. Devices, A.: ADP165 Datasheet and Product Info — Analog Devices. https://www.analog.com/en/products/adp165.html

19. Devices, A.: ADP5092 Datasheet and Product Info — Analog Devices. https://www.analog.com/en/products/adp5092.html?doc=ADP5091-5092.pdf#product-overview
20. Devices, A.: EVAL-ADP165-166 Evaluation Board — Analog Devices. https://www.analog.com/en/design-center/evaluation-hardware-and-software/evaluation-boards-kits/EVAL-ADP165-166.html
21. Devices, A.: EVAL-ADP509X Evaluation Board — Analog Devices. https://www.analog.com/en/design-center/evaluation-hardware-and-software/evaluation-boards-kits/EVAL-ADP509X.html#eb-overview
22. Dondi, D., Bertacchini, A., Brunelli, D., Larcher, L., Benini, L.: Modeling and optimization of a solar energy harvester system for self-powered wireless sensor networks. IEEE Trans. Industr. Electron. **55**(7), 2759–2766 (2008)
23. Eaton: Eaton PB-5R0H474-R. https://www.mouser.at/datasheet/2/87/eaton-pb_supercapacitors-cylindrical-pack-data-she-1608804.pdf
24. Fernández-Yáñez, P., Gómez, A., García-Contreras, R., Armas, O.: Evaluating thermoelectric modules in diesel exhaust systems: potential under urban and extra-urban driving conditions. J. Clean. Prod. **182**, 1070–1079 (2018). https://doi.org/10.1016/j.jclepro.2018.02.006. http://www.sciencedirect.com/science/article/pii/S095965261830310X
25. Gill, S.S., Buyya, R.: A Taxonomy and Future Directions for Sustainable Cloud Computing: 360 Degree View p. 68, December 2018
26. Güre, N.: Vibration energy harvesting from a railway vehicle using commercial piezoelectric transducers (2017). http://dspace.marmara.edu.tr/handle/11424/36590
27. Hande, A., Polk, T., Walker, W., Bhatia, D.: Indoor solar energy harvesting for sensor network router nodes. Microprocess. Microsyst. **31**(6), 420–432 (2007). https://doi.org/10.1016/j.micpro.2007.02.006. http://www.sciencedirect.com/science/article/pii/S0141933107000415
28. Harb, A.: Energy harvesting: state-of-the-art. Renewable Energy **36**(10), 2641–2654 (2011). https://doi.org/10.1016/j.renene.2010.06.014. http://www.sciencedirect.com/science/article/pii/S0960148110002703
29. Hartberger, T.: Algorithm implementation in HLS or HDL: power consumption and efficiency effects. Bachelor Thesis, TU Wien, November 2017
30. Isakovic, H., et al.: CPS/IoT Ecosystem: A platform for research and education. p. 8, October 2018
31. Jorge Martins, F.P. Brito, L.G.J.A.: Universidade do Minho: Thermoelectric exhaust energy recovery with temperature control through heat pipes, April 2011. http://hdl.handle.net/1822/15737
32. Kaur, T., Chana, I.: Energy Efficiency Techniques in Cloud Computing: A Survey and Taxonomy, October 2015. https://doi.org/10.1145/2742488
33. Leonov, V.: Thermoelectric energy harvesting of human body heat for wearable sensors. IEEE Sens. J. **13**(6), 2284–2291 (2013). https://doi.org/10.1109/JSEN.2013.2252526
34. Leonov, V., Vullers, R.J.M.: Wearable electronics self-powered by using human body heat: the state of the art and the perspective. J. Renew. Sustain. Energy **1**(6), 062701 (2009). https://doi.org/10.1063/1.3255465. http://aip.scitation.org/doi/10.1063/1.3255465
35. Mastelic, T., Brandic, I.: Recent trends in energy-efficient cloud computing. IEEE Cloud Comput. **2**(1), 40–47 (2015). https://doi.org/10.1109/MCC.2015.15. http://ieeexplore.ieee.org/document/7091782/

36. MFR, T.: TEG1-24111-6.0. https://thermoelectric-generator.com/product/teg1-24111-6-0/. library Catalog: thermoelectric-generator.com
37. Pi, R.: Raspberry Pi. https://www.raspberrypi.org, library Catalog. https://www.raspberrypi.org
38. Raghunathan, V., Schurgers, C., Park, S., Srivastava, M.: Energy-aware wireless microsensor networks. IEEE Signal Process. Mag. **19**(2), 40–50 (2002). https://doi.org/10.1109/79.985679
39. Raghunathan, V., Kansal, A., Hsu, J., Friedman, J., Srivastava, M.: Design considerations for solar energy harvesting wireless embedded systems. In: IPSN 2005. Fourth International Symposium on Information Processing in Sensor Networks, pp. 457–462, April 2005. https://doi.org/10.1109/IPSN.2005.1440973
40. Rose, K., Eldridge, S., Chapin, L.: The Internet of Things: An Overview, February 2015. https://www.internetsociety.org/wp-content/uploads/2017/08/ISOC-IoT-Overview-20151221-en.pdf
41. Samson, D., Kluge, M., Becker, T., Schmid, U.: Wireless sensor node powered by aircraft specific thermoelectric energy harvesting. Sens. Actuators A Phys. **172**(1), 240–244 (2011). https://doi.org/10.1016/j.sna.2010.12.020. http://www.sciencedirect.com/science/article/pii/S0924424710005182
42. Schlögl, P.: An Energy harvesting powered sensor node for machine condition monitoring. Ph.D. thesis (2018). http://repositum.tuwien.ac.at/obvutwhs/content/titleinfo/2962783
43. Shah, R.C., Rabaey, J.M.: Energy aware routing for low energy ad hoc sensor networks. In: 2002 IEEE Wireless Communications and Networking Conference Record. WCNC 2002 (Cat. No.02TH8609), vol. 1, pp. 350–355 (2002)
44. STMicroelectronics: B-L072Z-LRWAN1.   https://www.st.com/en/evaluation-tools/b-l072z-lrwan1.html, library Catalog: www.st.com
45. STMicroelectronics: STLM20. https://www.st.com/en/mems-and-sensors/stlm20.html, library Catalog: www.st.com
46. STMicroelectronics: X-NUCLEO-GNSS1A1.https://www.st.com/en/ecosystems/x-nucleo-gnss1a1.html, library Catalog: www.st.com
47. Rausch, T., Raith, P., Pillai, P., Dustdar, S.: A System for Operating Energy-Aware Cloudlets, November 2019. http://cpsiot.at/?p=235, library Catalog: cpsiot.at Section: News
48. Yan, R., Sun, H., Qian, Y.: Energy-aware sensor node design with its application in wireless sensor networks. IEEE Trans. Instrum. Meas. **62**(5), 1183–1191 (2013). https://doi.org/10.1109/TIM.2013.2245181

Inference Performance Comparison of Convolutional Neural Networks on Edge Devices

Sheikh Rufsan Reza$^{(\boxtimes)}$, Yuzhong Yan, Xishuang Dong, and Lijun Qian

Center of Excellence in Research and Education for Big Military Data Intelligence (CREDIT Center), Prairie View A&M University, Texas A&M University System, Prairie View, TX 77446, USA
sreza@student.pvamu.edu, {xidong,liqian}@pvamu.edu

Abstract. With the proliferation of Internet of Things (IoT), large amount of data are generated at edge devices with an unprecedented speed. In order to protect the privacy and security of big edge data, as well as reduce the communications cost, it is desirable to process the data locally at the edge devices. In this study, the inference performance of several popular pre-trained convolutional neural networks on three edge computing devices are evaluated. Specifically, MobileNetV1 & V2 and InceptionV3 models have been tested on NVIDIA Jetson TX2, Jetson Nano, and Google Edge TPU for image classification. Furthermore, various compression techniques including pruning, quantization, binarized neural network, and tensor decomposition are applied to reduce the model complexity. The results will provide a guidance for practitioners when deploying deep learning models on resource constrained edge devices for near real-time and on-site learning.

Keywords: Model compression · Edge device · Deep learning · Internet of Things

1 Introduction

The Internet of Things (IoT), with pervasive interconnected smart objects operating together, has become particularly popular with the rapid development of small low-cost sensors, wireless communication technologies, and new internet techniques [1]. It is anticipated that the number of connected IoT devices will reach nearly 50 billion in 2020. As a result, huge amount of data has been generated that needs to be processed. In this context, machine learning techniques can be applied to build models to process data and a popular architecture is shown in Fig. 1. In this case, the cloud will collect the data from different IoT sensors and devices and process it by machine learning algorithms. Typically, these models are deep neural networks (DNN) that require high computational power to train.

© ICST Institute for Computer Sciences, Social Informatics and Telecommunications Engineering 2021
Published by Springer Nature Switzerland AG 2021. All Rights Reserved
S. Paiva et al. (Eds.): SmartCity360° 2020, LNICST 372, pp. 323–335, 2021.
https://doi.org/10.1007/978-3-030-76063-2_23

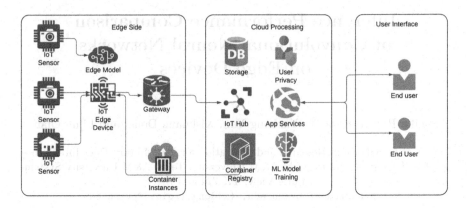

Fig. 1. Processing IoT data in cloud

Recently, the proliferation of IoT and the recent breakthroughs in deep learning have fueled a growing demand for intelligent edge devices featuring near real-time and on-site learning. Although centralized big data processing is mature, it is either not feasible to transmit all the data to a central location, or the delay incurred may exceed the tolerance of the time-sensitive applications [2], because of the densely deployed IoT devices and limited wireless communications bandwidth. In addition, there are security and privacy concerns when transmitting raw data that may contain private information [3]. Hence, mobile edge computing has been proposed to bring computing closer to the data [2]. Wireless edge networks provide highly sophisticated network and client nodes, equipped with rich sensing, computation, and storage resources. In this scenario, there is an opportunity to *leverage mobile edge devices as learning engines* which can use the locally collected data sets at edge nodes such as audio and video to derive local learning models (edge model, see Fig. 1) without sending the raw data to a central location. Compared to the centralized learning solutions, this approach reduces communication costs, improves latency, and preserves data privacy.

Let us consider the surveillance camera of an office as an example. If the camera captures videos and transmits them to the cloud, these videos can be attacked by hackers and transmitting these videos will require a large amount of bandwidth. On the contrary, if the camera connecting to an edge computing device and the monitoring software (edge model) can be run on the device without sending the raw videos to the cloud (and only send alarms with associated information when intrusion is detected), it will save a lot of bandwidth and be more secure.

However, the practical realization of such systems remains a challenge due to the limited computing and energy resources available at the edge devices, as well as the growing complexity of the state-of-the-art DNNs. There are some recent studies on the inference performance of popular deep learning models on edge devices. For example, it has been demonstrated that Jetson Nano can run MobileNet at 64 fps for the images with resolution 300 × 300 on TensorFlow framework, and be able to process larger images (960×544) at 5 fps by running a Resnet-18 SSD (single shot multibox detector) [4].

This paper presents a comprehensive comparison of inference performance of three convolutional neural networks (CNN) models, namely, MobileNet V1 [5], MobileNet V2 [6], and Inception V3 [7] by running image classification tasks on three edge devices, NVIDIA Jetson TX2, NVIDIA Jetson Nano, and Google Edge TPU. The models needs to be simplified before executing them on resource constraint devices. Now various compression techniques including pruning [8], quantization [9,10], binarized neural network [11,12], and tensor decomposition [13] are tested to reduce the model complexity. The goal is to evaluate the advantages and disadvantages of deep learning models when performing inference on different edge devices, and provide guidance on the practical choices of compressed DNNs vs. edge devices to achieve specifications of (particularly delay-sensitive) applications.

2   Deep Learning Models and Tools

2.1   Convolutional Neural Network Models

Convolutional neural network (CNN) [14] is a category of multilayer neural network including three main components: convolutional layer, pooling and non-linear layer, and lastly the fully connected layer, where the basic architecture of CNN for image classification is shown in Fig. 2. The convolutional layer is used to extract features by parsing small convolutional filters across the input. Afterwards a pooling layer is added between two convolutional layers to speed up the computation and decrease the size of input. The fully connected layer for the output is a feed forward layer which uses the softmax activation function to get the prediction probabilities of the input belonging to different classes. We can utilize CNN to build different kinds of applications such as image classification [15], object detection [16], object tracking [17] and many more.

This paper uses MobileNet V1 [5], MobileNet V2 [6] and Inception V3 [7] for performance comparison. These models were created to be suitable for edge devices by reducing the model complexity and computational cost. As a result, these models are not too complex yet they have good accuracy while reducing cost. MobileNet [5] is a popular neural network suitable for mobile and embedded based computer vision tasks. The aim was to achieve high accuracy with low computational cost. The main idea is to change the standard convolution into depth-wise convolution and 1×1 point-wise convolution. Width multiplier and resolution multipliers are additional to control the input widths. These approaches can significantly reduce the computational cost of the model. Equation (1) shows regular convolution operation (RCO) and Equation (2) shows depth-wise followed by point-wise convolution operation (PCO) [5].

$$Cost_{RCO} = D_K * D_F * M * N * D_K * D_F \tag{1}$$

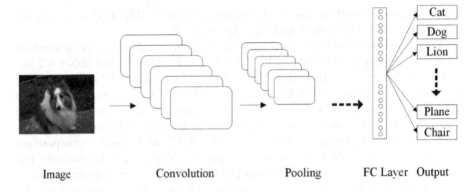

Fig. 2. An example convolutional neural network

$$Cost_{PCO} = D_K * D_F * M * D_K * D_F + M * N * D_F * D_F \tag{2}$$

where D_K and D_K are the height and width of filter while D_F and D_F are the height and width of input feature map size. Moreover, M is the number of input channel and N is the number of output channel. The comparison between these two convolution operations results in $1/N + 1/D_K^2$, which means PCO has less computation than the RCO [5].

MobileNet V2 [6] was introduced as the improved version of mobile models. The difference between MobileNet version 1 and 2 is that version 2 has a new layer which is 1×1 projection layer, which is observed in Fig. 3. It makes the number of channel smaller. It has 17 building blocks followed by 1×1 convolution, global average pooling and classification layer. In addition, when the number of channel though a layer is same, residual connection is introduced to help the flow of gradients through the network. The overall architecture is like the input comes in a low dimensional tensor which is expanded to higher dimension. Then the depth-wise layer is used to filter the data. Afterwards projection layer again compresses the data. The model was trained using 16 GPU with a batch size of 96. The version 2 is more lighter than the version 1 [6].

Inception v3 [7] uses approaches such as factorizing convolution, auxiliary classifier, grid size reduction to build a more robust and lighter model. For example, a large 5×5 filter is replaced by two 3×3 filters. The number of parameters is reduced from 25 to 18. Moreover, a 3×3 filter is replaced by 3×1 and 1×3 filter. The number of parameters is reduced from 9 to 6. Finally, the number of parameters is reduced from 25 to 6.

2.2   Model Compression

Considering the resource limitation of edge devices such as limited memory and low computational resources, regular CNN models have to be simplified before deploying in resource constrained devices [18]. Many simplification techniques are being developed where the tradeoff is between speed and accuracy [19]. The

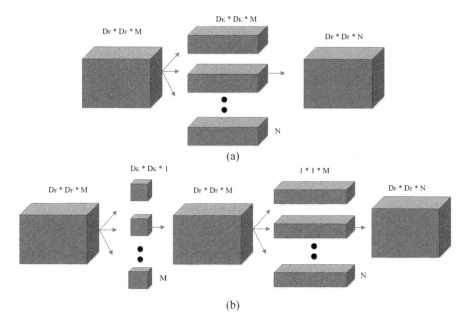

$D_F * D_F * M$

$D_K * D_K * M$

$D_F * D_F * N$

N

(a)

$D_F * D_F * M$

$D_K * D_K * 1$

$D_F * D_F * M$

$1 * 1 * M$

$D_F * D_F * N$

M

N

(b)

Fig. 3. (a): Regular convolution operation (RCO), (b): Point-wise convolution operation (PCO) [5]

goal is to reduce the memory required to store the weights. Pruning [8], quantization [10], data compression [20] are some of the popular techniques. The idea of pruning is to reduce the number of neurons by finding the less important neurons [8] in a network. Quantization method is used to reduce the number of floating or bit point operation [10], which speeds up the algorithm as lesser weight is transferred between memory and cores. If the floating point operation is reduced, memory consumption is also reduced. For example, binarized neural network is where activations and weights are represented in binary, can be easily implemented in a memory constrained device [11]. Another example is data compression technique. Parameters computed in the training phase are stored in compressed form where it is decompressed at runtime [20].

2.3   Software Tools

Tensorflow was the basic library used for this paper. TensorRT is a software development kit built on CUDA for high performance deep learning inference [21]. It can be used in many aspects as it can provide the maximum throughput as well as reduce the latency. TensorRT is compatible with frameworks such as TensorFlow or Matlab, and it supports model libraries of Keras, PyTorch and Caffe [22], which is illustrated in Fig. 4. TensorRT is capable of providing reduced bit point operations for image classification, natural language processing, object detection and so forth [21,23]. In our experiments, frozen graph was initially

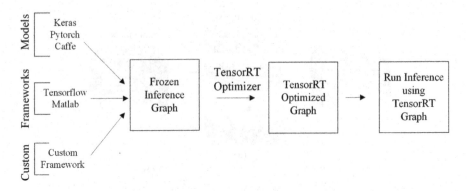

Fig. 4. TensorRT workflow [21]

created from the Keras application which operates on 32 bit operation. After-wards TensorRT converter is used to create the TensorRT graph which operates on 16 bit operation. Moreover Keras application [24] was used to execute the 32 bit point operations. Lastly the Edge TPU compatible file was derived from tensorflow Lite [25] which is the lighter version of tensorflow.

3   Edge Devices

As shown in Fig. 5, Nvidia Jetson hardwares have been used for this research. This is a good platform for DL/AI tasks. These have a lightweight GPU mounted on top of them making them run deep learning algorithm smoothly. Jetson TX2 and Nano both have a 4-core ARM A57 core where TX2 performs at 2 GHz. Both have 256-core Pascal and 128-core Pascal.

Edge TPU is the third device applied in this paper. Edge TPU devices help to deploy strong AI model on mobile devices, and it can be used in multiple application such as machine learning, robotics, medical, retail and many more [26]. Tensor Processing Units (TPUs) are custom-developed application-specific integrated circuits (ASICs) specially designed for machine learning task by Google Inc. Google has introduced this in both cloud and edge devices. The edge TPU devices are Google Coral Dev Board and USB Accelerator. This paper uses the USB Accelerator and referred as Edge TPU, as shown in Fig. 5. It supports TensorFlow lite and its hardware helps to run machine learning models faster than most other devices. Edge TPU supports only TensorFlow lite models are illustrated in Fig. 6. It uses 8-bit integer operation with TensorFlow Lite quantized models. This on-board coprocessor can perform fast image classification task. The TensorFlow Lite model is built with quantize-aware training. Edge TPU has a matrix processor designed such that it can compute hundreds of thousands of operations in a single clock cycle where a conventional GPU can only do tens of thousands. The hardware is designed in such a way that it was able to do matrix multiplication operations like operating thousands of multipliers and

Fig. 5. Left: Jetson TX2, Right (Top): Jetson Nano, Right (Bottom): Google Coral TPU USB Accelerator

Table 1. Edge device comparison

	Jetson TX2	Jetson Nano	Google Coral TPU USB Accelerator
Memory	8 GB	4 GB	NA
Storage	32 GB	16 GB eMMC	NA
Processor	Quad-Core ARM Cortex-A57 MPCore	Quad-core ARM Cortex-A57 MPCore	NA
AI Accelerator	256 Cuda Core (Pascal)	128 Cuda Cores (Maxwell)	Edge TPU

adders instantly from the operation without sending those to the memory [25]. The comparison of the three devices is presented in Table 1.

4   Experiment

4.1   Dataset

We employ ImageNet 2012 validation dataset consisting of 50,000 images and 1,000 classes for testing the accuracy [27]. We run pre-trained models created using TensorFlow framework on different devices for performance comparison.

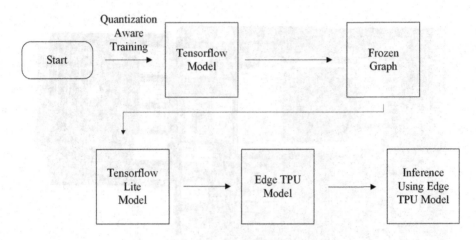

Fig. 6. TPU USB accelerator workflow [25]

4.2 Evaluation Metrics

We utilize different evaluation metrics for performance comparison. They are listed below.

- FP denotes floating point operation taken 32 bit and 16 bit for Jetson devices and 8 bit operation for Edge TPU.
- Accuracy refers to the ratio of number of correct predictions to the total number of testing samples.
- Memory denotes how much dynamic memory has been allocated by the python thread in mebibyte or MiB (1 MiB = 1024 × 1024 bytes).
- Load denotes the pre-trained model loading time in seconds.
- Time denotes the total time python script requires to execute the task.
- Average Inference (Avg Inf) is the average inference time of a single image in seconds.
- FPS (inf) represents the frame per second which is how many images can this model run in one second. Now FPS (inf) shows the rate of processing image while only considering inference whereas the last column FPS shows the rate of processing image while taking model loading, image preprocessing and inference into consideration.

Frame per second (FPS) and Frame per second (inf) are given in equation (3) and (4).

$$FPS = \frac{N}{M + \sum_{n=1}^{50000}(P_n + I_n)},$$ (3)

$$FPS(inf) = \frac{N}{\sum_{n=1}^{50000} I_n}.$$ (4)

Here N denotes the 50,000 validation images. M in the denominator is the model loading time, P is the time for preprocessing of images, and I is inference time.

The model loading occurs only once but preprocessing and inference occurs for all 50,000 images.

Table 2. Performance comparison on various edge devices with MobileNet V1.

Device	FP	Accuracy	Memory (MiB)	Load (sec)	Time (sec)	Avg. Inf. (ms)	FPS (inf)	FPS
TX2	32 bit	0.68364	1595.426	30.98	2582.42	40	25	19.36
TX2	16 bit	0.68374	2267.48	363.11	2033.77	20	50	24.58
Nano	32 bit	0.68362	1147.215	20.04	4591.97	70	14.29	10.89
Nano	16 bit	0.68372	2136.59	82.95	2151.96	20	50	23.23
TPU	8 bit	0.68008	108.516	3.06	1235.07	9.43	106.04	40.48

Table 3. Performance comparison on various edge devices with MobileNet V2.

Device	FP	Accuracy	Memory (MiB)	Load (sec)	Time (sec)	Avg Inf (ms)	FPS (inf)	FPS
TX2	32 bit	0.68048	1818.398	53.95	2799.24	40	25	17.86
TX2	16 bit	0.68048	1914.27	187.56	2278.44	20	50	21.94
Nano	32 bit	0.68048	1546.164	28.93	5471.34	90	11.11	9.14
Nano	16 bit	0.68084	2102.309	78.96	2206.76	20	50	22.66
TPU	8 bit	0.69026	103.078	3.07	1315.2	11.28	88.65	38.02

Table 4. Performance comparison on various edge devices with Inception V3.

Device	FP	Accuracy	Memory (MiB)	Load (sec)	Time (sec)	Avg Inf (ms)	FPS (inf)	FPS
TX2	32 bit	0.76276	1674.637	88.99	8860.52	150	6.67	5.64
TX2	16 bit	0.76284	3656.887	1945.94	4302.21	20	50	11.62
Nano	32 bit	0.76276	1044.277	47.38	17752.81	320	3.13	2.82
Nano	16 bit	0.76264	3213.441	469.4	4191.77	50	20	11.93
TPU	8 bit	0.7705	147.883	3.13	25463.41	490	2.04	1.96

4.3   Results and Analysis

We evaluate the performance of MobileNet V1, MobileNet V2 and Inception V3 with 32 bit, 16 bit and 8 bit operation running on Jetson devices and Edge TPU. Jetson devices were used to compute the 32 bit and 16 bit operation while Edge TPU was used to do the 8 bit operation.

Table 2 reflects the result of MobileNet V1, the 16 bit operation case takes more time to load the model but much less time to execute the entire python program than the 32 bit operation. The 32 bit operation and 8 bit operation pre-trained models are from their own application which are more optimized than the 16 bit operation in Keras pre-trained model. This could be the reason for the 16 bit operation to require more memory and more loading time. If we consider only the average inference time of a single image, then 16 bit operation is faster than the 32 bit operation. Execution time is significantly more in Nano than TX2 with TX2 having more memory consumption.

Table 3 shows that for MobileNet V2 the accuracies for different devices are almost the same. The memory consumption is more for the 16 bit operation probably because loading the library and model is the main source of memory consumption. It is also reflected on the model loading time column. In Jetson TX2, loading the model in 32 bit operation is almost 12 times faster. Also due to memory issue the validation dataset was loaded in SD card for the TX2 in all the experiments. Inference time and fps was better in 16 bit operation in TX2. The Edge TPU outperforms all the other devices by a great margin for two MobileNet models. Accuracy, memory consumption, execution time, fps is better than others.

Table 4 shows the performance of Inception V3 on various edge devices. The network structure of Inception V3 is much more complicated than MobileNet V1 and V2, with more layers and larger input image size. If we compare in terms of model size, MobileNet V2 has 4.5 MB and Inception V3 has 25.1 MB on Edge TPU. This architecture gave Inception V3 higher accuracy but slower average inference time. Similar to previous results, the inference time of 16 bit operation is faster than that of the 32 bit operation. The low FPS of the Edge TPU Coral USB Accelerator was caused by the testing environment, in which we connected TPU Coral USB Accelerator to the host CPU through USB 2.0 ports. If we ran the same model on TPU Coral Dev Board or switch to another host machine with USB 3.0 port connected to TPU Coral USB Accelerator, the average inference time is about 43.6 ms, or 22.94 FPS, nearly two times faster than NVIDIA Jetson TX2 and NVIDIA Jetson Nano. The speed up of running Inception V3 model on Edge TPU is consistent with MobileNet V1 and V2 models running on those edge devices.

5   Related Work

5.1   Model Compression

Model compression has been a popular research topic in recent years since it can reduce the model complexity significantly. For example, the specially designed convolution architecture in MobileNet was able to reduce the number of parameters by 7 times while losing the accuracy only by 1 percent. If this comparison is made with another popular model like VGG 16, then the number of parameters is reduced by almost 33 times [5]. Moreover, model compression can reduce the inference time in addition to the number of parameters. Jiaxiang et al. [9] presented that quantized convolution was able to speed up the inference 4 to 6 times and reduce the number of parameters 15 to 20 times. Han et al. [28] presented a three-stage pipeline containing pruning, quantization and huffman coding which can reduce the Alexnet model size from 240 MB to 6.9 MB.

5.2   Deep Learning Inference on Edge Devices

It is demonstrated in this paper that sophisticated deep learning models can be accommodated on resource constrained devices when applying model compression, which is consistent with studies in the literature. For instance, it has been shown that Jetson Nano runs MobileNet V2 at 64 frames per second, and Google Edge TPU Coral Dev Board runs the same model at 130 frames per second [4]. It takes a single 64-bit Intel(R) Xeon(R) Gold 6154 CPU at 3.00GHz with the coral Edge TPU USB Accelerator 2.4 ms to performs inference using MobileNet V1 or V2. Without TPU, it takes the same desktop CPU about 53 ms and 51 ms to perform the same task [29]. Taylor et al. [30] also presented an adaptive deep learning model selection for edge device which can achieve a 7.52 percent improvement in accuracy and 1.8 times reduction in inference time.

6   Conclusion

This paper presents a comprehensive comparison of the inference performance of several popular pre-trained convolutional neural networks on three edge computing devices. Specifically, MobileNet V1 & V2 and Inception V3 models have been tested on NVIDIA Jetson TX2, Jetson Nano, and Google Edge TPU for image classification. Furthermore, various compression techniques including pruning, quantization, binarized neural network, and tensor decomposition are applied to reduce the model complexity. Experimental results indicate that Edge TPU outperforms Nvidia Jetson TX2 and Nano in most experiments with faster inference speed and more accurate result. However, Edge TPU cannot work independently because it needs a host computer to complete the task. In addition, TX2 is better than Nano in most cases regarding most of the evaluation results, as expected. It is also observed that MobileNet V1 or V2 are the candidate models for speed while Inception V3 would be more accurate, which is another example of the tradeoff between inference time and prediction accuracy. It is also demonstrate that the choice of the edge computing device and the corresponding deep learning model should match the needs of the specific application. This is our first attempt to measure the inference performance of various DNNs, model compression, and edge device combinations, and we hope the results could serve as a guidance for practitioners when deploying deep learning models on resource constrained edge devices for near real-time and on-site learning.

Acknowledgment. This research work is supported by the U.S. Office of the Under Secretary of Defense for Research and Engineering (OUSD(R&E)) under agreement number FA8750-15-2-0119. The U.S. Government is authorized to reproduce and distribute reprints for governmental purposes notwithstanding any copyright notation thereon. The views and conclusions contained herein are those of the authors and should not be interpreted as necessarily representing the official policies or endorsements, either expressed or implied, of the Office of the Under Secretary of Defense for Research and Engineering (OUSD(R&E)) or the U.S. Government.

References

1. Atzori, L., Iera, A., Morabito, G.: The internet of things: a survey. Comput. Netw. **54**(15), 2787–2805 (2010)
2. Mao, Y., You, C., Zhang, J., Huang, K., Letaief, K.B.: A survey on mobile edge computing: the communication perspective. IEEE Commun. Surv. Tutorials **19**(4), 2322–2358 (2017)
3. Neshenko, N., Bou-Harb, E., Crichigno, J., Kaddoum, G., Ghani, N.: Demystifying IoT security: an exhaustive survey on IoT vulnerabilities and a first empirical look on internet-scale IoT exploitations. IEEE Commun. Surv. Tutorials **21**(3), 2702–2733 (2019)
4. Jetson nano: Deep learning inference benchmarks. https://developer.nvidia.com/embedded/jetson-nano-dl-inference-benchmarks
5. Howard, A.G., et al.: Mobilenets: efficient convolutional neural networks for mobile vision applications (2017). arXiv preprint arXiv:1704.04861
6. Sandler, M., Howard, A., Zhu, M., Zhmoginov, A., Chen, L.-C.: Mobilenetv 2: inverted residuals and linear bottlenecks. In: Proceedings of the IEEE Conference on Computer Vision and Pattern Recognition, pp. 4510–4520 (2018)
7. Szegedy, C., Vanhoucke, V., Ioffe, S., Shlens, J., Wojna, Z.: Rethinking the inception architecture for computer vision. In Proceedings of the IEEE Conference on Computer Vision and Pattern Recognition, pp. 2818–2826 (2016)
8. Molchanov, P., Tyree, S., Karras, T., Aila, T., Kautz, J.: Pruning convolutional neural networks for resource efficient inference (2016). arXiv preprint arXiv:1611.06440
9. Wu, J., Leng, C., Wang, Y., Hu, Q., Cheng, J.: Quantized convolutional neural networks for mobile devices. In: Proceedings of the IEEE Conference on Computer Vision and Pattern Recognition, pp. 4820–4828 (2016)
10. Zhou, A., Yao, A., Guo, Y., Xu, L., Chen, Y.: Incremental network quantization: towards lossless CNNS with low-precision weights (2017). arXiv preprint arXiv:1702.03044
11. Zhao, R., et al.: Accelerating binarized convolutional neural networks with software-programmable FPGAs. In: Proceedings of the 2017 ACM/SIGDA International Symposium on Field-Programmable Gate Arrays, pp. 15–24 (2017)
12. Courbariaux, M., Hubara, I., Soudry, D., El-Yaniv, R., Bengio, Y.: Binarized neural networks: Training deep neural networks with weights and activations constrained to+ 1 or-1 (2016). arXiv preprint arXiv:1602.02830
13. Cheng, T., et al.: Convolutional neural networks with low-rank regularization (2015). arXiv preprint arXiv:1511.06067
14. Krizhevsky, A., Sutskever, I., Hinton, G.E.: Imagenet classification with deep convolutional neural networks. Adv. Neural Inf. Process. Syst. **25**, 1097–1105 (2012)
15. Howard, A.G.: Some improvements on deep convolutional neural network based image classification (2013). arXiv preprint arXiv:1312.5402
16. Cai, Z., Fan, Q., Feris, R.S., Vasconcelos, N.: A unified multi-scale deep convolutional neural network for fast object detection. In: Leibe, B., Matas, J., Sebe, N., Welling, M. (eds.) ECCV 2016. LNCS, vol. 9908, pp. 354–370. Springer, Cham (2016). https://doi.org/10.1007/978-3-319-46493-0_22
17. Hong, S., You, T., Kwak, S., Han, B.: Online tracking by learning discriminative saliency map with convolutional neural network. In: International Conference on Machine Learning, pp. 597–606 (2015)

18. Yanai, K., Ryosuke Tanno, and Koichi Okamoto. Efficient mobile implementation of a cnn-based object recognition system. In: Proceedings of the 24th ACM International Conference on Multimedia, pp. 362–366 (2016)
19. Li, X., Zhou, Y., Pan, Z., Feng, J.: Partial order pruning: for best speed/accuracy trade-off in neural architecture search. In: The IEEE Conference on Computer Vision and Pattern Recognition (CVPR), June 2019
20. Makhzani, A., Frey, B.J.: Winner-take-all autoencoders. In: Advances in Neural Information Processing Systems, pp. 2791–2799 (2015)
21. Deep learning SDK documentation. https://docs.nvidia.com/deeplearning/sdk/tensorrt-developer-guide/index.html
22. Vanholder, H.: Efficient inference with tensorRT (2016)
23. Real-time natural language understanding with BERT using tensorRT. https://devblogs.nvidia.com/nlu-with-tensorrt-bert/
24. Géron, A.: Hands-On Machine Learning with Scikit-Learn, Keras, and TensorFlow: Concepts, Tools, and Techniques to Build Intelligent Systems. O'Reilly Media, Sebastopol (2019)
25. Tensorflow models on the edge TPU. https://coral.ai/docs/edgetpu/models-intro/#compatibility-overview
26. Internet of things. https://cloud.google.com/edge-tpu
27. Deng, J., Dong, W., Socher, R., Li, L.-J., Li, K., Li, F.-F.: Imagenet: a large-scale hierarchical image database. In: 2009 IEEE Conference on Computer Vision and Pattern Recognition, pp. 248–255. IEEE (2009)
28. Han, S., Mao, H., Dally, W.J.: Deep compression: compressing deep neural networks with pruning, trained quantization and Huffman coding (2015). arXiv preprint arXiv:1510.00149
29. Edge TPU performance benchmarks. https://coral.ai/docs/edgetpu/benchmarks/
30. Taylor, B., Marco, V.S., Wolff, W., Elkhatib, Y., Wang, Z.: Adaptive deep learning model selection on embedded systems. ACM SIGPLAN Notices **53**(6), 31–43 (2018)

Cognitive Computing and Cyber Physical Systems

A Non-intrusive IoT-Based Real-Time Alert System for Elderly People Monitoring

Hugo Martins[1], Nishu Gupta[2]([envelope]), and M. J. C. S. Reis[3]

[1] University of Trás-os-Montes e Alto Douro (UTAD), 5000-801 Vila Real, Portugal
[2] Chandigarh University, Chandigarh, India
[3] UTAD/IEETA, Vila Real, Portugal
mcabral@utad.pt

Abstract. Typically, elderly people may be living alone for part of the day or full time, and may have difficulties or problems with mobility, but they want to maintain their independence and autonomy. Internet of Things (IoT) technology may be used to contribute to increasing the degree of security of these people in their own homes, in a much more discreet and non-intrusive way than the typical commercially available systems, providing real-time data about the status of these people to their family members or caretakers. In this article, a non-intrusive IoT-based real-time alert system to be used by elderly people is proposed, using simple and low-cost "of the shelf" electronic components. It is also intended that this solution can integrate other monitoring devices already available on the market, such as bracelets, video cameras, robots, among others. Both laboratorial and house-hold tests have been conducted to prove the effectiveness of the system.

Keywords: IoT · Non-intrusive · Real-time alert system · Elderly people

1 Introduction

All over the world, people are living longer and it is prognosed that in Europe by 2060 one third of the population will be aged 65 and above, with many of them having some kind of disability or limitations, requiring different forms of care [10]. Unless a big change is introduced, the limited number of caregivers will not be able to respond to the care demands. As such, providing high quality care services is becoming one of the biggest challenges of contemporary societies. One possible solution is the use of assistive technologies to support people in their own homes or even in assisted living facilities. There are two main objectives in the Ambient and Assisted Living (AAL) research area: monitoring solutions providing information used for detection of emergency situations (e.g., a fall or illness) and/or for detection of symptoms indicating that such situations may happen

© ICST Institute for Computer Sciences, Social Informatics and Telecommunications Engineering 2021
Published by Springer Nature Switzerland AG 2021. All Rights Reserved
S. Paiva et al. (Eds.): SmartCity360° 2020, LNICST 372, pp. 339–357, 2021.
https://doi.org/10.1007/978-3-030-76063-2_24

in the future; and direct support of elderly people in their everyday life. The first one, monitoring, can be implemented using positioning systems, which may also deliver useful information about the elderly person health. Consequently, the development of monitoring systems should be made having in mind the aim and place where the system will operate. The resulting information can be used for different purposes, being activity monitoring one of the most used [8]. The collected data allows for the determination of physical activity periods. For example, information on walked paths can be useful for behavior analysis (e.g., determination of occupancy periods of particular rooms), and walking speed (e.g., analysis of data in the time domain). The information of the gait speed is very important, because it depends on the health status of the elderly. It should be noted that the elderly person gait speed is typically very low, usually not higher than $1.2\,m/s$, and values lower than $0.6\,m/s$ increase the likelihood of health issues (see, for example, [22,24] for the influence of various diseases on gait disorders). These systems can also be used in other type of impairments, such as wandering patterns [14,17].

Later data analysis helps to detect abnormal situations resulting from health problems or accidents. The processing of the collected data allows the comparison of the person's behavior against an assumed model. The difference between the model and the current person's behavior may be used to trigger alerts, that are usually sent to the caregivers of the monitored person [8]. The purpose of the collected data has crucial implications on the requirements concerning the tracking system's accuracy. For example, in case of activity or room occupancy evaluation, determination of position with room accuracy is sufficient. However, if the system is used for gait velocity tracking, positioning meter or even sub-meter accuracy is crucial, whereas for wandering detection the precision of localization results is of paramount importance.

The most important barriers concerning technology acceptance are discussed, for example, in [27]. The acceptance of the system is the most important and a crucial factor, determining the success of the monitoring. Preserving privacy, trust, declared functionality and low cost of the devices and services are on the top of the list of elderly users' and caregivers' acceptance criteria. If the devices performing the monitoring is to be wear by the elderly person, its use must be accepted by the user. One way to gain elderly users' acceptance is to provide the user with a wide variety of forms of tags and ways of wearing (e.g., simply carried around in a pocket, wristbands, pendants, devices attached to a waist belt). Obviously, the size and the weight of the devices should be minimized.

Obtrusivity of the system infrastructure is another very important factor. A typical infrastructure of the monitoring system consists of several "sensing nodes" (performing the measurements) and a "controller" (processing the measurement results, calculating the localizations of the elderly person—or, more precisely, the location of the tag, etc.). These systems are typically deployed in the already furnished homes, and so any changes to the interior design, such as connecting the devices with cables or moving the furniture, should be avoided.

Another important issue related to the system exploitation is the tag's energy consumption. However, because the system presented here does not rely on the use of any kind of tag, this issue will not be discussed here.

Requirements for positioning systems intended for AAL applications are discussed in [7]. The environment where the system is installed has a significant impact on the tracking accuracy and system reliability. For example, building materials, pieces of furniture and other interior design elements determine propagation conditions influencing signals delays and levels, which may reduce the performance of the system. In some cases, tracking errors can be reduced by changing "sensing nodes" locations.

The system proposed here aims at being a real-time, non-intrusive, IoT-based alert system for monitoring elderly people. Activity and room occupancy evaluation is its major concern, so that determination of position with room accuracy is sufficient. Additionally, the system is to be developed using simple and low-cost "of the shelf" electronic components. However, it is also intended that this solution can integrate other monitoring components commercially available on the market, such as electronic bracelets for measuring heart rate, video cameras, robots (e.g., medication intake), among others.

2   Related Work—Indoor Localization Systems

In [18] the authors use broadband ultrasonic signals to implement a high accuracy 3D indoor positioning system. They used low cost transducers to produce acoustic chirps of between 20 and 45 KHz as pulse signals. Then, by using synchronized ultrasonic anchor nodes and time division multiplexing to share the medium, they build a GPS-like system for indoor pervasive applications. They have performed a set of experiments to evaluate the proposed system and 3D position estimates were obtained with an absolute standard deviation less than 2.3 cm, and a position refresh rate of 350 ms.

Narrowband radio technologies are the most used radio positioning systems. Due to its low power consumption, Bluetooth Low Energy (BLE) seems to be one of the most popular. For example, the system described in [2] is based on wristbands and smartphones. The system uses "SensorTags" from Texas Instruments and it was tested in 17 elderly houses, and achieved a rate over 86% of correct room detections.

In the approach described in [16], the location of a smartphone is determined in respect to three BLE beacons. With the implementation of an algorithm based on Received Signal Strength Indicator (RSSI) and step detection, the authors achieved sub-meter accuracy. However, the measurements were performed in strictly defined conditions, with the smartphone kept in a fixed position.

Another popular class of tracking systems is based on the use of the Wi-Fi standard, which typically utilize a fingerprinting approach. In [4] a system of this class is presented, where a smartwatch is being localized using machine learning algorithms. The authors achieved room accuracy localization during tests in five flats. However, due to reception of Wi-Fi signals and intensive processing, the authors faced energy consumption problems. Sub-meter accuracy was achieved, using only static measurements carried out in a university building, in another example of a Wi-Fi positioning system presented in [25].

ZigBee-based systems for the localization of people and goods are also available. For example, three simple positioning algorithms, in-Max, Trilateration and Maximum Likelihood, were presented in [5]. The authors have conducted tests with ZigBee modules in five different environments, achieving few meters positioning errors. In [9] the localization of elderly people was simulated, and additionally using an artificial neural network. With these simulations the authors achieved positioning errors in the order of centimeters, assuming a propagation channel model.

A combination of these three technologies, ZigBee, Wi-Fi and Bluetooth, was investigated in [6], where multilateration and Viterbi algorithms were used for position calculation. The authors have performed tests in an industrial environment and a hospital. Measurements were performed in static conditions or with an autonomous vacuum cleaner positioning, and the localization errors were in the order of a few meters; the authors have not conducted any tests with persons carrying the tags.

Systems using Ultra Wideband Radio (UWB) to determine the positioning of people and goods are able to provide excellent localization accuracy. The laboratorial tests performed in [12] confirmed positioning errors lower than 0.2 m. In [11] the authors have performed tests in a nursing home with elderly people, and they were able to identify patients' behaviors. In [21] a radio frequency identification (RFID) reader was designed to simultaneously track multiple persons. The authors conducted experiments, and achieved positioning errors below 0.2 m.

The IEEE 802.15.4a standard and the availability of the compliant chips increased the interest in the UWB-based localization. The solution presented in [13] obtained sub-meter accuracy. In [19] the authors describe an implementation of a system that uses the transmission of combined chirps, also defined in the IEEE 802.15.4a standard. They achieved a localization error lower than 1 m, with a probability of 70%, in laboratory tests.

Energy consumption of these systems used for indoor tracking purposes of people and goods is a real issue, particularly if the system is to operate for long periods of time. Most of the systems require periodic battery recharging or replacement, this being a task very difficult to perform by elderly people. Only a few of the above cited systems addressed and discussed this problem. Additionally, although the systems presented above can collect useful information in AAL applications, the number of practical experiments performed in real scenarios is relatively small, with most of them being tested in laboratorial conditions.

In [26] a review of wearable technologies used for elderly persons tracking is presented. A comparison of available technological solutions, along with different criteria (e.g., accuracy, power consumption, need for the device on user side) is also presented. The number of published journal papers reviews every year in the field of indoor positioning technologies for the tracking of people and goods is very high. See, for example, [1,3,15,20] and [23], to name only a few.

The system described in the next section has no need for periodic battery recharging or replacement, and was tested in a real home scenario.

3   Conceptual Description of the System

As stated above, it is wanted to present a non-intrusive, IoT-based, real-time alert system to be used by elderly people, using simple and low-cost "of the shelf" electronic components. Additionally, it is also intended that the software component of this solution, described below, can integrate other monitoring devices already available on the market, such as bracelets, video cameras, robots, among others.

Figure 1 provides a general conceptual overview of the system. As can be seen, the detection sensors are wirelessly connected to the gateway controller. In the case presented in this figure, passive infrared (PIR) sensors, bed sensors and a Panic Button are all connected to the gateway controller. The gateway controller is connected to a cloud server. If no activity is detected for periods of time superior to the ones established and stored in the data base, an alert SMS will be sent by the server to the mobile application (App) installed in the smartphone of the caregiver. The caregiver uses this App to get real-time information about the status of every sensor, the latest detected activity, etc., and receive alert SMS. As can be seen, the system is conceptually divided in two main components: the hardware component and the software component.

In the hardware component all the different type of sensors and devices are included, like, for example, passive infrared (PIR) motion sensors, water flow sensors, switches sensors, door opining sensors, bed movement sensors, panic button, among other, and the gateway "controller", with pre-processing and communications capabilities. Note that the system is intended to work with all these and other sensors installed, or with just one type (e.g., PIR motion sensors). In fact, the results presented below were obtained with the system presented in Fig. 1, using only PIR motion sensors, one bed sensor, and a panic button. In Table 1 the components used, the manufactures, and the price of each IoT-based hardware component used in the experiments can be seen.

The software component was designed using a server-side application and a mobile (smartphone) application (App). The server-side application includes the databases, where all the data sent by the detection sensors are stored. The data stored in the data bases include the sensor's name, identification (ID), and its location, and for each activity detection the ID of the sensor who have triggered the detection, and the date and time of the detection are stored. Also included in the server-side application are the software modules responsible for the detection of potential alert situations, which trigger the sending of warning SMS to the

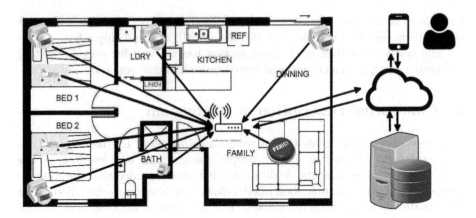

Fig. 1. General conceptual overview of the system (refer to the main text).

Table 1. Manufacturers, price, and type of the IoT hardware components used in the tests of the setting presented in Fig. 1.

Component reference	Manufacturer/Seller	Price (€)	Type
PIR motion sensor	DIGOO	7	Mandatory
Door opening sensor	DIGOO	5	Optional
Panic Button	DIGOO	3	Optional
Bed sensor			Optional
MPR121 board	NXP	3.38	—
RN2483	Microchip	11	—
0900AD54B2450E	Johanson Technology	3	—
AMS1117	Advanced Monolithic Systems	0.05	—
USB connector	TE Connectivity	1.74	—
Copper strips	—	0.20	—
Gateway controller			Mandatory
TTGO T-CALL V1.3	LILYGO	15	—
LM2596	Texas Instruments	0.50	—
RXB12 RF 433 MHz	EEant Technology	0.80	—
PIC16F1704-I/SL	Microchip	0.90	—
LoRa Module RFM95	RF Solutions	17	—
0900AD54B2450E	Johanson Technology	3	—

caregivers. For example, typically an elderly gets up in the morning, leaves the bed, goes to the bathroom, and then he/she goes to the kitchen to prepare its breakfast; if no activity is detected on the kitchen sensor after, say 15 min, nor any movement is detected in the bathroom at the end of this time, then an alert SMS is sent to the mobile App.

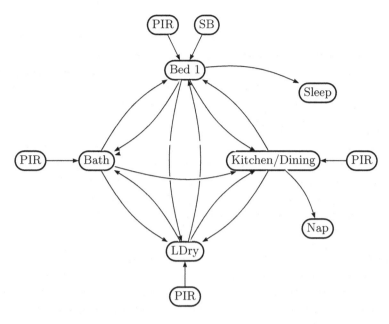

Fig. 2. State machine representing the potential alert situations that may occur to trigger the sending of SMS to the caregivers.

Figure 2 represents the state machine implemented during the tests presented below, reflecting the possible alert situations that can occur. For example, if the sensor bed "detects activity" and the corresponding PIR sensor (installed in the bedroom) detects no activity for a period longer than 5 min, the system enters the "sleep mode" state. This sate will be leaved only if the PIR bedroom sensor detects any activity or the total number of configured sleeping hours is achieved. In this last case, if no activity is detected by the PIR sensor and the total number of sleeping hours is exceeded, then an alert SMS is sent to the caregiver. Note that the state of sleep can also be entered, for example, after lunch, where typically the elderly person sits on their sofa to watch a little television and ends up falling asleep. However, in this situation the total sleeping time will be much lower, and the corresponding alert SMS will be sent if this different time threshold will be exceeded. Each of the individual sates has a different alert threshold time that triggers the sending of alert SMS when that value is exceeded. It should also be noted that the systems keeps periodically re-sending the alert SMS, if the "no activity detected" situation continues to be verified.

By using the mobile application the caregiver can check the status of the different sensors in real time, check for the last room in the house and time where activity was detected, set different threshold times for each of the states (rooms), receive/read the warning SMS, among other things.

4   Tests and Results

To test the principles and functioning of the proposed system we have implemented the practical situation depicted in Fig. 1, in a real house (flat); we have not used the sensors presented in bedroom 2 in this figure (in fact, the room was locked). The corresponding sate machine is represented in Fig. 2, and the IoT hardware components are the ones presented in Table 1.

In this particular case, all the detection sensors and controller use wireless communications. As such, there is no need for the installation of cables or any other kind of home works. All the sensors are powered by the grid network, using power adapters. These sensors can be battery powered, but then they have to be periodically replaced, with all the associated problems discussed above.

Figure 3 presents a diagram and Fig. 4 presents a photo of the gateway controller implemented, using only "of the shelf" IoT components. We have used GPRS, using a GSM modem with an IoT global operator (Things Mobile^{TM}) SIM-card, for the communications between the gateway controller and the server-side application, and the communications between the sensors and the gateway controller were implemented using RF 433 Mhz (RXB12 EEant Technology^{TM}) super-heterodyne receiver, with encoding EV1527. By using the Things Mobile^{TM} SIM-card there is no need for the installation of an "Internet pack service" by a communications provider, with a typical much higher cost.

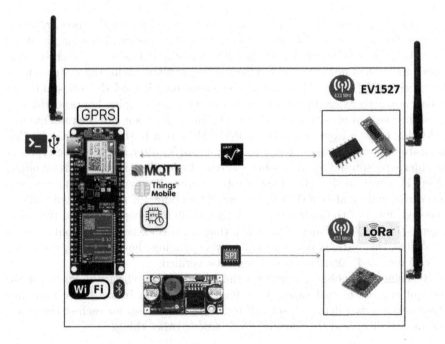

Fig. 3. Diagram of the gateway controller implemented, using only "of the shelf" IoT components.

Fig. 4. Photo of the actual gateway controller implemented, using only "of the shelf" IoT components.

Fig. 5. Picture of the actual PIR activity sensor implemented, using only "of the shelf" IoT components.

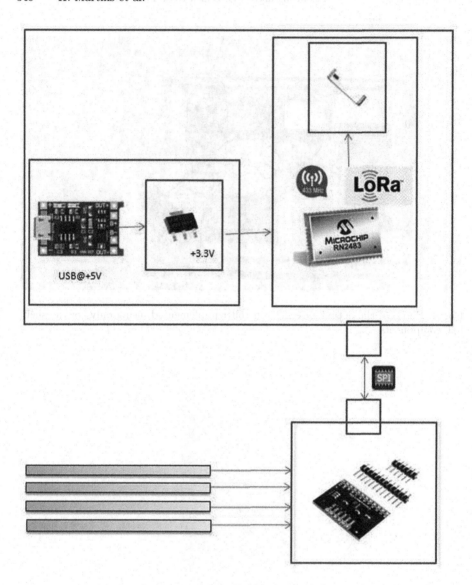

Fig. 6. Diagram of the bed activity sensor implemented, using only "of the shelf" IoT components.

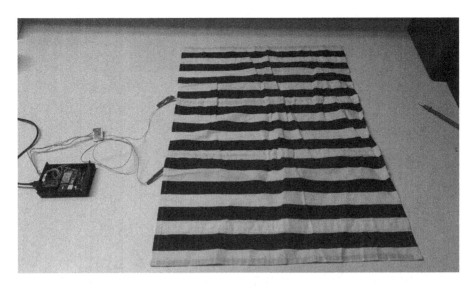

Fig. 7. Photo of the actual bed activity sensor implemented, using only "of the shelf" IoT components.

For example, in Portugal it typically costs 20 € per month, whereas the price of this solution is 2 € per month. However, if the house/flat has already installed an Internet pack service, the system can use it, because the board we are using (LILYGO™ TTGO T-CALL V1.3) has already a Wi-Fi embeded module. The total cost of the IoT-based hardware used in this experiment is approximately 87 €.

As stated above, we have implemented the system depicted in Fig. 1 in a real flat, but with bedroom 2 closed, and we have tested its functioning for a week. Figures 5 presents a picture of the actual PIR sensor used, and Figs. 6 and 7 present, respectively, a diagram and a photo of the bed activity sensor implemented.

In Fig. 2 the state machine of this test-bed can be seen. The threshold alert time parameters can be configured by the caregiver, in real time, using the mobile application.

Figure 8 shows a screen-shot of the mobile application page where the caregiver can see that the system is online", meaning it is working properly, Fig. 9 shows a screen-shot of the mobile application page where the caregiver can see the latest detected activity, Fig. 10 shows a screen-shot of the mobile application page where the caregiver can see that the bed sensor was activated, and in Fig. 11 the alert SMS sent by the system.

Fig. 8. Screen-shot of the mobile application page where the caregiver can see that the system "online" (working properly, first option; in Portuguese).

During the week of tests, we have monitored an elderly person's normal activity, by using a surveillance camera system, and there were no situations of false activity detections caused by the sensors (both PIR and bed sensors). Although the PIR sensors did not always detect the presence or movement of the elderly person in the room (where they are installed) at first, they always ended up detecting the presence of the elderly person following its subsequent

Fig. 9. Screen-shot of the mobile application page where the caregiver can see the last detected activity. In this case, it was detected movement in the "Kitchen/Dining" area (in Portuguese).

movements. This fact is not a problem for our system, since the presence of the elderly person in a given room of the house was, sooner or latter, always detected. For this reason, the number of times the PIR sensors did not detect movement at first was not counted.

Fig. 10. Screen-shot of the mobile application page where the caregiver can see that the bed sensor was activated (in Portuguese).

The panic button was also tested and it has functioned well; fortunately, the elderly person did not have no need to use it in a real situation. In Fig. 12 we can see a screen-shot of the app where the red sign indicates that the "Panic Button" was pressed.

We have also tested the changing of the threshold alert times in real-time and no errors occurred. Additionally, all the alert SMS were correctly sent.

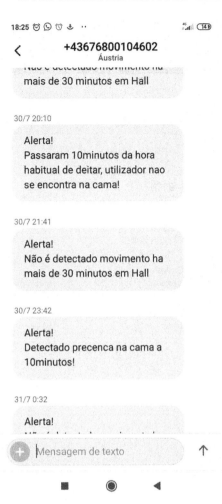

Fig. 11. Screen-shot of the mobile application page where the caregiver can read the alert SMS sent by the system (in Portuguese).

Fig. 12. Screen-shot of the mobile application page where the caregiver can see that "Panic Button" (in red) was pressed (in Portuguese).

5   Conclusions

A non-intrusive IoT-based real-time alert system for elderly people was presented. The system aims at being low-cost and made using "of the shelf" electronic components. The system is prepared to integrate other monitoring devices already available on the market, such as bracelets, video cameras, robots, among others.

The conducted tests, both laboratorial and house-hold tests, have prove the effectiveness of the system, and the system tested has a total price less than 100 €.

In the near future we want to integrate Convolutional Neural Networks (CNN) with Deep Learning algorithms in the system, in order to identify patterns of the behavior of the elderly person, and thus automatically adapt and fine-tune the individual threshold times of each state for the sending of alert SMS.

References

1. Alakhras, M., Oussalah, M., Hussein, M.: A survey of fuzzy logic in wireless localization. EURASIP J. Wirel. Commun. Netw. **2020**(1), 1–45 (2020). https://doi.org/10.1186/s13638-020-01703-7
2. Almeida, A., Mulero, R., Rametta, P., Urošević, V., Andrić, M., Patrono, L.: A critical analysis of an IoT-aware AAL system for elderlymonitoring. Future Gener. Comput. Syst. **97**, 598–619 (2019). https://doi.org/10.1016/j.future.2019.03.019. http://www.sciencedirect.com/science/article/pii/S0167739X18321769
3. Ashraf, I., Hur, S., Park, Y.: Smartphone sensor based indoor positioning: current status, opportunities, and future challenges. Electronics **9**(6) (2020). https://doi.org/10.3390/electronics9060891
4. Belmonte-Fernandez, O., Puertas-Cabedo, A., Torres-Sospedra, J., Montoliu-Colas, R., Trilles-Oliver, S.: An indoor positioning system based on wearables for ambient-assisted living. Sensors **17**(1) (2017). https://doi.org/10.3390/s17010036
5. Ciabattoni, L., et al.: Human indoor localization for AAL applications: an RSSI based approach. In: Cavallo, F., Marletta, V., Monteriù, A., Siciliano, P. (eds.) ForItAAL 2016. LNEE, vol. 426, pp. 239–250. Springer, Cham (2017). https://doi.org/10.1007/978-3-319-54283-6_18
6. De Poorter, E., Van Haute, T., Laermans, E., Moerman, I.: Benchmarking of localization solutions: guidelines for the selection of evaluation points. AdHoc Netw. **59**, 86–96 (2017). https://doi.org/10.1016/j.adhoc.2017.02.002. http://www.sciencedirect.com/science/article/pii/S1570870517300264
7. Eisa, S., Moreira, A.: Requirements and metrics for location and tracking for ambient assisted living. In: 2012 International Conference on Indoor Positioning and Indoor Navigation (IPIN), pp. 1–7 (2012). https://doi.org/10/ggcfbg
8. Eisa, S., Moreira, A.: A behaviour monitoring system (BMS) for ambient assisted living. Sensors **17**(9), 1946 (2017). https://doi.org/10/ggk8qb
9. Gharghan, S.K., et al.: Accurate fall detection and localization for elderly people based on neural network and energy-efficient wireless sensor network. Energies **11**(11) (2018). https://doi.org/10.3390/en11112866

10. Global Coalition on Aging: Relationship-based home care: a sustainable solution for Europe's elder care crisis. Technical report, Global Coalition on Aging, London (2018)
11. Grunerbl, A., Bahle, G., Lukowicz, P., Hanser, F.: Using indoor location to assess the state of dementia patients: results and experience report from a long term, real world study. In: 2011 Seventh International Conference on Intelligent Environments, pp. 32–39 (2011). https://doi.org/10.1109/IE.2011.22
12. Kearns, W.D., Algase, D., Moore, D.H., Ahmed, S.: Ultra wideband radio: a novel method for measuring wandering in persons with dementia. Gerontechnology 7(1), 48 (2008). https://doi.org/10/cv526s
13. Kolakowski, J., Djaja-Josko, V., Kolakowski, M.: UWB monitoring system for AAL applications. Sensors 17(9) (2017). https://doi.org/10.3390/s17092092
14. Kolakowski, M., Blachucki, B.: Monitoring wandering behavior of persons suffering from dementia using BLE based localization system. In: 2019 27th Telecommunications Forum (TELFOR), pp. 1–4 (2019). https://doi.org/10.1109/TELFOR48224.2019.8971136
15. Kunhoth, J., Karkar, A.G., Al-Maadeed, S., Al-Ali, A.: Indoor positioning and wayfinding systems: a survey. HCIS 10(1), 1–41 (2020). https://doi.org/10.1186/s13673-020-00222-0
16. Liang, P., Krause, P.: Smartphone-based real-time indoor location tracking with 1-m precision. IEEE J. Biomed. Health Inf. 20(3), 756–762 (2016). https://doi.org/10/ggcdf7
17. Lin, Q., Zhang, D., Chen, L., Ni, H., Zhou, X.: Managing elders' wandering behavior using sensors-based solutions: a survey. Int. J. Gerontol. 8(2), 49–55 (2014). https://doi.org/10.1016/j.ijge.2013.08.007. http://www.sciencedirect.com/science/article/pii/S1873959814000295
18. Lopes, S.I., Vieira, J.M.N., Albuquerque, D.: High accuracy 3D indoor positioning using broadband ultrasonic signals. In: 2012 IEEE 11th International Conference on Trust, Security and Privacy in Computing and Communications, pp. 2008–2014 (2012)
19. Lottis, A., Heß, D., Bastert, T., Röhrig, C.: Safe@home – a wireless assistance system with integrated IEEE 802.15.4a localisation technology. In: 2013 IEEE 7th International Conference on Intelligent Data Acquisition and Advanced Computing Systems (IDAACS), vol. 1, pp. 461–467 (2013). https://doi.org/10/ggk9tg
20. Maheepala, M., Kouzani, A.Z., Joordens, M.A.: Light-based indoor positioning systems: a review. IEEE Sens. J. 20(8), 3971–3995 (2020). https://doi.org/10.1109/JSEN.2020.2964380
21. Paolini, G., Masotti, D., Antoniazzi, F., Salmon Cinotti, T., Costanzo, A.: Fall detection and 3-D indoor localization by a custom RFID reader embedded in a smart e-health platform. IEEE Trans. Microwave Theory Tech. 67(12), 5329–5339 (2019). https://doi.org/10/ggk8qn
22. Pirker, W., Katzenschlager, R.: Gait disorders in adults and the elderly. Wien Klin Wochenschr 129, 81–95 (2017). https://doi.org/10/f9sgwd
23. Simoes, W.C.S.S., Machado, G.S., Sales, A.M.A., de Lucena, M.M., Jazdi, N., de Lucena Jr, V.F.: A review of technologies and techniques for indoor navigation systems for the visually impaired. Sensors 20(14) (2020). https://doi.org/10.3390/s20143935
24. Studenski, S., et al.: Gait speed and survival in older adults. JAMA 305(1), 50–58 (2011). https://doi.org/10/bf94g8

25. Varadharajan, V., Tupakula, U., Karmakar, K.: Secure monitoring of patients with wandering behavior in hospital environments. IEEE Access **6**, 11523–11533 (2018). https://doi.org/10/ggcvnn
26. Wang, Z., Yang, Z., Dong, T.: A review of wearable technologies for elderly care that can accurately track indoor position, recognize physical activities and monitor vital signs in real time. Sensors **17**(2) (2017). https://doi.org/10.3390/s17020341
27. Yusif, S., Soar, J., Hafeez-Baig, A.: Older people, assistive technologies, and the barriers to adoption: a systematic review. Int. J. Med. Inf. **94**, 112–116 (2016). https://doi.org/10.1016/j.ijmedinf.2016.07.004. http://www.sciencedirect.com/science/article/pii/S1386505616301551

A Smartphone Application Designed to Detect Obstacles for Pedestrians' Safety

Marios Thoma[1(✉)], Zenonas Theodosiou[1], Harris Partaourides[1], Charalambos Tylliros[1], Demetris Antoniades[1], and Andreas Lanitis[1,2]

[1] Research Centre on Interactive Media, Smart Systems and Emerging Technologies - RISE, Nicosia, Cyprus
{z.theodosiou,h.partaourides,c.tylliros,d.antoniades,
a.lanitis}@rise.org.cy
[2] Visual Media Computing Research Lab, Department of Multimedia and Graphic Arts, Cyprus University of Technology, Limassol, Cyprus

Abstract. Encouraging people to walk rather than using other means of transportation is an important factor towards personal health and environmental sustainability. However, given the large number of pedestrian accidents recorded every year, the need for safe urban environments is increasing. Taking advantage of the potential of citizen-science for crowdsourcing data and creating awareness, we developed a smartphone application for enhancing the safety of pedestrians while walking in cities. Using the application, citizens will monitor the urban sidewalks and update a crowdsourcing platform with the detected barriers and damages that hinder safe walking, along with their location on a city map. To help users assign the correct type of obstacle, and authorities to assess the urgency, a Convolutional Neural Network (CNN) model for barrier and damage recognition is embedded in the application. The results of a user evaluation, based on a group of volunteers who used the application in real conditions, demonstrate the potential of using the application in conjunction with a smart city framework.

Keywords: Pedestrian safety · Citizen-science · Crowdsourced data collection · Smart city · Obstacle recognition · Deep learning

1 Introduction

Walking is directly related to the quality of life, especially in modern urban environments where everyday life is becoming more and more demanding. The benefits it offers to the environment and natural resources, through the reduction of air pollutants and traffic noise, significantly improve the health of citizens. However, the growing number of barriers and damages that block pedestrian paths, often endanger the lives of pedestrians [10]. According to the World Health Organization (WHO), 26% of all road traffic deaths in 2016 involved pedestrians and cyclists [18]. Due to the human, social and economic dimensions of the problem, pedestrian safety has always been a grand challenge for local authorities

S. Paiva et al. (Eds.): SmartCity360° 2020, LNICST 372, pp. 358–371, 2021.
https://doi.org/10.1007/978-3-030-76063-2_25

to address. Keeping routes clear from static barriers (e.g. badly designed pavements, dustbins, furniture, etc.), short-term barriers (e.g. construction work, illegal parking, dense crowds, etc.) and damages (e.g. cracks, holes, broken pavers, etc.) is important for the easy, safe, well-maintained and secure pedestrian access to urban infrastructure environments (obstacle examples are shown in Fig. 1). In addition, it helps to improve the urban environment through the removal of items that cause pollution (i.e. litter and other rubbish on pavements).

Fig. 1. Examples of obstacles that impede pedestrian routes (a) Illegal parking; (b) Broken pavement; (c) Pavement blocked by bush; (d) Narrow pavement; (e) Illegal parking/parking prevention barrier, and (f) Roadworks.

Citizen-science has gained considerable attention in recent years, involving the active participation of citizens in scientific research activities related to real-world problems [3]. By exploiting the widespread and ubiquitous use of smartphones, a large number of citizen-science studies have focused on crowdsourced data collection, overcoming the problems and limitations of conventional collection methods [7]. Several smartphone applications have been developed for the collection and sharing of various categories of information, in both rural and urban areas. Among the most successful ones, *iNaturalist*[1] and *eBird*[2] allow users to share observations about biodiversity and bird sightings, respectively. Other applications have focused on improving the quality of life, for example the *Loss of the Night*[3] application which invites the citizens to measure and submit night sky brightness observations, and *NoiseTube*[4] that aims to monitor noise pollution by allowing citizens to measure and submit the level of noise in cities. Citizen science has played a significant role in the development of meaningful and democratic smart cities since human value allows for creating intelligent smart services [5]. Smart citizens are involved in the governance of their city helping to improve the quality of their daily lives.

Building on the idea that citizens can, and should, play the role of knowledge's carriers during their everyday activities for enhancing pedestrians' safety, a crowdsourcing platform can be used for reporting the barriers and damages which put the pedestrians' lives at risk. The proposed citizen-science platform will create awareness and build capacity in regard to pedestrian safety, by informing walkers and public authorities in real time. This paper presents the development and preliminary evaluation of a prototype smartphone application that aims towards this direction. The proposed application allows pedestrians to easily report any obstacle they encounter while walking in a city. A Convolutional Neural Network (CNN), trained specifically for recognising various barriers and damages [15], aids users in quickly choosing the correct type of barrier or damage. The evaluation of the prototype application involves 25 volunteers who tested the application in real conditions and answered an online questionnaire regarding user experience.

The rest of the paper is as follows: Sect. 2 presents the literature review; Sect. 3 describes the interactive platform hosting the proposed application; Sect. 4 presents the proposed smartphone application, while Sect. 5 describes the evaluation process and its results. Conclusions and future work prospects are explored in Sect. 6.

2   Literature Review

Several research efforts have focused on the development of smartphone applications to help pedestrians and fulfil their needs. Papageorgiou et al. [9] studied how an application can lead to sustainable walking and analysed the walking patterns of young people, concluding that a dedicated smartphone application on safer walking would encourage more young people to walk. *Walksafe*, presented by Wang et al. [17], is a smartphone application intended to help pedestrians cross the streets safely. The application combines the back camera of smartphones and a vehicle detection algorithm to alert users about possible hazards.

---

[1] https://www.inaturalist.org.
[2] https://ebird.org.
[3] https://www.globeatnight.org.
[4] http://www.noisetube.net.

mPASS combines georeferenced data related to urban accessibility with a user's profile and suggests personalised walking routes [8]. Other applications have been developed for enabling people with disabilities [13], collecting real data for walking routes via gamification [6], analysing users ability to see while walking after dark [1], etc. Similar *CIT2ADM*[5] is a smartphone application for pedestrians that allows reporting problems while walking in the neighbourhood, for immediate awareness of the local municipality and other neighbours.

The advances in wearable cameras and the enormous increase in the use of smartphones have aroused the interest of the research community [14] which has created a new field of Computer Vision that includes methods of analyzing data collected through portable cameras. This field is known as Egocentric or First-Person Vision. The analysis of egocentric data can give useful insights in several domains including health, security, entertainment, etc. Thus, a number of research efforts have been presented for indoor and outdoor applications related to the daily needs of the carriers including nutrition habits [2], automatic recognition of locations in the daily activities [4], digital memory [14], etc.

A method for the recognition of obstacles in egocentric data for pedestrians' safety was presented in [15]. The obstacle recognition was based on a CNN which was specifically trained to classify different obstacle types. For this purpose, a dedicated annotated dataset was used which consists of images collected using a smartphone camera while a pedestrian walked in urban areas. A total number of 1854 bounding boxes related to 15 different barriers and damages was utilized to train a well-known CNN deep algorithm using TensorFlow framework. More specifically, a variant of the VGG-16 architecture was used to classify 15 obstacle types, including *Hole/Pot-hole, Narrow Pavement, No Pavement, Light, Bin, Parking Meter, Plat Pot, Tree, Shrub, Mail Box, 4-Wheels, 2-Wheels, Safety Sign, Fence* and *Traffic Cone*.

Unlike *CIT2ADM*, the application we present in this work incorporates egocentric vision algorithms for the automatic recognition of barriers and damages, intended to aid users in reporting obstacles more quickly. Additionally, we evaluated the user experience, enabling the derivation of results related to the operation of the application that will allow its improvement to deal effectively with users' needs.

3   Smart City Digital Twin Platform

The smartphone application has been developed to connect to the interactive platform which is implemented within the *iNicosia*[6]. This project aims to create a Digital Twin of Nicosia city by integrating available data into a 3D model and visualising the real-time and future conditions of the city, simulating solutions to optimise planning activities and providing the best solutions in case of emergency scenarios. The project builds on top of the Nicosia Municipality Smart

---

[5] https://cit2adm.com.

[6] http://inicosia.rise.org.cy.

City infrastructure. Its ultimate goal is to setup the proper technical infrastructure that will enable the city digital transformation, as well as host data
and modules for real-life applications, advancing both the research capabilities
in the city as well as citizen quality-of-life. Such infrastructure will include the
data storage and standardisation modules that will transform the data originating from different services into standardised formats, enabling the integration
of the data. Furthermore, it includes modules for analysing and visualising the
data, as well as providing the data and/or results of the analysis to interested
stakeholders, either through well-formed Application Programming Interfaces
(APIs) or applications. The architecture of the platform is depicted in Fig. 2.

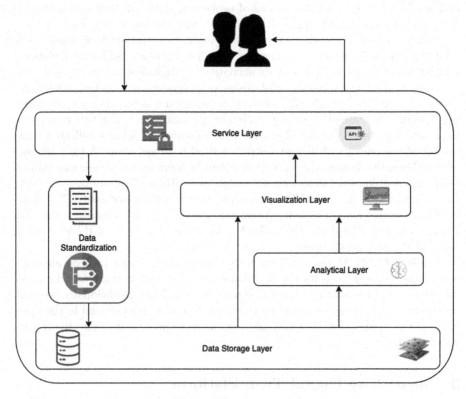

Fig. 2. High-level architecture of the interactive platform.

In addition to the crowdsourcing application for pedestrians safety, the platform so far hosts other applications and services including visualisation and
prediction of road traffic, as well as the visualisation of open data concerning
the city, such as the Quality of Life evaluation of various areas based on the priorities of citizens, and identification of micro-scale events happening around the
city from online Social Networks. Currently, the development team is working
towards the preparation of a 3D model of Nicosia city by utilising data from the

Department of Land and Survey of the Cyprus Government, and on a Mixed Reality collaboration app, where Virtual Reality and Augmented Reality users can communicate in real time and exchange information in the city to create valuable stories.

4 The Prototype Smartphone Application

The proposed mobile application has a single objective; to enable citizens that want to report obstacles they encounter during their journey in the city. To succeed on this objective it tries to make the reporting as easy as possible by incorporating advanced AI methods that aid the user during this process. Towards this end, the proposed application utilises the users' smartphone feature, i.e. camera, GPS and other sensors, to capture an image of the obstacle, enables the user to tag further details of the surroundings in the image and upload the information in a crowdsourcing platform for the further analysis.

In this section, we describe the main components and methodology of the mobile application prototype development. We provide an overview of the mobile architecture, details on the automatic obstacle classification embedded in the application, the information collected in the database and a demonstration of the application workflow.

4.1 Application Architecture

The application is based on the Model-View-ViewModel (MVVM) architecture paradigm [16]. MVVM, the recommended Android application development architecture, is structured around three main components:

- Model: Data access layer for retrieving and storing data
- View: Interacts with the rest of the application through the ViewModel
- ViewModel: Exposes streams of data

MVVM follows the principle of the "Separation of concerns", whereby the View contains strictly User Interface (UI) related logic, and is driven by the data contained in the DataModel, as exposed by the ViewModel. For our prototype, the View is structured around the Single Activity-Multiple Fragments pattern (Subsect. 4.2). Relevant information and user actions are gathered and stored in an on-device database. When there is an appropriate network connection (i.e. WiFi or LTE connection based on the user preferences) the application synchronises the reported obstacles with the Smart City Digital Twin platform presented in Sect. 3. The users have the option to use their mobile data for the synchronisation process. As per the latest guidelines and requirements of mobile application development, upon first launch of the application, the users are informed and give their consent for access to their devices' camera and GPS sensors by the application. A graphical representation of the architecture is shown in Fig. 3.

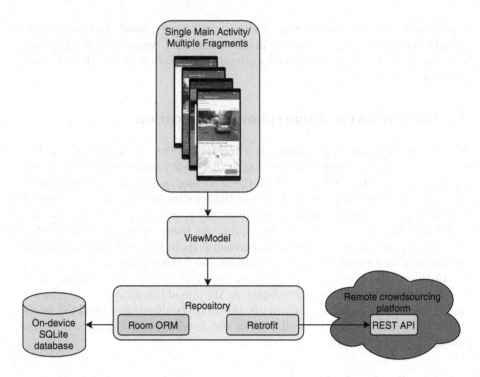

Fig. 3. Application architecture.

The application prototype was developed for the Android operating system, with the Kotlin programming language, and can run on devices with Android version 5.0 and up (SDK 21). Among others, the following libraries were used in the development process: the Navigation Component library[7], an on-device SQLite database accessed via the Object-Relational Mapping library Room[8], and the Retrofit HTTP client library[9] for communicating with the remote crowdsourcing platform.

Additionally, a Machine Learning (ML) algorithm that provides an automated list of obstacle type recommendations was embedded in the application. For this functionality, we utilised a related publicly available CNN model [15] that was tuned using transfer learning, based on a dedicated dataset of typical obstacles found in urban environments [15]. To incorporate the ML model in the application, we used the TensorFlow Lite converter Python library[10] to convert the CNN to the mobile compatible TensorFlow Lite format.

---

[7] https://developer.android.com/guide/navigation.

[8] https://developer.android.com/topic/libraries/architecture/room.

[9] https://square.github.io/retrofit/.

[10] https://www.tensorflow.org/lite/convert.

4.2   Obstacle Reporting Workflow

The View component of our MVVM architecture is structured around a single activity, that displays one of multiple fragments, depending on the task at hand. The general process consists of capturing a photo of an obstacle and storing relevant information about it in a database; this process is divided in four fragments.

1. Main: Start a new obstacle capture process and observe previous ones.
2. Obstacle capture: Take photos of the obstacles.
3. Obstacle type: An automated recommendation list of possible obstacle types.
4. Overview: An overview of the information gathered about the obstacle.

In the *main* fragment the user can start a new obstacle capture process or observe the ones they have already captured (see Fig. 4a). If the user chooses to start a new capture, the application directs them to the second fragment, *obstacle capture*, where the user's camera is initialised within the application. Here, the user can take a picture of the obstacle encountered in their urban walk (Fig. 4b). Following the capture, an *obstacle type* selection fragment is shown, where the user is presented with the five most probable obstacle types to choose from, with an additional option to show more types if the actual obstacle type is not included in the recommended types (Fig. 4c). For a full list of urban obstacle types used, see the list in [15]. In the scenario where the obstacle does not fall under any of the predefined types, the user has the option of entering the obstacle type manually.

Between the *obstacle capture* and the *obstacle type* fragments, the photos taken by the application are pre-processed and passed as inputs to the mobile adapted CNN model. The pre-processing includes a down-sampling to the resolution of $224 \times 224 \times 3$ pixels, and normalisation of the pixel values to the range of $[0, 1]$. The input is passed through the CNN in a feedforward manner, which outputs the probabilities of each obstacle class. We exploit these probabilities as a ranking mechanism for our automated obstacle recommendation list. The employed image classification function is implemented as a coroutine, that runs in a background thread, and passes the results to the main thread once the analysis is finished, to be displayed by the UI. Our employed image classification model takes a reasonable amount of time and does not impede the obstacle capturing process.

Once the user specifies the obstacle's type, they are presented with the *overview* fragment, which shows all information gathered about the obstacle by the application (Fig. 4d). To make obstacle reporting fast, efficient and effortless, we automatically gather as much information about the obstacle as possible with minimal user input, using all available sensors in the user's device, namely GPS, accelerometer, magnetometer and gyroscope. Hence, we are able to collect latitude, longitude, altitude and the orientation of the device. The current location is displayed in the *overview* screen using a Google Maps view. Users can edit the location using the map view, in case the location retrieved is erroneous, or can even input manually the location if their device does not have a working GPS

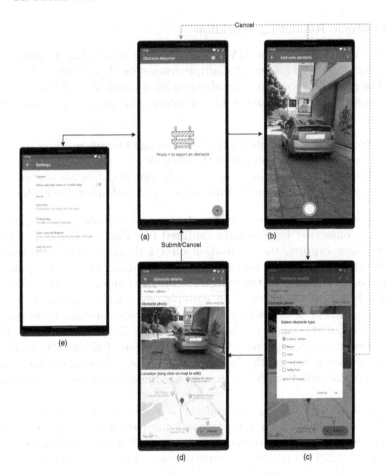

Fig. 4. Application workflow (a) Main screen; (b) Obstacle capture; (c) Obstacle type selection; (d) Overview; and (e) Settings.

sensor. To hinder malicious intent we store both the original and edited GPS coordinates. Additionally, the users are able to crop the captured photo for a better obstacle representation.

In parallel, information regarding the obstacle prediction model is collected. These include the user's obstacle type choice and the complete list of obstacle types along with their predicted probabilities. Once the users are satisfied with the collected information they can submit their report. The information is then automatically uploaded to the crowdsourcing platform when there is an available network connection. A graphical representation of the complete workflow is shown in Fig. 4.

5   Evaluation and Discussion

The preliminary evaluation of the application prototype regarding user experience (UX) was achieved with the aid of a group of volunteer users. The users were asked to use the application for at least 10 min while walking around the city, and to report at least 3 obstacles they encountered during their walk. Then, they were asked to complete an online questionnaire, which consisted of three parts: (A) Demographics, (B) Evaluation, and (C) Feedback.

Part A included demographic questions in regard to the gender, age, average walking time per day, and familiarity with smartphones and technology in general. In total 25 volunteers participated in the evaluation, 9 female and 16 male, aged between 16 and 60 years old (Fig. 5a and 5b, respectively). 10 participants stated that they walk 10 to 30 min every day on average, 10 participants that they walk from 30 to 60 min on average, while the remaining 5 stated that they walk less than 10 min per day (Fig. 5c). The majority of the participants answered that they are quite familiar with technology, with 15 stating that they are very familiar (Fig. 5d).

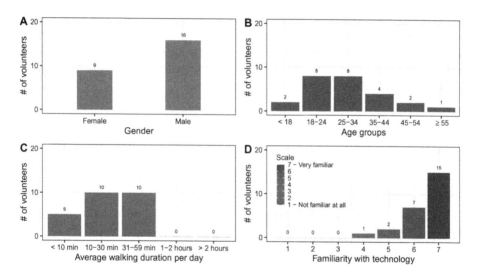

Fig. 5. Demographic information concerning the volunteers that participated in the app evaluation.

Part B was concerned with the UX evaluation and was based on a shortened version of the User Experience Questionnaire (UEQ) [11,12]. The questionnaire included 12 of the 26 UEQ questions, 2 for each one of the following 6 scales: Attractiveness, Dependability, Efficiency, Novelty, Perspicuity and Stimulation, as shown in Table 1.

The results of the UEQ evaluation are shown in Fig. 6. The prototype application received a positive evaluation, having all scores greater than 0.8 according

Table 1. UEQ scales used in the app evaluation, and their individual components.

Scale	Component 1	Component 2
Attractiveness	Attractive - unattractive	Friendly - unfriendly
Dependability	Meets expectations - Does not meet expectations	Obstructive - supportive
Efficiency	Fast - slow	Impractical - practical
Novelty	Conservative - innovative	Inventive - conventional
Perspicuity	Clear - confusing	Complicated - easy
Stimulation	Not interesting - interesting	Valuable - inferior

to the study of Schrepp et al. [12]. Based on the benchmark intervals provided by the same authors, the prototype application achieved *Excellent* evaluation for the scales of Attractiveness, Dependability, Efficiency, Novelty and Stimulation, while it scored *Above Average* for Perspicuity. The Perspicuity scale represents how easy it is for users to get familiar with the application and learn how to use it, indicating that the prototype application will greatly benefit if this is improved in its future versions.

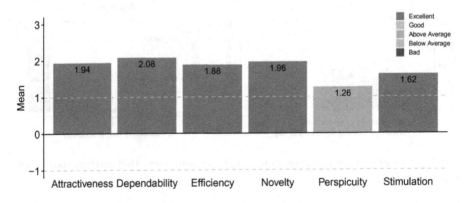

Fig. 6. Results from the UEQ evaluation.

The last part of the questionnaire (Part C) focused on collecting users' feedback on problems they may have faced during the evaluation procedure and possible improvements that they believe will help the prototype application to offer a better user experience. No major problems were reported, while a few minor issues reported were: (i) the quality of photos used in application's introductory tutorial, (ii) the slight delay during the photo analysis by the CNN, and (iii) the difficulty in translating the obstacle types in the users' native language. In regard to possible improvements, the users suggested the use of rewards in order to attract more pedestrians to use it during their everyday activities, and the availability of the application in their native language.

6   Conclusions and Future Work

This work presents the prototype Android application we have developed, aiming to enhance the pedestrians' safety. The application provides users with the opportunity to report obstacles which put pedestrians at risk for the creation of safe access in urban environments. An automatic recognition algorithm based on a CNN assists the users in choosing the appropriate type of the detected obstacles. The prototype was positively evaluated in regard to the user experience using the UEQ with 5 of the 6 sections having an *Excellent* score. The application has great potential to be used in a citizen-science crowdsourcing project, for reporting damages and barriers which endanger pedestrians. In addition, the application can be used for the creation of annotated first-person datasets, as an attempt to address the challenge of training deep learning algorithms for egocentric vision content analysis.

The feedback collected from users in the preliminary evaluation will help us to improve the application, and will be taken into account for its finalisation. Thus, future plans include, firstly, the enhancement of the application with a more accurate version of the obstacle recognition model, in order to improve the recognition accuracy during the reporting phase. Data collected through the application could be used to retrain the CNN periodically, and the improved CNN could be redistributed to the application via updates. Second, a new application introductory tutorial will be created based on better-quality images, and improved with more information, so as to help the users to become more familiar with the application. Third, the application will offer multi-language support, so that it is accessible to users from different countries. In addition, the application will be evaluated in a larger scale, including more volunteers and different scenario tests, before it is finalised and made available to the general public through app stores.

Acknowledgements. This project has received funding from the European Union's Horizon 2020 research and innovation programme under grant agreement No 739578 complemented by the Government of the Republic of Cyprus through the Directorate General for European Programmes, Coordination and Development.

References

1. Bierings, R., Jansonius, N.: Luminance and pedestrians' perceived ability to see after dark: mapping the Netherlands using a citizen science network of smartphone users. Light. Res. Technol. **51**(2), 231–242 (2019). https://doi.org/10.1177/1477153518758355

2. Bolaños, M., Radeva, P.: Simultaneous food localization and recognition. In: 23rd International Conference on Pattern Recognition (ICPR), pp. 3140–3145 (2016)

3. Bonney, R., et al.: Citizen science: a developing tool for expanding science knowledge and scientific literacy. Bioscience **59**(11), 977–984 (2009). https://doi.org/10.1525/bio.2009.59.11.9

4. Furnari, A., Farinella, G.M., Battiato, S.: Recognizing personal locations from egocentric videos. IEEE Trans. Hum.-Mach. Syst. **47**(1), 6–18 (2017)

5. Haklay, M.E.: Beyond quantification: a role for citizen science and community science in a smart city. In: Proceedings of the Data and City Workshop. Data and City Workshop, Meynooth University, Ireland (2015). https://discovery.ucl.ac.uk/id/eprint/1470344/

6. Kapenekakis, I., Chorianopoulos, K.: Citizen science for pedestrian cartography: collection and moderation of walkable routes in cities through mobile gamification. Hum.-Centric Comput. Inf. Sci. **7**(1), 10 (2017). https://doi.org/10.1186/s13673-017-0090-9

7. Maramis, C., et al.: Developing a novel citizen-scientist smartphone app for collecting behavioral and affective data from children populations. In: O'Hare, G.M.P., O'Grady, M.J., O'Donoghue, J., Henn, P. (eds.) MobiHealth 2019. LNICST, vol. 320, pp. 294–302. Springer, Cham (2020). https://doi.org/10.1007/978-3-030-49289-2_23

8. Mirri, S., Prandi, C., Salomoni, P.: Personalizing pedestrian accessible way-finding with mPASS. In: 13th IEEE Annual Consumer Communications & Networking Conference (CCNC), pp. 1119–1124. IEEE, Las Vegas (2016). https://doi.org/10.1109/CCNC.2016.7444946

9. Papageorgiou, G., Hadjigeorgiou, K., Ness, A.N.: Exploring the prospects of developing a smartphone application for pedestrians. In: 2020 19th International Symposium INFOTEH-JAHORINA (INFOTEH), pp. 1–5 (2020). https://doi.org/10.1109/INFOTEH48170.2020.9066287

10. Sas-Bojarska, A., Rembeza, M.: Planning the city against barriers. Enhancing the role of public spaces. Procedia Eng. **161**, 1556–1562 (2016). https://doi.org/10.1016/j.proeng.2016.08.626

11. Schrepp, M., Hinderks, A., Thomaschewski, J.: Applying the user experience questionnaire (UEQ) in different evaluation scenarios. In: Marcus, A. (ed.) DUXU 2014. LNCS, vol. 8517, pp. 383–392. Springer, Cham (2014). https://doi.org/10.1007/978-3-319-07668-3_37

12. Schrepp, M., Hinderks, A., Thomaschewski, J.: Construction of a benchmark for the user experience questionnaire (UEQ). Int. J. Interact. Multimed. Artif. Intell. **4**, 40–44 (2017). https://doi.org/10.9781/ijimai.2017.445

13. Smith, S.F., et al.: Connecting pedestrians with disabilities to adaptive signal control for safe intersection crossing and enhanced mobility: system requirements [year 2]. Technical report FHWA-JPO-19-751, U.S. Department of Transportation, Intelligent Transportation Systems Joint Program Office (2019). https://rosap.ntl.bts.gov/view/dot/43627

14. Theodosiou, Z., Lanitis, A.: Visual lifelogs retrieval: state of the art and future challenges. In: 2019 14th International Workshop on Semantic and Social Media Adaptation and Personalization (SMAP) (2019)

15. Theodosiou, Z., Partaourides, H., Atun, T., Panayi, S., Lanitis, A.: A first-person database for detecting barriers for pedestrians. In: 15th International Conference on Computer Vision Theory and Applications, VISAPP, vol. 5, pp. 660–666 (2020). https://doi.org/10.5220/0009107506600666

16. Verdecchia, R., Malavolta, I., Lago, P.: Guidelines for architecting android apps: a mixed-method empirical study. In: 2019 IEEE International Conference on Software Architecture (ICSA), pp. 141–150. IEEE, Hamburg (2019). https://doi.org/10.1109/ICSA.2019.00023

17. Wang, T., Cardone, G., Corradi, A., Torresani, L., Campbell, A.T.: Walksafe: a pedestrian safety app for mobile phone users who walk and talk while crossing roads. In: Proceedings of the Twelfth Workshop on Mobile Computing Systems & Applications - HotMobile 2012, p. 1. ACM Press, San Diego (2012). https://doi.org/10.1145/2162081.2162089

18. WHO: global status report on road safety 2018: summary. Technical report WHO/NMH/NVI/18.20. WHO, Geneva (2018). https://www.who.int/violence_injury_prevention/road_safety_status/2018/en/

Automatic Generation of Security Requirements for Cyber-Physical Systems

Jinghua Yu[1]($\boxtimes$) , Stefan Wagner[2] , and Feng Luo[3]

[1] Tongji University, Caoan Highway 4800, Shanghai 201804, China
yujinghua@tongji.edu.cn
[2] University of Stuttgart, Universitätsstraße 38, 70569 Stuttgart, Germany
stefan.wagner@iste.uni-stuttgart.de
[3] Tongji University, Caoan Highway 4800, Shanghai 201804, China
luo_feng@tongji.edu.cn

Abstract. Security is one of the essential properties in Cyber-Physical Systems (CPS). Attacking systems like autonomous vehicles and healthcare systems may lead to financial or privacy losses of stakeholders or even life threats. Security analysis, as an early activity in the system design, addresses security issues and identifies system vulnerabilities in advance to guide further security design. However, the security analysis is mostly performed manually requiring a high workload with human oversight. Besides, the manual analysis is not flexible for modification in later design stages and largely depends on expert knowledge and experience. Therefore, a new security analysis approach has been proposed in this paper to generate security requirements automatically, which is based on the System-Theoretic Process Analysis (STPA) framework and is applicable for data-flow-based CPSs. We have also developed a software prototype to support the implementation of this automatic approach and used it to obtain the security requirements of two CPSs in the automotive domain. Finally, we compared the automatically generated outcomes with the manually obtained ones and evaluated the proposed approach. Based on the experiment results, we found that the automatic way is efficient, effective and flexible. Furthermore, the proposed approach is also extensible. Analysts in a team can establish their own empirical repository to achieve accurate security requirements for their specific systems.

Keywords: Security analysis · STPA framework · Pattern matching · Empirical repository

1 Introduction

Cyber-Physical Systems (CPS) are built from, and depend on, the seamless integration of computation and physical components, which consist of computing

Supported by the China Scholarship Council and funds of the German Federal Ministry of Education and Research under grant number 16KIS0995.

S. Paiva et al. (Eds.): SmartCity360° 2020, LNICST 372, pp. 372–385, 2021.
https://doi.org/10.1007/978-3-030-76063-2_26

devices, actuation, sensing and network infrastructure as well as possible human interactions [7]. CPSs, like vehicular systems, medical and health-care systems, industrial control systems and smart grid [11], are indispensable nowadays and transforming the way people interact with engineered systems [7]. However, due to the high complexity and connectivity of CPSs and increasing applications in our daily life, securing CPSs is becoming much more significant, especially for safety- or security-critical systems. Adversaries may attack an insecure system to control it maliciously or eavesdrop on sensitive information, which leads to financial or even life losses. Therefore, security should be kept in mind during the whole life cycle of systems, particularly in the early design stage. Early security considerations can lower costs downstream in systems' life cycle, identify vulnerabilities before being exploited and adopt a proactive, rather than reactive, approach to security [4].

Security analysis, as an early design activity, addresses potential security issues and achieves security requirements, which are defined as conditions over the phenomenon of the environment that should be ensured to mitigate risks [13]. Standards or frameworks, like the SEA J3061 guideline [5] and the EVITA [14] framework in the automotive domain, have been published to achieve systematic security design of a target. Techniques proposed in these frameworks are normally threat-oriented, which start with system decomposition and threats identification. To strengthen the consideration of interactions among system components, System-Theoretic Process Analysis (STPA) has been proposed as a hazard analysis approach originally, which views losses as components interactions [20]. An extension of STPA for security (STPA-Sec) was then proposed [19] for security design.

However, the security analysis is normally performed by human analysts, which has the following limitations. First, the analysis process requires a high manual workload, especially for complex systems with a large number of components, which makes it easy for a human to make mistakes. Second, it is not friendly for modification. Once an error is detected or modification is required in later analysis phases, it's boring and time-consuming to correct every signal related detail in all previous documents manually. Furthermore, the analysis outcomes largely depend on the knowledge and expert experience, which means that to achieve trusted and useful results, it's necessary for analysts to be familiar with both the target system and knowledge in the security fields, which is sometimes not possible in a team.

To overcome the limitations of the manual analysis, we propose an approach based on an extension of STPA-Sec for data-flow-based systems (STPA-DFSec) to achieve security requirements automatically. Then, we develop a prototype by using Excel Visual Basic for Application (VBA) to implement our concept. Finally, we conduct experimental analyses of two CPSs in the automotive domain to evaluate the automated approach.

The rest of this paper is organized as follows. In Sect. 2, we introduce existing approaches for the automatic generation of security requirements and the STPA framework with its automated extensions. In Sect. 3, the automatic generation methodology is introduced, including the original STPA-DFSec steps, the automated generation process and a generator prototype. In Sect. 4, we present experimental analyses of two CPSs in the automotive domain, compare the experiment results and evaluate the proposed approach. Finally, we conclude the paper in Sect. 5.

2 Related Work

2.1 Existing Approaches for Automated Generation

We investigated the existing approaches for obtaining system security requirements automatically and classified them into the following classes.

The first class is permutations and combinations, which identifies variants in the requirement expressions, enumerates possible values and lists all combinations by the computer automatically. Thomas [16] established the system process model by determining context variants and their values to identify hazardous control actions for a system. Various context combinations are listed in a table but whether a concrete situation is hazardous for the system or not should be judged by human analysts. Gao and his colleagues [9] decomposed their spacecraft into subsystems and components with required variants and value ranges. By combining all possible pre-defined scenarios and objects with various parameters, a set of test cases is generated. This kind of approach can cover all possible cases efficiently and is also a common idea to generate test cases. However, the generated results may contain a number of meaningless combinations since the permutation and combination algorithm normally does not include a judgment process. Besides, if there are too many initial variants and values, the amount of the generated results may be too large to be processed manually.

The second class is recommendations, which uses machine learning to obtain recommended security requirements through training. Xu and his colleagues [18] proposed a co-occurrence recommendation model to get software security requirements. Relationships between security threats and requirements were established through training with the data extracted from security target documents. However, this approach is only for software products and may not be applicable to complex CPSs. Threats have to be extracted manually from security target documents but such documents may not even exist at the early design stages. Besides, it's also hard to ensure that the training data is proper and enough to make the recommendation system effective and trusted.

The third class is formal approaches, which use formal models to express the system and analyze it formally. Graa and his colleagues [10] modeled a system using a goal-oriented approach named Knowledge Acquisition in autOmated Specification (KAOS) and generated security policies with externally input security information. But the inputs including risk analysis results and security requirement specifications have to be obtained manually by analysts. Emeka and Liu [6] proposed a new framework based on the Structured Object-Oriented Formal Language (SOFL) to define security requirements. Yet, the authors didn't discuss the possibility of processing it automatically. Besides, the state machine model is commonly used to model a system and performs model check based on branching-time logic (e.g. Linear Temporal Logic (LTL) and Computation Tree Logic (CTL)) [2,3,17]. However, that research is about generating test cases and verifying systems according to predefined requirements. No study of deriving requirements by the state machine model has been found.

2.2 STPA Framework and Automated Extensions

System-Theoretic Process Analysis (STPA) is a hazard analysis approach based on the System-Theoretic Accident Model and Processes (STAMP) model, which treats system safety as a dynamic control problem rather than a failure prevention problem. Many evaluations and comparisons of STPA to traditional analysis methods have been done and show that STPA identified more, often software-related and non-failure, scenarios and it costs much less time and resources than the traditional processes [12]. Extensions have been proposed to conduct better analysis with the basic STPA idea, including the STPA for security (STPA-Sec) [19], the STPA for privacy (STPA-Priv) [15] and the STPA for co-analysis of both safety and security (STPA-SafeSec) [8]. The steps of the basic STPA is shown in Fig. 1.

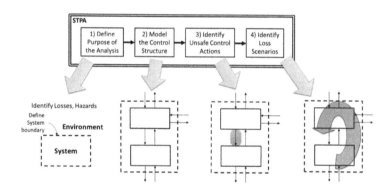

Fig. 1. Overview of the basic STPA steps [12]

To extend and automate the STPA for the requirement generation, Thomas [16] defined a formal structure underlying STPA and presented a method for automating both the STPA analysis and the requirements generation with a conflict detection feature. Abdulkhaleq [1] proposed an STPA-based safety engineering approach for software-intensive systems called STPA SwISs to conduct seamless safety analysis and software verification activities. A platform called XSTAMPP was developed to support identifying requirements, verifying practical implementation against SPTA-generated requirements by model checking tools and generating safety-based test cases automatically. These researches show the possibility of automating the STPA-based approaches to increase the efficiency and reliability of the analysis process.

In our previous research [21,22], we identified some limitations of the STPA-Sec, which is not effective for information-critical systems, and proposed a data-flow based extension of STPA-Sec (STPA-DFSec). Two case studies have been conducted manually to verify the effectiveness of the proposed approach comparing with other approaches. Nevertheless, we found that the manual processes required a high workload. Later modifications in the analysis documents were always boring and time-consuming. These manual analysis drawbacks motivate our research on the automatic way to achieve security requirements.

3   Methodology

3.1   Brief Introduction of STPA-DFSec

The data-flow-based STPA-Sec (STPA-DFSec) [21] follows the basic steps of the STPA framework and introduces some data-flow-related adjustments into it. The overview of STPA-DFSec steps is shown in Fig. 2.

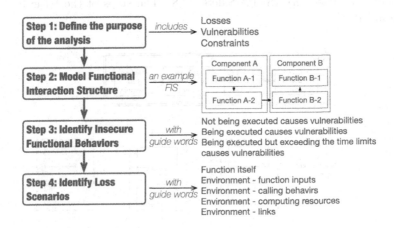

Fig. 2. Overview of the STPA-DFSec steps

First, the purpose of the analysis should be defined at a high level, including identifying system-level losses, vulnerabilities and constraints. Second, the Functional Interaction Structure (FIS) of the target system is modeled to interpret how the system works from the perspective of data flows. Functions, as the basic element of the FIS, are identified and linked with each other by data flows. Third, Insecure Function Behaviors (IFB), which lead to system vulnerabilities in a particular context, are identified with the help of guide words. Finally, Loss Scenarios (LS), describing the causal factors that lead to insecure function behaviors, are identified. Each loss scenario can be translated into system security requirements by simply inversing the conditions or defining what the system must do in case the incident occurs [12].

3.2   Automated Generation Process

The automated generation process complies with the STPA-DFSec and aims to achieve IFBs and LSs effectively and efficiently. Figure 3 is the overall workflow of the proposed generator. The automated process starts after the second step of STPA-DFSec, in which the system FIS has been created and functions have been defined. The human analysts need to fill in a questionnaire to provide information for the generator. Table 1 is the questionnaire template. Nine questions in the questionnaire are abstracted from the analysis results that we identified manually in the previous research and are closely related to the automated judgment.

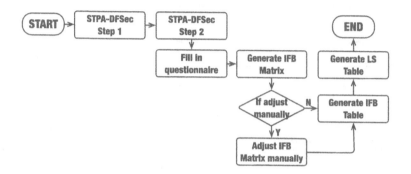

Fig. 3. Flowchart of the automatic generator

Table 1. Questionnaire template

Questions	Function1	
1. Is it related to confidentiality?	Y/N	...
2. Is it related to integrity?	Y/N	...
3. Is it related to availability?	Y/N	...
4. Is it possible to bypass the function?	Y/N	...
5. Does it return an execution result flag?	Y/N	...
6. Is its input from another components via physical links?	Y/N	...
7. Is its output to another components via physical links?	Y/N	...
8. Is it controlled by software algorithms?	Y/N	...
9. Is the supporting data (e.g. cryptography keys, system states, feedbacks on UIs) required for the execution?	Y/N	

Then, the IFB matrix is generated automatically. The flowchart of generating the IFB Matrix is shown in Fig. 4 (a). The generator checks the type conditions of each function and marks a 'Y' (Yes) or 'N' (No) in the matrix to indicate if a function contains a certain type of IFBs. The IFB types and their conditions are listed in Table 2. Whether a condition is matched or not is determined by the answer of a corresponding question in the questionnaire. The final IFBs and LSs will be generated on the basis of this IFB matrix, which can also be manually adjusted if necessary.

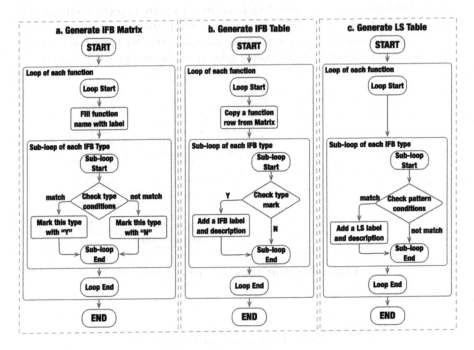

Fig. 4. Flowcharts of automatic generation

Table 2. IFB types and conditions

IFB types	Conditions (related questions)
Type1: Not being executed	It can be bypassed intendedly (4)
Type2: Being executed with information leakage risks	It is related to confidentiality (1)
Type3: Being executed with tempered data or algorithms	It is related to integrity (2)
Type4: Being executed but violating system specifications (e.g. timing limits)	It is related to availability (3)

Finally, IFBs and LSs are generated according to the workflow in Fig. 4 (b) and (c) respectively. To obtain an IFB table, the generator checks each type mark in the IFB matrix and add a concrete IFB label and description if the mark is 'Y'. To obtain LSs, the generator checks pattern conditions of identified IFBs and add labels with the corresponding descriptions if the conditions are matched. The LS patterns and their conditions are shown in Table 3.

Table 3. LS patterns and conditions

IFB types	LS patterns	Conditions (related questions)
Type1	Function is bypassed intendedly, which can be detected by user	Matched by default
	Function is bypassed intendedly and outputs fake results	Function should return a flag value (5)
Type2	No or inadequate mechanism is used to protect data confidentiality	Matched by default
	Physical input links are not protected, adversary eavesdrops data on links	There should be an input channel via physical links to function (6)
	Physical output links are not protected, adversary eavesdrops data on links	There should be an output channel via physical links from function (7)
	Algorithm is tampered maliciously to eavesdrop data during function execution	Function should by controlled by software algorithms (8)
	Supporting data is tampered, leading to execution with risks of information leakage	Some kinds of supporting data are required for function execution (9)
Type3	No or inadequate mechanism is used to protect data integrity	Matched by default
	Physical input links are not protected, adversary tampers data on links	There should be an input channel via physical links to function (6)
	Physical output links are not protected, adversary tampers data on links	There should be an output channel via physical links from function (7)
	Algorithm is tampered, which leads to unexpected behaviors of function	Function should by controlled by software algorithms (8)
Type4	Data is blocked on links or routed to an unexpected destination	There should be an output channel via physical links from function (7)
	Transmission is slowed down by additional mechanisms on links	There should be an output channel via physical links from function (7)
	Algorithm is tampered, which leads to unexpected behaviors (e.g. reject legal request)	Function should by controlled by software algorithms (8)
	Algorithm is tampered, which needs more computing resources	Function should by controlled by software algorithms (8)
	Computing resource is occupied to cause violation of execution timing limitations	Function should by controlled by software algorithms (8)
	Supporting data is tampered, which leads function being executed wrongly	Some kinds of supporting data are required for function execution (9)

3.3 Generator Prototype

To implement and verify the proposed approach in practice, a quick prototype has been developed using Excel VBA. After filling the questionnaire in the first sheet, an IFB matrix (in Fig. 5) is generated. Then, by clicking the 'Generate IFBs' and 'Generate LSs' buttons in the IFB matrix sheet (Fig. 5), the final IFB and LS tables are obtained in a second (shown in Fig. 6).

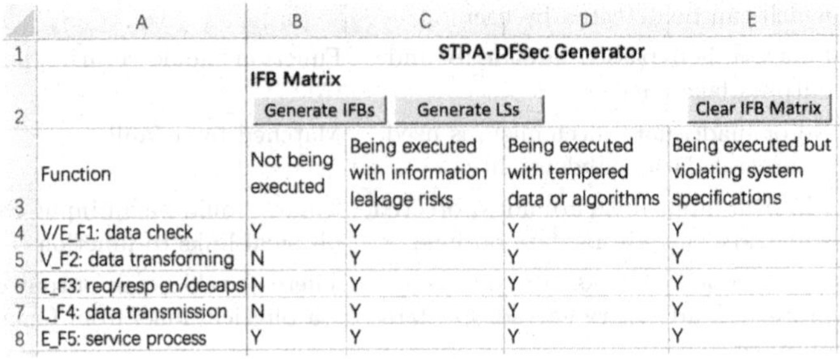

	A	B	C	D	E
1				STPA-DFSec Generator	
2		IFB Matrix			
		Generate IFBs	Generate LSs		Clear IFB Matrix
3	Function	Not being executed	Being executed with information leakage risks	Being executed with tempered data or algorithms	Being executed but violating system specifications
4	V/E_F1: data check	Y	Y	Y	Y
5	V_F2: data transforming	N	Y	Y	Y
6	E_F3: req/resp en/decaps	N	Y	Y	Y
7	L_F4: data transmission	N	Y	Y	Y
8	E_F5: service process	Y	Y	Y	Y

Fig. 5. Generated IFB matrix

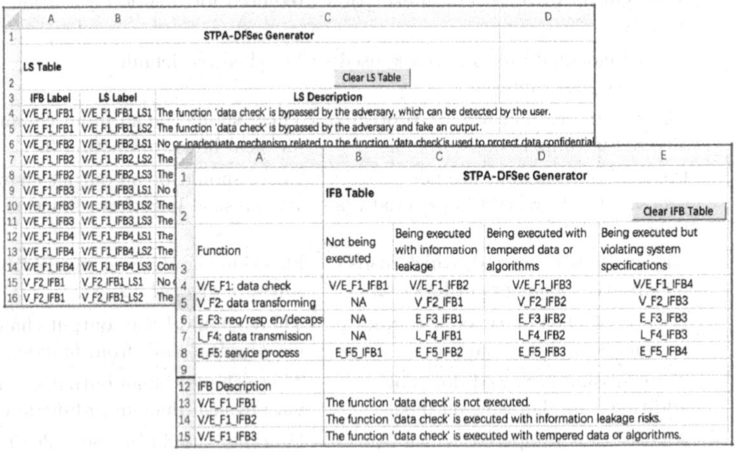

Fig. 6. Screenshots of the generated IFB table and LS table

3.4 Approach Conclusion

The main idea of this automated generation approach is to enumerate all possible IFBs and LS patterns at a general level and decide whether an enumerated item is matched to a particular function. The judgment is based on the input information obtained from the questionnaire. Other than the three classes introduced in the '2.1 Existing Approaches for Automated Generation' section, the proposed approach can be classified into a fourth 'pattern matching' class.

The complete sets of IFB types, LS patterns and corresponding conditions are established based on the original STPA theories and empirical conclusions in practices. These sets are regarded as empirical study repository, in which previously extracted IFB types and LS patterns are stored. This empirical repository is an open framework, into which newly recognized patterns can be added. Companies or specific teams can establish their own type and pattern repository to better support their specific target systems.

4   Experiments and Evaluation

4.1   Example Cases

To verify and evaluate the proposed approach, experiments have been conducted based on two example cases in the automotive field. In this sub-section, both cases are introduced briefly. More details about the example systems and the manual analysis processes are elaborated in the previous publications [21,22].

The first system (notated as Sys1) is an in-vehicle diagnostic and software update system, which transmits data via in-vehicle networks, like Controller Area Network (CAN) and Automotive Ethernet (AE), to achieve the diagnostics and software or configuration updates of electronic devices in vehicles. This system consists of a vehicle interface, in-vehicle networks and an end device (shown in Fig. 7 (a)). Due to the increasing interactions between the in-vehicle systems and the outside entities (e.g. handheld devices, manufacturer's cloud), such a system is security-critical and needs to be protected against hazards including eavesdropping on the device firmware or customer data and injecting malicious software. By using STPA-DFSec, 17 IFBs and 23 LSs were identified manually.

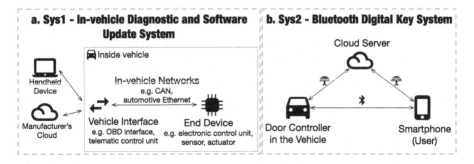

Fig. 7. System sketch of two example systems

The second system (notated as Sys2) is a Bluetooth digital key system of the vehicle consisting of three main physical components (shown in Fig. 7 (b)).

The user uses a smartphone to lock or unlock the vehicle doors via Bluetooth. A cloud server is required to support cryptographic mechanisms for secure communications between components. Such a digital key system should be protected against malicious actions including unlocking vehicle doors illegally and Denial-of-Service (DoS) attacks. 22 IFBs and 41 LSs were identified manually by STPA-DFSec.

4.2 Experiments and Comparison

We followed the workflow of the automated generator (Fig. 3) to obtain the IFBs and LSs of both Sys1 and Sys2 automatically. The time duration and the outcomes of the automated process are recorded and compared with the manual ones which we recorded in previous studies (see 'Sect. 4.1 Example Cases').

Figure 8 shows the time consumption of the analysis processes. For the automated process, the analysts took approximately 1.7 min per function to fill in the questionnaire, review and adjust the IFB Matrix when necessary. Then, IFBs and LSs were generated instantly by two clicks. By contrast, it took at least 50 mins to identify and write down all labels and descriptions of IFBs and LSs manually.

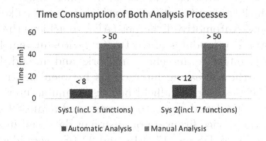

Fig. 8. Time consumption of both analysis processes

Outcomes have also been compared and shown in Table 4. We mapped each IFB achieved by both processes and found that one automatically obtained IFB may be related to several manually obtained IFBs. Besides, the understanding error also impacts the number of outcomes. The understanding of a system by a person is subjective. For example, expert A thinks function1 is related to confidentiality while expert B doesn't think so. Even the same person may have different ideas at different times. Therefore, to make the numbers comparable, the outcome differences caused by the understanding errors are removed. The comparison conclusion is listed in the final column of Table 4, which shows that the automated generation can achieve almost the same numbers of IFBs and obviously more LSs than those in the manual analysis. The reason may be that the number of IFBs is relatively small and can be handled well by the human mind, while it would be easy for human analysts to miss something when the number of items increases.

Table 4. Outcome comparison of both analysis processes

Item type	System	Number in automatic	Number in manual	Comparison conclusion (considering understanding errors)
IFB	Sys1	17	17	The number is the same
	Sys2	24	22	1 new IFB in the automatic one
LS	Sys1	42	23	5 new LSs in the automatic one
	Sys2	60	41	20 new LSs in the automatic one

Furthermore, the expressions generated automatically are more abstract and at higher levels, while the manually identified ones are sometimes more concrete with the detailed context in a specific case.

4.3   Evaluation and Discussion

Finally, the automated generation approach was evaluated based on three metrics, which are efficiency, effectiveness and flexibility.

As for the efficiency, the automated analysis requires much less time than the manual one, especially for complex systems with a large number of functions. The workload of human analysts is reduced significantly by the automated process.

As for the effectiveness, the generated IFBs and LSs cover all manually identified outcomes. Since the generation conditions are designed based on the empirical repository, which stores previous experience and knowledge collected in practice, the generated results are reliable. Note that the outcomes of security analysis, no matter they are identified by the proposed approach automatically or manually, are not able to be proven complete. In practice, analysis outcomes largely depend on the analysis emphasis, available system information and the knowledge and experience of the analysts who build the repository or perform the manual analysis. In our experiments, the same authors did the manual analyses and designed the generator with its repository, which makes the obtained IFBs and LSs comparable in our cases. Besides, the low workload also reduces the probability of making mistakes by a human. Complex systems and long working duration may cause mistakes and omitted points, while the automated process does not have such problems.

As for the flexibility, it's much easier to perform an iterated analysis or modify something at any design stage. The analysts can update the questionnaire and IFB matrix within at most 2 mins per function and then regenerate everything instead of modifying every related label and description by hand. Furthermore, the automated process is also a good way to deal with understanding errors, which are inevitable due to the knowledge and experience of the analysts, the description in system documents and personal understanding ability. Once an understanding error is identified even in the later design stage, the analysts only need to revise the questionnaire and get updated outcomes immediately.

Two limitations of the proposed generator have been identified. First, since the generation is based on the empirical repository, the quality of such a repository and the abstracted patterns is important for obtaining reliable outcomes.

It requires experienced experts and many practical case studies to build a high-quality repository, which will spend much time and effort for a new type of system at the beginning. However, once the corresponding repository is established, the work efficiency can be increased significantly. Second, the generated IFBs and LSs are described at a general level, which can not explain specific situations related to a particular system. Therefore, such general descriptions required further refinement by human analysts to support concrete design work later. However, the generated outcomes can be used as the outputs of a high-level analysis at early design stages, preliminary requirements of the system or the elicitation hints for more specific requirements with concrete details in the later design stage.

5 Conclusion

In this paper, we proposed an approach based on the STPA-DFSec to achieve system security requirements automatically and provided a prototype tool to support the implementation. We conducted the experiments of two CPSs in the automotive domain and compared the outcomes of both manual and automatic analyses. Finally, we evaluated the proposed approach from the perspective of efficiency, effectiveness and flexibility.

Comparing with the manual process, the automatic analysis requires less time and workload, obtains reliable outcomes based on previous empirical cases and is friendly for human analysts to perform iterations or modify analysis details even in the later design stages. Besides, the proposed approach is more reliable because the automated way reduces both the probability of human mistakes and the dependency on the knowledge and experience of analysts. Furthermore, this approach is an open framework for automatic generation. New patterns and conditions can be added to the repository to support specific and accurate requirement generation.

In the future, we will analyze more CPSs in practice to improve the pattern repository for a better generation of security requirements in various fields. Besides, a software tool will be designed based on the proposed prototype to support practical implementation in industries with better user experience features.

References

1. Abdulkhaleq, A.: A system-theoretic safety engineering approach for software-intensive systems. Ph.D. thesis (2017)
2. Abdulkhaleq, A., Wagner, S.: A systematic and semi-automatic safety-based test case generation approach based on systems-theoretic process analysis. arXiv preprint arXiv:1612.03103 (2016)
3. Aouadi, M.H.E., Toumi, K., Cavalli, A.: A formal approach to automatic testing of security policies specified in XACML. In: Cuppens, F., Garcia-Alfaro, J., Zincir Heywood, N., Fong, P.W.L. (eds.) FPS 2014. LNCS, vol. 8930, pp. 367–374. Springer, Cham (2015). https://doi.org/10.1007/978-3-319-17040-4_25

4. Carter, B.T., Bakirtzis, G., Elks, C.R., Fleming, C.H.: Systems-theoretic security requirements modeling for cyber-physical systems. Syst. Eng. **22**(5), 411–421 (2019)
5. SAE International: SAE J3061 - Cybersecurity Guidebook for Cyber-Physical Automotive Systems (2016)
6. Emeka, B.O., Liu, S.: Security requirement engineering using structured object-oriented formal language for m-banking applications. In: 2017 IEEE International Conference on Software Quality, Reliability and Security (QRS), pp. 176–183. IEEE (2017)
7. US National Science Foundation: Cyber-physical systems program solicitation (nsf 20–563) (2020). https://www.nsf.gov/pubs/2020/nsf20563/nsf20563.htm
8. Friedberg, I., McLaughlin, K., Smith, P., Laverty, D., Sezer, S.: STPA-SafeSec: safety and security analysis for cyber-physical systems. J. Inf. Secur. Appl. **34**, 183–196 (2017)
9. Gao, S., Lyu, J., Wuniri, Q., Meng, X., Ma, S.: Spacecraft test requirement description and automatic generation method. J. Beijing Univ. Aeronaut. Astronaut. **41**(7), 1275–1286 (2015)
10. Graa, M., et al.: Using requirements engineering in an automatic security policy derivation process. In: Garcia-Alfaro, J., Navarro-Arribas, G., Cuppens-Boulahia, N., de Capitani di Vimercati, S. (eds.) DPM/SETOP -2011. LNCS, vol. 7122, pp. 155–172. Springer, Heidelberg (2012). https://doi.org/10.1007/978-3-642-28879-1_11
11. Khaitan, S.K., McCalley, J.D.: Design techniques and applications of cyberphysical systems: a survey. IEEE Syst. J. **9**(2), 350–365 (2014)
12. Leveson, N.G., Thomas, J.P.: STPA Handbook (2018). https://psas.scripts.mit.edu/home/get_file.php?name=STPA_handbook.pdf
13. Matulevičius, R.: Fundamentals of Secure System Modelling. Springer, Cham (2017). https://doi.org/10.1007/978-3-319-61717-6
14. Ruddle, A., et al.: Deliverable D2.3: security requirements for automotive on-board networks based on dark-side scenarios. Technical report, EVITA (2009)
15. Shapiro, S.S.: Privacy risk analysis based on system control structures: adapting system-theoretic process analysis for privacy engineering. In: 2016 IEEE Security and Privacy Workshops (SPW), pp. 17–24. IEEE (2016)
16. Thomas, J.P.: Extending and automating a systems-theoretic hazard analysis for requirements generation and analysis. Ph.D. thesis, Massachusetts Institute of Technology (2013)
17. Wardell, D.C., Mills, R.F., Peterson, G.L., Oxley, M.N.: A method for revealing and addressing security vulnerabilities in cyber-physical systems by modeling malicious agent interactions with formal verification. Procedia Comput. Sci. **95**, 24–31 (2016)
18. Xu, Y., Ge, W., Li, X., Feng, Z., Xie, X., Bai, Y.: A co-occurrence recommendation model of software security requirement. In: 2019 International Symposium on Theoretical Aspects of Software Engineering (TASE), pp. 41–48. IEEE (2019)
19. Young, W., Leveson, N.G.: Systems thinking for safety and security. In: Proceedings of the 29th Annual Computer Security Applications Conference, pp. 1–8 (2013)
20. Young, W., Leveson, N.G.: Inside risks-an integrated approach to safety and security based on system theory: Applying a more powerful new safety methodology to security risks. Commun. ACM **57**(2), 232–242 (2014)
21. Yu, J., Wagner, S., Luo, F.: Data-flow-based adaption of the System-Theoretic Process Analysis for Security (STPA-Sec). PeerJ Comput. Sci. **7**, e362 (2021)
22. Yu, J., Wagner, S., Luo, F.: An STPA-based approach for systematic security analysis of in-vehicle diagnostic and software update systems. In: FISITA Web Congress 2020, F2020-VES-020 (2020)

Privacy-Preserving Blockchain-Based Solutions in the Internet of Things

Nikolaos Zapoglou[1], Ioannis Patsakos[1], George Drosatos[2(✉)],
and Konstantinos Rantos[1]

[1] Department of Computer Science, International Hellenic University, Kavala, Greece
{xizapog,iopatsa,krantos}@cs.ihu.gr
[2] Institute for Language and Speech Processing,
Athena Research Center, Xanthi, Greece
gdrosato@athenarc.gr

Abstract. Internet of Things (IoT) is a promising, relatively new technology that develops "smart" networks with a variety of uses and applications (e.g., smart cities, smart home and autonomous cars). The diversity of protocols, technologies and devices that IoT consists of, even though they add in value and utility, they create major privacy issues that can be exploited by malicious entities to benefit from or even violate privacy of IoT users. The special features of blockchain technology, such as immutability, transparency, accessibility, autonomy and decentralisation, has led the academics and the industry to search for further uses of it, besides financial applications (e.g., Bitcoin) that was initially applied. This paper is a survey on the existing literature regarding blockchain-based privacy-preserving solutions that have been proposed specifically for the IoT to address personal data protection and preserve user privacy.

Keywords: Internet of Things (IoT) · Blockchain technology · Privacy-preserving solutions

1 Introduction

In the past decade, a new technology named Internet of Things (IoT), has been introduced in most aspects of our modern life. Countless devices, such as meters, cameras and actuators, are connected to networks with the purpose to make our lives easier, our industry more efficient, our healthcare more patient-centric, our world "smarter" and much more [21]. Vast volumes of data, including personal ones, are being collected, generated, transferred and processed through IoT networks which mainly consist of devices with limited resources, where conventional security and privacy protection techniques do not work or are too expensive to adopt [38]. Given the sensitive nature of the data and the potentially harmful information that can be extracted from the IoT ecosystem, it soon became clear that effective and relatively easy ways to overcome these issues had to be invented.

© ICST Institute for Computer Sciences, Social Informatics and Telecommunications Engineering 2021
Published by Springer Nature Switzerland AG 2021. All Rights Reserved
S. Paiva et al. (Eds.): SmartCity360° 2020, LNICST 372, pp. 386–405, 2021.
https://doi.org/10.1007/978-3-030-76063-2_27

Blockchain technology, a decentralised immutable public "database", can solve or address sufficiently some of the user privacy issues and personal data protection in the IoT. It gained popularity due to the creation of the first digital cryptocurrency, Bitcoin [25]. There are a lot more applications than Bitcoin, where blockchain technology can be a pioneer and enhance existing technologies and their security and privacy properties.

The structure of a blockchain network, the use of advanced cryptographic mechanisms in a blockchain, and the use of smart contracts [5], are some of the key-factors that can contribute in upgrading/preserving privacy issues in various IoT networks. This paper provides a literature review of the various approaches and applications of blockchain technology to address privacy issues sourcing in the IoT ecosystem. The rest of this paper is organised as follows. Section 2 provides a brief background analysis on IoT and blockchain technologies. The methodology used in conducting this research is described in Sect. 3. Section 4 presents identified blockchain-based solutions that have been proposed for preserving users privacy in the IoT domain. Section 5 discusses the identified solutions and provides future research directions. Finally, Sect. 6 concludes the paper.

2   Background and Related Work

The IoT ecosystem comprises many applications and services that can be combined with other edge technologies, such as machine learning, big data and blockchain technology to provide the, so-called, smart environments with promising results. The amount of user-related personal data being generated, processed and transferred in the diversified IoT deployments (in terms of protocols, technologies, and devices), attract a lot of unwanted attention by threat agents who target, among others, users' personal data. Figure 1 depicts a typical example of a user IoT ecosystem with privacy challenges.

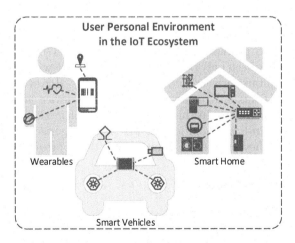

Fig. 1. Example of user personal environment in the IoT ecosystem.

Privacy is an ambiguous concept that cannot be clearly defined and can be affected by the individual's perception on the protection of its own personal environment. In compute science, it is recognised as data or information privacy, refers to the relationships between technology and the legal right to, or public expectation of, privacy in the collection and exchange of personal data [10]. Privacy restrictions typically stem from applicable legal frameworks. For example, in the European Union, the General Data Protection Regulation (GDPR) [12] has come into force to create an even higher level, than before, of privacy protection within the EU and gave citizens control over their personal data. Given the volume of the personal data being handled by IoT devices, it is easy to understand that the GDPR has many implications to many IoT domains.

Blockchain is an append-only decentralised digital public ledger based on cryptography. A record of all the transactions that take place inside the blockchain is being maintained in a chronological order (time-stamped) in a distributed database, in the form of blocks in a chain. All the participating nodes in this peer-to-peer network get a duplicated copy of the blockchain database.

When the participating nodes agree on the validity of a transaction and the requirements of the consensus algorithm have been satisfied, a time-stamped block is added to the blockchain. After a block becomes part of the blockchain it is nearly impossible to tamper with it [19]. Accordingly, the overall blockchain framework consists of three layers, as depicted in Fig. 2: the application layer, the data layer and the network layer [17]. The application layer includes all the features, applications and uses of blockchain. The data layer is self-explanatory and the network layer handles all the connectivity matters of blockchain.

The applications of blockchain vary and include financial services, healthcare, rights management, IoT and security. The key features of blockchains, such as decentralisation, transparency, open source, accessibility, autonomy and immutability [19] make them very attractive to many environments, as they can successfully address significant security requirements. Still though, there are privacy challenges that need to be considered when applying blockchain technology [13].

Although blockchain technology has been extensively studied in the IoT [7, 31] and proposed to protect privacy for IoT devices [47], to the best of our knowledge, there has been only one similar work [43] reviewing blockchain-based methods that facilitate privacy preservation in IoT. However, Sharma et al. [43] in their work focus only on two issues, i.e. the device authentication and the decentralised identifiers. In this paper, we present a wider range of privacy preserving blockchain-based solutions in IoT and categorise them according to the topic in which they proposed a solution and the approach they used.

3   Research Methodology

The methodology that we followed consists of two main steps:

1. Extensive search in the research literature maintained in Scopus search engine (www.scopus.com), a certified academically approved tool. The goal

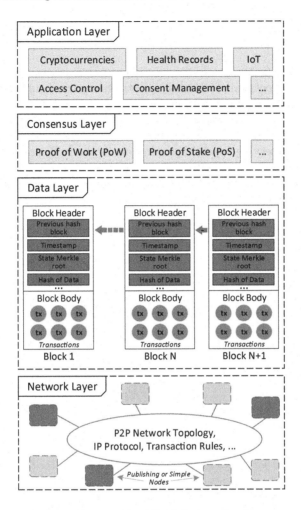

Fig. 2. Framework of blockchain technology.

of our search was to find explicitly the related keywords of "privacy" and "blockchain" in the title of the papers and the related keywords of "IoT" in the title, abstract and keywords. The exact query which was used in April 2020 and returned us 96 relevant papers, was the following:

```
TITLE((Privacy OR "Personal Data") AND (Blockchain OR "Distributed
    Ledger")) AND TITLE-ABS-KEY(IoT OR "Internet of Things" OR
                        "Internet-of-Things")
```

2. By studying the Title – Abstract – Conclusion parts of each of the above papers we were able to narrow down even more the relevant, to our subject, papers. In this step we excluded papers that were addressing specific sectors of IoT networks (e.g., apply only in VANET, MIoT, UAV technology, healthcare,

etc.) and we focused on papers that had potential solutions in wider and more generalised application in IoT.

Figure 3 shows (i) the yearly distribution of publications that deal with privacy solutions in blockchain technology (i.e. the first part of our query in methodology), (ii) the number of publications per year that we focus on this paper based on the query of our methodology, and (iii) the percentage of (ii) in (i) for each year. This demonstrates the interest that the research community shows on the use of privacy-preserving blockchain solutions in the IoT ecosystem. Based on these statistical results we infer that the global interest in this kind of solutions is rising and gaining ground fast, with the amount of relevant to the matter papers almost doubling each year, since the publication of the first research paper in 2017.

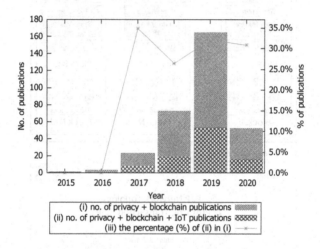

Fig. 3. Number and percentage of publications per year in Scopus.

4   Privacy Preserving Blockchain-Based Solutions in IoT

This section presents, in a chronological order, the solutions that were identified in the literature by using the methodology described in Sect. 3. The subsections below provide a brief description about the functionality, usage, and the privacy preserving nature of each of the identified solutions. Table 1 summarizes some of their properties.

4.1   FairAccess

FairAccess is a privacy-preserving blockchain-based access control framework for IoT, introduced by Ouaddah et al. [28,29], which combines access control

Table 1. Comparison of privacy preserving blockchain-based solutions in the IoT.

Proposed solution	IoT area	Blockchain infrastructure	Privacy-preserving provided service	Underlying privacy mechanism	Implementation
FairAccess [28]	IoT	Bitcoin	Access control	Encrypted authorization tokens with ECC	Proof of concept
BC Gateways [6]	IoT	Ethereum	Access control	Smart contracts & preference policies	Proposal
PPB-ABE [34]	IoT	Public blockchain	Access control	Attribute-based encryption (ABE)	Numerical analysis
CapChain [20]	IoT	Monero	Access control	Capability obfuscation & ring signature	Proof of concept
PPDAC [27]	IoT	Public blockchain	Access control	DMCP-ABE & zk-SNARKs	Proposal
ADVOCATE [37]	IoT	Public blockchain	Consent management	Data minimization & hashing	Proof of concept
SecureSVM [44]	Smart City	–	Machine learning	Paillier homomorphic encryption	Experimental
TrustChain [18]	IoT	New permissioned blockchain	Distributed ledger	ZKP, encryption & anonymization	Proposal
PBEM-SGN [16]	Smart grid	Permissioned blockchain	Energy transactions	Group signatures & covert channel authorization	Experimental
PrivySharing [23]	Smart City	Hyperlegder Fabric	Access control & data sharing	Smart contracts & access control rules	Experimental
Xyreum [40]	IIoT	–	Multi-factor authentication & key establishment	T-ZKPK & authenticated encryption	Experimental
Hy-Bridge [15]	Smart grid	Pysimplechain	Energy transactions	k-anonymity, suppression & data generalization	Simulation
BFL-PPDS [22]	IIoT	Permissioned blockchain	Data sharing	Federated learning & differential privacy	Experimental

and cryptocurrency mechanisms. Through the use of encrypted authentication tokens (data structures transferred from peer to peer via transactions) enforced by smart contracts [5], an IoT device owner can manage access rights and policies (get, revoke, update, etc.) in a flexible and easy to apply manner. The encryption of token is performed using the built-in elliptic-curve cryptosystem (ECC).

FairAccess addresses several IoT privacy and security requirements, such as decentralisation, lightweightness, identification (allowing thing-to-thing interactions), fine-grained and user-driven access control, transparency, unlikability and pseudonymity [27]. Although, some issues in IoT are successfully addressed thanks to FairAccess, some other critical issues emerged: (1) There is a discrepancy between the sensitive and private nature of access control policies and the transparent and public nature of blockchain technology. (2) Traceability, allowing third parties to detect thing-to-thing communication patterns and authorisation functionality patterns.

FairAccess is experimentally implemented with a Raspberry Pi 2 device and a local Bitcoin network (regression test mode) [28].

4.2   BC Gateways

Cha et al. [6] propose the usage of blockchain connected gateways (BC Gateways) to preserve users' privacy by providing access to the data of IoT devices according to a given preference policy. These gateways store user privacy preferences of IoT devices in a blockchain infrastructure. The blockchain gateways play the role of a mediator between users and IoT devices.

Users can acquire the information and privacy policies of an IoT device connected to a blockchain gateway and access the device via the blockchain gateway rather than accessing the device directly. Consequently, the blockchain gateway impede the device from obtaining personal data unless users accept the device's privacy policies. The data stored in a blockchain infrastructure is tamper-resistant, thus, user's preferences can be utilised to resolve disputes between users and IoT service providers. Finally, the above-mentioned system utilises Ethereum [5] to support its idea utilising smart contracts.

4.3   Privacy-Preserving Blockchain Based IoT Ecosystem Using Attribute-Based Encryption (PPB-ABE)

Rahulamathavan et al. [34] proposed a solution that uses decentralised attribute-based encryption (ABE) to preserve confidentiality and privacy of transaction data in blockchain-based IoT applications. Their method, which is followed a similar approach with [9], utilises more powerful devices (e.g., smartphones and home routers) than IoT sensors as *cluster heads* to perform computationally expensive operations on behalf of IoT sensors. These operations are mainly data aggregation and encryption required in the generation of transaction data. The encryption of transaction data is performed by cluster heads and in such a way that can only be seen and verified by entities who have the *right attributes*.

Satisfying the requirements of ABE, the entities involved in the proposed scheme are (1) cluster heads, responsible of the aforementioned processing, (2) blockchain miners who verify transactions and contribute to the blockchain, (3) attribute authorities (AAs) and (4) the blockchain with blocks of transactions. The cluster head encrypts data wisely to target the particular miners with the right attributes. The blockchain miners verify the transacted data and the transaction itself. After that, they mine, add new blocks to the blockchain and get rewarded with tokens. The AAs have to verify and issue credentials for distinct users and miners according to their attributes. Finally, the authors provide a numerical analysis to estimate the added complexity of ABE in the blockchain.

4.4   CapChain

Le and Mutka proposed CapChain [20], a privacy preserving access control framework for pervasive environments that is based on blockchain technology.

CapChain allows users to share access rights to devices they own by managing capabilities, i.e. tokens that represent access rights to IoT devices. Capabilities are generated and encrypted by the device's owner, and transferred by appropriate anonymous transactions that take place on a public blockchain. The latter serves as a public immutable ledger that records capabilities authorisations.

Device owners have full control over the delegations they provide as they can assign expiration dates on them, can track and revoke the whole chain of the delegations they provided, and control capabilities from multiple domains with the use of a single account. Participants identities and transaction details are protected. To ensure their privacy, CapChain adapts well-established techniques, such as obfuscation to hide capability ID and ring signature to avoid unauthorised capability commitment. An overview of the access rights delegation process is shown in Fig. 4.

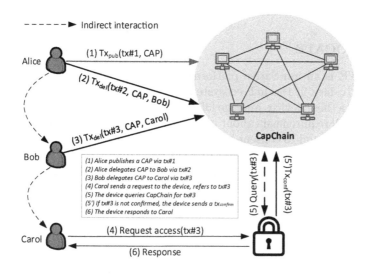

Fig. 4. CapChain overview [20].

CapChain employs a similar idea to transfer authorisation tokens through transactions such as FairAccess [28]. Simultaneously, it is affected by anonymous cryptocurrencies such as CryptoNote [39], Monero [26] and ZeroCash [41] since it proposes a token named CAP to get access in IoT device. In addition, the authors analyse their scheme as a case study under the consensus of an adapted proof-of-work (PoW) from Monero.

4.5 PPDAC

Ouaddah proposed a privacy-preserving distributed access control scheme that is called PPDAC [27]. PPDAC is a lightweight and privacy-preserving access control framework based on the rising blockchain technology, mainly the unlicensed and public type, to assure in-depth access control functions for IoT devices with strong anonymity guarantee for IoT end-users. The proposed scheme preserves the merits of blockchain to meet IoT security and privacy arising needs while overcoming the challenges in integrating blockchain to IoT. PPDAC is integrated over FairAccess [28] that successfully ensures IoT's security and privacy requirements. The reason why the author has developed PPDAC scheme was to strengthen users' anonymity and to maintain transparency features in FairAccess. More precisely, it is developed a policy-hiding access control scheme that protects both sensitive attributes and policies using a white box of distributed multi-authority ciphertext policy attribute-based encryption (DMCP-ABE) [3]. Additionally, to enable untraceability of authorisation tokens, it is introduced a zero-knowledge succinct non-interactive arguments of knowledge (zk-SNARKs) protocol [4]. To sum up, the provided approach respects principles, such as security through transparency, user-driven policy, privacy by design and edge intelligence.

4.6   ADVOCATE

ADVOCATE is an innovative platform that addresses the problem that users are bound to face in the IoT ecosystem with managing their devices, and the personal data these devices manage [35, 37]. The proposed solution tries to satisfy the GDPR [12] requirements about users being able to control their personal data and be informed and to consent to processing by third parties. It also helps third parties wishing to access such data to meet the requirements of the Regulation, such as informing users in a transparent and unambiguous manner about the data they manage, their purposes and the processing periods.

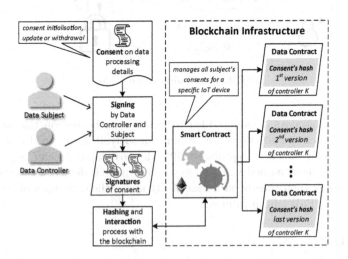

Fig. 5. The steps followed by the ADVOCATE to secure a consent [37].

ADVOCATE focuses on the management of devices that users own, and on allowing the latter to formulate and easily manage their personal data protection policy and consents. An Intelligent Policies Analysis Mechanism utilises intelligent adaptive technologies to identify contradictory or conflicting rules and policies related to the disposal of private information and ensure that these cannot be used for user profiling [8, 36].

The consents management component responsible for providing integrity, versioning control, non-repudiation and validity of data subjects' consents and data controllers' commitments is based on a blockchain. Signed consents to data controllers are added to the ledger without however, disclosing any details about the users' identities or the devices they handle (Fig. 5).

The authors do not bind their architecture to a specific Blockchain solution. They rather focus on the consensus algorithm and they suggest the use of a Proof-of-Authority (PoA) one, which requires less messages exchanges and offers better performance.

4.7 SecureSVM

Shen et al. [44] proposed SecureSVM, a privacy-preserving Support Vector Machine (SVM) training scheme over blockchain-based encrypted IoT data. SecureSVM addresses the challenging task of incorporating blockchain into a machine learning training process. The first challenge was to design an appropriate training data format that could be easily accommodated by a blockchain solution while preserving the data privacy of each individual provider. The second challenge lied with the elaboration of a training algorithm that constructs accurate SVM classifiers using the data recorded on the blockchain without disclosing sensitive data.

The proposed supervised learning process consists of two phases, i.e. the training phase and the classification phase. In comparison to previous works, [46, 48] and [33], SecureSVM combines the Paillier cryptosystem [30] (an efficient additive homomorphic encryption system) with blockchain techniques to address the concerns about data privacy, integrity, and ownership, during training SVM classifiers with IoT data originating from different providers. Thus, the proposed privacy-preserving SVM training algorithm can be used without the need of a trusted third party and is able to train SVM classifiers without accuracy loss. The authors concluded that with the use of SecureSVM, each data provider is unable to acquire any knowledge regarding the data of other providers, while the data analyst's model parameters are also kept hidden from data (data providers encrypt their data locally by using their own private keys).

The authors do not provide details about the types of blockchains that their proposed solution requires. Moreover, the experimental results they provide are about the performance of secureSVM in terms of accuracy and efficiency through experiments they conducted using real-world datasets, without however, experimenting on a specific blockchain solution.

4.8   TrustChain

A privacy-preserving permissioned blockchain, named TrustChain, is proposed by Jayasinghe et al. [18] to overcome issues related to energy consumption and delays found in traditional blockchain architectures. IoT devices do not have the enormous energy resources required to verify each block of data in the blockchain.

TrustChain does so by combining the power of blockchains with trust concepts. This research work studies how TrustChain can evolve in edge computing environments with dissimilar levels of enhancements to efface delays and privacy concerns associated with centralised processing and to maintain resources in IoT ecosystem. TrustChain is designed to increase the privacy of its participants while improving the effectiveness of services. The main difference of TrustChain to other convectional blockchains is the application of computational trust on realising various functions inside the provided distributed ledger service. It develops a novel lightweight consensus management protocol by combining this trust with the Byzantine Fault Tolerance (BFT) protocol [45]. Indicatively, to evaluate the provided trust, it measures the reliability of participating parties before creating smart contracts and initiating interactions among them. Additionally, TrustChain delegates the edge computing architecture of IoT due to its durability with low storage and computing resources. Finally, TrustChain embeds unique techniques to improve privacy when dealing with sensitive personal data and complies with GDPR legislation [12] by applying techniques, such as zero knowledge proof (ZKP), encryption, and anonymization.

4.9   PBEM-SGN

Gai et al. [16], utilised a permissioned blockchain to address privacy protection and energy security in smart grids. The proposed system provides transparency and traceability on users' energy usage, without, however, revealing participating nodes identities. Users are identified in the blockchain by the use of pseudonyms.

Storing data on the permissioned blockchain facilitates data protection, while access authorisation is secured by the use of traditional access control methods, such as attribute-based authorisation, as well as Covert Channel Authorisation (CCA) techniques [42]. Edge node/user identities are registered with the use of a group signature algorithm and validated by a super node using CCA. The use of group signatures for edge nodes facilitates anonymity as nodes in the group do not know each other's identity but only the identity of the super node which is responsible for organising resource allocation. Figure 6 depicts the main activities that take place in the PBEM-SGN proposed blockchain.

The authors provided a practical proof of their proposed scheme on Ethereum, using the standalone client Geth and Ethereum Wallet.

4.10   PrivySharing

Makhdoom et al. [23], proposed a blockchain-based framework, called PrivySharing, that aims to facilitate data-sharing in smart cities while protecting users'

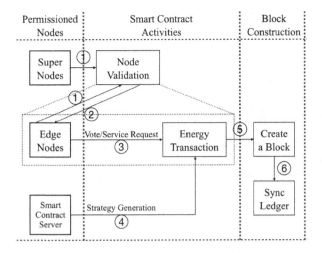

Fig. 6. Main activities in the PBEM-SGN blockchain system [16].

privacy and providing data security. The authors utilise the channels mechanism of the Hyperledger Fabric platform [2] to control access to specific types of data, such as health and smart energy, by a group of authorised organisations. The adoption of multiple channels provides increased privacy of user data but also scalability to their proposed solution. Fine-grained access control to user data is further secured by the adoption of access control rules in the smart contracts, which allows data exposure to stakeholders, on the need-to-know basis.

Moreover, PrivySharing complies with some of the most significant data security and privacy requirements of the GDPR [12], such as the "right to forget". The methodology is based on agile blockchain application development guidelines [24], for reducing the transaction settlement time for real-time applications. Furthermore, the solution provides data integrity, tamper-resistance, and non-repudiation.

PrivySharing grants secure client access to the blockchain network through a REST API. It also defines a reward system for users sharing their data with stakeholders or third parties, with a local digital token named PrivyCoin. Finally, their experimental results verified that a multi-channel blockchain solution scales better than a single channel blockchain system.

4.11 Xyreum

Xyreum, proposed by Sani et al. [40], is a scalable high-performance blockchain scheme providing security and privacy for the Industrial Internet of Things (IIoT). The model aims to overcome problems in IIoT, such as high computational complexity and latency challenges, which are considered inappropriate for this environment. Their proposed Mutual Multi-factor Authentication and Key

Establishment (MMFA-KE) protocol uses a Time-based Zero-Knowledge Proof of Knowledge (T-ZKPK) [14] scheme combined with authenticated encryption.

In the nodes registration phase, Xyreum relies on Pedersen commitments [32] (it supports homomorphic operations and can provide perfect hiding of real message with the same trapdoor) to assign them digital identities. Also, it authenticates nodes using T-ZKPK and derives shared secret session keys for securing transactions. The T-ZKPK usage mitigates eclipse attacks where proof of work (PoW) and proof of stake (PoS) are vulnerable.

A local blockchain, accessible by all nodes for verification purposes and managed by a master node, is used to record all transactions. Xyreum allows the use of multiple such local blockchains in a distributed system, each with its own master node. Figure 7 depicts the block and transaction structures in a local blockchain.

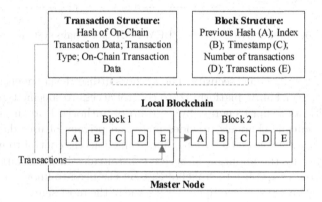

Fig. 7. Xyreum's local blockchain [40].

Furthermore, the authors explain how to use their scheme to strengthen security and privacy of the REMME protocol (https://remme.io), a blockchain-based security protocol, which they use as a case study. The experimental results reveal that Xyreum has low computational complexity compared to existing relevant schemes and, in terms of latency, it meets the required IIoT latency target.

4.12   Hy-Bridge

Firoozjaei et al. [15] propose a hybrid blockchain scheme for trustful billing and charging transactions in IoT energy and utility markets. The infrastructure consists of a main blockchain, which is used for billing and charging transactions, and subnetwork blockchains which are used for isolated Peer-to-Peer (P2P) energy transactions between neighbours in microgrids.

The introduced bridge, which links the main blockchain to its subnetworks, isolates users' P2P transactions and provides user anonymity. The bridge performs k-anonymity protection which allows IoT users access shared services anonymously in a credit-sharing group. As such, it helps avoid user profiling and identification by entities of the upper-layer of the smart-grid. An overview of the proposed scheme is depicted in Fig. 8.

P2P transactions within credit-sharing groups in microgrids are handled by local blocks which accommodate an additional header, namely credit header, which is used for authorising IoT devices and enforcing the credit-sharing policy. The authors simulated a use case scenario of a smart building to evaluate the performance of their proposed solution. The blockchain used for this purpose is a Python blockchain package, available on GitHub [1].

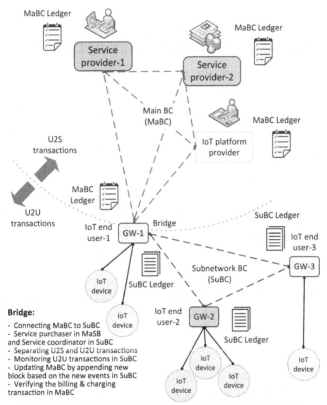

MaBC: *Main blockchain,* **SuBC:** *Subnetwork blockchain,* **U2U:** *User-to-user transaction,*
U2S: *User-to-server transaction,* **GW:** *Gateway in IoT end user's network*

Fig. 8. Hy-Bridge Architecture [15].

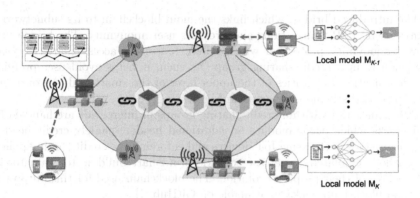

Fig. 9. Architecture of BFL-PPDS [22].

4.13   Blockchain and Federated Learning for Privacy-Preserved Data Sharing in Industrial IoT (BFL-PPDS)

Lu et al. proposed a differentially private multiparty data sharing model for machine learning purposes in IIoT applications, that is based on permissioned blockchain [22]. In their approach, the actual raw data is not directly shared among the parties but used for building data models based on federated learning algorithms.

Additionally, the authors present a blockchain-based architecture that allows collaborative data sharing over the multiple parties located distributively in order to reduce data leakage risks. This decentralised architecture continues to support data owners to keep the control of their data and to provide selectively access to it. An overview of BFL-PPDS architecture is presented in Fig. 9.

In order to enrich further the provided privacy, differential privacy methods [11] are integrated into federated learning by adding appropriate noise in the local raw data. Also, the proposed approach is evaluated for its effectiveness in two real-world datasets for data categorisation. The results show that the increase in data providers has little effect on the accuracy, while the running time is obviously increasing. Nevertheless, the authors do not provide experiments with any custom or real blockchain infrastructure.

5   Discussion

In this section, a short discussion is being conducted regarding the aforementioned privacy-preserving blockchain-based solutions in IoT based on their corresponding analysis. There are several issues emerging from our work that can be useful to future research.

As it is presented in Table 1, the majority of the proposed solutions focus on access control as a privacy-preserving provided service utilising public blockchain infrastructures. These solutions include FairAccess [28], BC Gateways [6], PPB-ABE [34], CapChain [20] and PPDAC [27]. PrivySharing [23], on the other hand, provides the same service, based on permissioned blockchain. All of these solutions lack evaluation with the exception of PrivySharing which provides both a security analysis and extended experimental results.

Another group of solutions, are more application oriented, and focus on privacy in energy transactions, like Hy-Bridge [15], which uses algorithmic techniques such us data suppression and generalisation, and PBEM-SGN [16] which uses group signatures. Both solutions provide sufficient experimental results, however, evaluation on a large scale would provide a better feasibility assessment.

Privacy-preserving solutions for machine learning in IoT data is proposed in SecureSVM [44] and BFL-PPDS [22]. SecureSVM [44], utilises homomorphic encryption to achieve user data privacy, a most frequently used method amongst the proposed methodologies. BFL-PPDS [22], introduces a new approach, which utilises federated learning and differential privacy. Both of the proposed services provide only partial experimental results which need to be expanded to also cover blockchain technology aspects.

Finally, there are other proposed solutions in the literature, which look at the investigated topic, each of them, from a different point of view, such as ADVO-CATE [37], which utilises blockchain technology to provide consent management of IoT data, Xyreum [40], which looks at distributed multi-factor authentication in IIoT, and TrustChain [18], which proposes a permissioned blockchain in IoT. Each of these topics needs to be further explored by the research community and requires extended evaluation.

6   Conclusions

In this survey paper, we presented privacy-preserving blockchain-based solutions in the IoT that address personal data protection and preservation of user privacy. In our analysis, we described the identified solutions and we compared them in regards to the focused IoT area, the applied blockchain infrastructure, the provided privacy-preserving service, the utilized underlying privacy mechanisms and the implementation level.

Blockchain technology, as revealed from the results of this paper, is recently adopted as a solution to cover various privacy issues related to the IoT, and so it is not odd that many of the proposed solutions are still in theoretical or early development/experimentation stage, with less than 50% providing implementation details. Thus, it is paramount that in order to provide viable solutions and attain a better grasp to the matter, further research and exploration has to be conducted from the research community.

Acknowledgement. This work was supported by the MPhil program "Advanced Technologies in Informatics and Computers", hosted by the Department of Computer Science, International Hellenic University, Kavala, Greece.

References

1. Alcaide, E.: Pysimplechain (2017). https://github.com/EricAlcaide/pysimplechain. Accessed on 5 June 2020
2. Androulaki, E., et al.: Hyperledger fabric: a distributed operating system for permissioned blockchains. In: 13th European Conference on Computer Systems (EuroSys). ACM, New York, NY, USA (2018). https://doi.org/10.1145/3190508.3190538
3. Bethencourt, J., Sahai, A., Waters, B.: Ciphertext-policy attribute-based encryption. In: IEEE Symposium on Security and Privacy (SP), pp. 321–334. IEEE (2007). https://doi.org/10.1109/SP.2007.11
4. Bitansky, N., Chiesa, A., Ishai, Y., Paneth, O., Ostrovsky, R.: Succinct non-interactive arguments via linear interactive proofs. In: Sahai, A. (ed.) Theory of Cryptography. pp. 315–333. Springer, Berlin, Heidelberg (2013). https://doi.org/10.1007/978-3-642-36594-2_18
5. Buterin, V.: A next-generation smart contract and decentralized application platform (2014). https://github.com/ethereum/wiki/wiki/White-Paper. Accessed on 5 June 2020
6. Cha, S., Tsai, T., Peng, W., Huang, T., Hsu, T.: Privacy-aware and blockchain connected gateways for users to access legacy IoT devices. In: IEEE 6th Global Conference on Consumer Electronics (GCCE), pp. 1–3. IEEE (2017). https://doi.org/10.1109/GCCE.2017.8229327
7. Christidis, K., Devetsikiotis, M.: Blockchains and smart contracts for the Internet of Things. IEEE Access **4**, 2292–2303 (2016). https://doi.org/10.1109/ACCESS.2016.2566339
8. Demertzis, K., Rantos, K., Drosatos, G.: A dynamic intelligent policies analysis mechanism for personal data processing in the IoT ecosystem. Big Data Cogn. Comput. **4**, 9 (2020). https://doi.org/10.3390/bdcc4020009
9. Dorri, A., Kanhere, S.S., Jurdak, R.: Towards an optimized blockchain for IoT. In: IEEE/ACM Second International Conference on Internet-of-Things Design and Implementation (IoTDI), pp. 173–178. IEEE (2017)
10. Drosatos, G.: Utilization and protection of personal data in ubiquitous computing environments. Ph.D. thesis, Department of Electrical and Computer Engineering, Democritus University of Thrace, University Campus, Xanthi 67100, Greece (2013). https://doi.org/10.12681/eadd/30085
11. Dwork, C.: Differential privacy: a survey of results. In: Agrawal, M., Du, D., Duan, Z., Li, A. (eds.) Theory and Applications of Models of Computation, pp. 1–19. Springer, Berlin, Heidelberg (2008). https://doi.org/10.1007/978-3-540-79228-4_1
12. European Parliament and Council: Regulation (EU) 2016/679 of 27 April 2016 on the protection of natural persons with regard to the processing of personal data and on the free movement of such data, and repealing Directive 95/46/EC (General Data Protection Regulation). Official Journal of the European Union, pp. 1–88 (2016)
13. Feng, Q., He, D., Zeadally, S., Khan, M.K., Kumar, N.: A survey on privacy protection in blockchain system. J. Netw. Comput. Appl. **126**, 45–58 (2019). https://doi.org/10.1016/j.jnca.2018.10.020
14. Fiat, A., Shamir, A.: How to prove yourself: Practical solutions to identification and signature problems. In: Odlyzko, A.M. (ed.) Advances in Cryptology - CRYPTO '86, pp. 186–194. Springer (1987). https://doi.org/10.1007/3-540-47721-7_12

15. Firoozjaei, M., Ghorbani, A., Kim, H., Song, J.: Hy-Bridge: a hybrid blockchain for privacy-preserving and trustful energy transactions in Internet-of-Things platforms. Sensors **20**(3), 928 (2020). https://doi.org/10.3390/s20030928
16. Gai, K., Wu, Y., Zhu, L., Xu, L., Zhang, Y.: Permissioned blockchain and edge computing empowered privacy-preserving smart grid networks. IEEE Internet Things J. **6**(5), 7992–8004 (2019). https://doi.org/10.1109/JIOT.2019.2904303
17. Huynh, T.T., Nguyen, T.D., Tan, H.: A survey on security and privacy issues of blockchain technology. In: International Conference on System Science and Engineering (ICSSE), pp. 362–367. IEEE (2019). https://doi.org/10.1109/ICSSE.2019.8823094
18. Jayasinghe, U., Lee, G.M., MacDermott, Á., Rhee, W.S.: Trustchain: a privacy preserving blockchain with edge computing. Wirel. Commun. Mobile Comput. **2019** (2019). https://doi.org/10.1155/2019/2014697
19. Joshi, A.P., Han, M., Wang, Y.: A survey on security and privacy issues of blockchain technology. Math. Found. Comput. **1**, 121–147 (2018). https://doi.org/10.3934/mfc.2018007
20. Le, T., Mutka, M.W.: CapChain: A privacy preserving access control framework based on blockchain for pervasive environments. In: IEEE International Conference on Smart Computing (SMARTCOMP), pp. 57–64 (2018). https://doi.org/10.1109/SMARTCOMP.2018.00074
21. Lee, M.J.W.: Guest editorial: special section on learning through wearable technologies and the internet of things. IEEE Trans. Learn. Technol. **9**(4), 301–303 (2016). https://doi.org/10.1109/TLT.2016.2629379
22. Lu, Y., Huang, X., Dai, Y., Maharjan, S., Zhang, Y.: Blockchain and federated learning for privacy-preserved data sharing in industrial IoT. IEEE Trans. Industr. Inf. **16**(6), 4177–4186 (2020). https://doi.org/10.1109/TII.2019.2942190
23. Makhdoom, I., Zhou, I., Abolhasan, M., Lipman, J., Ni, W.: PrivySharing: a blockchain-based framework for privacy-preserving and secure data sharing in smart cities. Comput. Secur. **88** (2020). https://doi.org/10.1016/j.cose.2019.101653
24. Marchesi, M., Marchesi, L., Tonelli, R.: An agile software engineering method to design blockchain applications. In: 14th Central and Eastern European Software Engineering Conference Russia (CEE-SECR). ACM, New York, NY, USA (2018). https://doi.org/10.1145/3290621.3290627
25. Nakamoto, S.: Bitcoin: A peer-to-peer electronic cash system (2008). https://bitcoin.org/bitcoin.pdf. Accessed on 5 June 2020
26. Noether, S., Mackenzie, A.: Monero research lab: ring confidential transactions. Ledger **1**, 1–18 (2016). https://doi.org/10.5195/ledger.2016.34
27. Ouaddah, A.: A blockchain based access control framework for the security and privacy of IoT with strong anonymity unlinkability and intractability guarantees. In: Kim, S., Deka, G.C., Zhang, P. (eds.) Role of Blockchain Technology in IoT Applications, Advances in Computers, vol. 115, pp. 211–258. Elsevier (2019). https://doi.org/10.1016/bs.adcom.2018.11.001
28. Ouaddah, A., Abou Elkalam, A., Ait Ouahman, A.: FairAcces: a new blockchain-based access control framework for the Internet of Things. Secur. Commun. Netw. **9**(18), 5943–5964 (2016). https://doi.org/10.1002/sec.1748
29. Ouaddah, A., Elkalam, A.A., Ouahman, A.A.: Towards a novel privacy-preserving access control model based on blockchain technology in IoT. In: Rocha, Á., Serrhini, M., Felgueiras, C. (eds.) Europe and MENA Cooperation Advances in Information and Communication Technologies, pp. 523–533. Springer, Cham (2017). https://doi.org/10.1007/978-3-319-46568-5_53

30. Paillier, P.: Public-key cryptosystems based on composite degree residuosity classes. In: Stern, J. (ed.) Advances in Cryptology - EUROCRYPT '99, pp. 223–238. Springer, Berlin, Heidelberg (1999)

31. Panarello, A., Tapas, N., Merlino, G., Longo, F., Puliafito, A.: Blockchain and IoT integration: a systematic survey. Sensors **18**(8), 2575 (2018)

32. Pedersen, T.P.: Non-interactive and information-theoretic secure verifiable secret sharing. In: Feigenbaum, J. (ed.) Advances in Cryptology - CRYPTO '91, pp. 129–140. Springer, Berlin, Heidelberg (1992). https://doi.org/10.1007/3-540-46766-1_9

33. Rahulamathavan, Y., Phan, R.C., Veluru, S., Cumanan, K., Rajarajan, M.: Privacy-preserving multi-class support vector machine for outsourcing the data classification in cloud. IEEE Trans. Dependable Secure Comput. **11**(5), 467–479 (2014). https://doi.org/10.1109/TDSC.2013.51

34. Rahulamathavan, Y., Phan, R.C., Rajarajan, M., Misra, S., Kondoz, A.: Privacy-preserving blockchain based IoT ecosystem using attribute-based encryption. In: IEEE International Conference on Advanced Networks and Telecommunications Systems (ANTS), pp. 1–6. IEEE (2017). https://doi.org/10.1109/ANTS.2017.8384164

35. Rantos, K., Drosatos, G., Demertzis, K., Ilioudis, C., Papanikolaou, A.: Blockchain-based consents management for personal data processing in the IoT ecosystem. In: 15th International Joint Conference on e-Business and Telecommunications (ICETE) - Volume 2: SECRYPT, pp. 572–577. SCITEPRESS (2018). https://doi.org/10.5220/0006911007380743

36. Rantos, K., Drosatos, G., Demertzis, K., Ilioudis, C., Papanikolaou, A., Kritsas, A.: ADvoCATE: A consent management platform for personal data processing in the iot using blockchain technology. In: Lanet, J.L., Toma, C. (eds.) Innovative Security Solutions for Information Technology and Communications, vol. 11359 LNCS, pp. 300–313. Springer, Cham (2019). https://doi.org/10.1007/978-3-030-12942-2_23

37. Rantos, K., Drosatos, G., Kritsas, A., Ilioudis, C., Papanikolaou, A., Filippidis, A.P.: A blockchain-based platform for consent management of personal data processing in the IoT ecosystem. Secur. Commun. Netw. **2019**, 1–15 (2019). https://doi.org/10.1155/2019/1431578

38. Roman, R., Zhou, J., Lopez, J.: On the features and challenges of security and privacy in distributed Internet of Things. Comput. Netw. **57**(10), 2266–2279 (2013). https://doi.org/10.1016/j.comnet.2012.12.018

39. van Saberhagen, N.: CryptoNote v2.0 (2013). https://cryptonote.org/whitepaper.pdf. Accessed on 5 June 2020

40. Sani, A.S., et al.: Xyreum: A high-performance and scalable blockchain for iiot security and privacy. In: IEEE 39th International Conference on Distributed Computing Systems (ICDCS), pp. 1920–1930 (2019). https://doi.org/10.1109/ICDCS.2019.00190

41. Sasson, E.B., et al.: Zerocash: Decentralized anonymous payments from Bitcoin. In: IEEE Symposium on Security and Privacy, pp. 459–474. IEEE (2014). https://doi.org/10.1109/SP.2014.36

42. Shah, G., Molina, A., Blaze, M.: Keyboards and covert channels. In: 15th USENIX Security Symposium (USENIX-SS) - Volume 15. USENIX Association, USA (2006)

43. Sharma, M., Lim, J.: A survey of methods guaranteeing user privacy based on blockchain in Internet-of-Things. In: 2nd International Conference on Data Science and Information Technology (DSIT), pp. 147–153. ACM, New York, NY, USA (2019). https://doi.org/10.1145/3352411.3352435

44. Shen, M., Tang, X., Zhu, L., Du, X., Guizani, M.: Privacy-preserving support vector machine training over blockchain-based encrypted iot data in smart cities. IEEE Internet Things J. **6**(5), 7702–7712 (2019). https://doi.org/10.1109/JIOT. 2019.2901840

45. Sousa, J., Bessani, A., Vukolic, M.: A byzantine fault-tolerant ordering service for the hyperledger fabric blockchain platform. In: 2018 48th Annual IEEE/IFIP International Conference on Dependable Systems and Networks (DSN), pp. 51–58. IEEE (2018). https://doi.org/10.1109/DSN.2018.00018

46. Wang, W., Vong, C.M., Yang, Y., Wong, P.K.: Encrypted image classification based on multilayer extreme learning machine. Multidimension. Syst. Signal Process. **28**(3), 851–865 (2017). https://doi.org/10.1007/s11045-016-0408-1

47. Yu, Y., Li, Y., Tian, J., Liu, J.: Blockchain-based solutions to security and privacy issues in the Internet of Things. IEEE Wirel. Commun. **25**(6), 12–18 (2018). https://doi.org/10.1109/MWC.2017.1800116

48. Zhu, H., Liu, X., Lu, R., Li, H.: Efficient and privacy-preserving online medical prediagnosis framework using nonlinear SVM. IEEE J. Biomed. Health Inform. **21**(3), 838–850 (2017). https://doi.org/10.1109/JBHI.2016.2548248

Sensor Systems and Software

Assessment of Video Games Players and Teams Behaviour via Sensing and Heterogeneous Data Analysis: Deployment at an eSports Tournament

Alexander Korotin, Anton Stepanov, Andrey Lange, Dmitry Nikolaev, Simon Abramov, Nikita Klyuchnikov, Evgeny Burnaev, and Andrey Somov(✉)

Center for Computational and Data-Intensive Science and Engineering (CDISE), Skolkovo Institute of Science and Technology, Moscow, Russia
a.somov@skoltech.ru

Abstract. eSports is video gaming where individual players or teams oppose their physical, psychological and emotional conditions in the game context to achieve a specific goal by the end of the game. However, neither players nor teams have been studied in real scenarios. In this paper, we report on the deployment of sensing system for collecting a player biometric data (a computer mouse and keyboard), voice data, and heart rate in an eSports 'Team Fortress 2' tournament. Upon the data analysis we demonstrate that an increased heart rate has a negative impact on the player performance. At the same time, successful teams communicate more during the game. Moreover, team communication in positive tone has a positive contribution in the overall team performance.

Keywords: eSports · Intelligent sensing · Data analysis · Deployment

1 Introduction

eSports is a quickly developing area of video gaming where individuals or teams compete within a game environment for achieving a specific goal by the end of the game. Currently, eSports audience involves around 1.5 billions players worldwide [1], eSports is recognized as sport in many countries, lots of local and international tournaments are regularly organized and followed by visitors and via online broadcasts or streams. By playing games, the eSports players are involved in continuously changing context where they have to take decisions quickly. It results in stress situations during the games which influence their psychological and emotional conditions. At the same time, eSports specific injuries could be identified in advance and therefore avoided. Performance of individual players and teams depends on these factors drastically.

However, eSports players have not been studied in real conditions. From the research point of view eSports is in its infancy and is limited within in-game

© ICST Institute for Computer Sciences, Social Informatics and Telecommunications Engineering 2021
Published by Springer Nature Switzerland AG 2021. All Rights Reserved
S. Paiva et al. (Eds.): SmartCity360° 2020, LNICST 372, pp. 409–421, 2021.
https://doi.org/10.1007/978-3-030-76063-2_28

data analysis or modelling players [25]. Although myriads of research works have been published on the data collection in sport [9], finding correlation between the stress/fatigue and physiological parameters [7], identification of specific movement pattern [15] they still have not been adapted to the eSports domain. This domain is quite specific in terms of decision taking in a short period of time, constantly changing game context, stress environment. Moreover, there is a lack of eSports deployments which could help for data collection in real scenarios and further data analysis. Indeed, the deployment related studies allow for testing particular testbeds, technologies, and getting feedback on proposed research ideas in terms of their practical feasibility [3,19].

The problem of players assessment and their behavior analysis has been approached theoretically and in lab conditions from (i) psychological point of view and (ii) physiological point of view when a certain dataset was collected using various sensors fixed on the player.

Regarding psychology, there is a bunch of works combining the studies on both psychological self-reports from players and log files based on the in-game events are generated into a meta-synthesis player types profile [11]. Another research direction deals with the general psychological motivation of human to play digital games [10]. Relevant data-driven approaches aiming at a player modeling were discussed in [14]. The authors emphasize a variety of machine learning methods applied to the analysis of in-game actions of player behavior. Also, there is a study combining both psychological and physiological assessment of players in terms of their reaction time. It is assessed through the gaze tracking and personality traits [17]. While combining both psychological and physiological methods is promising, there is still a lack of this research since it requires truly multidisciplinary research team.

As for the physiology related research in eSports, a number of sensing technologies have been used so far. We note here that for physiological data collection unobtrusive sensing technologies are welcome by professional players who a highly sensitive to any kind of discomfort during the game and training routine. Unobtrusive technologies include the usage of keyboard and computer mouse during the data collection, an eye tracker placed on top or below a display [24], a gaming chair equipped with the sensors [22] as well as the video game recordings (demo files) [21] collected during the game. As noticed earlier, some sensing technologies, e.g. wearable sensing technologies, may cause unpleasant experience for the players. This kind of discomfort may result in the performance reduction. An Electroencephalography (EEG) headset [8], a heart rate sensor and wearables [13] is a typical source of discomfort for the players. At the same time, using some sensing technologies, e.g. EEG, it is a non-trivial task to collect high quality data. EEG measurements are characterized by a number of artefacts heavily influencing the measurements quality. As a result, the gaze tracking is among the popular research trends in eSports. In [4,16] the authors studied the differences between an amateur and Pro players using an eye tracker and the data collected from the computer keyboard and mouse. As a result, the authors demonstrated the patterns of gaze information from the players with different experience level.

The players behaviour can be assessed using the movement related sensors integrated in a gaming chair [22]. Feature engineering and machine learning have helped identify specific features describing the players with different level. It is worth noting that the research reported in [16,22] involved the data collection from professional players in lab conditions. As noticed earlier, the eSports related deployments, e.g. data collection and players assessment in real conditions, are missing so far.

In this work, we report on a sensor network deployment at an eSports tournament. The goal of this deployment is to collect the eSports data including game events (computer keyboard, mouse), voice (microphone), heart bit (wireless heart rate monitor) for assessing the players and teams behaviour in real conditions. To the best of our knowledge, it is the first deployment at an eSports tournament. The results obtained in this work are essential for both eSports players and researchers - they demonstrate which data are relevant for analysis and how the team and players can develop their professional qualities, communication in the team, and control certain physiological parameters. Moreover, this study is highly important in the situations when the eSports team formation is in progress [6] and for the analysis of the professional eSports athletes' work [20].

The paper is organized as follows: we present the eSports deployment in Sect. 2 where we provide the details on the tournament, game discipline, sensing system, and the data collection procedure. We then demonstrate the analysis of collected data in Sect. 3 by focusing on our results in voice, heart rate and game events analysis. Finally, we provide concluding remarks and discuss our future work in Sect. 4.

2   Deployment

Prior to dig deeper into details of the deployment scenario and the sensor network used for data collection, we stress the point that this deployment was carried out at a tournament in real conditions. It means that this event was featured by the tight schedule, there were real participants, and a reasonable prize pool. That is why (i) the deployment preparation must be perfectly organized, (ii) there must be the data backup system, and (iii) the entire deployment and each single sensor must be unobtrusive for the players as it may have a negative impact on their performance.

2.1   Scenario

Tournament. Moscow LAN is the annual Team Fortress 2 (TF2) tournament which helds in Moscow, Russia. 2020 tournament was cancelled due to Covid-19 pandemic. 7 teams participated in 2019 TF2 Moscow LAN tournament[1]. The tournament lasted for 2 d at Winstrike Arena: the qualify stage in the first day and the quarter-final with the grand final during the second day. 7 teams double

---

[1] TF2 Moscow LAN official website https://match.tf/tournaments/44.

elimination bracket was used for the qualify stage. During the tournament an online stream on Twitch platform was organized. Heart rate monitors performing the team captains heart bits were also streamed as an overlay and were always visible to the Twitch streamers (Fig. 1).

Fig. 1. TF2 Moscow LAN 2019.

Competitive play in TF2 refers to the organized gaming according to Highlander – a standard competitive format shared by the majority of leagues. This set of rules assumes that the game should be played in a prescribed list of maps and regimes (King of the Hill, Payload, Capture Point, Timed Capture the Flag) with some disabled options (critical hits, damage spread, and customization). Most players that follow the standard competitive format use the standard competitive lineup made up of the following game classes (Medic, Demoman, Pocket, Roamer, and Utilities). Therefore each team at the tournament is composed of 5 players in total leaded by their captain.

Game. TF2 is a First Person team-based online multiplayer game available on the PC and other platforms[2]. It is one of oldest games on Steam with intriguing concept and small, but passionate competitive community. The original version

---

[2] C.Moore 'Hats of affect: A study of Affect, Achievements and Hats in Team Fortress 2', available at http://gamestudies.org/1101/articles/moore.

of this game was a modification (mod) of Quake made by id Software in 1996 and reworked by Valve. It became highly popular among gamers seeking the alternative options from the individualistic deathmatch style of play that dominated early multiplayer FPS games.

Players of two teams respawn near their fortresses after loosing all their character hitpoints. Each player belongs to the nine different player classes which are divided into three categories: assault, defence and support. The tactical combinations of these classes produce a complex formulae for matching different elements in different sequences. Effective communication and coordination, synergy between the players, accomplishment of their character abilities make the teamwork the most important aspect for winning.

The core of combat system is the rules of interaction between nine different classes divided by Valve in three categories: offense, defense, and support. Each class has the unique attributes that determine its strengths and weakness: health, movement speed, weaponry, and other innate abilities such as health regeneration or the ability to Double Jump.

2.2   Hardware and Sensor Network

The tournament infrastructure included 40 high performance PCs connected through 1 Gbps local network were used during TF2 Moscow LAN tournament. 35 PCs were occupied by the eSports players, 1 PS was used for game hosting, 2 PCs were used for Twitch online-stream and 2 PCs were in hot reserve. One additional computer (Intel NUC) was used as a FTP and NTP server. Custom made data collection software was used on every gaming PC. This software enable recording of keyboard pressings, mouse movements, microphone sound capture during the game sessions. At server PC full log was enabled for all the in-game events. Wireless sensor network was used for heart-rate data collection. The captain of each team was equipped with a HRM belt connected to Raspberry PI SBC. Heart-rate was measured by HRM belt. Raspberry PI captured signal from the local HRM belt, decoded it and than transferred to Twitch stream PC. The PC used for online-streaming was featured by a specific software effectuating the hear-rate data visualisation and video overlay software (Fig. 2).

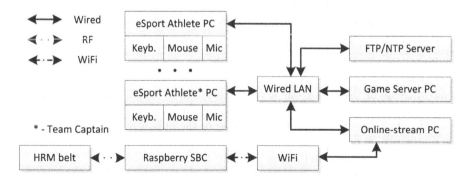

Fig. 2. Block diagram of sensor network for eSports data collection.

It should be noted that our aim was to ensure unobtrusive sensing and avoid potential situations where the sensors could disturb the players or create any kind of interference to gaming procedure in the scope of tournament. That is why we had to give up on the idea to use as much sensing technologies as we have tested earlier in the lab conditions [22,23].

2.3 Data Collection

All the gaming PCs and the game server were synchronized with accuracy up to 10 ms. To do this special software settings were applied and the dedicated NTP server was used [23]. Data collection software performs continuous recording of keyboard, mouse and voice during the course of tournament. Players were able to switch the PC to another one between the tournament stages. The game server performs the full logging of in-game events including IP addresses of each connected player and his player-id and nickname. These allows us to cut the continuous recorded timeseries to the chunks correlated with the particular game and particular player. Due to time synchronization across all the computers different timeseries were synchronized and ready for the analysis.

We note here that our future plans include the collection and analysis of game recording (video) files. This activity requires extra efforts in improving the experimental testbed by adding data center facility [5].

3 Data Analysis

In terms of data analysis, a few months before the deployment we have discussed with the TF2 players and managers the metrics of interest for this particular discipline. It appeared that the motor skills could be developed, i.e. trained, and are not that important for the team performance. As for the heart rate, most of the players were aware of the point that it does have an impact on the performance and can be controlled using specific techniques. At the same time, the team speak, i.e. communication in the team during the game, is much more important in terms of the overall team performance and requires research efforts.

3.1 Game Events

Along with modern biometric indicators, the logs of in-game events remain a significant part of the analysis. In this study, we performed the analysis of the movements and rotations of players' avatars using the data of their 'virtual' behavior. One of the issues was about association of virtual and real world: if the motion intensities can characterize the team or a certain player, how these characteristics depend on the map, the level of the opponent team and whether the match is final or it is still qualification. The intensities for yaw and distance were calculated as the sum of their absolute changes per second.

As shown in Fig. 3a, the intensity of player's avatar rotation is more a characteristic of a player or his/her role in the game because within-player differences

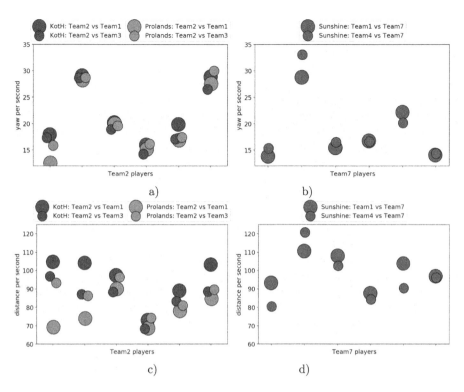

Fig. 3. a) and c) - respectively, the yaw and movement velocities for Team2 players in two matches with Team1 (the match in grand final with the winner) and in two matches with Team3 (also strong team) on two different maps: *KotH* and *Prolands*; b) and d) - respectively, the yaw and the movement velocity for the players of Team7 (has hot won any match) with Team1 and Team4 (has not played in final) on the map *Sunshine*.

look smaller than the between-player differences for two maps and matches versus two different teams. This remains true also for Team7 that did not win any match: rotation intensities do not depend on the opponent teams significantly, although Team1 and Team4 have different professional levels (see Fig. 3b).

However, the velocity of the avatar movement demonstrates significant differences with respect to the map (see Fig. 3c). Interestingly that all the players of Team2 demonstrated higher intensities for both yaw and distance for the map *KotH* than for the map *Prolands* in the matches with the champion Team1. The velocity of the movement also depends on the opponent team and this is different for different maps (see Fig. 3c).

Although both movement and rotation velocities depend on the opponent team, their average values over the team players do not depend significantly on the team level: the values for Team7 (see Fig. 3b and Fig. 3d) are comparable with the values for Team2 (see Fig. 3a and Fig. 3c, respectively).

3.2   Heart Rate

To qualify for the final of the tournament, there were two competing teams Team3 and Team1. As expected, the fight turned out to be hot. This can be judged not only by the fact that the battle was long, but also according to how the heart rate of the team captains changed. With each new map, the stress and pressure were growing. Figure 4 shows the heart rate range (bits per minute) of the team captains on three different maps. Upon reaching the score 1 : 1 on the maps, the captain of the blue team (Team3) was stressed enough. On the last map, his average heart rate increased by as much as 25 bits/min and reached a record 135 bits/min. At the same time, the captain of the red team (Team1) was much calmer. Playing at a heart rate of about 125 bits/min on the second and the third maps, he made a significant contribution to team play. We tend to think, it was his deadly concentration in the game that brought the team to the final of the tournament.

In the final game, the situation is different. Team2 captain was in constant pressure throughout the game. Team1 captain, on the other hand, was clearly relaxed in the first two rounds, having the heart rate 20–30 bits per minute lower. The situation changed when, with the score 1 : 1 on the maps, the control stage of the game for winning the final began. The average heart rate of team1 captain increased by 10–15 bits and nearly reached the heart rate of his opponent captain. However, in such a stressful situation, it was team1 which won the tournament. Here, the skillful sniper of the winning team also made an invaluable contribution to win the game.

3.3   Voice

To analyse players' communication during the game, we automatically labeled the emotions for every players' voice record. This was done by training a machine learning emotions classifier on a publicly available dataset and applying it to the collected dataset for recognising emotions.

As the base classification model, we used Random Forest classifier [2] trained on Mel Frequency Cepstral Coefficient features (MFCC, see [12]). These coefficients are extracted from each 3 s interval (with time period 0.5 s) of each recording, so each interval is a training/testing object. We used 40 MFC coefficients.

To train Random Forest for emotions classification, we used publicly available Ryerson Audio-Visual Database of Emotional Speech and Song (RAVDESS) [18]. Originally, the database consists of >1000 recordings for 24 actors with 8 types of emotions: neutral, calm, happy, sad, angry, fearful, disgust, surprised. In our case, it is not reasonable to discern 'neutral', 'calm' and 'sad' classes in eSports audio data: all these emotions represent some kind of passivity. Empirically, we also noted that 'disgust' and 'surprised' classes turned to be not typical for considered tournament's audio. Thus, for the reason of classifier training we considered only the most representative classes: 'calm', 'happy', 'angry', 'fearful'. To make classifier robust, we also artificially (manually) collected 30 crops of

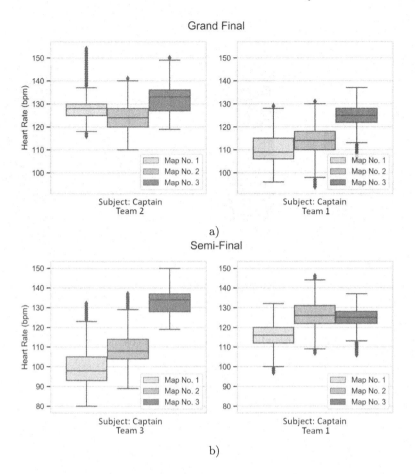

Fig. 4. Heart rate of team captains during a) final game, and b) semi-final game.

background sound from the tournament's audio dataset and added them to the train set with an artificial label 'background noise'. The final trained classifier provided 92.7% balanced accuracy score for 5-class classification on the 3-fold cross validation on the extended RAVDESS dataset.

We applied the obtained emotion classifier (MLP) to our eSports dataset, i.e. classified emotions of each player for every 3 s interval of the dataset. We define the player's **emotional passivity level** as follows.

$$EP = \frac{\text{Calm} + \text{Background Noise duration}}{\text{Game duration}} \quad (1)$$

It is the fraction of time when the player was calm during the game. In the same way, we define the fraction of time when a player was 'happy' as follows.

$$PT = \frac{\text{Positive tone's duration ('happy')}}{\text{Game duration}} \quad (2)$$

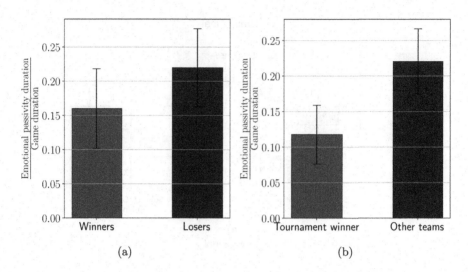

Fig. 5. Emotional passivity level for a) all winners vs all losers, b) the winner of the tournament vs all the others.

It is the fraction of time when a player was 'sad' by

$$NT = \frac{\text{Negative tone's duration ('angry')}}{\text{Game duration}} \tag{3}$$

We depict the average values (averaged over the players in teams and over the matches) of EP, PT, NT for both winning and losing team in Figs. 5 and 6.

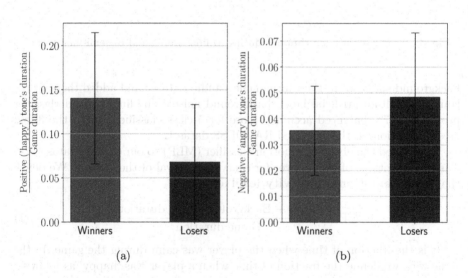

Fig. 6. Comparison of emotional tone of teams' conversations a) positive tone, b) negative tone.

From Figs. 5 and 6 we extract the following insights:

- More successful teams communicate more;
- The communication of more successful teams is in a more positive tone.

Both observations have reasonable explanations: the proper team communication improves chances to win, and winning improves team's morale, providing more positive communication tone.

4 Conclusions

eSports research is a developing area lacking the players assessment in real conditions. In this work, we have reported on a deployment of sensing system at a real tournament followed by the data analysis. We have ensured the data collection from the computer keyboard and mouse, microphone, and heart rate sensor for performing the analysis of game events, heart rate and voice, respectively. These sensors were used intentionally for guarantying unobtrusive sensing during the competition.

Our results have demonstrated that rotation velocities depend on the opponent rather on the current team skill level. Also, our next finding (a reasonably straightforward one) was connected with the heart rate of the players (we assume here that all the players are equally healthy) - those players who managed to control their heart bit had success in their games. As for the voice communication, i.e. team speak, we came to two conclusions: (i) successful teams naturally speak more during the game, and (ii) the communication of successful teams is in positive tone.

As for the future work, we plan to add a data center facility for storing and performing the analysis of game video recording (demo files) as well as involve extra sensors, e.g. an eye tracker, the sensors for environmental monitoring, which ensure both unobtrusive sensing and provide more insights for the data analysis and making consequent inference on the players behavior and their performance.

Acknowledgments. The reported study was funded by RFBR according to the research project No. 18-29-22077\19.

Authors also thank the organizers of 'Team Fortress 2' Moscow LAN 2019 for technical support during the data collection and fruitful discussions of the game insights.

References

1. Anderson, C.G.: Understanding esports as a stem career ready curriculum in the wild. In: 2018 10th International Conference on Virtual Worlds and Games for Serious Applications (VS-Games), pp. 1–6 (2018)
2. Breiman, L.: Random forests. Mach. Learn. **45**(1), 5–32 (2001)
3. Ceriotti, M.: Monitoring heritage buildings with wireless sensor networks: the torre aquila deployment. In: 2009 International Conference on Information Processing in Sensor Networks, pp. 277–288 (2009)

4. Choi, G., Kim, M.: Eye gaze information and game level design according to fps gameplay beats. J. Inform. Commun. Convergence Eng. **16**, 189–196 (2018)

5. Dupont, C., Hermenier, F., Schulze, T., Basmadjian, R., Somov, A., Giuliani, G.: Plug4green: A flexible energy-aware vm manager to fit data centre particularities. Ad Hoc Netw. **25**, 505–519 (2015)

6. Freeman, G., Wohn, D.Y.: Understanding esports team formation and coordination. Comput. Support. Coop. Work **27**(3–6), 1019–1050 (2018)

7. Garcia-Ceja, E., Osmani, V., Mayora, O.: Automatic stress detection in working environments from smartphones' accelerometer data: a first step. IEEE J. Biomed. Health Inform. **20**(4), 1053–1060 (2016)

8. Guo, J., Zhou, R., Zhao, L., Lu, B.: Multimodal emotion recognition from eye image, eye movement and eeg using deep neural networks. In: 2019 41st Annual International Conference of the IEEE Engineering in Medicine and Biology Society (EMBC), pp. 3071–3074 (2019)

9. Haladjian, J., Schlabbers, D., Taheri, S., Tharr, M., Bruegge, B.: Sensor-based detection and classification of soccer goalkeeper training exercises. ACM Trans. Internet Things **1**(2), 1–20 (2020)

10. Hamari, J., Keronen, L.: Why do people play games? A meta-analysis. Int. J. Inf. Manage. **37**(3), 125–141 (2017)

11. Hamari, J., Tuunanen, J.: Player types: a meta-synthesis. Trans. Digital Games Res. Assoc. **1**(2), 29–53 (2014). https://doi.org/10.26503/todigra.v1i2.13

12. Hasan, M.R., Jamil, M., Rahman, M., et al.: Speaker identification using mel frequency cepstral coefficients. Variations **1**(4) (2004)

13. Heinz, E.A., Kunze, K.S., Gruber, M., Bannach, D., Lukowicz, P.: Using wearable sensors for real-time recognition tasks in games of martial arts - an initial experiment. In: 2006 IEEE Symposium on Computational Intelligence and Games, pp. 98–102 (2006). https://doi.org/10.1109/CIG.2006.311687

14. Hooshyar, D., Yousefi, M., Lim, H.: Data-driven approaches to game player modeling: a systematic literature review. ACM Comput. Surv. **50**(6) (2018). https://doi.org/10.1145/3145814

15. Jeyakumar, J.V., Lai, L., Suda, N., Srivastava, M.: Sensehar: a robust virtual activity sensor for smartphones and wearables. In: Proceedings of the 17th Conference on Embedded Networked Sensor Systems, pp. 15–28. SenSys '19, Association for Computing Machinery, New York, NY, USA (2019). https://doi.org/10.1145/3356250.3360032

16. Khromov, N., Korotin, A., Lange, A., Stepanov, A., Burnaev, E., Somov, A.: Esports athletes and players: a comparative study. IEEE Pervasive Comput. **18**(3), 31–39 (2019)

17. Koposov, D., Semenova, M., Somov, A., Lange, A., Stepanov, A., Burnaev, E.: Analysis of the reaction time of esports players through the gaze tracking and personality trait. In: 2020 IEEE 29th International Symposium on Industrial Electronics (ISIE), pp. 1560–1565 (2020). https://doi.org/10.1109/ISIE45063.2020.9152422

18. Livingstone, S.R., Russo, F.A.: The ryerson audio-visual database of emotional speech and song (ravdess): a dynamic, multimodal set of facial and vocal expressions in north american english. PloS one **13**(5), e0196391 (2018)

19. Meyer, M., et al.: Event-triggered natural hazard monitoring with convolutional neural networks on the edge. In: Proceedings of the 18th International Conference on Information Processing in Sensor Networks. pp. 73–84. IPSN '19, Association for Computing Machinery, New York, NY, USA (2019). https://doi.org/10.1145/3302506.3310390

20. Paravizo, E., de Souza, R.R.L.: Playing for real: an exploratory analysis of professional esports athletes' work. In: Bagnara, S., Tartaglia, R., Albolino, S., Alexander, T., Fujita, Y. (eds.) Proceedings of the 20th Congress of the International Ergonomics Association (IEA 2018), pp. 507–515. Springer International Publishing, Cham (2019)

21. Sifa, R., Drachen, A., Bauckhage, C.: Large-scale cross-game player behavior analysis on Steam. In: Proceedings of the 11th Conference on Artificial Intelligence and Interactive Digital Entertainment (2015)

22. Smerdov, A., Burnaev, E., Somov, A.: esports pro-players behavior during the game events: Statistical analysis of data obtained using the smart chair. In: 2019 IEEE SmartWorld, Ubiquitous Intelligence Computing, Advanced Trusted Computing, Scalable Computing Communications, Cloud Big Data Computing, Internet of People and Smart City Innovation (SmartWorld/SCALCOM/UIC/ATC/CBDCom/IOP/SCI), pp. 1768–1775 (2019)

23. Stepanov, A., Lange, A., Khromov, N., Korotin, A., Burnaev, E., Somov, A.: Sensors and game synchronization for data analysis in esports. In: 2019 IEEE 17th International Conference on Industrial Informatics (INDIN), vol. 1, pp. 933–938 (2019)

24. Velichkovsky, B.B., Khromov, N., Korotin, A., Burnaev, E., Somov, A.: Visual Fixations Duration as an Indicator of Skill Level in eSports. In: Lamas, D., Loizides, F., Nacke, L., Petrie, H., Winckler, M., Zaphiris, P. (eds.) INTERACT 2019. LNCS, vol. 11746, pp. 397–405. Springer, Cham (2019). https://doi.org/10.1007/978-3-030-29381-9_25

25. Yannakakis, G.N., Togelius, J.: Modeling Players, pp. 203–255. Springer International Publishing, Cham (2018)

A Feature-Fusion Transfer Learning Method as a Basis to Support Automated Smartphone Recycling in a Circular Smart City

Nermeen Abou Baker(✉) ⓘ, Paul Szabo-Müller ⓘ, and Uwe Handmann ⓘ

Computer Science Institute, Ruhr West University of Applied Sciences, Lützowstrasse 5, 46236 Bottrop, Germany

{nermeen.baker,paul.szabo-mueller,uwe.handmann}@hs-ruhrwest.de

Abstract. In this paper, we present how Artificial Intelligence (AI) could support automated smartphone recycling, hence, act as an enabler for Circular Smart Cities (CSC), where the Smart City paradigm could be linked to the Circular Economy (CE), which is a leading concept of the sustainable economy. While business and society strive to gain benefits from automation, the ongoing rapid digitalization, in turn, accelerates the mass production of Waste Electric and Electronic Equipment (WEEE), often called E-Waste. Therefore, E-Waste is the fastest growing waste stream in the world and comes up with several negative environmental and social impacts. In our research, we show an AI technique (particularly, Transfer Learning) that could become an enabler for the CSC and the CE in general and supporter of automated recycling, specifically. However, research on this topic is emerging only recently, and practical applications are lacking even more. For instance, object recognition has extensive research, whereas smartphone classification nevertheless has rare attention. Our main contribution is a Transfer Learning (TL) approach based on visual-feature extraction to classify smartphones; as a result, it supports automated smartphone recycling independently of brands and even without any ex-ante information about product designs. Our findings show that the main advantages of using TL, are reducing the size of the training-set, computation time, and significant enhancements without designing a completely new network from scratch. This may ease the automated recycling of smartphones as well as other E-Waste, hence, contribute to the development of the CE and CSC.

Keywords: Feature fusion · Transfer learning · Smartphone recycling · Circular economy · Automation systems · Smart city · Sustainability · E-waste management · Circular city

1 Introduction

1.1 Motivation and Challenges

The interplay of emerging digital technologies such as AI, Smart City development, CE opportunities, and challenges associated with E-Waste brings us to our research question

© ICST Institute for Computer Sciences, Social Informatics and Telecommunications Engineering 2021
Published by Springer Nature Switzerland AG 2021. All Rights Reserved
S. Paiva et al. (Eds.): SmartCity360° 2020, LNICST 372, pp. 422–441, 2021.
https://doi.org/10.1007/978-3-030-76063-2_29

Fig. 1: How can AI (particularly, TL) be applied in order to enable automated smartphone recycling, hence, contribute to the development of CSC?

In particular, this paper addresses the problem of smartphone recycling and applies a feature-fusion TL method to classify smartphones without any ex-ante information about product designs. In our interdisciplinary research in cooperation with digitalization and sustainability, we embed this deep investigation in the wider framework of Smart City development and CE.

Cities around the world are looking for strategies to become more sustainable places. On one hand, economic prosperity, environmental quality, and social wellbeing should go hand in hand. On the other hand, cities try to cope with global and local challenges, such as; climate change, air pollution, biodiversity loss, social inequality, and resource depletion. These visions of sustainable city convergence with digital technologies, like AI, 3D Printing, Big Data Analysis, and the Internet of Things (IoT) in the smart city concept and almost all areas of life [1–3].

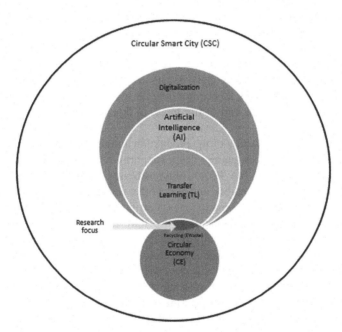

Fig. 1. Our cooperative interdisciplinary research with digitalization and CE in the framework of Smart City

Particularly, AI could become the fundamental driver of CE and CSC. Despite that, the smart city concept faces some challenges concerning the security and privacy issues, and the rising of infrastructure costs, there are still ubiquitous areas of application, such as; enhancing the city's security level by recognizing people' faces [43, 44] to access restricted areas [8–10], improving traffic flows by partly autonomous drones and vehicles [11–13], traffic management and smart tracking, assistance systems [14, 15], predictive maintenance [16, 17], and last but not least, smart waste management, such as [18];

installing sensors on waste bins to enhance the collection, smart disposal segregation, sorting and disassembling, and maximizing materials use.

Some smart city initiatives also aim to become circular cities by picking up elements of the CE, to magnify benefits from smarter use of resources [4]. The CE concept proposes low-emission and resource-saving modes of production and consumption by closing material loops and extending product life-cycles. In the combination of the smart city and the CE concept, we see a kind of new category or focus of action, respectively, which we call a Circular Smart City (CSC).

In general, digital technologies could pull down some existing barriers to the CE, like lacking knowledge about the location and condition of obsolete products or included as well as currently higher costs of their treatment compared to 'non-circular' ones [5, 6]. By doing so, digitalization could support the application of CE strategies, for example, some of the so-called R-Strategies like the redesign, reuse, redistribution, refurbishment and maintenance, repair, remanufacturing, as well as recycling of materials [7].

However, while businesses and society strive to get advantages from the ongoing rapid digitalization, it comes with several side-effects. Figures from the latest Global E-Waste Monitor [19] indicate that digitalization currently accelerates the mass production of E-Waste and will speed up more in the future. E-Waste is the fastest growing waste stream in the world, with an annual growth rate of 3 to 4%. From 2014 to 2019, it grew by 21%. Nonetheless, only 17.4% of global E-Waste was officially documented and properly recycled in 2019. On one hand, this comes up with several negative environmental and social impacts, not only at the end-of-life-phase of those products but along the whole value chain.

A closer look at the evolution of the production and use of digital devices, such as; smartphones, which we investigate in deep, support our argumentation. Smartphones play a vital role in our daily life. People and businesses use them for communication, shopping, navigation, entertainment, and many other activities with few screen touches. The continuous consumption of smartphones contributes to a scarcity of non-renewable resources since smartphone manufacturers use Rare Earth Element (REE) and other precious metals. According to [32], only about 1% of smartphones are recycled, and one reason behind this extremely low-rate is the technological complexity to recycle REE. On the other hand, the raw material value of E-Waste offers vast economic opportunities. It is estimated [20] to be 5100 tons of smartphone content of precious and critical metals in units put on the market by 2035 comparing to 1500 tons by 2020.

A periodic table that demonstrates the scarcity of elements used in smartphones was demonstrated in 2019 on the 150th anniversary of the creation of the original periodic table [33]. Modern smartphones contain more than 30 different elements, in which gold, silver, and copper are used for wiring and lithium and cobalt for the battery, and other REE, including yttrium, terbium, and dysprosium. Even though having fractions of grams is considered endangered. Many concerns are raised because about 17 elements needed to manufacture smartphones are finite, and the continuous depletion of these resources is alarming due to limited supplies, lack of recycling, or the location in conflict zones. A study by Yale University [34], tried to find possible replacements. However, they found 12 metals and metalloids, namely rhenium, rhodium, lanthanum, europium, dysprosium, thulium, ytterbium, yttrium, strontium, thallium, magnesium, and manganese, have no replacement at all because the substitution will be inadequate and will decrease the performance.

But how to make use of these resources with the help of digital technologies such as AI? So far this is still an open question [21], but this is a prerequisite for smart(er) smartphone recycling, which is a significant component of smarter E-Waste management.

The remainder of the paper is organized as follows. First, we further elaborate on our motivation and challenges to make AI an enabler to CE in terms of E-Waste Management, we present the state of the art of automated waste management, and to narrow our focus on smartphone recycling. Second, we present a TL method to classify smartphones based on feature extraction. Third, our implementation of the TL is described in detail, followed by demonstrating our experimental results and discussion of optimizing the classification performance. Finally, we draw our conclusion and future work.

1.2   State of the Art of Automated Waste Management and Smartphone Recycling

Waste Management

Traditional waste recycling has many drawbacks: It uses intense manual labor leading to high operation costs, and workers are exposed to these harmful substances through inhalation, skin contact, or ingestion [22]. Moreover, many industrial and household appliances contain hazardous toxic materials like mercury that damages the human brain.

Digital technologies could enhance waste management. It could do so not only the end-of-life-phase of products but it could also extend their life-time and enhance their product-life-cycle. To overcome these barriers and to gain CE benefits, many waste management companies now understand the increasing need for smart Waste Management Systems (WMS) and the automated disassembly of products to maintain sustainability or stimulate eco-design products. Digital solutions are increasingly used to meet the requirements of processing massive waste streams, e.g. identifying waste container loads, tracking vehicle routes, etc. Real-time processing of a large volume of data with the minimum human intervention will certainly support industrial decision-making. Applying AI, including deep learning techniques, will enable building smart WMS. This includes but is not limited to; E-Waste collection, recognizing waste patterns, sorting and evaluating the material status, and estimating the behaviors of waste generators, thereafter to support CE. All in all, we think that AI-enhanced E-Waste Management will contribute to the development of CSC.

Smartphones Recycling

Smartphones are a specific type of E-Waste and there is also potential, but also a need for further research on smart E-Waste management in this area. This is indicated by the fact that the above-mentioned challenges drive leading smartphone manufacturers (Apple, Samsung, and Huawei) to take further measures to adopt a closed-loop system and assess design sustainability, hence to develop and implement CE strategies.

Apple developed two disassembly robots, Liam, followed by Daisy, as a closed-loop supply chain. The company announced that Daisy could recover all the materials like Gold and REE used to manufacture its smartphones [35]. Apple claimed that Daisy can disassemble 15 different iPhone models at 200 devices per hour, which is more efficient than any traditional recycling. They assemble devices by breaking down and separating components to recover materials from iPhones. Daisy can disassemble 2 million devices per year and recycle them automatically.

Samsung announced that the Re+ program has its sustainable promise to support CE. According to [36], the company collected 3.55 million tons of end-of-life products between 2009 and 2018 through this program. It stated that the material compositions of smartphones are: plastic, aluminium, steel, copper, cobalt (the primary resource used in batteries), and gold and other materials, with the percentage of 35.1%, 20.2%, 10.6%, 10.0%, 8.6%, 15.5% respectively. Their new vision is to allow the company to design the devices to be easy to repair, disassemble, and recycle, which will expand the life span of products and improve durability.

Huawei also takes part in supporting CE through its Green Action program. Its service centers took back almost 60 tons of spare parts every month in 2019 and involved its customers in a credit-based recycling program [37]. Furthermore, hundreds of thousands of smartphone batteries were replaced each month of 2019 through the battery replacement program at a fixed price, and they improve their maintenance quality through discounted repair programs and even the EMUI 10.1 system that improves the file fragmentation to prevent phones from freezing up for 18 months. Eventually, the customers can use the product longer with fewer resources in the long term.

These companies can make products from recycled or renewed materials only by using their own product design knowledge as a core prerequisite of recycling. It is worth mentioning that modular phones like ARA by Google, G5 by LG, the Dutch FairPhone, or the German ShiftPhone are examples of modular smartphones. They are considered as best-practice in sustainable design and durability. These phones are easily disassembled, contain less hazardous substances, long time warranty (mostly five years) as well a transparent cost-breakdown [38]. Unfortunately, they fail to take a big market share because of their high costs in relation to lower-technical feasibility compared with conventional smartphones.

2   Method: Transfer Learning Approach - Extraction of Information Based on Visual Features

While describing the potentials of AI for smart E-Waste Management is easy, the development of the respective solutions is a rather sophisticated task. Concerning the technical challenges that face AI solutions, building an entire Neural Network (NN) is a challenge even to AI experts. Therefore, rather than reinventing the wheel, we used AlexNet [24] as a pre-trained model on a large-scale dataset, fine-tuned the model on a new, relatively small training-set of smartphone images, and transferred the learned characteristics to classify smartphones.

Challenges for smartphone classification emerge as their designs look similar recently in terms of shape and size, especially when keypads, big antennas, buttons, screen flips, and slides are abdicated. Instead, big touchscreens, all-glass front, multi-cameras, and adjusted size to fit in hands became the typical design, in order to satisfy users' preferences.

The extraction of information based on visual features is often solved based on NN [39]. Convolutional Neural Networks (CNN) application has significant success in object recognition and classification [40]. Therefore, our method is designed to extract information based on visual features.

2.1 Transfer Learning Method

It is labor-intensive to train NN from scratch because a huge data set is needed. Alternatively, an approach like TL could help to solve classification problems, e.g. different smartphone models. Bear in mind that TL is considered as a supplement but not a replacement to learning techniques. To successfully implement TL, why, how, and when to transfer should be clear beforehand.

Why Transfer Learning

In AI, new knowledge could be obtained by starting from scratch, but it needs a tremendous amount of training data. The TL technique has verified its efficacy against the scratch method's training to tackle this problem. TL is a relatively new topic in the AI domain. It is used when the source and target datasets have different features, and it works efficiently when the target dataset has a small amount of data. The main concept is to reuse specific parts of source samples into target samples to improve the attained learning in a new task. Thus, our method is based on extracting features using a TL approach that seeks good feature representation in the source and leads to better smartphone classification accuracy and less error. Later in the implementation, we will test the advantages of TL.

How to Transfer and Why AlexNet is Used?

Image classification is one domain area in the field of deep learning [15]. Using TL techniques (Fine-tuning AlexNet, specifically) have impressive success in many fields that underpin modern AI-enabled technology, to name but a few; biometrics [25], medical images [26], fault diagnosis in the industry [27], natural language processing [28]. However, smartphone classification received less attention.

Performing TL means choosing a pre-trained model that leverages the required task as a starting point and then fine-tune it to achieve the desired results. AlexNet has been used intensively in many applications as a leading model that uses TL for the following reasons:

- First, it is considered a deep NN because it has many hidden layers of non-linear feature extractors, as we will describe them further in the network structure section.
- Second, it outperformed the other Non-deep learning method in the ImageNet Large Scale Visual Recognition Challenge (ILSVRC) in 2012 [26].

- Third, it has a high-performance trade-off between accuracy and speed, thanks to Rectified Linear Units (ReLU) that accelerates the convergence of the NN than using saturation function like Tanh or Sigmoid [41].

Therefore, we used AlexNet in our approach, and we will describe the architecture in Sect. 3.1.

When to Transfer?

Even though TL has superior benefits, it is not merely a plug-and-play model. To decide what features are maintained in the network is an open challenge. The pre-trained model should be well understood before proceeding with any modifications.

3   Implementation

3.1   Classifying Smartphones

In the implementation, we pass the training data to the network, and setting the options of the training algorithm; then, we will train the network and optimize the performance. Figure 2, shows the system flowchart of the total implementation. The computing environment was Matlab since it has a suitable deep learning toolbox, which allows us to comprehensively customize solutions by creating, editing, visualizing, and analyzing the CNN, on a core i5 Intel laptop with 16 GB RAM. An Allied GigE camera is used for real-time testing.

We used the TL concept to classify 14 models of smartphones from different brands. We start by building our dataset; then, we fine-tune the traditional AlexNet structure to fit with our target output. Next, we set the training options to trigger the early stop. After training the network, we monitor the performance, and we suggest to perform controlling the error rate and data augmentation to enhance the generalization capabilities. A technical description of the procedure is delivered in the following section.

Network Architecture

In this paper, we suggest a fine-tuning of the pre-trained model of AlexNet. First, the standard AlexNet is analyzed here. It has eight learned layers, as follows:

- Five convolutional layers (conv1–conv5), which are basically used to extract features. The information extracted from (conv1–conv3) represents the generic features with different colors, texture, and intensity. Whereas, the next layers (conv4–conv5) extract the more refined features (or local patterns) like those with different sizes and shapes.
- Three pooling layers, usually to downsample the features to implement faster computation.
- Three Fully Connected (FC) layers: (FC6–FC7) who are mainly used for features that are more task-specific and prevent the model from overfitting while training, (FC8) combines the previous features to present the output 1000 labels.

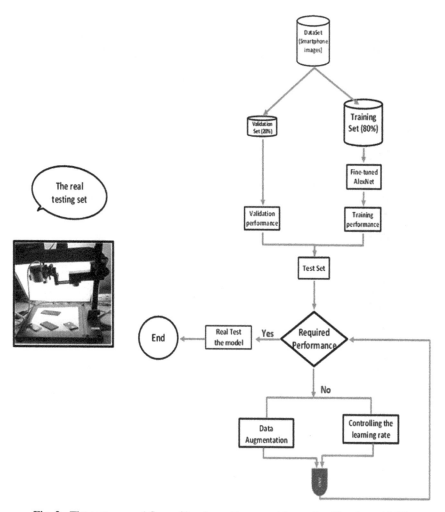

Fig. 2. The system workflow of implementing smartphone classification with TL

AlexNet is a large CNN that has successfully classified 1.2 million images with 1000 object labels, so this abundant data is rich with a wide variety of feature representations. In the original pre-trained AlexNet architecture, the last third layer is configured to map the extracted features from the previous layers to 1000 output classes; then, the softmax layer acts as a normalization step to turn the raw values of the 1000 classes into a probability distribution of the image belongs to that class; thus, the sum of all elements in this vector is equal to 1. Finally, the last layer takes the most probability and returns the most likely class as a network output. We propose a network modification by freezing

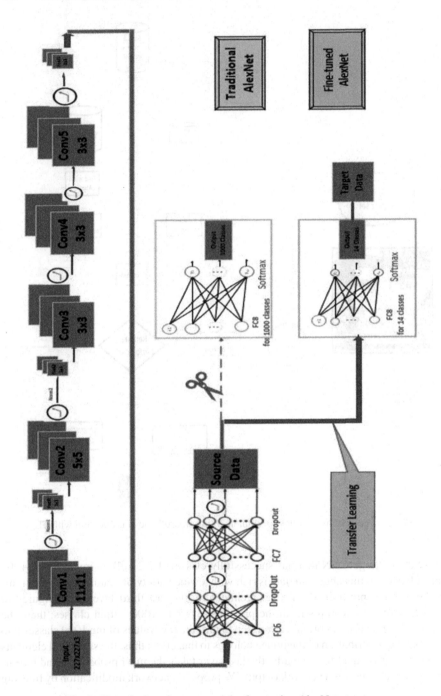

Fig. 3. Transfer learning approach by fine-tuning AlexNet structure

the last three layers, replace them with (an FC layer, a softmax layer, a classification output layer) to suit the new training-set, then retrain them, as illustrated in Fig. 3.

Training Algorithm

We control the behavior of the training algorithms to gain better training performance. We split the dataset as 80% (320 images) for the training-set and 20% (80 images) for the validation. We used the Stochastic Gradient Descent with Momentum (SGDM) method as a training algorithm because it converges faster towards lower minima, and it oscillates less. We set the mini-batch size to 20 and we found that the accuracy and loss factor stabilize when the max epoch is equal to 20, where in each iteration one mini-batch is trained and the number of epochs represents the number of times that the network sees the entire dataset. We control the early stop when the validation error no more improves to set a trade-off between the training time and accuracy. Following the training, we evaluate the network performance using the validation-set during training. It is an important step to check overfitting.

3.2 Training the Network

After preparing the three previous components, we are ready to train our network. We demonstrate different metrics to evaluate the classification efficiency; accuracy, and loss function. Besides that, the confusion matrix of validation testing and real-time testing will be conducted later to test the model performance. The accuracy represents the percentage of the correctly classified trained images during an iteration to the number of the entire dataset, which calculates the Root-Mean-Squared-Error (RMSE) in the model gradients function. The error between the predictions and the true known class is called the loss function. It defines the extent to which the actual outputs are correctly predicted; practically, it represents the mini-batch loss. In the NN we aim to minimize the loss function (see Fig. 4).

4 Results and Discussion

After training the network, we found that the validation accuracy is equal to 86.4%, and it is stabilizing to be less than the training accuracy, which is not adequate. We recommend the following steps to modify some training options to gain a better performance.

4.1 Controlling the Learning Rate

Choosing the learning rate is one of the challenging tasks in learning a CNN. In our method, we schedule the learning rate by reducing updating the weights by slowing down the learning rate initially to maintain the useful features, but then we speed up the learning features. We set the dropout factor as 0.5 to obtain maximum regularization [42]. We found that the validation accuracy is 88.7%, but the model is underfitting (Fig. 5).

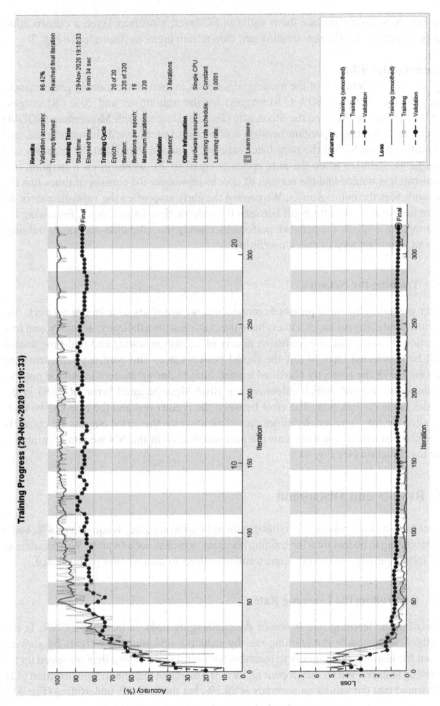

Fig. 4. The network performance before improvement

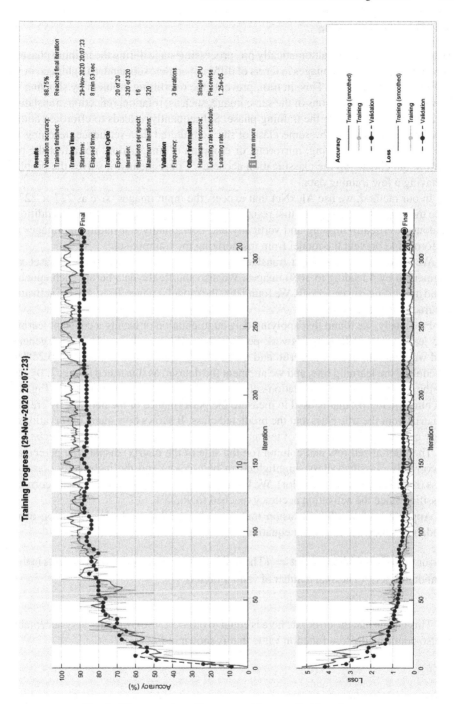

Fig. 5. The network performance with controlled learning rate

4.2 Data Augmentation

Data augmentation is an automatically pre-processing stage during the training phase, to cope with the imperfect images in terms of different angles, substandard lightings, or not well-cropped or framed. This, in turn, prevents the overfitting problem by showing the network, different variations of the same image, such as; rotation, reflection, translation, shear, and scaling during the training phase. Subsequently, it leads to effortless adding multiple viewpoints of the same class of the non-altered data-set hence, teaching the network that minor shifting, mirroring, or cropping of images does not affect the prediction, but enhancing the classification accuracy. Consequently, it solves the problem of having a few training data.

In our method, we use AlexNet that expects the input images' size as $227 \times 227 \times 3$, so the training-set should be first resized to feed the first layer. Besides that, additional randomly vertically flipping and vertically and horizontally translating the images are performed to prevent the model from memorizing the training-set.

We perform reflection and translation on the X and Y axis, so our dataset was augmented by 4 leading to 1680 images. We also shuffle the data before each epoch to avoid discarding it every epoch. We found that the model is generalized, but the activation accuracy is 86.25% (Fig. 6).

Previously, we found that applying data augmentation or having a constant learning rate leads to non-adequate network performance. We found that the model generalized well without over or underfit, and the accuracy is enhanced to become 96.25% by scheduling the learning rate, and we augment the dataset, as illustrated in Fig. 7. By testing the (80 images) in the validation-set, a confusion matrix is demonstrated in Fig. 8. It is a numeric matrix that is used to measure the performance of the network by creating a matrix from the true class and the predicted class. It shows how many observations in every cell, where the diagonal of the matrix shows the correctly classified objects.

The normalized row and column (on the side of the matrix) display the percentage of correctly classified class (highlighted in blue color) and the incorrectly classified class (highlighted in orange color). We found that most of the smartphones are correctly classified since the activation accuracy reached to 96.25%.

Apparently, from the confusion matrix we can calculate the loss function of the validation-set, as the following equation:

Error rate of the ValidationSet = (The number of incorrectly classified objects in the validationSet)/(The total number of validationSet)

$$(1)$$

This means that the error rate here is equal to 0.0375 (3/80), which is very acceptable. It also confirms the loss function value that is shown in Fig. 7.

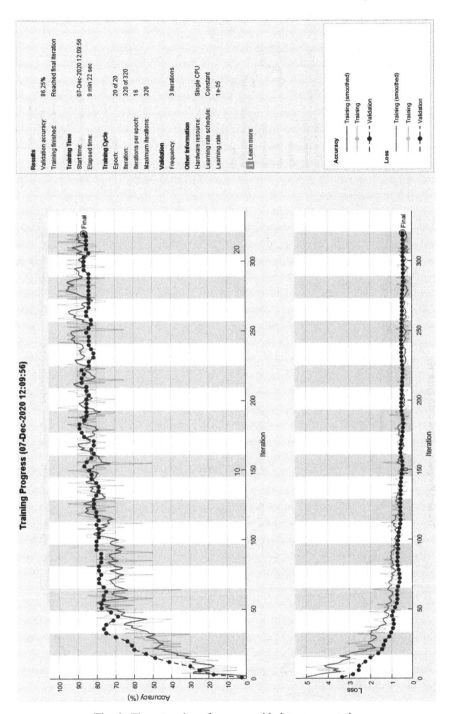

Fig. 6. The network performance with data augmentation

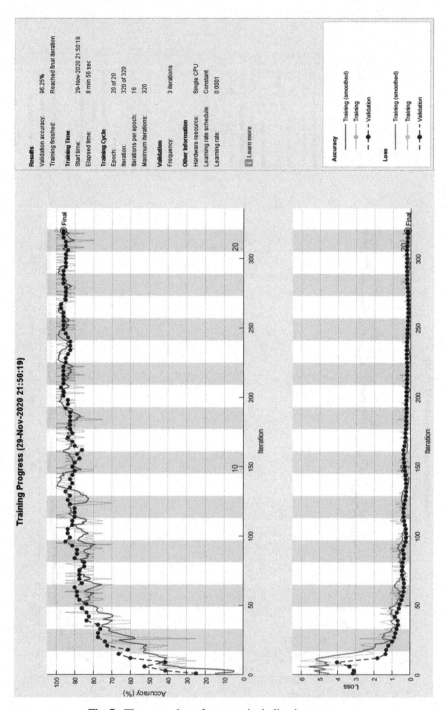

Fig. 7. The network performance including improvements

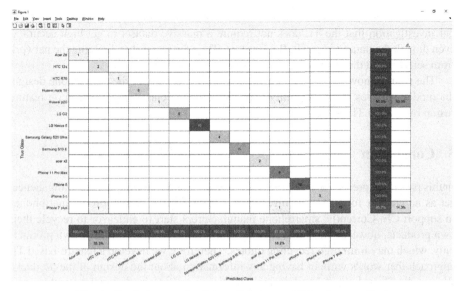

Fig. 8. Confusion matrix of the validation set (Color figure online)

4.3 Real-Time Smartphone Classification

By using the real-testing set, illustrated in Fig. 2, we conducted a real-time smartphone classification, by using the Allied GigE Camera and four examples of smartphone models. Figure 9, shows that a high testing accuracy has been achieved based on visual features only, with our proposed TL approach.

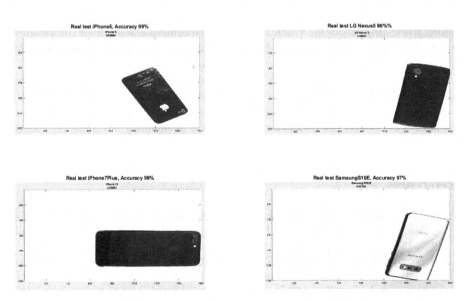

Fig. 9. Real testing on four smartphone models

We found that the model leads to considerable results. Furthermore, this confirmed our investigation that the TL does not require a massive dataset to get high accuracy, even though the dataset is small. Besides that, TL is far easier than building the network from scratch, and the training time is greatly reduced.

The results show that despite having no information about the smartphone design, the model achieves good feasibility of the smartphone classification based on feature fusion by using a TL technique.

5 Conclusion

In this paper, we present how AI could support automated smartphone recycling, hence, act as an enabler for CSC. We investigate a feature-based extraction of smartphones to support CE. Currently, smartphone manufacturers start to endeavor to recycle their own products, however, their recycling programs are designed to fit their own products only, which may limit high recycling quotes. Therefore, we develop a feature-based TL approach that works without having any information about the design of the products. We use the TL technique, by choosing AlexNet as a pre-trained model, to perform our test, and to gain the advantages of TL techniques, as easier and faster way than training the NN from scratch, which we prove in our results.

In consequence, we conclude that AI and CE could conjointly be applied to achieve smart sustainability successfully. As we find that AI can help in transforming the E-Waste management infrastructure into a closed-loop system, we conclude that AI can pave the way towards CSC.

However, further research is needed. Smartphone recognition still faces more challenges even with state-of-the-art image classification methods, especially for the recent smartphone models due to the high similarity in visual characteristics.

Future research will address these shortcomings. We suggest conducting non-destructive testing outside the visible light to detect the internal smartphone components, e.g. the battery, camera, ID sensors, that helps in material recognition, by using a fusion of sensors in different wavelengths to support automated recycling, hence the CE.

Last but not least, we argue that a fully-sustainable system would require rethinking and changing behaviors of customers and smartphone manufacturers, respectively. This would include, for instance, avoiding the replacement of smartphones every couple of years unless they need maintenance and thinking in maintaining raw materials needed by eco-design of future products.

References

1. Albino, V., Berardi, U., Dangelico, R.M.: Smart cities: definitions, dimensions, performance, and initiatives. J. Urban Technol. **22**(1), 3–21 (2015). https://doi.org/10.1080/10630732.2014. 942092
2. de Jong, M., Joss, S., Schraven, D., Zhan, C., Weijnen, M.: Sustainable–smart–resilient–low carbon–eco–knowledge cities; making sense of a multitude of concepts promoting sustainable urbanization. J. Clean. Prod. **109**, 25–38 (2015). https://doi.org/10.1016/j.jclepro.2015.02.004

3. Dameri, R.P. (ed.): Smart City Implementation: Creating Economic and Public Value in Innovative Urban Systems. Springer, Cham (2017). https://dx.doi.org/10.1007/978-3-319-45766-6
4. Prendeville, S., Cherim, E., Bocken, N.: Circular cities: mapping six cities in transition. Environ. Innov. Soc. Transit. **26**, 171–194 (2017). https://doi.org/10.1016/j.eist.2017.03.002
5. Antikainen, M., Uusitalo, T., Kivikytö-Reponen, P.: Digitalisation as an enabler of circular economy. Procedia CIRP **73**, 45–49 (2018). https://doi.org/10.1016/j.procir.2018.04.027
6. Ritzén, S., Sandström, G.Ö.: Barriers to the circular economy – integration of perspectives and domains. Procedia CIRP **64**, 7–12 (2017). https://doi.org/10.1016/j.procir.2017.03.005
7. Kirchherr, J., Reike, D., Hekkert, M.: Conceptualizing the circular economy: an analysis of 114 definitions. Resour. Conserv. Recycl. **127**, 221–232 (2017). https://doi.org/10.1016/j.resconrec.2017.09.005
8. Thalesgroup: Facial recognition in 2020 (7 trends to watch). https://www.thalesgroup.com/en/markets/digital-identity-and-security/government/biometrics/facial-recognition. Accessed 04 Oct 2020
9. Hommel, S., Grimm, M.A., Malysiak, D., Handmann, U.: APFel - fast multi camera people tracking at airports, based on decentralized video indexing. Science 2 - Safety and Security, Homeland Security UG, Hemer, Germany, vol. 2, pp. 48–55 (2014)
10. Zengeler, N., et al.: Person tracking in heavy industry environments with camera images. In: 10th EAI International Conference on Sensor Systems and Software, Braga, Portugal, pp. 324–336 (2020)
11. Schreurs, M.A., Steuwer, S.D.: Autonomous Driving - Political, Legal, Social, and Sustainability Dimensions. Springer, Heidelberg (2015). https://doi.org/10.1007/978-3-662-45854-9_8
12. Mallozzi, P., Pelliccione, P., Knauss, A., Berger, C., Mohammadiha, N.: Autonomous vehicles: state of the art, future trends, and challenges. In: Dajsuren, Y., van den Brand, M. (eds.) Automotive Systems and Software Engineering, pp. 347–367. Springer, Cham (2019)
13. Handmann, U., Kalinke, T., Tzomakas, C., Werner, M., Seelen, W.V.: An image processing system for driver assistance. Image Vis. Comput. **18**(5), 367–376 (2000). https://doi.org/10.1016/S0262-8856(99)00032-3
14. Rabie, A., Handmann, U.: NFC-based person-specific assisting system in home environment. In: Proceeding of the 11th World Congress on Intelligent Control and Automation. IEEE (2014)
15. Kopinski, T., Sachara, F., Handmann, U.: A deep learning approach to mid-air gesture interaction for mobile devices from time-of-flight data. In: Proceedings of the 13th International Conference on Mobile and Ubiquitous Systems: Computing, Networking and Services - MOBIQUITOUS 2016, pp. 1–9. ACM Press, New York (2016)
16. Nieß, C., Fey, J., Schwahlen, D., Reimann, M., Handmann, U.: Applying step heating thermography to wind turbine rotor blades as a non-destructive testing method, Telford, UK (2017)
17. Fey, J., Djahan, C., Mpouma, T.A., Neh-Awah, J., Handmann, U.: Active thermographic structural feature inspection of wind-turbine rotor. In: 2017 Far East NDT New Technology & Application Forum (FENDT). IEEE (2017)
18. ITU: End of life management for ICT equipment (2012). https://www.itu.int/dms_pub/itu-t/oth/4B/04/T4B0400000B0013PDFE.pdf
19. Baldé, C.P., Forti, V., Gray, V., Kuehr, R., Stegmann, P.: The global e-waste monitor 2017: quantities, flows, and resources. United Nations University (UNU); International Telecommunication Union (ITU); International Solid Waste Association (ISWA), Bonn/Geneva/Vienna. Accessed 14 Dec 2017

20. Gurita, N., Fröhling, M., Bongaerts, J.: Assessing potentials for mobile/smartphone reuse/remanufacture and recycling in Germany for a closed loop of secondary precious and critical metals. J. Remanuf. **8**(1–2), 1–22 (2018). https://doi.org/10.1007/s13243-018-0042-1

21. Pagoropoulos, A., Pigosso, D.C.A., McAloone, T.C.: The emergent role of digital technologies in the circular economy: a review. Procedia CIRP **64**, 19–24 (2017). https://doi.org/10.1016/j.procir.2017.02.047

22. Julander, A., et al.: Formal recycling of e-waste leads to increased exposure to toxic metals: an occupational exposure study from Sweden. Environ Int. **73**, 243–251 (2014). https://doi.org/10.1016/j.envint.2014.07.006

23. Ellen MacArthur Foundation (EMF) and Google: Artificial intelligence and the circular economy (July 2020). https://www.ellenmacarthurfoundation.org/publications/artificial-intelligence-and-the-circular-economy. Accessed 17 July 2020

24. Krizhevsky, A., Sutskever, I., Hinton, G.E.: ImageNet classification with deep convolutional neural networks. Commun. ACM **60**, 84–90 (2017). https://doi.org/10.1145/3065386

25. Almisreb, A.A., Jamil, N., Din, N.M.: Utilizing AlexNet deep transfer learning for ear recognition. In: 2018 Fourth International Conference on Information Retrieval and Knowledge Management (CAMP), Kota Kinabalu, Malaysia, pp. 1–5 (2018)

26. Shin, H.-C., et al.: Deep convolutional neural networks for computer-aided detection: CNN architectures, dataset characteristics and transfer learning. IEEE Trans. Med. Imaging **35**(5), 1285–1298 (2016). https://doi.org/10.1109/TMI.2016.2528162

27. Shi, X., Cheng, Y., Zhang, B., Zhang, H.: Intelligent fault diagnosis of bearings based on feature model and Alexnet neural network. In: 2020 IEEE International Conference on Prognostics and Health Management (ICPHM), Detroit, MI, USA, pp. 1–6 (2020)

28. Almodfer, R., Xiong, S., Mudhsh, M., Duan, P.: Enhancing AlexNet for Arabic handwritten words recognition using incremental dropout. In: 2017 IEEE 29th International Conference on Tools with Artificial Intelligence (ICTAI), Boston, MA, pp. 663–669 (2017)

29. Uçar, E., Le Dain, M.-A., Joly, I.: Digital technologies in circular economy transition: evidence from case studies. Procedia CIRP **90**, 133–136 (2020). https://doi.org/10.1016/j.procir.2020.01.058

30. Barletta, I., Johansson, B., Cullbrand, K., Bjorkman, M., Reimers, J.: Fostering sustainable electronic waste management through intelligent sorting equipment. In: 2015 IEEE International Conference on Automation Science and Engineering (CASE), Gothenburg, Sweden, pp. 459–461 (2015)

31. AMP Robotics: AMP Neuron—AMP Robotics. https://www.amprobotics.com/amp-neuron. Accessed 1 Oct 2020

32. Nygaard, A.: Specific investments in closed loop-technology instead of "Blood Metals" (2019)

33. EuChemS: Element Scarcity - EuChemS Periodic Table - EuChemS. https://www.econstor.eu/bitstream/10419/195114/1/103236680X.pdf. Accessed 3 Oct 2020

34. YaleNews: For metals of the smartphone age, no Plan B. https://news.yale.edu/2013/12/02/metals-smartphone-age-no-plan-b. Accessed 1 Oct 2020

35. Apple Newsroom: Apple expands global recycling programs. https://www.apple.com/newsroom/2019/04/apple-expands-global-recycling-programs/. Accessed 1 Oct 2020

36. Samsung levant: Resource Efficiency | Environment | Sustainability | Samsung LEVANT. https://www.samsung.com/levant/aboutsamsung/sustainability/environment/resource-efficiency/. Accessed 1 Oct 2020

37. Huawei: Green Pipe - Huawei Sustainability. https://www.huawei.com/en/sustainability/environment-protect/circular-economy. Accessed 1 Oct 2020

38. Proske, M., Schischke, K., Sommer, P., Trinks, T., Nissen, N.F., Lang, K.-D.: Experts view on the sustainability of the Fairphone 2. In: 2016 Electronics Goes Green 2016+ (EGG), Berlin, pp. 1–7 (September 2016)

39. Handmann, U., Lorenz, G., Schnitger, T., von Seelen, W.: Fusion of different sensors and algorithms for segmentation. In: IEEE International Conference on Intelligent Vehicles 1998, Stuttgart, Germany (1998)
40. Sachara, F., Kopinski, T., Gepperth, A., Handmann, U.: Free-hand gesture recognition with 3D-CNNs for in-car infotainment control in real-time. In: 2017 IEEE 20th International Conference on Intelligent Transportation Systems (ITSC): Free-hand Gesture Recognition with 3D-CNNs for In-car Infotainment Control in Real-time, Yokohama, pp. 959–964 (October 2017)
41. Chatfield, K., Simonyan, K., Vedaldi, A., Zisserman, A.: Return of the devil in the details: delving deep into convolutional nets (2014). https://arxiv.org/pdf/1405.3531
42. Kingma, D.P., Salimans, T., Welling, M.: Variational dropout and the local reparameterization trick (2015). https://arxiv.org/pdf/1506.02557
43. Wiegand, S., Igel, C., Handmann, U.: Evolutionary optimization of neural networks for face detection. In: 12th European Symposium on Artificial Neural Networks, ESANN 2004, Bruges, Belgium, Proceedings, pp. 139–144 (2004)
44. Wiegand, S., Igel, C., Handmann, U.: Evolutionary multi-objective optimization of neural networks for face detection. Int. J. Comput. Intell. Appl. 4(3), 237–253 (2004)

Are Neural Networks Really the Holy Grail? A Comparison of Multivariate Calibration for Low-Cost Environmental Sensors

Xinwei Fang$^{(\boxtimes)}$, Iain Bate, and David Griffin

Department of Computer Science, University of York, York, UK
{Xinwei.Fang,Iain.Bate,David.Griffin}@york.ac.uk

Abstract. Data obtained from low-cost environmental sensors can have various issues such as low precision and accuracy and incompleteness. A calibration process is often applied to address such issues. With the recent advances in artificial intelligence, we have seen an increased number of applications that starts to use an artificial neural network (ANN) to calibrate the sensors, and their results are promising. In this work, we used a six-months worth of real hourly data to demonstrate that the ANN may not always be the best choice of a calibration method. Our evaluation compares an ANN-based method with a simple regression-based method in various aspects. The result shows that the ANN-based method does not consistently outperform the regression-based method. More interestingly, in the comparison, our results suggest that the performance of a calibration can be more sensitive to some of the factors (e.g. training and testing data, model parameters) than the use of different calibration methods. Even though the results may not be generalised in other sensors or datasets, our evaluation provides evidence showing that inappropriate use of a calibration method can compromise the calibration result, and the use of the ANN will not magically solve that problem.

Keywords: Low-cost sensors · Sensor calibration

1 Introduction

Low-cost environmental sensors have been widely used in monitoring of urban environment as they can provide much better spatial and temporal resolutions than the regulatory monitoring instruments [3,4,9,15]. However, the low-cost sensors are prone to temporary failure and are sensitive to the environmental interference, which results in the obtained data being much less structural in term of size, completeness and integrity [11]. More importantly, the data quality from these low-cost sensors is often reported to be insufficient and requires pre-processing [3,13,19,24].

Sensor calibration is one of a process to improve data quality. In this paper, sensor calibration is to determine a model that transfers the data of low-cost

© ICST Institute for Computer Sciences, Social Informatics and Telecommunications Engineering 2021
Published by Springer Nature Switzerland AG 2021. All Rights Reserved
S. Paiva et al. (Eds.): SmartCity360° 2020, LNICST 372, pp. 442–461, 2021.
https://doi.org/10.1007/978-3-030-76063-2_30

sensors to minimise the difference with the data from the co-located reference instruments. According to the literature, the state-of-the-art in-field sensor calibrations often use multiple variables to calibrate a sensor, which is referred to as multivariate calibration [7–10]. Multivariate calibration means the calibration model is constructed using not only the parameter of interest but also other supporting parameters, e.g. including temperature when calibrating NO_2 [18]. The intuition is if the response of NO_2 is related to or affected by the temperature, a more accurate calibration of NO_2 can be determined if it includes the temperature and accounts for the related effects.

Multivariate calibration can be accomplished in many ways, and the two most prominent methods seen in current literature are a simple regression-based method and and artificial neural networks (ANNs) based method [7,9,10,12,19]. With the recent advance in machine learning, we have seen an increased number of applications that starts to use an ANN-based method to calibrate the sensors, and their results are promising. This makes us wonder if the ANN-based methods can also work better on the *imperfect* data (e.g. the small size, noisy data) and whether the ANN-based method should always be the first choice when comes to the selection of a calibration method.

This paper presents a systematic comparison of those two calibration techniques (i.e. a regression-based method and an ANN-based method) using a real dataset, and focuses on determining how their calibration results can be affected under various conditions. This work not only compares the calibration accuracy but also analyses the sensitivity of each method to different settings of training and testing dataset. This gives us an evidence and insight to reason weather the ANN-based method is really the holy grail in the calibration of low-cost sensors.

Main contribution: Even though a few existing works have demonstrated the comparison of the calibration methods for calibrating low-cost sensors, to the best of our knowledge, this paper is the first work that focus on the sensitivity of the calibration methods with respect to various scenarios (e.g. *imperfect* data). With the main contribution, the following additional contributions are made:

- **Reality:** Real hourly data from 6-month worth of deployment was used to simulate the calibration of sensors for a short deployment.
- **Practicality:** The selection of model parameters are demonstrated to show the variability of the calibration process, which are often ignored in the existing comparison.
- **Sensitivity:** Both models are trained and tested under different settings to gain an in-depth knowledge on the sensitivity of the methods.

After the review of the existing comparison of multivariate calibrations in Sects. 2, 3 explains how the calibration models can be constructed using both approaches and what the model parameters need to be determined; Sect. 4 illustrates the determination of the model parameters for both approaches; Sects. 5, 6, and 7 compare the approaches in conditions of model generation, varying training and testing dataset and varying data characteristic respectively. Section 8 concludes the paper.

2   Related Work

We have seen an increasing number of sensor calibration starts to use an ANN-based method to calibrate a low-cost sensor [19,24]. However, to the best of our knowledge, a little work has done to demonstrate a systematic comparison of different calibration methods, especially when calibrated data are *imperfect*.

A prominent existing comparison, such as [24], is limited to comparing the calibration result in terms of calibration accuracy, which is often represented as the averaged error between the model predictions and the reference, e.g. root-mean-squared error (RMSE) or mean-absolute error (MAE). Since two identical averaged errors may represent different error distributions, using an averaged error as the only metric for the comparison would not help us to gain an insight of the performance. Further, while a focus on aggregate measures allows us to characterise the mean error of different methods, such metrics can be skewed by outliers and hence are insufficient to determine which method is most likely to give the best results.

To solve that issue, authors in [7,10] provided a more detailed comparison for multivariate calibration approaches. In their work, the approaches were cross-compared not only for the calibration accuracy (determined by the mean absolute error) but also for the capability of dealing with different training scenarios. In work [10], the calibration result was compared by varying a different number of training and testing samples with more than 40000 instances in total. However, it is noted that the variation of the training and testing samples were divided by a cut-off value. Since a cut-off value can change the size of both the training and testing dataset, it difficult to determine which changes are responsible for the variation of the result.

Devito et al. [7] analysed how the calibration accuracy was affected by using different model parameters. For example, Devito et al. compared the calibration accuracy by varying the certain model parameters in the ANN network. In that case, Devito et al. would have to assume that the model parameters of the ANN are independent or partially dependent. However, this assumption does not hold in our evaluation as demonstrated in Sect. 4.3.

3   Determine the Calibration Models

Sensor calibration is a process of finding a calibration model that minimises the difference between the model output and the reference. In this section, we demonstrate how calibration models can be constructed using both methods, and discuss what model parameters are important for each of the methods. For the demonstration, we assume that calibrating X_1 to its reference $\tilde{X}_1$ requires X_2 and X_3 as the supporting parameters. Then, we further assume that all the parameters, including the reference, have the same number of samples taken during the same time window.

3.1   Calibration Using an ANN-Based Method

A mathematical representation of an ANN can be extremely complicated, as discussed in [5]. Hence, instead of a detailed mathematical construct, we use more abstract notations of ANN's. The training process determines the calibration model. The model would provide an approximation of the calibrated $\tilde{X}_1$ given the uncalibrated inputs, X_1, X_2 and X_3. According to the literature, there are a number of model parameters are important for the ANN-based method [22], which are summarised in Table 1.

Table 1. Model parameters to be needed for an ANN-based method

Model parameters	Examples
Activation function	Sigmoid, ReLU [21], SeLU [17], etc.
Number of neurons	1 to $+\infty$
Number of layers	1 to $+\infty$
Type of neurons	Dense, LSTM, etc.
Batch size	1 to the total number of training samples
Epoch	1 to $+\infty$
Loss function	Mean squared error, mean absolute error, etc.
Optimisation method	Gradient descent, Adam, etc.

3.2   Calibration Using a Regression-Based Method

In contrast to the ANN-based method, a regression-based method is easier to be presented mathematically, and it does not require many pre-determined parameters [12,19]. For example, a linear calibration model to calibrate X_1 using the corresponding coefficients β_i can be constructed based on Eq. 1.

$$\tilde{X}_1(i) = \beta_0 + \beta_1 \cdot X_1(i) + \beta_2 \cdot X_2(i) + ... + \beta_n \cdot X_n(i) + \varepsilon(i) \tag{1}$$

In Eq. 1, ε stands for the error term and the i indicates that the measurements are taken from the same time frame. $\tilde{X}_1$ is the reference of X_1; X_2 to X_n are the supporting parameters of the calibration. The calibration model is then to determine the coefficient β based on the Eq. 2.

$$\mathcal{E} = minimise \sum_{i=1}^{N} \varepsilon(i)^2 \tag{2}$$

Note that the example in Eq. 1 uses a linear combination of first order terms to describe the relationship between the inputs variables and output (i.e. linear). If a more complex non-linear relationship needs to be utilised in the model, a pre-determination of the model is required (e.g. including non-linear terms or applying a non-linear transformation). Therefore, we consider the relationship between input variables and output as the only model parameter for the regression based method.

4   Determining the Model Parameters

In this section, we demonstrate the determination of the model parameters, and discuss the practical issues encountered during the process. Firstly, we present the data and programming environment used for this experiment. Then, we demonstrate the process for both methods respectively.

4.1   Data and Programming Environment

An ELM unit, a product from Perkin Elmer [23], is used as low-cost sensor in this work. The unit was situated at York, UK, next to a busy junction. It measures multiple parameters: nitrogen dioxide (NO_2), ozone (O_3), nitrogen oxide (NO), temperature (T), humidity (H). The ELM unit was co-located with a regulatory monitoring instrument from [6], and the hourly NO_2 data from this instrument was used as the reference for the sensor calibration in this work. Due to restrictions on reporting the data, we are unable to provide information on the exact quantities, including units, but all data are comparable.

The collected data is pre-processed in advance, which aggregates the ELM data into the same temporal resolution as the reference (hourly) and excludes data gaps in the averaged data. The process ensures the consistent samples in the dataset and it is required by the method. After the process, the dataset has 4000 samples with a temporal resolution of one hour.

The regression based method was programmed in Matlab, and the ANN-based method was programmed in Python using *Keras* library [16] and TensorFlow [26].

For the selection of model parameters, the entire dataset was divided sequentially into two equally sized partitions. The first 2000 samples are used as training (i.e. the first half of sensor's operative time span) and the rest of the samples are used as testing. This is to simulate the situation where only 2000 samples were available (i.e. a short development with 3-month worth of data) for training the model. Furthermore, as calibrating NO_2 is often reported to be problematic and would require multivariate calibration to compensate [18,20,24], the calibration of NO_2 is used as an example for this paper.

4.2   Model Parameters for a Regression Based Method

Most of the existing works for the regression based method utilise the linear relationship to construct the calibration model [12,19]. This experiment is to determine whether using a more complex relationship (e.g. non-linear) would improve the calibration accuracy. The complex relationship is referred to as adding higher order terms into the existing linear model.

For the experiment, the calibration errors from using different models are illustrated in Fig. 1. The calibration error is defined as the difference between the model output (y) and the reference (Y), given by Eq. 3. It is noted that i indicates the number of samples.

$$error(i) = Y(i) - y(i) \tag{3}$$

In the figure, the number in the X-axis differentiate calibration models. The first model uses a linear combination of first order terms, which is identical to Eq. 1, and expressed as $f(NO_2, O_3, NO, T, H)$. The following models are constructed by gradually including a second order term into the existing model as well as their interactions [14]. We express the second model as $f(NO_2, O_3, NO, T, H, (NO_2)^2)$ and the last model as $f(NO_2, O_3, NO, T, H, (NO_2)^2, (O_3)^2, (NO)^2, (T)^2, (H)^2)$. The experiment tests all the possible combinations, i.e. $\binom{0}{5} + \binom{1}{5} + \binom{2}{5} + \binom{3}{5} + \binom{4}{5} + \binom{5}{5}$, which have 32 models in total. In the figure, X-axis (1) indicates the linear model; whereas X-axis (2) to (32) indicates non-linear model in which one or more higher order terms were introduced.

Figure 1 shows that utilising a more complex relationship in the calibration model does not appear to improve the calibration result. Therefore, a linear relationship is used for the model of the regression based method.

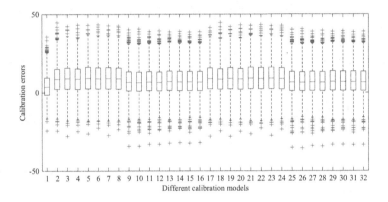

Fig. 1. The error distributions for different model settings

4.3   Model Parameters for an ANN-Based Method

It is noted that the determination of the model parameters for an ANN-based method, which is also known as hyperparameter optimisation [2], is still an open challenge, and the trial by error is currently the best practice for this purpose [1]. Since the parameters often need to be selected from a large parameter space, it would be impractical to test all possible combinations. Therefore, the selection of the parameters in this paper is tested in a certain range only, for which the decision is made based on either existing works or expert knowledge. This also reflects the disadvantage of using ANN.

Activation function. The Sigmoid, RuLU, and SeLU are tested. It is clear that each neuron can have a different activation function. However, since it is impractical to test the combination of activation functions, the same activation function is applied to all neurons in a network setting.

Type of neurons. Dense and LSTM are tested. As above, due to the exponential cost of varying each neuron, the same type of neurons are used in all neurons in the network.

Number of neurons and layers. We vary the number of neurons in each layer as [5 20 35] and the number of layers in [1 2 3 4 5]. The same number of neurons are used in each layer. These test ranges was chosen as the similar range of the parameters was used in [7].

Batch size and epoch. We test the number of batch size in [1 6 11 16 21 26] and epoch in [1 6 11 16 21 26], which is 1 to 26 with an increment of 5, as no significant different in results can be determined with further increase of the batch and epoch sizes.

Loss function. We test the Mean Absolute Error (MAE), Poisson and Mean Squared Error (MSE) as the loss function in the experiment as they are often used as the evaluation of sensor calibrations.

Optimization method. Gradient descent, RMSprop and Adam are tested in the experiment.

In the experiment, we vary all eight model parameters. As a result, the model parameters would be selected from eight dimensional parameter space. The selection is based on the Root Mean Squared Error (RMSE) between the reference and the model output. We use determination of the loss function as example to demonstrate how the model parameter is selected.

We classify all networks into three groups with respect to the use of the loss functions. Then, we determine the percentage of the model in each group that the error in terms of RMSE is below an RMSE threshold. The RMSE threshold varies from small to large, and the process is applied to all three groups. The result would indicate the difference between the loss function. We consider the optimal parameters as the one that has the highest percentage with the lowest RMSE threshold. The result is showing in Fig. 2.

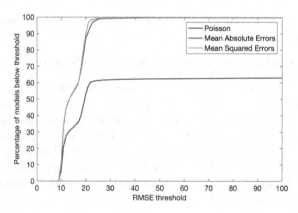

Fig. 2. Percentage of model below threshold for different loss functions

In addition, we perform a statistical test to determine the probability that one method is more likely to produce a better result than another. This is accomplished by fixing parameters of a given test apart from the parameter of interest. Once the data is gathered, a null hypothesis test [25] is conducted with the null hypothesis being that the varying the parameter between two values has no effect. If the evidence supports the alternative hypothesis, that one of the parameter values has consistently better performance, we can reject the null hypothesis for this configuration. By repeating this experiment across all possible values of other parameters, we can derive an estimate for the probability that a parameter is more likely to produce a better result; this is shown in Table 2 for the Loss function, where we can conclude Mean Squared Error has highest chance of producing the best result from the three loss functions. The result is also in-line with Fig. 2.

Table 2. Probability of dominance when varying loss function

	Mean squared error	Mean absolute error	Poisson
Mean squared error		42%	63%
Mean absolute error	37%		61%
Poisson	27%	24%	

The same process is applied to all eight parameters. We summarise the parameters used in this work in Table 3.

Table 3. The parameters used in the ANN-based method

Model parameters	Parameter used
Activation function	ReLU
Number of neurons	20
Number of layers	1
Type of neurons	LSTM
Batch size	26
Epoch	21
Loss function	MSE
Optimisation method	Adam

5   Variability of Model Generation

In this section, we want to understand how the model output would be affected by the model generation process. Hence, we train the model with identical parameters multiple times and compare their model outputs, with the only difference being the random seed used for training the ANNs.

The training and testing datasets used in this experiment are identical to the previous experiment, which have been discussed in Sect. 4.1. The RMSE of the calibrated results is shown in Fig. 3.

Figure 3-b shows the 100 model outputs obtained from the regression based method. It is clear that the regression based method provides a consistent result as long as the model settings and the use of the data are identical as the RMSE for the regression based method shows no variation over the 100 iterations. Figure 3-a presents the 100 model outputs obtained from the ANN-based method. In comparison to the regression based method, Fig. 3-a indicates that the ANN-based method is sensitive to the model generation process as the variation of the model output can be observed. While the ANN-based method does produce a slightly better RMSE, it does not produce a significant advantage.

While there is a clear variation in the RMSE of the ANN-based method, it is comparatively small when compared to the variation in the RMSE from changing the model parameters. Given this, we assume that provided the model parameters are set correctly, the variation in ANN models due to the training process is largely insignificant. Hence for the remainder of this work we will ignore the random effects of training the ANN model.

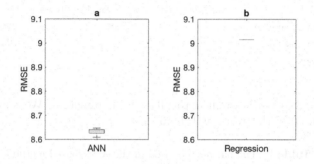

Fig. 3. Comparing the variation of RMSE over 100 repetitions

This section demonstrate that the regression based method would provide a consistent calibration result for the model generation; however, the model generation would introduce a variation in the calibration result for the ANN-based method.

6   Comparing the Model Under Different Training and Testing Scenarios

This section compares the difference between in performance of the methods using different settings of training and testing dataset. The first experiment varies the size of training dataset, and then with varying the size of testing dataset.

6.1   Varying the Training Dataset

This experiment is designed to understand how the increasing size of training dataset would affect the calibration result for both methods. In the experiment, the same dataset used previously is divided sequentially and evenly into to 10 partitions with each partition having 10% of the data and following the temporal dimension. The calibration model is determined by using the training dataset that gradually increasing the data size; and the result of the calibration is evaluated in the same testing dataset. This could help us to understand how to size of training data plays in the calibration process. The classification and the use of the training and testing dataset are illustrated in Fig. 4.

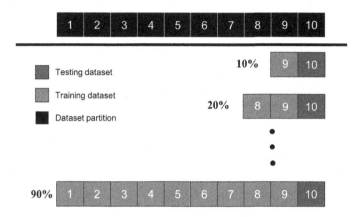

Fig. 4. Varying the training datasets

Figure 4 shows how the data is divided into ten equal partitions, numbered from (1) to (10). For the testing dataset, the last partition (10) is used; and for the training dataset, different combinations of the partitions are applied. As illustrated in Fig. 4, the training dataset steadily increase from 10% of the data to 90% of the data with each step being 10%. In order to preserve the temporal dependencies of the data, the first experiment uses Partition (9) for the training dataset (to preserve the dependencies with Partition (10)). More data is added to the later experiments by going backwards from Partition (9) e.g. the second experiment uses Partitions (8) and (9). We label the use of the different training datasets as 10% to 90% to simplify the labelling in the later plots.

The calibration errors from using the different training datasets are illustrated in the boxplots in the Fig. 5. Comparing the boxplots in the figure, the difference between the methods as well as the effect of increasing size the training dataset is not obvious. Therefore, we plot the mean value of the errors with the confidence interval in Fig. 6 to analyse it further.

In Fig. 6, the bars show the mean of the errors, the error bars indicate the confidence level of the mean. The color of the bar differentiates the calibration methods. The figure shows that the regression-based method would over predict when the training dataset is relatively small, and under predict when the training dataset is relatively large. Whereas, the ANN-based method over predict in all circumstance. The result suggests that the change of the training dataset does have significant impact on the calibration results.

While the averaged errors allow us to determine a general accuracy of the calibration, they do not indicate which method is most likely to give the best result. To accomplish this we perform a null-hypothesis test [25] on the output data of the models, using the null-hypothesis that the two methods are equal -

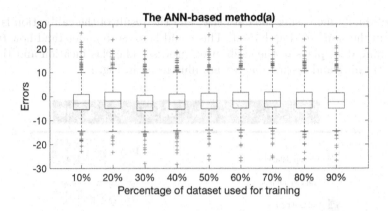

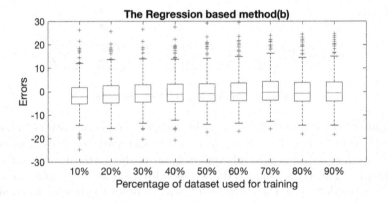

Fig. 5. The errors when using different training datasets

i.e. that for a given input vector, the regression-based method has a 50% chance of producing a lower error than the ANN-based method. We then compute the probability of the actual result of the experiment under the null-hypothesis, and if this probability is sufficiently unlikely, we can reject the null-hypothesis. This method allows us to have statistical confidence in our claim of which method is most likely to produce the lowest error. Our degree of confidence is derived by the standard method of determining how many standard deviations (σ) from the mean of the null-hypothesis deviation the observed result is [25]. At confidence levels above 3σ, we can claim that a method is better, and that at 5σ, we are certain that a method is better. The result is shown in Table 4.

Table 4 shows that the ANN-based method provide consistent better results when a larger training dataset is used. It suggests that an ANN-based method would potentially benefit from using a larger training dataset.

6.2 Varying the Testing Dataset

This experiment is designed to understand how the calibration result is affected by increasing the size of the testing dataset, which may reflect on how long a

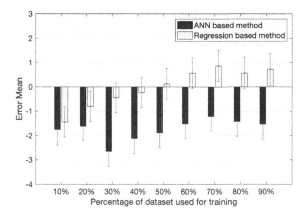

Fig. 6. Error mean with the confidence interval (Color figure online)

Table 4. Significance between calibration results when varying training dataset

Training dataset	P-value	Significance of P-value
10%	0.0976	No significant difference (1σ)
20%	0.0554	ANN potentially better (2σ)
30%	0.9708	Regression better (3σ)
40%	0.5000	No significant difference (0σ)
50%	0.0815	No significant difference (1σ)
60%	0.0063	ANN better (3σ)
70%	0.0083	ANN potentially better (2σ)
80%	0.0035	ANN better (3σ)
90%	0.0010	ANN better (3σ)

Low P-values indicate ANN is better, High P-values indicate regression is better. Results given to 4 decimal places

calibration function can hold. For this experiment, the same dataset is divided into the partitions as in the previous experiment in Sect. 6.1, but the training and testing datasets are utilised differently as illustrated in Fig. 7.

The errors between the model output and the reference when utilising different testing datasets are illustrated in Fig. 8. The boxplots represent the error distribution and x-axis indicate the testing dataset increases from 10% to 90% of the dataset according to Fig. 7. In the figure, using 10% of the data shows the best result for both methods in comparison to using other testing datasets. It suggests that the calibration function would obtain a better result if the testing dataset and the training dataset are close in time and have a similar data size. Furthermore, comparing Fig. 8-a to b, the errors for the ANN-based method contain more extreme values than the regression-based method.

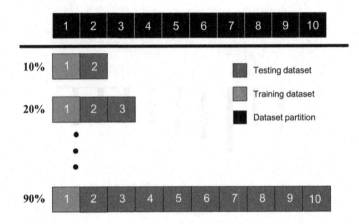

Fig. 7. Training models by varying the testing datasets

Table 5. Significance between calibration results when varying testing dataset

Testing dataset	P-value	Significance of P-value
10%	0.4210	No significant difference (0σ)
20%	0.9880	No significant difference (1σ)
30%	0.9998	Regression better (3σ)
40%	0.9999	Regression better (4σ)
50%	1.0000	Regression certainly better (5σ)
60%	1.0000	Regression certainly better (5σ)
70%	1.0000	Regression certainly better (5σ)
80%	1.0000	Regression certainly better (5σ)
90%	1.0000	Regression certainly better (5σ)

Low P-values indicate ANN is better, High P-values indicate Regression is better. Results given to 4 decimal places

We further plot the mean of the errors with the confidence interval in Fig. 9, which show the error mean and 95% confidence interval from the experiment. The figure shows that the error mean for both methods gradually increase with more testing data used. It suggests that both calibrations would degrade over time with a similar tend, and the performance of the calibration can be more sensitive to the testing dataset than the calibration method.

We also apply the statistical analysis for this experiment, again using the null-hypothesis that the methods are equal. The result is shown in Table 5. The table shows the regression-based method is consistently better than the ANN-based method with the increasing size of the testing dataset. This implies that the degradation of the calibration for the regression-based method is much less significant than the ANN-based method.

7 Influence from the Data Characteristics

In previous section, we have seen that the size of training and testing dataset can have a large impact on the calibration result for both methods. In this section, we investigate how the performance of the calibration methods is sensitive to the change of data characteristics. The experiment was performed using the same dataset as the previous experiments. However, the training dataset was selected based on indices that randomly selected from 50% of the data, and the rest of the data are used for testing. This process is to ensure that the data characteristics between the training and testing datasets are consistent (e.g. training and testing data are from the same distribution). Then, we artificially manipulate the characteristics of the testing datasets to create a different data characteristics. It is clear that the data characteristics can be different in many ways. In this experiment, we consider three properties as they are commonly observed in the low-cost sensors [13]: (1) a sensor outputing a constant value, (2) a sensor outputing an offset value and (3) a sensor outputing values with a greater spread (represented as a higher standard deviation).

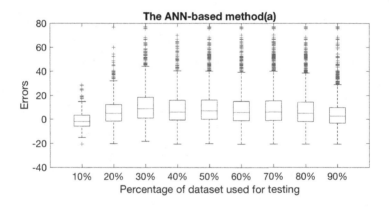

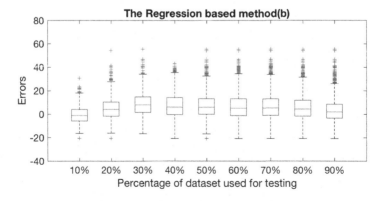

Fig. 8. The errors of both methods when using different testing datasets

Table 6. Different configurations for varying the test data characteristics

Constant value	STD	= 0
	Mean	Not changed
Offset mean	STD	Not changed
	Mean	2*mean
Higher standard deviation	STD	2*STD
	Mean	Not changed

The modification of the testing dataset was performed according to Table 6. The changes of mean and standard deviation are with respect to the original testing data. For the constant value, all samples in the testing dataset are replaced by the mean value of the testing dataset. The offset mean doubles the mean value of the the testing dataset but the standard deviation of the data remains the same. The higher standard deviation changes the standard deviation of the testing dataset but the mean remains. Since different parameters may contribute to the calibration result differently, the modification was performed on all parameters. It is noted that there only one parameter being modified for every calibration.

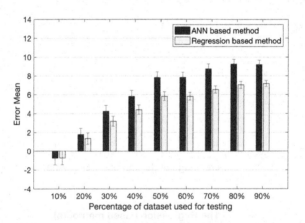

Fig. 9. Error mean with the confidence interval

Table 7. Significance of the calibration result (constant value)

Constant value		
Modified parameter	P-value	Significance of P-value
NO_2	0.9999	Regression better (4σ)
O_3	0.4115	No significant confidence (0σ)
Humidity	0.0006	ANN better (3σ)
Temperature	0.0006	ANN better (3σ)
NO	1.0000	Regression certainly better (5σ)

Low P-values indicate ANN is better, High P-values indicate Regression is better. Results given to 4 decimal places

Table 8. The calibration results when using the testing dataset with constant value

Constant value		Original	NO_2	O_3	H	T	NO
ANN based method	RMSE	9.10	8.51	7.17	6.53	6.53	11.74
	Mean	5.33 ± 0.47	-2.22 ± 0.45	-2.55 ± 0.38	-1.33 ± 0.37	-1.33 ± 0.37	-4.61 ± 0.58
Regression based method	RMSE	6.65	7.86	7.12	6.94	6.94	9.28
	Mean	-0.12 ± 0.37	-0.12 ± 0.42	-0.12 ± 0.39	-0.12 ± 0.38	-0.12 ± 0.38	-0.12 ± 0.52

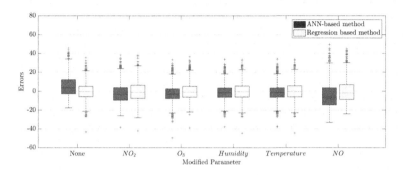

Fig. 10. The calibration errors when using the testing dataset with constant value

Table 9. Significance of the calibration result (offset mean)

Offset mean		
Training dataset	P-value	Significance of P-value
NO_2	1.0000	Regression certainly better (5σ)
O_3	0.9463	ANN potentially better (2σ)
Humidity	1.0000	Regression certainly better (5σ)
Temperature	1.0000	Regression certainly better (5σ)
NO	1.0000	Regression certainly better (5σ)

Low P-values indicate ANN is better, High P-values indicate Regression is better. Results given to 4 decimal places

Table 10. Significance of the calibration result (higher standard deviations)

Higher standard deviation		
Training dataset	P-value	Significance of P-value
NO_2	0.9780	Regression potentially better (2σ)
O_3	0.9239	No significant difference (1σ)
Humidity	0.8683	No significant difference (1σ)
Temperature	0.9413	No significant difference (1σ)
NO	0.9999	Regression better (3σ)

Low P-values indicate ANN is better, High P-values indicate Regression is better. Results given to 4 decimal places

Figures 10, 11 and 12 show the calibration results when the testing dataset of one parameter is modified according to Table 6. The figures differentiate the different modifications, i.e. offset, constant value and higher standard deviation. The boxplots in each figure represent the calibration errors, with the label on the X-axis indicating which parameter (if any) is modified (Table 10).

Figure 10 and Table 8 presents the results when one parameter of the testing data becomes constant. Figure 10 shows no observable difference in terms of the errors, which suggests that the constant value would only have a small impact on both calibration methods. The table indicates that the constant value only causes a small variation in RMSE, and it has even less impact on the error mean, especially for the regression-based method.

The result of the statistical analysis is summarised in Table 7, which shows that the ANN-based method is more sensitive to the NO_2 and NO readings becoming constant, and regression-based method is more sensitive to Humidity and Temperature becoming constant. This indicates that both calibrations may assign different weight to the input parameters when constructing a calibration model.

Figure 11 and Table 11 illustrate the calibration result when the mean value of one parameter is doubled than the original testing dataset. Figure 11 shows a large variation in the errors when the mean value of the testing dataset is modified, which suggests the change of the mean value would have significantly higher impact on the calibration result. Table 11 shows that most of the RMSE and error mean are significantly worse than the result using the unmodified data. The results suggests the change of mean value of the testing dataset would have a great impact on the calibration result. The statistical test is shown in Table 9,

Table 11. The calibration results when using the testing dataset with offset mean

Offset mean		Original	NO_2	O_3	H	T	NO
ANN based method	RMSE	9.10	14.68	7.53	11.02	18.34	13.04
	Mean	5.33 ± 0.47	−12.23 ± 0.53	−3.4 ± 0.41	−9.02 ± 0.40	−17.91 ± 0.43	−7.36 ± 0.59
Regression based method	RMSE	6.65	9.76	7.64	6.71	13.67	9.88
	Mean	−0.12 ± 0.37	−6.36 ± 0.42	4.53 ± 0.39	1.39 ± 0.37	13.18 ± 0.38	−2.80 ± 0.15

Table 12. The calibration results when using the testing dataset with a large standard deviation

Higher standard deviation		Original	NO_2	O_3	H	T	NO
ANN based method	RMSE	9.10	7.87	6.95	6.87	7.21	8.94
	Mean	5.33 ± 0.47	−1.83 ± 0.45	−1.78 ± 0.38	−1.52 ± 0.38	−2.05 ± 0.39	−1.56 ± 0.53
Regression based method	RMSE	6.65	7.55	6.96	6.66	7.01	8.53
	Mean	−0.12 ± 0.37	−0.13 ± 0.44	−0.13 ± 0.40	−0.12± 0.37	−0.13 ± 0.39	−0.12 ± 0.53

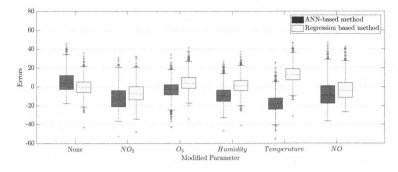

Fig. 11. The calibration errors when using the testing dataset with offset mean

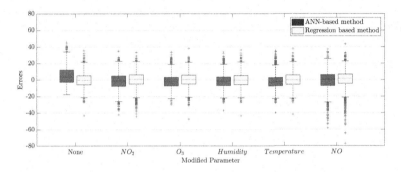

Fig. 12. The calibration errors when using the testing dataset with higher standard deviation

which suggests that the regression-based method is significantly better than the ANN-based method most of the time. It implies that both methods can have different tolerance to drift of mean, and the regression-based method seems to have a better tolerance based on our result.

Figure 12 and Table 12 show the calibration results when one parameter in the testing data have a higher standard deviation. The figure shows that the higher standard deviation in the testing dataset would also have a small impact on the calibration result as the variation of the errors between using modified data and non-modified data is not significant.

Cross-comparing the results above, we conclude that the difference between the training and testing dataset in terms of data characteristics does have a higher impact on the calibration result than the methods itself. However, in general, the ANN-based method is more sensitive to these influences than the regression-based method. Among the different data characteristics, both methods can cope well with the constant value and the higher data standard deviations, but not for the offset mean. This implies that a re-calibration of sensors may be needed if actual training and testing dataset are significantly different in the mean value.

8 Conclusions

This paper provided a systematic comparison between two of the most popular calibration methods, regression-based method and ANN-based method, with detail sensitivity analysis under various conditions.

The comparison shows that the calibration results are extremely sensitive to some of the factors such as the use of hyperparameters in the calibration models or different training and testing datasets. The calibration result can be more sensitive to some of those factors than the use of different calibration methods. In addition, in our comparison, the ANN-based method did not consistently show a better calibration result compared to the regression-based method, and in some of the conditions, it performed much worse than the regression-based method. The result suggests that the ANN-based method may not always be the best option for calibrating a low-cost sensor as the its performance is sensitive to many factors.

Even though some of the results obtained in this study may not be generalised in or directly applied to other sensors or datasets, we have a good reason to believe based on our evaluation that the performance of a sensing calibration is not only dependent on the use of a method but also heavily related to many associated factors (e.g. the training and testing data, the selection of model parameter, the characteristic of the monitored data). Therefore, understanding the key factors and their influence can be important for selecting an appropriate calibration method.

Acknowledgement. This work is funded by the European Union's Seventh Framework Programme for research, technological development and demonstration under grant agreement no. 608014 (CAPACITIE).

References

1. Bashiri, M., Geranmayeh, A.: Tuning the parameters of an artificial neural network using central composite design and genetic algorithm. Scientia Iranica **18**(6), 1600–1608 (2011)
2. Claesen, M., De Moor, B.: Hyperparameter search in machine learning (2015)
3. Castell, N., et al.: Can commercial low-cost sensor platforms contribute to air quality monitoring and exposure estimates? Environ. Int. **99**, 293–302 (2017)
4. Cheng, Y., et al.: Aircloud: a cloud-based air-quality monitoring system for everyone. In: Proceedings of the 12th ACM Conference on Embedded Network Sensor Systems, pp. 251–265. ACM (2014)
5. Coolen, A.: A beginners guide to the mathematics of neural networks. In: Landau, L.J., Taylor, J.G. (eds.) Concepts for Neural Networks, pp. 13–70. Springer, London (1998). https://doi.org/10.1007/978-1-4471-3427-5_2
6. Department for Environment Food & Rural Affairs: Monitoring networks (2017). https://uk-air.defra.gov.uk/networks/
7. Devito, S., et al.: Calibrating chemical multisensory devices for real world applications: an in-depth comparison of quantitative machine learning approaches. Sens. Actuators, B Chem. **255**, 1191–1210 (2018)

8. Devito, S., Piga, M., Martinotto, L., Difrancia, G.: co, no_2 and no_x urban pollution monitoring with on-field calibrated electronic nose by automatic Bayesian regularization. Sens. Actuators, B Chem. **143**(1), 182–191 (2009)

9. Esposito, E., Devito, S., Salvato, M., Bright, V., Jones, R., Popoola, O.: Dynamic neural network architectures for on field stochastic calibration of indicative low cost air quality sensing systems. Sens. Actuators, B Chem. **231**, 701–713 (2016)

10. Esposito, E., De Vito, S., Salvato, M., Fattoruso, G., Di Francia, G.: Computational intelligence for smart air quality monitors calibration. In: Gervasi, O., et al. (eds.) ICCSA 2017. LNCS, vol. 10406, pp. 443–454. Springer, Cham (2017). https://doi.org/10.1007/978-3-319-62398-6_31

11. Fang, X., Bate, I.: Issues of using wireless sensor network to monitor urban air quality. In: Proceedings of the First ACM International Workshop on the Engineering of Reliable, Robust, and Secure Embedded Wireless Sensing Systems (FAILSAFE). ACM (2017)

12. Fang, X., Bate, I.: Using multi-parameters for calibration of low-cost sensors in urban environment. In: International Conference on Embedded Wireless Systems and Networks (EWSN) (2017)

13. Fang, X., Bate, I.: An improved sensor calibration with anomaly detection and removal. Sens. Actuators, B Chem. **307**, 127428 (2020)

14. Hayes, A.: Introduction To Mediation, Moderation, and Conditional Process Analysis: A Regression-Based Approach. Guilford Press, New York (2013)

15. Heimann, I., et al.: Source attribution of air pollution by spatial scale separation using high spatial density networks of low cost air quality sensors. Atmos. Environ. **113**, 10–19 (2015)

16. Keras: The Python deep learning library. https://keras.io (2017)

17. Klambauer, G., Unterthiner, T., Mayr, A., Hochreiter, S.: Self-normalizing neural networks. arXiv e-prints (2017)

18. Lewis, A., et al.: Evaluating the performance of low cost chemical sensors for air pollution research. Faraday Discuss. **189**, 85–103 (2016)

19. Maag, B., Saukh, O., Hasenfratz, D., Thiele, L.: Pre-deployment testing, augmentation and calibration of cross-sensitive sensors, pp. 169–180. ACM (2016)

20. Mueller, M., Meyer, J., Hueglin, C.: Design of an ozone and nitrogen dioxide sensor unit and its long-term operation within a sensor network in the city of Zurich. Atmos. Meas. Tech. **10**(10), 3783–3799 (2017)

21. Nair, V., Hinton, G.: Rectified linear units improve restricted Boltzmann machines. In: Proceedings of the 27th International Conference on Machine Learning, pp. 807–814 (2010)

22. Nielsen, M.A.: Neural Networks and Deep Learning. Determination Press (2015). http://neuralnetworksanddeeplearning.com/

23. Perkin Elmer: ELM sensor. https://elm.perkinelmer.com/map/ (2015)

24. Spinelle, L., Gerboles, M., Villani, M., Aleixandre, M., Bonavitacola, F.: Field calibration of a cluster of low-cost available sensors for air quality monitoring part a: ozone and nitrogen dioxide. Sens. Actuators, B Chem. **215**, 249–257 (2015)

25. Stephens, L.J.: Schaum's Outlines: Beginning Statistics, 2nd edn. McGraw-Hill, New York (2006)

26. Tensorflow: An open-source software library for machine intelligence. https://www.tensorflow.org (2017)

MOBIUS: Smart Mobility Tracking with Smartphone Sensors

Daniele Di Mitri[1]([✉]), Khaleel Asyraaf Mat Sanusi[1], Kevin Trebing[2],
and Stefano Bromuri[1]

[1] Open University of The Netherlands, Valkenburgerweg 177,
6419 AT Heerlen, The Netherlands
{daniele.dimitri,khaleel.asyraaf,stefano.bromuri}@ou.nl
[2] Maastricht University, Minderbroedersberg 4-6,
6211 LK Maastricht, The Netherlands
k.trebing@student.maastrichtuniversity.nl

Abstract. In this paper we introduce MOBIUS, a smartphone-based system for remote tracking of citizens' movements. By collecting smartphone's sensor data such as accelerometer and gyroscope, along with self-report data, the MOBIUS system allows to classify the users' mode of transportation. With the MOBIUS app the users can also activate GPS tracking to visualise their journeys and travelling speed on a map. The MOBIUS app is an example of a tracing app which can provide more insights into how people move around in an urban area. In this paper, we introduce the motivation, the architectural design and development of the MOBIUS app. To further test its validity, we run a user study collecting data from multiple users. The collected data are used to train a deep convolutional neural network architecture which classifies the transportation modes using with a mean accuracy of 89%.

Keywords: Smart mobility · Human-activity recognition ·
Smartphone data · Mobility tracking

1 Introduction

With the spread of the Covid-19 pandemic, and with new policies to ensure the physical distance between people, there is a stronger request from regional authorities to have a better overview and understanding of citizen's mobility in urban areas to prevent overcrowded areas and redistribute traffic more efficiently. The idea of MOBIUS, which stands for *MOBIlity for Urban Sustainability*, aims at addressing the mobility knowledge gap by automatically detecting citizen's mode of transportation at a different time of the day. In the MOBIUS project, we take as an example the municipality of Heerlen, a city in the south of The Netherlands. The hypothesis of the local government is that many people still prefer cars over bikes as compared to other Dutch cities. This behaviour is not energy efficient since the city of Heerlen can count on highly viable bike paths and

© ICST Institute for Computer Sciences, Social Informatics and Telecommunications Engineering 2021
Published by Springer Nature Switzerland AG 2021. All Rights Reserved
S. Paiva et al. (Eds.): SmartCity360° 2020, LNICST 372, pp. 462–475, 2021.
https://doi.org/10.1007/978-3-030-76063-2_31

that most of the destinations within the municipality are within seven kilometres of distance. With the purpose of better understanding the citizens' mobility behaviour, the municipality of Heerlen, therefore, initiated a city-wide survey, in which it invited randomly its citizens to retrospectively declare what mode of transport they use at what time of the day. This post-hoc data collection is not optimal and can lead to biased or inaccurate reports.

In this paper, we introduce the MOBIUS app, an Android-based application that can continuously gather multiple smartphone sensors such as accelerometer, gyroscope, and GPS coordinates without heavily draining the battery of the smartphone. The MOBIUS app can also record self-reported annotations on the modality of transportation used. The sensor and self-report data are stored on a web-server into a cloud repository. The MOBIUS app can be used to collect a data corpus that can later be used for training Convolutional Neural Networks (CNN). Based on the collected data, these CNNs can automatically differentiate between different transportation classes: Stationary, Walking, Running, Biking, Train/Bus, and Car. The MOBIUS app is to be considered a research tool which can be used by multiple users for gathering their mobility data. It can be used also as *citizen crowd-sourcing* app for studying the mobility patterns in the city and better devise transportation policies. This paper contributes advancing the research in transportation mode classification by introducing the MOBIUS, an open source application that uses scalable approach for collecting sensor data and users' annotations.

This paper is organised as follows: in Sect. 2, we review the related work in the area of transportation mode detection using smartphone's sensor data. In Sect. 3, we detail the methodological approach adopted for developing the MOBIUS app. In Sect. 4, we describe the pilot data collection of the app and the preliminary results of the classification. In Sect. 6, we summarise the proposed work and we describe the limitations and additional features that the MOBIUS app can entail in the future.

2   Related Work

Nowadays almost every citizen carries a smartphone in their pocket. Since smartphones have many in-built sensors, such as accelerometer, gyroscope, magnetometer, and GPS. These sensors could help to classify the transportation method of their user. We looked for systems that allow for collecting smartphone sensor data from multiple users for citizen crowd-sourcing.

Early work in transportation mode detection using smartphones relied on change of cell tower signal strength [1,15] which is not using the internal sensors of the smartphone. They classified three different classes: stationary, walking, and driving. Although the authors achieved an accuracy of 80% and 85%, respectively, the models rely on cell phone signal coverage, which may vary in different places on earth and the classified classes are quite basic. The authors of [12] extend the classification task to differentiate between still, walk, run, bike, and motor. Furthermore, they use the internal GPS and accelerometer sensor of the smartphone to create custom features which they feed into their Decision Tree in conjunction with a Hidden Markov Model. Their approach achieves an accuracy of 93.6%.

Extending the classes even further by differentiating different motorised vehicles the authors of [16] use the GPS sensor of the smartphone to create additional features such as average speed, average acceleration, and average heading change. Additionally, they created maps of bus-stops, rail stops and rail-lines of Chicago, Illinois, USA together with publicly available real-time GPS locations of buses in Chicago to help classify the user's transportation mode. Using a Random Forest Classifier they achieved an accuracy of 93.5%. A drawback of this approach is that it is limited to the area of Chicago and that the user required to have a constant GPS signal which they noted is draining a lot of battery power.

By using only the accelerometer of the smartphone the authors of [6] achieved an accuracy of 80% on the classes stationary, walk, bus, train, metro, and tram while using a very small power demanding sensor. Their classifier of the transportation methods consists of multiple sub-classifiers that each uses different features from the accelerometer sensor.

Similar to [6], the authors of [10] use only the energy efficient accelerometer sensor of the phone for classifying. They use a deep convolutional neural network to differentiate the classes stationary, walk, bicycle, bus, car, train, and subway. In order to feed only important information to their CNN they remove the gravity component in their accelerometer data and apply a filter to the signal that removes different movements of the phone and user, such as picking up the phone. The accelerometer sensor is sampled 50 Hz and the CNN is trained on data from about two hours of every transportation mode. Their final accuracy score is 94.48%.

Also using a deep neural network, [5] use a Multilayer Perceptron (MLP) to differentiate the five classes: still, walk, run, bike, and vehicle. Additionally to the accelerometer, they used gyroscope and magnetometer sensors that are all sampled at 30 Hz. They achieved an accuracy of 95%.

Since sensor readings are time-series, the use of a long short-term memory (LSTM) network [7] is self-evident as LSTMs have some kind of memory of the input signal that is helpful when working with these kind of signals. This memory is useful for identifying important features and trends of the input signal. The authors of [17] use an extended LSTM version: a bi-directional LSTM. Their model can differentiate between the transportation modes stationary, walk, run, bike, bus, and subway. In addition to using an accelerometer, the authors extended the sensor attributes by including a gyroscope sensor from the smartphone to classify the transportation modes. Furthermore, both sensors are sampled at a rate of 50 Hz. By splitting the dataset into only training and test sets, they achieved an accuracy of up to 92.8%.

The authors of [8] used a hybrid deep learning model, namely Deep Convolutional Bi-directional-LSTM (DCBL), which combined convolutional and bi-directional LSTM layers. They trained this model on smartphone sensor data for classifying the following transportation modes: car, bus, train, subway, walk, run, bike, and stationary. Additionally, the sensors used were accelerometer, gyroscope, magnetometer, linear acceleration, gravity, orientation, and ambient pressure. They compared their model to Supervised Vector Machine (SVM) and MLP models on extracted features. As a result, DCBL performs better than the traditional machine learning approaches. Furthermore, they used an ensemble of DCBL on trained raw sensor data using the different combination of sensors and window sizes and achieved an F1-score of 0.96.

3   Methodology

In the light of the related experiments, we derived five functional requirements (FRs) for the software architecture of the MOBIUS app with the aim to accomplish the overarching objective of this study *automatically classifying modes of transportation using smartphone sensor data.* The functional requirements are summarised as follows.

(FR1) Data Collection. The MOBIUS app should be able to continuously collect the accelerometer, gyroscope, and GPS sensor data. Meanwhile, the MOBIUS app should have the GPS sensor set off by default, leaving it optional for the user to activate it, if needed. The data collection should feature in the background, in case the user locks the smartphone or accidentally closes the MOBIUS app. The accelerometer and gyroscope data should be sampled at 60 Hz (60 updates per seconds) while the GPS coordinates should be sampled every 10 s, as found in the literature. The data collection should be able to last for long periods of time, i.e. also the entire day, if necessary. The data gathering should affect the battery consumption as little as possible.

(FR2) Data Storing. The sessions should be stored into a compressed format that can be easily sent via the Wi-Fi network to the server. Along with the smartphone client there needs to be a back-end application running on a server, where each Mobius client can store the session recordings and which can be queried for later retrieval.

(FR3) Data Annotation. The MOBIUS app should collect user's self-reports. The user should be able to activate a toggle for each mode of transportation multiple times in one journey and for multiple journeys without limitations. Given the fact the self-reports are prone to mistakes, the user-annotations should be editable with a post-processing tool.

(FR4) Data Analysis. The collected data and corresponding user's annotations should be processed and transformed in a suitable representation for machine learning.

(FR5) Privacy. The app should ensure the privacy of its user, all the participants should use it after signing informed consent. The user should be able to deactivate the GPS coordinate tracking, without affecting the performance of

the transportation mode detection. For the final users of the MOBIUS app, the classification model will run on the phone itself without the need of uploading the sensor readings on the server. Instead, it will only upload the anonymized transportation modes.

3.1 System Architecture

To fulfil the five FRs we designed a the System Architecture represented graphically in Fig. 1. The MOBIUS system architecture consists of four main software components, two of which were developed from the ground up, while, the remaining two, adapted from previous experiments. All the components are developed as Open Source software released with Creative Commons license.

(1) Mobius Client. Is an Android application developed in Java. Each final user installs and runs one instance of the Mobius Client app. The app is responsible for continuous collection of sensor data and user's transportation self-reports[1].

(2) Mobius Server. A Python web application running on the Azure Cloud, implementing some basic API functionalities to which the clients connect to. The MOBIUS Server is responsible for storing and converting the sessions received by each client[2].

(3) Visual Inspection Tool (VIT). A web-based tool developed in Javascript and HTML5, which allows the visual inspection and the annotation of multimodal datasets encoded with MLT-JSON data format [3]. VIT was modified to deal with geo-location data[3].

(4) SharpFlow. A data analysis toolkit for time-series classification using deep and recurrent neural networks [4]. SharpFlow can be used both for offline model training as well as for online classification[4].

3.2 Data Collection

The MOBIUS application is intended to run in the background for long periods of time. We launch a background service that constantly listens to the accelerometer, gyroscope, and GPS sensor without being interrupted by the operating system as long as the user starts the recording. During the recording, the accelerometer and gyroscope sensor are activated, while the GPS sensor is set to off and can only be activated by the user. Once the recording has been stopped, the background service will be terminated. We show screenshots of the MOBIUS app in Fig. 2. Both accelerometer and gyroscope data are sampled at 60 Hz, which gives

---

[1] Code available at Mobius_client.
[2] Code available at Mobius_server.
[3] Code available at Visual Inspection Tool.
[4] Code available at Sharpflow.

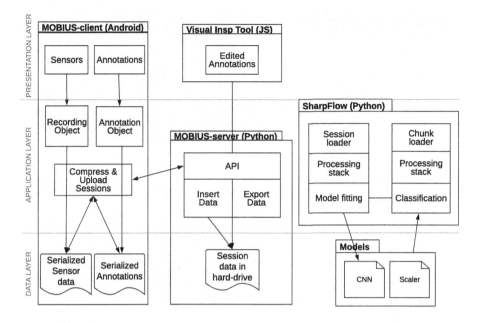

Fig. 1. System architecture of Mobius app

us 60 updates per second. Meanwhile, the GPS data is sampled every 10 s for an update on coordinate values and speed, only when the GPS detects changes on the location. Self-report data, on the other hand, is entered by the user manually. The user chooses one of the following modes of transportation: Stationary, Walking, Running, Car, Train/Bus, and Biking. By doing so, the user annotates the data which is crucial for later classification.

To ensure that we have adequate data, the system will prompt the user when a certain speed threshold is broken, which means the wrong transportation mode is selected during sensor recordings. Prompting the user also works when no transportation mode is selected as we attempt to reduce the "Stationary" data as much as possible.

3.3 Data Storing

Each recorded session is finally sent via HTTP Post to the Mobius Server. For security purposes the server only accepts files from users that have a valid ID. The Mobius server implements a basic API interface which serialises the data into zip folders. The compressed file of each session is saved with a filename with the following format: *ID_-api-key-_YYYY-MM-DDTHH-MM-SS.zip*. The sensor data is saved in a comma-separated value (CSV) format. GPS is in an independent CSV file, while both accelerometer and gyroscope share the same CSV document.

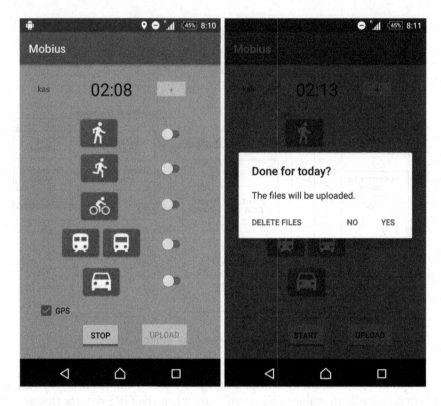

Fig. 2. Screenshots of the MOBIUS app.

```
1    Time,Latitude,Longitude
2    2020-05-28T16:18:08.541,50.877411127,5.9587547178
3    2020-05-28T16:18:18.542,50.877393466,5.9587584740
4    2020-05-28T16:18:28.543,50.877327296,5.9583815937
5    2020-05-28T16:18:38.544,50.877291249,5.9578777499
6    ...
```

Listing 1.1. Example GPS coordinates in the CSV dataformat

MLT Data Format. The *Meaningful Learning Task* MLT-JSON data format, introduced by [14] was adopted to describe an instance of human activity with a clear 'start' and 'end'. The MLT data format was chosen to ensure backward compatibility with the VIT. An example entry of the MLT-JSON data format may look like the following:

```
1    {
2        "recordingID": "2020-05-28T16-13-37-819",
3        "applicationName": "gps",
4        "frames": [
```

```
 5        {
 6             "frameStamp": "00:04:30.722",
 7             "frameAttributes": {
 8                 "Latitude": 50.8774111277,
 9                 "Longitude": 5.9587547179
10             }
11        }, ...
12    ]
13 }
```

Listing 1.2. GPS coordinate file in the MLT data format

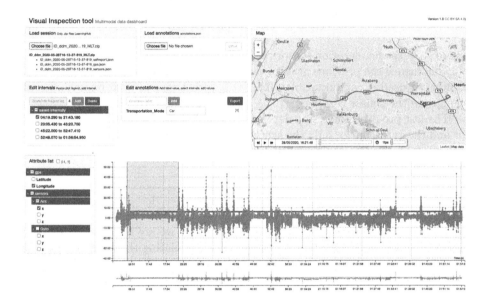

Fig. 3. One recorded MLT session loaded in the VIT.

3.4   Data Annotation

The self-reported annotations were improved using the VIT. In Fig. 3, we show a screenshot of the VIT. The MLT sessions can be loaded and the journey visualised as blue line on the map (top-right corner). At the same time, the plots are visualised (bottom) when the sensor attributes are selected which are hierarchically sorted in the Attribute list (bottom-left).

Using the VIT allowed us to fix wrongly annotated sensor readings by recognising for example long intervals of no sensor readings despite annotated as a transportation mode or having a bicycle annotation while driving faster than 90 km/h on the highway.

3.5   Data Processing

Using the annotated data files we created our dataset in which the samples are 512 sequential sensor measurements each with the corresponding transportation mode as label. The window of 512 was chosen to have the same dimension as [10] and also to have a long enough time window that we believe is needed for the classification. In our case 512 sensor readings cover roughly 8.7 s. This window was moved over the recorded sessions in an interval of 64 readings (ca. 1 s) resulting in a total dataset size of 168476 samples.

Additionally, we pre-processed the data in the same way [10] did by removing gravity from the accelerometer sensors and applying a smoothing on each sensor stream[5]. We estimated gravity by the following equation,

$$G_t = \alpha \cdot G_{t-1} + (1 - \alpha) \cdot A_t \qquad (1)$$

where A_t is the acceleration sensor reading and α is a value that determines how much influence the previous gravity value has. We chose a value of 0.8 for α. As a filter we used a Savitzky-Golay-filter [13] with a size of 5 to remove abrupt changes in the sensor readings.

The last pre-processing step depends on whether we use both the accelerometer and the gyroscope or only the accelerometer. When using only the accelerometer we can calculate the magnitude of the three dimensions of the sensor for every time point:

$$Acc_{magnitude_t} = \sqrt{Acc_{x_t}^2 + Acc_{y_t}^2 + Acc_{z_t}^2} \qquad (2)$$

When using both the accelerometer and gyroscope we are using the smoothed values of all dimensions of the sensors without calculating their magnitude. We tried both approaches, because [10] used the accelerometer magnitude and we hypothesised that we get better performance using more sensor readings.

3.6   Machine Learning Model for Automated Classification

We tried two different machine learning approaches for automated transport mode detection. One approach uses a convolutional neural network and the other approach a bi-directional long short term memory.

The CNN architecture that we used is based on the convolutional neural network of [10]. The network consists of six 1D convolutions with max-pooling followed by a hidden-layer and a final output layer. The exact architecture structure is shown in Fig. 4. The first convolution has a kernel size of 15, the next two of 10 and the last three have a size of 5. Following every convolutional operation we apply the ELU activation function [2] followed by a max-pooling operation with kernel size 4 and stride 2. After the last operation we flatten the signal

---

[5] After the collection of the data we found an option to record sensor readings without gravity directly on Android devices.

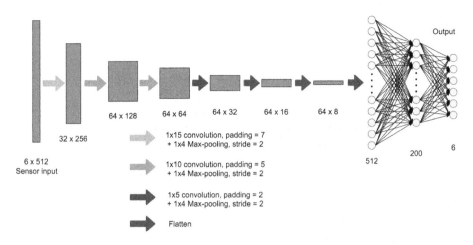

Fig. 4. The network architecture for automated transportation mode detection.

and feed it into a multilayer perceptron with 200 hidden neurons and 6 output neurons. The resulting architecture has 229,918 trainable parameters.

The bi-directional LSTM consists of two bi-directional LSTM layers with 64 neurons and 32 neurons, respectively, followed by a multilayer perceptron with 32 hidden neurons and 6 output neurons. This LSTM architecture has 79,078 trainable parameters.

We compare our two approaches to two dummy classifiers from the sklearn-package [11]: the first one predicts a label with respect to the training set's class distribution (sklearn calls it "stratified") and the second one always predicts the most frequent label, named "most frequent". These classifiers used all six smoothed sensor readings.

3.7 Training

We trained our models for maximally 200 epochs with a batch size of 1024. We used the Adam optimiser with a learning rate of 1e–4 for the CNN and 1e–3 for the LSTM and for both a weight decay of 1e–3 was used [9]. Furthermore, we used early stopping if the validation loss did not decrease for 30 epochs and a learning rate scheduler that reduced the learning rate to a tenth of the current learning rate if the validation loss did not decrease for 5 epochs. The model that had the lowest validation loss in the training run was chosen as the best performing model and its performance was assessed on the test set.

4 Results

For the user test of the Mobius app, the research team (4 users) collected roughly 47 h recordings for all transportation modes combined. The data was collected using four different Android smartphones with the Mobius app installed in the course of two weeks time. The resulting dataset has over 168000 samples and can be seen in Table 1.

Table 1. Collected data samples for the Mobius user test.

Class	Amount	Hours	Proportion
Stationary	49703	13.80	29.50%
Walking	34969	9.71	20.76%
Running	5452	1.51	3.24%
Car	42747	11.87	25.37%
Train/bus	10108	2.81	6.00%
Biking	25497	7.08	15.13%
Total	168476	46.80	100%

As previously mentioned, we tried different input data configurations. Firstly, using the accelerometer magnitude (as done in [10]); secondly, the smoothed sensor readings from the accelerometer; and thirdly, smoothed sensor readings from both the accelerometer and gyroscope. The results can be seen in Table 2. The table shows that using all six sensor readings achieves best results in almost all scores. Interestingly, we did not achieve very good results when using the accelerometer magnitude as reported in [10]. Using only the accelerometer sensor resulted in the same overall accuracy of 89% as when using both accelerometer and gyroscope. Nonetheless, other metrics such as F1 score are minimally better for most classes when using both sensors. The approach using a bi-directional LSTM achieves a mean accuracy of 81%, which is better than the CNN using the accelerometer magnitude, but worse than using the smoothed accelerometer readings.

Table 2. Skill scores of the models on the different classes. Best scores of class are in bold.

Model	F1-score of classes						Mean accuracy
	Stationary	Walking	Running	Car	Train/Bus	Biking	
Dummy (Stratified)	0.29	0.22	0.02	0.26	0.06	0.16	0.22
Dummy (most frequent)	0.45	0.00	0.00	0.00	0.00	0.00	0.29
CNN (Acc-magnitude)	0.61	0.61	0.79	0.79	0.94	0.77	0.70
Bi-LSTM (Acc)	0.72	0.71	0.84	0.91	0.93	0.89	0.81
CNN (Acc)	**0.85**	**0.82**	**0.89**	0.94	0.95	0.94	**0.89**
CNN (Acc + Gyro)	**0.85**	**0.82**	0.88	**0.96**	**0.96**	**0.95**	**0.89**

5   Discussion

The results in Table 2 show that our CNN approach using both the accelerometer and gyroscope data results in the best accuracy for almost all transportation modes. The difference in performance to using only accelerometer data is only minor (max is 2% worse F1-score in *car* mode), but this approach has the advantage that it requires only half the amount of sensor readings and therefore less space and also power from the smartphone. Furthermore, this shows us that the gyroscope sensor only seems to have a minor performance impact on the overall performance. Therefore, for further experiments we recommend using only the accelerometer sensor to extend the phones battery life and storage space. Our bi-directional LSTM approach achieves better accuracy than the CNN model from [10] using the accelerometer magnitude, but worse results than the CNN model using the same input as the LSTM (smoothed sensor readings).

As previously mentioned, we did not achieve good results when using the accelerometer magnitude as was done in [10]. Furthermore, replicating the bi-directional LSTM model from [17] did not yield an accuracy of over 90% as claimed by the authors. A possible reason for this is that they used a smaller time window (2.56 s) with a sampling rate of 50 Hz as input to the model unlike our longer time window of 8.7 s sampled at 60 Hz. Nevertheless, these approaches outperform the two baselines by a big margin.

A possibility for the CNN outperforming the LSTM approach could be that the cyclic nature of the transportation methods, such as running, walking and biking, is easy to spot by the spatially invariant kernels of the convolutions. A LSTM does not have these kind of kernels that can look at a slice of the signal simultaneously, instead it gets the signal fed in one at a time, which makes it harder for the LSTM to recognize these cyclic patterns. Indeed, when looking at Table 2 again, we can see that the discrepancy between the F1-scores of the LSTM model and CNN model for cyclic motions such as walking, running and biking is largest, whereas for car and train/bus they are quite close together.

6   Conclusions and Future Works

In this paper, we have introduced MOBIUS, a smartphone-based system for automatic classification of citizens' transportation mode. The MOBIUS app collects smartphone's sensor data such as accelerometer and gyroscope, with the inclusion of self-report and GPS data. These sensor readings were used to classify users' transportation modes. Based on the results, using both gyroscope and accelerometer sensor readings achieved the highest classification rate, therefore increasing the potential of using the MOBIUS system to better understand the citizens' mobility behaviour.

While the classification accuracy achieved using CNN reached results comparable to the state of the art analysed in Sect. 2, this paper introduces a open-source and scalable infrastructure which can collect both crowd-sourced sensor data from multiple users and corresponding annotations of the mode of transportation used. The open-sourced released components can be the base for developing further smart-mobility applications for devising better policies for mobility and health. Especially with the recent Covid-19 pandemic, future developments works could explore the possibility of using the MOBIUS as citizens tracking application that allows identifying the potential virus outbreaks. Similarly MOBIUS can be used for smarter urban and transportation planning, for example for identifying or suggesting car-sharing opportunities.

The transportation mode classification took into account only accelerometer and gyroscope data and not GPS coordinates. The GPS tracking feature that enables the user to record the itineraries, was set off by default whenever the user started a new session. The GPS coordinate tracking was primarily used for the sake of improving the annotations of the training dataset. Future users do not have to enable the GPS tracking to be able to classify the transportation mode with MOBIUS. We believe that with this approach, MOBIUS can better safeguard the privacy of the user. To further improve the user's privacy, future works can look on how to embed the trained model in the MOBIUS-client app. In this way, the MOBIUS app will not have to push the collected data to the server and the users' privacy will be preserved.

Additional improvements can also be made to the MOBIUS-client to become more user-friendly for future users. The usage of smartwatch devices for the collection of sensor and self-report data can be investigated, for extending the smartphone application into a smartwatch application. In addition to being able to retrieve similar attributes as the smartphone, the smartwatch can obtain extra data such as heart rate and step count. Not only does this allow us to gain more understanding about the behaviour but also helps to monitor the health status of the user.

References

1. Anderson, I., Muller, H.: Practical activity recognition using GSM data (2006)
2. Clevert, D.A., Unterthiner, T., Hochreiter, S.: Fast and accurate deep network learning by exponential linear units (ELUs). arXiv preprint arXiv:1511.07289 (2015)
3. Di Mitri, D., Schneider, J., Klemke, R., Specht, M., Drachsler, H.: Read between the lines: an annotation tool for multimodal data for learning. In: Proceedings of the 9th International Conference on Learning Analytics & Knowledge - LAK19, pp. 51–60. ACM, New York USA (2019). https://doi.org/10.1145/3303772.3303776
4. Di Mitri, D., Schneider, J., Trebing, K., Sopka, S., Specht, M., Drachsler, H.: Real-time multimodal feedback with the CPR tutor. In: Bittencourt, I.I., Cukurova, M., Muldner, K., Luckin, R., Millán, E. (eds.) AIED 2020. LNCS (LNAI), vol. 12163, pp. 141–152. Springer, Cham (2020). https://doi.org/10.1007/978-3-030-52237-7_12
5. Fang, S.H., Fei, Y.X., Xu, Z., Tsao, Y.: Learning transportation modes from smartphone sensors based on deep neural network. IEEE Sens. J. 17(18), 6111–6118 (2017)
6. Hemminki, S., Nurmi, P., Tarkoma, S.: Accelerometer-based transportation mode detection on smartphones. In: Proceedings of the 11th ACM Conference on Embedded Networked Sensor Systems, pp. 1–14 (2013)

7. Hochreiter, S., Schmidhuber, J.: Long short-term memory. Neural Comput. **9**(8), 1735–1780 (1997)
8. Jeyakumar, J.V., Lee, E.S., Xia, Z., Sandha, S.S., Tausik, N., Srivastava, M.: Deep convolutional bidirectional LSTM based transportation mode recognition. In: Proceedings of the 2018 ACM International Joint Conference and 2018 International Symposium on Pervasive and Ubiquitous Computing and Wearable Computers, pp. 1606–1615 (2018)
9. Kingma, D.P., Ba, J.: Adam: a method for stochastic optimization. arXiv preprint arXiv:1412.6980 (2014)
10. Liang, X., Zhang, Y., Wang, G., Xu, S.: A deep learning model for transportation mode detection based on smartphone sensing data. IEEE Trans. Intell. Transp. Syst. **21**, 5223–5235 (2019)
11. Pedregosa, F., et al.: Scikit-learn: machine learning in Python. J. Mach. Learn. Res. **12**, 2825–2830 (2011)
12. Reddy, S., Mun, M., Burke, J., Estrin, D., Hansen, M., Srivastava, M.: Using mobile phones to determine transportation modes. ACM Trans. Sens. Netw. (TOSN) **6**(2), 1–27 (2010)
13. Savitzky, A., Golay, M.J.: Smoothing and differentiation of data by simplified least squares procedures. Anal. Chem. **36**(8), 1627–1639 (1964)
14. Schneider, J., Di Mitri, D., Limbu, B., Drachsler, H.: Multimodal learning hub: a tool for capturing customizable multimodal learning experiences. In: Pammer-Schindler, V., Pérez-Sanagustín, M., Drachsler, H., Elferink, R., Scheffel, M. (eds.) EC-TEL 2018. LNCS, vol. 11082, pp. 45–58. Springer, Cham (2018). https://doi.org/10.1007/978-3-319-98572-5_4
15. Sohn, T., et al.: Mobility detection using everyday GSM traces. In: Dourish, P., Friday, A. (eds.) UbiComp 2006. LNCS, vol. 4206, pp. 212–224. Springer, Heidelberg (2006). https://doi.org/10.1007/11853565_13
16. Stenneth, L., Wolfson, O., Yu, P.S., Xu, B.: Transportation mode detection using mobile phones and GIS information. In: Proceedings of the 19th ACM SIGSPATIAL International Conference on Advances in Geographic Information Systems, pp. 54–63 (2011)
17. Zhao, H., Hou, C., Alrobassy, H., Zeng, X.: Recognition of transportation state by smartphone sensors using deep Bi-LSTM neural network. J. Comput. Netw. Commun. **2019**, Article ID 4967261 (2019)

An Attack-Resistant Weighted Least Squares Localization Algorithm Based on RSSI

Yitong Liu[1], Jun Peng[2], Xingcheng Liu[2,3(✉)], Yi Xie[1], and Zhao Tang[2]

[1] School of Computer Science and Engineering, Sun Yat-sen University, Guangzhou, China
{isslxc,xieyi5}@mail.sysu.edu.cn
[2] School of Electronics and Information Technology, Sun Yat-sen University, Guangzhou, China
[3] School of Information Science, Guangzhou Xinhua University, Guangzhou, China

Abstract. As an important part of the Internet of things (IoT), wireless sensor networks (WSNs) have been applied in many fields. Most applications require accurate location information, hence node localization is one of the important issues in WSNs. It is very important to ensure the security of localization when WSNs are under attack. A new attack-resistant weighted least squares (ARWLS) algorithm based on RSSI was proposed in the paper. The algorithm is oriented to the problem solution for the situation that the attacker influences the system by tampering with the transmitting power in the localization mechanism. The proposed algorithm can be used in the attack scenarios. Simulations results show that, compared with other algorithms, the proposed algorithm has merits in localization accuracy and robustness to resisting the tampering activities of attackers.

Keywords: Wireless sensor networks · Malicious nodes · Secure localization · Sequential probability ratio test · Weighted least squares

1 Introduction

With the continuous development of related technologies, the Internet of Things (IoT) is playing an increasingly important role in people's daily lives in recent years [1]. As an important part of the IoT, a wireless sensor network (WSN) has a high research value [2]. It has been used in many fields, such as national defense, environmental monitoring, medical health, mechanical fault diagnosis and so on [3,4]. Most applications require accurate location information, and the

The work was supported by the Joint Key Program of the National Natural Science Foundation of China and Guangdong Province of China(Grant No. U2001204), by the National Natural Science Foundation of China (Grant Nos. 61873290, 61972431 and 61572534), and by the Science and Technology Program of Guangzhou, China (Grant No. 202002030470).

S. Paiva et al. (Eds.): SmartCity360° 2020, LNICST 372, pp. 476–494, 2021.
https://doi.org/10.1007/978-3-030-76063-2_32

information collected by the sensor nodes cannot be processed correctly without location information of themselves. Equipping the node with a global positioning system(GPS) device or deploying the node in a predetermined location is the direct mean to obtain the location information. However, the resources of WSNs are limited, the power consumption of equipping each node with GPS devices is too high. In addition, under nonline-of-sight (NLOS) conditions, the error caused by GPS becomes larger [5,6]. What's more, WSNs are often deployed in harsh and dynamically changing environments, and it is not practical to deploy each sensor node in a specific location. In practice, only part of the node's location information is known, which is called the anchor node. It is a critical technique in WSN to estimate the location of the target node by using prior information. Currently, the localization algorithms can be divided into two categories: the range-based [7–10] and the range-free [11–13] localization algorithms. For the range-based algorithm, the distance or angle values are directly measured and computed through the physical ranging technologies. For the range-free localization algorithms, the location estimate of the target node relies on the connectivity of the whole network topology.

1.1   Related Works

In recent decades, various security strategies have been proposed to address the node location in malicious attack environments. The strategies for resisting attacks vary according to the application scenarios. The attack-resistant localization strategies proposed in literatures can be divided into three categories: malicious anchor node detection algorithms [14–16], robust localization algorithms [17–20] and location verification strategies [21–23].

In the process of location estimation of the target node, the information provided by the anchor node is required, so the reliability of the anchor node largely determines the reliability of the location result. The method of malicious anchor node detection is designed to filter the information provided by the malicious anchor node by analyzing the network model and the behavior characteristics of the malicious anchor node, and then to estimate the location of the target node with the anchor node with high reliability. To this end, a malicious node detection algorithm based on clustering and consistency evaluation (MNDC) [14] was proposed. The algorithm takes advantage of the consistency between the distance measurements of ToA and RSSI. The differences between the distance measurements of ToA and RSSI are taken as the basis of the detection. With the aid of the designed scheme, the anchor nodes under malicious attack when using ToA are eliminated. However, the limitation of this algorithm lies in the need to ensure that RSSI measurements are always protected from attack. Grag. et al. proposed an efficient Gradient Descent (GD) approach [15]. The approach is divided into two stages. In the first stage, the least squares solution is searched by gradient descent method. When the sum of the gradients of anchor nodes exceeds the preset threshold, the selection pruning stage is entered. 50% anchor nodes with larger gradient are regarded as malicious, while the remaining anchor nodes are adopted to continue the iteration.

The ability of the algorithm to tolerate attacks can be improved by improving the robustness of the distance measurement stage and the position calculation stage. Improving the robustness of distance measurement is usually achieved through time or space constraints. Distance-Bounding Protocol [17] was proposed, which can prevent distance shortening attacks caused by early response of nodes. However, there is a big limitation in the distance boundary protocol. The protocol is based on the time of arrival of the RF signal, leading to an extremely high requirement on the accuracy of the recorded time. The nanosecond error in the time is represented as a difference of tens of centimeters in the distance. At present, most localization algorithms adopt Least Squares (LS) in the final estimation of position calculation stage. The essence of the LS algorithm is to find the coordinates of the target nodes corresponding to the minimum sum of residual of all anchor nodes. LS is sensitive to outliers. Once an anchor node is under attack, it may cause a relatively large deviation in the estimated location. To avoid that, Li et al. [18] divided the anchor nodes into several subsets, and in each subset Least Median Squares (LMS) is used to get the corresponding location candidate values. The candidates with the minimum residual value is regarded as the location estimation. In addition, they proposed an adaptive LS and LMS positioning mechanism, among which the LS has the computational advantage in the absence of attacks. To solve the secure localization problem, a weighted Least Squares (WLS) algorithm [19] was proposed based on RSSI. To go further, an attack-resistant localization algorithm [20], was proposed. The consistency of multiple anchor nodes can be used in the same network to achieve secure localization. Meanwhile, a voting-based localization algorithm [20] was presented to treat the problem. According to the coverage of each anchor node, the area to be detected can be partitioned into grids. The grids are judged and rated with a vote. Finally, the center of the grid with the highest number of votes is selected as the final location estimation of the target node.

Location verification system is also used to improve the security of the networks. The location anomaly detection (LAD) algorithm [23] determines whether the node is malicious by judging whether the error between the estimation and the real location is within a certain threshold. If the difference value does not exceed the threshold, then a decision is made that the node is benign. However, the prior information of node distribution is required. Therefore, LAD does not work in many scenarios, the final solution of which is to be resolved.

1.2 Contributions

In order to solve the security problem of range-based localization mechanism under attack, we proposed an attack-resistant weighted least squares (ARWLS) localization algorithm. ARWLS algorithm operation consists of an anchor node screening stage and a final location calculation stage. In the proposed algorithm, the main contributions can be summarized as follows:

- A scheme is proposed to identify the malicious anchor nodes.
- The quasi-Newton [24] method is used to determine the reference anchor nodes, and the initial location estimate, which is the basis of the followed detection, but not the whole detection itself.
- The estimate of the initial location is used to approximate the real location of the target node. Then the power difference information is used as the sample of sequential probability ratio test (SPRT).

Compared with other secure localization algorithms, the proposed algorithm guarantees the security of location estimation from the two aspects: eliminating or decreasing the malicious anchor nodes and improving the robustness of the location calculation. In addition, the proposed algorithm has no requirement of prior information or additional hardware facilities.

The rest of the paper is organized as follows. The network model and the localization problem formulations under malicious attack are demonstrated in Sect. 2. The idea and the specific process of the proposed algorithm are described in detail in Sect. 3. Then the simulation results and corresponding analysis are presented in Sect. 4. Finally, Sect. 5 summarize the work of the paper.

2 Network Model and Problem Formulations

2.1 Network Model

We consider a two-dimensional localization system in which all anchor nodes in the region are randomly distributed. It is assumed that the system satisfies the following conditions.

1) The network is stable and the locations of all the sensor nodes are not changed after deployed;
2) All anchor nodes are within the communication range of the target node, so the target node can receive signals from all anchor nodes.

2.2 Problem Formulations

It is assumed that there are N anchor nodes with known locations in the network. The location of the i-th anchor is denoted by $\mathbf{A}_i = [x_i, y_i]^T, i = 1, 2 \cdots N$. Among the N anchor nodes, M of them are malicious, which will send false messages to interfere with the localization process. Assume that there is a target node to be located in the system, and its real position is denoted by $\mathbf{T} = [x_t, y_t]^T$. Assuming that the anchor nodes send messages at a fixed power level, the target node is located according to the received signal strength indication and the location of the anchor nodes. The true distance between the anchor node and the target node is represented with $d = [d_1, d_2, \cdots d_N]^T$, where $d_i = \|\mathbf{A}_i - \mathbf{T}\|$. For RSSI ranging, the distance between the anchor nodes and the target node can be estimated through the path loss in the transmission process, which is related to the specific transmission model. In this paper, the log-distance model is adopted, and the received power can be modeled as Eq. (1) [25]:

$$p^r = p_0^t - 10a \log_{10}(d). \tag{1}$$

where p_0^t(dBm) represents the transmitting power of the anchor node at a reference distance, p^r represents the received power of the anchor nodes, a denotes the path loss exponent, and d is the distance between the anchor node and the target node. Equation (1) describes the received power under ideal conditions. The target node receives P packets from the i-th anchor node, and the corresponding received power can be denoted by $\mathbf{p}_i^r = [p_{i1}^r, p_{i2}^r, \ldots, p_{iP}^r]^T, i = 1, 2, \ldots, N$. Given the transmitting power p_0^t and received power p_{ij}^r, the corresponding distance measurement ed_{ij} can be estimated, as shown in Eq. (2):

$$ed_{ij} = 10^{\frac{p_0^t - p_{ij}^r}{10a}}, i = 1, 2, \ldots, N, j = 1, 2, \ldots, P. \tag{2}$$

According to Eq. (2), transmitting power transmitting power p_0^t, received power p_{ij}^r and the path loss exponent a all have an impact on the distance measurement. Based on Eq. (2), it can be inferred that the relationship between the received signal power and the measured distance is nonlinear.

Noncoordinated Attacks. In a noncoordinated attack environment, the attacker acts alone on each captured anchor node, tampering with its transmitting power, and the target node is unaware whether the transmitting power of the anchor node has been changed. In this paper, we model this attack scenario by reporting the received signal power of the target node. Under noncoordinated attack, the received signal power at the target node can be defined as Eq. (3):

$$(p_i^r)^{(nc)} = \begin{cases} p_0^t - 10a \log_{10}(d_i) + n_i, & \text{if } M_i = 0 \\ p_{m_i}^{nc} - 10a \log_{10}(d_i) + n_i, & \text{if } M_i = 1 \end{cases} \tag{3}$$

where $M_i = 0$ denotes the case that the i-th anchor node is benign, and $M_i = 1$ denotes the i-th anchor node is malicious. p_0^t represents the predefined transmitting power, and all the benign anchor nodes broadcast packets. A zero-mean Gaussian random variable n_i is used to model measurement noise, and the variance of n_i is σ^2, i.e. $n_i \sim \mathcal{N}(0, \sigma^2)$. n_i is influenced by environmental factors. The transmitting power of the malicious anchor node is tampered to p_m^t by the attacker. $p_{m_i}^{nc}$ is defined as $p_{m_i}^{nc} = p_0^t + \kappa$, where κ is a Gaussian random variable with a mean of zero and variance of σ_{att}^2, i.e. $\kappa \sim \mathcal{N}(0, \sigma_{att}^2)$. The number of malicious anchor nodes, m, and the standard deviation of attack term, σ_{att}, will affect the degree of attack to the whole network.

Coordinated Attacks. In a coordinated attack environment, the attacker may specify a position, which may be randomly selected, or a position that is determined to be favorable to the attacker. The specified position can be denoted by $\mathbf{T}_{mal} = [x_m, y_m]^T$. Multiple malicious anchor nodes communicate with each

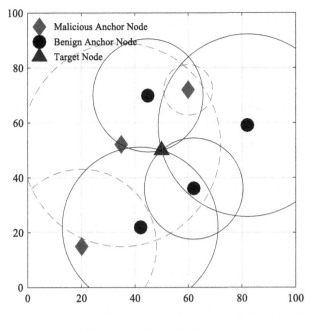

(a) Noncoordinated Attacks

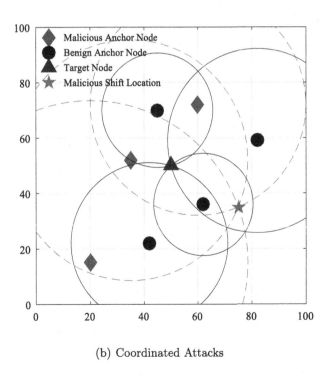

(b) Coordinated Attacks

Fig. 1. Attacks caused by malicious anchors in a WSN with 7 anchor nodes and 3 of them are malicious, ignoring the measurement noise n.

other to reach cooperation and attempt to locate the target node to $\mathbf{T}_{mal}$. In this scenario, the received power $(p_i^r)^c$ can be modeled as:

$$(p_i^r)^{(c)} = \begin{cases} p_0^t - 10a\log_{10}(d_i) + n_i, & \text{if } M_i = 0 \\ p_{m_i}^c - 10a\log_{10}(d_i) + n_i, & \text{if } M_i = 1 \end{cases} \tag{4}$$

where $p_{m_i}^c$ is defined by the distance between $\mathbf{T}_{mal}$ and $\mathbf{T}$. We define $d_a = \|\mathbf{T}_{mal} - \mathbf{T}\|$. Therefore, $p_{m_i}^c$ can be defined as $p_{m_i}^c = p_0^t - 10a\log_{10}(\frac{\|\mathbf{T}_{mal} - \mathbf{A}_i\|}{d_i})$. In fact, the goal of the coordinated attack is to change the distance measurements from the malicious anchor nodes to the target node $\mathbf{T}$ into the distance to the specified position $\mathbf{T}_{mal}$ by tampering with the transmitting power. The degree of coordinated attack can be represented by the value of d_a.

Figure 1 shows the models of the uncoordinated attack and coordinated attack, where the measurement noise is 0. Suppose that there are seven anchor nodes in the system, three of which are malicious. In Fig. 1(a), the three malicious anchor nodes act alone. In Fig. 1(b), the three malicious anchor nodes attempt to shift the target node to the specified location.

3   Proposed Algorithm for Secure Localization

Aiming at the situation that the attacker tampers with the transmitting power of anchor node based on RSSI, we proposed an attack-resistant weighted least squares (ARWLS) to achieve secure localization.

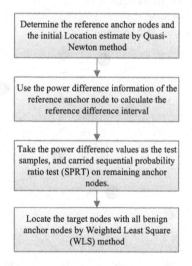

Fig. 2. Main steps of ARWLS algorithm

The main steps of ARWLS algorithm are shown in Fig. 2. The algorithm can be divided into two stages. The first stage is the anchor node screening. At this stage, we remove the detected malicious anchor nodes. This stage consists of three steps. First, assuming that there is no malicious anchor node, the residual sum of all nodes is taken as the objective function and the quasi-Newton method is adopted to obtain the initial location estimate of the target node. According to the characteristics of the initial location estimate, which is close to the real location of the target node, the anchor nodes with smaller gradients are regarded as the reference anchor nodes. Then, based on the distance measurements and the initial location estimate, the approximate value of the difference between the real transmitting power and the transmitting power in the non-attacking state can be calculated. According to the power difference information of the reference anchor nodes, a reference error interval can be calculated, and the judgment of the remaining anchor nodes is regarded as a hypothesis testing problem [26,27]. The power difference values are taken as the test samples, with which the method of sequential probability ratio test (SPRT) [28] is adopted to detect the remaining anchor nodes. In the second stage, the benign anchor nodes are used for positioning. The mean value and variance of multiple measurements are used to calculate the corresponding weight of each benign anchor node, and the weighted least square method is used for the final location estimate of the target node.

In the first stage, the malicious anchor nodes are eliminated to prevent the false information from being used in the localization of the target nodes and improve the capability of the algorithm in resisting attacks. In the second stage, the robustness of location calculation is improved. Even if some malicious anchor nodes are not removed in the first stage and then allowed to participate in the localization process, the final location estimate will not be greatly affected. Therefore, the algorithm improves the security of location from the above two aspects. Next, we will elaborate on each step in detail. Figure 3 is the flow chart of the whole ARWLS algorithm.

3.1 Anchor Nodes Screening Stage

In this stage, the received power information corresponding to all anchor nodes is collected. Therefore, the average measured distance corresponding to each anchor node $\overline{ed}_i, i = 1, 2, \ldots, N$ can be calculated. The satge consists of the following three steps: the reference anchors determined, the reference interval computed, and the SPRT operation performed.

Determine the Reference Anchor Nodes and the Initial Location Estimate. Firstly, the BFGS which is one of quasi-Newton methods is used to obtain the LS solution when all anchor nodes participate in the localization of the target nodes. The BFGS algorithm has a superlinear convergence speed, which can converge to the LS solution faster than the gradient descent (GD) algorithm. Assuming there is no malicious anchor node, the BFGS algorithm is then used

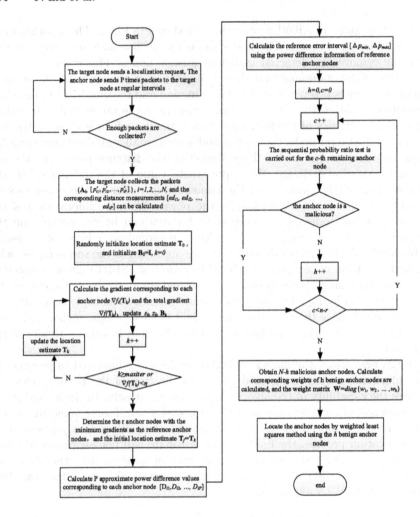

Fig. 3. Flowchart of ARWLS algorithm

to iteratively search the LS solutions. The residual sum of all anchor nodes is taken as the objective function, as shown in Eq. 5:

$$\hat{\mathbf{T}} = \arg\min_{\mathbf{T}} \sum_{i=1}^{N} (\|\mathbf{A}_i - \mathbf{T}\| - \overline{ed}_i)^2 = \arg\min_{\mathbf{T}} f(\mathbf{T}). \tag{5}$$

According to the BFGS algorithm, we have,

$$\mathbf{B}_{k+1}\left[\nabla f(\mathbf{T}_{k+1}) - \nabla f(\mathbf{T}_k)\right] \approx \mathbf{T}_{k+1} - \mathbf{T}_k, \tag{6}$$

where k denotes the number of iterations, $\mathbf{B}_k$ is approximately positive definite matrix of the inverse of the Hessian matrix $\mathbf{H}_k^{-1}$, $\nabla f(\mathbf{T}_k)$ represents the total gradient corresponding to the location of k-th iteration.

According to the relevant properties of the BFGS algorithm, the update formula of the location estimate $\mathbf{T}_k$ is shown in Eq. (7)

$$\mathbf{T}_{k+1} = \mathbf{T}_k - \lambda \nabla f(\mathbf{T}_{k+1}), \tag{7}$$

where λ denotes the step size for searching.

Calculate the Power Difference Reference Interval. Since the initial location estimate $\mathbf{T}_f$ is close to the real position of the target node, it can be used to approximate the real location of the target node $\mathbf{T}$. Given the received power p_{ij}^r and the approximate location of the target node $\mathbf{T}_f$, the j-th transmitting power of the i-th anchor can be approximately inferred with Eq. (8) if the measurement noise is ignored,

$$p_{ij}^t \approx 10a \log_{10}(\|\mathbf{A}_i - \mathbf{T}_f\|) + p_{ij}^r. \tag{8}$$

All anchor nodes send P packets at regular intervals. Then, each anchor node gets the corresponding P distance measurements. Given the distance measurements ed_{ij} and the predefined transmitting power p_0^r, the j-th transmitting power of the i-th anchor can be approximately inferred with Eq. (9) if the measurement noise is ignored,

$$\hat{p}_{ij} \approx 10a \log_{10}(ed_{ij}) + p_{ij}^r. \tag{9}$$

Therefore, the power difference value can be calculated as Eq. (13):

$$\begin{aligned} D_{ij} &\approx \hat{p}_{ij} - p_{ij}^t \\ &= 10a \log_{10}(\frac{ed_{ij}}{\|\mathbf{A}_i - \mathbf{T}_f\|}). \end{aligned} \tag{10}$$

For benign anchor nodes, the difference is only affected by the error of the LS solution and measurement noise in the first stage. Compared with the error introduced by the malicious anchor nodes, this difference is very small. The set of reference anchor nodes is a subset of all anchor nodes. Based on the premise that the reference anchor nodes are benign, the difference information of the reference anchor node is taken as the basis for establishing the detection model. The power difference values are taken as the samples. Suppose a reference anchor node is an individual, then for the i-th individual, the mean value $\overline{D}_i$ and the variance s_i^2 of the individual can be calculated as follows:

$$\overline{D}_i = \frac{\sum_{j=1}^{P} D_{ij}}{P}, \tag{11}$$

$$s_i^2 = \frac{\sum_{j=1}^{P}(D_{ij} - \overline{D}_i)^2}{P - 1}. \tag{12}$$

Averaging the mean values of the different individuals, the mean value of total samples can be calculated as Eq. (16):

$$\overline{D} = \sum_{i=1}^{r} \frac{D_i}{r}. \tag{13}$$

Next, the differences between individuals of each reference anchor node are analyzed, and the variation s_e^2 of the mean value $\overline{D}_i$ between individuals can be expressed as Eq. (14):

$$s_e^2 = \sum_{i=1}^{r} \frac{(\overline{D}_i - \overline{D})^2}{r-1}. \tag{14}$$

The variance between individuals s_a^2 is given in Eq. (15):

$$s_a^2 = \sum_{i=1}^{r} \frac{P-1}{N-r} s_i^2, \tag{15}$$

where $N = P \cdot r$ is the total number of samples. Based on the analysis of the s_i^2 and s_a^2, the population distribution of the sample can be described, and the population variance of the sample can be expressed as Eq. (16):

$$s_t^2 = s_e^2 + (1 - \frac{1}{m_h}) s_a^2, \tag{16}$$

where m_h is the harmonized mean of the numer of the measured times. Since each anchor node sends P packets at regular intervals, $m_h = \frac{r}{\frac{1}{P \cdot r}} = P$. Based on the above analysis, the reference error interval of the power difference between reference anchor nodes can be calculated as Eq. (17) and Eq. (18) when the significance level is ϵ:

$$D_{min} = \overline{D} - (z_{1-\frac{\epsilon}{2}}) \times \sqrt{s_t^2}, \tag{17}$$

$$D_{max} = \overline{D} + (z_{1-\frac{\epsilon}{2}}) \times \sqrt{s_t^2}, \tag{18}$$

where $z_{1-\frac{\epsilon}{2}}$ is the upper quartile of $1 - \frac{\epsilon}{2}$ of the standard normal distribution.

Sequential Probability Ratio Test (SPRT). According to the reference difference interval obtained in the previous step, a Bernoulli random variable Z_{ij} can be established for the difference information D_{ij} of the remaining anchor nodes, which is given in Eq. (19),

$$Z_{ij} = \begin{cases} 0, & D_{min} < D_{ij} < D_{max} \\ 1, & others \end{cases}. \tag{19}$$

Define the probability of D_{ij} exceeding the reference difference interval as p, i.e. $P(Z_{ij} = 1) = p$. So the probability that D_{ij} is within the reference difference interval is $1 - p$, i.e. $P(Z_{ij} = 0) = 1 - p$. Two hypotheses H_0 and H_1 can be established:

- H_0: the detected anchor node is benign, $p \leq p_0$,
- H_1: the detected anchor node is malicious, $p > p_1$,

where p_0 and p_1 are preset thresholds.

Through the above test, the malicious anchor nodes can be screened out, and the information provided by them will be eliminated, which is helpful to improve the localization accuracy.

3.2   Location Calculation Stage

For benign anchor nodes, there exists a nonlinear relationship between the received power and the distance measurements. For the anchor node which is far from the target node, the noise of the same size will cause more fluctuation in distance measurements. Therefore, it can be concluded that the anchor nodes close to the target node are more robust to noise [19]. For the malicious nodes, its transmitting power is affected by the extra attack item, so its fluctuation range of the distance measurements is larger.

Firstly, the selected benign anchor nodes are relabeled as $1, 2, \cdots, h$, and the corresponding coordinates are denoted as $(x_i, y_i), i = 1, \cdots, h$. We use the variance of the squares of distance measurements $\mathbf{ed}_i^2 = [ed_{i1}^2, ed_{i2}^2, \ldots, ed_{iP}^2]^T, i = 1, 2, \ldots, N$ as the standard to measure the reliability of anchor nodes. The variance $Var(ed_{ij})^2$ can be calculated as Eq. (20):

$$Var(ed_{ij}^2, \overline{ed}_i^2) = \frac{\sum_{j=1}^{P}(ed_{ij}^2 - \overline{ed}_i^2)^2}{P - 1}. \tag{20}$$

Each anchor node can be weighted by the variance of the square of the distance measurements $Var(ed_{ij})^2$, where the weight of the i-th anchor node can be calculated as Eq. (21)

$$w_i = \frac{1}{Var(ed_{ij}^2, \overline{ed}_i^2)}. \tag{21}$$

The weight matrix can be defined as $\mathbf{W} = diag[w_1, w_2, \ldots, w_h]$. We can use a modified version of the least squares (LS) which is called weighted least squares (WLS) to make the final calculation. The final estimate of the location of the target node can be calculated by $\mathbf{WAt} = \mathbf{b}$, where the matrixes (vectors) are given in Eq. (22)

$$\mathbf{A} = \begin{bmatrix} -2x_1 & -2y_1 & 1 \\ -2x_2 & -2y_2 & 1 \\ \vdots & \vdots & \vdots \\ -2x_h & -2y_h & 1 \end{bmatrix}, \mathbf{b} = \begin{bmatrix} \overline{ed}_1 - x_1^2 - y_1^2 \\ \overline{ed}_2 - x_2^2 - y_2^2 \\ \vdots \\ \overline{ed}_h - x_h^2 - y_h^2 \end{bmatrix}. \tag{22}$$

4   Performance Evaluation

The proposed algorithm is experimently compared with two existing secure localization methods, namely, the Gradient Descent (GD) [15] and the Weighted Least Squares (WLS) [19] in this paper. The GD algorithm includes fix-step Gradient Descent (GD_f) algorithm and variable-step Gradient Descent (GD_v) algorithm, both of which have similar performance in localization accuracy. Here, we only show the performance of GD_f algorithm in this section. In WLS scheme, the prior information of the standard deviation of noise σ is required. In this section, the complexity of the algorithm is also discussed.

4.1   Experimental Platform and Parameters Setting

In this paper, all of the simulation experiments were performed on Mathworks MATLAB 2016a. The simulation environment is as follows: Intel Core I7-8700 CPU @3.20GHZ and 16GB RAM running with Windows 10 64-bit operating system. The parameters setting in the experiment is shown in Table 1 [19], except stated otherwise.

Table 1. Parameters setting

Symbols	Meanings	Values
N	Number of anchor nodes	30
M	Number of malicious anchor nodes	9
r	Number of reference anchor nodes	3
p_0^t	Predifined transmitting power	$-10\,\mathrm{dBm}$
σ	Std deviation of measurement noise	$2\,\mathrm{dBm}$
σ_{att}	Std deviation of attack	$8\,\mathrm{dBm}$
d_a	Distance between the malicious shift location and the target node	$12\,\mathrm{m}$
a	Path loss exponent	4
η	Gradient threshold	$1.8\,\mathrm{m}$
λ	Step size	0.5
P	Number of packages	20
p_0	Null hypothesis threshold	0.1
p_1	Alternative hypothesis threshold	0.9
α	False positive rate	0.01
β	False negative rate	0.01

4.2   Simulation Results

The localization performance of the schemes under noncoordinated and coordinated attacks is demonstrated in this part.

Noncoordinated Attacks. The localization error of different algorithms varying with the std deviation of attack σ_{att} under different levels of noise σ is shown in Fig. 4. This figure shows the localization performance at $\sigma = 2\,\mathrm{dBm}$ and $\sigma = 6\,\mathrm{dBm}$ in Figs. 4(a) and 4(b), respectively. As is shown in the figure, the performance of the proposed ARWLS algorithm in positioning error is more stable than any other algorithms. Even if σ_{att} increases, the proposed algorithm can still ensure relatively high localization accuracy. This is because the proposed ARWLS algorithm eliminates the malicious anchor nodes in the screening stage

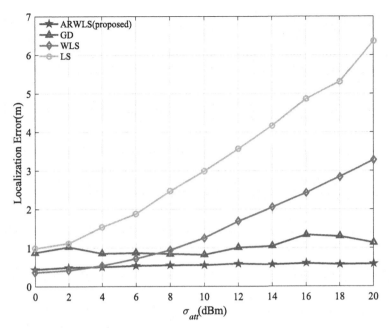

(a) Localization error with varied deviation of attacks at measurement noise σ=2dBm

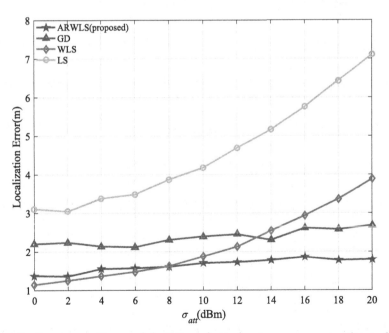

(b) Localization error with varied deviation of attacks at measurement noise σ=6dBm

Fig. 4. Localization error with varied std deviation of attacks, σ_{att}, at different levels of noises, σ.

and improves the robustness in the location calculation stage. When the attack strength (σ_{att}) increases, the proposed scheme will introduce large errors to the localization results once a malicious anchor node participates in the location calculation stage. At the same time, it is more likely that the power difference samples of the malicious anchor node exceed the reference error interval. Therefore, the probability of the malicious anchor nodes being eliminated also increases. Accordingly, the fluctuation range of the localization error becomes relatively small.

In contrast, the information provided by anchor nodes is taken into account for the WLS algorithm. The participation of malicious anchor nodes in localization will inevitably affect the performance of the localization mechanism. For the GD algorithm, it directly eliminates 50% of anchor nodes, leading to a part of benign anchor nodes unable to participate in the final localization. As is shown in Fig. 4(b), when $\sigma > \sigma_{att}$, the localization error of the proposed algorithm is slightly larger than the error of the WLS algorithm. However, when σ_{att} continues increasing, the localization error of the proposed algorithm keeps lower than 2 m till $\sigma_{att} = 20$ dBm, while the error for other three algorithms grows much faster.

In the above experiments, the location of the target node is deployed randomly each time. For the fixed location of the target node, Fig. 5 shows the localization performance of the algorithms. Figure 5(a) shows the performance of the localization error of the algorithms with the standard deviation of the attack σ_{att} when the target node is fixed at the center of the deployment area, (50, 50) and the anchor nodes are randomly distributed, while Fig. 5(b) shows that when the target node is fixed at the edge of the area, (10, 90). Compared with the curves in Fig. 5, the localization error of the proposed ARWLS algorithm is always kept below others, specifically, below 0.5 m and 1 m when the location of the target node is fixed at the center or near the boundary of the deployment area, respectively. Further, compared with other three algorithms, the ARWLS algorithm is less affected as the attack strength increases, demonstrating a strong robustness.

Coordinated Attacks. The case of coordinated attacks is rather complicated. To explain the influence of coordinated attacks, we provide experiments to explain. In our experiments, the percentage of the malicious anchor nodes is 30%. Figure 6 compares the localization performance of the algorithms with a varying distance between the real location of the target node **T** and the shifted location, $\mathbf{T}_{mal}$, tampered by the attacker under coordinated attacks. It is observed that the performance of the WLS is similar to that of the LS. Such a result means that the WLS does not greatly improve the security of the network under coordinated attacks. When $d_a < 20$ m, the localization error of the proposed algorithm is slightly higher than the GD algorithm. This is because the accuracy of anchor node screening stage of the proposed algorithm is relatively low when the value of d_a is small. However, when d_a continues increasing, the proposed algorithm outperforms others, which shows the excellence of the proposed ARWLS algorithm most of the time.

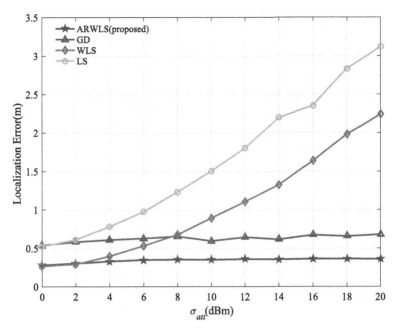

(a) Localization error with the target node fixed at (50, 50), the center of the deployment area

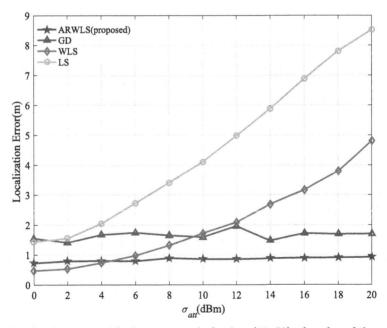

(b) Localization error with the target node fixed at (10, 90), the edge of the area

Fig. 5. Localization error with varied std deviation of attacks, σ_{att}, under noncoordinated attacks.

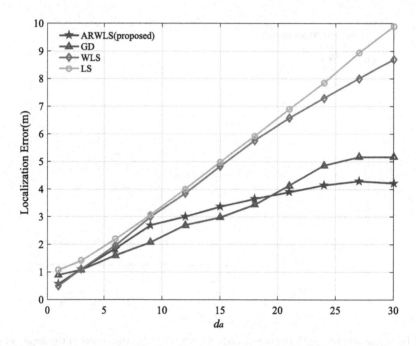

Fig. 6. Localization error with the distance between the real location of the target node and the shifted location d_a under coordinated attacks.

5   Conclusion

Malicious anchor nodes may tamper transmitting power and launch non-coordinated or coordinated attack to the network, which badly affects the estimate accuracy in the RSSI-based localization mechanism. In order to solve the problem of node localization in such a malicious environment, a localization algorithm named ARWLS is proposed in this paper. The algorithm can be implemented without requiring prior information or additional hardware support. The proposed ARWLS algorithm is performed in two stages: the anchor nodes screening stage and the location calculation stage. In the algorithm, the quasi-Newton method is used to determine the reference anchor nodes and the initial location estimate. The approximately calculated power difference is obtained and used as the sample of the SPRT for further screening. Finally, the weighted least squares method is used to improve the robustness of location calculation. The proposed algorithm is compared with the existing algorithms in the performance of localization accuracy. The simulation results show that the proposed algorithm is superior to others, especially in the case of the non-coordinated attacks.

References

1. Khan, I., Belqasmi, F., Glitho, R., Crespi, N., Morrow, M., Polakos, P.: Wireless sensor network virtualization: a survey. IEEE Commun. Surv. Tutor. **18**(1), 553–576 (2016)
2. Liu, X., Li, W., Han, F., Xie, Y.: An optimization scheme of enhanced adaptive dynamic energy consumption based on joint network-channel coding in WSNs. IEEE Sens. J. **17**(18), 6119–6128 (2017)
3. Lu, W., Gong, Y., Liu, X., Wu, J., Peng, H.: Collaborative energy and information transfer in green wireless sensor networks for smart cities. IEEE Trans. Ind. Informat. **14**(4), 1585–1593 (2018)
4. Zhang, Y., Sun, L., Song, H., Cao, X.: Ubiquitous WSN for healthcare: recent advances and future prospects. IEEE Internet Things J. **1**(4), 311–318 (2014)
5. Zhou, B., Chen, Q.: On the particle-assisted stochastic search mechanism in wireless cooperative localization. IEEE Trans. Wirel. Commun. **15**(7), 4765–4777 (2016)
6. Liu, D., Xu, Y., Huang, X.: Identification of location spoofing in wireless sensor networks in non-line-of-sight conditions. IEEE Trans. Ind. Informat. **14**(6), 2375–2384 (2018)
7. Liu, X., Yin, J., Zhang, S., Ding, B., Guo, S., Wang, K.: Range-based localization for sparse 3-D sensor networks. IEEE Internet Things J. **6**(1), 753–764 (2019)
8. Sun, Y., Zhang, F., Wan, Q.: Wireless sensor network-based localization method using TDOA measurements in MPR. IEEE Sens. J. **19**(10), 3741–3750 (2019)
9. Xiong, H., Peng, M., Gong, S., Du, Z.: A Novel hybrid RSS and TOA positioning algorithm for multi-objective cooperative wireless sensor networks. IEEE Sens. J. **18**(22), 9343–9351 (2018)
10. Wu, Y.I., Wang, H., Zheng, X.: WSN localization using RSS in three-dimensional space-a geometric method with closedform solution. IEEE Sens. J. **16**(11), 4397–4404 (2016)
11. Zhao, Y., Liu, X., Han, F., Han, G.: Recovery of hop count matrices for the sensing nodes in Internet of Things. IEEE Internet Things J. **7**(6), 5128–5139 (2020)
12. Ahmadi, Y., Neda, N., Ghazizadeh, R.: Range free localization in wireless sensor networks for homogeneous and non-homogeneous environment. IEEE Sens. J. **16**(22), 8018–8026 (2016)
13. Fan, J., Hu, Y., Luan, T.H., Dong, M.: DisLoc: a convex partitioning based approach for distributed 3-D localization in wireless sensor networks. IEEE Sens. J. **17**(24), 8412–8423 (2017)
14. Liu, X., Su, S., Han, F., Liu, Y., Pan, Z.: A range-based secure localization algorithm for wireless sensor networks. IEEE Sens. J. **19**(2), 785–796 (2019)
15. Garg, R., Varna, A.L., Wu, M.: An Efficient gradient descent approach to secure localization in resource constrained wireless sensor networks. IEEE Trans. Inf. Forens. Secur. **7**(2), 717–730 (2012)
16. Liu, D., Ning, P., Wenliang, D.: Detecting malicious beacon nodes for secure location discovery in wireless sensor networks. In: 25th IEEE International Conference on Distributed Computing Systems (ICDCS 2005), pp. 609–619, Columbus (2005)
17. Brands, S., Chaum, D.: Distance-bounding protocols. In: Helleseth, T. (ed.) EUROCRYPT 1993. LNCS, vol. 765, pp. 344–359. Springer, Heidelberg (1994). https://doi.org/10.1007/3-540-48285-7_30
18. Li, Z., Trappe, W., Zhang, Y., Nath, B.: Robust statistical methods for securing wireless localization in sensor networks. In: Fourth International Symposium Information Processing in Sensor Networks, pp. 91–98, April 2005

494   Y. Liu et al.

19. Mukhopadhyay, B., Srirangarajan, S., Kar, S.: Robust range-based secure localization in wireless sensor networks. In: IEEE Global Communications Conference (GLOBECOM). Abu Dhabi, United Arab Emirates 2008, pp. 1–6 (2018)
20. Liu, D., Ning, P., Du, W.K.: Attack-resistant location estimation in sensor networks. In: IPSN: Fourth International Symposium on Information Processing in Sensor Networks, 2005, Boise, ID, USA 2005, pp. 99–106 (2005)
21. Capkun, S., Rasmussen, K., Cagalj, M., Srivastava, M.: Secure location verification with hidden and mobile base stations. IEEE Trans. Mob. Comput. **7**(4), 470–483 (2008)
22. Capkun, S., Hubaux, J.: Secure positioning in wireless networks. IEEE J. Sel. Areas Commun. **24**(2), 221–232 (2006)
23. Du, W., Fang, L., Ningi, P.: LAD: localization anomaly detection for wireless sensor networks. In: 19th IEEE International Parallel and Distributed Processing Symposium, pp. 1–15, CO, Denver (2005)
24. Jin, L., Zhang, Y.: Discrete-time zhang neural network for online time-varying nonlinear optimization with application to manipulator motion generation. IEEE Trans. Neural Netw. Learn. Syst. **26**(7), 1525–1531 (2015)
25. Rappaport, T.S.: Wireless Communications: Principles and Practice. Prentice-Hall, Upper Saddle River (2002)
26. Koh, J.Y., Nevat, I., Leong, D., Wong, W.: Geo-spatial location spoofing detection for Internet of Things. IEEE Internet Things J. **3**(6), 971–978 (2016)
27. Zhang, P., Nagarajan, S.G., Nevat, I.: Secure location of things (SLOT): mitigating localization spoofing attacks in the Internet of Things. IEEE Internet Things J. **4**(6), 2199–2206 (2017)
28. Ho, J., Wright, M., Das, S.K.: ZoneTrust: fast zone-based node compromise detection and revocation in wireless sensor networks using sequential hypothesis testing. IEEE Trans. Dependable Secure Comput. **9**(4), 494–511 (2012)

Smart Governance for Sustainable Smart Cities

Promotion as a Tool of Smart Governance in Cities

Katarína Vitálišová[(✉)] [iD], Anna Vaňová, Kamila Borseková, and Darina Rojíková

Faculty of Economics, Matej Bel University, Tajovského 10, 97590 Banská Bystrica, Slovakia
{katarina.vitalisova,anna.vanova,kamila.borsekova,
darina.rojikova}@umb.sk

Abstract. The aim of the paper is to identify the promotion tools used as a part of smart governance in the city and verify its utilization in the cities of the Slovak Republic. The paper defines the tools of smart governance and its interconnections with the promotion tools of the cities based on the theoretical review. Subsequently, the defined tools are verified by the empirical research in 141 cities of the Slovak Republic. The research findings are supplemented by the examples of good practice in smart communication from the Slovak cities. Based on the discussion of the research results the strengths, weaknesses and challenges of promotion tools' utilization in smart governance are formulated.

Keywords: Smart governance · Promotion · Tools

1 Introduction

We live in a time when the communication is strongly influenced by modern technologies, such as laptops, tablets and smart phones. The vast majority of people also use these devices to browse the information on websites and share the ideas via social media. These changes in the communication reflects also the new tools of smart governance in cities. The focus is on regular and multi-channel communication with all relevant stakeholders including the virtual space.

The new forms of communication with stakeholders make easier to actively involve them into the local governance, access information and co-create local policy. In the paper, we focus on the promotion tools used as a part of smart governance in the city and verify its utilization in the cities of the Slovak Republic.

The paper is divided into three chapter. The theoretical part defines the promotion tools and its specifics as a part of smart governance. In part Material and methodology we explain how the research was done and which material was used. In the fourth chapter, we present the research results of realized empirical research on mapping the utilization of promotion tools in the Slovak cities, which is supplemented by the examples of best practices. To conclude the paper we summarizes the strengths, weaknesses and challenges of promotion tools' utilization in smart governance.

© ICST Institute for Computer Sciences, Social Informatics and Telecommunications Engineering 2021
Published by Springer Nature Switzerland AG 2021. All Rights Reserved
S. Paiva et al. (Eds.): SmartCity360° 2020, LNICST 372, pp. 497–510, 2021.
https://doi.org/10.1007/978-3-030-76063-2_33

2 Smart Governance in Cities and Its Tools

The development of new technologies influences all spheres of society including public sector. The most evident is an impact at the lowest level of public administration, which is the closest to citizens, so it means in cities, towns and villages.

The transformation of public administration at local level in line with the technological progress, digitalization and "smartness" in decision making has resulted in a new phenomenon smart governance within the smart city ecosystem.

Based on the deep literature and research studies analysis one of the most complex definition provides Ruhlandt (2018, p. 10). He defines smart governance as "a processual interplay among a diverse set of stakeholders, equipped with different roles and responsibilities, organized in various external and internal structures and organization, driven and facilitated by technology and data, involving certain types of legislation, polices and exchange arrangements, for the purpose of achieving either substantive outputs for cities or procedural changes."

Smart governance brings smart cities initiatives to citizens, supports their participation in transparent decision-making process including implementation, monitoring and evaluating these initiatives and strengths the collaboration of stakeholders in these activities by ICT (Albino et al. 2015; Misuraca et al. 2011; Baccarne et al. 2014; Scholl and Scholl 2017; Osella et al. 2016; Guendeuz et al. 2017).

Smart governance in cities includes management of:

– city infrastructure containing free access to information and presence of technologies. They are a key element of smart governance implementation. The government in smart city aims to harmonize management, governance and policy with other factors below to define and implement public policies based on sharing visions and strategies with the relevant stakeholders (Nam and Pardo 2011; Mellouli et al. 2014).
– the resources necessary for the development of smart cities (financial, material, technological, natural, human etc.) including performance assessment (Maheshwari and Janssen 2014; Nam and Pardo 2014).
– human assets and other immaterial capital (networks, intellectual capital, knowledge, data, etc.) (Lee and Lee 2014; Lombardi et al. 2011).

The importance of these factors as a core of smart governance was confirmed also by Castelnovo et al. (2015) and Pereira et al. (2018).

All activities within smart governance can be divided into two groups - participation in public policy processes (including informing) and involvement in improving services in the city (co-creation of smart city services). Participation of stakeholders increases openness, transparency, accountability of local authority and thus the quality of relations between stakehodlers and local governments. Governments use and share data, information and knowledge to support evidence-based decision-making that enables governments to make more informed decisions and improve the effectiveness of public policies and programs. There can be used the traditional tools of participation as well as their innovative forms or new one (Castelnovo et al. 2015). Co-creation of smart city services can help increase the city's competitiveness and citizens' quality of life, through the use of ICT in city planning and management. Innovative services provide citizens with information, knowledge and actions related to various aspects of their city life (Lee and Lee 2014).

The central use of ICT-based participation tools in public policy as well in creation of city services is confirmed by many authors (inter alia Díaz-Díaz and Pérez-González 2016; Pereira et al. 2017; Kleinhans et al. 2015; Castelnovo et al. 2015; Khan et al. 2015; Navarro-Galera et al. 2016). These tools increase stakeholders' ability to participate in governance, in all phases of public policy, including public service delivery processes at various stages of preparation such as planning, decision-making, implementation and evaluation. It can help decision-makers make better decisions that meet the needs of the population. It leads to the concept of participatory government, which is strongly linked to a governance model that promotes communication, interaction, cooperation, participation in governance and direct democratization (Pereira et al. 2017) The Internet and ICT have enabled citizens to reduce the gap or even connect with political elites and thus influence policy-making, especially today, when traditional participation is in decline. The local governments have become to be aware of the value of the opportunities given by ICTs (Nam and Pardo 2014).

However, to use ICTs for the purposes below it is necessary to publish and share transparently all data and information about the local municipality (e.g. their strategical, financial, legislative documents, statistics etc.). The link between transparency and smart cities lies in both technology and also in information that is truly transparent and digitized, making it easier to find and use. Different categories of transparency allow citizens to use government data to create new and useful applications that focus on to citizens, solve their problems and thus improve life in the city. Thus, digital information can help address the goals of a smart city for a more informed and participatory citizen (Chourabi et al. 2012).

Based on the study of literature and research studies (inter alia Macintosh 2005; Castelnovo et al. 2015; Estevez and Janowski 2013; Chourabi et al. 2012; Wijnhoven et al. 2015; Gil-Garcia et al. 2015; Johannessen and Berntzen 2018) to the modern forms of e-participation and e-democracy belong electronic e-voting, e-petition, e-referendum, e-panel, discussion forums and chatting rooms, electronic community, electronic civil boards. To support the decision-making process very efficient tools are electronic advisory elections, simulation of decision making, quick polls and surveys. To the tools that strongly influence the activity of stakeholders to participate belong various forms of promotion tools and communication channels (websites, social media, PR, blogs, etc.) as well as mobile applications and various digital platforms, which are the subject of our deeper study in the paper.

Even though, the internet and modern ICT bring new opportunities for local municipalities, the challenge is a lack of knowledge and skills of citizens or other stakeholders as their users. That is why it is necessary to combine the traditional and modern tools of smart governance, to increase awareness and develop the skills of stakeholders to become an equal partner in relationship with local government.

2.1 Modern Forms of Promotion in Smart Governance

Nowadays, new modern forms of promotion play an important role in increasing citizen involvement and support the development of new governance models (Jaeger 2003;

Stamati et al. 2015). To the most progressive and more and more frequently used tools belong websites, discussion forums, blogs, social media, mobile applications, influencers activities, various kinds of events (real or virtual), etc. Implementation of these tools in practice has several positive effects, such as improving cooperation and communication between government and citizens, empowering citizens, transparency and openness of government, and final co-governance with all relevant stakeholders (Stamati et al. 2015; Linders 2012; Jaeger 2003). They can be key drivers of new strategies for managing public consultation and interaction in public policy-making.

From the theoretical point of view these tools that use local municipalities as a part of marketing activities are also a part of smart governance tools. Promotion mix used by cities informs about the products or other activities of the cities and in synergy with other marketing tools it influences the behavior of target groups to perceive them positively, to buy or to consummate the product. The communication should also provide feedback and the ability to correct the errors. Feedback is a source of impulses and the basis of collective learning (Ježek et al. 2007). Active utilization of internet in the promotion of cities strengths its role also as a part of smart governance tools. It allows the global coverage, low distribution costs and interactivity, thanks to which consumers have the opportunity to react retrospectively to the city's suggestions, plans or strategies as a part of local policy.

The summary of promotion tools used by the cities including these ones which are based on modern ICTs and internet presents Table 1.

Table 1. Tools of promotion by Vaňová et al. (2017).

Tool	Aims	Forms
Public relations	Increasing trust, changing attitudes and behavior, persuading of subjects, building an image	Direct (interpersonal communication, meetings, informal meetings, publications), indirect (media, events, annual reports, sponsorship, lobbying, information services, bulletins, etc.)
Advertising	Present and promote the city's product (s) through the media for fee	Communication channels (internet, printed materials, multimedia), promotional materials (leaflets, brochures, maps, calendars, postcards, publications, posters, tourist guides, videos, banners, etc.)
Sales promotion	Support the goals of the communication mix with short-term incentives aimed at activating of will to buy or sell	Price benefits for entrepreneurs, participation in exhibitions and fairs, presentations to journalists, removal of bureaucratic barriers, etc.
Persona communication	To offer the area to potential visitors, residents, investors, entrepreneurs, etc. through a verbal presentation	Creating and maintaining personal relationships, formal or informal presentation, sales contracts, personal friendships, etc.

(continued)

Table 1. (*continued*)

Tool	Aims	Forms
Events	Increase customer and media interest in the city	Social (balls), cultural (concerts, theaters), sports (tournaments), corporate (company days), historical (festivities), gastronomic (food preparation), business (exhibitions), educational (conferences), information (open days) and other events
Virtual communication	Communicate with customers with precise targeting	Blog, banner, text links, e-mail, chat, audiovisual communication, social networks
Direct mail	Address a precisely defined target segment	Telephone, post office, internet, e-mail, teleshopping
Word-of-mouth	Exchange information with a direct link to the territory and its products	Communication between persons
Buzz communication	Make a buzz	Interesting, unusual and often controversial topics that would have the potential to cause excitement between consumers and the media
Virtual communication	Achieve exponential growth of product awareness by non-managed dissemination of information among people on the internet	A message (in the form of an image, animation, video) with promotional content that attracts so much attention from consumers that they send it and spread it
Guerilla	Rise an attention	A surprising, original and unconventional campaign with a low budget
Product placement	Promote the city intentionally and for fee	Placing the territory in a positive context in an audiovisual work
Mobil communication	Communicate fast with the customers	Phone calls, SMS messages, applications

For the empirical research in the Slovak cities we selected following modern tools of promotion, that belong also to the tools of smart governance in cities:

Social networks – they consist of the community of users, people or organizations that have something in common. For instance, it can be real friendship, kinship, employment, hobby, interests, or a particular social problem. Such users are interconnected and share information. Communication takes place on the Internet with the access from a computer or a mobile phone. Today, the most popular international social networks include Facebook, Twitter, YouTube, Instagram, Linked In, etc.

Social networks provide a lot of opportunities for interaction with citizens through plug-in applications, groups and fanpages. Each social network is specific and has its specific users. Social media give the users a chance to share their ideas, contents and relationships online. The user can create, comment and post their own content and share it with the others. The users' posts can have the form of a text, a video, animation, images, photos, etc. The concept of social networking creates vast possibilities for presentation. Creative and interactive communication brings the product, place or brand to attention. On the other hand, customers can attach videos, photos or comments to their profiles. They can also have discussions managed and possibly entered by the discussion group administrators. In this way information is spread to people who would probably not get it otherwise.

Chat and audio-visual communication - The Internet is used for visual and voice communication, so it enables arranging video conferences, discussion forums, IP telephoning, instant messaging (ICQ, g-talk, skype). All these technology options make communication faster and allow better cooperation between various entities. The great advantage is a quick immediate response. Chat allows electronic communication between the Internet users in real time, or on-line discussions with several users at the same time.

Blog is a form of Internet communication, that allows publication of promotional texts, attaching audio files available to a greater number of stakeholders– we can speak of millions –practically free of charge.

Mobile communication includes various formats and principles of use of mobile marketing communication through text messaging or applications. The advantage of mobile marketing communication is a possibility of accurate targeting of a campaign (information about the consumer's identity, behaviour, personal preferences and geographic location), the ability of mediate direct interaction between the advertiser and recipient, high operability in real time, simple and quick updating, high user comfort, low cost, large scale use and, last but not least, simple measurability (Vaňová et al. 2017).

Websites and website promotion are a part of internet marketing. There are different synonyms of the term used in literature, e.g. on-line marketing or web marketing. Website is a collection of texts, multimedia components, images, etc., arranged in a document which is placed on a web server and made available via the internet (Stuchlík and Dvořáček 2000). The purpose of a website is to a build a brand, to provide information about products and activities for all interest groups. They also provide a selling advertising space, products and services over the Internet (Janouch 2010). To the form of selling advertising space belong banners, that are linked to something exceptional on the homepage. **Banners** can be static, animated or interactive. A specific form of banner is a button. It is usually placed in the upper part of the website and is used for promotion of other web servers. To make the banner successful, it needs to have an attractive headline and provide a simple and quick approach to the message. The other possibility is an **I-Candy** - graphic type of internet advertising. It takes the form of an animation or game. They are smiling and sometimes a bit cheeky icons and banners that expand when clicked on them. A new website will be launched with interesting graphics and impressive music. **Intermercial** is a graphic type of advertising on website, in a size of the entire screen. It is an intrusive animated advertisement that appears in the content of individual websites, while acting as a television spot. But unlike a TV spot, intermercial allows, after playing, a visit to the corresponding website. **Subvert** is an advertisement accessible on the Internet. If the user clicks on the ad, they will see about 20 s of images and audio about the product/brand/activity being promoted, and then automatically return to the website they started on. The last possibility is **a screensaver**, which is a type of poster advertising on the computer. The screen saver is used by most computer users and is therefore a potential place for advertising.

3   Material and Methodology

The paper deals with the actual topic of smart governance tools and role of communication in them. The aim of the paper is to identify the promotion tools used as a part of smart governance in the city and verify its utilization in the cities of the Slovak Republic.

For the definition of smart governance tools and promotion tools we use the method of literature review of foreign and domestic scientific papers and books. It helps us to categorize the tools and identify mutual penetrations of both tools categories (promotion x smart governance). The defined tools we verified by the empirical research in all 141 cities of the Slovak Republic during 1. 4. – 25. 6. 2020. We collected data on used promotion tools from the cities websites, published official reports by the cities and profiles on social networks. We use the method of observation, analysis, comparison, synthesis and deduction.

The research sample consists of 141 cities of the Slovak Republic within 7 size categories (Table 2) from 1000 inhabitants to more as 100 000 inhabitants.

Table 2. Number of the Slovak cities by the size categories by Slovak Statistical Office (2019)

Size categories of the cities	Number of cities	Share of the cities
100000+	2	1,42%
50000–99999	8	5,67%
20000–49999	29	20,57%
10000–19999	33	23,40%
5000–9999	45	31,91%
2000–4999	22	15,60%
1000–1999	2	1,42%
Total	141	100,00%

The research findings on mapping the utilization of promotion tools in the Slovak cities are supplemented by the examples of best practices in the Slovak cities. To conclude the paper we summarizes the strengths, weaknesses and challenges of promotion tools' utilization in smart governance.

4   Exploitation of Modern Promotion Tools in Slovak Cities

There are no doubts about the important role of communication within the implementation of smart governance in cities. From the marketing point of view, the communication is a core of city promotion. The tools of city promotion are strongly influenced by the development of new technologies. Referring to the theoretical framework of the paper we researched in the Slovak city the implementation of following tools: social networks (Facebook, Twitter, Instagram, Youtube, etc.); websites; mobile application; location placement; events; discussion forum, chats; digital advertisement. The exploitation of these tools by all Slovak cities presents Fig. 1.

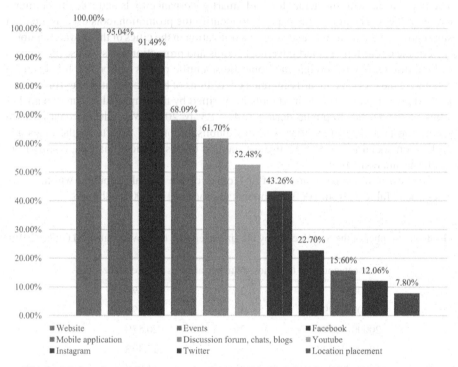

Fig. 1. Modern forms of promotion implemented in Slovak cities. Source: own research

The Fig. 1 shows that the most used tools is a website. All Slovak cities have their own website presented the city, its services and government. The second most used tool is an organisation of event (95.04%; 134 cities). The highest share of Facebook exploitation in cities confirms the fact that the Facebook is the most used social network in Slovakia. More than 50% of cities use also mobile application, discussion forums, chats and blogs as well as Youtube. To the least exploited tools belongs digital advertisement and location placement.

The detailed analysis of social networks exploitation is illustrated in Fig. 2. It presents the utilization of the social networks by size categories of the cities.

All bigger cities (with inhabitants more than 50 000) use for promotion Facebook, Instagram, Youtube. Both biggest cities – Bratislava (capital city) and Košice use also Twitter, LinkedIn and Tumbrl. Bratislava has even two profiles on Facebook and Instagram, one oriented on the citizens of Bratislava, the second one is oriented on tourists. The higher number of followers is indicated in case of tourism profile of the city.

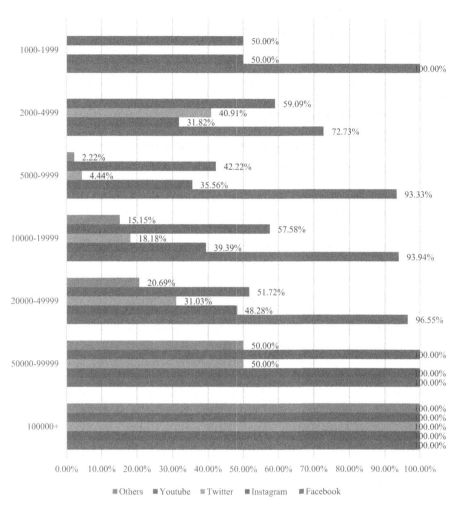

Fig. 2. Exploitation of the social networks by Slovak cities regarding the size category. Source: own research

The most used social network in cities of all sized categories is Facebook (more than 90% of cities in each size category except cities with 2000 – 4999 inhabitants). More than 50% of cities in each size category use also channels on Youtube except cities with 5000 – 9999 inhabitants. Twitter and Instagram are not so popular networks in cities from 1000 to 49 999 inhabitants (Instagram - from 31,82% to 50%; Twitter – from 0 to 40,91%). To the other exploited social networks by small number of cities belong Pinterest, LinkedIn, Tumbrl, Gmail, Yahoo.

The implementation of other modern forms of promotion in cities by size categories presents Fig. 3.

The second most used tool, almost in all cities beside the size category 2000 – 4999 inhabitants, is an organization of events. Still more and more cities has also own mobile application for various purposes – for citizens, tourists, for parking, for buying travel

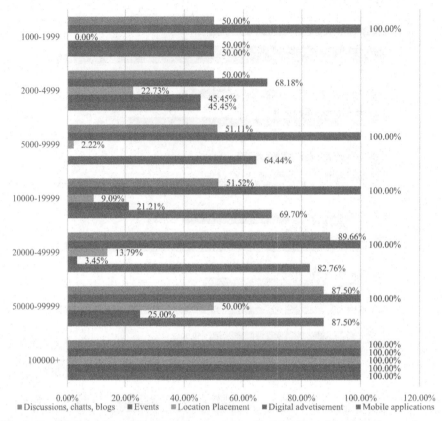

Fig. 3. Exploitation of the other forms of promotion by Slovak cities and the size category. Source: own research

tickets etc. The share of cities with the mobile application is lower in smaller cities – from 45,45% till 69,70% in cities to 19 999 inhabitants. Only cca ½ of these cities uses also discussion forums, chats and blogs. In bigger cities (from 20 000 inhabitants) are these forms of promotion used more frequently (cca 90% of cities). Digital advertisement and location placement are the least used forms of promotion.

The characterization of the current state of art in utilization of promotion tools as a part of smart governance in the Slovak republic we supplemented by some best practices from the Slovak cities.

One of the pioneers in building smart city is Trnava, the site of the Trnava region. In 2020 the city launched the project Trnava smart city. In the first stage of the project the core activity is a integrated platform in a form of mobile application and website smart.trnava.sk that provide the current reports on weather, air quality, noise levels, traffic situation, filling of large-capacity semi-underground containers in the city and also on the activities of the municipality. The application will be developed, and new functionalities will be added. The total expected costs of the project will be €116,000.

The second example is a Smart City - Chatbot A.I. preparing for city Trenčín based on elements of artificial intelligence. Smart City - A.I. chatbot is a computer program that simulates a normal conversation between people. It can communicate with several inhabitants at once in real time and in large volumes. It can adapt and personalize communication according to the context of conversation, behavior or preferences of the population. The essence of the chatbot will be interactive personalized communication between Trenčín and residents on the main topics of the city such as news, invitations to cultural events, changes in the organization of transport, notifications of repairs, comments on the official board and information from the city council. Citizens will be able to choose the information they prefer to receive via "chat" in the Messenger application as well as in a web chat. Implementation costs are estimated at €65,000.

The last example presents a mobile application SOM. It operates currently in more than 21 towns in Slovakia. It is the first platform in which residents will find all important city services in one place. Anyone who downloads an application of its city on the mobile phone will get up-to-date information about what's happening in the city. The application is available for Android and iOS devices for free. Inhabitants can find online newspapers and important phone numbers that can be dialed directly from the application, neighborhood exchange etc. Basically, the application is developed as a complex platform for communication online in one device - the web, social networks, online newspapers, notifications, the official board, reporting problems, the neighborhood exchange, but also bus departures and arrivals. The application is used by the cities of all size categories including the city districts of Bratislava, the sites of regions as Nitra, Žilina, Trnava, small cities as Trstená, Žiar nad Hronom, Moldava nad Bodvou, Lučenec and villages Zavar, Veľké Kostolany and others.

The research results show that the implementation of new modern promotion tools in Slovak cities is developing. It copies the global trends in marketing of cities as well as in smart governance. It includes the necessity to deliver information via own website of the city; to create an open and friendly environment also in virtual space by communication via social networks, blogs, chats or discussion forums. The importance of these new promotion tools was confirmed by more research studies (inter alia The American Advanced Learning Institute 2015; Castelnovo et al. 2015; Gil-Garcia et al. 2015; Johannessen and Berntzen 2018; Tran 2019). The great benefits of this communication include saving funds, active involevment of stakeholders, and usefulness in crisis situation and in building trust with the public, space for the test links and improving the local services based on the citizen's experience; authenticity and transparency.

There are still various possibilities to improve this area what declares the pioneer examples of best practice from the Slovak cities. The tools should be more combined to achieve the integrated and multichannel led communication. The utilization of mobile applications in local governance as well as in delivering local services should be strengthened. The orientation of the mobile application content is currently oriented more on travel guides, parking or selling travel tickets, but the offer of services should be gradually broaden and integrated also with various form of participative planning, budgeting or delivering the wider offer of public services.

The strength of the modern promotion in Slovak cities is an organization of various kinds of events in cities. They include the traditional ones (fair trades, market of local craft works or local food), sport, cultural, informative events etc.

To the less used tools belong forms of digital advertisement and location placement. It can be caused also by orientation of local municipalities on interactive forms of communication, what is also confirmed by the content of smart governance tools. That is why it is difficult to identify it as strength or weakness. Because of the restrictions in public sector there is not possibility to use the potential of these forms fully, but only in accustomed form (e.g. not as a paid advertisement by some identified sponsor on the city website).

The implementation of modern tools of promotion and smart governance face with the global challenges as continual and fast development of new technologies and technics, the increasing interests of stakeholders to participate online and offline instead of personal contact and to be informed permanently. In case of Slovakia also by the challenges at the national level as weak awareness about the importance of smart city concept and its part - smart governance, the difficulty to gain the financial support for smart cities strategies implementation caused by the bureaucracy, length of the public procurement process and other restrictions given by law, and at the local level inadequate skills of the responsible employees in the cities and their resistance to changes as well as misunderstanding of benefits of these tools for both sides of communication.

5 Conclusion

The implementation of new trends in local governance and policy is an essential precondition to be competitive among cities at the national and international level. The new forms of promotion which are gradually involve into the original agenda of the cities can be seen as a good starting point to implement smart governance approach. The aim of the paper was to identify the promotion tools used as a part of smart governance in the city and verify its utilization in the cities of the Slovak Republic. We oriented on the researching of following tools: social networks (Facebook, Twitter, Instagram, Youtube, etc.); websites; mobile application; location placement; events; discussion forum, chats; digital advertisement. The Slovak cities use the majority of investigated tools but there is still please to develop the old promotion tools as well as to introduce the new ones or even better these ones that are verified by the practice in foreign cities (Berlin, Vienna, Amsterdam, Stockholm, Oulu, Tallinn) as the beneficial ones.

The paper presents the partial outputs of project VEGA 1/0213/20 Smart Governance in Local Municipalities.

References

Albino, V., Berardi, U., Dangelico, R.M.: Smart cities: definitions, dimensions, performance and initiatives. J. Urban Technol. **22**, 3–12 (2015)

American Advanced Learning Institute: Seven benefits of using social media for government communications (2015). https://www.aliconferences.com/social-media-for-government-communications/. Accessed 17 Aug 2019

Baccarne, B., Mechant, P., Schuurman, D.: Empowered cities? An analysis of the structure and generated value of the smart city Ghent. In: Dameri, R.P., Rosenthal-Sabroux, C. (eds.) Smart City, pp. 157–182. Springer, Cham (2014). https://doi.org/10.1007/978-3-319-06160-3_8

Castelnovo, A., et al.: Smart cities governance. The need for a holistic approach to assessing urban participatory policy making. Soc. Sci. Comput. Rev. **34**(6), 724–739 (2015)

Chourabi, H., Nam, T., Walker, S., Gil-Garcia, J.R., Mellouli, S., Nahon, K., et al.: Understanding smart cities: an integrative framework. In: Proceedings of the Annual Hawaii International Conference on System Science, pp. 2289–2297 (2012)

Díaz-Díaz, R., Pérez-González, D.: Implementation of social media concepts for e-government: case study of a social media tool for value co-creation and citizen participation. J. Organ. End User Comput. **28**(3), 18 (2016)

Estevez, E., Janowski, T.: Electronic governance for sustainable development—conceptual framework and state of research. Gov. Inf. Q. **30**, 94–109 (2013)

Gil-Garcia, J.R., Pardo, T.A., Nam, T.: What makes a city smart? Identifying core components and proposing an integrative and comprehensive conceptualization. Inf. Policy **20**, 61–87 (2015)

Guendeuz, A.A., Mettler, T., Schedler, K.: Smart government – participation and empowerment of citizens in the era of big data and personalized algorithms. HMD Praxis Der Wirthschaft informatik **53**(4), 447–487 (2017)

Jaeger, P.T.: The endless wire: E-government as global phenomenon. Gov. Inf. Q. **20**(4), 323–331 (2003)

Janouch, V.: Internetový marketing: Prosaďte se na webu a sociálních sítích. Computer Press, Brno (2010)

Ježek, J., et al.: Manuál pro potreby praxe: Marketingový management obcí, mest a regionu. Ostravská univerzita, Ostrava (2007)

Johannessen, M.R., Berntzen, L.: Smart Technologies for Smart Governments: Transparency, Efficiency and Organizational Issues. Springer, Heidelberg (2018)

Khan, Z., Anjum, A., Soomro, K., Tahir, M.: Towards cloud based big data analytics for smart future cities. J. Cloud Comput. **4**(1), 1–11 (2015). https://doi.org/10.1186/s13677-015-0026-8

Kleinhans, R., Ham, M., Evans-Cowley, J.: Using social media and mobile technologies to foster engagement and self-organisation in participatory urban planning and neighbourhood governance. Plann. Pract. Res. **30**(3), 237–247 (2015)

Lee, J., Lee, H.: Developing and validating a citizen-centric typology for smart city services. Gov. Inf. Q. **31**(1), 93–105 (2014)

Linders, D.: From e-government to we-government: defining a typology for citizen coproduction in the age of social media. Gov. Inf. Q. **29**, 446–454 (2012)

Lombardi, P., Giordano, S., Farouh, H., Wael, Y.: An analytical network model for Samrt cities. In: Proceedings of the 11th International Symposium on the Analytical Hierarchy Process, Sorrento, Italy (2011)

Macintosh, A., et al.: E-methods for public engagement. Bristol City Council, Bristol (2005)

Maheshwari, D., Janssen, M.: Reconceptualizing measuring, benchmarking for improving interoperability in smart ecosystems: the effect of ubiquitous data and crowdsourcing. Gov. Inf. Q. **31**, 84–92 (2014)

Mellouli, S., Luna-Reyes, L.F., Zhang, J.: Smart government, citizen participation and open data. Inf. Polity **19**, 1–4 (2014)

Misuraca, G., Reid, A., Deakin, M.: Exploring emerging ICT-enables governance models in European cities: analysis of the mapping survey to identify key city governance policy areas most impacted by ICTs. Serville: European Commission. JRC Technical Notes (2011)

Nam, T., Pardo, T.A.: The changing face of a city government: a case study of Philly31. Gov. Inf. Q. **31**, 1–9 (2014)

Nam, T., Pardo, T.A.: Conceptualizing smart city with dimensions of technology, people, and institutions. In: Proceedings of the 12th Annual International Conference on Digital Government Research, College Park, MD, pp. 282–291 (2011)

Navarro-Galera, A., Alcaraz-Quiles, F.J., Ortiz-Rodríguez, D.: Online dissemination of information on sustainability in regional governments. Effects of technological factors. Gov. Inf. Q. **33**, 53–66 (2016)

Osella, M., Ferro, E., Pautasso, M.E.: Toward a methodological approach to assess public value in smart cities. In: Gil-Garcia, J., Pardo, T., Nam, T. (eds.) Smarter as the New Urban Agenda, pp. 129–148. Springer, Cham (2016). https://doi.org/10.1007/978-3-319-17620-8_7

Pereira, G.V., Parycek, P., Falco, E., Kleinhaus, R.: Smart governance in the context of smart cities: a literature review. Inf. Polity **23**(2), 1–20 (2018)

Pereira, G.V., Cunha, M.A., Lampoltshammer, T.J., Parycek, P., Testa, M.G.: Increasing collaboration and participation in smart city governance: a cross-case analysis of smart city initiatives. Inf. Technol. Dev. **23**(3), 526–553 (2017)

Ruhland, R.W.S.: The governance of smart cities: a systematic literature review. Cities **81**, 1–23 (2018)

Scholl, H.J., Scholl, M.C.: Smart governance: a roadmap of research and practice. In: Iconeference 2017 Proceedings (2017)

Stamati, T., Papadopoulos, T., Anagnostopoulos, D.: Social media for openness and accountability in the public sector: cases in the Greek context. Gov. Inf. Q. **32**, 12–29 (2015)

Stuchlík, P., Dvořáček, M.: Marketing na internetu. Praha, Grada (2002)

Tran, T.: Social media in government: Benefits, challenges, and how it's used (2019). https://blog.hootsuite.com/social-media-government/. Accessed 17 Aug 2019

Vaňová, A., Vitálišová, K., Borseková, K.: Place marketing. Belianum, Banská Bystrica (2017)

Wijnhoven, F., Ehrenhard, M., Kuhn, J.: Open government objectives and participation motivations. Gov. Inf. Q. **32**(1), 30–42 (2015)

Identity Inclusion: A Digital National Identification for All

Andrew Amstrong Musoke[1], Patrick Dushimimana[1], and Martin Saint[1,2](✉) (iD)

[1] Department of Information and Communications Technology,
Carnegie Mellon University Africa, Kigali, Rwanda
{amusoke,pdushimi}@andrew.cmu.edu, msaint@cmu.edu
[2] Kigali Collaborative Research Centre, Kigali, Rwanda
http://www.africa.engineering.cmu.edu, http://www.kcrc.rw

Abstract. Governments offer civil services to their citizens if the citizen can identify themselves using a government-issued identification document. Several documents are often required, such as a national ID and driving license. These identification documents do not share data, or even validity, between different civil entities. Organizations like Sovrin, SecureKey, and ShoCard have presented solutions to ease identification using digital identification based on blockchain technology because of the benefits of immutability, transparency, reliability, and secure sharing of identity data. The solutions, however, all require the use of Internet-enabled devices to access the solution. To accommodate developing countries where smartphones and computers are not prevalent, we designed a proof of concept digital national identification based on the Ethereum blockchain that utilizes Unstructured Supplementary Service Data (USSD) for end-user communications. The solution gives governments control over lawfully required data while allowing the citizen to retain sovereignty over personal data using trust zones. Consequently, a citizen can use a single identity across multiple civil service providers, even with a feature phone.

Keywords: Digital identity · National identity · Blockchain 2.0 · Smart contract · Ethereum · Digital assets · E-infrastructure · E-government

1 Introduction

The ISO/IEC 24760-1 specification for IT Security and Privacy defines identity as a set of attributes related to an entity [1]. A digital identity is an identity in an online or networked environment that represents a real-world entity like a person or business.

A digital identity enables institutions like governments, banks, and telecommunication service providers to incorporate secure digital services into their operations. In the digital realm, any assertion we make about ourselves, the identity owner, is called a claim. Claims can be anything from the name of the

S. Paiva et al. (Eds.): SmartCity360° 2020, LNICST 372, pp. 511–525, 2021.
https://doi.org/10.1007/978-3-030-76063-2_34

identity owner to the school from which they graduated. These claims can be nearly impossible to verify, unlike in the physical world, where possession of an acceptable document is considered sufficient proof of identity. For this reason, organizations like the Sovrin Foundation have embarked on digital identification implementations using blockchain technology, as explained in the Sovrin white paper [2].

A blockchain is a distributed, decentralized, public ledger. Private or permissioned versions are also possible. It is a record-keeping technology with a distributed network of participating nodes that maintain a majority-consensus of the state of the entries in the ledger. Records kept in the ledger are considered immutable due to the infeasibility of altering records across a large number of independently distributed nodes. These properties make a blockchain a desirable technology for the implementation of digital identity due to the transparency, immutability, and global nature of a blockchain network.

Here, the term *government* is used to collectively refer to the executive, legislative and judiciary branches including ministries, local governments, public sector offices, etc.

1.1   Background

A national identification document or card is a government-issued portable document given to each citizen or resident in some countries that serves as legal proof, for government and many other services, that the person is whom they claim to be. Taking the case of the country of Rwanda, for instance, the first Rwandan national ID was issued during the Belgian colonial period starting in 1930 and was paper-based and written by hand. A new plastic laminated national identity card system was implemented in 2008, improving both durability and the system for issuing identity documents [3].

To get a national identity card in Rwanda, the citizen must be above the age of 15. Rwanda has an online platform called IREMBO that helps citizens access different e-government services such as national identity document issuance, birth certificates, insurance payments, and police declarations.

To get the national identity card in Rwanda, a citizen needs to get both an application number from their residential sector office and a biometric data form with information such as fingerprints. They then apply online [4]. The application cost is 500 Rwandan Francs (about $0.53 US at the time of this writing), and a card is issued within one month and sent to the applicant's sector office for them to pick up.

Each Rwandan identity card has a National Identity Number (NIN) that can serve as a unified interface between a unique individual and any civil service availed by the government. The card is also legal identification for hospitals that keep patient details, banks, school registration, and when accessing government services like birth certification, driving permits, and land permutation [5].

1.2 Problem Statement

Despite holding the national identity card, for a Rwandan to access different forms of civil services, they may require different forms of identification. For example, a citizen needs to show a driver's permit to access traffic control services, despite having a national ID that duplicates much of the same information. Despite being "national", the current physical identity card system is challenged by a lack of interoperability amongst civil service providers. Even in cases where integration is attempted, this is done in silos for different services as opposed to a single integration platform with a unified interface to ease and accelerate integration. The physical card is also subject to loss or damage, forgery, and fraud. A physical document does not interface well with an increasingly digital world and the proliferation of e-government and online services.

In this paper, we demonstrate a technical approach to implementing a secure digital identity system using the Ethereum blockchain. This system is appropriate for Africa because it requires little in the way of new infrastructure and builds upon a well-accepted blockchain platform. We also address a problem not well explored in other papers: implementation in the context of a country with a prevalence of feature phones over smartphones or computers. While we use the case of Rwanda in our examples, our approach is appropriate for many African countries or developing nations where citizens rely primarily on feature phones to access the Internet or digital services. We focus on demonstrating the technology without attempting to address the myriad of policy and socio-economic challenges that come with a blockchain-based national identity scheme. It is not our intent to minimize the non-technical challenges. Instead, they exist outside of the scope of this paper.

1.3 Objectives

Considering the digital identity problems mentioned in the prior section, we define the following objectives for our solution:

1. Build a robust and resilient platform that is sufficiently reliable to be used nationally.
2. The solution must be distributed for robustness and flexible enough to be deployed despite civil service providers' heterogeneity.
3. The solution should be usable by citizens who own only a feature phone.
4. As a national identity, the solution should be under the control of the government.

2 Literature Review

There are several approaches to providing digital identity for individuals using a blockchain. The Sovrin Foundation is an open-source project working toward creating a digital identity that is entirely controlled by the user, a concept called self-sovereignty. Here, the user chooses which attributes to share. The architecture, however, requires trusted and authorized organisations called stewards to provide resources towards the network and intermediaries like trust anchors that control how you acquire your identity [2]. The concept of self-sovereign identity would present challenges in a government setting where a user is mandated by law to share identification information. For a national identity, the government should retain control over the identity attributes and issuing or revoking a national ID [2,6].

Another project that does not utilize the self-sovereignty principle is called ShoCard. A citizen takes a picture of an existing verified credential, like a passport, in a process called bootstrapping [7]. The credential is then bound to a cryptographic identity, and this forms their digital ID. ShoCard then acts as a trusted third party that stores the credentials and interactions with a party requesting a user's ID. This system's reliance on a third party voids certain benefits of decentralization, such as the resiliency of a distributed network, should the company go out of business. Dunphy and Petitcolas compare Sovrin and ShoCard against the Facebook Connect digital identity solution, which does not utilize blockchain technology [8]. Their work concluded that the blockchain-based digital identity systems suffered from poor user experience, which is a barrier to uptake because users have to understand cryptographic key management in both cases.

Mudliar et al. proposed a framework to integrate an existing national identity system in India, the Aadhar number, into the blockchain [9]. They explore the benefits of migrating to a decentralized national ID, such as voting or healthcare, where one simply scans a barcode to be identified. Under this system, officials have access to all information, and a record of all actions performed with the identity is kept on a public ledger.

Other work, using the country of Columbia as an example, suggested using three aspects to identify a citizen [10]. The proposed model introduces a digital identity that provides strong authentication comprising something the user has, like a physical smart card, something the user knows, like a personal identification number (PIN), and something the user is, like a fingerprint.

A paper by Wolfond discusses how Canada has used a digital ID to improve their service delivery in both the public and private sectors in a completely decentralised model [11]. Current systems of identification are either too cumbersome, like passwords, or less secure and harder to validate, like driving licenses. Another drawback of traditional systems is the inherent vulnerability of relying on a centralized system with a single point of failure and audit. Centralization affects both the system's resilience and user privacy, since all user transactions may be tracked through one application if compromised. The author concludes with the perceived benefits of using a blockchain, such as reduced wait times, quick verifiability of third party documents, and improved citizen privacy protection when delivering government services.

Some of the previous work mentioned relies on physically issued identification or does not lend itself to solving the interoperability challenge. Other work builds upon the self-sovereignty principal, which is inappropriate for a government-controlled identification. Finally, because many developing countries have a low prevalence of smartphones, for instance, about 15% of the population in a country like Rwanda, most of the solutions mentioned would be infeasible due to the need for a smartphone or computer. In a developing nation context, these solutions would exclude the majority of the population from using them [12].

In this work, we present a proof of concept digital national identity based on the Ethereum blockchain. It serves as a single personal data and identification store to ease government service providers' interoperability while reaping the benefits of a robust decentralized database. We utilize an Unstructured Supplementary Service Data (USSD) interface accessible on both feature phones and smartphones. Using this combination of platforms enables a solution that requires little in the way of new infrastructure and is appropriate for a government identity solution in developing countries.

3 Methodology

We develop our identity application using the Ethereum blockchain platform. Ethereum is a decentralized computing resource that allows users to develop applications and then deploy them on the Ethereum network. Ethereum employs smart contracts, which are programs stored on the networked computing resource that can perform defined functions based on specific inputs. Smart contracts store user data and provide the logic for modifying that data. In our case, the citizen's biometric data. Guided by the earlier objectives, the goal is to create a decentralized platform that citizens can use to procure civil services seamlessly with a single identity.

3.1 Developing the Prototype

For our prototype application, we focus on government and hospital services, demonstrating how a national digital ID is used with both services without carrying a physical ID.

3.2 Identity Trust Zones

An essential contribution of our system is the inclusion of trust zones in the ID. We define trust zones as predefined boundaries that group entities wishing to access a citizen's attributes. More highly trusted entities are closer to the center zone. This model enables using a single national ID for heterogeneous use cases.

The different trust zones are shown in Fig. 1. In the first trust zone lies the citizen, who has access to all the data represented by, or linked to, the national ID. The second trust zone will have the government and its trusted third parties, like document issuing agencies. Second zone entities have limited access to the citizen's data, but the citizen will be mandated to declare data required for civic service delivery. In the third and fourth zones, the citizen has full control over the data that they declare. The fourth zone may be made more restrictive or limited to particular data to provide greater security and privacy.

A health care center would belong to the third trust zone. A citizen would retain the right to share information that they agree is necessary. Of course, this could affect the level of service they would be able to receive, given the individual health center's policies.

Trust zones are implemented in the logic of the smart contract. Entities are placed in trust zones by the government institutions at the point of registration. Citizens decide what data to share with entities in trust zones three and four through the USSD interface.

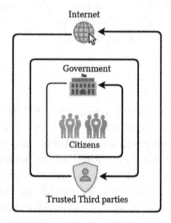

Fig. 1. Identity trust zones for citizen national ID.

3.3 Test Prototype

After building the code base for the smart contracts, we tested their functionality offline. We used a combination of the MetaMask Ethereum account manager and Rinkeby test network, a free public network for testing smart contracts before deployment to the Ethereum network [13,14].

3.4 Smart Contract Deployment

In the final step, we deploy the smart contract to the test Ethereum network. Our front end interacts with the smart contract using the Web3.js API. The deployment includes running an end to end demonstration of the healthcare use case to prove interoperability.

4   Implementation

Following our methodology, in this section, we describe the implementation of our system. First, we explain the proposed architecture and compare it with the setup used in the testing phase. Finally, we describe the process flow between the entities of the system. Our prototype's codebase is hosted in a GitHub repository at https://github.com/patrickdushimimana/national_ID.

4.1   Architecture

Communication between the different systems is shown in Fig. 2. Civil service providers interact with a web browser-based user interface that communicates with a government-owned server. The server hosts the logic to communicate with a mobile network operator (MNO), which communicates with the citizen's feature phone via a USSD API. The USSD protocol can take up to 182 characters which is enough to list a menu of queries [15]. The server, which also houses the application and database backend, also communicates with the Ethereum blockchain network where the smart contract and a hashed reference to the citizen registration data are stored. Here, the term server is used as a stand-in for a secure, reliable and scalable application and database infrastructure.

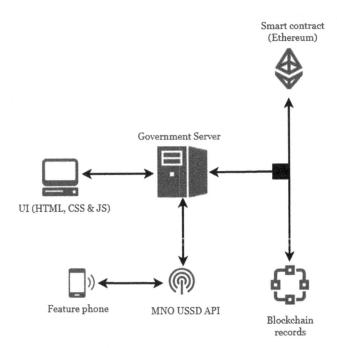

Fig. 2. Architecture for the national ID system.

4.2   Test Setup

The following tools were utilized to create and test the application.

- *Ganache* is a personal blockchain for Ethereum development that is used to deploy contracts, develop the applications, and run tests [16].
- *Truffle* is "a development environment, testing framework and asset pipeline for blockchains using the Ethereum Virtual Machine (EVM)" [17].
- *MetaMask* allows running Ethereum distributed applications (dApps) in a browser without running a full Ethereum node [13].
- *Node.js* is a server-side platform built on the Google Chrome JavaScript Engine [18].
- *Web3.js* is a collection of libraries to interact with a local or remote Ethereum node using a HTTP or IPC connection [19].
- *Ethereum* is a distributed public blockchain network that focuses on running programming code of any decentralized application [20].
- *HTML* is the HyperText Markup Language for creating web pages [21].

The blockchain technology, Ethereum, on which our solution is based, has been tested for performance and scalability in previous works. Therefore, we focus on the proof of concept within our test environment [22].

4.3   Process Flow

The proposed system considers three actors, all of whom may interact directly with one another or indirectly through the logic of Ethereum smart contracts. We consider a citizen as the identity owner, a government institution as the trusted identity verifier, and a public hospital as the civil service provider. For this work, we demonstrate the feasibility of our solution in the context of only one civil service provider, a health care center.

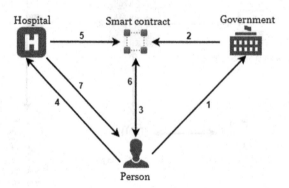

Fig. 3. Process flow diagram for the national ID system.

Unlike Fig. 2, which details interactions between the system components, Fig. 3 depicts the logical flow of interactions between the different actors, abstracting away the system. The flow is described as follows:

1. A citizen physically registers with an official government institution, for example Rwanda's National ID Agency (NIDA).
2. The institution verifies the citizen's information and registers the citizen's data to the blockchain. This is done through a portal interfacing with our Ethereum smart contract.
3. The citizen receives a prompt to input a four digit personal identification number (PIN). This prompt is received through a USSD application interfacing with our smart contract. Entering the PIN will confirm the registration process.
4. The citizen requests a service from a health care center.
5. The health care center requires the identifying information of the citizen. The health care center will also require national insurance information. The health care center requests the citizen's phone number, and through a portal, sends a request for the required data to the smart contract.
6. The citizen receives a prompt to input their PIN and authorize the release of their insurance, biometric, and medical history data to the health care center specified. USSD enables menu functions that would allow the aggregated authorization to all data requested by the health care center, or allow the citizen to approve only certain pieces or subsets of the requested data.
7. Upon authorization, the health care center can then confirm the identity of the citizen and proceed to offer the requested services.

In addition to requesting a citizen's information to authorize the provision of health care services, a health worker can then record the citizen's health data and link it to their identification. This data can then be stored privately on the blockchain. When the citizen visits the same or a different health care center, they can opt to share previously stored medical information, effectively having an immutable and readily available medical history that is not dependent on the health care center's information system.

In the case where a citizen does not posses their phone, they can still be identified with their National ID number. This benefits from the fact that developing countries like Rwanda have established National ID frameworks that can be extended. The National ID number will act as a reference to one's biographical and biometric data that the government and related trusted third parties have access to anyway. Verification then proceeds with biometric data like facial images, fingerprint, or voice-print identification.

4.4   Implementation Overview

This section shows some of the primary functions of the implemented project.

Individuals already registered for the national ID are shown in Fig. 4. They can access available services.

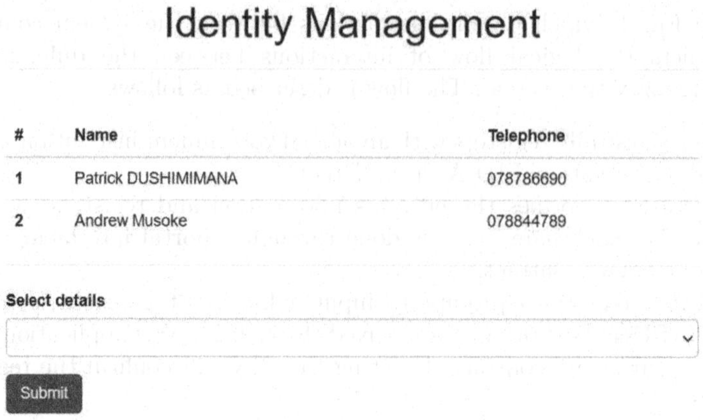

Identity Management

#	Name	Telephone
1	Patrick DUSHIMIMANA	078786690
2	Andrew Musoke	078844789

Select details

[⌄]

[Submit]

Fig. 4. Sample list of individuals registered for the national ID.

Individuals who have provided their insurance information as requested by the health center, are shown in Fig. 5. The document registration is recorded as a transaction in Ethereum.

The cost, in Ether, Ethereum's native cryptocurrency, charged for transactions related to registering insurance, is shown in Fig. 6. The account balance prior to a series of transactions is 100 Ether and 99.80 after.

5   Discussion

We implemented a proof of concept system that can serve as a foundation for a more sophisticated digital national identification platform in a developing country with low smartphone technology penetration. The system has two user interfaces, a web-based one for a government entity or civil service provider interaction, and another USSD-based one for a citizen. Compared to the current alternative, where citizens have to carry multiple forms of physical identities which can be lost or damaged, our system requires them to carry nothing but a phone to receive civil services from many different providers. Even without a phone, having a national ID or national ID number is sufficient to begin the verification process. Civil service providers can be held accountable for the use or misuse of citizen personal data since each request and use of this data is recorded as an immutable and transparent transaction on the blockchain. This can expedite audits of government entities and authorized third parties against data protection policies. It can also significantly reduce the cases of fraudulent identification claims.

5.1   The Issue of Cost

The system contains two levels of charges: (1) the *Ethereum gas* fee, in Ether, which is the cost of making a transaction on the Ethereum network, and (2) the

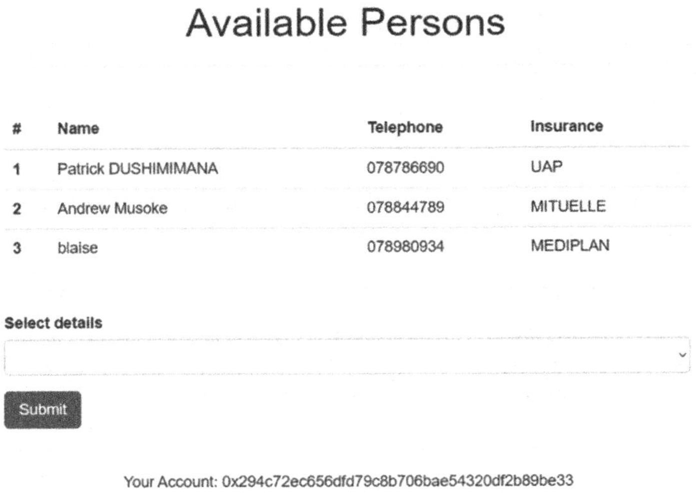

Available Persons

#	Name	Telephone	Insurance
1	Patrick DUSHIMIMANA	078786690	UAP
2	Andrew Musoke	078844789	MITUELLE
3	blaise	078980934	MEDIPLAN

Select details

Submit

Your Account: 0x294c72ec656dfd79c8b706bae54320df2b89be33

Fig. 5. List of individuals and their insurance providers.

Fig. 6. Ether (cost) charged for the transactions.

USSD cost, paid to the MNO per USSD session. Our tests show that registering one citizen on the Ethereum network costs approximately 19 USD at the time of writing. The cost per USSD session is estimated through the pricing of an integrator like *Africa's Talking*, with charges of approximately 0.014 USD [23]. The USSD cost is low enough to be of minimal concern, but the Ethereum cost would be prohibitive in most applications. However, our implementation assumes on-chain storage of citizen data. Storing a hash of the off-chain data on-chain and keeping the actual data itself off-chain would reduce the majority of the Ethereum cost. Data storage alternatives are also under active development by the Ethereum Foundation, as this is a general problem for all applications.

5.2   The Issue of Centralization

The architecture proposed introduces some aspects of centralization, where the government is seen as the single point of contact. We worked under the assumption that the country has a government whose majority membership is trusted to offer its citizens civil services. The system, however, makes no assumption about the trustworthiness of any one individual. From this perspective, the system can still be viewed as decentralised because no one person can control the blockchain network without consensus from the majority of the trusted government.

An authorized individual can still perform malicious activity, like unauthorized access of citizen data. Without the ability to control the blockchain network, however, and given the immutable and transparent nature of the blockchain, such malicious actors will be deterred when faced with inevitable discovery by the trusted government.

5.3   Adoption of the Solution

The proposed solution does not require the invention or engineering and testing of a scalable and reliable framework that includes auditing and integration. The Ethereum blockchain is a tested platform that provides these features by default, reducing the cost of development and maintenance. Our proposal also utilizes existing infrastructure that is already familiar to citizens, the USSD interface.

As a precursor for the move to a Smart Government, Rwanda has invested heavily in the provision of Internet, with 4G coverage available in 95% of the entire country [24]. Indeed, the International Telecommunication Union reports that in 2019, 97% of the world's population lived within range of a mobile phone signal [25]. Rwanda has also automated and delivered selected civil services online through a platform called Irembo for several years [26]. Those who cannot get online directly can do so at a government service center in most villages.

5.4   Tradeoffs

Our system is not a genuinely decentralized application, as is typically characteristic of applications built using the blockchain. Our system trades decentralization for ease of governance. We assumed that a government using the system would require centralized control over the process of acquiring a digital national identity. As a result, the system introduces centralization, since the citizen must appear in person before an appropriate government entity for verification and then registration.

For usability reasons, we traded the security of the public-private key pair typically used for interacting with a blockchain application. Due to the introduction of a PIN, citizens have an easier method of authenticating to the application that is consistent with other USSD applications. However, a four-digit PIN is less secure than the cryptographically secure keys typically used by blockchain apps. In the event of a mismanaged identity, such as a PIN that is lost or stolen, our system allows the issuer to block access as soon as it is reported. Rwanda's major telecom service provider, MTN, established precedent by requiring their users to secure their mobile money wallets with PIN authentication, so this approach to securing sensitive data in a developing country is not untested [27]. Work is underway to enable more novel forms of two-factor authentication, like voice-print technology, which is already being offered by companies like Phonexia [28] and implemented by organizations like Chase Bank [29].

Finally, we traded self-sovereignty, also for ease of governance. Citizens own their identities, but do not have full control over what portions of the data they can share with different entities, as explained in the methodology section. If citizens had full control over their data, they could deny government entities and related trusted third parties legally required information. As a compromise, we introduced the concept of trust zones, so that different categories of entities have different levels of access to citizen's information.

6   Conclusion

Citizens in countries with national identification systems require multiple forms of identification to access different civil services like police records or national healthcare. We proposed a blockchain-based national identification that would ensure interoperability among the different government entities and trusted third parties when providing civil services to citizens. Although a significant amount of work has been completed in the area of digital IDs, they do not address the nuances of a digital national identity in a country with low adoption of smartphone technology. We developed and described a proof of concept national ID system appropriate to the context of government service while using the concept of trust zones to retain a measure of self-sovereignty for the citizen.

For the future, we suggest further work on ways of reducing the cost of operating the system, such as off-blockchain storage of data and use of private blockchain networks. Future work could also include improving authentication methods, for example, by using fingerprint or voice-print scanners. Developing further use cases in more detail or a test deployment in a real-world setting would also be logical next steps.

References

1. ISO: IT security and privacy–a framework for identity management–part 1: terminology and concepts. International Standard ISO/IEC 24760–1:2019(E), ISO (the International Organization for Standardization) and IEC (the International Electrotechnical Commission), Geneva, Switzerland, 2nd Ed, May 2019
2. The Sovrin Foundation: Sovrin: a protocol and token for self-sovereign identity and decentralized trust. White paper, Sovrin Foundation, Provo, Utah, USA, March 2018. https://sovrin.org/wp-content/uploads/2018/03/The-Inevitable-Rise-of-Self-Sovereign-Identity.pdf
3. Times Reporter: National ID launch today. The New Times, Online, July 2008. https://www.newtimes.co.rw/section/read/4519. Accessed 05 July 2020

4. Republic of Rwanda: e-service, application for national ID. Irembo. https://
   irembo.gov.rw/rolportal/en/web/nida/application-for-national-id?menu-
   highlight=CAT#NIDA.IDAPP. Accessed 05 July 2020
5. Atick, J.J.: The identity ecosystem of Rwanda: a case study of a performant
   ID system in an African development context. White paper, ID4Africa, Kigali,
   Rwanda, May 2016. https://www.id4africa.com/2016/files/ID4Africa2016_The_
   Identity_Ecosystem_of_Rwanda_eBooklet.pdf
6. Khovratovich, D., Law, J.: Sovrin: digital identities in the blockchain era. White
   paper, Sovrin Foundation, Provo, Utah, USA, December 2016. https://sovrin.org/
   wp-content/uploads/AnonCred-RWC.pdf
7. El Haddouti, S., Kettani, M.: Analysis of identity management systems using
   blockchain technology. In: 2019 International Conference on Advanced Communication Technologies and Networking (CommNet), pp. 1–7, Rabat, Morocco, April
   2019. https://doi.org/10.1109/COMMNET.2019.8742375
8. Dunphy, P., Petitcolas, F.A.P.: A first look at identity management schemes on
   the blockchain. IEEE Secur. Priv. **16**(4), 20–29 (2018). https://doi.org/10.1109/
   MSP.2018.3111247
9. Mudliar, K., Parekh, H., Bhavathankar, P.: A comprehensive integration of national
   identity with blockchain technology. In: 2018 International Conference on Communication Information and Computing Technology (ICCICT), pp. 1–6. IEEE, IEEE,
   Mumbai, India, February 2018. https://doi.org/10.1109/ICCICT.2018.8325891
10. Juan, M.D., Andrés, R.P., Rafael, P.M., Gustavo, R.E., Manuel, P.C.: A model
    for national electronic identity document and authentication mechanism based on
    blockchain. Int. J. Model. Optim. **8**(3), 160–165 (2018). https://doi.org/10.7763/
    IJMO.2018.V8.642
11. Wolfond, G.: A blockchain ecosystem for digital identity: improving service delivery
    in Canada's public and private sectors. Technol. Innov. Manage. Rev. **7**(10), 35–40,
    October 2017. https://doi.org/10.22215/timreview/1112
12. Adepoju, P.: Rwanda's Kagame bemoans country's low smartphone penetra-
    tion rate. ITWeb Africa, October 2019. http://www.itwebafrica.com/more-
    countries/rwanda/246560-rwandas-kagame-bemoans-countrys-low-smartphone-
    penetration-rate. Accessed 06 July 2020
13. MetaMask: a crypto wallet & gateway to blockchain apps. https://metamask.io/.
    Accessed 06 July 2020
14. Rinkeby.io: Rinkeby: ethereum testnet. https://www.rinkeby.io. Accessed 15 Oct
    2020
15. 3rd Generation Partnership Project: digital cellular telecommunications sys-
    tem (phase 2+) (GSM); universal mobile telecommunications system (UMTS);
    unstructured supplementary service data (USSD); stage 1. Technical Specification
    3GPP TS 22.090 version 16.0.0 Release 16, 3rd Generation Partnership Project
    (3GPP), Sophia Antipolis, France, August 2020. https://www.etsi.org/deliver/
    etsi_ts/122000_122099/122090/16.00.00_60/ts_122090v160000p.pdf
16. Truffle Blockchain Group: Ganache overview. https://www.trufflesuite.com/docs/
    ganache/overview. Accessed 05 July 2020
17. Truffle Blockchain Group: Truffle overview. https://www.trufflesuite.com/docs/
    truffle/overview. Accessed 05 July 2020
18. OpenJS foundation: about node.js. https://nodejs.org/en/about/. Accessed 06
    July 2020
19. Ethereum Foundation: Web3.js Ethereum Javascript API. https://web3js.
    readthedocs.io/en/v1.2.9/. Accessed 06 July 2020

20. Ethereum Foundation: Ethereum is a global, open-source platform for decentralized applications. https://ethereum.org/. Accessed 06 July 2020
21. WHATWG Community: HTML living standard, July 2020. https://html.spec. whatwg.org/multipage/. Accessed 06 July 2020
22. Schäffer, M., di Angelo, M., Salzer, G.: Performance and scalability of private ethereum blockchains. In: Di Ciccio, C., et al. (eds.) BPM 2019. LNBIP, vol. 361, pp. 103–118. Springer, Cham (2019). https://doi.org/10.1007/978-3-030-30429-4_8
23. Africa's Talking: USSD API – build mobile apps accessible everywhere. https:// africastalking.com/ussd#pricing. Accessed 06 July 2020
24. Tashobya, A.: Four years later, 95% of Rwanda covered with 4G Internet. The New Times, May 2018. https://www.newtimes.co.rw/news/four-years-later-95-rwanda-covered-4g-internet
25. International Telecommunication Union: Facts and figures 2019: Measuring digital development. Report, International Telecommunication Union (ITU), Geneva, Switzerland (2019). https://itu.foleon.com/itu/measuring-digital-development/home/
26. Government of Rwanda: Smart rwanda 2020 master plan. Report, Government of Rwanda, Kigali, Rwanda, October 2015. https://nyamasheke.gov.rw/fileadmin/templates/DOCUMENT_Z_ABAKOZI/SMART_RWANDA_MASTER_PLAN_FINAL.pdf
27. MTN: MTN mobile money service terms and conditions. Kigali, Rwanda. https:// www.mtn.co.rw/wp-content/uploads/2019/11/MOMO-TERMS-CONDITIONS.pdf
28. Phonexia: voice biometrics platform. https://www.phonexia.com/en/product/voice-biometrics/. Accessed 15 Oct 2020
29. JPMorgan Chase & Co.: With voice ID, we can verify you by the sound of your voice. https://www.chase.com/personal/voice-biometrics. Accessed 15 Oct 2020

Computer Vision Assisted Approaches to Detect Street Garbage from Citizen Generated Imagery

Hye Seon Yi[✉] and Sriram Chellappan

University of South Florida, Tampa, FL 33620, USA
{hsyi,sriramc}@usf.edu

Abstract. The basis of smart governance is to leverage state-of-the-art technologies to improve lives of citizens. With the rapid permeance of smart-phone technologies today, citizens are increasingly active now in collaborating with public officials for improved quality of life. However, for effective utility, public officials must be empowered with optimal tools that can best leverage citizen participation. In this paper, we present the design and details of computer vision techniques to automatically detect and localize street garbage from citizen generated imagery, and analyze the performance of multiple techniques. Our dataset is mined from (citizen-generated) images in the well-known 311 service deployed in San Francisco, which is actually a service citizens use to report civic issues. Using a dataset of $2,500$ images (containing $6,474$ objects) evenly distributed between those containing street garbage and those that do not, we design and compare convolutional neural network techniques to detect and localize sources of garbage in the images. Results from our evaluations show that our system can be a vital cog towards next generation smart governance systems geared towards cleaner and healthier neighborhoods. Since identifying, collecting and disposing of street garbage is a critical aspect of governance across the globe, we believe that our work in this paper is critical, timely and may have global impact.

Keywords: Object detection · Garbage detection · Public health · Smart governance · Transfer learning · Computer vision

1 Introduction

Across the globe, there are urgent efforts now to rethink governance from the ground up to tackle various challenges including rising populations, keeping them healthy, combating climate change, managing rising floods, ensuring availability of food and water, providing education, and so much more. Unfortunately, the challenges are only mounting. In this context, and especially with the ubiquity and affordability of smartphones and network connectivity, citizens are now increasingly able to support local governance efforts. Furthermore, with the advent of social media, most gaps between officials and citizens are only

© ICST Institute for Computer Sciences, Social Informatics and Telecommunications Engineering 2021
Published by Springer Nature Switzerland AG 2021. All Rights Reserved
S. Paiva et al. (Eds.): SmartCity360° 2020, LNICST 372, pp. 526–541, 2021.
https://doi.org/10.1007/978-3-030-76063-2_35

shrinking even further. There is hence a rich set of emerging literature on leveraging citizen generated data for improving governance efforts across many fronts including water management, public health, law enforcement, intelligent transportation and much more.

In this context, a critical service provided by governmental agencies across the globe, is keeping localities cleaner and free from garbage. Needless to say, excess or abandoned garbage has serious repercussions to society today including attracting criminals, attracting pests and dangerous animals, low property assessments, contaminated soil, foul odors and so much more. Unfortunately, despite best efforts, there are always sources of abandoned garbage even in high-income countries today, and the problem is much worse in medium and low income countries. In this paper, we present the design and details of using Artificial Intelligence (Computer Vision) techniques to provide an automated mechanism to detect and localize multiple sources of garbage (cardboard boxes, loose garbage, garbage can and garbage can overflow) from images generate by citizens themselves.

Table 1. Communication preferences of 311 requests among citizens in San Francisco

Communication channel	311 Requests	With image	No image
Phone	1,777,585	6,279	1,771,306
Mobile/Open311	1,213,300	952,014	261,286
Website	564,849	38,266	526,583
Third party agency	123,907	2	123,905
Twitter	31,776	8,101	23,675
Other	6,953	6	6,947
Total	3,718,370	1,004,668	2,713,702

The dataset for our problem is generated from publicly available 311 services that citizens in San Francisco [1] use to report civic problems. While, we present more details later, 311 services are available at most big US cities [2], and serves as the primarily customer service center for civic problems. In San Francisco, the service is available via phone calls, a mobile app, a dedicated website, and Twitter. Citizens can call to report problems, and also use the app, website and Twitter to do the same, while also uploading picture of problems they see. As of Aug 2019 in San Francisco alone, there are more than 3.7 million citizen generated civic reports, and there are more than 1 million images that citizens have uploaded so far. Table 1 presents details of 311 use in San Francisco alone, from where we see that Internet based platforms (app, website, Twitter) are very popular among citizens. From this dataset, we utilized 2, 500 images (containing 6, 474 objects) for the current study focusing specifically on designing computer vision techniques for automatic identification and localization of garbage within an image.

We design, analyze and compare two pre-trained CNN models for our problem in this paper. The techniques are a) Faster R-CNN [3] and b) RetinaNet [4], both of which are successful object detection models with high performance [5]. Basically, in Faster R-CNN technique, feature maps are extracted from our training images using convolutional neural networks. The class to be learnt for our problem comprises of cardboard boxes on roads, loose garbage, garbage cans and overflowing garbage cans. Subsequently, and in order to localize objects of interest in an image, we train a simple neural network to learn features embedded within annotated objects of interest in the training images, and from the feature maps derived earlier in the previous step. Subsequently, these steps are repeated during the testing phase, wherein, once an image comes in, our model will identify and report either a) no garbage class is present; or b) garbage class is present, and also localize where the detected object of interest is present in the image via bounding boxes. RetinaNet on the other hand is a single network that is comprised of a backbone network and two task-specific sub-networks, The backbone network computes a convolutional feature map over an entire input image and is an off-the-self CNN. The first sub-network performs classification on the output of the backbone, while the second sub-network performs convolution bounding box regression.

Table 2. Categorical columns sorted by 311 requests with images.

#	Service_name	Service_subtype	Service_details	Requests	Percent
1	Street and Sidewalk Cleaning	general_cleaning	other_loose_garbage	177,897	17.82%
2	Encampments	encampment_reports	encampment_cleanup	88,822	8.90%
3	Street and Sidewalk Cleaning	bulky_items	furniture	57,364	5.75%
4	Street and Sidewalk Cleaning	human_or_animal _waste	human_or_animal _waste	48,356	4.84%
5	Street and Sidewalk Cleaning	bulky_items	boxed_or_bagged _items	42,341	4.24%
6	Abandoned Vehicle	abandoned_vehicles	dpt_abandoned _vehicles_low	30,168	3.02%
7	Graffiti	graffiti_on_other _enter_additional _details_below	other_enter _additional_details _below_offensive	27,836	2.79%
8	Street and Sidewalk Cleaning	bulky_items	mattress	22,020	2.21%
9	Graffiti	graffiti_on_building _commercial	building_commercial _not_offensive	21,163	2.12%
10	Street and Sidewalk Cleaning	city_garbage_can _overflowing	city_garbage_can _overflowing	21,056	2.11%
11	Illegal postings	illegal_postings _affixed_improperly	affixed_improperly	19,088	1.91%

To the best of our knowledge, we are not aware of any study that specifically focuses on detecting and localizing garbage from citizen generated imagery. We believe that our work is practical, and can be an important tool for next generation smart and automated governance systems across the globe (especially as it pertains to detection of a variety of garbage sources). The comparisons we do between the two CNN techniques we employ in this paper are expected to benefit policy-makers in real-time when attempting to use AI techniques for citizen science applications.

2   Our Dataset Consisting of 311 Images

The 311 service is popular in large cities in the US, wherein citizens can report civic related issues and complaints for rapid addressing. Across the US, these services are available to citizens via phone, websites, apps, and sometimes through third party web based intermediaries. When a citizen contacts 311 via any medium, it creates a 311 request. These requests are all available to the public. For the specific case of San Francisco - one of the biggest cities in the US - the information on all reports is available on DataSF, a San Francisco open data portal (https://datasf.org/opendata/). DataSF uses Socrata [6] platform for their data management, which provides APIs to access its data programmatically.

Using the Socrata APIs, we were able to collect the total of 3,718,370 requests dated from July 1, 2008 to August 28, 2019. Among those requests, there were 1,004,668 requests that had images uploaded by citizens. Tables 2, 3 and 4 present details on the dataset. Table 2 presents details of various requests in San Francisco with images from citizens, categorized by type of service requested. Table 3 provides a simpler to visualize categorization of the same, and finally, Table 4 provides details on the dataset for our problem in this study, that comprises of 6,474 objects (in 2,500 images) in total, out of which 5,745 were used for designing our AI models, and 729 were used for validating and testing the AI models. Figures 1 and 2 shows a snapshot of images in our dataset for clarity.

Table 3. Service names sorted by 311 requests with images.

#	Service_name	Requests	Percent
1	Street and Sidewalk Cleaning	423,485	42.15%
2	Graffiti	219,384	21.84%
3	Encampments	96,417	9.60%
4	Parking enforcement	41,241	4.10%
5	Abandoned vehicle	30,313	3.02%
6	Illegal postings	26,482	2.64%
7	Sign repair	20,777	2.07%

Table 4. Number of objects used in the train and test datasets.

Class	Total	Training (%)	Validation and Testing (%)
cardboard_box	1,490	1,319 (89%)	171 (11%)
garbage	3,244	2,856 (88%)	388 (12%)
garbage_can	864	775 (90%)	89 (10%)
garbage_can_overflow	876	795 (91%)	81 (9%)
Total	6,474	5,745 (89%)	729 (11%)

Fig. 1. Examples of garbage and cardboard boxes in our dataset

3 Our Proposed Methodology for Object (Garbage) Detection and Localization

For the purposes of this study, we chose four classes, namely "garbage", "garbage_can", "garbage_can_overflow", and "cardboard_box", for object detection. Note that these were all categorized as "Street and Sidewalk Cleaning" in 311 dataset which was the most requested service with images in San Francisco. Table 4 shows details of number of images in our dataset.

3.1 Images and Labeling

After deciding the four classes for object detection, we need to create ground truth data for the study. First, we downloaded related images containing those four class objects. We picked out about 2,500 images for object detection, that contained 6,474 objects of interest (in Table 4), since in many images more than one object of interest was present. Then, we labeled those images manually using LabelImg, which is one of the widely used image annotation tools for labeling images [7]. Figure 3 is the screenshot of LabelImg. Essentially, the task here is manually emplacing bounding boxes around the object of interest, so that the algorithm designed learns to detect the object of interest (if present) in an image, and also localize it by emplacing bounding boxes. In this manner, even minor

Fig. 2. Examples of garbage cans and overflowing garbage cans in our dataset

garbage boxes could be detected better from the perspective of a human operator that is viewing these images in run-time.

We divided these 2,500 labeled ground truth images with 6,474 objects for training, validation and testing datasets. For training, we used 90% and for validation and testing, we used 10% of images [8]. Table 4 presents details of training, validation and testing.

3.2 Transfer Learning with Pre-trained Object Detection Models

Many of the current state-of-the-art object detection models are based on deep convolutional neural networks (CNN) which are one of the commonly used deep learning methods [9–11]. CNNs can automatically extract meaningful features from images whereas traditional object detection models used feature-based and statistical machine learning methods [12]. However, training CNN models from scratch is not an easy task because it requires a lot of labeled data and computing power. Moreover, creating labeled image data is time consuming and expensive because each image has to be examined and labeled manually. To remedy this problem, transfer learning is a highly recommended alternate approach. The idea of transfer learning is to train a model using the knowledge learned from excellent pre-trained models, that work for a broad class of problems. These pre-trained models were trained using large existing labeled image dataset, such as ImageNet [13] and KITTI [14]. In this study, we used two pre-trained object detection models namely Faster R-CNN and RetinaNet.

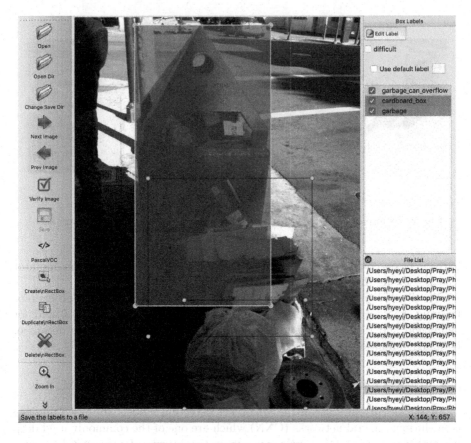

Fig. 3. Screenshot of LabelImg

Faster R-CNN. Faster R-CNN proposed by Ren [3] is one of well-known and successful object detection models [12,15]. This model accomplished the highest accuracy on PASCAL VOC in 2007 and 2012 and the models based on Faster R-CNN won 1st place in several tracks in ILSVRC and COCO competitions in 2015 [16]. [3] describes Faster R-CNN as follows. Faster R-CNN is composed of two modules: a Region Proposal Network (RPN) and the Fast R-CNN detector [17]. A RPN is a fully convolutional network which proposes regions. Fast R-CNN is a predecessor of Faster R-CNN and the Fast R-CNN detector uses the proposed regions for object detection. RPNs generate region proposals with different scales and aspect ratios by using anchor boxes. RPNs and Fast R-CNN share convolutional layers to enhance the running time. Figure 4a shows that both a RPN and Fast R-CNN use the convolutional feature maps. Figure 4b demonstrates that anchor boxes with different scales and aspect ratios. To deploy Faster R-CNN, we used the code base from https://github.com/tensorflow/models/tree/master/research/object_detection.

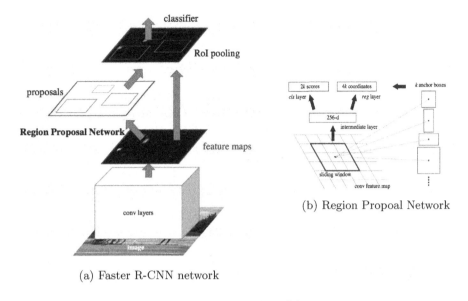

(a) Faster R-CNN network

(b) Region Propoal Network

Fig. 4. Faster R-CNN [3]

RetinaNet. RetinaNet is proposed by Lin [4]. It tackles the problem that one-stage object detection models fall behind in their accuracy compared to two-stage object detection models. However, one-stage object detection models usually surpass in speed and efficiency to their counterparts. The authors of [4] introduce Focal Loss which is focusing on training hard and incorrectly classified examples by down-weighting easy examples. With the use of Focal Loss, RetinaNet was able to achieve the speed of one-stage detectors without damaging the accuracy.

Figure 5 compares Focal Loss and Cross Entropy Loss. Cross Entropy Loss is a standard loss function commonly used in many of two-stage object detection models such as R-CNN, Fast R-CNN, and Faster R-CNN.

[4] explains cross entropy for binary classification as follows.

$$CE(p,y) = \begin{cases} -log(p) & \text{if } y = 1 \\ -log(1-p) & \text{otherwise} \end{cases} \quad (1)$$

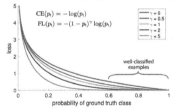

Fig. 5. Focal Loss [4]

From the above, $y \in \{-1, 1\}$ is ground truth class and $p \in [0, 1]$ is the predicted probability of the class. [4] define p_t:

$$p_t = \begin{cases} p & \text{if } y = 1 \\ 1 - p & \text{otherwise} \end{cases} \quad (2)$$

and restate $CE(p, y) = CE(p_t) = -log(p_t)$. The blue curve in Fig. 5 denotes the cross entropy loss.

The focal loss is as defined below and Fig. 5 plots focal loss with different γ values ranging from 0 to 5 [4]:

$$FL(p_t) = -(1 - p_t)^\gamma log(p_t) \tag{3}$$

Thus, when $\gamma = 0$, $CE(p_t) = FL(p_t)$. From Fig. 5, the loss is not trivial with easy examples ($p_t \geq 0.5$), and this means that the loss from these easy examples can overwhelm the loss from hard examples when there are much more easy examples than hard examples in the data [4]. [4] found that the results were best when $\gamma = 2$ from their experiments.

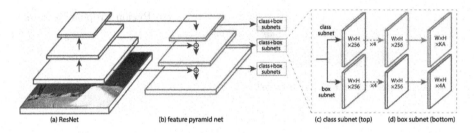

Fig. 6. RetinaNet network architecture [4]

Figure 6 is the architecture of RetinaNet. RetinaNet deploys a Feature Pyramid Network (FPN) on top of ResNet [18] which is a CNN architecture to detect features with deep layers (a). The (b) part depicts FPN constructing a multi-scale feature pyramid and the (c) and (d) parts show the FPN is connected to two sub-networks: one for classification of anchor boxes (Classification Subnet) and the other for regression of anchor boxes (Box Regression Subnet) [4]. To deploy RetinaNet, we used the code base from https://github.com/fizyr/keras-retinanet.

4   Results

4.1   Evaluation Metrics

In object detection, the most common metrics to measure the performance of an object detection model is mean average precision (mAP). mAP is the mean of average precision (AP) of classes which the model try to detect. AP of each class can be calculated using precision-recall curve. Precision-recall curve is plotted with precision and recall values which are calculated using Intersection over Union (IoU) between ground truth bounding boxes supplied from the dataset and predicted bounding boxes from the model. IoU is defined as the following.

$$IoU = \frac{Intersection}{Union} \tag{4}$$

After the object detection model predicts bounding boxes, each predicted bounding box's IoU against its corresponding ground truth bounding box is calculated. If the calculated IoU is greater than the IoU threshold, the predicted bounding box is counted as a true positive (TN). In this study, 0.5 was used for the IoU threshold. However, the predicted bounding box is counted as a false positive (FP) if its calculated IoU is less than the IoU threshold or there is a mismatch with the class between the predicted bounding box and the corresponding ground truth bounding box. Also, if there are more than one predicted bounding box to a ground truth bounding box, the predicted bounding box with the highest IoU with the correct class is counted as a true positive whereas the remaining predicted bounding boxes are counted false positives. The ground truth bounding boxes with no detection are counted as false negatives (FN). For object detection, true negatives (bounding boxes with no object) are not counted because there can be so many possible true negatives in an image. Due to this reason, precision and recall, instead of accuracy, are used to evaluate the performance of a model in object detection. Precision and recall are calculated with TP, FP and FN like the below.

$$Precision = \frac{TP}{TP + FP} = \frac{\text{correct predictions}}{\text{all predictions}} \tag{5}$$

$$Recall = \frac{TP}{TP + FN} = \frac{\text{correct predictions}}{\text{all ground truth objects}} \tag{6}$$

Then, the predicted bounding boxes are sorted according to their confidence value, which is calculated by the object detection model, in descending order (boxes with the highest confidence first). This confidence value is the probability whether the predicted bounding box contains an object of the classes which the object detection model attempts to detect. With each prediction bounding box, the precision and recall is calculated and they are plotted in the precision-recall curve. AP of an object class is calculated by "averaging precision across recall values from 0 to 1" [19]. There are two ways to find AP, namely 11-point interpolation and all point interpolation. We used all point interpolation to find AP. After finding an AP for an object class, mAP is found by averaging APs of object classes. [19] contains more details how to calculate AP and mAP.

4.2   Loss and mAP of Faster R-CNN

Figure 7a plots mAP while training the Faster R-CNN model whereas Fig. 7b plots the loss. The highest mAP for Faster R-CNN was 0.78, which was lower than mAP from RetinaNet. The object detected images (Fig. 8 and Fig. 9) displayed were generated from Faster R-CNN. The left-side images labeled as detected are detection images from Faster R-CNN while the right-side images labeled as ground-truth are ground-truth images. Figure 8 shows images with correctly detected objects while Fig. 9 shows images with some incorrectly detected objects.

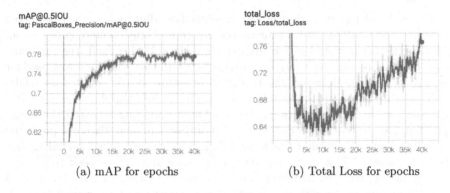

(a) mAP for epochs   (b) Total Loss for epochs

Fig. 7. Training results for epochs of Faster R-CNN network with ResNet101

Fig. 8. Object detected images with no error generated from Faster R-CNN

4.3   Loss and mAP of RetinaNet

Figure 10a plots mAP while training the RetinaNet model whereas Fig. 10b plots
the loss. Figure 11 are precision recall curves and APs of the object classes. The
precision recall curves were plotted using a tool available from https://github.
com/rafaelpadilla/Object-Detection-Metrics. Also, [20] is the paper about the
tool. RetinaNet converges early. At Epoch 3, training mAP reached 0.87 which
was the higest mAP. From this results, we found that RetinaNet returns the
better results than Faster R-CNN. The object detected images (Fig. 12 and

Fig. 9. Object detected images with errors generated from Faster R-CNN

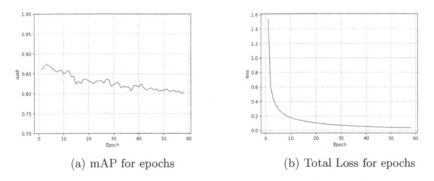

(a) mAP for epochs

(b) Total Loss for epochs

Fig. 10. Training metrics for epochs of RetinaNet with ResNet152

Fig. 13) displayed were generated from RetinaNet. The bounding boxes in the images were color-coded according to ground truth (blue), true positive (green), false positive (red) and false negative (yellow). Figure 12 shows images with correctly detected objects while Fig. 13 shows images with some incorrectly detected objects.

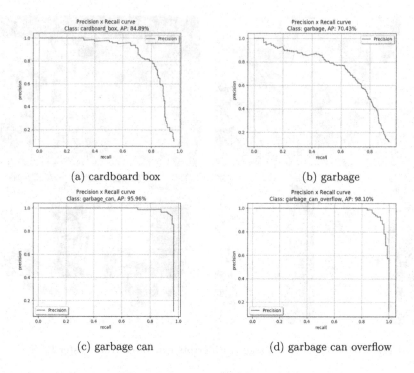

(a) cardboard box

(b) garbage

(c) garbage can

(d) garbage can overflow

Fig. 11. Precision Recall curves

Fig. 12. Object detected images with no error generated from RetinaNet (Color figure online)

Fig. 13. Object detected images with some error generated from RetinaNet (Color figure online)

5   Discussions, Conclusions and Future Work

Citizen science today is becoming extremely useful for a variety of applications that target the greater good. The ubiquity of the Internet, smart-phones and connectivity are natural enablers for citizen-science. While there are services using citizen science to monitor disease outbreaks [21,22], protecting bio-diversity [23,24], pollution monitoring [25,26] and many more, we are not aware of any particular work that focuses on citizen-science and image processing techniques for civic engagement like the ones we are focusing on in this paper. This is the gap, we address in this paper.

Many large cities in the United States employ the 311 service to allow their citizens to report non-emergent issues or to inquire city-related information with various communication channels such as phone, mobile apps, website and Twitter. With these various communication channels, 311 users can not only report an issue but also upload related images. We observed from SF 311 (San Francisco 311) that there are many garbage related images uploaded by its users. With these garbage related images, we implemented object detection with two pre-trained models, namely Faster R-CNN and RetinaNet, to detect four object classes, which are garbage, garbage cans, garbage can overflow and cardboard boxes. RetinaNet outperformed Faster R-CNN with mAP = 0.87 while Faster R-CNN's mAP was 0.78. This object detection on garbage can be used to facilitate automatic garbage detection.

Our future work is to include more classes to detect, and expand our model and database of image to other cities. Looking at GPS locations, will also enable us generate new results and studies related to factors like racial, socio-economic, crime propensity and other important aspects of civic life, as it pertains to quality of civic engagement and how to improve it. But the AI techniques we design in this paper are still robust foundations for such a study. Presenting our studies to policy makers, and getting their feedback using sound HCI designs, and using lessons learned for tangible action is part of our on-going work also.

References

1. Home, SF311: https://sf311.org/home. Accessed 4 May 2020
2. What is 311? https://www.govtech.com/dc/articles/What-is-311.html. Accessed 2 May 2020
3. Ren, S., He, K., Girshick, R., Sun, J.: Faster R-CNN: towards real-time object detection with region proposal networks (2016). arXiv:1506.01497
4. Lin, T., Goyal, P., Girshick, R., He, K., Dollar, P.: Focal loss for dense object detection (2018). arXiv:1708.02002
5. State of the Art Object Detection - use these top 3 data augmentations and Google Brain's optimal policy for training your architecture: https://medium.com/@lessw/state-of-the-art-object-detection-use-these-top-3-data-augmentations-and-google-brains-optimal-57ac6d8d1de5. Accessed 23 Nov 2020
6. Socrata, Data & Insights: https://www.tylertech.com/products/socrata. Accessed 5 May 2020
7. LabelImg · PyPI: https://pypi.org/project/labelImg/. Accessed 8 May 2020
8. Training Custom Object Detector - TensorFlow Object Detection API tutorial documentation: https://tensorflow-object-detection-api-tutorial.readthedocs.io/en/latest/training.html. Accessed 8 May 2020
9. Jiao, L., Zhang, F., Liu, F., Yang, S., Li, L., Feng, Z., Qu, R.: A survey of deep learning-based object detection. IEEE Access **7**, 128837–128868 (2019)
10. Liu, L., Ouyang, W., Wang, X., Fieguth, P., Chen, J., Liu, X., Pietikäinen, M.: Deep learning for generic object detection: a survey (2018). arXiv:1809.02165
11. Zhao, Z., Zheng, P., Xu, S., Wu, X.: Object detection with deep learning: a review (2019). arXiv:1807.05511
12. Cai, W., Li, J., Xie, Z., Zhao, T., Lu, K.: Street object detection based on faster R-CNN. In: Proceedings of the 37th Chinese Control Conference, pp. 9500–9503. Wohan, China (2018)
13. Krizhevsky, A., Sutskever, I., Hinton, G.: ImageNet classification with deep convolutional neural networks. In: Neural Information Processing Systems (2012)
14. Geiger, A., Lenz, P., Urtasun, R.: Are we ready for autonomous driving? The KITTI vision benchmark suite. In: Conference on Computer Vision and Pattern Recognition (2012)
15. Chen, Y., Li, W., Sakaridis, C., Dai, D., Gool, L.: Domain adaptive faster R-CNN for object detection in the wild (2018). arXiv:1803.03243
16. Fan, Q., Brown, L., Smith, J.: A closer look at faster R-CNN for vehicle detection. In: Proceedings of 2016 IEEE Intelligent Vehicles Symposium (IV), Gothenburg, Sweden (2016)
17. Girshick, R.: Fast R-CNN. In: IEEE International Conference on Computer Vision (ICCV) (2015)

18. He, K., Zhang, X., Ren, S., Sun, J.: Deep residual learning for image recognition (2015). arXiv:1512.03385
19. Evaluating Object Detection Models: Guide to Performance Metrics: https://manalelaidouni.github.io/manalelaidouni.github.io/Evaluating-Object-Detection-Models-Guide-to-Performance-Metrics.html. Accessed 29 July 2020
20. Padilla, R., Netto, S., Silva, E.: A survey on performance metrics for object-detection algorithms. In: 2020 International Conference on Systems, Signals and Image Processing (IWSSIP), pp. 237–242 (2020)
21. Shahid, F., Ony, S., Albi, T., Chellappan, S., Vashistha, A., Islam, A.: Learning from tweets: opportunities and challenges to inform policy making during dengue epidemic. In: Proceedings of the ACM on Human-Computer Interaction, vol. 4, CSCW1, Article 65 (2020)
22. Wiggins, A., Wilbanks, J.: The rise of citizen science in health and biomedical research. Am. J. Bioeth. **19**(8), 3–14 (2019). https://doi.org/10.1080/15265161.2019.1619859
23. Tweddle, J., Robinson, L., Pocock, M., Roy, H.: Guide to citizen science: developing, implementing and evaluating citizen science to study biodiversity and the environment in the UK. Natural History Museum and NERC Centre for Ecology & Hydrology for UK-EOF (2012)
24. Nugent, J.: iNaturalist: citizen science for 21st-century naturalists. Sci. Scope **41**(7), 12–14 (2018). National Science Teachers Association
25. Huddart, J., Thompson, M., Woodward, G., Brooks, S.: Citizen science: from detecting pollution to evaluating ecological restoration. In: Wiley Interdisciplinary Reviews Water, vol. 3, issue 3, pp. 287–300. Wiley, Great Britain (2016)
26. Jerrett, M., et al.: Validating novel air pollution sensors to improve exposure estimates for epidemiological analyses and citizen science. Environ. Res. **158**, 286–294 (2017). https://doi.org/10.1016/j.envres.2017.04.023

Smart Governance in Urban Mobility Process

Ralf-Martin Soe[✉]

FinEst Twins Smart City Center of Excellence, Tallinn University of Technology, Tallinn,
Estonia
ralf-martin.soe@taltech.ee

Abstract. This paper is interested in the interplay between smart governance and
urban mobility planning in the context of smart city. Mobility is one of the key
urban domains, thus, it is crucial to analyze the governance models behind it, especially from two perspectives: participation of stakeholders and decision-making
procedures. More specifically, this project takes a closer look at the European
approach to rather top-down initiated Sustainable Urban Mobility Plans (SUMP)
and analyses how they are designed and implemented in the Baltic Sea region,
with an in-depth focus on the city of Tallinn where interviews with city officials
and mobility stakeholders were conducted. The results indicate that the top-down
approach has not been taken over effectively by the city officials and thus, creating
the lack of ownership on the local level. The Tallinn SUMP involved key stakeholders into the planning process including satellite areas and various interests'
groups. On the other hand, technology-enabled participation of citizens remains
weak.

Keywords: Smart city · Urban mobility · Smart governance · SUMP ·
Participation

1 Related Work: Smart Governance and Mobility

The smart city governance as a term is evolving and there are several definitions among
researchers and practitioners without widespread consensus (Bolívar and Meijer 2016;
Ruhlandt 2018). Smart governance, as one key dimension of smart cities (Bolívar and
Meijer 2016; Lopes 2017), helps to reshape administrative processes and structures
across multiple city agencies (Alawadhi and Scholl 2016). Involving stakeholders is seen
as a prerequisite to successful smart city initiatives (Alawadhi and Scholl 2016) that also
can be more broadly conceptualized as smart collaboration (Viale Pereira et al. 2017).
Tomor et al. (2019) define, based on the systematic literature review, smart governance as
"*technology-enabled collaboration between citizens and local governments to advance
sustainable development,*" applied as a working definition in this analysis.

In the case of urban mobility, the main challenges have been related to the growing
demand for passenger and freight transport due to urbanization, resulting in increased
congestion, pollution and quality of life (Kiba-Janiak and Witkowski 2019). In Europe,
this has triggered the European Commission (EC) to promote the concept of Sustainable

S. Paiva et al. (Eds.): SmartCity360° 2020, LNICST 372, pp. 542–552, 2021.
https://doi.org/10.1007/978-3-030-76063-2_36

Urban Mobility Plans (SUMP), especially for the capital city regions. According to Maria et al. (2018), SUMPs are not new in Europe but go back decades and have several precedents in larger countries like France, UK, Italy and Germany; the aim of SUMP is to propose a strategy to reduce the increasing dependency on private cars and thus also reduce Carbon dioxide (CO_2) emissions; these plans are usually designed for ten to fifteen years.

Several authors propose methodology for SUMP, analyse specific cities and/or propose integration models for multilevel transports system planning (Maria et al. 2018; May 2015; Okraszewska et al. 2018). Zawieska and Pieriegud (2018) take more global perspective on sustainable governance of transport systems and they investigate CO_2 emissions for different potential scenarios in the case of Warsaw (Poland) using the United Nations' ForFITS model and also evaluating the additional impact on CO_2 in the case of mobility. According to Zawieska and Pieriegud (2018), meeting the reduction targets set by European Union 2011 whitepaper (precedent of SUMP guidance) is challenging. There is also a question how SUMPs contribute to broader key societal challenges such as the United Nations Sustainable Development Goals. In general, SUMPs are non-existing concepts in the most European member states (Arsenio et al. 2016).

In the context of central-local government collaboration models, May (2015) has developed recommendations that enable governments to support their cities in developing SUMPs based on the EC guidelines and tested them against current practice in six European countries (Belgium, France, Germany, Italy, Netherlands, Norway and UK) resulting in 9 recommendations in 20 criteria. As there is limited literature on the topic, Maria et al. (2018) propose a methodology to evaluate SUMPs from the cost-effectiveness perspective (in the case of Burgos, Spain). Another group of authors (Okraszewska et al. 2018) propose that the process of SUMP should be involved into a transport modelling framework. They analyse the efficacy of the Multilevel Model of Transport Systems for the SUMP process, considering behavioral aspects, and test it empirically in the city of Gdynia (Poland).

May (2015), when analyzing the size of cities of SUMPs, claims that since the EC guidance paper was published (European Commission 2013), the number of cities preparing for SUMP increased substantially. May (2015) covers the preparation of this guidance both at an European level and also at national level in Belgium, France, Germany, Italy, Poland, Scandinavia, Spain and the UK and identifies the weaknesses in the preparation of SUMPs and reviews the research which has been undertaken to overcome barriers. It is also important that having a SUMP is linked to future European Union funding into cities, which is seen as one of the key top-down initiated triggers.

Conceptually, there seems to be no direct link between smart cities and SUMPs, although there are several attempts to link these indirectly. One approach is proposed by Melo et al. (2017) that see urban traffic management systems as digital solutions that can transform cities to smart cities. The authors also develop a performance evaluation of re-routing for all types of vehicles in the case of city of Lisbon and analyse this from the urban network level. That type of digital tools can be enabled in order to reduce congestion that is one of the key goals of SUMPs. When linking the SUMP to digital methods and Intelligent Transport Systems (ITS), Cledou et al. (2018) claim that smart mobility initiatives require specialized and contextualised policies addressing the needs and interests of many stakeholders involved. They propose a global taxonomy for planning and designing smart mobility services. Docherty et al. 2018 in parallel propose a model for smart mobility governance based on the public value theory.

1.1 Key Characteristics of the SUMPs in Europe

According to the EC, Sustainable Urban Mobility Planning is the most important topic in the Urban Mobility Package (European Commission 2013). The SUMP concept foresees that plans are developed in cooperation across different policy areas and sectors, across different levels of government and administration and in cooperation with citizens and other stakeholders.

The EC has actively promoted this concept for several years with pre-developed guidelines, which provide local authorities a framework for the development and implementation of such a plan. However, Member States (central governments) need to promote those practices at national level and to ensure the right legislative and support conditions for their local authorities.

The EC plans to continue to support the development of SUMPs through funding instruments and is continuously expending its SUMP-specific information hub Eltis urban mobility observatory (www.eltis.org). According to the Eltis city database tool, there are over 400 SUMPs published online from different European countries.

According to the EC concept for sustainable urban mobility plans, the key characteristics of the SUMP are:

- A SUMP has a central goal improving accessibility of urban areas and providing high-quality and sustainable mobility and transport to, through and within the urban area. It regards the needs of the 'functioning city' and its hinterland rather than a municipal administrative region. The plan is accessible and meets the basic mobility needs of all users;
- A SUMP presents, or is linked to an existing, long-term strategy for the future development of the urban area and, in this context, for the future development of transport and mobility infrastructure and services.
- A SUMP equally includes a delivery plan for short-term implementation of the strategy. This should also include timetable (3–10 years) for implementation as well as a budget plan.
- The development of a SUMP should be build on a careful assessment of the present and future performance of the urban transport system. This is expected to involve suitable performance indicators, specific performance objectives and targets.
- A SUMP fosters a balanced development of all relevant transport modes, while encouraging a shift towards more sustainable modes. The plan puts forward an integrated set of technical, infrastructure, policy-based, and soft measures to improve performance and cost-effectiveness with regard to the declared goal and specific objectives. This includes, among others, a plan for improving public transport and also non-motorised transport.
- The development and implementation of SUMP follows an integrated approach with a high level of cooperation, coordination and consultation between the different levels

of government and relevant authorities. The Local Planning Authority is expected to put in place appropriate structures and procedures.

- A SUMP follows a transparent and participatory approach.
- The implementation of a SUMP should be closely monitored.
- Local Planning Authorities should have mechanisms to ensure the quality and validate compliance of the SUMP with the requirements of the concept.

1.2 SUMPs in Helsinki and Riga

The European Baltic Sea Cities of Helsinki and Riga have developed their SUMPs earlier than Tallinn, although with limited focus towards smart governance. In the case of Helsinki, the need for joint planning of transport system and land use with the need for participatory decision-making tool is emphasized, although not entirely applied. In the case Riga, the process has been more top-down, led by the Ministry of Transport, with international mobility experts involved. However, there is no specific focus on how to involve citizens into the process using the technology.

The Helsinki Region Transport System Plan (HLJ) was published in 2015 and it is a long-term strategic plan that represents the common will for transport policy and the development of the transport system in the region. The plan has been prepared in close cooperation with the regional land use plan (MASU) developed in accordance with the Letter of Intent on Land use, Housing and Transport (MAL) in the Helsinki region. The goals of HLJ are based on MAL goals and they emphasize the accessibility of the region, flow of traffic as well as social, economic and ecological sustainability. The HLJ is a plan whose environmental impacts have to be assessed as stipulated in the Act on the Assessment of the Impacts of the Authorities' Plans and Programmes on the Environment (SEA Act 200/2005). Assessments have been conducted throughout the HLJ and MASU process as part of the planning.

According to the HLJ 2015, measures derived from the policies effectively address challenges in different parts of the region within the limits of funding available. The key is to make the region more effective and competitive by utilizing the existing structure to the full and investing in the public transport trunk network and its service level. Measures are primarily targeted to support a more coherent urban structure and they are expected to improve the overall performance of the transport system and support land use development in which construction is primarily concentrated in the broad main center of the region and in the existing and emerging rail corridors. The use of the transport system is made a more responsible by making efficient use of traffic management tools and examining vehicular traffic pricing as a steering and financing tool.

The HLJ and MASU together are expected to contribute to socio-economic efficiency, accessibility of the region and more coherent urban structure with improving overall accessibility. Prior to 2025, the accessibility is expected to improve in particular along the existing rail corridors. By 2040 the improvement in accessibility is expected to spread quite evenly across the whole region. However, new developments have been located in areas with no competitive public transport supply in both the metropolitan area and the surrounding municipalities. In future, more attention should be paid on utilizing areas with good accessibility in particular when planning beyond 2025.

The preparation of and negotiations on the next MAL Letter of Intent are a vital part of the implementation of the transport system decision. The various parties are expected to promote measures set out in the transport system decision and the Letter of Intent and make provisions for planning and implementation conformable with them in their own financial and operational planning. The HLJ also states the need to consider developing transport system planning into a continuous process. The joint planning of transport system and land use and decision-making need to be even more closely coordinated and tools for them developed together regardless of the future administrative model or organizational structure.

The mobility plan and action program for Riga and Pieriga was published late 2010 by a consortium of international consultancies for the Ministry of Transport of Latvia (Ministry of Transport Republic of Latvia (2010)). The Riga SUMP is meant to create an overall framework in which all existing and new plans for construction and improvement of the traffic and transport system in Riga and Pieriga are evaluated and prioritised. Professional expertise and ideas of the consultant team have been combined with existing plans and information in the development. The plan provides solutions for the traffic and transport problems which the Ministry of Transport of Latvia is facing, contributing to spatial, ecological, economical, social and institutional optimization.

The Riga and Pieriga Mobility Plan (RPMP) has the following overall goal: 'To determine a vision and necessary actions in order to promote unified transport system development in Riga and Pieriga, thus improving accessibility of the territory'. The RPMP objectives are:

- to make effective use of the existing transport system of Riga and Pieriga and prefer soft measures (management, organisation, ITS) over hard measures (infrastructure development) where possible;
- develop an efficient, attractive and competitive public transport system, with priority for electric and railway modes;
- to create a coherent network with clear road and street classifications and prioritisation of modes, by eliminating bottlenecks in the road and street network;
- increase the level of road safety, without hampering accessibility;
- provide multi modal accessibility to different places;
- ensure good and reliable connections between the Riga Freeport, Riga and other national and international (TEN-T) transport infrastructure networks;
- ensure good and reliable connections between the Riga international airport, Riga and other main regional centres in a sustainable way.

2 Research Method

This is a qualitative case study of the city of Tallinn (capital of Estonia) SUMP process based on the document analysis (both public and internal documents) coupled with expert interviews (both face to face or online) of the key stakeholders, see annex 1. Conceptually, the design-reality cap method is applied, developed by Richard Heeks which is mainly used in the field of e-government, with some modifications for this research paper. In the context of this analysis, the "Design" means the model or conceptions and assumptions built into the project's design (*ex ante*) and the "Reality" represents the actual realities of the situation (*ex post*). The success and failure therefore depends on the size of gap that exists between 'realities' and 'design of the project'. The larger this design-reality gap, the greater the risk of failure. Equally, the smaller the gap, the greater the chance of success. According to Heeks (2003), seven dimensions – summarized by the ITPOSMO acronym – are necessary and sufficient to provide an understanding of design-reality gaps:

- Information
- Technology
- Processes
- Objectives and values
- Staffing and skills
- Management systems and structures
- Other resources: time and money

3 The Case of Tallinn SUMP

3.1 SUMP Design

The Tallinn SUMP was initiated under the EU-financed project, Finest Smart Mobility. According to the initial project plan, the Tallinn SUMP is a pre-requisite for future transport infrastructure projects in the Tallinn capital region, as the EC plans to demand SUMP-s for all future Cohesion Fund investments. When preparing the SUMP, public sector officials were expected to analyse the mobility needs of their region and have set the sustainable transport priorities for its transport investments. As the SUMP design includes review phase after implementation, this is expected to guarantee the continuity of the mobility planning in the Tallinn capital region. In addition, Tallinn planned to learn from Helsinki region mobility plan process (HLJ (2015)), where already second SUMP was approved before Tallinn started its process. The Tallinn SUMP was expected to be a role-model process for other Estonian cities and urban regions, as all of them have to start to prepare for the future EC transport infrastructure and mobility investments requirements (where an existing and high-quality SUMP is a key element). Importantly, stakeholders and participants were expected to be invited to the process of developing the plan and various digital technologies were planned to be applied. In addition, the approval of SUMP in the city councils of participating municipalities ensures that commitments are followed in the activities phase of the SUMP.

Interestingly, the Tallinn Region mobility plan was planned to be harmonized with the Helsinki Region transport strategy and plans. This was supposed to allow for planning and management of international aspects of the traffic as well as cross-border traffic between the countries and regions. Issues like intensive goods and truck traffic through both cities and Estonian private car approaches to Helsinki airport in Finland were planned to be addressed jointly.

The Tallinn SUMP had an initial timeline:

- Sept 17: Mobility Surveys (planning, procurement, surveys, conclusions).

- Dec 17: Introducing the Tallinn capital region mobility scenarios to stakeholders.
- March 18. Consultations with Helsinki, Vantaa and international transport stakeholders; negotiations of the investment plan of SUMP with neighboring municipalities of Tallinn.
- June 18: Public hearings of Tallinn Region Mobility Plan, preparations to discuss the SUMP in the councils of participating municipalities.
- Dec 18: Tallinn Region Mobility Plan discussed in the councils of participating municipalities with the aim to start with first activities in 2019.
- April 19: Tallinn Region Mobility Plan 2025 is accepted in the city council.

3.2 SUMP Reality

According to the final publication of SUMP, introduced publicly April of 2019, the city of Tallinn contributes to 50% of total mileage, CO2 emissions and traffic accidents in the entire Estonia. This trend is projected to increase as the population of Tallinn is foreseen to increase 9% by 2035 whereas the Estonia in general does not grow in population, rather is projected to decrease. The key challenges are related to increased costs of mobility, deepening dependency from private cars, too high risks of injuries of pedestrians and cyclists and negative health impact due to congestion. Most importantly, if no strategic decisions are made, CO2 emissions are expected to continue that are already now 40% above the Estonian target for 2030. In this light three scenarios were modelled until 2035 (with results on the Fig. 1):

1. **Business as Usual (BAU 2035)**

   - No major intervention and change in policy.
   - Number of private cars continues to grow.
   - Need for major investments into roads.
   - Financial Penalty for missing CO2 target is unavoidable.

2. **Public Transport Prioritization (PT 2035)**

   - Priority of investments is to improve accessibility and service quality of the Public Transport.
   - Planning hubs for better links between different modes.
   - Prioritising public transport on main directions in city center.
   - Improving walkability and cycling opportunities

3. **HELSINKI SUMP projected to TALLINN (HEL 2035):**

   - The SUMP goals of neighboring capital city of Finland (Helsinki) projected to Tallinn

In order to analyse the SUMP process in the context of smart governance and the ITPOSMO framework, interview results are presented below (see annex 1 for interviewed stakeholders A-E).

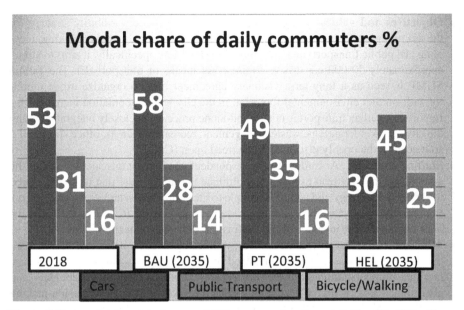

Fig. 1. Tallinn modal change in the case of different scenarios. Source: Tallinn City/ Pirko Konsa presentation.

- **Information**: urban mobility information was central to the SUMP planning; therefore, various mobility data was gathered, including typical daily routes of citizens (e.g. home to kindergarten to work), means of transport (public transport, car, walking/cycling) and also other aspects (e.g. parking) (D). The SUMP utilized some digital data-collection tools (e.g. mobile positioning for tracking urban mobility, people-tracking sensors in Public Transport), although some remained unused (satellite-based parking lots mapping) (A). On the other hand, there was no digital decision-making tool applied before the final stage when the process was sent to the local council in Tallinn (where all decisions are open for online consultations and later published online). Therefore, during the preparation period, the information stayed within the core project team, although it should have been more widely spread (C).
- **Technology**: the initial aim was to provide a decision-making tool based on the measurable mobility indicators (A; B; D), which did not succeed fully. More broadly, the Tallinn SUMP wanted to provide novel technologies for mobility (e.g. electric or hydrogen buses, local electricity generation) and for the infrastructure (if there is not fast public transport or network of pedestrian/bicycle roads then citizens will use cars instead) (E) – which both remained mainly at the "wishful-thinking" level. It is also important to note that the city of Tallinn has been piloting automated shuttle buses (Soe, Müür 2020; Soe 2020)
- **Processes**: Tallinn SUMP included too complex decision-making process with vague responsibilities (A; B). In theory, the process was well planned but it lacked political and high-level ownership and strategic management competences (C). It was also stated that there was too limited involvement of key city departments and stakeholders (D).

- **Objectives and values**: The key objective was to provide a mobility strategy for the entire region (A; C) with a focus on environment-friendly goals (walking, bicycling and public transport) and multimodality (B). More specifically, it aims to attract approximately 50 000 car drivers to use other means of transport (E). The Tallinn SUMP is seen as a long-term visionary agreement how to organize urban mobility with smaller environmental footprint, in the city where population increases (E). Importantly, urban transport is not a stand-alone process but closely integrated within the city (e.g. kindergartens, waste management, recreational areas, office spaces etc.) so it needs to be openly discussed and agreed upon (C; D).

- **Staffing and skills:** According to one respondent, the biggest miscalculation was the assumption that one lead expert can coordinate the full process that triggered a need to change the strategy and add more people to the coordination and analysis team (A). Importantly, the role of the government was underestimated (C, E) – they are be the ones to make larger investments into infrastructure and new technologies.

- **Management systems and structures**: According to several interviewed experts, the City Council was effectively involved in the last stage; it was also good to have morning seminars, although there was too limited involvement of stakeholders, and also limited use of digital technologies for the involvement and decision-making purposes. It also came out that city and government executive decision makers should have been more involved (e.g. Mayor's office, department heads). It was commonly stated that there were too limited Steering Committee meetings and open discussions with stakeholders (A; B; C). Despite of the lack of strategic management, the wish was to bring the mobility management on a new qualitative level via internal process innovation (B, C). Unfortunately, city decision-makers did not have a clear ownership in this process, only last period a Deputy-Mayor was briefed once in three weeks (C).

- **Other resources**: There was too strict timeline – it took Helsinki 15 years and now it was expected Tallinn to deliver a strategic mobility plan in 2 years. In addition, there is too big internal planning fragmentation – there are also other mobility related action plans (parking, bicycle roads, car logistics etc.) (A). The SUMP is also linked to the EC funding in the new period – cities without SUMP might have difficulties (B; D).

4   Conclusions

This paper is analyzing the governance processes within urban mobility strategy setting, with additional interest in the application of ICT-enabled tools. The European Commission has initiated Sustainable Urban Mobility Plans initiative from the top-down approach with a claim that future mobility investments are directed only towards cities with accepted SUMPs. This also triggered a development of SUMP Tallinn – the case this paper was interested in. As a research approach, an ITPOSMO framework was applied, that has been used within the e-governance projects evaluation. The data was collected via document analysis of the project files and by conducting expert interviews with the key actors in the process. The results indicate that the SUMP Tallinn was planned with wide stakeholder involvement including the use of digital tools. The reality, however, was different – most of the activities remained within the small project team with too limited internal (political and top-level involvement from the city executives) and external involvement (neighboring regions, central government, companies, NGOs, universities, and most importantly, citizens). In addition, the adaption of digital tools for analyzing the mobility of citizens, remained significantly weaker than planned (e.g. instead of validation and GPS data positioning of mobility of people and parking spaces, most data were gathered via traditional telephone mass surveys and physical observations).

5 Annex: List of Interviews

1. A, SUMP Project Manager, City of Tallinn, 8.5.2019
2. B, SUMP Project Manager, Road Administration, 20.5.2019
3. C, Head of Strategy, City of Tallinn, 15.5.2019
4. D, Head of Department, City of Tallinn, 20.5.2019
5. E, Outsourced Mobility Expert by the City of Tallinn, 21.5.2019

Acknowledgements. This work has been supported by the European Commission through the Baltic Sea Interreg project Finest Smart Mobility (CB359) and the H2020 project Finest Twins (grant No. 856602).

References

Alawadhi, S., Scholl, H.J.: Smart governance: a cross-case analysis of smart city initiatives. In: Proceedings of the Annual Hawaii International Conference on System Sciences, pp. 2953–2963 (2016). https://doi.org/10.1109/HICSS.2016.370

Arsenio, E., Martens, K., Di, F.: Research in transportation economics sustainable urban mobility plans: bridging climate change and equity targets? Res. Transp. Econ. **55**, 30–39 (2016). https://doi.org/10.1016/j.retrec.2016.04.008

Bolívar, M.P.R., Meijer, A.J.: Smart governance: using a literature review and empirical analysis to build a research model. Soc. Sci. Comput. Rev. **34**(6), 673–692 (2016). https://doi.org/10.1177/0894439315611088

Cledou, G., Estevez, E., Barbosa, L.S.: A taxonomy for planning and designing smart mobility services. Gov. Inf. Q. **35**(1), 61–76 (2018). https://doi.org/10.1016/j.giq.2017.11.008

Docherty, I., Marsden, G., Anable, J.: The governance of smart mobility. Transp. Res. Part A **115**, 114–125 (2018). https://doi.org/10.1016/j.tra.2017.09.012

European Commission: A Concept for Sustainable Urban Mobility Plans. European Union, pp. 1–5 (2013)

Heeks, R.: Most e-Government-for-Development Projects Fail How Can Risks be Reduced? (2003)

HLJ: Helsinki region Transport System Plan (2015). https://doi.org/10.1145/3132847.3132886

Kiba-Janiak, M., Witkowski, J.: Sustainable urban mobility plans: How do they work? Sustainability **11**(17) (2019). https://doi.org/10.3390/su11174605

Lopes, N.V.: Smart governance: a key factor for smart cities implementation. In: 2017 IEEE International Conference on Smart Grid and Smart Cities, ICSGSC 2017, pp. 277–282 (2017). https://doi.org/10.1109/ICSGSC.2017.8038591

Maria, J., Lopez-lambas, M.E., Gonzalo, H., Rojo, M., Garcia-Martinez, A.: Methodology for assessing the cost effectiveness of Sustainable Urban Mobility Plans (SUMPs). The case of the city of Burgos. J. Transp. Geogr. **68**, 22–30 (2018). https://doi.org/10.1016/j.jtrangeo.2018.02.006

May, A.D.: Case studies on transport policy encouraging good practice in the development of sustainable urban mobility plans. Case Stud. Transp. Policy **3**(1), 3–11 (2015). https://doi.org/10.1016/j.cstp.2014.09.001

Melo, S., Macedo, J., Baptista, P.: Research in transportation economics guiding cities to pursue a smart mobility paradigm: an example from vehicle routing guidance and its traffic and operational effects. Res. Transp. Econ. **65**, 24–33 (2017). https://doi.org/10.1016/j.retrec.2017.09.007

Ministry of Transport Republic of Latvia: Mobility Plan and Action Program for Riga and Pieriga SEA Report (2010)

Okraszewska, R., Romanowska, A., Wołek, M., Oskarbski, J., Birr, K., Jamroz, K.: Integration of a multilevel transport system model into sustainable Urban mobility planning. Sustainability **10**(2), 1–20 (2018). https://doi.org/10.3390/su10020479

Ruhlandt, R.W.S.: The governance of smart cities: a systematic literature review. Cities **81**, 1–23 (2018). https://doi.org/10.1016/j.cities.2018.02.014

Zawieska, J., Pieriegud, J.: Smart city as a tool for sustainable mobility and transport decarbonisation. Transp. Policy **63**, 39–50 (2018). https://doi.org/10.1016/j.tranpol.2017.11.004

Tomor, Z., Meijer, A., Michels, A., Geertman, S.: Smart governance for sustainable cities: findings from a systematic literature review. J. Urban Technol. **26**(4), 3–27 (2019). https://doi.org/10.1080/10630732.2019.1651178

Viale Pereira, G., Cunha, M.A., Lampoltshammer, T.J., Parycek, P., Testa, M.G.: Increasing collaboration and participation in smart city governance: a cross-case analysis of smart city initiatives. Inf. Technol. Dev. **23**(3), 526–553 (2017). https://doi.org/10.1080/02681102.2017.1353946

Soe, R.-M.; Müür, J.: Mobility acceptance factors of an automated shuttle bus last-mile service. Sustainability **12**, 5469 (2020). https://doi.org/10.3390/su12135469

Soe, R.-M.: Mobility in smart cities: will automated vehicles take it over?. In: Lopes, N. (ed.) Smart Governance for Cities: Perspectives and Experiences. EAISICC, pp. 189–216. Springer, Cham (2020). https://doi.org/10.1007/978-3-030-22070-9_10

A Theoretical Framework for GIS-Enabled Public Electronic Participation in Municipal Solid Waste Management

Irene Arinaitwe$^{(\boxtimes)}$, Gilbert Maiga, and Agnes Nakakawa

School of Computing and Informatics Technology, Makerere University, Kampala, Uganda
irene.arinaitwe@mak.ac.ug

Abstract. Population growth, urbanization and industrialization are increasing the amounts of solid waste generated in municipalities globally. Municipal solid management (MSWM) is complex and requires active and broader stakeholder participation to achieve sustainable solutions. However, existing solutions to MSWM challenges lack public participation. Although public participatory geographic information systems (PPGIS) may be used to solicit stakeholders' views in planning for spatial environmental issues, there is a need to develop robust theoretical frameworks to guide their development and use. This study sought to extend the adaptive structuration theory-2 (EAST-2) to develop a comprehensive theoretical framework for the use of PPGIS applications to ensure effective public participation and social inclusion in MSWM. Additional constructs as suggested in literature were added to the existing EAST-2 framework. Data were collected cross-sectionally from MSWM stakeholders in central-Uganda and analyzed using partial least squares structural equation modelling. In the revised framework, participant influences, technology influences and task influences influence GIS-enabled participatory decision-making processes. The revised framework could be used to guide GIS-enabled participatory processes in different environmental problems in similar resource-constrained settings.

Keywords: Geographic information systems · Participatory planning · Municipal solid waste management · Uganda

1 Introduction

Globally, the high population growth, urbanization and industrialization have tremendously increased waste generation in municipalities. Annually, 2.01 billion metric tons of wastes are generated globally [1]. In Sub-Saharan Africa, 62 million tons of waste are generated annually [2]. Therefore, efficient, and effective municipal solid waste management (MSWM) is a global priority. However, current MSWM systems are not well planned [3] and are therefore inefficient and not effective [2].

Several strategies to address MSWM challenges have been proposed. These include Life Cycle Assessment [4], Cost-Benefit Analysis [5], Multi-criteria Decision Analysis (MCDA) [6], and MCDA integrated with Geographic Information Systems (GIS).

© ICST Institute for Computer Sciences, Social Informatics and Telecommunications Engineering 2021
Published by Springer Nature Switzerland AG 2021. All Rights Reserved
S. Paiva et al. (Eds.): SmartCity360° 2020, LNICST 372, pp. 553–567, 2021.
https://doi.org/10.1007/978-3-030-76063-2_37

Regardless of the strategy adopted, public participation is central to achieving sustainable solutions [7]. Public participation ensures that MSWM challenges are identified and addressed [8].

Public participation in government administrative process can be supported by different tools such as public hearings, focus groups, and public education, interviews, electronic mails, faxes, volunteered Geographic Information (VGI), PPGIS, discussion forums and chat rooms [9]. However, other participation methods, other than PPGIS, reach fewer participants and are ineffective for gathering useful information for planning [10]. PPGIS is one of the e-participation tools that have been specifically developed to support the solicitation of public views for planning purposes [11]. However, there are concerns that PPGIS lack theoretical and conceptual foundations [12]. Theoretical concepts and foundations help to reduce the complexity associated with GIS use in collaborative decision making [13].

This study sought to develop a comprehensive theoretical framework that supports the implementation of PPGIS in MSWM in resource-limited settings (RLS). To this end, the Enhanced Adaptive Structuration Theory (EAST-2) was adapted, and modifications made to increase public participation. The development and testing of the proposed framework were guided by design science. Design science is preferred over other methods of framework development because it clearly specifies the two major processes of "build" and "evaluate", which are important in developing frameworks [14]. Additionally, it is a flexible method which can be combined with other methods such as action research, case studies in order to enhance its contribution to theory [15].

After the introduction, the remainder of this paper is structured as follows. Section 2 covers the key literature review on MSWM, public participation, and theories for ICT-enabled collaborations. Section 3 explains the research methods for this study. Section 4 presents the study findings while Sect. 5 presents the discussion and the conclusions.

2   Related Work

2.1   Municipal Solid Waste Management in the Ugandan Context

Municipal solid waste management (MSWM) involves the control of generation, storage, collection, transport, processing and disposal of solid waste materials in a way that best ensures public health and environmental safety [16]. Therefore, MSWM is a core service that municipalities should offer to its inhabitants in order to minimize the potential health and environmental hazards [17].

In Uganda, the amount of waste generated is increasing due to rapid population growth and industrialization. The management of solid is a function of local government and urban councils (UCs); municipal authorities are therefore responsible for the collection, transportation and disposal of all waste [18]. However, MSWM is largely inefficient and ineffective due to limited funding and poor infrastructure [17]. Therefore, there is limited coverage of MSWM, waste transportation routes are not planned [19], and there is indiscriminate and illegal waste dumping [18, 20]. These gaps are compounded by inadequate public participation in MSWM decision making [19]. Therefore efficient MSWM approaches, including public participation, are needed for across municipalities [21, 22].

2.2   The Role of Public Participation in Municipal Solid Waste Management

Public participation in environmental decision making is one of the strongest pillars for sustainable development. Environmental issues are better handled by ensuring broader stakeholder participation [7, 24], including citizens at all levels [23]. Public participation ensures that popular decisions and policies are implemented [24]. However, public participation in MSWM has received less attention [25]. In Uganda, inadequate MSWM is attributable to the lack of public participation [20]. Therefore, public participation should be incorporated and evaluated at all stages of solid waste management [26].

2.3   Methods of Public Participation

Public participation in governmental administrative processes can be implemented using both traditional and ICT-enabled methods (E-participation). Traditional public participation involves the use of physical participatory mechanisms such as surveys, public meeting, and interviews [9]. On the other hand, E-participation involves using modern two-way modern techniques such as PPGIS, Web GIS, volunteered geographic information, social media, discussion forums and chat rooms, games, collaborative software, and 3D virtual animations [27]. E-participation enhances and is complementary to traditional participation activities [28].

2.4   Public Participatory Geographic Information Systems (PPGIS)

PPGIS involves the use of GIS for public participation [29]. Its goal is to ensure the participation of stakeholders who would have otherwise been left out by the traditional tools [30, 31]. PPGIS decision-making includes discussions between stakeholders to clarify and resolve existent spatial MSWM challenges. PPGIS integrates people, GIS data, exploratory tools in order to maximize the participation of all stakeholders [32].

2.5   Theories for Analyzing E-Participation

E-participation is best analyzed using structural frameworks [33]. Structural frameworks help to deconstruct the decision support system into components that can be accomplished by appropriate tools and technologies. Examples of structural frameworks used for e-participation include Adaptive Structuration Theory [34], Enhance Adaptive Structuration Theory (EAST) [35], and Enhanced Adaptive Structuration Theory (EAST-2) [36].

2.6   Enhanced Adaptive Structuration Theory (EAST-2)

In this study, EAST-2 was selected for modification because it was specifically developed for analyzing group decision making and use of PPGIS [36]. The framework comprises of constructs and aspects that describe participatory decision making. The constructs show the structure and aspects that address the content of participatory decision making [37]. The EAST-2 framework is divided into three construct categories that characterize the complex decision-making processes of public participatory GIS

(PPGIS). The construct categories are convening, process and the outcome constructs. In these three construct categories, eight influences are prescribed: social-institutional influences, group-participant influence, PGIS influence, appropriation, group process, emergent influence, task outcomes, and social outcomes [36]. Thus, EAST-2 categorizes 'participation' into 25 aspects, and eight constructs.

2.7 Extending the Adaptive Structuration Theory-2

As shown in Fig. 1, the EAST-2 framework was adapted to develop an extended version that provides a robust theoretical framework for PPGIS adoption in RLS. The aspects and constructs that have been previously been found to be important in GIS-enabled collaborative decision making were systematically included to the original EAST-2.

Task Influence was added on the existing three convening constructs. The influence of task on the utilization of technology in social interaction is well described [34] and considers the content of a task as a source of structures that affect the actual use of technology in participation. In addition, the nature of the task influences the choice of technology and its use [38].

To ensure spatial MSWM planning, reading background information, generating alternatives, evaluating alternative, 'discuss plan' and collaboration among participants were added to the original decision process construct [39]. In addition, the process of participation benefits from the dynamic capabilities orchestrated by ICTs [40]. The dynamic capabilities from the dynamic capabilities theory that are important for public participation - ubiquitous participation and monitoring of the process [40] were added onto the "decision process construct".

Organizational aspects that enhance PPGIS were identified from the literature and added on the "social-Institutional influence" construct. These include (1) availability of resources [41], (2) access to spatial data [42], (3) assess the impact and outcomes of PPGIS [12] and (4) procedures for integrating public input in the final decision [12]. The participant influence aspects that were added to this construct include motivation and incentives [43], skills and experience [41], collaboration and knowledge sharing [43] and perceptions of other peoples' knowledge [12].

EAST-2 does not consider aspects related to the evaluation of the decision outcomes [44]. Therefore the evaluation parameters of efficiency finance, equity, accountability, conformance to values and sustainability [45], were added to the decision outcome construct.

2.8 Study Hypotheses

Based on the nine constructs in the extended EAST-2 framework, eight null hypotheses were tested:

1. H_1: PPGIS influence has a positive significant effect on the appropriation of PPGIS in a participatory decision process.
2. H_2: Social-Institutional Influences have a positive significant effect on the appropriation of PPGIS influences in a participatory decision process.

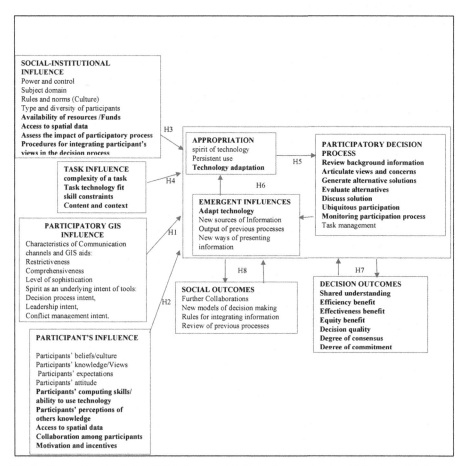

Fig. 1. Proposed extended EAST-2 framework* Note: the constructs which were added to the revised framework are in bold.

3. H$_3$: Public Participant Influences have a positive significant effect on the appropriation of PPGIS influences in a participatory decision process.

4. H$_4$: Task influence has a positive significant effect on the appropriation of PPGIS Influence in a participatory decision process.

5. H$_5$: Appropriation has a positive significant effect on the participatory decision process.

6. H$_6$: participatory decision process has a positive significant effect on the social outcomes of a participatory decision process.

7. H$_7$: Appropriation has a positive significant effect on the decision outcomes of a participatory decision process.

8. H$_8$: Appropriation has a positive significant effect on the social outcomes of a participatory decision process.

3   Methodology

3.1   Study Design and Survey Participants

A cross-sectional survey was conducted among stakeholders in MSWM in Uganda's rapidly growing urban areas of Kampala, Wakiso, Entebbe, Mukono, Mbarara and Busia. In the Ugandan context, stakeholders included residents, solid waste officers, health inspectors, environmental officers, landfill officers, waste recyclers, physical planners, and waste pickers.

3.2   Data Collection and Data Collection Tools

A Likert scale-based self-administered questionnaire was used to collect data to measure the nine latent variables. The questionnaire consisted of two parts. The first part consisted of questions on the nine variables in the proposed framework. Questions were arranged basing on the constructs in the proposed framework. The scale had 5 points, 1 (strongly disagree) to 5 (strongly agree). An option for 'not sure' was provided to avoid forced responses. The questionnaire was pretested on 15 respondents to determine reliability and validity and the suggested improvements were made before the survey. The second part of the questionnaire collected respondent demographics, including gender, age, the highest level of education and years of experience.

Stratified random sampling approach was used to select participants. The prospective study population was divided into municipal staff, the staff of agencies contracted for MSWM and the public. The study participants were then randomly from these groups.

3.3   Data Processing and Analysis

Partial least squares structural equation modelling (SEM) using SmartPLs 3.2.8 [46], was used to test the relationships between the measures and to fit the final structural model. Variables with loadings and path coefficients lower than the recommended values were omitted from the final model. Path coefficients for the trimmed model were then tested. Internal consistency was measured by Cronbach alpha and the recommended acceptable value (0.70) was used [47]. Convergent validity was measured by the average variance extracted (AVE) and a validity threshold of 0.50 used. The structural model included unobservable latent variables and their theoretical relationships [48].

4   Results

4.1   Characteristics of the Participants

Overall, 500 participants were enrolled, the majority of whom were male (65.2%), with at least diploma level education (58.3%). However, 97% had working experience for less than 10 years (Table 1).

Table 1. Demographics of participants (n = 500)

Characteristics	Frequency	Per cent
Gender		
Female	105	34.8
Male	195	65.2
Level of education		
Primary	39	12.9
Secondary	87	28.8
Diploma	86	28.5
Degree and above	90	29.8
Years of experience		
0-10 years	293	97.0
10-20 years	7	2.5
≥20 years	2	0.7

Table 2. Reliability results

Constructs	Cronbach's alpha	Composite reliability	AVE
Appropriation	0.724	0.844	0.644
Emergent structures	0.779	0.858	0.602
Organizational influence	0.880	0.907	0.582
Participatory decision process	0.774	0.848	0.529
Decision outcomes	0.856	0.888	0.499
Participant influence	0.850	0.883	0.487
Social outcomes	0.769	0.852	0.591
Task influence	0.767	0.851	0.588
Technology influence	0.806	0.861	0.510

4.2 Measurement Model

Overall, there was high internal consistency. The values of Cronbach's alpha, composite reliability, and AVE for the nine latent variables ranged from 0.724 to 0.856, 0.844 to 0.907, and 0.510 to 0.644, respectively (Table 2).

Additionally, the square roots of the AVEs were greater than the off-diagonal elements in their corresponding column (Table 3). Thus, most of the constructs in this study were valid.

Table 3. Discriminant validity

Construct	Appropriation	Emergent structures	Institutional influence	Participatory decision process	Decision outcomes	Participant	Social outcomes	Task	Tech influence
Appropriation	0.802								
Emergent structures	0.631	0.776							
Organizational influence	0.491	0.592	0.763						
Participatory decision process	0.697	0.748	0.575	0.727					
Decision outcomes	0.647	0.714	0.590	0.734	0.706				
Participant influence	0.510	0.606	0.724	0.542	0.610	0.698			
Social outcomes	0.575	0.660	0.572	0.633	0.727	0.545	0.769		
Task influence	0.527	0.643	0.535	0.607	0.557	0.560	0.524	0.767	
Technology influence	0.582	0.670	0.665	0.658	0.665	0.625	0.600	0.549	0.714

4.3 Structural Model

Coefficient of Determination (R2): Figure 2 shows the validated structural model, with the path coefficients and coefficient of determination (R2). The path coefficients indicate the strength of the relationships between the variables. Together, participant technology, task and institutional explain 46.1% of the variance in the appropriation of technology. All path coefficients were positive. Technology appropriation explains 64.3% of the variance in the participatory decision-making process. Also, participatory decision-making process explains 40.0% and 53.9% variances in social outcomes and participatory decision-making task outcomes, respectively.

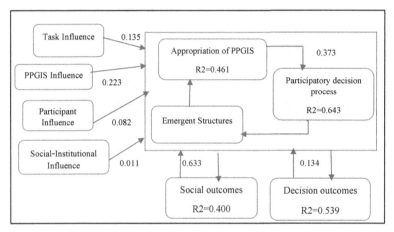

Fig. 2. Structural model

Significance of Factors and Path Coefficients: To test for the significance of path coefficient, we used bootstrapping and two-tailed test to generate estimates of t-values and p-values for the indicators and path coefficients (Table 4).

4.4 Hypothesis Testing Results

Overall, there was statistically a significant relationship between Appropriation and Participatory decision process (*p-value* < 0.001). Similarly, there was statistically a significant relationship between emergent structures and participatory decision process (*p-value* < 0.001) and appropriation (*p-value* < 0.001). Similarly, there is a statistically significant relationship between participatory decision process and decision outcomes (*p-value* < 0.001) as well as social outcomes (*p-value* < 0.001). In addition, there was a statistically significant relationship between technology influence and appropriation (*p-value* < 0.002). However, there was no statistically significant relationship between the appropriation of technology and participant influence (*p-value* = 0.220), as well as with organizational influence (*p-value* = 0.882). Additionally, there was a weak but not statistically significant relationship between task influence and appropriation of technology, but this relationship was not statistically significant (*p-value* = 0.066).

Table 4. Significance of path coefficient

Relationship between variables	SD	t-statistic	P-value
Appropriation → Participatory decision process	0.047	8.02	<0.001
Emergent structures → Appropriation	0.079	4.27	<0.001
Emergent structures → Participatory decision process	0.050	10.23	<0.001
Organizational influence → Appropriation	0.072	0.15	0.882
Participatory decision process → Decision outcomes	0.034	21.90	<0.001
Participatory decision process → Social outcomes	0.039	16.06	<0.001
Participant influence → Appropriation	0.066	1.23	0.220
Task influence → Appropriation	0.073	1.84	0.066
Technology Influence → Appropriation	0.072	3.11	0.002

Note: SD means standard deviation

5 Discussion and Conclusion

This study developed a comprehensive theoretical framework for guiding the implementation of GIS-enabled participatory processes to support planning and decision making in MSWM. The developed framework extended the EAST-2 framework to include the spatial planning process, decision outcome, evaluation, and social aspects. These aspects have previously been reported to influence the use of PPGIS in governmental administrative process. Nine relationships between variables were tested, six of which were statistically significant. This study validated the impact of technology influence on appropriation. Similarly, the impact of emergent structures on appropriation and participatory decision process was validated. In addition, the impact of participatory decision process on social and decision outcomes was also validated. Finally, there was also a relationship between appropriation and the participatory decision process. However, the social aspects such as those related to the individual participants, institutions and task influence did not have an impact on the appropriation of technology in a participatory decision process. This is potentially due to the infancy stage of utilization of technology to support participatory MSWM processes.

5.1 Relationships Among Variables

This study suggests that the characteristics and intent of a technology have a direct bearing on how the participatory process is conducted and ultimately on the outcomes. This finding is consistent with prior research. Schmitz *et al.* [49] found that the use and adaptation of technology enhance job performance. Similarly, technology enhances decision making in virtual teams and ultimately increases the amount of work accomplished [50].

Concerning Task influence, our study found a positive relationship between the nature of a task and the technology used. These findings are in line with Zigurs and Buckland [51] who supported the argument that task characteristics, such as complexity, are important in Group decision support systems.

Regarding the appropriation of PPGIS influences, there was a significant relationship between participatory decision process and decision outcomes. This finding is consistent with previous literature findings which have shown that ICT is necessary for group decision making [52]. The ICT tools that can potentially enhance group decision making include groupware, decision support systems (DSS), and telecommunications that are needed for quick and yet sustainable decision making. ICTs improve group and individual performance [53], quality and type of decisions [35, 54].

Regarding social outcomes, we found a relationship between Appropriation of PPGIS in a participatory decision process and the social outcomes. Group decision processes not only result in task-related outcomes but also for the strong ties between participants and organizations responsible for these processes [36, 55].

However, the study was unable to find a relationship between Social-institutional influence and appropriation in a participatory decision process This finding is inconsistent with prior literature that suggests that social influences affect uptake and utilization of technology in group support systems (GSS) and within an organization [37, 56]. Additionally, the literature suggests that social-institutional influences affect the use of technology in collaborative processes [35, 56]. The lack of relationship between social-Institutional influence and appropriation in this study may be attributed to the differences MSWM in most RLS and developed countries. Whereas public participation could be in advance stages in developed countries, developing countries are yet to embrace citizen engagement in governmental decision making [57].

Regarding participant influence, we did not find a significant effect of appropriation of PPGIS influence in a participatory process. This finding is inconsistent with prior literature that has reported the relationships between individual characteristics and technology use when executing a task [58]. The null finding in this study may be explained by the poor attitude towards MSWM initiatives by citizens and limited adoption of technology in MSWM process [25].

5.2 Application of the Extended EAST-2 Framework

The field of PPGIS is still evolving and faces social, political, and economic challenges, especially in RLS. Thus, the salient social, political, and economic factors identified in this study have a potential to contribute to the successful adoption and implementation of PPGIS applications in RLS. Also, the recent developments including COVID-19 pandemic make traditional PPGIS approaches unfeasible. The identified factors include establishing guidelines and procedures for evaluating public participation, access to spatial information, integrating generated data, and solicitation of financial and human resources.

The results of this study suggest that municipalities and cities intending to involve the public in MSWM should ensure equitable access to information, training, public participation, formulation of guidelines for conducting and evaluating participatory process.

5.3   Limitations

This study was conducted in urban areas therefore the performance of the framework should be investigated in rural settings. However, across many RLS, waste management is more challenging in urban settings. Additionally, in most RLS the use of spatial technologies and other ICT in MSWM is still in the infancy phase. Therefore, there is a need to study the adoption process and establish a clear understanding of the different stages, activities, expertise, and the social-economic dynamics of the field. This study relied on data from a survey among stakeholders. The results should be validated through a field experiment.

5.4   Conclusion

This study developed and tested a framework to support GIS-enabled public participation implementations for MSWM especially in RLS. The study validated the positive relationships between hitherto investigated aspects and PPGIS. The revised EAST-2 framework may comprehensively ensure public participation in MSWM. The findings of this study contribute to the implementation of PPGIS especially in RLS where PPGIS is in infancy stages. The revised framework could accelerate the adoption of PPGIS in RLS amidst the ongoing COVID-19 epidemic that has threatened traditional public participation avenues in most developing countries.

References

1. Kaza, S., Yao, L., Bhada-Tata, P., Van Woerden, F.: What a waste 2.0: a global snapshot of solid waste management to 2050 (2018). https://doi.org/10.1596/978-1-4648-1329-0
2. Kawai, K., Tasaki, T.: Revisiting estimates of municipal solid waste generation per capita and their reliability. J. Mater. Cycles Waste Manag. **18**(1), 1–13 (2015). https://doi.org/10.1007/s10163-015-0355-1
3. Vergara, S.E., Tchobanoglous, G.: Municipal solid waste and the environment: a global perspective. Annu. Rev. Environ. Resour. **37**, 277–309 (2012). https://doi.org/10.1146/annurev-environ-050511-122532
4. Tulokhonova, A., Ulanova, O.: Assessment of municipal solid waste management scenarios in Irkutsk (Russia) using a life cycle assessment-integrated waste management model. Waste Manag. Res. **31**, 475–484 (2013). https://doi.org/10.1177/0734242X13476745
5. Zhou, C., Gong, Z., Hu, J., Cao, A., Liang, H.: A cost-benefit analysis of landfill mining and material recycling in China. Waste Manag. **35**, 191–198 (2015). https://doi.org/10.1016/j.wasman.2014.09.029
6. Soltani, A., Hewage, K., Reza, B., Sadiq, R.: Multiple stakeholders in multi-criteria decision-making in the context of municipal solid waste management: a review. Waste Manag. **35**, 318–328 (2015). https://doi.org/10.1016/j.wasman.2014.09.010
7. Garnett, K., Cooper, T., Longhurst, P., Jude, S., Tyrrel, S.: A conceptual framework for negotiating public involvement in municipal waste management decision-making in the UK. Waste Manag. **66**, 210–221 (2017). https://doi.org/10.1016/j.wasman.2017.04.022
8. Ndururi, J., Muriithi, J., Ochola, S.: The influence of stakeholder participation strategies on domestic waste management in Biashara residential area, RUIRU. ijssit.com (2019)
9. Kingston, R.P.: Public participation in local policy decision-making: the role of Web-based mapping. Cartogr. J. **44**, 138–144 (2007). https://doi.org/10.1179/000870407X213459

10. Kahila-Tani, M., Broberg, A., Kyttä, M., Tyger, T.: Let the citizens map—public participation GIS as a planning support system in the Helsinki master plan process. Plan. Pract. Res. **31**, 195–214 (2016). https://doi.org/10.1080/02697459.2015.1104203

11. Nooshery, N.R., Taleai, M., Kazemi, R., Ebadi, K.: Developing a web-based PPGIS, as an environmental reporting service. In: International Archives of the Photogrammetry, Remote Sensing and Spatial Information Sciences - ISPRS Archives, pp. 115–121. International Society for Photogrammetry and Remote Sensing (2017). https://doi.org/10.5194/isprs-archives-XLII-2-W7-115-2017

12. Brown, G., Kyttä, M.: Key issues and research priorities for public participation GIS (PPGIS): a synthesis based on empirical research. Appl. Geogr. **46**, 122–136 (2014). https://doi.org/10.1016/j.apgeog.2013.11.004

13. Nyerges, T., Jankowski, P.: Enhanced adaptive structuration theory: a theory of GIS-supported collaborative decision making. Geogr. Syst. **4**, 225–260 (1997)

14. Järvinen, P.: Action research is similar to design science. Qual. Quant. **41**, 37–54 (2007). https://doi.org/10.1007/s11135-005-5427-1

15. Weber, S.: Design science research: paradigm or approach? In: AMCIS 2010 Proceedings (2010)

16. Environmental Protection Agency: Waste classification (2014)

17. Mukama, T., et al.: Practices, concerns, and willingness to participate in solid waste management in two urban slums in Central Uganda. J. Environ. Public Health (2016). https://doi.org/10.1155/2016/6830163

18. Nyakaana, J.B.: solid waste management in urban centers: the case of Kampala city—Uganda. East Afr. Geogr. Rev. **19**, 33–43 (1997). https://doi.org/10.1080/00707961.1997.9756235

19. Kinobe, J.R., Gebresenbet, G., Niwagaba, C.B., Vinnerås, B.: Reverse logistics system and recycling potential at a landfill: a case study from Kampala City. Waste Manag. **42**, 82–92 (2015). https://doi.org/10.1016/j.wasman.2015.04.012

20. NEMA: State of the Environment Report for Uganda 2006/2007. Environment (2007)

21. Ministry of Water and Environment: Water and environment sector performance report 2013, Kampala (2013)

22. Garnett, K., Cooper, T.: Effective dialogue: enhanced public engagement as a legitimising tool for municipal waste management decision-making. Waste Manag. **34**, 2709–2726 (2014). https://doi.org/10.1016/j.wasman.2014.08.011

23. Macnaghten, P., Jacobs, M.: Public identification with sustainable development. Glob. Environ. Chang. **7**, 5–24 (1997). https://doi.org/10.1016/s0959-3780(96)00023-4

24. Wiedemann, P.M., Femers, S.: Public participation in waste management decision making: analysis and management of conflicts. J. Hazard. Mater. **33**, 355–368 (1993). https://doi.org/10.1016/0304-3894(93)85085-S

25. Okot-Okumu, J., Nyenje, R.: Municipal solid waste management under decentralisation in Uganda. Habitat Int. **35**, 537–543 (2011). https://doi.org/10.1016/j.habitatint.2011.03.003

26. Kirunda, M.P.: A case of Kira town council, Uganda: public participation in solid waste management: challenges and prospects. Master thesis Public Particip. Solid Waste Management Challenges Prospect (2009). https://doi.org/10.3389/fmicb.2011.00098

27. Liu, T.: Internet-based public participation GIS in environmental management. Community Reg. Plan. Progr. Student Proj. Theses (2013)

28. Macintosh, A.: Characterizing e-participation in policy-making. In: Proceedings of the Hawaii International Conference on System Sciences (2004). https://doi.org/10.1109/hicss.2004.1265300

29. Steinmann, R., Krek, A., Blaschke, T.: Can online map-based applications improve citizen participation? In: Böhlen, Michael, Gamper, Johann, Polasek, Wolfgang, Wimmer, Maria A. (eds.) TCGOV 2005. LNCS (LNAI), vol. 3416, pp. 25–35. Springer, Heidelberg (2005). https://doi.org/10.1007/978-3-540-32257-3_3

30. Radil, S.M., Jiao, J.: Public participatory GIS and the geography of inclusion. Prof. Geogr. **68**, 202–210 (2016). https://doi.org/10.1080/00330124.2015.1054750

31. Floreddu, P., Cabiddu, F., Pettinao, D.: Public participation in environmental decision-making: the case of PPGIS. In: Information Technology and Innovation Trends in Organizations - ItAIS: The Italian Association for Information Systems, pp. 37–44. Physica-Verlag (2011). https://doi.org/10.1007/978-3-7908-2632-6_5

32. Wang, X., Yu, Z., Cinderby, S., Forrester, J.: Enhancing participation: experiences of participatory geographic information systems in Shanxi province China. Appl. Geogr. **28**, 96–109 (2008). https://doi.org/10.1016/j.apgeog.2007.07.007

33. Metla, J.A.: Participation technologies: a framework for the development of an online interactive GIS application (2008)

34. DeSanctis, G., Poole, M.S.: Capturing the complexity in advanced technology use: adaptive structuration theory. Organ. Sci. **5**, 121–147 (1994). https://doi.org/10.1287/orsc.5.2.121

35. Nyerges, T.L., Jankowski, P.: Enhanced adaptive structuration theory: a theory of GIS-supported collaborative decision making. Geogr. Syst. **4**, 225–260 (1997)

36. Jankowski, P.T.N., Nyerges, T.L.: Toward a framework for research on geographic information-supported participatory decision-making. URISA J. **15**, 9–17 (2003)

37. Jankowski, P., Nyerges, T.: GIS-supported collaborative decision making: results of an experiment. Ann. Assoc. Am. Geogr. **91**, 48–70 (2001). https://doi.org/10.1111/0004-5608.00233

38. Strong, D.M., Dishaw, M.T., Brent Bandy, D.: Extending task technology fit with computer self-efficacy. Data Base Adv. Inf. Syst. **37**, 96–107 (2006). https://doi.org/10.1145/1161345.1161358

39. Simão, A., Densham, P.J., Haklay, M.M.: Web-based GIS for collaborative planning and public participation: an application to the strategic planning of wind farm sites. J. Environ. Manag. **90**, 2027–2040 (2009). https://doi.org/10.1016/j.jenvman.2007.08.032

40. Porwol, L., Ojo, A., Breslin, J.G.: An ontology for next generation e-participation initiatives. Gov. Inf. Q. **33**, 583–594 (2016). https://doi.org/10.1016/j.giq.2016.01.007

41. Reynard, D.: Five classes of geospatial data and the barriers to using them. Geogr. Compass **12**, e12364 (2018). https://doi.org/10.1111/gec3.12364

42. Sieber, R.: Public Participation Geographic Information Systems: A Literature Review and Framework. Wiley, Hoboken (2006). https://doi.org/10.1111/j.1467-8306.2006.00702.x

43. Brown, G.: An empirical evaluation of the spatial accuracy of public participation GIS (PPGIS) data. Appl. Geogr. **34**, 289–294 (2012). https://doi.org/10.1016/j.apgeog.2011.12.004

44. Walker, B.B., Rinner, C.: A qualitative framework for evaluating participation on the Geoweb. URISA J. **25**, 15–24 (2013)

45. Nigussie, Z., et al.: Applying Ostrom's institutional analysis and development framework to soil and water conservation activities in north-western Ethiopia. Land Use Policy **71**, 1–10 (2018). https://doi.org/10.1016/j.landusepol.2017.11.039

46. Hair, J.F., Ringle, C.M., Sarstedt, M.: PLS-SEM: indeed a silver bullet. J. Mark. Theory Pract. **19**, 139–152 (2011). https://doi.org/10.2753/MTP1069-6679190202

47. Jr. Hair, J.F.: Essentials of Business Research Methods (2015). https://doi.org/10.4324/9781315704562

48. Hair, J.F., Black, W.C., Babin, B.J., Anderson, R.E.: Multivariate Data Analysis (2010). https://doi.org/10.1016/j.ijpharm.2011.02.019

49. Schmitz, K.W., Teng, J.T.C., Webb, K.J.: Capturing the complexity of malleable IT use: adaptive structuration theory for individuals. MIS Q. Manag. Inf. Syst. **40**, 663–686 (2016). https://doi.org/10.25300/MISQ/2016/40.3.07

50. Nordbäck, E.: The influence of emergent technologies on decision making process in virtual teams. In: 19th Americas Conference on Information Systems, AMCIS 2013 - Hyperconnected World: Anything, Anywhere, Anytime (2013)

51. Zigurs, I., Buckland, B.K.: A theory of task/technology fit and group support systems effectiveness. MIS Q. Manag. Inf. Syst. **22**, 313–334 (1998). https://doi.org/10.2307/249668
52. Karehka, R.: The Role of Information Technology in Group Decision Making (2014). https://useoftechnology.com/role-information-technology-group-decision-making/
53. Schmitz, K., et al.: Impact of lay health worker programmes on the health outcomes of mother-child pairs of HIV exposed children in Africa: a scoping review. PLoS One **14**, e0211439 (2019)
54. Cano, A.R.: Effects of technological support on decision making performance of distributed groups (1997)
55. Gopal, A., Bostrom, R.P., Chin, W.: Modelling the process of GSS use: an adaptive structuration perspective. In: Proceedings of the Hawaii International Conference on System Science (1992). https://doi.org/10.1109/hicss.1992.183432
56. Nyerges, T.L., Ramsey, K.S., Wilson, M.W.: Design considerations for an Internet portal to support public participation in transportation improvement decision making. In: Collaborative Geographic Information Systems (2006). https://doi.org/10.4018/978-1-59140-845-1.ch012
57. Denhardt, J., Terry, L., Delacruz, E.R., Andonoska, L.: Barriers to citizen engagement in developing countries. Int. J. Public Adm. **32**, 1268–1288 (2009). https://doi.org/10.1080/01900690903344726
58. Goodhue, D.L., Thompson, R.L.: Task-technology fit and individual performance. MIS Q. Manag. Inf. Syst. **19**, 213–236 (1995). https://doi.org/10.2307/249689

IoT in Urban Space

A Crowd-Sourced Obstacle Detection and Navigation App for Visually Impaired

Edward Kim, Joshua Sterner, and Afra Mashhadi[(✉)]

Computing Software System, University of Washington, Bothell, WA, USA
{edkim84,sternerj,mashhadi}@uw.edu

Abstract. Individuals with sight impairments rely heavily on various types of travel-aid when navigating their ways across their neighborhoods. Recently, there have been many breakthrough technologies that focus on the visually impaired by providing solutions such as wearable bands and optical wearable devices. However, such technologies are costly and not suited for the general market. Others have started investigating smartphone applications as a much more widely available solution but with limited applicability on outdoor barriers and obstacles that these groups of people face in their day to day journeys. In this work, we propose GeoNotify, a smartphone application which is tailored to detect unexpected temporary obstacles that could cause injury to visually impaired people. We present how advances in Convolutional Neural Networks merged with crowd-sourcing methodologies could be used to build more accurate models capable of recognizing wide representations of the real-world obstacles.

Keywords: Crowd-sourcing · Navigation system · Federated learning

1 Introduction

People with *partial* sight loss face daily challenges getting around their local area for accessing local shops or visiting their local general practitioners. Currently in the UK alone over two million people live with sight loss, and this number has been forecasted to reach to four million by 2050. In a recent report published by *Royal Institute of Blind People* [1], sidewalk obstacles have been identified as the biggest concern of visually impaired when walking in their local neighborhood. Indeed in 95% of cases, blind and partially sighted people have collided with an obstacle over a three month period with nearly third of those being seriously injured. The most common obstacles are reported to be bins of all kinds (e.g., household), street furniture (e.g., restaurants outdoor table and chairs), advertising boards, and hanging baskets.

Recently, smartphone-based navigation systems for the blind has attracted much attention with some commercial key players. For example Blindways[1] is

---

[1] https://www.perkins.org/access/inclusive-design/blindways, last accessed June 5, 2020.

© ICST Institute for Computer Sciences, Social Informatics and Telecommunications Engineering 2021
Published by Springer Nature Switzerland AG 2021. All Rights Reserved
S. Paiva et al. (Eds.): SmartCity360° 2020, LNICST 372, pp. 571–579, 2021.
https://doi.org/10.1007/978-3-030-76063-2_38

an application that helps users get to their bus stop once they are within 30 ft of the bus stop location. This application provides the concept of using 'clues' to help users find the bus stop post through a crowd-sourcing methodology. Eye-D[2] provides speech feedback to communicate to the user where they are currently located. "Seeing AI"[3] uses artificial intelligence to assist the user with varities of tasks and tools including object recognition and optical character recognition, face recognition, but does not offer navigation information to the user. Blind-square[4] is a navigation application for the blind/visually impaired that provides detailed points of interest and intersections. These details are gathered from Foursquare and OpenStreetMaps and they use algorithms to determine what information would be useful for the user.

In this paper we propose Geo-Notify, a crowd-sourcing smart-phone application that is designed to assist visually impaired with their walking navigation by notifying them of the obstacles that are placed in their path. Geo-Notify relies on the participation of users to create a dataset of hazardous obstacles. We demonstrate that the current image recognition models fail to recognize the ordinary obstacles due to the lack of data available for this specific task and the real-world diversity in the presentation of obstacle images. We show that by using transfer learning, we can achieve a high accuracy of improving obstacle recognition by relying on as little as 20 images per class of the obstacles. Finally, we report the viability of our approach in a distributed setting where the model is trained locally on the user's smartphone device by leveraging the Federated Learning paradigm. The contributions of this paper are as follows:

- We design an outdoor smart-phone navigation application that enables visually impaired to receive notifications of hazardous obstacles on their route, and re-route them accordingly.
- We propose a crowd-sourcing mechanism whereby images of obstacles can be contributed to our convolutional neural network model so to learn the task specific and context dependent representations of images. We report the result of our experimental analysis under both centralized and distributed setting.
- We produce the first curated dataset of images of sidewalk obstacles that are reported as main sources of injuries by the Royal Institute of Blind People, and share it with future researchers.

2   Related Work

Recently, the navigation assisting systems for the visually impaired has attracted much attention [6,8]. Navigation assisting technologies try to guide the user to a destination or provide in-situ information about user's current surroundings. For example in [8] authors present a campus navigation system for visually impaired people that includes a smartphone and a sonar device. Smartphone

---

[2] Last accessed June 5, 2020 https://eye-d.in/.

[3] https://www.microsoft.com/en-us/ai/seeing-ai, last accessed June 5, 2020.

[4] https://www.blindsquare.com/, last accessed June 5, 2020.

is used to obtain GPS data by the built-in GPS receiving module, and sonar device is employed to detect obstacles on the road. A cloud based server is queried and updated to the user's location. The sonar device however is unable to distinguish the types of obstacles as it functions independently of the mobile device. In [19], authors proposed a guidance system for the blind by relying on the OpenStreetMap [9] through vibration feedback. Several applications are designed to provide information regarding nearby POIs [4]. A main challenge that is faced in providing contextual information in outdoor environment is managing the quantity of audio information by balancing the quantity of information against distracting or overwhelming the user [16].

Some research efforts try to complement these limitations by detecting elements that are relevant for navigation, such as crosswalks and bus stops using computer vision [6,10,14,17]. However these approaches are limited to the identification of the fixed structures as opposed to temporary obstacles. Moreover, previous studies [3,5] on uncovering the information needs of visually impaired have identified *interactivity* and the ability to *pull* information on surrounding environment as an important component that often goes missing in spatial in-situ navigation systems.

The closest work to ours is by Chen et al. [6] who integrated obstacle detection and GPS navigation into one system. The authors study the obstacle detection based on MobileNetV2 [12]. To this end, the authors manually collect a set of 4500 images from four specific class of *cars, pedestrians, bicycles* and *electric bicycles*. They present that the trained model performance ranges between 69%–96% accuracy across various categories, with cars identified as the most accurate classification class and people as the least. Our work differs, as we perform not only object detection on the mobile device but also use the crowd-sourced images for training of the convolutional neural network model. Indeed, most available approaches assume that an accurate model is previously trained on the representation of images of the possible obstacles and thus the model is used only for inference on the device. In contrast, in our work we illustrate how such assumption does not hold and propose a continuous learning model which is capable of learning new obstacles through a crowd-sourced mechanism.

3   Application Design

In this section we briefly describe the application design and system architecture of GeoNotify and functionalities of its various components.

3.1   User Interface

To design for accessibility, we followed the previous guidelines by [2,11,18]. In so doing, we utilize the whole screen to maximize on the space for each button. With the maximized space, we can provide large letters for each button as demonstrated in Fig. 1. We use a black background and white text to create contrast and provide large descriptive icons to help moderately visually impaired users find the right button. We also use dark mode as suggested by [11,18], to make it easier for mild to moderate visually impaired to read the text. There is also an option to provide speech feedback to let the user know which screen they are currently on. To navigate the application, the user just taps a button to choose an option, or swipes right to go back to the previous screen. We also provide a voice navigation button where the user can tell the application the screen they want to navigate.

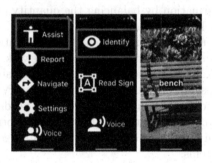

Fig. 1. Work flow (highlighted in red) of the Assist functionality of our application which is designed to help users to contextualize their surrounding environment. (Color figure online)

3.2   System Architecture

GeoNotify is composed of three main components (Navigate, Assist, and Report) with the overarching goal of providing a sense of additional safety for visually impaired users. Figure 2 presents the overall architecture of our system. The functionalities include object recognition, safety/obstacle monitor during navigation through notifications, as well as providing means for reporting issues through crowd-sourcing images. All these functions play a role in gathering data on the users' surroundings. The data gathered are stored into AWS relational database, which acts as proxy between the client and server. AWS Lambda[5] is a serverless compute service that acts as the access point to read and write to the database. For client application to be able to execute these lambda functions, we use AWS API Gateway. API Gateway creates an endpoint made available to the public where clients can make CRUD (Create, Read, Update, Delete) requests. API Gateway also seamlessly connects to AWS lambda functions by passing the data from the client to the lambda function[6].

3.3   Navigate

Our application provides the user with live information on the reported obstacles that are within their proximity. We rely on Google Maps API tool set to create

---

[5] https://aws.amazon.com/lambda/, last accessed June 5, 2020.

[6] https://aws.amazon.com/api-gateway/, last accessed June 5, 2020.

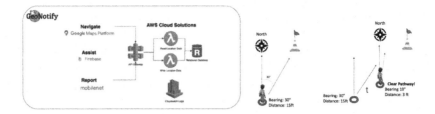

Fig. 2. The system architecture including the three main component of the GeoNotify application: Navigate, Assist and Report (left). Situating position of the obstacle by calculating the delta bearing angle (right).

a navigation path. The Navigate component takes the users current location and makes a get request to the API Gateway. When approaching any obstacle, the Navigate function uses push notification to warn the user about the obstacle and create an alternative route. In order to avoid obstacles, we calculate the bearing angle of the user with the nearby reported obstacles at every t time interval (Fig. 2). If the bearing stays the same for two consecutive time intervals we can infer that the user is heading towards the obstacle and reinforce the audio notification.

3.4   Assist and Report

The main underlying foundation of the Assist and Report component of our system is image recognition. The Assist component enables user to enhance their understanding of their surrounding environment. This module allows user to either request information about their surrounding by using Voice module which describes the nearby POIs to the user through audio, or alternatively to take a photo of their surrounding in order to read a sign or describe the objects in their proximity (Fig. 1). The Report module enables the users to voluntarily report obstacles thus contributing to the crowd-sourced dataset. The Report module also supports both audio and visual data. Through microphone integration, users are able to dictate the type of encountered obstacle on their path, which is then stored along with the GPS coordinate into our crowd-sourced database. Alternatively users can report any obstacles by take a photo of the nearby object. The photo is then classified using the obstacle detection component (as we describe in details next) and is recorded along with the GPS information.

4   Obstacle Detection

We use advances in Convolutional Neural Networks (ConvNet) to train a classifier that is able to identify the obstacles in the side walks. In particular we focus on two existing models that are lightweight and suitable for mobile device computation, MobileNet [12] and SqueezeNet [13]. MobileNetV2 proposed in 2018 by Google is a lightweight ConvNet that replaces standard convolution with

depthwise separable convolution. With the improvement of convolution structure, the convolution computational complexity has been shown to be reduced
significantly. SqueezeNet [13], is another state of the art lightweight ConvNet
which has shown to achieve the same accuracy as AlexNet but 50 times faster.

In doing so we follow the user study by [1], which interviewed 500 visually
impaired participants over the period of three months. This report identifies
four most common obstacles that impact visually impaired daily: cars parked
on the pavement, advertising-boards, bins and recycling boxes on pavements,
street furniture (such as chair and tables). Some of these classes (e.g., chair and
table) are common objects that are labeled in image recognition datasets such as
ImageNet [7] and thus are detectable using existing ConvNet models. However,
the presentations of these common objects across the world can vary significantly.
Others such as boards, sidewalk signs and potholes are specific to the context
of our study. We thus curated a dataset corresponding to 5 aforementioned
common obstacles. Figure 3 presents the sample images in each category as well
as the average in-class inference accuracy when the pre-trained MobileNet and
SqueezeNet are applied on 100 test images from each category.

Fig. 3. Five classes of the obstacles that are identified as most common source of
injuries for partially impaired.

As we rely on user contributions to construct our obstacle dataset, it is important to quantify the number of images that are required to train the model to
learn the representation of an object. To this end, we rely on transfer learning,
where we use the pre-trained MobileNet and SqueezeNet models and freeze the
learning on the earlier layers where the weights are transferred across the network, and retrain the fully connected (FC) layer to learn the representations
of our domain specific images. We evaluated these two models on a manually
curated dataset. Our dataset consists of 5 classes where each class has x number
of training images that we vary in our experiments, and 100 validation images.
Figure 4 presents the validation accuracy and loss results over the 10 training
epochs. This result suggests that using transfer learning both pre-trained networks are able to accurately learn the representation of the new obstacle objects
(maximum validation accuracy of 0.9) when relying on as few as 20 training
images per category.

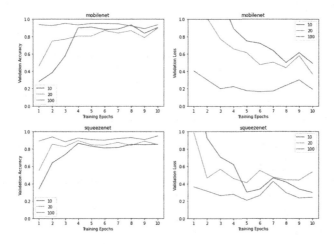

Fig. 4. Validation accuracy and loss for MobileNet and Squeezenet when applied under transfer learning setting to datasets of varying $x = 10, 20$ and 100 images per class.

To further assess the viability of relying on a crowd-sourced approach for obstacle detection, we also test both MobileNet and SqueezeNet using a Federated Learning [15] methodology. Federated learning is a recent machine learning paradigm where participants volunteer to collaboratively train a model under the orchestration of a central server, while keeping the training data on their own devices at all time. By following the principles of focused data collection and minimization, we rely on the users to contribute to the pre-trained global models (i.e., MobileNet and SqueezeNet that are pre-trained on ImageNet). In so doing, each user contributes a set of images across the five categories of obstacles to the retrain the final fully connected layer of the global model. As the training is done locally on the devices, the updated network weights are shared with the federated server and aggregated to Table 1 presents the average maximum validation accuracy and the average minimum loss for 5 cross-fold evaluation of the MobileNet using 10 epochs and batch size 20 (same hyper-parameters as the centralized setting).

Table 1. Maximum average validation accuracy and validation loss for varying number of images and contributors.

	No. images	No. users	$ValAccuracy$	$ValLoss$
MobileNet	20	20	0.86	1.18
		10	0.86	1.17
	100	20	0.93	0.9
		10	0.93	0.72

5   Conclusion

In this paper we proposed GeoNotify, a navigation and obstacle detection system for visually impaired users. We examined the viability of using crowd-sourcing approach to improve the obstacle detection model to recognize domain specific representation of new objects. We evaluated and reported the result of two ConvNet models, MobileNet and Squeezenet, when applied in a centralized setting using transfer learning, as well as preliminary results on when using a federated learning methodology.

We believe applications such as ours which rely on the crowds to build and improve the underlying models are needed as cities around the world go through rapid transformations. An example of such transformation is apparent across the world in the current pandemic where previous sidewalks and footpaths have been transformed to accommodate for businesses, thus creating a major hurdle for visually impaired. In our future work, we will expand our dataset to include more categories of obstacles and more number of images from across the world.

References

1. The royal institute for blind people (2016). https://www.rnib.org.uk/sites/default/files/who
2. Antunes, A.C., Silva, C.: Designing for blind users: guidelines for developing mobile apps for supporting navigation of blind people on public transports. In: User-Centered Software Development for the Blind and Visually Impaired: Emerging Research and Opportunities, pp. 1–25. IGI Global (2020)
3. Banovic, N., Franz, R.L., Truong, K.N., Mankoff, J., Dey, A.K.: Uncovering information needs for independent spatial learning for users who are visually impaired. In: Proceedings of the 15th International ACM SIGACCESS Conference on Computers and Accessibility, pp. 1–8 (2013)
4. Blum, J.R., Bouchard, M., Cooperstock, J.R.: What's around Me? Spatialized audio augmented reality for blind users with a smartphone. In: Puiatti, A., Gu, T. (eds.) MobiQuitous 2011. LNICST, vol. 104, pp. 49–62. Springer, Heidelberg (2012). https://doi.org/10.1007/978-3-642-30973-1_5
5. Brock, A.M., Truillet, P., Oriola, B., Picard, D., Jouffrais, C.: Interactivity improves usability of geographic maps for visually impaired people. Hum. Comput. Interact. **30**(2), 156–194 (2015)
6. Chen, Q., Wu, L., Chen, Z., Lin, P., Cheng, S., Wu, Z.: Smartphone based outdoor navigation and obstacle avoidance system for the visually impaired. In: Chamchong, R., Wong, K.W. (eds.) MIWAI 2019. LNCS (LNAI), vol. 11909, pp. 26–37. Springer, Cham (2019). https://doi.org/10.1007/978-3-030-33709-4_3
7. Deng, J., Dong, W., Socher, R., Li, L.J., Li, K., Fei-Fei, L.: Imagenet: a large-scale hierarchical image database. In: 2009 IEEE Conference on Computer Vision and Pattern Recognition, pp. 248–255. IEEE (2009)
8. Dutta, S., Barik, M.S., Chowdhury, C., Gupta, D.: Divya-Dristi: a smartphone based campus navigation system for the visually impaired. In: 2018 Fifth International Conference on Emerging Applications of Information Technology (EAIT), pp. 1–3. IEEE (2018)

9. Haklay, M., Weber, P.: Openstreetmap: user-generated street maps. IEEE Pervasive Comput. **7**(4), 12–18 (2008)

10. Hara, K., Azenkot, S., Campbell, M., Bennett, C.L., Le, V., Pannella, S., Moore, R., Minckler, K., Ng, R.H., Froehlich, J.E.: Improving public transit accessibility for blind riders by crowdsourcing bus stop landmark locations with google street view: An extended analysis. ACM Trans. Accessible Comput. (TACCESS) **6**(2), 1–23 (2015)

11. Hersh, M.: Mobility technologies for blind, partially sighted and deafblind people: design issues. In: Mobility of Visually Impaired People, pp. 377–409. Springer (2018)

12. Howard, A.G., et al.: Mobilenets: efficient convolutional neural networks for mobile vision applications (2017). arXiv:1704.04861

13. Iandola, F.N., Han, S., Moskewicz, M.W., Ashraf, K., Dally, W.J., Keutzer, K.: Squeezenet: Alexnet-level accuracy with 50x fewer parameters and ¡0.5 mb model size (2016). arXiv:1602.07360

14. Mascetti, S., Ahmetovic, D., Gerino, A., Bernareggi, C.: Zebrarecognizer: pedestrian crossing recognition for people with visual impairment or blindness. Pattern Recogn. **60**, 405–419 (2016)

15. McMahan, H.B., Moore, E., Ramage, D., y Arcas, B.A.: Federated learning of deep networks using model averaging. corr abs/1602.05629 (2016). arXiv:1602.05629

16. Panëels, S.A., Olmos, A., Blum, J.R., Cooperstock, J.R.: Listen to it yourself! evaluating usability of what's around me? for the blind. In: Proceedings of the SIGCHI Conference on Human Factors in Computing Systems, pp. 2107–2116 (2013)

17. Shangguan, L., Yang, Z., Zhou, Z., Zheng, X., Wu, C., Liu, Y.: Crossnavi: enabling real-time crossroad navigation for the blind with commodity phones. In: Proceedings of the 2014 ACM International Joint Conference on Pervasive and Ubiquitous Computing, pp. 787–798 (2014)

18. Sierra, J.S., Togores, J.: Designing mobile apps for visually impaired and blind users. In: The Fifth International Conference on Advances in Computer-Human Interactions, pp. 47–52. Citeseer (2012)

19. Velazquez, R., Pissaloux, E., Rodrigo, P., Carrasco, M., Giannoccaro, N.I., Lay-Ekuakille, A.: An outdoor navigation system for blind pedestrians using GPS and tactile-foot feedback. Appl. Sci. **8**(4), 578 (2018)

An Ecosystem Approach to the Design
of Sensing Systems for Bicycles

Ricardo Cabral⊙, Eduardo Peixoto⊙, Carlos Carvalho⊙, and Rui José(✉)⊙

Algoritmi Research Centre, University of Minho, Braga, Portugal
rui@dsi.uminho.pt

Abstract. Bicycles equipped with sensors, processing capacity and communications can be a promising source of data about the personal and the collective reality of urban cycling. While this concept has been attracting considerable interest, the key assumption is the design of a closed system where a uniform set of sensing bicycles, with a concrete set of sensors, is used to support a specific service. The core challenge, however, is how to generalise sensing approaches so that they can be collectively supported by many heterogeneous bicycles, owned by a multitude of entities, and integrated into a common ecosystem of urban data. In this work, we provide a comprehensive analysis of the design space for on-bike sensing. We consider a diverse set of sensing alternatives, the potential value propositions associated with their data, and the collective perspective of how to optimise sensing by exploring the complementarities between heterogeneous bicycles. This broader perspective should inform the design of more effective sensing strategies that can maximise the overall value generated by bicycles in smart cycling ecosystems and enable new cycling services.

Keywords: Smart mobility · Cycling data · Sensing bicycle

Smart cycling is a very broad concept encompassing the many paths through which cycling is being incorporated into the connected and smart transport networks of the future. It can be described as the shared, real-time and collaborative application of data, communication technologies, products, and services through both private and public actors, to help best move people individually, and collectively, across the urban environment [1, 2]. The application of Information Technologies in this domain is already a dominant factor for the successful adoption of shared bicycles [3], where they provide some of the collective features that characterise those services, such as the ability to find nearby bicycles or seamless pay per use. We can envision the evolution of this paradigm, with increasingly more bicycles being instrumented in ways that can add value to the entire ecosystem.

In this study, we analyse the role that bicycles equipped with sensors, processing capabilities and communications might have as a valuable source of data about the personal and the collective reality of urban cycling. Sensing systems for bicycles have been explored in many different ways [4–7], but the key assumption is always the design of a closed system where a uniform set of bicycles, with a concrete set of sensors, is

S. Paiva et al. (Eds.): SmartCity360° 2020, LNICST 372, pp. 580–595, 2021.
https://doi.org/10.1007/978-3-030-76063-2_39

used to support a specific service. Regardless of the technical merits of any particular systems, the larger challenge is how to generalise sensing approaches so that they can be collectively supported by many heterogeneous bicycles, owned by a multitude of entities, and operated under a common ecosystem of cycling data. This is a problem that goes beyond the existence of a single platform or the usage of standard protocols for data representation. It also involves the data collection procedures, the types of sensors used, data processing algorithms, the operation of sensors or even the details of how the sensors are deployed on the bicycles. Closed systems lack the generalization that is needed to allow different designs to be explicitly expressed in a way that describes their similarities, their differences and their contributions to a common cycling ecosystem.

1 Research Objectives

A smart cycling approach should allow sensing systems from multiple bicycles to compete for the best way to address specific data collection goals and to complement each other to serve broader data needs. Rather than assuming uniformity, the model should explore heterogeneity as the best way to allow these sensing systems to serve the very diverse set of data needs associated with Smart Cycling.

In this work, we aim to explore this path by providing a comprehensive analysis of the design space of bicycle sensing systems. Our research objectives can be summarized by these fundamental research questions:

- What is the range of sensors that should be integrated into the sensing systems of bicycles to provide a comprehensive view of urban cycling activity and its context?
- What are the key trade-offs involved in the design of sensing bicycles and how can they be optimised to reach the most effective results in the context of broader smart cycling ecosystems?

To explore the possible answers to these questions, we have started by developing our own prototype of a bicycle sensing system. Using this prototype as a research context, we have experimented different designs by creating multiple variants of sensing systems. This provided a key learning context to understand the sensitivities associated with this sensing context and assess the real value that can be obtained from various types of sensors. This experimental work was complemented with an analysis of the sensing design space for bicycles. This analysis was organised around 3 layers, more specifically the universe of viable sensors, the value propositions offered by those services through the services they enable and the collective perspective of how to combine heterogeneous sensing systems to optimise their value to the whole ecosystem. This broader perspective should provide new insights for the development of sensing systems for bicycles and the understanding of their role in the larger context of urban cycling services.

2 Related Work

Previous work has already explored many variants of bicycles equipped with various types of sensors. The smart e-bike monitoring system (SEMS) [8] is a platform for the real-time acquisition of usage data from electrically assisted bikes. The system collects e-bike data including location, rider control data and power data. The SEMS data feeds an online interface for data analysis, for riders to view their own data and sharing on social media. BikeNet [9] is a mobile sensing system for mapping the cyclist experience. BikeNet uses a number of sensors embedded into the bicycle so that it collects data about the cyclist's ride. BikeNet uses two approaches for data synchronization: an opportunistic approach where it uploads data when the bicycle opportunistically finds a wireless access point; and real time synchronization using the cellular data channel of the cyclist's mobile phone. SensorBike [7] is mainly focused on capturing data that influences security and comfort while cycling. It includes power sensors, vital sensors, accelerometers and vibration sensor, environmental sensors, distance sensors and cameras. The goal is to understand the cyclist's perspective and contribute to the future of cycling planning. The Smart e-bike [11] explores the combination of sensors associated with the physical characteristics and physical condition of the rider with the motor control system. The aim is to help the cyclist in situations when the values of his physical condition or the parameters of the environment are critical. The system includes pulse sensors, gyroscope/accelerometer, speedometer and GPS.

In addition to special bike configurations, there are also add-ons that include a major sensing functionality. The See.Sense system [10] is a set of augmented cycling products with the capability to collect and share trip information. The See.Sense smart bike lights include a GPS, accelerometers and GSM communication service. The system can collect data from cycling trips and alert cyclists when they are entering a more dangerous zone. The device is able to register 800 data points per second, enabling it to monitor road conditions and even alert the owner when the bicycle is being moved or stolen.

Air quality has been particularly popular as an application domain for sensing on bicycles. The motivation for using bicycles in this context is the possibility to collect data from many locations, many of which might not be reachable by car, and also the fact that the bicycle is not an air pollutant itself and therefore does not interfere with measurements.

Aeroflex [4] is a sensing bicycle for mobile air quality measurements. The system measures Ultra Fine Particles, Particle Matter, Black Carbon and CO. It also collects GPS location, sound, images, vertical acceleration, temperature and relative humidity. The Sniffer bike [6] is equipped with a particulate matter sensor developed in collaboration with the Utrecht Province to be attached to bicycles. It measures air quality every ten seconds and shares data with the Civity data platform every minute. The Copenhagen Wheel [5] is an electric bicycle system developed to transform any bicycle into a smart bicycle by replacing the rear wheel with the Copenhagen Wheel. The wheel is able to collect the location data of the bicycle and other data to improve cycling and cyclists' experience. It also collects data about air (CO_2, NO) and noise (db) pollution, congestions, road conditions, relative humidity as well as temperature.

Bike sharing companies also use different forms of sensing on their bicycles [12] They typically collect data related with position and timing from routes made by their users. The primary purpose of this data collection is for pricing processes, but it also enables the construction of data related to the users' profile so that the system can be optimized for them. Accordingly, they work on this data to improve efficiency and increase user satisfaction.

These systems demonstrate the variety of approaches that can be explored when combing sensors with bicycles. What differentiates our work in mainly the broader perspective on bicycle sensing. Rather than aiming to propose yet another sensing bicycle, our work aims to uncover the key technical trade-offs and design sensitivities associated with sensing bicycles. The ultimate goal is to allow a heterogeneous and open-ended set of sensing bicycles to coexist, while improving their capability to operate as complementary approaches under a common cycling ecosystem.

Regarding data usage, route characterisation has always been one of the most common goals for on-bike data collection. There is a vast research literature on the main determinants in cyclist's decisions to cycle or to decide where to cycle. These are important indicators for data that should be widely available in cycling ecosystem. Ehrgott et al. [13] observed that some cyclists prefer to travel longer distances in order to include cycle facilities on their routes. The shortest route is not necessarily the most attractive route to cyclist, making route selection a bi-objective routing problem, where the aim is to generate a set of compromise solutions that is considered efficient. A route is called efficient if, given the same travel time, there will be no route with higher level of suitability and given the same level of suitability, there will be no route with shorter travel time. In another study by Winters et al. [14] a group of cyclists answered 73 survey items, grouped into 15 factors that might influence their likelihood of cycling. These factors highlight the importance of the location and design of bicycle networks. In another survey with 65 commuter cyclists, Segadilha et al. [15] asked participants to classify the importance of 18 cycling factor in a scale from 1 to 5. The factors identified as the most important were grouped in these 5 categories: road, traffic, environment, trip and route as a whole. A survey conducted by Felix [16] with cyclists and non-cyclists has sought to understand their motivators, triggers and barriers towards cycling. Results have shown that both groups consider the issues related to the perception of safety, physical effort, lack of a safe cycling network, and bicycle ownership as important barriers to take up cycling. Broach et al. [17] developed a GPS model to collect data from cyclists so that stakeholders could answers questions about types of infrastructures, preferences and the links between bicycle infrastructures and cycling behaviour. Su et al. [18] identified some online bicycle trip planners and concluded that these online trip planners rarely provide the complete set of route selection criteria required for a bicycle trip planner including fast, safe, simple and attractive routes. These studies provided us important insights on the very diverse set of goals that may be relevant when collecting cycling data and on the identification of key target services for cycling.

3 A Prototype of Sensing System for Bicycles

Our own prototype of a sensing system for bicycles was an important research tool in this work. More than a goal in itself, this bicycle allowed us to experiment many sensing alternatives and uncover multiple challenges associated with sensors on bicycles. The bicycle design is not attached to any particular form of sensing or any particular usage of the data collected. Instead, the system is designed to support a broad range of sensing possibilities and be instantiated in various ways, according to the requirements of specific research goals. Therefore, there is not a unique prototype specification, but rather a set of diverse prototype instances created throughout the project to study specific perspectives of sensing bicycles.

These various instances may differ in many ways, such as their specific set of sensors, the way those sensors are physically deployed or the specifics of the data collection process. The structured exploration of these many possibilities provides a broader view of the whole range of on-bike sensing possibilities and creates actionable knowledge on how to define specific sensing strategies for specific sensing goals. It also creates a context where it can be possible to compare multiple competing alternatives for similar forms of sensing. To improve the generalization of the results, we also avoid any major assumptions about the ways in which a system like this could be embedded into a common bicycle, e.g. embedded directly on the bike or attached as a removable add-on. We will however, try to explicitly identify any effects associated with sensor positions or with other design decisions that may also impact on the viability of particular deployment approaches.

3.1 Bicycle Instrumentation

Our prototype bicycle was based on an electrical bike equipped with a Bosch motor. Figure 1 shows an instance of our sensing bicycle with a common combination of sensors and their deployment positions.

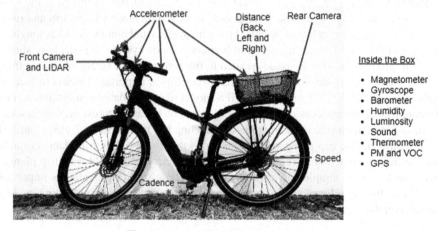

Fig. 1. Sensing Bicycle instrumentation

The instrumentation of the bicycle essentially involved the selection of specific positions for particular sensors and for the central control unit, as well as the installation of cables to support the connections between them. To facilitate deployment, a rear basket was added. This is where the central control unit was placed, together with most sensors and the power battery. To support the cable connection between the central unit in the rear basket and the various sensors that needed to be placed at the front of the bicycle, two small plastic tubes were attached to the bicycle frame and wrapped with black fabric.

3.2 System Architecture

The system follows a centralized architecture with a single control unit connected to multiple sensors via cable connections. In this integrated design, all core functionality is provided as part of a single system, developed and deployed by a single entity.

The system comprises an Arduino UNO R3, a shield with Qwiic extension ports, a micro-SD storage shield, a LED to signal the system status, a 12 V battery and a number of sensors controlled from the Arduino board. Figure 2 represents a particular instantiation of the system with four distance sensors, two accelerometers, one environmental sensor, one light sensor and one sound sensor.

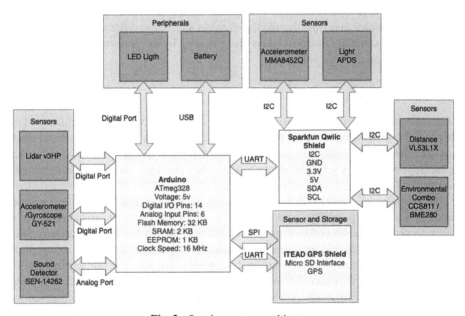

Fig. 2. Sensing system architecture

Since all the sensors are connected with cables, their maximum number is limited by the number of available connections. However, this has not been a major problem at this stage, because for each prototype instance there is normally a specific goal, for which only a particular sub-set of the potential sensors is needed.

3.3 Sensor Sampling Algorithm

The control software running on the Arduino board executes all the necessary tasks for continuously collecting sensor data and writing it to an output file in the SD Card. The sensor sampling algorithm begins with the setup phase, which involves the activation and initialization of the sensors. A LED light on the bicycle handlebar provides basic awareness about the current system status and will be on if all sensors defined as critical are operational. Once the setup is successfully completed, the system enters a data collection loop to obtain data from the various sensors. Given the specific properties of the Arduino Board, each cycle is a sequential process which needs to go through all the system's sensors to obtain their data.

Even though there is a single data collection cycle, we need to accommodate very different requirements regarding the sampling rates of various sensors. Accelerometers will typically have the highest rate. For example, for road anomaly detection in a car driving at 50 km/h, Silva et al. suggest a 50 Hz sampling rate [19]. On the contrary, for GPS data a single sample per second can already be seen as intensive tracking. To address these different sampling rates, we allocate to each sensor a variable that defines the respective frequency.

These sampling frequencies are determined by the envisioned usage of the data, which affects the potential relevance of higher sampling rates, and by the specifications of the sensors, which may limit the maximum rate at which data can actually be produced. The maximum sampling rate possible is also bounded by the performance of the board and the execution time of each cycle.

3.4 Data Collection

Data collection is the ultimate goal of any sensing system and is therefore a critical part of this research on sensing bicycles. Our data collection process is structured around three complementary data collection processes, as represented in Fig. 3. They are distinct processes because they serve different goals, but they also have many interdependencies and shared steps.

Urban data collection is what we envision as a generic, large scale data generation process, where a large number of different types of sensing bicycles are in operation to regularly produce the data needed to support various types of urban cycling services. This is the most generic process supported by the sensing bicycle and essentially corresponds to the normal execution of the software on the control board unit. The raw sensor data is a CSV file containing the data collected from sensors during a trip. The data is structured in a Tidy Data format [20], with each sensor output being registered as a new observation, consisting of line with a time stamp, the data context and the respective value. This format provides the flexibility needed to operate the system under multiple sensing bicycle configurations, each with its own particular set of sensors. It also provides a simple solution to address the very different sensing rates of the various sensors in our system, as each sensor is free to output its data to the file without any dependencies on the others. At the end of the process, data is exported to OGC SensorThings format [21]. This json format provides the necessary self-description of the data, allowing it to be processed without the need for further information, other than what is described in the file itself.

The sensing bicycle can also be used to produce training data for machine learning models. In this case, data collection should be done under a more structured protocol to control the specific variables involved and facilitate the annotation of relevant events. Videos can be used to support this annotation process. They show the concrete situations

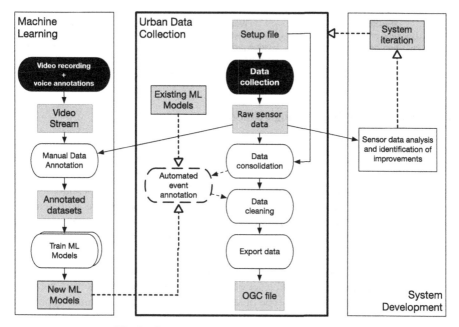

Fig. 3. Complementary data collection processes

being experienced during the ride and they will normally include voice descriptions of the events made by the rider. Each study will conduct whatever specific data manipulation processes it may need to produce specific Machine Learning models. Those ML models may at some point integrate the normal data processing flow to support the automated identification of such events during the ride and shared them as an additional data stream produced by the bicycle.

4   What to Sense in a Sensing Bicycle

A central research question in our work is how to determine the set of sensors that should be available on bicycles to support their role as sensing entities. Our experimental work on sensing systems for bicycles may provide us with many insights about the implications of certain design decisions or about the use of concrete sensors, but it does not take us closer to the answer to this question. This is a very open-ended question, which would normally be easier to answer if made in the context of a concrete systems with specific sensing goals. Trying to provide a generic answer can be much harder, as it requires the generic exploration of sensing possibilities, their viability in the cycling context and also the potential value of the respective data for concrete application domains in the cycling ecosystem. The overall process can be seen as involving three successive layers of analysis, which progressively reduce the set of sensors to be considered, as represented in Fig. 4.

The following sub-sections will explore each of these perspectives in more detail.

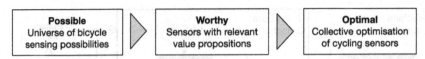

Fig. 4. Layers of analysis in the selection of sensors

4.1 Universe of Cycling Sensing Possibilities

The starting point in this analysis is the universe of bicycle sensing possibilities, which we define as the range of physical phenomena that are measurable, meaningful in the cycling domain and viable. Sensor viability is determined by their cost and by the practical implications of their deployment on the bicycles, such as dependability, size, volume, mass, and longevity [10]. For the purpose of this study, we will assume a loose interpretation of viability, and consider that the universe of sensing possibilities corresponds to all the sensors previously suggested for this purpose in other studies and market products.

Given the wide range of sensor possibilities and their various applications domains, we structured this analysis around a set of sensing profiles, which represent particular sensor types that share the same type of sensing phenomena and a similar application domain. This profile structure explores the fact that the various sensor possibilities are not independent between each other. Similar sensors will typically be used for similar purposes and most of the time will just be alternative solutions to the same problem. By treating them as a whole, we significantly reduce the complexity of the analysis, while still maintaining the capability to make meaningful connections between sensors and their value propositions. We will now present the proposed list of 8 sensing profiles:

Position Profile. The position profile assumes the existence of position sensors that can determine the position of the bicycle. Position data play a major role in the sensing process, not just as a core data itself, but also as a way to georeference data generated by others sensors. This profile may thus be often used in combination with other profiles. Position sensors rank high on viability as they can be low-cost, discrete and pose no major processing requirements, especially when no real-time data is involved. Whenever there is the need to determine the position of the bicycle on a regular basis, a GPS receiver is the common solution.

Motion Profile. Motion measurements can provide key data to understand the smoothness of the ride. When properly analysed by machine learning models this data can produce high-level knowledge about the motion patterns of a ride, including the driving style or the identification of riding events, such as braking, turning, road bumps or irregular tracks. This type of data can serve many relevant purposes, including those related with safety. The motion profile is mainly composed by IMU sensors, such as 3-axis accelerometers, 3-axis gyros and 3-axis magnetometers. these sensors can be low-cost. However, they produce large volumes of data that needs to be processed locally or otherwise transferred to a server. either way, this may introduce additional requirements regarding processing capability, storage or network connectivity.

Environmental Profile. Environmental sensors can measure a wide range of environmental characteristics, such as gas concentrations, particles in the air, light intensity, humidity level, atmospheric pressure or temperature. In the cycling domain, this data can be useful to inform each cyclist about the level of exposure to hazards elements experienced during daily rides and to complement information about route quality, E.G. The presence of certain particles can be a predictor for heavy motor traffic. This data can also be very useful beyond the cycling context, as bicycles are frequently recognized as ideal vehicles for mobile environmental data collection [4, 22, 23]. These sensors do not place many new additional requirements, but some of these sensors can be particularly expensive and require specific installation settings or calibration procedures that may not be compatible with large scale crowdsourcing data collection.

Surrounding Profile. The surrounding profile includes distance sensors to provide a perspective of route quality and safety. Distance between the bicycle and nearby objects defines the free surrounding space, which can be an important indicator for the safety risks associated short distances to other vehicles or to potential obstacles. Common distance sensors, possibly pointing into different directions, may provide simple data about nearest objects. A more sophisticated perception of the surrounding space can be created with data obtained from Lidar and Radar devices, as they offer the additional capability to make 3d representations and identify object sizes. However, LIDAR and Radar Sensors, can be much more demanding in regard to their deployment on the bicycle and their data processing requirements.

Rider. The rider is at the centre of the cycling experience and therefore data from the rider can also provide key insights about that experience. The heart beat rate is commonly used in sports contexts, but it may also be used as proxy for the level of stress experienced during the Ride. A cadence sensor can measure the rotations per minute performed by the rider on the pedal and therefore the effort the cyclist is making.

Video. With proper processing capability, video can be a powerful form of sensing, but the automated collection of data from computer vision processes is not common on bicycles, mainly due to the strong processing requirements. For the purpose of this study, we will embrace video mainly as a source of ground truth data through the creation of autonomous video streams for later annotation of relevant events. In this context, we can expect the video profile to be used mainly in the context of professional data collection activities.

Sound Profile. While potentially a form of environmental sensing, sound can be used to support more advanced interpretations of the cycling context. The level of sound obtained from a simple sound level sensor may be used as a proxy for traffic levels. Sound data obtained with a microphone may enable machine learning methods that explore the particular sound frequencies associated with riding events, E.G. different types of surface will typically produce distinct combinations of sound frequencies and being overtaken by a car may also produce a unique sound signature.

Proximity. Proximity sensors enable bicycles to detect the presence of nearby entities without any physical contact. This is not concerned with the physical proximity to surrounding objects as is the case with distance sensors. This is about logical proximity to recognisable entities, such as other bicycles, cars or bike counters, that are able to identify themselves and possibly engage in more sophisticated communications. Bluetooth, BLE or RFID are commonly used for this purpose.

These 8 profiles do not correspond to specific bicycle instances. They are meant to be combined in many different ways. In particular, the position profile can be expected to be often included when one of the other profiles is also included. By describing sensing systems from the perspective of the supported sensing profiles, it becomes possible to have a common framework to discuss many different sensing bicycle designs.

4.2   Sensors with Relevant Value Propositions

The universe of cycling sensors can be very large, but any realistic cycling sensing setup will have to be shaped by the worthiness of the data produced. Worthiness is essentially determined by the demand side and the concrete value propositions that can be associated with the data produced by those sensors. To scope this analysis, we will focus on cycling routes as the core data entity in our model. Our problem can thus be defined as identifying the types of data that are the most relevant to characterise cycling mobility on a given route network. We mainly consider two major types of data: trips that define movement, i.e. where bicycles are passing and at what speed; and route annotations that characterise routes, i.e. what type of road surface is there or what types of riding events are generated. These two dimensions can be combined with the individual and the collective perspective. For example, combining trips with the collective perspective corresponds to route traffic measurements, i.e. volume metrics. From and individual perspective, trip information can be used to track individual progress and achievements. The combination of these dimensions and their key results are depicted in Fig. 5.

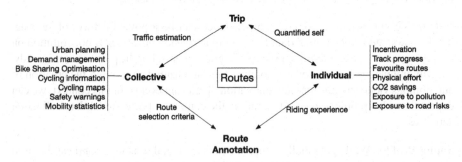

Fig. 5. Simplified model of cycling data needs

We can explore worthiness by exploring the possible associations between the many types of sensors and these different types of data needs. Trip information is largely provided by GPS devices, which generate a time series of positions along with the respective speed and orientation information. Usage of this type of data is very common with Traffic Management services for motorized vehicles where many of these same metrics are intensively explored to produce a general perspective of urban traffic, supporting the generation of live traffic maps and accurate and dynamic estimations of travel times. While there are many commonalities to be explored, cycling data differs from those models in that real-time data is not as relevant as it is with cars. A major goal with cars is to manage ongoing traffic and avoid congestion. With bicycles, volume is also very important, but mainly to understand demand trends and adjust accordingly. We can thus consider trip information as strongly relevant, even if it does not need to be shared in real-time.

On the contrary, route annotation data is very unique and much more relevant for bicycles than it is for cars. With cars, the navigation focus is very strongly on the fastest route. With bicycles, route selection requires a much broader set of data about routes, particularly in regard to safety, comfort or road gradient. Data collected by bicycles should thus be able to support the generation of indicators that represent complex and multi-criteria route selection processes.

The research literature includes a vast body of research on route selection criteria [13–18], which we have used to match sensing possibilities to worthy data applications. In particular, we have considered data services along the various layers of the Bicycle Pyramid model proposed by the BITS project [24]. The pyramid model is derived from Maslow's pyramid of needs and is also organized according to the principle that the needs at the bottom of the pyramid need to be met before the next level becomes relevant. The five proposed layers, from bottom to top, include Safety & Reliability, Speed, Convenience, Comfort and Experience. This is an extensive and prioritized view of multiple elements that can shape cycling activities and ultimately determine its adoption, and therefore provides a good framework for matching data with the value it can generate. Once again, we will use the abstractions offered by sensing profiles to facilitate the association between any specific sensing bicycle designs and concrete urban cycling services. The result is summarised in Table 1, which describes the mapping between different sensing profiles and particular sets of services.

Table 1. Mapping sensing profiles to specific services

Profile	Service
Position	Cycling Maps, Network planning, Volume estimations, Quantified self, Cycling network hierarchy, A -> B patterns, Travel times
Motion	Ridding Conditions, Road surface classification, Automated cyclist profile, Bump detection, Riding flow metrics
Environment	Local pollution levels, Traffic level estimations
surrounding	Safety index based on free surrounding Space
Rider	Physical condition, Riding stress, Exertion
Video	Route annotation. Data interpretation
Sound	Road surface classification, Surrounding traffic, Sound level
Proximity	Bicycle count, symbolic positioning

By providing a perspective of the mapping between sensing system and key data-centric services this table should help developers to consider which profiles to include to obtain specific services, or, given a set of profiles, to understand what can realistically be achieved with the available data.

4.3   Collective Optimisation of Cycling Sensors

The final layer in the analysis is to move beyond the individual bicycle and consider how to optimise an entire cycling sensing ecosystem. Ideally, once we define the target services and identify the sensor profiles that need to be included to support those services, we would like to have all the bicycles equipped with all sensors for all those profiles. In reality, this assumption is challenged by multiple effects, which occur across the various parts of the system and are common to any sensing bicycle design. These effects represent a design trade-off between the quantity and quality of the data that needs to be collected and the costs and hassles involved in that data collection process, as represented in the conceptual map in Fig. 6.

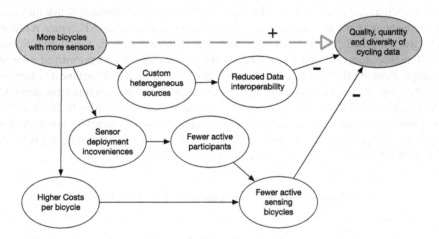

Fig. 6. Key design trade-offs

The key design decision regards the sensing profiles to deploy on each bicycle. In our work with the prototype bicycle, we found, from our many integration attempts, that the number and range of sensors deployed on a particular bicycle seems to have a major impact across a number of other key design goals, particularly cost, convenience and heterogeneity. The first two, cost and convenience, will significantly impact the number of bicycles that one can expect to be involved in the sensing system. The impact of cost is self-explanatory. The impact of sensor diversity is mainly associated with the potentially strong increase in system complexity. There will be more complex integration issues, and especially, there will be more and more specific deployment requirements, leading to all sorts of hindrances, such as specific pre-ride operations, additional cables on the bicycle, special configurations, regular maintenance or sensors placed at inconvenient positions in the bicycle. These will impact negatively on the cycling experience and would probably be enough to drive cyclists away from any form of sensing.

While previous work has often assumed sensing bicycles as part of a uniform fleet equipped with a specific set of sensors, this analysis led us to the opposite conclusion. Future smart cycling ecosystems are much more likely to be composed by a very heterogeneous set of bicycles with various combinations of sensing profiles. This will be even more the case, whenever we consider that a broad range of services, and consequently a broad range of sensing profiles, should be available. This is also much more aligned with an ecosystem view which naturally assumes the existence of many stakeholders with very different needs and, consequently, with different priorities on what sensors to include in their bicycles. Ultimately, each individual cyclist will also be making his or her own decisions on what sensing add-ons to use when cycling.

Therefore, rather than pushing for more uniform bicycles, we leverage heterogeneity as an opportunity to explore complementarities between large numbers of heterogeneous bicycles in an urban ecosystem. More specifically, we envision an ecosystem where different proportions of different types of sensing bicycles would be complementing each other to produce a balanced vision of the cycling reality and guarantee the necessary data while avoiding unnecessary redundancies. A larger number of low-cost sensing bicycles, with a basic sensing profile could collect large volumes of data, especially data that requires higher spatial and temporal coverage, e.g. traffic volume. These would be complemented with a few, more sophisticated, bicycles that could combine two or more sensing profiles and collect data that is updated only occasionally, such as route characterisation. Additionally, one or very few probe bicycles could be deployed for professional data collection regarding more critical data. These probe bicycles could include multiple sensing profiles, but its most distinctive property would be the professional nature of the data collection process, which could thus involve more rigorous processes and more credible data. The quantitative relation between specific sensing profiles and the proportion of bicycles where they should be included to produce the data needed by their target services is not addressed in this work, but becomes a relevant research topic for future work.

While bicycle heterogeneity may hold the key for sensing in urban cycling, it also raises interoperability issues that may negatively affect the value of the data generated by the whole system. In a context of heterogeneity, there are many design possibilities regarding the specific sensor model, the way it is deployed, its position on the bicycle or even the bicycle itself, that may affect the data generated. These challenges may go beyond the usual issues of standard data representations. They may also involve the explicit description of the data collection circumstances, which in some cases might be crucial for the correct interpretation of data. If these relevant elements are not considered, the ability to aggregate data from multiple sources and consequently the value that could be obtained from combining heterogeneous bicycles, can be compromised. This suggest the need for a reference design for sensing bicycles that allows many different bicycles to be used together as part of one common ecosystem, while explicitly dealing with any relevant deployment sensitivities.

5 Conclusions and Future Work

Sensors and bicycles are a powerful combination that is attracting significant attention from research and industry perspectives. While many technical approaches have already been explored, there is a gap on how to approach this topic from an ecosystem perspective where many stakeholders can be involved and data is being collected by very diverse sensing bicycles all of which with their own technology and sensing concepts. The novelty of this contribution is in the broader and more generic perspective of this study, which aimed to pursue a more explicit and thorough analysis of the various dimensions shaping the key trade-offs for cycling sensing systems.

5.1 Future Work

This is an ongoing work, where we are plan to develop further research to provide more thorough indications on how to design, describe and combine very diverse sets of sensing bicycles. In particular, we plan to explore the quantification of the size and relative proportion of the samples needed to offer the services associated with each sensing profile. This knowledge is crucial to support the planning of smart fleets of heterogeneous bicycles where the combination of the various profiles is optimized according to the target services. We also plan to evolve the definition of a reference design for sensing bicycles. This should offer a common reference for describing the sensing affordances of a particular bicycle design, from the simplest ones to a full-fledged probe bicycle for professional data collection. This should allow those sensing possibilities to be combined in many different ways, while allowing their results to be analysed consistently. With this model, it should become possible to relate multiple sensing bicycle designs as variants of a common model and it should be easier to integrate data generated from different instances into shared datasets.

Acknowledgements. This work is supported by: European Structural and Investment Funds in the FEDER component, through the Operational Competitiveness and Internationalization Programme (COMPETE 2020) [Project n° 039334; Funding Reference: POCI-01–0247-FEDER-039334].

References

1. Stratta, P.: Towards a Smarter Cycling. On the brink of a Smart (R)evolution. https://ecf.com/what-we-do/cycling-new-technologies/towards-smarter-cycling
2. Nikolaeva, A., te Brömmelstroet, M., Raven, R., Ranson, J.: Smart cycling futures: charting a new terrain and moving towards a research agenda. J. Transp. Geogr. **79**, 102486 (2019)
3. Lee, J., Leem, Y.T., Lee, S.H.: Categorizing u-bike service and assessing its adoptability under it. In: 12th World Conference on Transportation and Research, pp. 1–10 (2010)
4. Elen, B., et al.: The Aeroflex: a bicycle for mobile air quality measurements. Sensors (Switzerland) **13**, 221–240 (2013)
5. Outram, C., Ratti, C., Bitterman, A.: The Copenhagen Wheel: An innovative electric bicycle system that harnesses the power of real-time information and crowd sourcing. In: Mayor's Summit at the COP15 United Nations Climate Change Conference (2009)

6. SODAQ: SODAQ- Sniffer Bike. https://sodaq.com/projects/sniffer-bike/
7. Wirtschaft, W., S. des Van der H.K.– T. und: Feintuning für die Radverkehrsplanung, https://www.hs-karlsruhe.de/presse/feintuning-fuer-die-radverkehrsplanung/
8. Kiefer, C., Behrendt, F.: Smart e-bike monitoring system: real-time open source and open hardware GPS assistance and sensor data for electrically-assisted bicycles. IET Intell. Transp. Syst. **10**, 79–88 (2016)
9. Eisenman, S.B., Miluzzo, E., Lane, N.D., Peterson, R.A., Ahn, G.S., Campbell, A.T.: BikeNet: a mobile sensing system for cyclist experience mapping. ACM Trans. Sens. Networks. 6 (2009)
10. See.Sense: See.Sense. https://seesense.cc/
11. Makarova, I.V., Boyko, A.D., Shubenkova, K.A.: Cycling intellectualization in Smart Cities. EAI Endors. Trans. Smart Cities **2**, 153498 (2017)
12. Shen, S., Wei, Z.Q., Sun, L.J., Su, Y.Q., Wang, R.C., Jiang, H.M.: The shared bicycle and its network—internet of shared bicycle (IoSB): a review and survey. Sensors (Switzerland) **18**, 1–24 (2018)
13. Ehrgott, M., Wang, J.Y.T., Raith, A., Van Houtte, C.: A bi-objective cyclist route choice model. Transp. Res. Part A Policy Pract. **46**, 652–663 (2012)
14. Winters, M., Davidson, G., Kao, D., Teschke, K.: Motivators and deterrents of bicycling: Comparing influences on decisions to ride. Transportation (Amst) (2011)
15. Segadilha, A.B.P., Sanches, S.D.P.: Identification of Factors that Influence, Cyclistś, Route Choice. Procedia Soc. Behav. Sci. **160**, 372–380 (2014)
16. Félix, R.: Barriers and motivators to bicycle in low cycling maturity cities: Lisbon case study, 259 (2019)
17. Broach, J., Dill, J., Gliebe, J.: Where do cyclists ride? A route choice model developed with revealed preference GPS data. Transp. Res. Part A Policy Pract. **46**, 1730–1740 (2012)
18. Su, J.G., Winters, M., Nunes, M., Brauer, M.: Designing a route planner to facilitate and promote cycling in Metro Vancouver, Canada. Transp. Res. Part A Policy Pract. **44**, 495–505 (2010)
19. Silva, N., Soares, J., Shah, V., Santos, M.Y., Rodrigues, H.: Anomaly detection in roads with a data mining approach. Procedia Comput. Sci. **121**, 415–422 (2017)
20. Wickham, H.: Tidy data. J. Stat. Softw. **59** (2014).
21. Liang, S., Huang, C.Y., Khalafbeigi, T.: OGC SensorThings API Part 1: sensing. open geospatial consortium. Implement. Stand. 1–105 (2016)
22. Liu, X., Xiang, C., Li, B., Jiang, A.: Collaborative bicycle sensing for air pollution on roadway. In: Proceedings - 2015 IEEE 12th International Conference on Ubiquitous Intelligent Computing, 2015 IEEE 12th International Conference on Advanced Trusted Computing, 2015 IEEE 15th International Conference on Scalable Computing and Communication, vol. 20, pp. 316–319 (2016)
23. Corno, F., Montanaro, T., Migliore, C., Castrogiovanni, P.: SmartBike: an IoT crowd sensing platform for monitoring city air pollution. Int. J. Electr. Comput. Eng. **7**, 3602–3612 (2017)
24. Boot, M.: A digital future for cycling: the role of data and ITS in encouraging more cyclists. https://www.intelligenttransport.com/transport-articles/78216/digital-future-cycling-data-its-encouraging-cyclists/

Calibration of Low-Cost Particulate Matter Sensors with Elastic Weight Consolidation (EWC) as an Incremental Deep Learning Method

Rainer Schlund[1], Johannes Riesterer[1], Marcel Köpke[1], Michal Kowalski[2], Paul Tremper[1], Matthias Budde[1(✉)], and Michael Beigl[1]

[1] TECO/Pervasive Computing Systems, Karlsruhe Institute of Technology (KIT), Karlsruhe, Germany
budde@teco.edu
[2] Helmholtz Zentrum München, German Research Center for Environmental Health (HMGU), Neuherberg, Germany
https://www.teco.edu

Abstract. Urban air quality is an important problem of our time. Due to their high costs and therefore low spacial density, high precision monitoring stations cannot capture the temporal and spatial dynamics in the urban atmosphere, low-cost sensors must be used to setup dense measurement grids. However, low-cost sensors are imprecise, biased and susceptible to environmental influences. While neural networks have been explored for their calibration, issues include the amount of data needed for training, requiring sensors to be co-located with reference stations for extensive periods of time. Also re-calibrating them with new data can lead to catastrophic forgetting. We propose using Elastic Weight Consolidation (EWC) as an incremental calibration method. By exploiting the Fisher-Information-Matrix it enables the network to compensate for different sources of error, both pertaining to the sensor itself, as well as caused by varying environmental conditions. Models are pre-calibrated with data of 40 h measurement on a low-cost SDS011 PM sensor and then re-calibrated on another SDS011 sensor. Our evaluation on 1.5 years of real world data shows that a model using EWC with a time period of data of 6 h for re-calibration is more precise than models without EWC, even those with longer re-calibration periods. This demonstrates that EWC is suitable for on-the-fly collaborative calibration of low-cost sensors.

Keywords: Incremental learning · Elastic Weight Consolidation · Sensor calibration · Particulate matter · Air quality

1 Introduction

Urban air quality has become one of the most important problems of our time. The air we breathe is directly related to the quality of people's lives. Particulate

S. Paiva et al. (Eds.): SmartCity360° 2020, LNICST 372, pp. 596–614, 2021.
https://doi.org/10.1007/978-3-030-76063-2_40

matter pollution is one of the largest risks to health worldwide and also contributes to environmental problems such as acid rain, ozone layer depletion and global climate change [23,30].

In industrialized countries, there is on average one official monitoring station per 100,000 inhabitants in cities, whereas in developing countries with high levels of air pollution there is one monitoring station per millions of residents [35]. These classic measurement grids are unsuitable to capture the spatial and temporal dynamics of air pollution in the urban atmosphere [27]. More than ten years ago, the first projects emerged that aimed to bridge this gap using mobile and/or low-cost sensors: the *MESSAGE* project [29,33], *Common Sense* [11], or *OpenSense* [16,20] to name a few.

However, low-cost sensors have some inherent disadvantages and challenges that still have not been adequately addressed. They are generally much more sensitive to changes of environmental conditions such as temperature, wind, humidity and others. They often exhibit sensor drift and may lose sensitivity over time due to aging of their components and therefore need to be re-calibrated frequently [6,8,16]. An established approach to mitigate systematic errors is calibration. Neural networks can be trained to minimize deviations in comparison to reference instruments [23]. The disadvantage of neural networks is the large amount of data required for training in order to later yield sufficient quality [13], which usually means a long time span for data acquisition. This is especially true for Particulate Matter (PM) sensing, as many different environmental factors influence measurement [5]. Additionally, individual low-cost sensors often a-priori exhibit significant inconsistencies between one another [5]. Therefore, learned models cannot simply be transferred from one sensor to another. Instead, each sensor must be calibrated individually [7] over a long period of time to learn how it is influenced by meteorological factors like wind, temperature, humidity, etc., which strongly limits practical application.

This paper presents an approach that uses Elastic Weight Consolidation (EWC) in order to mitigate this limitation. EWC is an algorithm for the training of neural networks which enables them to learn similar tasks incrementally. The calibration of different individual sensors can be considered as a sequence of similar tasks. We show that neural networks can be trained incrementally with the EWC algorithm in order to transfer their calibration to further sensors. By transferring the calibration from one sensor to others the required amount of data and the length of training periods can be significantly reduced. Thus mitigating the limitations described above, when training each sensor individually.

2 Related Work

Spinelle et al. [36] compared the performance of different methods for field calibration of O_3 and NO_2 sensors and found that simple methods such as linear and multivariate linear regression were sufficient for the O_3 sensors, but an artificial neural network yielded better results for NO_2. They included wind and air pressure in addition to temperature and humidity. The neural network was trained with the hourly data of one week (168 data sets).

Yamamoto et al. [37] calibrated low-cost temperature sensors installed at three different locations, but they were not in the immediate vicinity of the references. For the experiment, hourly recorded data were collected over a period of 305 days. A neural net with a hidden layer was used, which had as input parameters the measured temperature, the radiation value of the sun, the humidity, the azimuth value and the altitude above sea level. In the evaluation the neural network shows clear advantages over a simple linear regression and is even able to compensate for measurements influenced by direct solar radiation.

Hojaiji et al. [17] describe the calibration of a fine dust sensor under artificial conditions simulating indoor and outdoor climate. They achieve good results with a simple correction algorithm, which is supposed to compensate influences of temperature and humidity. However, the algorithm was only tested over a period of one day, so that no statements can be made about the long-term behaviour. Also how the calibration behaves under real outdoor conditions has not been investigated.

A calibration using a sensor array for ozone is described in [1]. The array is calculated to a virtual calibrated sensor using linear regression. The influences of temperature and humidity were also taken into account. After removing outliers, 450 hourly measurements from a period of 3–4 weeks were used for calibration. Since some nonlinearities are shown in scatterplots, it is pointed out under Future work, that the root of the mean square error (RMSE) can possibly be further improved with the use of nonlinear calibration models, to which neural networks belong.

In [8] the sensors were first calibrated in the vicinity of a reference instrument. Various Matlab functions for nonlinear regression were used, which processed about 13000 data recorded in minute intervals. The calibrated sensor was then validated at another location over a period of several months. However, the validation was only performed with an hourly resolution, but showed good performance compared to the reference.

The ability of a system to transfer knowledge and acquired skills from one task to another is called transfer learning. Traditional machine learning methods learn tasks always anew without relying on existing knowledge. Transfer learning techniques, on the other hand, attempt to transfer what has been learned from one task or domain to another, assuming the tasks have similarities between each other [22]. Prahm et al. [34] show that thigh prostheses can be controlled by simple myoelectric signals from muscle groups that are still present. However, this control is susceptible to electrode displacement, sweat, fatigue and other influences. This means that continuous recalibration of the control signals is necessary. The prostheses are first trained in an interference-free system. In the application they are then incrementally recalibrated daily with small data sets of less than one minute, based on the initial training, by transfer learning.

In recent years some new learning techniques by transferring known knowledge using neural networks have been developed. One of them is the Elastic Weight Consolidation Algorithm [18]. This algorithm is the foundation of this work.

In order to effectively build sensor networks, [24] proposes an approach using a cross sensor calibration based on sensor rendezvous. If two sensors fall below a certain distance from each other, a calibration process is initiated provided that one of the two sensors has sufficient validity for its measurement data. Various regression methods are used, for which neural networks could be a potential alternative.

Cheng et al. [9] follow a cloud-based approach in which the network's sensors send their data to a central database via the Internet. From there, the data is calibrated using a neural network and can then be transferred to apps for health care, for example.

3 Design

An aspect of neural networks is their ability to learn different tasks by training them simultaneously. This leads to problems if not all tasks are already previously known [18,31]. Sequential learning can be achieved if the data of a training session is stored in an episodic memory and presented to the network again for the next task. However, the data from the memory must be presented to the network again in each training run [19,25].

There is evidence that biological systems anchor what they have learned by consolidating the synapses that are essential for a learned task, which means that they are less plastic and therefore remain stable over longer periods of time [2,12]. Following theses insights, the Elastic Weight Consolidation (EWC) algorithm developed by Kirkpatrick et al. [18] consolidates the weights which are important for a specific task. For a neural network, there is not only one optimal configuration of the weights, but many that lead to comparable results. This set of weights can be viewed as a subset of the space of all possible weights. This suggests that for two similar tasks A and B, such as calibrating two sensors, there are weight distributions θ_A and θ_B that are similar and suitable for both. The EWC algorithm forces the development of the weights in training for task B into the (if available) intersection $\theta_A \cap \theta_B$, shown schematically in Fig. 1. After training, the newly calculated weights are therefore in an area that performs optimally for both tasks A and B [18].

3.1 Mathematical Foundations of the EWC-Algorithmus

Looking at neural networks from a probability theory point of view, a training is the search for the weights that best describe a given data set $\mathcal{D}$. In the case of a regression this means that the expected value of the unknown distribution $p(\theta|\mathcal{D})$ is a minimum for a loss function [18,28]. For this conditional distribution, Bayes theorem in logarithmic form can be applied:

$$\log p(\theta|\mathcal{D}) = \log p(\mathcal{D}|\theta) + \log p(\theta) - \log p(\mathcal{D}) \tag{1}$$

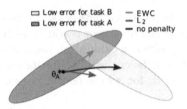

Fig. 1. The EWC algorithm ensures that the weights learned in task B are still suitable for task A by rewarding movements in the direction of the red arrow. The green arrow shows that uniform forcing in any direction is too restrictive. The blue arrow shows the development of the weights without EWC [18]. (Color figure online)

So if one wants to find the optimal weights for two consecutive tasks, then $\mathcal{D} = \mathcal{D}_A \cup \mathcal{D}_B$ with $\mathcal{D}_A \cap \mathcal{D}_B = \emptyset$ and we compute using the log version of Bayes theorem:

$$
\begin{aligned}
\log p(\theta|\mathcal{D}) &= \log p(\theta|\mathcal{D}_A \cup \mathcal{D}_B) \\
&= \log p(\mathcal{D}_A \cup \mathcal{D}_B|\theta) + \log p(\theta) - \log p(\mathcal{D}_A \cup \mathcal{D}_B) \\
&= \log(p(\mathcal{D}_A|\theta) * p(\mathcal{D}_B|\theta)) + \log p(\theta) - \log(p(\mathcal{D}_A) * p(\mathcal{D}_B)) \\
&= \log p(\mathcal{D}_B|\theta) - \log(p(\mathcal{D}_B)) + \underbrace{\log p(\mathcal{D}_A|\theta) + \log p(\theta) - \log(p(\mathcal{D}_A))}_{=\log p(\theta|\mathcal{D}_A)} \\
&= \log p(\mathcal{D}_B|\theta) + \log p(\theta|\mathcal{D}_A) - \log(p(\mathcal{D}_B))
\end{aligned}
\tag{2}
$$

The distribution for the model of task A is the only term which dependents on $\mathcal{D}_A$ is. This means that all information about task A is contained in this distribution. Assuming that some weights θ_A^* are close to the optimal weights, they are a good estimator for the expected value of $\log p(\theta|\mathcal{D}_A)$. An estimator for a parameter, on the other hand, is the better the smaller the variance of its distribution function is. In the example of the normal distribution, a small variance leads to a narrower and higher bell curve, so the interval for values with high probability becomes narrower. What the EWC algorithm wants to achieve is that only weights that are good estimators for task A are chosen for task B [18].

The a posteriori distribution for task A can be estimated by a Laplace approximation

$$
p(\theta|D_A) = \frac{1}{Z}e^{-E(\theta)},
\tag{3}
$$

where $E(\theta) = \log p(\theta, D_A)$ is called energy function with $Z = p(\mathcal{D}_A)$ [28]. If the Taylor series of the energy function around some weights θ_A^* is formed up to the second degree, the first gradient of the approximation is zero, since θ_A^* is a minimum for task A and we get:

$$
p(\theta|D_A) = e^{-E(\theta_A^*)}e^{[-\frac{1}{2}(\theta-\theta_A^*)^T H(\theta-\theta_A^*)]}
\tag{4}
$$

where H is the Hesse matrix of the energy function. The negative value of H is known as the observed information matrix F and its expected value $\mathbb{E}(F)$ is known as the Fisher matrix [28]. If we assume $e^{-E(\theta_A^*)}$ to be of constant value λ, which will be the case if task A has already been trained, and apply the logarithm to Eq. (4), we get:

$$\log p\left(\theta|\mathcal{D}\right) = \log p\left(\mathcal{D}_B|\theta\right) - \frac{\lambda}{2}\left(\theta - \theta_A^*\right)^T F_{\theta_A^*}\left(\theta - \theta_A^*\right) + C \tag{5}$$

where $C := -\log(p(\mathcal{D}_B)$ is constant with respect to the weights. To reduce the computational effort for computing the Fisher matrix, it is assumed to be a diagonal matrix (which also might be achieved by a change of basis) and in this case Eq. (5) simplifies to

$$\log p\left(\theta|\mathcal{D}\right) = \log p\left(\mathcal{D}_B|\theta\right) - \frac{\lambda}{2}F_{\theta_A^*}\left(\theta - \theta_A^*\right)^2 + C. \tag{6}$$

The Fisher matrix has two interesting properties. It can be used to assess the quality of an estimator and the inner product $(\theta - \theta_A^*)^T F_{\theta_A^*}(\theta - \theta_A^*)$ defines a metric that can be used to calculate a local distance between estimators [32]. In this metric, all optimal estimators for task A have a small distance between them. If the training for task B results in an estimator becoming less optimal for task A, the distance between these two estimators increases. This distance calculated with $\frac{\lambda}{2}F_{\theta_A^*}\left(\theta - \theta_A^*\right)^2$ is therefore suitable as a penalty term within the loss function of task B defined by

$$\mathcal{L}(\theta) = \mathcal{L}_B(\theta) + \frac{\lambda}{2}F_{\theta_A^*}(\theta - \theta_A^*)^2. \tag{7}$$

$\frac{\lambda}{2}$ is thereby a proportionality factor (EWC-factor), which is trained as a hyperparameter during training and determines how large the resistance is, for a change of the weights determined by the first task [28] and [18,21].

A neural network is described by the output function $t = y\left(x,\theta\right)$ with $x \in \mathcal{D}_A$. In case of a linear activation function, for the distribution $p(\mathbf{t}|\mathbf{x})\ \mathbf{x} \in D_A$ one can assume a normal distribution centered around $y(x,\theta)$ with a variance β^2 [18]. This distribution coincides with the distribution of $p(\theta|\mathcal{D}_A)$, since $p(t|x) = p(\theta|x)$. Assuming t_i to be conditionally independent we conclude:

$$p_\theta\left(t|x\right) = \prod_{i=1}^{o} N\left(t_i|y(\mathbf{x},\theta)_i, \beta^2\right) \tag{8}$$

The definition of the Fisher matrix is:

$$I(\theta) := \mathrm{E}_\theta(S_\theta^2) \tag{9}$$

In this case the scoring function S_θ is the first derivative of the log-likelihood function of the normal distribution in 8. Thus, following [32] the Fisher can be computed by:

$$F = \beta^2 \mathrm{E}\left[\sum_{i=1}^{0}\left(\frac{\partial y_i}{\partial \theta}\right)^T\left(\frac{\partial y_i}{\partial \theta}\right)\right] \tag{10}$$

The Fisher matrix is thus a diagonal matrix whose diagonal contains the sum of the derivatives of the output function of the net $y(x, \theta)$ with respect to all data points. The Fisher matrix describes an expected value. Since the average of the results obtained from a large number of trials approaches the mean value, the matrix is calculated by taking the mean value for a selected set of n data points from $\mathcal{D}_A$.

3.2   Construction of the Neural Networks

Deeper neural networks have a higher parameter efficiency, i.e. they can model complex functions with exponentially fewer neurons than flat ones and can therefore be trained more quickly [13]. Hence a simple backpropagation net with seven input parameters, three hidden layers and one output layer with one neuron was chosen as model with a linear activation function as output layer. But as these configuration is not chosen by profound experience, this must be further evaluated in future work. The input parameters are the sensor reading in $\mu g/m^3$, the temperature in degrees Celsius, the relative humidity in percent, the wind speed in meters per second, the precipitation in millimeters, the air pressure in millibar and the day of the year (1-365). As minimization function the mean squared error (MSE) was used because it' higher sensitive to outliers (unusually high or low values) [26]. Hyper parameters of the network are number of neurons per layer, activation function per layer, optimization function, learning rate, batch size. The values of all parameters were deliberately restricted as little as possible, since there is hardly any experience to date in the selection of hyperparameters with regard to the EWC algorithm for a regression task. The number of neurons is selected from the interval $[10, 1000]$. The following activation functions are available: Sigmoid function, Rectified linear unit (*Relu*), Leaky_Relu, Exponential linear unit (*Elu*) and Tangent hyperbolic function. The selection of optimization functions consists of Adam, Adagrad and RMSProp. The learning rate can take values between 0.0001 and 0.2, the batch size values from 8 to 128.

3.3   Bayesian Optimization

For a defined model, the Bayesian algorithm searches exploratively and exploitatively for the best possible values for the hyperparameters which minimize the loss function for training runs on the data [3]. To limit the time required for the search, the model is trained with a smaller number of epochs using the MSE as a loss function. The relationship between exploitation and exploration is determined by the so-called acquisition functions. The one that was chosen (UCB) is the one that works with the upper limit of the confidence interval for the prediction. The ratio between exploitation and exploration is determined with the parameter Kappa, which can have values from 0.1 to 10. A mean value of 1.0 was chosen for this parameter. Other parameters that are set are the number of randomly selected points used as a starting point for the exploration and the number of iterations of a search. In total five optimization runs with different parameter combinations were performed.[1]

3.4 Trial Procedure

The entire test series consists of three consecutive steps (see also Table 1):

Bayesian Optimization. In this step a pre-selection of models suitable for further training is made. A total of 252 different models have been generated in five runs. For each sensor/data combination, the six models with the lowest MSE value were included in the second step.

Pre-selection. The nets selected in the Bayesian optimization are trained in the pre-selection with a larger number of epochs and more repetitions on differently sized training data sets. On the basis of the ratio between the MSE for the training data, the MSE for the test data and the absolute values of the MSE for the test data, an estimation should be made of the minimum amount of data with which a successful training for the net can be performed. Of all the runs performed on all the training data, the three models with the lowest MSE are selected again for the final training with the EWC algorithm.

Final Training with EWC. Finally, the initial training and then the subsequent training are carried out for the networks with and without EWC according to the encoding Table 2. Before the nets are trained, they are evaluated on the test data from the sensors for the follow-up training to determine how well the predictions improve in the follow-up training.

All final training are carried out in the follow-up training with different amounts of data in order to estimate, as in the pre-selection, with which minimum amount of data a successful training for the networks can be carried out. These data are then used to evaluate the test. Table 1 shows an overview of the parameter values used for the training runs in the different test sections.

4 Evaluation

We evaluated our approach on the data of six NovaFitness SDS011 PM1 sensors, which were operated for more than 1.5 years under real world conditions on the roof on an air quality and weather measurement station (see Fig. 2). In laboratory tests (cmp. Budde et al. [5]), these sensors showed good linear behaviour, but with a systematic misinterpretation of the actual concentration. It was also shown that the measured values in certain areas are strongly dependent on environmental factors such as relative humidity. The SDS011 recorded data with a

---

[1] As basis for our implementation, we used the GitHub repositories https://github.com/fmfn/BayesianOptimization (Bayesian Optimization) and https://github.com/ariseff/overcoming-catastrophic (EWC algorithm).

Table 1. Overview of the value ranges of the training parameters

Bayesian search				
Run	Exploitation/exploration coefficient Kappa	Initial points	Iterations	Epochs
1	1	20	40	400
2	1	20	40	400
3	1	20	40	500
4	1	200	400	700
5	1	400	500	700
Backpropagation network				
Hidden layer 1		10–1000		
Hidden layer 2		10–1000		
Hidden layer 3		10–1000		
Activation function layer 1		sigmoid, tanh, elu, relu, leaky_relu		
Activation function layer 2		sigmoid, tanh, elu, relu, leaky_relu		
Activation function layer 3		sigmoid, tanh, elu, relu, leaky_relu		
Optimization functions		RMSProp, Adam, Adagrad		
Pre-selection and test for required data volume				
# selected models from bayesian optimization		6		
# datasets (1 dataset equals 74 min of data)		8, 16, 64, 200, 400, 600, all		
# epochs		500, 1500		
# training runs per model		8		
Final training				
# selected models from pre-selection		3		
# datasets for EWC algorithm		5, 20, 80, all		
# epochs audited		50, 100, 500, 800, 2000		
# epochs for training the initial sensor		1500		
# training runs per model		3		
EWC factor		150000		

frequency of 1 reading every 3 min in several separate periods between October 22nd, 2017 and April 1st, 2019. A total of approx. 100,000 usable data points, spanning all four seasons, was recorded. There was no removal of incorrect measured values or outliers. There are areas where the sensors underestimate as well as overestimate values, which indicates a nonlinear behaviour of the sensors.

A Grimm EDM180 particle counter was used as reference device [14]. Additionally, every minute one value measuring temperature, humidity, air pressure, precipitation and wind speed each was recorded. The day of the year was added to these values as a further date in order to be able to adjust for whether this seasonal information had an effect on the quality of the calibration.

Fig. 2. Data collection setup: Six NodeMCU platforms with an SDS011 PM sensor and a BME280 temperature/humidity sensor (yellow rectangle) were operated for a period of 1.5 years. They were installed on top of an air quality measurement container in Augsburg, Germany (as part of the SmartAQnet project [4]) within a well-ventilated instrument shelter (red rectangle). (Color figure online)

Since the data points were collected at different frequencies, the values from the reference station were combined to form three-minute averages. For the precipitation data, the sum was calculated instead. In order to be able to assign the two time series to each other, the values of the reference values were replenished to minute cycles, so that three copies of each measured value were made. The two time series were merged again by a join operation. Since there was a small period of time in which the reference did not record any values, this was subsequently removed. At the end of the process, there is a measurement in the data again for every third minute, except in the periods in which the sensors did not measure.

Measurements were taken for the two particle sizes PM10 and PM2.5. Since neural networks often work better on normalized data all data sets of the SDS011 sensors have been normalized. No normalized files were generated from the reference values, in this case the output layer maps back to the original value range. In the Table 2 the color coding for the trained neural networks and the different data sets of the sensors is shown. The six sensors available for the experiment are divided into two groups. With the first group (sensors 1, 2 and 3) the nets are trained in the initial training without using the EWC (marked black in Table 2).

The nets are then trained with the data from the second group of sensors (sensors 4, 5 and 6) with and without EWC in a subsequent training (blue markings in Table 2). For the training, all data sets used have been split in the ratio $\frac{4}{9}$ training, $\frac{3}{9}$ test, and $\frac{2}{9}$ validation. The nets are first trained on training data and then evaluated with the test data. Good models with low mean square error are selected based on the results they produce on the test data. Since the

Table 2. Color coding of all data-sensor combinations of the neural networks trained in the experiments.

		Initial Training 🛰	Sensors	
			Follow-up Training 🛰	
			without EWC	with EWC •
Data	PM10	🗄🛰	🗄🛰	🗄🛰
	PM2.5	🗄🛰	🗄🛰	🗄🛰

selection is made in several successive training runs, the trained models are no longer completely independent of the test data and have to be tested once on completely unknown data, the validation data set, in the end.

Before looking at the evaluation data, we present the mean squared error (MSE) of the raw (unprocessed) measurements of the six SDS011 sensors compared to the reference in Fig. 3. It is noticeable that the values for the particle size PM10 shown significantly higher MSE values and also a greater range of variation than the values for PM2.5. This is in line with findings from related work that showed that the SDS011 is much more susceptible to errors in the PM10 channel [5].

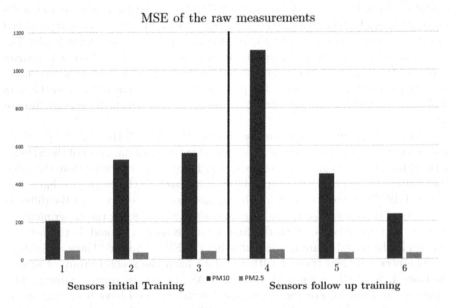

Fig. 3. Mean squared error (MSE) values for all sensors. MSE in $(\mu g/m^3)^2$

In total 7,290 models were trained. 2,430 of them were trained on initial sensors (sensors 1, 2, 3 marked black) without EWC (see column *Initial training* in Table 2). Originating from those all models were subsequently trained on follow-up sensors with and without EWC (columns *Follow-up Training without EWC* and *Follow-up Training with EWC* in Table 2 respectively).

4.1 Description of Evaluation Data

All following results are carried out as mean values aggregated over all sensors, since the basic properties of the EWC should not be dependent on a selection of sensors. In order to get an estimation of the amount of data needed for the training with EWC, we trained with different amount of data and also with different number of epochs. Furthermore, the evaluations is only presented for networks that meet a given quality standard. In Table 3, only nets with an MSE lower than one hundred are considered. The evaluation is divided into two sections.

1. The initial training 🐾. The trained nets are evaluated on:
   (a) the validation data of the initial training for PM10 🗄 and PM2.5 🗄
   (b) the test data of the sensors of the follow-up training for PM10 🗄 and PM2.5 🗄
2. The follow-up training for the networks initialized in 1. once with 🐾 and once without EWC 🐾. The nets are evaluated in each case on:
   (a) the validation data of the follow-up training for PM10 🗄 and PM2.5 🗄
   (b) the validation data for initial training for PM10 🗄 and PM2.5 🗄.

During training, the EWC tries to keep the weights in an optimal range for both tasks. To estimate how well the data of the initial training will be evaluated after the follow-up training, one has to compare the MSE from (1.a) with the MSE from (2.b). This shows how well the networks can continue to predict the measured values of the initial sensor after the follow-up training. (2.a) and (2.b) shows how well the nets can predict the measured values for both sensors. The comparison between 2. With and without EWC shows how well the nets trained with EWC perform compared to those without.

4.2 Validation

1. Networks trained with and without EWC: It is shown that the nets trained with EWC are able to make very good predictions for both sensors, with significantly better values than the nets trained without EWC (comparison of columns 2 and 3 respectively columns 4 and 5).
2. Prediction for initial sensor: Also only slight losses are shown in the comparison of the nets trained with EWC on both sensors compared to the nets trained only on the data of the initial sensor (columns 1 and 3).

Table 3. MSE for PM10 over all sensor pairs. Selection of the networks: MSE for follow-up training on initial data in the validation with (column3) or without (column 2) EWC less than 100. Models trained with EWC show clearly better results than those without for both evaluation data sets.

Data fraction	# epochs					
		training on				
		evaluation on				
5	50	63	82	76	71	64
	200	63	86	77	73	68
	500	60	87	79	74	67
	800	60	86	79	75	68
	1200	59	86	79	72	67
20	50	62	81	74	70	63
	200	61	81	74	63	60
	500	69	82	77	63	61
	800	61	80	75	66	64
	1200	62	81	76	64	63
80	50	61	83	74	66	60
	200	61	80	73	64	59
	500	63	78	75	60	58
	800	63	77	75	60	59
	1200	62	79	75	59	59

Initial training   Follow-up training   Follow-up training with EWC   Data initial training/test   Data follow-up training/test

3. Amount of data: Looking at the results for the different data sets in columns 3 and 5, it can be seen that the results for five and ten data units respectively could be of good enough quality for sensor training. This corresponds to a period between 6 h and 12 h for the measurements. This value is still below the value in test section 2 Fig. 4 estimated value of 32 units = 38 h.

The same picture can be seen in Table 4 for the particle size PM2.5, for which the quality measure is an MSE smaller than forty.

To investigate whether there is a significant difference in the mean values of MSE in training with and without EWC on the validation data of the initial and the follow-up sensors, only models with a maximum MSE of 100 for PM10 are considered for both qualities, for PM2.5 the limit is 40.

Table 5 shows that the mean values of the MSE on nets trained with EWC are better for both particle sizes than without. The standard deviation and standard error are of a similar order of magnitude on the compared nets.

Table 6 shows the correlation between the nets trained with and without EWC. Finally, we need to check if the differences in the MSE are significant. Since this test involves dependent samples with parameterized data, Student's t-test for dependent samples is used for the test. A prerequisite for the test is a normal distribution of the MSE values, but this can be neglected for large data sets. What is given when the sample size is over 500 values for both PM2.5 and PM10 [10].

Table 4. MSE for PM2.5 over all sensor pairs. Selection of the networks: MSE for follow-up training on initial data in the validation with (column 3) or without (column 2) EWC less than 40. Models trained with EWC show clearly better results than those without for both evaluation data sets.

Data fraction	# epochs					
	training on					
	evaluation on					
5	50	16	21	16	23	18
	200	16	24	19	25	20
	500	16	25	20	25	20
	800	16	25	20	25	21
	1200	16	26	21	26	21
20	50	16	21	16	21	17
	200	16	21	17	21	18
	500	16	21	18	21	18
	800	16	21	18	21	18
	1200	16	22	18	21	19
80	50	16	20	16	20	17
	200	16	19	16	19	17
	500	16	18	16	17	16
	800	17	19	16	18	16
	1200	16	18	16	17	16

Initial training   Follow-up training   Follow-up training with EWC   Data initial training/test   Data follow-up training/test

Table 5. Descriptive statistics on the nets trained with and without EWC on task 2 for the two particle sizes PM2.5 and PM10. The upper half shows the evaluation on the data of the initial sensors, the lower half on the data of the subsequent sensors.

Sensors	Class	Training	Validation	N	mean	stddev	stderr
	PM2.5			760	21.90	5.03	0.77
				760	18.09	3.40	0.66
	PM10			603	82.02	9.57	3.34
				603	76.04	9.38	3.10
	PM2.5			760	21.67	5.59	0.77
				760	18.45	4.36	0.66
	PM10			603	66.50	17.47	3.34
				603	62.82	16.04	3.10

Initial training   Follow-up training   Follow-up training with EWC   Data initial training/test   Data follow-up training/test

The values in Table 6 confirm that the differences between the MSE values of nets trained with EWC on the data of the initial sensors (task 1) and the differences on the data of the subsequent sensors (task 2) are significant. This means that the nets trained with EWC are better able to calibrate the data of the initial sensors as well as the data of the subsequent sensors.

Table 6. Pearson correlation (PCC) and t-Test on the significance of the differences in the mean values of the MSE (each for the nets trained with and without EWC, for both particle sizes on the data of the initial and subsequent sensors). (* significance level 5%)

Sensors	Class	Training Validation		Pearson correlation		t-Tests	
				PCC	Significance*	Test statistics	p-Value*
	PM2.5			0.69	<0.05	-28.85	<0.05
	PM10			0.69	<0.05	-19.80	<0.05
	PM2.5			0.75	<0.05	-24.36	<0.05
	PM10			0.93	<0.05	-14.10	<0.05

Initial training   Follow-up training   Follow-up training with EWC   Data initial training/test   Data follow-up training/test

No trends can be identified for the hyperparameters trained in the optimization. The values for the batch size are usually above 80, and there is no recognizable trend for the activation functions of the hidden layers and the learning rate. The number of neurons per layer is usually over 100, but there are also individual nets that manage with a total number of less than 100 neurons and provide good values. Also for the different optimizers no preference of a particular one can be recognized.

All in all, the optimization indicates that there are many different parameter combinations that are suitable for calibrating the sensors in the experimental setup chosen here. From the Bayesian optimization, the 24 best models per sensor were taken over into the preselection.

4.3 Preselection and Data Volume

Test runs that do not have a value better than 100 in at least one of the MSE values for test and training data, or a value greater than 300 in one of the two, were rejected as unsuccessful training runs. The test runs were performed with 1500 and 500 epochs. Since the results are almost identical for both, only the data for 1500 epochs are presented here.

To estimate the amount of data required, the mean value of the MSE for training was calculated for all sensors. The values are shown separately for the two particle sizes PM10 and PM2.5 in Fig. 4.

The curves for both particle sizes show a large difference between the MSE for the test data and the MSE for the training data up to 32 data units. This is an indication that the network is overtrained for these values. In addition, it can be seen that the MSE on the test data tends to improve further with larger amounts of data.

These are good indications that the smallest amount of data required is at least greater than 32 units. 32 units correspond to 768 measurements performed at a frequency of three minutes, i.e. about 38 h.

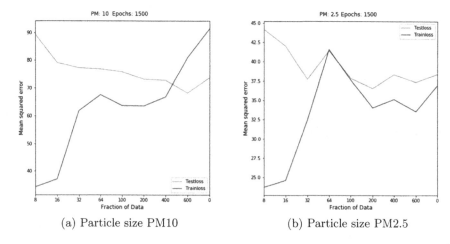

(a) Particle size PM10   (b) Particle size PM2.5

Fig. 4. Comparison of the development of the MSE for test- and training data, the data set 0 corresponds to a training with all data.

It is noticeable that the mean of the MSE for the training data of the particle size PM10 is significantly higher for the data units 600 and 0 (0 = all data) than for the test data, although for a mean value over all training runs it could rather be expected that the opposite case is realized. Investigations of the reference data have shown that some unusually high readings occurred in these areas that the network could not compensate for through training and explain this difference.

5   Conclusion and Future Work

In this work, we presented a method of transferring calibration models from one low-cost particle sensor to another. By exploiting Elastic Weight Consolidation (EWC), we demonstrated that this can be done using substantially less training data – and thereby time – than with previous approaches.

For this, we trained neural network based calibration models on a low cost sensor and subsequently continue to train them on a second one with and without using the EWC algorithm. In order to study the ability of the two approaches to learn the second calibration while recognizing the first, we evaluated various models on several pairs of sensors that collected data under real-world conditions for more than 1.5 years. It turned out that even with a small data set containing only 120 measured values (approx. 6h) for the second sensor, the training with EWC shows very good results and in comparison to training without EWC the MSE values are significantly better on both sensors.

The exploration of models in this work was quite restricted. For example, the EWC factor is not trained as a hyperparameter, but with a fixed value, since it has shown itself to be relatively insensitive to changes over a wide range of values in test runs. The number of hidden layers was also not optimized as a hyperparameter. The potential of a detailed optimization of the hyperparameters could therefore still be investigated. Possibilities for improvement might also lie in the selection of a different net typology. LSTM nets, for example, are particularly suitable for time series, such as measurement data from sensors [13]. It might also be interesting to check whether an initial training of the networks on several instead of only one sensor can lead to further improvements.

In this paper was not examined, how far a sensor can be moved away from the reference station and still delivers reliable data and how long the measurements remain reliable over time. These are points that should be addressed in future work.

The original work on the EWC itself sees room for improvement by using a point estimator for the a posteriori estimation of variance, which could be further improved by using a Bayesian neural network [18].

In [21] it is described how the performance of the EWC can be further improved by a reparameterization that leads to a rotation of the parameter space.

In this context, it could be examined to what extent such networks are suitable for approaches like on-the-fly or collaborative calibration [15,24]. Therefore it might be possible to train sensors cumulatively using the presented method with even smaller amounts of data and thus keep the individual length of stay at the reference device small.

Acknowledgements. This work has been partially funded by the German Federal Ministry for Traffic and Digital Infrastructure (BMVI) as part of project SmartAQnet [4] (grant number 19F2003B).

References

1. Barcelo-Ordinas, J.M., Garcia-Vidal, J., Doudou, M., Rodrigo-Muñoz, S., Cerezo-Llavero, A.: Calibrating low-cost air quality sensors using multiple arrays of sensors. In: 2018 IEEE Wireless Communications and Networking Conference (WCNC), pp. 1–6. IEEE (2018)
2. Benna, M.K., Fusi, S.: Computational principles of biological memory. arXiv preprint arXiv:1507.07580 (2015)
3. Brochu, E., Cora, V.M., De Freitas, N.: A tutorial on Bayesian optimization of expensive cost functions, with application to active user modeling and hierarchical reinforcement learning. arXiv preprint arXiv:1012.2599 (2010)
4. Budde, M., et al.: SmartAQnet: remote and in-situ sensing of urban air quality. In: Proceedings of SPIE Remote Sensing of Clouds and the Atmosphere XXII, vol. 10424, p. 104240C (2017)
5. Budde, M., et al.: Potential and limitations of the low-cost SDS011 particle sensor for monitoring urban air quality. ProScience 5, 6–12 (2018)
6. Budde, M., Zhang, L., Beigl, M.: Distributed, low-cost particulate matter sensing: scenarios, challenges, approaches. ProScience 1, 230–236 (2014)
7. Castell, N., et al.: Can commercial low-cost sensor platforms contribute to air quality monitoring and exposure estimates? Environ. Int. 99, 293–302 (2017)
8. Cavaliere, A., et al.: Development of low-cost air quality stations for next generation monitoring networks: calibration and validation of PM2.5 and PM10 sensors. Sensors 18(9), 2843 (2018)

9. Cheng, Y., et al.: AirCloud: a cloud-based air-quality monitoring system for everyone. In: Proceedings of the 12th ACM Conference on Embedded Network Sensor Systems, pp. 251–265. ACM (2014)
10. Diaz-Bone, R.: Statistik für Soziologen. UTB GmbH (2018)
11. Dutta, P., et al.: Common sense: participatory urban sensing using a network of handheld air quality monitors. In: Proceedings of the 7th ACM Conference on Embedded Networked Sensor Systems, SenSys 2009, pp. 349–350. Association for Computing Machinery, New York (2009). https://doi.org/10.1145/1644038.1644095
12. Fusi, S., Drew, P.J., Abbott, L.F.: Cascade models of synaptically stored memories. Neuron 45(4), 599–611 (2005)
13. Géron, A.: Hands-On Machine Learning with Scikit-Learn and TensorFlow: Concepts, Tools, and Techniques to Build Intelligent Systems. O'Reilly Media, Inc., Newton (2017)
14. Grimm Aerosol Technik: Model EDM180. https://www.grimm-aerosol.com/products-en/environmental-dust-monitoring/approved-pm-monitor/edm180/
15. Hasenfratz, D., Saukh, O., Sturzenegger, S., Thiele, L.: Participatory air pollution monitoring using smartphones. Mob. Sens. 1, 1–5 (2012)
16. Hasenfratz, D., Saukh, O., Thiele, L.: On-the-fly calibration of low-cost gas sensors. In: Picco, G.P., Heinzelman, W. (eds.) EWSN 2012. LNCS, vol. 7158, pp. 228–244. Springer, Heidelberg (2012). https://doi.org/10.1007/978-3-642-28169-3_15
17. Hojaiji, H., Kalantarian, H., Bui, A.A., King, C.E., Sarrafzadeh, M.: Temperature and humidity calibration of a low-cost wireless dust sensor for real-time monitoring. In: 2017 IEEE Sensors Applications Symposium (SAS), pp. 1–6. IEEE (2017)
18. Kirkpatrick, J., et al.: Overcoming catastrophic forgetting in neural networks. Proc. Natl. Acad. Sci. 114(13), 3521–3526 (2017)
19. Kumaran, D., Hassabis, D., McClelland, J.L.: What learning systems do intelligent agents need? Complementary learning systems theory updated. Trends Cogn. Sci. 20(7), 512–534 (2016)
20. Li, J.J., Faltings, B., Saukh, O., Hasenfratz, D., Beutel, J.: Sensing the air we breathe—The OpenSense Zurich dataset. In: Twenty-Sixth AAAI Conference on Artificial Intelligence (2012)
21. Liu, X., Masana, M., Herranz, L., Van de Weijer, J., Lopez, A.M., Bagdanov, A.D.: Rotate your networks: Better weight consolidation and less catastrophic forgetting. In: 2018 24th International Conference on Pattern Recognition (ICPR), pp. 2262–2268. IEEE (2018)
22. Lu, J., Behbood, V., Hao, P., Zuo, H., Xue, S., Zhang, G.: Transfer learning using computational intelligence: a survey. Knowl.-Based Syst. 80, 14–23 (2015)
23. Maag, B., Zhou, Z., Thiele, L.: A survey on sensor calibration in air pollution monitoring deployments. IEEE Internet Things J. 5(6), 4857–4870 (2018)
24. Markert, J.F., Budde, M., Schindler, G., Klug, M., Beigl, M.: Private rendezvous-based calibration of low-cost sensors for participatory environmental sensing. In: Proceedings of the Second International Conference on IoT in Urban Space, pp. 82–85. ACM (2016)
25. McClelland, J.L., McNaughton, B.L., O'Reilly, R.C.: Why there are complementary learning systems in the hippocampus and neocortex: insights from the successes and failures of connectionist models of learning and memory. Psychol. Rev. 102(3), 419 (1995)
26. Mertens, P., Rässler, S.: Prognoserechnung. Springer, Heidelberg (2005). https://doi.org/10.1007/b138143

27. Monn, C.: Exposure assessment of air pollutants: a review on spatial heterogeneity and indoor/outdoor/personal exposure to suspended particulate matter, nitrogen dioxide and ozone. Atmos. Environ. **35**(1), 1–32 (2001)
28. Murphy, K.P.: Machine Learning: A Probabilistic Perspective. MIT Press, Cambridge (2012)
29. North, R., Richards, M., Cohen, J., Hoose, N., Hassard, J., Polak, J.: A mobile environmental sensing system to manage transportation and urban air quality. In: 2008 IEEE International Symposium on Circuits and Systems (2008)
30. World Health Organization: Who releases country estimates on air pollution exposure and health impact (2016). https://goo.gl/G4uqFE
31. Parisotto, E., Ba, J.L., Salakhutdinov, R.: Actor-mimic: deep multitask and transfer reinforcement learning. arXiv preprint arXiv:1511.06342 (2015)
32. Pascanu, R., Bengio, Y.: Revisiting natural gradient for deep networks. arXiv preprint arXiv:1301.3584 (2013)
33. Polak, J.: Mobile environmental sensor systems across a grid environment-the message project. ERCIM News **2007**(68) (2007)
34. Prahm, C., Paassen, B., Schulz, A., Hammer, B., Aszmann, O.: Transfer learning for rapid re-calibration of a myoelectric prosthesis after electrode shift. In: Ibáñez, J., González-Vargas, J., Azorín, J.M., Akay, M., Pons, J.L. (eds.) Converging Clinical and Engineering Research on Neurorehabilitation II. BB, vol. 15, pp. 153–157. Springer, Cham (2017). https://doi.org/10.1007/978-3-319-46669-9_28
35. Rai, A.C., et al.: End-user perspective of low-cost sensors for outdoor air pollution monitoring. Sci. Total Environ. **607**, 691–705 (2017)
36. Spinelle, L., Gerboles, M., Villani, M.G., Aleixandre, M., Bonavitacola, F.: Field calibration of a cluster of low-cost available sensors for air quality monitoring. Part A: ozone and nitrogen dioxide. Sens. Actuators, B Chem. **215**, 249–257 (2015)
37. Yamamoto, K., Togami, T., Yamaguchi, N., Ninomiya, S.: Machine learning-based calibration of low-cost air temperature sensors using environmental data. Sensors **17**(6), 1290 (2017)

Person-Flow Estimation with Preserving Privacy Using Multiple 3D People Counters

Yoshiteru Nagata$^{(\boxtimes)}$ ⓘ, Takuro Yonezawa ⓘ, and Nobuo Kawaguchi ⓘ

Nagoya University, Nagoya, Aichi, Japan
teru@ucl.nuee.nagoya-u.ac.jp

Abstract. The spread of mobile phones made it easy to estimate person-flow for corporate marketing, crowd analysis, and countermeasures for disaster and disease. However, due to recent privacy concerns, regulations have been tightened around the world and most smartphone operating systems have increased privacy protection. To solve this, in this study, we propose the person-flow estimation technique with preserving privacy. We use 3D People Counter which can record only the time and direction of passing people, a person's height, and walking speed, therefore it preserves privacy from the moment of collecting data. To estimate people's in-out data, we propose four methods and they use some of the sensor data above in different combinations. We compared these methods and the height-based method could estimate about 79% of the sensor data as in-out data. Additionally, we also created a system to interpolate in-out data into person-flow data and to visualize it. By using this method, we believe that it can be used for the purposes described in the beginning.

Keywords: Person-flow estimation · Privacy · 3D People Counter

1 Introduction

There are many situations where person-flow data can be used in the real world. For example, in a shopping mall, shop owners can measure how long people stay in a place and which corridors are frequently visited to improve their sales. More recently, person-flow data has also been used to counter the coronavirus outbreaks by analyzing the number of people in public places.

To obtain person-flow data, we can use various methods described below. Global Positioning System (GPS) is the most well-known method to obtain a personal location and is used by some smartphone applications. On the other hand, mobile network operators collect their user's device location. Also, Wi-Fi packets or Bluetooth packets are useful to track a person's move. However, the operating system (OS) of modern smartphones has made it more difficult to get personal location data. For example, Android OS makes users possible to select when the application can use their location data [2]. Furthermore,

© ICST Institute for Computer Sciences, Social Informatics and Telecommunications Engineering 2021
Published by Springer Nature Switzerland AG 2021. All Rights Reserved
S. Paiva et al. (Eds.): SmartCity360° 2020, LNICST 372, pp. 615–634, 2021.
https://doi.org/10.1007/978-3-030-76063-2_41

several smartphones have a function to randomly set the MAC addresses when connecting to a Wi-Fi access point in the OS, therefore we cannot track people who have such a smartphone.

Moreover, many countries around the world are rethinking the protection of privacy. Particularly, in the European Union (EU), EU General Data Protection Regulation (GDPR) has been set in place [14]. The GDPR requires organizations that want to use personal location data for their services to treat them in the same way as personal information. However, in general, person-flow estimation requires the acquisition of personal location data from people's smartphones, therefore it is a problem to ensure their anonymity.

Based on this situation, in this study, we propose a person-flow estimation technique with preserving privacy by multiple 3D People Counters. Similar sensors and cameras have already become popular, but the sensor only collects people passing data and does not save stereo images captured. Therefore, unlike other techniques, this method can preserve privacy from the time collecting data. Using this sensor, we aim to estimate person-flow in any area where all gates have a sensor. If the area looks like a long rectangle and has only two gates at both short sides of the rectangle, we can estimate person-flow easily. However, many areas in the real world look like various shapes and have multiple gates in general, therefore it is difficult to estimate person-flow in such an area.

To solve this, we propose the three-step person-flow estimation method including in-out estimation, interpolation, and visualization. Firstly, we estimate the people's in-out data by analyzing the sensor data including passing time, person's height, and duration to go through the sensing area in four ways. The first in-out estimation method uses only passing time. The next method uses passing time and height. In this method, we can convert about 79% of the passing data to person-flow data and it seems to be the best in this paper. The third replaces people's height data with walking speed data, and the last uses all data, and we tried two strategies. After in-out estimation, we interpolate the in-out data into person-flow data to visualize realistically. We used the customized RVO2 Library [3] to interpolate person-flow data more realistic in that people in the area do not collide with each other and hit obstacles. Finally, we visualize the person-flow data using Harmoware-VIS and evaluate the effectiveness of the interpolation. As a result, we could estimate person-flow and visualize it in reality.

The contributions of the paper are followings:

- We defined the problem of how we estimate person-flow with preserving privacy.
- We proposed and implemented the method which has three steps including in-out estimation, interpolation, and visualization to solve the problem.
- We evaluated and confirmed the effect of the proposed method.

2   Related Work

2.1   Work About Location Acquisition Techniques and Person-Flow Estimation Methods

Location acquisition techniques and person-flow estimation methods have already been widely studied and some of them are put to practical use. Here we introduce some of them and discuss the pros and cons of them.

GPS. Generally, GPS estimates a personal location by calculating the propagation time of radio waves from three satellites or more. Thanks to the signal from satellites, its estimation error is a few meters outdoors anywhere on earth. However, we can rarely use GPS in rebar buildings or undergrounds because radio waves from satellites are greatly attenuated. Furthermore, GPS uses long length radio waves and requires 4 satellite signals to estimate location accurately. Therefore, to get continuous location data it consumes big electric power, and it results in a decrease of uptime of mobile devices.

Mobile Network. We can estimate personal location by the strength of radio waves and the location of a mobile base station to which a mobile device is connected. Related to a person-flow estimation, the method above has been considered to be able to use a survey of traffic volume.

In the study by Ratti et al. [13], the usage data of mobile phones in an urban area was collected by mobile base stations chronologically. Then they estimated person-flow in the city by creating a heatmap of this data. Besides, they mentioned that results could provide a new approach to improve urban systems. In the study by Caceres et al. [7], they utilized a characteristic that a cell phone communicates to a base station when the phone enters or leaves the communication range of the station. Thanks to their method, they demonstrated that traffic data could be collected at a lower cost. In the study by Ng et al. [12], they estimated location data by focusing on the attenuation of a signal of mobile network in Hong Kong.

In general, these methods have a lower cost than others because most of them use existing equipment. However, they use privacy-sensitive data such as call histories possessed by a mobile network operator after anonymization. Therefore, if these data are not handled properly, it can be a big problem in terms of privacy protection.

Wi-Fi Packet Sensors. In the study of Fukazaki et al. [8,9], they conducted person-flow estimation by anonymized MAC address in prove requests from smartphones collected by multiple Wi-Fi packet sensors. However, because several people may have two or more smartphones, they compared people count from packet sensors with that from more reliable sensors to estimate more accurate person-flow only by packet sensors. In the study of Kawaguchi et al. [11], they also compared people count from packet sensors with that from cameras and examined a ratio of randomized MAC addresses to all MAC addresses collected by packet sensors individually. They concluded that these ratios seem to depend on the location of a sensor and will not change over time. Therefore, we can estimate person-flow only by packet sensors statically by examining environments of the location of a sensor in advance. In the study of Xu et al. [21] and Fukazaki et al. [9], they utilized the Received Signal Strength Indication (RSSI) value to estimate a more accurate location.

Bluetooth. There are mainly two estimation methods using Bluetooth. The First is collecting an inquiry response packet from a smartphone to which a Bluetooth device sends a connection inquiry. In the study of Schauer et al. [15], they used the method above but the estimation accuracy of this method was lower than that of the Wi-Fi method because recent smartphones do not replay to a connection inquiry by default and it causes the decrease in detectable smartphones by Bluetooth.

The Second is collecting packets from a Bluetooth Low Energy (BLE) tag by multiple BLE scanner. In the study of Urano et al. [18,19], they distributed BLE tags to event participants and tested the method. Furthermore, they proposed a tandem scanner to avoid packet loss and introduced three-point positioning and particle filter to improve estimation accuracy.

Person-Flow Camera. There are many studies to improve obtaining person-flow using cameras. In the study by Bartolini et al. [6], they created robust people counting method to be able to be applied in buses. Their system can deal with vibrations, lighting fluctuations, and environmental variations. Also, Terada et al. [17] introduced a stereo camera to realize people counting in a crowd where a conventional method cannot deal with. In the study by Abuarafah et al. [5], they developed the crowd density estimation system using a thermal camera. On the other hand, Satyam et al. [16] created a robust crowd estimation method using texture features. Also, Ibrahim et al. [10] reviewed some optical flow techniques for motion estimation of crowd flow.

2.2   The Position of This Study in Comparison with Related Work

Figure 1 shows the relation between our work and related works. We can track person-flow in wide areas by GPS and Mobile Network at a lower cost. However, the use of GPS is restricted by a modern smartphone OS. Also, location data from Mobile Networks contains a user's information like a phone number. Therefore, there is great concern about privacy when we use them for person-flow estimation. On the other hand, Wi-Fi and Bluetooth can collect only a user device's MAC address, therefore there is less concern about privacy. However, a tracking area is generally narrower than that by GPS or Mobile Network. Moreover, cameras may be able to track the narrowest area than other methods and the cost of equipment will be high if we install many cameras in order to cover a wide area.

Fig. 1. Compared to related works.

In order to realize the person-flow estimation method which can be applied to a wide area and consider privacy, we introduce multiple 3D People Counters. This sensor only obtains photos of the head of people, therefore the sensitiveness of the privacy is considered to be lower than other methods. Also, the cost to use this method in a wide area seems to be better than a method that uses cameras installed in an entire area. The person-flow is estimated by examining the correlations of the sensor data, including a person's height which can be obtained by a stereo camera but not by a single-lens camera. It is expected that our works can be applied to commercial marketing in stores and disaster countermeasures.

3   Person-Flow Estimation in Open Space

3.1   Target Environment

In this paper, we aim to estimate person-flow in an area like Fig. 2. A target area has multiple gates and thousands of people enter and leave the area from them every day. For example, a station, an underground mall, an airport terminal, and a shopping mall are one of them. If we can obtain person-flow data in such an area, there are many merits for us. For example, in a shopping mall, shop owners can measure how long people stay in a place and which corridors are frequently visited. These customer behavior data are useful to improve their sales. Also, there is much public transportation including trains, buses, and taxis at a station or an airport terminal, therefore we can estimate the time-series trend of usage of public transportation. More recently, person-flow data has also been used to counter the coronavirus outbreaks by analyzing the number of people in public places such as stations. Therefore, obtaining person-flow data in target areas is a significant problem.

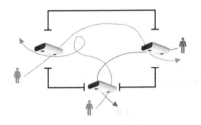

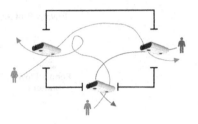

Fig. 2. The example of an estimation target area.

Fig. 3. 3D People Counter (VC-3D by Vitracom GmbH.)

3.2 Problem Definition

To estimate person-flow in an area like Sect. 3.1, we install 3D People Counters shown in Fig. 3 and Table 1 at ceilings of every gates. Each sensor can collect a passing time, direction, person's height, and duration to go through the area. However, sensor data is only passing data and does not represent a person-flow in the area. Therefore, we estimate people's in-out data by analyzing the correlations of some of the sensor data, including time, height, and duration. After estimation, we interpolate the in-out data into person-flow data in order to obtain what route do people walk in the area. Finally, we visualize the person-flow data to be able to be easily understood by a human and utilize for the aim described at the beginning of the introduction.

3.3 Procedure of Person-Flow Estimation

In this study, we estimate person-flow by following steps shown in Fig. 4. First of all, 3D People Counters capture stereo images and analyze them to output sensor data. Sensor data consist of individual people data including when to pass the gate, how long to pass through the sensing area, the direction to which they passed, and their height. The captured images are discarded and not included in the sensor data. After that, we store the sensor data to our server in real-time and retrieve them for person-flow estimation lately.

Before estimation, we calibrate sensor data to eliminate the error derived from the condition of the installed place of a sensor and the characteristic of an individual stereo camera. To do this, we first shift all sensor's height data so

Table 1. The specification of 3D People Counter.

Installation height	2.4 to 6.0 m
Monitoring area	Up to 10.0 × 7.0 m
Counting line	Up to 5 lines
Power Supply	Power over Ethernet (PoE)

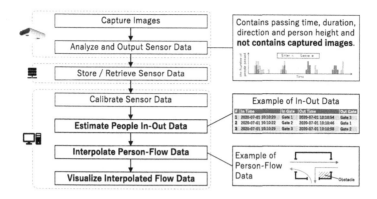

Fig. 4. Procedure of person-flow estimation in this study.

that the average is the same value (in this paper, this value is 160.) Next, we align them so that the variance is the same (15 in this paper.)

Using calibrated data, we can estimate person-flow by our proposed method described in Sect. 4. To begin with, we estimate people in-out data from sensor data by four methods in Sect. 4.1. This procedure can also be conducted for non-calibrated real-time sensor data and results can be obtained with about 2–5 min delay (depends on the size of the area.) However, if we simply visualize the in-out data so that people walk in linear from an entrance to an exit, several of them may collide with each other or hit an obstacle. To solve this problem, we interpolate the in-out data into person-flow data so that each person in the area do not collide with each other and not hit an obstacle. Finally, we visualize the person-flow data.

4 Details of Proposed Method

4.1 In-Out Estimation

In our study, we propose mainly four methods for estimating in-out data in order to compare the conversion rate between sensor data and in-out data and the reliability of in-out data. Each method uses different data set from sensor data and their calculation cost are different from each other, therefore we should select the most cost-effective method among them when using them in a new area where we want to estimate person-flow. In the following sections, these methods will be explained respectively and the area like Fig. 2 is the estimation target.

Method A: Using Passing Time and Direction Data. In this method, we estimate in-out data by comparing the temporal changes in the number of people passing by each sensor. For example, in Fig. 5, the sensor data shows that 10 people entered the area from the Sensor 1 gate around 10:10:00, 4 people left from Sensor 2 around 10:10:30, and 6 people left from Sensor 3 around 10:10:45. In addition, nobody enters or leaves the area between 10:10:00 and 10:10:50. Therefore, we estimate that 4 people move from the Sensor 1 gate to Sensor 2 in about 30 s and 6 people move from Sensor 2 to Sensor 3 in about 45 s.

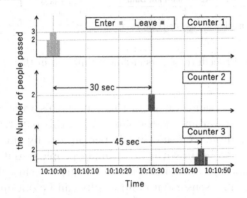

Fig. 5. The sample sensor data used in the method using passing time and direction data.

Method B: Using Passing Time, Direction and Person Height Data. In this method the each person's in-out data is estimated using the height of the passing person as a key. First of all, we roughly calculate the required time to move from one sensor gate to another in all combinations. In the calculation, we use the result from the previous section's method or the division of distances between gates and average human walking speed. Next, we determine the following time duration parameters for all sensor combinations. These parameters are used to eliminate the wrong flow which is too fast or slow for people to walk, thus we have not to determine them strictly.

- $d_{min(a \to b)}$ The minimum required time to move from Sensor a to Sensor b
- $d_{ave(a \to b)}$ The average required time to move from Sensor a to Sensor b
- $d_{max(a \to b)}$ The maximum required time to move from Sensor a to Sensor b.

In addition, we introduce a fourth parameter h_d which represents the range that allows for height error. This is because although we calibrated height data, there are remaining errors that can never be eliminated. In our experience, this error is about 2–4 cm between entrance and leaving, therefore we use $h_d = 5$ [cm] in this paper. (For the convenience of explanation, the error with h_d [cm] or more is considered to be a different person.)

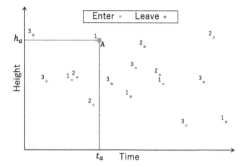

Fig. 6. The graph showing time, height, direction of passing people. (Color figure online)

Finally, we define the Flow Reality Matrix (FRM) as the fifth parameter. The FRM is a matrix that defines how likely person-flow is to occur between each sensor. The value of each element of the FRM is defined as $fr_{a,b}$: the reality of occurrence of person-flow from the gate of sensor a to b. Each $fr_{a,b}$ is a value between 0 and 1 and the higher $fr_{a,b}$ is, the more likely it is to occur person-flow from sensor a to b. This matrix is defined from information known in advance about the target area in order to avoid estimation errors. For example, in a public place such as a station terminal, we define a smaller $fr_{a,a}$ value (same sensor) for all sensors because it is unlikely that people will enter and exit the same gate. We also reduce $fr_{a,b}$ for other gates that are eventually connected to the same destination.

Given the five parameters above, the estimation is conducted by the following steps.

1. Shown in Fig. 6, we consider a graph of the time axis and height axis, and each point is classified by sensor No. and the color that represents entry or exit. For example the Point A surrounded with a blue circle represents that a person whose height is h_a entered the target area from the Sensor 1 gate at the time of t_a.

2. For all points that represent entry to the area in Fig. 6 (define as $P_1 \ldots P_m$ in chronological order), calculate the probability of the same person as all points that represent leaving from the area (define as $Q_1 \ldots Q_n$ in chronological order.) At this time, the score for the flow from P_i to Q_j is defined as $s_{i,j}$, and the passing time, height and sensor No. for P_i is defined as t_{P_i}, h_{P_i} and c_{P_i} respectively. (Therefore, $t_{P_1} \leq t_{P_2} \leq \ldots \leq t_{P_m}$ and $t_{Q_1} \leq t_{Q_2} \leq \ldots \leq t_{Q_n}$.) The calculation of $s_{i,j}$ is performed like below.

   (a) Define the degree of height similarity between P_i and Q_j as $h_{i,j}$ and calculate $h_{i,j}$ as below.

$$h_{i,j} = 1 - \left(\frac{min(|h_{P_i} - h_{Q_j}|, h_d)}{h_d} \right)^2 \tag{1}$$

   Note: Define the minimum value between a and b as $min(a, b)$.

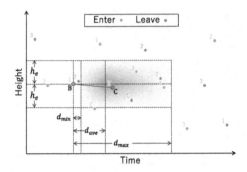

Fig. 7. The search of combinations of a entering data and a leaving data. (Color figure online)

(b) For P_i and Q_j, let $t_{i,j}$ be the degree of probability that the flow from the Sensor c_{P_i} gate and Sensor c_{Q_j} can occur on the time basis. In addition, define following variables: $d_{i,j} = t_{P_i} - t_{Q_j}, d_{min} = d_{min(c_{P_i} \to c_{Q_j})}, d_{ave} = d_{ave(c_{P_i} \to c_{Q_j})}, d_{max} = d_{max(c_{P_i} \to c_{Q_j})}$ and calculate $t_{i,j}$ like below

$$
t_{i,j} = \begin{cases} 1 - \left(\dfrac{d_{ave} - d_{i,j}}{d_{ave} - d_{min}}\right)^2 & (d_{min} \le d_{i,j} \le d_{ave}) \\[2mm] 1 - \left(\dfrac{d_{ave} - d_{i,j}}{d_{ave} - d_{max}}\right)^2 & (d_{ave} \le d_{i,j} \le d_{max}) \\[2mm] 0 & (otherwise) \end{cases} \tag{2}
$$

(c) Calculate $s_{i,j}$ as follows.

$$
s_{i,j} = h_{i,j} t_{i,j} fr_{c_{P_i}, c_{Q_j}} \tag{3}
$$

For example the color density in Fig. 7 is proportional to the score for Point B.

3. Using the score $s_{1,1}, \ldots, s_{1,n}, s_{2,1}, \ldots, s_{m,n}$ obtained above, explore combinations of P_i and Q_j from the perspective that each of them is considered to be right as a one person's entrance and leaving. First of all, we start exploration with $i = 1$ and do the following:
   - If P_i is already combined with any of Q_j, do nothing.
   - If $s_{i,j}$ is bigger than all of $s_{i,1}, s_{i,2}, \ldots, s_{i,j-1}, s_{1,j}, s_{2,j}, \ldots, s_{i-1,j}$, consider P_i and Q_j is the right combination and set $s_{i,1}, s_{i,2}, \ldots, s_{i,j-1}$, $s_{1,j}, s_{2,j}, \ldots, s_{i-1,j} = 0$.
   - If $s_{i,j}$ is smaller than any of above, do nothing.

After that, repeat above with $i = 2$ and continue until $i = m$. Once finished, go back to $i = 1$ and repeat the whole procedure until a new combination will not be found in a procedure. In short first priority is given to early entry, and the second priority is given to the height similarity and duration probability. For example, Point B in Fig. 7 should be combined with Point C.

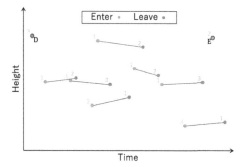

Fig. 8. The estimation result from Fig. 6.

After exploration, the entry and leaving points in Fig. 6 are combined like Fig. 8. Using Fig. 8, we can estimate the number of people who have moved to a specific entrance and exit and the time required to move between gates.

Method C: Using Passing Time, Direction and Walking Speed Data. In this method we replace person height in Sect. 4.1 with walking speed. Similarly define the walking speed of P_i as v_{P_i}, the degree of walking speed similarity between P_i and Q_j as $v_{i,j}$ and the range that allows for walking speed error as v_d. After that, calculate $v_{i,j}$ as following.

$$v_{i,j} = 1 - \left(\frac{min(|v_{P_i} - v_{Q_j}|, v_d)}{v_d} \right)^2 \tag{4}$$

Also $s_{i,j}$ is calculated like Formula 3.

$$s_{i,j} = v_{i,j} t_{i,j} f r_{c_{P_i}, c_{Q_j}} \tag{5}$$

Method D: Using Passing Time, Direction, Person Height and Walking Speed Data. In this method, we introduce two strategies: AND strategy and OR strategy. In AND strategy (hereinafter called "method D-1"), we use both height and walking speed as a condition to distinguish one person from another. Therefore, we calculate $s_{i,j}$ like below.

$$s_{i,j} = h_{i,j} v_{i,j} t_{i,j} f r_{c_{P_i}, c_{Q_j}} \tag{6}$$

On the other hand, in OR strategy (hereinafter called "method D-2"), we first use the method in Sect. 4.1 and use the method in Sect. 4.1 with remaining data. In other words, we use height data mainly and use walking speed data as backup.

4.2 Interpolation of People In-Out Data

After an in-out estimation, we can see when and how many people move between specific gates. However, we cannot determine what route did they walk in the area from in-out data. If we think that they walk linear in the area, several people may collide with each other and pass through an obstacle.

To solve this, we added the interpolation step before visualization and introduced a customized RVO2 Library [3] for interpolation. RVO2 Library is an open-source implementation of Optimal Reciprocal Collision Avoidance (ORCA) [20] formulation. ORCA guarantees that agents in the simulation (i.e. people) have collision-free navigation. In addition, we created the new feature to add or remove agents while the simulation is running by RVO2. This feature represents the people's entrance and exit in the target area.

4.3   Visualization

In this study, we developed the visualization system using Harmoware-VIS [1] in order to easily understand the estimated person-flow by a human. Harmoware-VIS is the Spatio-Temporal Visualization Library using Deck.GL being developed by our Laboratory. To make use of Harmoware-VIS, we also created Synerex [4] provider that import person-flow data created in Sect. 4.2 and send it to Harmoware-VIS. In addition, we customized the size of moving agents (i.e. people in the area) to be suitable for people.

5   Experiment

In this experiment, we compared four proposed in-out estimation methods to find which method is the best for the sensor data. The target area in this experiment is Access Plaza in Chubu Centrair International Airport shown in Fig. 9. This plaza is connected to the train station, bus stops, taxi zone, the hotel, two airline terminals, and the parking and has an area of about 120 m by 70 m. We use one hour of data clipped from one day of calibrated sensor data. Also, we compared the visualization results between in-out data and interpolated person-flow data in order to validate the effectiveness of interpolation.

5.1   In-Out Estimation in Open Space

In this experiment, we installed 20 people sensors in the target area and grouped them into 7 groups by directions.

The parameter for this experiment is described below. We set $d_{min(a \to b)}$, $d_{ave(a \to b)}$, $d_{max(a \to b)}$ using the distance between Sensor a to Sensor b (define as $dist_{a,b}$) as follows:

- $d_{min(a \to b)} = dist_{a,b}/5.5$ (five times faster than below.)
- $d_{ave(a \to b)} = dist_{a,b}/1.1$ (slightly slower than the average walking speed because there are obstacles in the real space.)
- $d_{max(a \to b)} = dist_{a,b}/0.55$ (two times slower than above.)

We also set $h_d = 5$, $v_d = 0.1$ and $fr_{a,b} = 1$ for all sensor pairs at first. (To confirm the effectiveness of fr, we change this parameter later and compare the estimation results.)

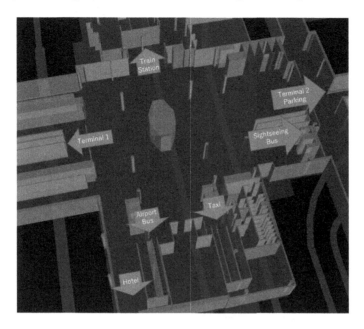

Fig. 9. Access Plaza in Chubu Centrair International Airport.

Method A: Using Passing Time and Direction Data. Figure 10 shows the sensor data used in this method. In the figure, the exit count surrounded by red squares in Group 1 and 2 emerged after the entry count surrounded by red squares in Group 7 emerged. In addition, the exit count ratio between Group 1 and 2 is about 9:1. Therefore, we can estimate that 90% of people entered from Group 7 moved to Group 1 in about 30 s and 10% of them moved to Group 2 in about 60 s.

However, the data not surrounded by red squares have few changes in people count and it causes difficulty in estimation. For example, the data between :10 and :15 are mostly counted in Group 1 and 2, therefore we can estimate people entered from Group 2 moved to Group 1 but a duration to move between them can hardly be estimated. In addition, the data in Group 3–6 have too few people count for estimation.

Method B: Using Passing Time, Direction and Person Height Data. Figure 11 shows the estimation result obtained from this method. In contrast to the previous result, we can estimate in-out data from the sensor data between :10 and :15. Furthermore, several data in Group 3–6 can also be converted to in-out data. In this method, we could convert about 78.6% of the sensor data to the estimated in-out data. The remaining sensor data seem to be derived from a sensor error or a person's behavior who stay in the area longer than we expected.

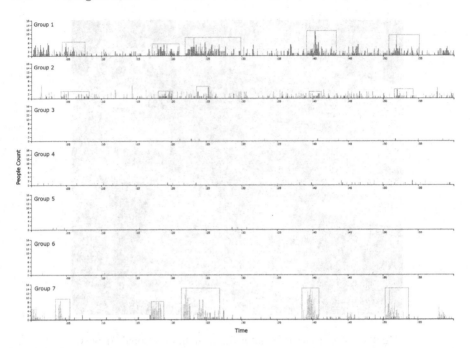

Fig. 10. The sensor data and estimation result by the method A. (Color figure online)

Method C: Using Passing Time, Direction and Walking Speed Data.
Figure 12 shows the estimation result obtained from this method. We expected
that we can obtain similar results and conversion rates as the previous method
because we use the same procedure with different sensor data. However, we could
convert only 57.1% of the sensor data to the flow. This is because much data
seem to be an error in the passing duration data. For example, several people
walked faster than 10 m/s according to several sensor's data although common
people cannot walk (run) at the speed. In addition, several person's walking
speed was not be able to obtain from sensor data.

**Method D: Using Passing Time, Direction, Person Height and Walk-
ing Speed Data.** In Figs. 13 and 14, a radius of each entrance/leaving point
represents the walking speed for the person.

AND Strategy (Method D-1). Figure 13 shows the estimation result obtained
from this strategy. This strategy is the most strict one among other proposed
methods, therefore we could only convert about 30.1% of the data. However, it
seemed that 30% of people are more likely to move as estimated in-out data in
real.

OR Strategy (Method D-2). Figure 14 shows the estimation result obtained from
this strategy. The conversion rate for this strategy is about 82.6%, therefore

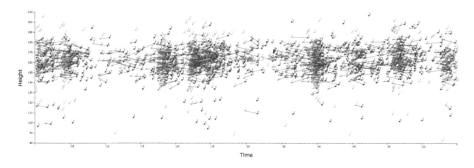

Fig. 11. The estimation result by the method B.

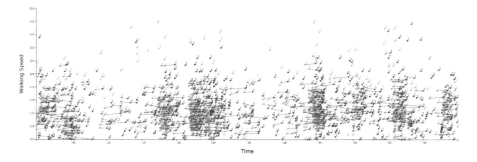

Fig. 12. The estimation result by the method C.

about 4% of the estimated in-out data is obtained from the previous method (using walking speed.) However, a height error for that flow is sometimes too big to consider the flow is occurred by the same person. Therefore, the estimation result of this strategy is a lack of reliability.

Introduction of Flow Reality Matrix. As Described in Sect. 4.1, we introduced Flow Reality Matrix to reduce estimation miss. To confirm its effectiveness, here we set Flow Reality Matrix as follows:

- $fr_{a,a} = 0.25$ for all sensors (a flow between a same sensor)
- $fr_{a,b} = 0.5$ for a sensor pair in a same group (a flow between a same direction)
- $fr_{a,b} = 1$ for others.

Using the parameter above, we conducted the estimation method using passing time, direction, and person height data. The estimation result of this is shown in Fig. 15 and the comparison of In-Out table is shown in Tables 2 and 3. It is said that several people who considered to enter and leave from the same Group if $fr_{a,b} = 1$ for all sensors were estimated to move between different Groups after the Flow Reality Matrix was changed. Therefore, the effectiveness of the Flow Reality Matrix is somewhat confirmed but we should check the validity of this by comparing it with the ground truth in-out data.

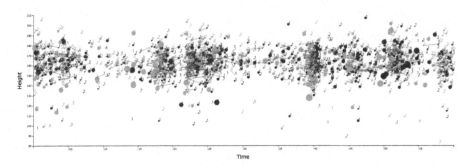

Fig. 13. The estimation result by the method D-1.

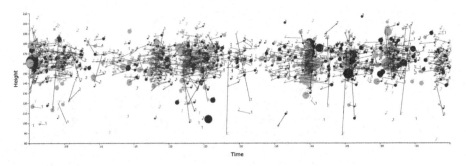

Fig. 14. The estimation result by the method D-2. (Blue lines in this figure represent person-flow estimated by walking speed.) (Color figure online)

5.2   Interpolation and Visualization

We examined the effectiveness of interpolation by visualizing the interpolated result by Harmoware-VIS. Figure 16 shows frames clipped from the video of our previous visualization. The video frames start at the upper left and are arranged to the right, then go to the bottom left and end at the bottom right. Each green point represents people and the blue square is an obstacle. In this figure, one person is hit by the obstacle and several people hit each other. However, we cannot go through obstacles and not frequently hit other people in the real world.

In contrast to the above, Fig. 17 shows frames of the visualization using interpolated data. People in this figure do not collide with obstacles and other people, therefore it is said that this visualization is more realistic than the previous one.

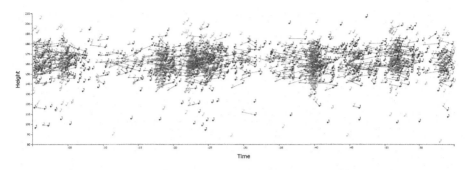

Fig. 15. The estimation result by the method using passing time, direction and person height with optimized Flow Reality Matrix.

Table 2. The In-Out table from Fig. 11.

In Out	Group 1	Group 2	Group 3	Group 4	Group 5	Group 6	Group 7
Group 1	20	34	1	1	2		11
Group 2	257	8	2	1	1		20
Group 3	1	2					
Group 4	16	5					1
Group 5	2	1					
Group 6	2	1					
Group 7	339	74	4	14	3		14

Table 3. The In-Out table from Fig. 15.

In Out	Group 1	Group 2	Group 3	Group 4	Group 5	Group 6	Group 7
Group 1	17	37	1	1	2		11
Group 2	259	6	2	1	1		20
Group 3	1	2					
Group 4	16	5					1
Group 5	2	1					
Group 6	2	1					
Group 7	341	74	4	14	3		11

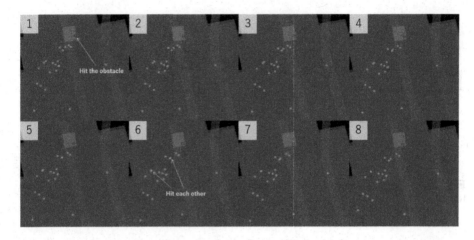

Fig. 16. The visualization result without interpolation by RVO2. (Color figure online)

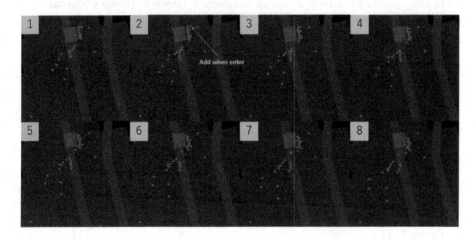

Fig. 17. The visualization result with interpolation by RVO2.

6   Conclusion

In this paper, we have proposed a method of person-flow estimation using multiple 3D People Counters. We have proposed four estimation methods to associate one's in-out data. Also, we have provided the interpolation and visualization method for the estimation result.

Using the second in-out estimation method, which uses passing time, direction, and person height data, we could have converted about 79% of the sensor data into people in-out data. Furthermore, Flow Reality Matrix could have reduced the in-out data that seems to be wrong to some extent.

Also, we have customized the RVO2 Library to be able to add or remove agents as time goes by for interpolation. Finally, we have visualized the interpolated person-flow data by Harmoware-VIS.

However, it has been difficult to obtain accurate walking speed data, therefore it has been hardly possible to estimate person-flow accurately. In the future, we would like to examine a method of acquiring person-flow from walking speed.

In addition, we have been unable to evaluate the validity of the results of the person-flow estimation in this study because we were unable to prepare ground truth person-flow data. Also, we could not experiment in a very crowded situation due to COVID-19. In the future, we would like to evaluate the validity of the proposed method by collecting additional data and comparing it with data obtained by other methods such as a spherical camera.

As a future issue, we would like to estimate person-flow in more complicated places that have multiple areas and gates such as a shopping mall and an office. We think it can be done by connecting the results of in-out estimation data for all areas. Furthermore, we have already installed sensors in several contiguous areas and we are going to create the estimation system in such places.

Acknowledgement. This research is supported by the Commissioned Research of National Institute of Information and Communications Technology (NICT) and MIC SCOPE (No. 191506001).

References

1. Harmoware/harmoware-vis: Spatial-temporal visualization library using deck.gl. https://github.com/Harmoware/Harmoware-VIS. Accessed 11 July 2020
2. Request location updates—Android developers. https://developer.android.com/training/location/request-updates. Accessed 30 June 2020
3. Rvo2 library - reciprocal collision avoidance for real-time multi-agent simulation. http://gamma.cs.unc.edu/RVO2/. Accessed 12 July 2020
4. Synerex project. https://github.com/synerex. Accessed 30 June 2020
5. Abuarafah, A.G., Khozium, M.O., AbdRabou, E.: Real-time crowd monitoring using infrared thermal video sequences. J. Am. Sci. **8**(3), 133–140 (2012)
6. Bartolini, F., Cappellini, V., Mecocci, A.: Counting people getting in and out of a bus by real-time image-sequence processing. Image Vis. Comput. **12**(1), 36–41 (1994)
7. Caceres, N., Wideberg, J., Benitez, F.: Deriving origin-destination data from a mobile phone network. IET Intell. Transp. Syst. **1**(1), 15–26 (2007)
8. Fukuzaki, Y., Mochizuki, M., Murao, K., Nishio, N.: A pedestrian flow analysis system using Wi-Fi packet sensors to a real environment. In: Proceedings of the 2014 ACM International Joint Conference on Pervasive and Ubiquitous Computing: Adjunct Publication, pp. 721–730 (2014)
9. Fukuzaki, Y., Mochizuki, M., Murao, K., Nishio, N.: Statistical analysis of actual number of pedestrians for Wi-Fi packet-based pedestrian flow sensing. In: Adjunct Proceedings of the 2015 ACM International Joint Conference on Pervasive and Ubiquitous Computing and Proceedings of the 2015 ACM International Symposium on Wearable Computers, pp. 1519–1526 (2015)

10. Kajo, I., Malik, A.S., Kamel, N.: Motion estimation of crowd flow using optical flow techniques: a review. In: 2015 9th International Conference on Signal Processing and Communication Systems (ICSPCS), pp. 1–9. IEEE (2015)
11. Kawaguchi, N., et al.: Wi-Fi human behavior analysis and BLE tag localization: a case study at an underground shopping mall. In: Proceedings of the 13th International Conference on Mobile and Ubiquitous Systems: Computing, Networking and Services, pp. 151–159 (2016)
12. Ng, J.Y., Chan, S., Kan, K.: Providing location estimation within a metropolitan area based on a mobile phone network, pp. 710–715 (2002). https://doi.org/10.1109/DEXA.2002.1045981
13. Ratti, C., Frenchman, D., Pulselli, R.M., Williams, S.: Mobile landscapes: using location data from cell phones for urban analysis. Environ. Plann. B. Plann. Des. **33**(5), 727–748 (2006)
14. Regulation, G.D.P.: Regulation (EU) 2016/679 of the European parliament and of the council of 27 April 2016 on the protection of natural persons with regard to the processing of personal data and on the free movement of such data, and repealing directive 95/46. Off. J. Eur. Union (OJ) **59**(1–88), 294 (2016)
15. Schauer, L., Werner, M., Marcus, P.: Estimating crowd densities and pedestrian flows using Wi-Fi and bluetooth. In: Proceedings of the 11th International Conference on Mobile and Ubiquitous Systems: Computing, Networking and Services, pp. 171–177 (2014)
16. Srivastava, S., Ng, K.K., Delp, E.J.: Crowd flow estimation using multiple visual features for scenes with changing crowd densities. In: 2011 8th IEEE International Conference on Advanced Video and Signal Based Surveillance (AVSS), pp. 60–65. IEEE (2011)
17. Terada, K., Yoshida, D., Oe, S., Yamaguchi, J.: A counting method of the number of passing people using a stereo camera. In: IECON 1999, Conference Proceedings, 25th Annual Conference of the IEEE Industrial Electronics Society (Cat. No. 99CH37029), vol. 3, pp. 1318–1323. IEEE (1999)
18. Urano, K., Hiroi, K., Kaji, K., Kawaguchi, N.: A location estimation method using BLE tags distributed among participants of a large-scale exhibition. In: Adjunct Proceedings of the 13th International Conference on Mobile and Ubiquitous Systems: Computing Networking and Services, pp. 124–129 (2016)
19. Urano, K., Kaji, K., Hiroi, K., Kawaguchi, N.: A location estimation method using mobile BLE tags with tandem scanners. In: Proceedings of the 2017 ACM International Joint Conference on Pervasive and Ubiquitous Computing and Proceedings of the 2017 ACM International Symposium on Wearable Computers, pp. 577–586 (2017)
20. Van Den Berg, J., Guy, S.J., Lin, M., Manocha, D.: Reciprocal n-body collision avoidance. In: Pradalier, C., Siegwart, R., Hirzinger, G. (eds.) Robotics Research. STAR, vol. 70, pp. 3–19. Springer, Heidelberg (2011). https://doi.org/10.1007/978-3-642-19457-3_1
21. Xu, Z., et al.: Pedestrain monitoring system using Wi-Fi technology and RSSI based localization. Int. J. Wirel. Mob. Netw. **5**, 17–34 (2013)

Quality and Reliability Metrics for IoT Systems: A Consolidated View

Matej Klima[1] , Vaclav Rechtberger[1] , Miroslav Bures[1]([⊠]) ,
Xavier Bellekens[2] , Hanan Hindy[3] , and Bestoun S. Ahmed[1,4]

[1] Department of Computer Science, FEE, Czech Technical University in Prague,
Prague, Czechia
{klimama7,miroslav.bures}@fel.cvut.cz
[2] Department of Electronic and Electrical Engineering, University of Strathclyde,
Glasgow, UK
[3] Division of Cyber Security, Abertay University, Dundee, UK
[4] Department of Mathematics and Computer Science, Karlstad University,
Karlstad, Sweden
http://still.felk.cvut.cz/

Abstract. Quality and reliability metrics play an important role in the evaluation of the state of a system during the development and testing phases, and serve as tools to optimize the testing process or to define the exit or acceptance criteria of the system. This study provides a consolidated view on the available quality and reliability metrics applicable to Internet of Things (IoT) systems, as no comprehensive study has provided such a view specific to these systems. The quality and reliability metrics categorized and discussed in this paper are divided into three categories: metrics assessing the quality of an IoT system or service, metrics for assessing the effectiveness of the testing process, and metrics that can be universally applied in both cases. In the discussion, recommendations of proper usage of discussed metrics in a testing process are then given.

Keywords: Internet of Things · IoT · Quality · Metrics · Testing · Reliability · Verification

1 Introduction

To evaluate the output quality and reliability of a System Under Test (SUT), various characteristics and metrics are commonly used [1,21,22,26]. For example, we can give the ratio of the number of known defects in an SUT to the code lines number, the number of defects occurring in a production run of an SUT, or a ratio of time when a service provided by the SUT is available without being blocked by a defect. Thus, quality and reliability metrics can serve several purposes including, but not limited to: (1) monitoring the quality of a created SUT during the later development and testing phases; (2) evaluating the effectiveness of the testing and debugging process; (3) serving as the exit criteria between test levels

© ICST Institute for Computer Sciences, Social Informatics and Telecommunications Engineering 2021
Published by Springer Nature Switzerland AG 2021. All Rights Reserved
S. Paiva et al. (Eds.): SmartCity360° 2020, LNICST 372, pp. 635–650, 2021.
https://doi.org/10.1007/978-3-030-76063-2_42

and the acceptance criteria at the end of system development; (4) evaluating the reliability of a system in its production run.

Despite the fact that the field of measurements and metrics has been adequately discussed for various aspects of software systems (for instance [8,9,12, 14,17,22,37,38]), no consolidated overview of the reliability and quality metrics focused on an Internet of Things (IoT) system from a high-level perspective has been published to the best of our knowledge.

In the field of IoT quality and reliability metrics, only studies focusing on individual aspects of quality and reliability of IoT systems have been published, which will further be explored in Sect. 2.

IoT systems differ from software systems in a number of aspects, which brings specific quality assurance challenges [2,25,28]. As some examples, we can give (1) larger heterogeneity of used technologies, protocols and devices, creating a significantly higher number of possible configurations of a system to be tested, (2) higher demands on interoperability and flawless integration, (3) current lower level of standardization of communication protocols or (4) various privacy and security issues of the current IoT systems. Because of these differences, we consider it relevant to approach the IoT domain separately to the software domain and analyze the relevant quality and reliability metrics accordingly.

Similar consolidation work on the quality characteristics of IoT systems was recently carried out [10] by the authors and was supplemented by another recent study by White *et al.* Specifically, [40] studied and summarized the available literature focused on quality of services (QoS) in IoT systems. The study primarily focused on quality characteristics and the architectural perspective; however, it does not discuss particular quality metrics.

General quality characteristics differ from quality and reliability metrics by their level of detail and domain applicability.

A *quality metric* provides detailed information expressed by a number and is typically defined by a formula that is based on the quantification of SUT elements, the SUT model (e.g., a number of defects on a line of code), and/or quantified information from the testing and test management process (e.g., a number of found defects).

We understand the *quality characteristic* to be a general property of the SUT that can be used to carry the test planning, test strategy or test reporting; e.g., functional correctness, security, usability, or maintainability [10]. Differently to quality metrics, quality characteristics are usually not expressed by particular formulas that allow for the quantification of a measured property by a concrete number.

This paper is organized as follows. Section 2 analyzes the existing literature related to the quality metrics of both software and IoT systems. Section 3 provides a consolidated view on IoT-related quality and reliability metrics with references to sources originally discussing these metrics. Section 4 discusses the consolidated overview and possible limits of this work. The last section concludes the paper.

2   Related Work

In the field of IoT systems, several studies discussing individual quality metrics have been published. These are analyzed and discussed within this section. However, these studies unequivocally lack the quality and reliability metrics applicable to IoT.

To distinguish the quality of cloud services providers, Zheng *et al.* define a quality model for cloud services CLOUDQUAL [41]. The model consists of six different quality dimensions and metrics: availability, reliability, usability, responsiveness, security, and elasticity. Despite focusing on cloud services, some metrics are broad enough to be adapted to IoT systems.

A study by Li *et al.* proposes availability, together with currency and validity, as quality metrics for measuring the data quality in pervasive environments [27]. We consider the data availability component of this work to be relevant to IoT systems.

Sollie [36] discusses metrics for assessing the security and usability of authentication systems. From these metrics, the *"Rate of User Error"* is relevant to the IoT domain.

In the recent studies by Kim [23] and Kim *et al.* [24], quality models for the evaluation of IoT applications and services are presented. Kim discusses particular definitions of metrics and identifies four criteria: functionality, reliability, efficiency, and portability, for which various metrics are presented [23].

In the field of QoS measurements for IoT systems, certain quality characteristics have been categorized by Singh *et al.* [34]. Three main types of QoS measurements are identified: the QoS of communication, the QoS of things, and the QoS of computing. However, although the authors use the term metrics, the paper actually discusses quality characteristics (formulas defining metrics are not provided in this study). Snigdh *et al.* published a similar categorization for wireless sensor network areas in which more metrics are discussed [35].

A comprehensive literature study of the QoS for IoT systems has been conducted by White *et al.* [40]. This study discusses three aspects of the QoS: (1) layers of the IoT architecture, which are the most frequent subject of QoS research; (2) the quality factors are measured; (3) the types of research conducted in the field. In this study, consolidated high-level quality characteristics can be found. However, no consolidated view on quality metrics with their definitions is provided, as such overview is beyond the scope of the study.

The quality of end devices in IoT systems have also been the subject of some investigation; for example, actuators in [5]. In this study, concrete measurements of quality parameters are presented, and the authors conclude that the main factors impacting perceived quality were *"average delay"* and *"packet loss"* [5]. These factors could also be applied to other IoT components.

One study by Staron *et al.* [37] contains metrics for measuring the quality of the system architecture, such as the number of coupled components, the number of changes in architecture per time unit, or the number of interfaces. However, the *"Design Stability"* description discusses metrics that can also be applied in the IoT environment.

Baggen *et al.* discuss a set of software code metrics impacting maintainability [6], thereby extending the previous list of metrics proposed by Heitlager *et al.* [18]. We consider these metrics to be relevant in different parts of IoT systems. The authors list the volume of the code, its redundancy, the size of its units, complexity, unit interface size, and the extent of component coupling. Although no particular definition of metrics is given in the study, they can be easily defined from these suggestions.

Besides coupling and code complexity, Pantiuchina *et al.* discuss other code quality metrics; cohesion and code readability in particular. Formulas to compute cohesion are also provided in [32]. The lack of code cohesion and coupling indicators is examined by Chaparro *et al.*, and detailed formulas to quantify the properties are provided in their study [11].

Code quality impacts the potential reliability and quality of an IoT system. High-quality decreases the presence of flaws in the system and positively impacts the maintainability and ease of extending the system. However, it is difficult to identify the relations between high-level quality metrics typically based on defects found in a system or the failures of the system and code quality metrics.

Defining quality metrics is generally inspired by related work focusing on more general quality characteristics. As examples of quality characteristics, we can give an overview of Sogeti's test management approach (TMap) methodology, which focuses on software[1] and, following the recent trends, on IoT systems[2] [39].

Regarding the security aspects, the metrics that are utilized for general-purpose networks and apply to IoT networks are extensively discussed by Hindy *et al.* [19]. Specifically focusing on IoT security, Bonilla *et al.* [7] proposed a particular metric for the measurement of the security level of IoT devices that we later include in our overview.

Following the literature review, it is apparent that there is a lack of comprehensive studies focusing on IoT-related quality metrics. Such a study is the subject of this paper.

3   Metrics Overview

In the following section, we provide a consolidated overview of the quality and reliability metrics applicable to IoT systems.

The scope of this study approaches the quality metrics problem from the overall view of an IoT system. Considering this scope as the delimitation, this study does not focus specifically on QoS metrics, as their goal is primarily to evaluate the performance of the network layers of such systems. Thus, the overview provided does not focus on general test coverage criteria and specific code quality metrics. We explain the reasons and provide the literature for these fields in Sect. 4.

---

[1] https://www.tmap.net/wiki/quality-characteristics.

[2] https://www.tmap.net/wiki/quality-characterstics-iot-environment.

3.1 Methodology of This Overview

Seven publisher databases and indexing services were used for the review: IEEE Xplore, ACM Digital Library, Springer Link, Elsevier ScienceDirect, Web of Science, Scopus, and Google Scholar.

The generic search string (adopted in accord with the local specifics of individual databases and indexing services) is:

('Quality Metrics' AND IoT) OR ('Quality Metrics' AND 'Internet of Things') OR ('Quality Measurement' AND IoT) OR ('Quality Measurement' AND 'Internet of Things') OR ('Quality Model' AND IoT) OR ('Quality Model' AND ''Internet of Things')

where apostrophes serve to denote an exact string that must be searched for. No publication time span was set during the search.

The papers found were assessed for their relevance to the discussed topic based on the abstract and a full reading. The process was conducted using "two pairs of eyes" verification, to minimize possible errors during the search phase.

As a consequence of the full-text reading of relevant papers, we conducted a snowball sampling process to acquire other relevant papers discussing the topic. The quality metrics found in the papers were then consolidated.

In this study, we divide the metrics into three categories: (1) metrics relating to the quality of an IoT system, product, or service; (2) metrics relating to the effectiveness of the testing process of an IoT system; and (3) metrics applicable to both previous aspects. Each of these categories is discussed in a separate subsection.

It is important to mention that the same name in the literature can refer to practically different quality metrics. For example, the availability defined by Li *et al.* [27] describes the availability of data in a system; the availability defined by Zheng *et al.* [41] describes the general availability for an IoT service. In such cases, the differences are discussed in the explanation of the metrics.

3.2 Quality Metrics to Evaluate an IoT System or Service

The quality and reliability of an IoT system or service can be measured in different aspects, that can be expressed by particular metrics.

Availability. To measure the availability of a service or an IoT system [41], a metric based on the uptime ratio of the service during a specified time interval can be used:

$$AV = \frac{t_{up}}{t},$$

where t_{up} is the time the service was available, and t is the time interval the availability was measured. The metric values range from 0 to 1, with 1 representing a 100% availability of the service.

A similar metric can be defined for the *availability of data* provided as a part of the service as proposed by Li *et al.* [27], which can be defined as:

$$DAV = 1 - \frac{\sum_{i=1}^{n} max(0, t_i - T^{exp})}{OP},$$

where OP denotes the observation period, n denotes the number of data objects received during OP, t_i is the interval between the ith and the $i + 1$th updates, and T^{exp} is expiration time [27].

Flaws over Time. To measure the system reliability, a ratio of the number of critical flaws found in the system over a period during a review or after system deployment can be used:

$$FVT = \frac{n_{failure}}{n_{total}},$$

where $n_{failure}$ is the total number of failed operations and n_{total} is the total number of operations that have occurred in a time interval [23]. The metric value ranges from 0 to 1 with 0 indicating that there have been no flaws observed in the system during the measured time.

Reliability. Alternatively, we can use an inverse metric expressing the extent to which the system is free from hardware and software defects (or other defects) that can lead to system failures [41]. Thus,

$$R = 1 - FVT.$$

The closer the Reliability value is to 1, the more reliable the system. FVT represents the time-related flaws metric as previously defined.

Functional Correctness. The alternative reliability metric describes an error rate of the system in the sense of functional defects affecting the system processes and the procedures handling the data stored in the system [10]:

$$FC = \frac{n_{failure} - n_{total}}{n_{total}},$$

where $n_{failure}$, and n_{total}, are the number of failed and total operations that have occurred in a time interval.

Mean Time Between Failures. To measure reliability of continuously running services, the mean time between failures (MTBF) [15,41] can be used as follows:

$$MTBF = \frac{\sum_{i=1}^{n} t_i - t_{i-1}}{n}$$

where n is the number of detected failures in a set and t_i is the (date) times of the individual SUT failures.

Rate of User Error. User interaction with a system also plays an important role for the evaluation of its reliability. Thus, we can base a corresponding metric on the extent to which the user encounters errors or is required to perform an action arising from a system error:

$$RUE = \frac{n_{user\_failure} - n_{total}}{n_{total}},$$

where $n_{user\_failure}$ is the number of failed user operations and n_{total} is the total number of user operations that have occurred in a time interval [36].

Responsiveness. To express the extent to which the system respond to the requests during a time interval, the responsiveness function suggested by Zheng et al. [41] can be used:

$$RESP = 1 - \frac{f_{i=1}^n(t_i)}{t_{max}},$$

where t_i is the time between the submission and the completion of ith request, t_{max} denotes the maximal acceptable time to complete a request, and the function f is an abstraction for a function expressing the tendency of the observed data, e.g., the mean or median [41]. A value of $RESP$ closer to 1 means better system responsiveness.

Security. For a high-level expression of the security of an IoT system, metrics based on *Flaws over Time* can be employed:

$$SEC = 1 - FVT_{sec},$$

where FVT_{sec} is the FVT metric capturing the security flaws and defects. This metric ranges from 0 to 1, where 1 implies the highest security level. An alternative option can use the *mean time between failures*. In this case, the definition of $MTBF$ can be maintained; only the failures taken into account are considered security breaches and incidents detected during the run time of the system.

To further analyse the security of an IoT system, Bonilla et al. suggest grouping the security flaws per IoT layer (i.e. perception, network and application) to assist in a deeper understanding [7]. The authors define the security of level i as

$$SEC_i = \left(\sum_{j=1}^{k_i} V_{ij} \cdot T_{ij} \cdot E_{ij}\right) \cdot A_i,$$

where i is the IoT layer, k_i is the number of known vulnerabilities in layer i, for each vulnerability j in layer i, Search Results Web result with site links Common Vulnerability Scoring System (CVSS) base score [29], the weight of the vulnerability class and the vulnerability exploitability factor are represented as V_{ij}, T_{ij}, and E_{ij} respectively. Finally, the authors define A_i is the asset weight for layer i, which is determined based on its number of vulnerabilities [7].

3.3   Metrics to Evaluate Effectiveness of the Testing Process

For the expression and measurement of the performance of the testing process of an IoT system, several metrics can be used. Compared to standard software development, in this area, established metrics can be reused, as discussed specificity of IoT systems does not play a more substantial role here.

Test to Defect Ratio. To measure the quality of the IoT system, a metric based on a number of discovered defects per executed test case can be used:

$$TDR = \frac{n_{defects}}{n_{steps}},$$

where $n_{defects}$ denotes the number of defects discovered in a defined time period (typically the testing phase of a test level) and n_{steps} denote number of test steps in the test cases executed in a given time period. Alternatively, if the test management process does not allow for the tracking of the individual steps of the test cases, number of test cases must be used instead of n_{steps}. The high value of the TDR indicates the high relative density of the defects in an actual version of the examined system.

Test Execution Productivity. To measure the time effectiveness of test execution, a metric for the amount of labor required to execute the test cases can be used [31]:

$$TEP = \frac{TS + TS_{retested}}{E},$$

where TS denotes the number of total executed test steps in a given time period, $TS_{retested}$ denotes the number of additional retested steps in the given period, and E denotes the labor required to conduct these test steps, measured in personnel hours.

Defect Rejection Rate. Due to the poor reporting quality of the found defects, some of them were rejected by the development team, which caused additional overhead in the system development and testing process (such defects must be verified by a tester, reported again with an improved description, and re-analyzed by the development team). On large scale projects, the increase in overhead caused by such sub-optimal processes can be significant. The defect rejection rate is expressed as:

$$DR = \frac{n_d}{n_{rd}} \cdot 100\%$$

where n_{rd} denotes the number of rejected defects, and n_d denotes the number of total reported defects for a given period or module of the system [31]. Alternatively, defect acceptance can be defined when n_{rd} is substituted by the number of defects accepted by the development team to be fixed [31].

Test Scripting Productivity. The effectiveness of the test case creation in a test preparation phase (or during the testing) is expressed as:

$$SP = \frac{n_{test\_steps}}{E},$$

where n_{test_steps} is the number of created test steps, and E denotes the labor required to create them, measured in personnel hours. Alternatively, the number of test cases can be used instead of the number of test steps; however, because the test cases might differ in length and level of detail, the accuracy of such metric might be lower.

Requirement Coverage. To measure the extent to which the system functionality is covered by the test cases, the requirements gathered in the requirement phase should be mapped to those test cases. If such traceability [1] is available, the coverage can be quantified as:

$$RC = \frac{n_{mapped\_rq}}{n_{total\_rq}} \cdot 100\%,$$

where n_{mapped_rq} denotes the requirements that are mapped to any test case and n_{total_rq} denotes the number of total requirements. This metric can serve as the main indicator of basic flaws in the test coverage; a value below 100% generally requires further investigation.

As each requirement can be covered by a set of test cases, more detailed test coverage metrics can be used to obtain more accurate insight into the test coverage. However, such an overview is out of the scope of our study, and we recommend further literature on this topic in Sect. 4.

Defect Discovery vs Defect Fix Rate. To support managerial decisions regarding releasing an IoT system or establishing the transition between individual test levels, the speed at which the new defects can be repaired by the development team can be evaluated as:

$$DD = \frac{dd_{c/h/m}}{dr_{c/h/m}},$$

where $dd_{c/h/m}$ is the number of defects discovered in the last N days that are of critical, high, or medium severity, and $dr_{c/h/m}$ is the number of closed and rejected defects (defects that are considered fixed after proper retesting or rejected by a test manager or the development team) in the last N days that are of critical, high, or medium severity.

A lower DD value indicates a higher quality of the developed system, as well as, a better prospective capacity of the development team to fix the remaining defects. This metric can also be used separately for defects of different severity (critical, high, or medium) or the numbers of defects can be evaluated cumulatively.

Test Execution Rate. To monitor the test progress, the following metric can be used:

$$TER = \frac{n_{tests\_not\_executed}}{n_{tests\_planned}} \cdot 100\%,$$

where $n_{tests\_not\_executed}$ is the number of tests not executed and $n_{tests\_planned}$ is the total number of planned tests. The metric can be used for continuous monitoring of testing progress or for the evaluation of tests that were executed at the end of a test level [31].

Test Case Reuse in Regression Tests. For high-level quantification of the conducted regression tests, metrics expressing the reuse of test cases can be applied:

$$TCR = \frac{n_{tc\_used\_in\_rt}}{n_{tc\_total}} \cdot 100\%,$$

where $n_{tc\_used\_in\_rt}$ denotes the number of test cases used in the regression tests and n_{tc_total} denotes the number of all test cases created during the system creation.

A low value of TCR indicates the inability to reuse previously created test cases in regression testing; hence, a low level of regression tests is probable, which might be sub-optimal from a test management viewpoint.

Defect Re-open Rate. The effectiveness of the removal of defects from a system can be measured as:

$$DRR = \frac{n_{reopened}}{n_{fixed}},$$

which is a ratio of inadequately fixed defects reopened during retesting ($n_{reopened}$) and fixed defects that have been successfully retested (n_{fixed}) [31].

In practical terms, DRR describes the quality of the defect fixes and the quality of the defect reporting, as vague defect reports might lead to weak defect fixes. The high value of DRR indicates the ineffectiveness of the defect fixing process.

Defect Density of Test Case Review. To ensure the quality of created test cases, their review is recommended during the test preparation phase. The review results indicating quality of created test cases can be expressed as:

$$RDD = \frac{n_{rd}}{n_{rtsur}},$$

which is the ratio of total reviewed test case defects or flaws (n_{rd}) to the total of raw test steps under review (t_{rtsur}); the lower the RDD value, the more efficient the test script creation team.

3.4 Metrics Applicable to both Previous Aspects

Some metrics measure both the quality of the IoT products and the test process performance. In this section, we suggest that such metrics are applicable to IoT systems.

Defect Leakage. To express the extent to which the defects are not detected in certain test levels and are discovered in the following test level (or in a production run of a system after its release), the defect leakage can be defined as:

$$DL = \frac{n_{i+1}}{n_i + n_{i+1}} \cdot 100\%,$$

where n_{i+1} is the number of valid defects detected in phase $i + 1$, and n_i is the number of valid defects detected in phase i. The phase $i + 1$ can be considered as the production run of the system after its rollout.

In addition to expressing the actual state of the tested system, the DL also indirectly indicates the effectiveness of the testing team and testing process, along with the quality of the created test cases.

There are alternative names or definitions of this metric in the literature. Nirpal *et al.* refer to this metric as test efficiency [31] and Chen *et al.* provide a similar metric called *Test Effectiveness* [13], defined as:

$$TE = \frac{n_T}{n_{TP} + n_F} \cdot 100\%,$$

where n_T is the number of defects detected during the product cycle, n_{TP} is the number of defects detected during the test phases, and n_F is the number of defects detected in the system in its production run [13].

Effective Defect Density. As not all detected defects have the same significance, a metric using a weighted number of defects can be used for better reporting accuracy; this is defined as:

$$EDD = \frac{n_{wd}}{n_{steps}},$$

where n_{wd} can be computed as the mean of the number of defects weighted by their severity, and n_{steps} is the number of test case steps [31].

For better accuracy, EDD shall not be used for the system as a whole, as different parts of the system can contain a significantly different number of defects. Instead, EDD shall be computed for individual system parts.

Valid Defects. As reported, the defects are exchanged between the testers and the development team, and some of the defects can be rejected by developers during the overall process (which can be expressed by the *Defect Rejection Rate* metric). The goal is to make the defect fixing process more effective and objective for all involved parties; hence, the review of reported defects must be conducted by a dedicated test manager or, in later test levels, a representative of prospective users from a user acceptance testing team. Such reviews can also eliminate the duplication of reported defects. A metric based on a ratio of valid defects can be used to support such a process, defined as:

$$VD = \frac{n_{valid\_defects}}{n_{total\_defects}},$$

where $n_{valid\_defects}$ denotes the number of relevant defects and $n_{total\_defects}$ is the total number of reported defects.

Quality of Code. To evaluate quality of a software part in an IoT system, a metric using the number of defects and the amount of newly added code can be used:

$$QC = \frac{D_{TP} + D_F}{KCSI},$$

where D_{TP} is the number of defects found in the testing phases, D_F is the number of defects found in a production run of the system, and $KCSI$ is the number of new lines of source code or changed code in a development phase, scaled in thousands [13]. Chen *et al.* suggest using $KCSI$ instead of the total number of code lines to emphasize actual quality achieved in a particular development phase [13].

4   Discussion

In this study, we consolidated the available reliability and quality metrics applicable to IoT systems, as no previous attempt had been made for a high-level reliability view in this domain.

However, this list might not be exhaustive for several reasons. Because of the scope selection, we have not covered several specific areas or domains of metrics, which may be considered, even indirectly, relevant to the problem.

Namely, we have not focused on the *QoS* field, as the QoS is measured in the lower levels of an IoT system and this area has already been covered in the literature [30,34,35,40]. However, there are overlaps between the scope definition used in our study and the QoS field; typically, the *Availability* and *Responsiveness* metrics could be influenced by the QoS on the lower levels of an IoT system.

In addition, it is up to debate, if *test coverage* of the created test cases shall be discussed in the context of metrics related to a performance of the testing process. When properly applied, test coverage metrics generally provide a conception of the potential of created test cases to detect some defects. However, as a number of test coverage criteria have been defined for different types of tests and this problem has also been covered in the literature [3,4,16,33], we decided to approach this problem using the *Requirement Coverage* metric as it best fit the high-level viewpoint previously mentioned.

Moreover, another class of metrics that might be potentially relevant when discussing the quality and reliability of an IoT system are metrics related to *Code Quality*. Poor code quality can negatively impact the effectiveness of the testing process and the quality and reliability of the created IoT system. However, to maintain viewpoint consistency and because this topic has been sufficiently discussed in the literature [6,11,18,20,32], we decided not to include specific code quality metrics in the presented overview. The only exception is the high-level metric *Quality of Code* suggested by Chen *et al.* [13], which we considered to fit well with the high-level framework used here.

Another area to be discussed is the application of the presented metrics. In particular, certain concerns can be raised regarding the unsuitable application of some metrics for evaluating the effectiveness of the testing process (see Sect. 3.3). Generally, these metrics can be useful in such measurements; however, when they are applied to team key performance indicators (KPIs), individual performance evaluations, or individual KPIs, or contractual conditions, negative side effects are possible.

When incorrectly applied to monitor the test preparation phase, the *Test Scripting Productivity* metric can lead to a higher amount of brief test cases, which are quickly prepared without the necessary in-depth analysis of the particular situations to be tested. Logically, the potential to detect defects of such test cases might be lower as a consequence. Hence, the use of such metrics should be balanced by test case revisions (that can be supported by *Test Case Review Defect Density* metric) or the parallel application of another metric focusing on the defect detection capacity of created test cases, such as *Test to Defect Ratio*.

Likewise, the overemphasis on *Test Execution Productivity* may have an adverse effect, as the testers focus only on the exact scenario described in a test case and are discouraged from trying more data combinations or alternative situations, which could lead to the discovery of more relevant defects. This metric can be balanced, for example, by a total number of found relevant defects.

Finally, a misplaced emphasis on the *Defect Rejection Rate* may discourage testers from reporting defects, the relevance of which may be unclear. Thus, they may report only the defects in which the actual SUT functionality explicitly contradicts a scenario given in a test case, and valuable information about other potential defects might be systematically lost during the testing process. This metric can be balanced when used together with the total number of reported defects or a metric capturing the relevance of the found defects (*Valid Defects*, as mentioned in Sect. 3.4).

5 Conclusion

In this paper, we analyzed the contemporary literature dedicated to the quality measurements and metrics for IoT systems and consolidated applicable metrics to a unified view. To our knowledge, such a view has not yet been proposed for IoT systems.

In this unified view, we have taken a high-level perspective on the functionality, reliability, and related quality aspects of IoT systems. To maintain consistency with this overview, the QoS metrics and low-level code metrics were deliberately not examined here. These specific metrics are detailed in the existing literature, which we provided in Sect. 4.

We divided the consolidated metrics into three categories: metrics for measuring system reliability and quality, metrics for evaluating the testing processes of IoT systems, and metrics that can be applied for both purposes.

The list of metrics provided here might not be exhaustive, as a wide variety of current IoT systems also imply their domain specificity, and we deliberately did not address specific lower-level fields such as QoS, test coverage, and code quality. However, we believe that we have covered the majority of the important high-level quality metrics of IoT systems, and the provided overview will be useful for both researchers and testing practitioners in the field.

Acknowledgements. This research is conducted as a part of the project TACR TH02010296 Quality Assurance System for the Internet of Things Technology. The authors acknowledge the support of the OP VVV funded project CZ.02.1.01/0.0/0.0/16_019/0000765 "Research Center for Informatics". Bestoun S. Ahmed has been supported by the Knowledge Foundation of Sweden (KKS) through the Synergi Project AIDA - A Holistic AI-driven Networking and Processing Framework for Industrial IoT (Rek:20200067).

References

1. van der Aalst, L., Roodenrijs, E., Vink, J., Baarda, R.: TMap NEXT: business driven test management. Uitgeverij kleine Uil (2013)
2. Ahmed, B.S., Bures, M., Frajtak, K., Cerny, T.: Aspects of quality in Internet of Things (IoT) solutions: a systematic mapping study. IEEE Access **7**, 13758–13780 (2019)
3. Ammann, P., Offutt, J.: Introduction to Software Testing. Cambridge University Press, Cambridge (2016)
4. Ammann, P., Offutt, J., Xu, W.: Coverage criteria for state based specifications. In: Hierons, R.M., Bowen, J.P., Harman, M. (eds.) Formal Methods and Testing. LNCS, vol. 4949, pp. 118–156. Springer, Heidelberg (2008). https://doi.org/10.1007/978-3-540-78917-8_4
5. Aráuz, J., Fynn-Cudjoe, T.: Actuator quality in the Internet of Things. In: 2013 IEEE International Workshop of Internet-of-Things Networking and Control (IoT-NC), pp. 34–42 (2013)
6. Baggen, R., Correia, J.P., Schill, K., Visser, J.: Standardized code quality benchmarking for improving software maintainability. Softw. Qual. J. **20**(2), 287–307 (2012)
7. Bonilla, R.I., Crow, J.J., Basantes, L.S., Cruz, L.G.: A metric for measuring IoT devices security levels. In: 2017 IEEE 15th International Conference on Dependable, Autonomic and Secure Computing, 15th International Conference on Pervasive Intelligence and Computing, 3rd International Conference on Big Data Intelligence and Computing and Cyber Science and Technology Congress (DASC/PiCom/DataCom/CyberSciTech), pp. 704–709 (2017)
8. Bures, M.: Framework for assessment of web application automated testability. In: Proceedings of the 2015 Conference on Research in Adaptive and Convergent Systems, pp. 512–514 (2015)

9. Bures, M.: Metrics for automated testability of web applications. In: Proceedings of the 16th International Conference on Computer Systems and Technologies, pp. 83–89 (2015)

10. Bures, M., Bellekens, X., Frajtak, K., Ahmed, B.S.: A comprehensive view on quality characteristics of the IoT solutions. In: José, R., Van Laerhoven, K., Rodrigues, H. (eds.) Urb-IoT 2018. EICC, pp. 59–69. Springer, Cham (2020). https://doi.org/10.1007/978-3-030-28925-6_6

11. Chaparro, O., Bavota, G., Marcus, A., Di Penta, M.: On the impact of refactoring operations on code quality metrics. In: 2014 IEEE International Conference on Software Maintenance and Evolution, pp. 456–460. IEEE (2014)

12. Chawla, M.K., Chhabra, I.: A quantitative framework for integrated software quality measurement in multi-versions systems. In: 2016 International Conference on Internet of Things and Applications (IOTA), pp. 310–315. IEEE (2016)

13. Chen, Y., Probert, R.L., Robeson, K.: Effective test metrics for test strategy evolution. In: Proceedings of the 2004 Conference of the Centre for Advanced Studies on Collaborative Research, pp. 111–123 (2004)

14. Chidamber, S.R., Kemerer, C.F.: A metrics suite for object oriented design. IEEE Trans. Softw. Eng. **20**(6), 476–493 (1994)

15. Conte, S.D., Dunsmore, H.E., Shen, Y.: Software Engineering Metrics and Models. Benjamin-Cummings Publishing Co., Inc., San Francisco (1986)

16. Dias Neto, A.C., Subramanyan, R., Vieira, M., Travassos, G.H.: A survey on model-based testing approaches: a systematic review. In: Proceedings of the 1st ACM International Workshop on Empirical Assessment of Software Engineering Languages and Technologies: Held in Conjunction with the 22nd IEEE/ACM International Conference on Automated Software Engineering (ASE), pp. 31–36 (2007)

17. Dromey, R.G.: A model for software product quality. IEEE Trans. Softw. Eng. **21**(2), 146–162 (1995)

18. Heitlager, I., Kuipers, T., Visser, J.: A practical model for measuring maintainability. In: 6th International Conference on the Quality of Information and Communications Technology (QUATIC 2007), pp. 30–39. IEEE (2007)

19. Hindy, H., et al.: A taxonomy of network threats and the effect of current datasets on intrusion detection systems. IEEE Access **8**, 104650–104675 (2020)

20. Jiang, Y., Cuki, B., Menzies, T., Bartlow, N.: Comparing design and code metrics for software quality prediction. In: Proceedings of the 4th International Workshop on Predictor Models in Software Engineering, pp. 11–18 (2008)

21. Jung, H.W., Kim, S.G., Chung, C.S.: Measuring software product quality: a survey of ISO/IEC 9126. IEEE Softw. **21**(5), 88–92 (2004)

22. Kan, S.H.: Metrics and Models in Software Quality Engineering. Addison-Wesley Longman Publishing Co., Inc., Boston (2002)

23. Kim, M.: A quality model for evaluating IoT applications. Int. J. Comput. Electr. Eng. **8**(1), 66 (2016)

24. Kim, M., Park, J.H., Lee, N.Y.: A quality model for IoT service. In: Park, J.J.J.H., Pan, Y., Yi, G., Loia, V. (eds.) CSA/CUTE/UCAWSN 2016. LNEE, vol. 421, pp. 497–504. Springer, Singapore (2017). https://doi.org/10.1007/978-981-10-3023-9_77

25. Kiruthika, J., Khaddaj, S.: Software quality issues and challenges of internet of things. In: 2015 14th International Symposium on Distributed Computing and Applications for Business Engineering and Science (DCABES), pp. 176–179. IEEE (2015)

26. Koomen, T., Broekman, B., van der Aalst, L., Vroon, M.: TMap next: for result-driven testing. Uitgeverij kleine Uil (2013)

27. Li, F., Nastic, S., Dustdar, S.: Data quality observation in pervasive environments. In: 2012 IEEE 15th International Conference on Computational Science and Engineering, pp. 602–609. IEEE (2012)
28. Marinissen, E.J., et al.: IoT: source of test challenges. In: 2016 21th IEEE European Test Symposium (ETS), pp. 1–10. IEEE (2016)
29. Mell, P., Scarfone, K., Romanosky, S.: Common vulnerability scoring system. IEEE Secur. Priv. 4(6), 85–89 (2006)
30. Ming, Z., Yan, M.: A modeling and computational method for QoS in IoT. In: 2012 IEEE International Conference on Computer Science and Automation Engineering, pp. 275–279. IEEE (2012)
31. Nirpal, P.B., Kale, K.: A brief overview of software testing metrics. Int. J. Comput. Sci. Eng. 3(1), 204–2011 (2011)
32. Pantiuchina, J., Lanza, M., Bavota, G.: Improving code: the (mis) perception of quality metrics. In: 2018 IEEE International Conference on Software Maintenance and Evolution (ICSME), pp. 80–91. IEEE (2018)
33. Pezzè, M., Young, M.: Software Testing and Analysis: Process, Principles, and Techniques. Wiley, Hoboken (2008)
34. Singh, M., Baranwal, G.: Quality of Service (QoS) in Internet of Things. In: 2018 3rd International Conference On Internet of Things: Smart Innovation and Usages (IoT-SIU), pp. 1–6 (2018)
35. Snigdh, I., Gupta, N.: Quality of service metrics in wireless sensor networks: a survey. J. Inst. Eng. (India): Ser. B 97(1), 91–96 (2016)
36. Sollie, R.S.: Security and usability assessment of several authentication technologies. Master's thesis (2005)
37. Staron, M., Meding, W.: A portfolio of internal quality metrics for software architects. In: Winkler, D., Biffl, S., Bergsmann, J. (eds.) SWQD 2017. LNBIP, vol. 269, pp. 57–69. Springer, Cham (2017). https://doi.org/10.1007/978-3-319-49421-0_5
38. Staron, M., Meding, W., Karlsson, G., Nilsson, C.: Developing measurement systems: an industrial case study. J. Softw. Maint. Evol. Res. Pract. 23(2), 89–107 (2011)
39. Van de Ven, T., Bloem, J., Duniau, J.P.: IoTMap: testing in an IoT environment. Uitgeverij kleine Uil (2016)
40. White, G., Nallur, V., Clarke, S.: Quality of service approaches in IoT: a systematic mapping. J. Syst. Softw. 132, 186–203 (2017)
41. Zheng, X., Martin, P., Brohman, K., Da Xu, L.: CLOUDQUAL: a quality model for cloud services. IEEE Trans. Ind. Inform. 10(2), 1527–1536 (2014)

Author Index

Printed in the United States
by Baker & Taylor Publisher Services